Image Processing Computer Vision Masterclass with Python

Learn advanced image processing techniques, computer vision fundamentals, and applications

---

2nd Edition

Sandipan Dey

bpb

www.bpbonline.com

Second Revised and Updated Edition 2025

First Edition 2021

Copyright © BPB Publications, India

ISBN: 978-93-65890-037

LIMITS OF LIABILITY AND DISCLAIMER OF WARRANTY

To View Complete
BPB Publications Catalogue
Scan the QR Code:

Dedicated to

*In loving memory of my dad,
my inspiration, my strength,
and the one who encouraged me
to write this book.
Without him, I am nothing.
Without him, none of this
would have been possible.*

About the Author

Sandipan Dey is an author and data science enthusiast with a wide range of interests, including machine learning, deep learning, image processing, and computer vision. He has worked across various domains in data science, such as recommender systems, predictive modeling for the events industry, sensor localization, sentiment analysis, and device prognostics. He holds a master's degree in computer science from the University of Maryland, Baltimore County, and has published research papers in several IEEE data mining conferences and journals. With over 10 years of work experience as a data scientist in the software and IT industry, he has also authored multiple books on image processing, published by international publishing houses. He has completed over 500 MOOCs from leading institutions worldwide, covering a wide range of subjects including data science, machine learning, deep learning, generative AI, image processing, natural language processing, artificial intelligence, algorithms, statistics, mathematics, and related fields. A passionate advocate for machine learning education, he frequently shares his insights, research, and projects on his blog.

Acknowledgement

I offer my deepest love, eternal gratitude, and cherished remembrance to my beloved dad, who is no longer with me. Not a day passes without feeling the ache of your absence, yet your love surrounds me still, steady, guiding, and everlasting. Your unwavering love, strength, and belief in me continue to inspire every step I take. Everything I am, everything I have achieved, carries a part of you. You were my greatest inspiration, the heart behind this journey and the reason these pages exist. Though you are no longer here, your spirit lives in every word. This book is for you and is a tribute to your spirit and to the bond we will always share.

I express my deepest gratitude to my beloved mother, whose endless love, strength, and blessings have been the foundation of everything I do.

I am also grateful to BPB Publications for their guidance and expertise in bringing this book to fruition. It was a long journey of revising this book, with valuable participation and collaboration of reviewers, technical experts, and editors.

I would also like to acknowledge the immense learning opportunities provided by MOOCs on platforms such as Coursera and edX. The wide range of courses I undertook in image processing, computer vision, machine learning, deep learning, generative AI, and related fields played a crucial role in shaping the knowledge required to write this book. Additionally, my years of experience working in the tech industry have been invaluable, offering practical insights and lessons that deeply informed and enriched this work.

Finally, I would like to thank all the readers who have taken an interest in my book and for their support in making it a reality. Your encouragement has been invaluable.

Preface

This book was conceived to address the growing demand for a practical, problem-oriented resource that guides learners through advanced topics in modern computer vision. It was written to build upon foundational knowledge and to offer readers a hands-on journey through a diverse set of techniques—from classical image processing to cutting-edge deep learning and generative AI models.

A deliberate choice was made to follow a problem-first approach, where real-world challenges are introduced and then explored through a variety of methods. In computer vision, there is rarely a single correct way to solve a problem. Instead, solutions are often shaped by factors such as application context, data constraints, and performance needs. Thus, this book aims not to prescribe the most optimal or efficient method in every case, but rather to expose readers to a broad spectrum of techniques. The goal is to help them develop the insight and flexibility to choose—or even design—the best solution for their own unique scenario.

Each chapter is structured to include the necessary background theory, followed by well-explained Python code demonstrations using widely adopted libraries such as OpenCV, scikit-image, SimpleITK, PyTorch, TensorFlow, Keras, and more. Readers are encouraged to treat the hands-on examples not as fixed templates, but as launchpads for experimentation, adaptation, and deeper learning.

Given Python's dynamic and ever-evolving ecosystem, it is acknowledged that some functions or APIs used in this book may be deprecated or modified in the future. However, readers should not be discouraged by such changes. Once the core concepts are understood, tweaking, debugging, and adapting code to evolving libraries becomes not only manageable but also an excellent learning opportunity. It is in this iterative process of troubleshooting and discovery that one's true expertise begins to flourish.

This book assumes that readers are already comfortable with Python programming and possess foundational knowledge in image processing, machine learning, deep learning, and mathematical disciplines such as linear algebra, calculus, and probability. For readers who wish to build or reinforce this foundation, it is strongly recommended to explore the companion book *Image Processing Masterclass with Python*, authored by the same writer.

Ultimately, the aim of this book is to guide, inspire, and empower. The solutions presented are stepping stones, not finish lines. It is hoped that readers will not only gain practical skills but also develop a sense of joy and fascination in solving visual problems. The journey through image processing and computer vision is rich, challenging, and immensely rewarding—may you enjoy every step of it.

Welcome to the masterclass. Let the journey begin.

Chapter 1: Image Restoration and Inverse Problems in Image Processing - This chapter introduces fundamental concepts in image restoration and inverse problems. It begins with the mathematical formulation of degradation models and explores various denoising and deblurring techniques, both classical and modern. Key techniques include weighted median filtering, non-blind and blind deconvolution (for example, Richardson-Lucy), total variation minimization, wavelet-based denoising, non-local means, bilateral filtering, MAP Bayesian estimation with MRF priors, and kernel PCA-based denoising—all demonstrated in Python.

Chapter 2: More Image Restoration and Image Inpainting - Building on the previous chapter, this section dives deeper into image restoration using neural techniques. It covers autoencoder-based denoising, GAN-based blind deblurring (DeblurGAN), and multiple approaches to image inpainting. Topics include anisotropic diffusion filtering, simple deep image painting using Keras, and semantic inpainting using DCGANs, with rich code examples to reinforce learning.

Chapter 3: Image Segmentation - Segmentation is a core problem in vision. This chapter introduces foundational segmentation techniques, including gray-level and bitplane slicing, thresholding methods, and clustering-based segmentation. It also covers advanced algorithms like MeanShift, watershed, GrabCut, RandomWalk, and SLIC/NCut segmentation using Python libraries like OpenCV, scikit-learn, and scikit-image.

Chapter 4: More Image Segmentation - This chapter extends segmentation to more advanced and applied topics. It covers human skin detection using classical binary classifiers, labeling connected components, and video background separation using Gaussian Mixture Models. Deep learning-based segmentation techniques such as DeepLabV3+, ENet, and Detectron2 are explored, along with practical tasks like background replacement in images/videos and outlier detection with autoencoders.

Chapter 5: Image Feature Extraction and Its Applications: Image Registration - Feature detection is a critical building block for many applications. This chapter reviews keypoint detection and description methods, and focuses on feature-based image alignment and registration. Topics include rigid and deformable registration with tools like pystackreg, pyelastix, SimpleITK, and the deep learning-based VoxelMorph model using TensorFlow/Keras.

Chapter 6: Applications of Image Feature Extraction - This chapter showcases how feature extraction powers real-world applications. Examples include image panorama stitching with OpenCV, facial feature analysis using NMF, LBPH, and Gabor filters, and pedestrian detection using HOG and HAAR-Cascade features. Each use case is backed by end-to-end Python code.

Chapter 7: Image Classification - Image classification forms the foundation of many AI systems. This chapter walks through the entire pipeline—from classical machine learning approaches for classifying Fashion-MNIST to deep learning models using TensorFlow/Keras. It also demonstrates transfer learning with PyTorch and training classifiers on custom datasets using pre-trained models.

Chapter 8: Object Detection and Recognition - Delve into object localization with deep learning. Topics include using pre-trained models, YOLOv4 with transfer learning, instance-level tasks like selective coloring using Mask R-CNN, face verification with DeepFace, and barcode/QR detection. Hands-on examples provide a strong basis for object detection projects.

Chapter 9: Application of Image Processing and Computer Vision in Medical Imaging - Explore the rich world of medical image analysis. This chapter covers handling and visualizing DICOM and NIfTI formats using libraries like pydicom, nibabel, and ITK. It includes segmentation of brain MRIs, 3D rendering, CT reconstruction, and pneumonia classification using deep CNNs—highlighting the real impact of vision in healthcare.

Chapter 10: Application of Image Processing and Computer Vision in Medical Imaging and Remote Sensing - This dual-topic chapter covers both medical and remote sensing applications. Medical topics include COVID-19 detection, prostate segmentation, and brain tumor segmentation using nnUNet and U-Net. Remote sensing topics include segmentation of satellite images (for example, FloodNet, SN7), and landcover classification using ResNet101 with Fastai. It illustrates how vision systems solve problems beyond consumer devices.

Chapter 11: Miscellaneous Problems in Image Processing and Computer Vision - This final chapter brings together innovative and creative applications of vision. Topics include deep dreaming, neural style transfer, image colorization, visualizing CNN features with t-SNE, generating 3D point clouds, AR with OpenCV, video editing with MoviePy, image generation from text with GAN-CLS, seamless cloning, and DALL-E-based generation—pushing the boundaries of what is possible in computer vision.

Code Bundle and Coloured Images

Please follow the link to download the
Code Bundle and the *Coloured Images* of the book:

https://rebrand.ly/j4mhx9r

The code bundle for the book is also hosted on GitHub at
https://github.com/bpbpublications/Image-Processing-and-Computer-Vision-Masterclass-with-Python-2nd-Edition.
In case there's an update to the code, it will be updated on the existing GitHub repository.

We have code bundles from our rich catalogue of books and videos available at **https://github.com/bpbpublications**. Check them out!

Errata

We take immense pride in our work at BPB Publications and follow best practices to ensure the accuracy of our content to provide with an indulging reading experience to our subscribers. Our readers are our mirrors, and we use their inputs to reflect and improve upon human errors, if any, that may have occurred during the publishing processes involved. To let us maintain the quality and help us reach out to any readers who might be having difficulties due to any unforeseen errors, please write to us at :

errata@bpbonline.com

Your support, suggestions and feedbacks are highly appreciated by the BPB Publications' Family.

Did you know that BPB offers eBook versions of every book published, with PDF and ePub files available? You can upgrade to the eBook version at www.bpbonline. com and as a print book customer, you are entitled to a discount on the eBook copy. Get in touch with us at :

business@bpbonline.com for more details.

At **www.bpbonline.com**, you can also read a collection of free technical articles, sign up for a range of free newsletters, and receive exclusive discounts and offers on BPB books and eBooks.

Piracy

If you come across any illegal copies of our works in any form on the internet, we would be grateful if you would provide us with the location address or website name. Please contact us at **business@bpbonline.com** with a link to the material.

If you are interested in becoming an author

If there is a topic that you have expertise in, and you are interested in either writing or contributing to a book, please visit **www.bpbonline.com**. We have worked with thousands of developers and tech professionals, just like you, to help them share their insights with the global tech community. You can make a general application, apply for a specific hot topic that we are recruiting an author for, or submit your own idea.

Reviews

Please leave a review. Once you have read and used this book, why not leave a review on the site that you purchased it from? Potential readers can then see and use your unbiased opinion to make purchase decisions. We at BPB can understand what you think about our products, and our authors can see your feedback on their book. Thank you!

For more information about BPB, please visit **www.bpbonline.com**.

Join our Discord space

Join our Discord workspace for latest updates, offers, tech happenings around the world, new releases, and sessions with the authors:

https://discord.bpbonline.com

Table of Contents

CHAPTER 1

Image Restoration and Inverse Problems in Image Processing

Introduction

Image restoration is the process of recovering a degraded image to enhance its quality by reducing noise, blur, or other distortions. The goal of image restoration is to undo or compensate for the elements that corrupt or degrade an image. Degradation can be caused because of sensor noise, motion blur, defocus blur (camera misfocus), optical aberrations, and environmental distortions. When an image is corrupted with some kind of blur, the actual blurring function — typically modeled as a **Point Spread Function** (**PSF**) — can be estimated, and the blur can be undone to restore the original image through deconvolution techniques. Similarly, noise degradation—whether caused by electronic interference, low-light conditions, or compression artifacts—requires denoising methods such as total variation regularization, wavelet-based filtering, or deep-learning-based restoration to recover image details.

Recent advancements in AI-driven image restoration leverage transformer-based models, **generative adversarial networks** (**GAN**), and self-supervised learning to enhance image quality beyond traditional techniques. These methods have demonstrated superior performance in handling complex degradations, blind restoration scenarios, and real-world applications.

In this chapter, we shall explore and implement fundamental and modern image restoration techniques, analyzing their effectiveness for different types of degradation while considering the latest developments in image processing and computational imaging.

Structure

In this chapter we shall explore the following topics:

- Mathematical model for image restoration
- Inverse problems in image processing
- Denoising with weighted median filtering
- Non-blind deconvolution for image restoration
- Blind deconvolution with Richardson-Lucy algorithm
- Total variation denoising
- Image denoising with wavelets
- Denoising using non-local means with opencv-python
- Denoising with bilateral filter
- Denoising with MAP Bayesian with an MRF prior
- Denoising images with kernel PCA

Objectives

By the end of this chapter, we will be able to understand the fundamental concepts of image restoration, including the types of degradation (for example, noise, blur) that affect images and how restoration techniques aim to reverse these effects. We will also identify the difference between denoising and deblurring problems in image restoration and how these are handled by various algorithms, implement non-linear spatial filtering techniques such as the weighted median filter to effectively reduce noise in an image, apply non-blind deconvolution techniques using Python libraries (for example, **opencv-python**, **SimpleITK**) to restore images affected by motion blur or defocus blur, leveraging methods like the Wiener filter and inverse filter, explore blind deconvolution methods, including the Richardson-Lucy algorithm, to restore images when the blur kernel is unknown, use **total variation** (**TV**) denoising to preserve important features like edges while removing noise, using Python libraries such as **scikit-image** or **SimpleITK**, and implement wavelet denoising to remove noise at multiple frequency levels using the **pywt** library. Understand and implement **non-local means** (**NLM**) filtering and bilateral filtering, which consider spatial and intensity differences for efficient denoising while preserving edges. Additionally, we will explore Bayesian denoising techniques with **Markov Random Field** (**MRF**) priors for probabilistic image restoration, utilizing kernel **Principal Component Analysis** (**PCA**) for denoising, which applies dimensionality reduction techniques to image restoration problems, and use popular Python libraries like **scikit-image**, **opencv-python**, **SimpleITK**, **scipy.ndimage**, and **matplotlib** to implement these techniques and visualize the results.

By mastering these topics, you will have a strong grasp of how to restore corrupted images using various modern techniques and how to implement them effectively in Python for practical applications.

Mathematical model for image restoration

To formalize the image restoration process, let us begin by examining its underlying mathematical model, which describes how an observed image is formed through degradation mechanisms. The general form of the image degradation model is shown in the following figure:

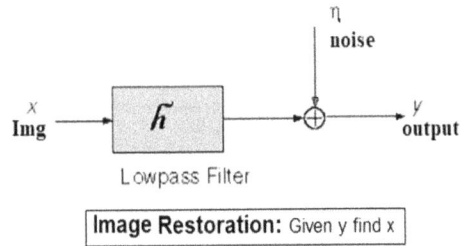

Figure 1.1: Schematic diagram for image restoration problem

Figure 1.1 represents the generative model $g(x,y) = f(x,y) \circledast h(x,y) + n(x,y)$, where:

- $f(x,y)$ is the original image (represented by x in the aforementioned figure)
- $h(x,y)$ is the PSF, a convolution kernel
- $\circledast$ is the convolution operation
- $n(x,y)$ is the noise signal
- $g(x,y)$ is the convolved output image (represented by y in the figure)

When the noise is not present in the preceding model, the problem reduces to deblurring; there are several techniques for non-blind and blind deblurring (a few of them we shall implement).

When the blur kernel is absent, the problem reduces to denoising, typically done by spatial / frequency domain filters, let us start with a generalized form of one such non-linear spatial filter.

Inverse problems in image processing

Inverse problems in image processing refer to the task of estimating the original image from its degraded observation by mathematically reversing the effects of distortions such as blur, noise, and occlusions. It is called an inverse problem because instead of directly observing the cause (for example, motion blur), we infer unknown parameters from the degraded image, essentially inverting the degradation process. While image restoration is a subset of inverse problems, inverse problems in imaging also encompass tasks like super-resolution, image inpainting, and tomography, making it a broader concept beyond just restoring images. In this section, we shall focus on restoration of a degraded image.

As discussed in the introduction section, image degradation can be represented by a convolution of an image with a PSF, combined with the addition of noise [4], so that it can be mathematically modeled as $g = Af_{true} + \eta$, where A is matrix that represents a two-dimensional convolution with a Gaussian blur (with standard deviation σ), and η represents the additive noise (of standard deviation θ).

Here f_{true} is the original image (not available to us), all we have is the degraded image g and the convolution matrix A (for non-blind convolution). We want to obtain an estimate $\hat{f}_{true}$.

The class of problems is often known as an inverse problem in image processing, where we aim at the data estimation from inadequate or noisy observations, and it is often encountered in practice. It is an ill-posed problem, and the solution is non-unique due to noise and lack of information. Hence, we aim to obtain an approximate solution.

In this section we shall use **normal equations** (with **regularization**) to obtain an estimate for the original image.

Let us start by importing all the required libraries using the following code snippet:

```
%matplotlib inline
import numpy as np
import matplotlib.pyplot as plt
from scipy.ndimage.filters import gaussian_filter
from skimage.metrics import peak_signal_noise_ratio as psnr
from scipy.sparse.linalg import LinearOperator, gmres
import warnings
warnings.filterwarnings('ignore') # ignore warnings
```

Let us define the convolution process with Gaussian blur kernel with variance σ^2, using the **gaussian_filter()** function from **scipy.ndimage.filters** module.

Implement the degradation process with the function **degrade()**, which first applies the convolution, followed by addition of a standard normal noise of variance θ^2, as shown in the following code block.

Initialize σ and θ variables.

```
def A(f, sigma):
    return gaussian_filter(f, sigma)

def degrade(f, sigma, theta):
    g = A(f, sigma)
    g += theta*np.random.randn(g.shape[0], g.shape[1])
    return g

sigma, theta = 0.15, 0.075
f_true = rgb2gray(imread('images/beans.jpg'))
g = degrade(f_true, sigma, theta)
```

From the degradation equation, we can see that it can be represented as an optimization (**minimization**) problem with the classic **OLS loss function** along with a **Ridge (L_2) penalization** term as:

$$\min_f (g - Af)^T(g - Af) + \alpha f^T f$$

The true image is restored by solving the preceding normal equation (prove it):

$$f = (A^T A + \alpha I)^{-1} A^T g$$

The process of reversing the degradation effects to restore the true image f_α from the observed degraded image g, as a solution to $(A^T A + \alpha I)f_\alpha = A^T g$, is generally known as **deconvolution**.

We can solve the preceding problem using a **Krylov** solver such as the **Generalized Minimal Residual Method (GMRES)**.

Since the explicit matrix representation of A is infeasibly large, pass the solver instead of a function that computes $(A^T A + \alpha I)f_\alpha$:

$$z = A^T A(f, \alpha)$$

It performs the following two-step process:

$$y = A(f)$$
$$z = A^T(y) + \alpha f$$

The following code snippet solves the preceding equation with the function **gmres()** from **scipy.sparse.linalg** module and obtains an estimate for $\hat{f}$ for the original image. Invoke **gmres($A^T A + \alpha I$, $A^T g$)**, to use **GMRES** iteration for solving the linear system of equations given by $(A^T A + \alpha I)f = A^T g$, to find $\hat{f}$.

```
def ATA(f, alpha=1e-2):
    y = A(f, sigma)
    z = A(y, sigma) + alpha*f
    return z
h, w = g.shape
AL = LinearOperator((w*h,w*h), ATA)
ATg = np.ravel(A(g, sigma))
f_hat = np.reshape(gmres(AL, ATg)[0], (h,w))
```

Plot the degraded image and the restored one with the following code block:

```
plt.figure(figsize=(20,10))
plt.subplot(121), plt.imshow(g), plt.title('degraded, PSNR: {:.02f}' \
               .format(psnr(f_true, g)), size=20), plt.axis('off')
plt.subplot(122), plt.imshow(f_hat), plt.title('restored, PSNR: {:.02f}' \
               .format(psnr(f_true, f_hat)), size=20), plt.axis('off')
plt.tight_layout()
plt.show()
```

Once you run the aforementioned code snippet, you should obtain the following figure:

Figure 1.2: Image restoration with the GMRES method

Denoising with weighted median filtering

When an image (a 2D or 3D signal) is transmitted over some distance over a communication channel, it frequently gets contaminated by noise. The simplest model for the acquisition of noise by a signal is additive noise, with the form:

$$\underset{\text{degraded signal}}{g(x,y)} \quad = \quad \underset{\text{original signal}}{f(x,y)} \quad + \quad \underset{\text{noise signal}}{\eta(x,y)}$$

The basic assumptions for noise signal $\eta(x, y)$ are the following:

- Noise is **additive**.
- Noise is a **random** signal (with white Gaussian noise having **0** mean).
- Noise is a **high-frequency** signal.

Again, our objective of denoising is to remove noise $\eta(x, y)$ from the noisy image $g(x, y)$, while retaining most of the important signal features. Here, we shall use a weighted median filter to achieve the same.

A simple **median filter** is a **nonlinear** spatial filter that replaces each pixel with the median from a set in a window (patch) surrounding the pixel. This has the effect of minimizing the absolute prediction error. The output of the filter can be written as follows:

$$Y_s = \underset{\theta}{argmin} \sum_{k \in w(s)} |X_k - \theta|$$

Where $w(s)$ is a window surrounding pixel s. It can be shown that Y_s is minimum when $\theta = \underset{k \in w(s)}{median}(X_k)$ (see question 1 in the exercise and reference [1]).

The **median** filter is particularly very useful for removing the **salt and pepper (s&p)** noise (a type of image noise, where random pixels are replaced with black or white values, resembling scattered salt and pepper grains) from an image. The **weighted median filter** generalizes the median filter by allowing some pixels in the window to have more influence on the output than others. Here, the output is written as follows:

$$Y_s = \underset{\theta}{argmin} \sum_{k \in w(s)} \alpha_{s-k} |X_k - \theta|$$

Where α_{s-k} are **weighting factors** which determine the relative influence pixels in $w(s)$ have on the output. A typical set of weights is shown as follows:

1	1	1	1	1
1	2	2	2	1
1	2	2	2	1
1	2	2	2	1
1	1	1	1	1

Figure 1.3: Sample weights for a weighted median filter

This weight mask allows the pixels closer to the current pixel to have a stronger influence on the output.

In this section, we shall implement the weighted median filter function and apply it to denoise an **Integrated Circuit (IC)** grayscale image, degraded with s&p noise.

Let us start by importing the required libraries by using the following lines of code:

```
import cv2
from skimage.util import random_noise
```

Now, let us implement the function **weighted_median()** that applies the **Weighted Median Filter (WMF)** on an image. The function accepts a (noisy) input image and a **weight mask** for the WMF. The following is a step-by-step breakdown of how the algorithm works:

1. It slides a kernel window across the image (a standard way to implement a spatial filter).

2. Next, for each position of the window, it sorts the pixels in the window in descending order. Then it places the corresponding pixel weights in the same order as the sorted pixels.

$$X_{(1)}, X_{(2)}, \dots, X_{(p)}$$

$$\alpha_{(1)}, \alpha_{(2)}, \dots, \alpha_{(p)}$$

3. Finally, it determines the weighted median $X_{(i_m)}$ by incrementing the index i_m until the following holds true.

$$\sum_{i=1}^{i_m} \alpha_{(i)} \geq \sum_{i=i_m+1}^{p} \alpha_{(i)}$$

Let us implement the aforementioned algorithm using the python function **weighted_median()**, as shown in the next code snippet. The function **np.argsort()** is used to obtain the sorted indices of the pixels in a window. The function **np.cumsum()** is used to compute the cumulative sum of the weight mask values in the following implementation.

```python
def weighted_median(im, mask):
    h, w = im.shape
    sz = mask.shape[0]
    im1 = im.copy()
    mask1 = mask.ravel()
    for i in range(h-sz+1):
        for j in range(w-sz+1):
            win = im[i:i+sz, j:j+sz].ravel()
            indices = np.argsort(win)[::-1]
            win, mask1 = win[indices], mask1[indices]
            csum1, csum2 = np.cumsum(mask1), np.cumsum(mask1[::-1])[::-1]
            k = 0
            while csum1[:k].sum() < csum2[k:].sum():
                k += 1
            im1[i+sz//2, j+sz//2] = win[k]
    return im1
```

Now, read the input gray-scale image. Add impulse (**s&p**) noise to the input image using the function **random_noise()** from **skimage.util** module to obtain the noisy image.

Construct the weight mask aforementioned, using **numpy slicing**, as done in the next code snippet. Subsequently, apply the weighted median filter function to denoise (smooth) the degraded image, by invoking the **weighted_median()** function on the corrupted image:

```python
im = cv2.imread('images/ic.jpg', 0)
im = im / im.max()
noisy_im = random_noise(im, mode='s&p')
weight_mask = np.ones((5,5))
weight_mask[1:-1,1:-1] = 2
denoised_im = weighted_median(noisy_im, weight_mask)
```

Plot the original input image, the noisy (degraded) image, and the denoised (restored) output image side-by-side. Use `skimage.util` module's `peak_signal_noise_ratio()` function to compute the **Peak Signal-to-Noise Ratio** (**PSNR**, which measures the quality of a reconstructed image by comparing it to the original and computed using the formula

PSNR = 10 $\log_{10}\left(\frac{MAX^2}{MSE}\right)$, where **MAX** is the maximum pixel value and **MSE** is the **Mean Squared Error**) of the noisy and denoised images and observe that PSNR improved a lot after restoration. You should obtain a figure as follows:

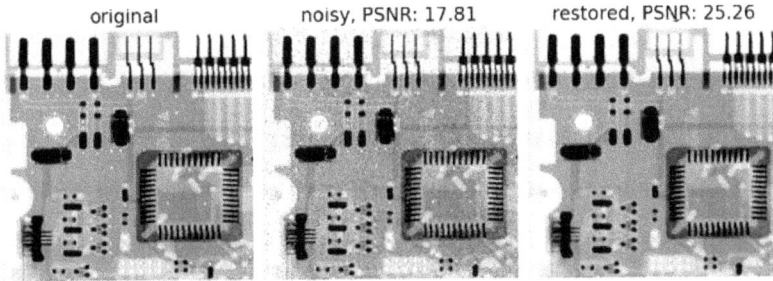

Figure 1.4: Image restoration with weighted median filter

Non-blind deconvolution for image restoration

Deconvolution is an operation inverse to convolution, it is a computationally intensive image processing technique for image restoration. In general, the objective of deconvolution is to find an (approximate) solution for f from a convolution equation of the form: $g = f \circledast h + \epsilon$, given g and the convolution kernel h. In this section, we shall discuss a few deconvolution algorithms with the assumption that the deconvolution is **non-blind**, i.e., the **PSF**, which describes how a single point source of light is blurred by an imaging system, modeling the system's response to an ideal point input, and the **convolution kernel** $h(.)$ is known.

Image deconvolution with inverse filter

The **inverse** filter is the most straightforward **deconvolution** method. Considering that the **convolution** of two images in the **spatial domain** is equivalent to **multiplication** of the **Fourier transforms** of the two images in the frequency domain (by the **convolution theorem**), the inverse filter attempts to invert the multiplication.

If in the spatial domain, the convolution operation is represented as $g(x,y) = f(x,y) \circledast h(x,y)$, in the frequency domain it can be represented by a simple multiplication $G(u,v) = F(u,v) \times H(u,v)$, where F, H and G represent the 2D **Discrete Fourier Transform** (**DFT**, which converts a spatial-domain image into its frequency components, computed in 2D as $F(u,v) = \sum_{i=0}^{M-1} \sum_{j=0}^{N-1} f(x,y)\, e^{-2\pi i\left(\frac{ux}{M} + \frac{vy}{N}\right)}$) of f (the original $M \times N$ image), h (the convolution kernel) and g (the convolved image), respectively (note that we are ignoring the noise here, the impact of noise on inverse filter is left as an exercise). A naive approach for image restoration is to multiply the DFT of the blurred image by inverse of $H(u, v)$:

$$\hat{F}(u, v) = \frac{G(u, v)}{H(u, v)} = F(u, v) \times \frac{H(u, v)}{H(u, v)} = F(u, v)$$

The next step is to apply the 2D **IDFT** (**Inverse Discrete Fourier Transform**, converts an image back to spatial domain from its frequency domain representation, and it is computed in 2D as: $\hat{f}(x, y) = \frac{1}{MN} \sum_{i=0}^{M-1} \sum_{j=0}^{N-1} \hat{F}(u, v) e^{2\pi i \left(\frac{ux}{M} + \frac{vy}{N} \right)}$) to obtain the restored image $\hat{f}$ from its frequency domain representation.

The aforementioned method is called **inverse filtering**, where $\frac{1}{H(u,v)}$ is the **inverse** filter. However, the problem in this formulation is that $\frac{1}{H(u,v)}$ may not exist / it may be computationally impossible to compute $\frac{1}{H(u,v)}$ (for example, when $H(u, v) \approx 0$). The ideal (more stable) inverse filter (also known as **pseudo-inverse filter**) can be approximated as follows:

$$\hat{F}(u, v) = \begin{cases} \frac{G(u,v)}{H(u,v)}, & \text{if } |H(u, v)| \geq \epsilon \\ 0, & \text{otherwise} \end{cases}$$

Figure 1.5: Pseudo-inverse filter

Where ϵ is a small threshold.

Another way to compensate for the values close to zero in H is just to get rid of high-frequency components beyond a cutoff threshold (for example, $u^2 + v^2 > \eta$) with naive inverse filtering with the deconvolution operator $\frac{1}{H(u,v)}$ as follows:

$$\hat{H}(u, v) = \frac{1}{H(u, v)}$$
$$\hat{H}(u, v) = 0, \quad \text{if } u^2 + v^2 > \eta$$
$$\hat{F}(u, v) = G(u, v) \hat{H}(u, v)$$

Figure 1.6: Another implementation of the inverse filter

Where η is a high frequency threshold.

In this section, we shall implement the pseudo-inverse filter using the aforementioned two approaches and restore a degraded image. Let us start by importing the required libraries using the following lines of code:

```
from scipy import signal
import scipy.ftpack as fp
from skimage.io import imread
from skimage.color import rgb2gray
from mpl_toolkits.mplot3d import Axes3D
from matplotlib.ticker import LinearLocator, FormatStrFormatter
```

Let us implement the frequency domain convolution using the function **convolve2d()**, notice that before performing the convolution as multiplication in the frequency domain, we must ensure that the **PSF** (convolution **kernel**) is padded properly to have shape exactly equal to the image shape. Let us also implement the **pseudo-inverse filter** and use the post-processing cutoff, as shown in the next code snippet:

```
def convolve2d(im, psf, k):
    M, N = im.shape
    freq = fp.fft2(im)
    assert(k % 2 == 1 and k > 0 and k <= min(M,N))
    # assumption: min(M,N) >= k > 0, k odd, kxk kernel
    psf = np.pad(psf, (((M-k)//2,(M-k)//2+(1-M%2)), ((N-k)//2,(N-k)//2+(1-N%2))),\
                                                        mode='constant')
    freq_kernel = fp.fft2(fp.ifftshift(psf))
    return np.abs(fp.ifft2(freq*freq_kernel))

def inverse_filter_cutoff(y, h, eta):
    Hf = fp.fft2(fp.ifftshift(h))
    M, N = Hf.shape
    u, v = np.meshgrid(range(N), range(M))
    indices = np.sqrt(u**2 + v**2) <= eta
    Hf[indices] = np.ones((M,N))[indices] / Hf[indices]
    Hf[np.sqrt(u**2 + v**2) > eta] = 0
    Yf = fp.fft2(y)
    I = Yf*Hf
    im = np.abs(fp.ifft2(I))
    return im, Hf

def pseudo_inverse_filter(y, h, epsilon):
    Hf = fp.fft2(fp.ifftshift(h))
    M, N = Hf.shape
    Hf[(np.abs(Hf)<epsilon)] = 0
    indices = np.where((np.abs(Hf)>=epsilon))
    Hf[indices] = np.ones((M,N))[indices] / Hf[indices]
    Yf = fp.fft2(y)
    I = Yf*Hf
    im = np.abs(fp.ifft2(I))
    return im, Hf
```

Let us define the following functions to plot the frequency **spectrums**, both in 2D (as **heatmap**) and 3D (as **surface plot**):

```
def plot_freq_filter(F, title, size=20):
    plt.imshow(20*np.log10( 0.01 + np.abs(fp.fftshift(F))), cmap='inferno')
    plt.title(title, size=size), plt.colorbar(orientation='horizontal')

def plot_freq_spec_3d(freq):
    fig = plt.figure(figsize=(10,10))
    ax = fig.gca(projection='3d')
    Y = np.arange(-freq.shape[0]//2,freq.shape[0]-freq.shape[0]//2)
    X = np.arange(-freq.shape[1]//2,freq.shape[1]-freq.shape[1]//2)
    X, Y = np.meshgrid(X, Y)
    Z = (20*np.log10(0.01 + fp.fftshift(freq))).real
    surf = ax.plot_surface(X, Y, Z, cmap=plt.cm.inferno, linewidth=0, \
                            antialiased=True)
    ax.zaxis.set_major_locator(LinearLocator(10))
    ax.zaxis.set_major_formatter(FormatStrFormatter('%.02f'))
    plt.show()
```

Now, let us create a couple of degraded (grayscale) images with two different types of blur kernels, first with a **Gaussian blur** and then using a **motion blur** kernel, and restore the degraded versions in each case using the **pseudo-inverse** filters (using the functions **inverse_filter_cutoff()** and **pseudo_inverse_filter()**), compare the quality of the denoised images with **PSNR** metric and plot the frequency spectrums, using the following code snippets.

Gaussian blur kernel

Gaussian blur kernel (in image processing) is a kernel (a matrix or a 2D array) used to smooth (or blur) an image by averaging pixel values with a Gaussian distribution, reducing noise and detail. It applies a weighted average to the surrounding pixels, with the center pixel having the highest weight and decreasing weights for pixels farther from the center, following the shape of a Gaussian (bell curve).

Mathematically, a 2D Gaussian function is defined as:

$$G(x,y) = \frac{1}{2\pi\sigma^2} e^{-\frac{x^2+y^2}{2\sigma^2}}$$

Where:

- x, y are the pixel coordinates relative to the center of the kernel
- σ is the standard deviation (controls the extent of blurring)
- $G(x,y)$ gives the weight for each pixel based on its distance from the center

The kernel values are derived from this Gaussian function and normalized so that they sum to 1, ensuring no change in image brightness. The image is convolved with this kernel to produce the blurred effect. The following Python code snippet shows how a degraded image (blurred with Gaussian kernel is restored using an inverse filter):

```
(M, N), k, sigma2, nsigma2 = im.shape, 15, 0.125, 0.0025

im = rgb2gray(imread('images/house.jpg'))
kernel = np.outer(signal. windows.gaussian(k, sigma2), \
                signal. windows.gaussian(k, sigma2))
im_blur = convolve2d(im, kernel, k) #, mode='same')
im_cor = random_noise(im_blur, var=nsigma2)
freq = fp.fft2(im_cor)
epsilon = 1e-3
eta = 1 / epsilon
kernel = np.pad(kernel, (((M-k)//2,(M-k)//2+1), ((N-k)//2,(N-k)//2+1)), \
                mode='constant')
im_res_cutoff, F_cutoff = inverse_filter_cutoff(im_cor, kernel, eta)
im_res_pseudo, F_pseudo = pseudo_inverse_filter(im_cor, kernel, epsilon)
```

The preceding Python code demonstrates image restoration by applying an **inverse** filter to a degraded image. The following is a breakdown of how it works:

- **Defining image parameters**:
    - o **M, N**: Dimensions of the image.
    - o **k**: Size of the blur kernel.
    - o **sigma2**: Standard deviation for generating the Gaussian kernel (controls blur intensity).
    - o **nsigma2**: Variance of the noise added to the blurred image.

- **Image loading and conversion**: The image is loaded and converted to grayscale using **rgb2gray(imread(.))**.

- **Generating the blur kernel**: A Gaussian blur kernel is created using **signal. windows.gaussian()**, which generates a 1D Gaussian, and **np.outer()** forms a 2D kernel, by exploiting the **separability** of the Gaussian function in 2D.

- **Blurring the image**: The image is blurred by convolving it with the Gaussian kernel using **convolve2d()**, where convolution (in 2D) is mathematically defined as: $(f \circledast h)(x, y) = \sum_m \sum_n f(m, n) h(x - m, y - n)$, with f and h representing the image and the kernel, respectively.

- **Adding noise**: Random noise with variance **nsigma2** is added to the blurred image using **random_noise()**, to simulate a noisy, degraded image.

- **FFT of the corrupted image**: The corrupted (blurred and noisy) image is transformed into the frequency domain using the **Fast Fourier Transform (FFT)** with **fp.fft2()**.

- **Inverse filter application**:

  o **Kernel padding**: The kernel is padded to match the image size using `np.pad()`.

  o **Inverse filter**: The following two variations of the inverse filter are applied:

    ▪ **Cutoff inverse filter (`inverse_filter_cutoff()`)**: This applies a frequency domain cutoff to limit high-frequency noise using the inverse of the kernel (with a threshold **eta**).

    ▪ **Pseudo-inverse filter (`pseudo_inverse_filter()`)**: This uses a regularized pseudo-inverse approach to stabilize the inversion, avoiding divisions by small values using **epsilon**.

Both filters attempt to undo the blur and noise degradation, thereby restoring the image. If you run the preceding code snippet and plot the degraded and restored images (along with the magnitude of the frequency spectrums) using the aforementioned two implementations, you should obtain a figure as follows:

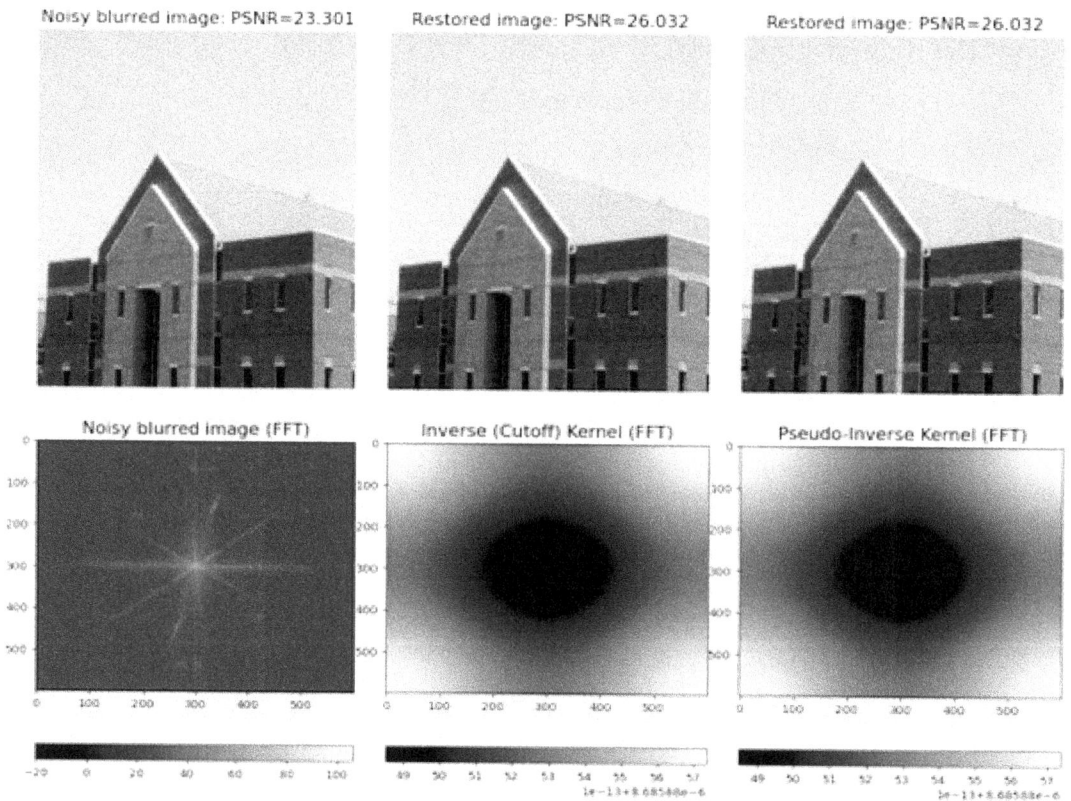

Figure 1.7: *Image restoration with (pseudo) inverse filter*

If you plot the magnitude of frequency spectrums in 3D, you will obtain a figure like the next one:

`plot_freq_spec_3d(fp.fft2(im_cor))`   `plot_freq_spec_3d(fp.fft2(im_res_cutoff))`

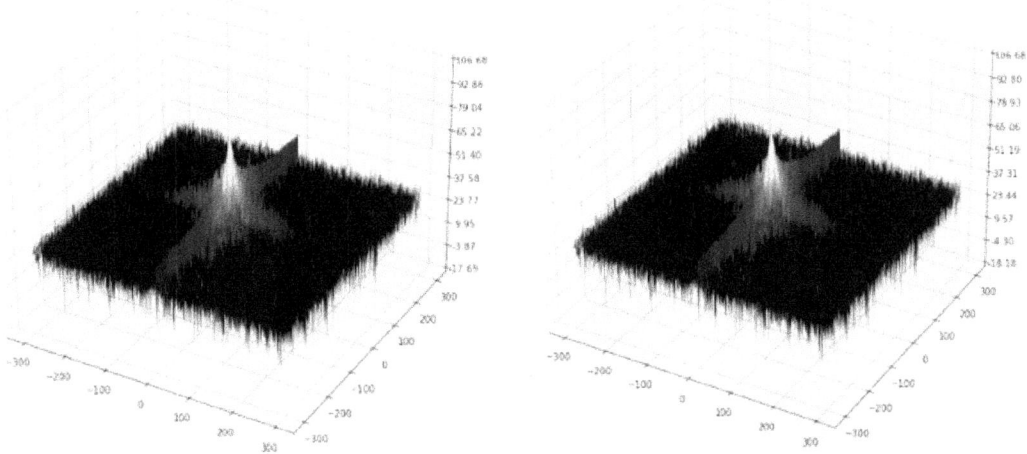

Figure 1.8: Frequency spectrum of the degraded vs. restored image

As we have seen in the last section, **Gaussian blur** kernel applies a symmetric, **isotropic** smoothing effect to an image by convolving it with a 2D Gaussian function, which assigns higher weights to pixels closer to the center. It is commonly used to reduce noise or create a soft-focus effect. In contrast, a **motion blur** kernel simulates the effect of object motion or camera shake by averaging pixel intensities along a specific direction and distance. Unlike Gaussian blur, **motion blur** is directional and **anisotropic**, resulting in elongated streaks that mimic the perceived motion. They serve distinct purposes: Gaussian blur focuses on uniform smoothing, while motion blur captures the directional nature of movement.

Motion blur kernel

A motion blur kernel in image processing is used to simulate the effect of camera or object movement during exposure, causing the image to appear smeared along the direction of motion. It is a **linear filter** that averages pixel values along a straight line in the direction of the blur, giving the appearance of motion.

Mathematically, a **motion blur** kernel is often represented as a 2D matrix where non-zero values form a line with equal weights in the **direction** of the **blur**. For example, a simple horizontal motion blur kernel of size N×N can be written as the following matrix (with the first row as all ones and all the elements of the rest of the matrix as zeros):

$$K = \frac{1}{N}\begin{bmatrix} 1 & \cdots & 1 \\ \vdots & \ddots & \vdots \\ 0 & \cdots & 0 \end{bmatrix}$$

In the preceding example, the kernel has N non-zero elements (all equal to $1/N$) in the first row, simulating uniform averaging along a horizontal path of length N. The image is convolved with this kernel, which results in a blurring effect along the specified motion direction.

For vertical or diagonal motion blur, the non-zero values in the kernel would be arranged along a vertical or diagonal line, respectively. The general motion blur can be extended to other directions by adjusting the orientation of the kernel.

Let us now degrade an image using motion blur and restore (**deblur**) using the **inverse filter**, using the following code snippet:

```python
im = rgb2gray(imread('images/car.jpg'))
(M, N), k = im.shape, 21  # k x k kernel
kernel = np.zeros((k, k)) # construct a 21 x 21 motion-blur kernel
kernel[int((k-1)/2), :] = np.ones(k) # fill middle row of kernel matrix with 1s
kernel = kernel / k

im_blur = convolve2d(im, kernel, k)
im_cor = im_blur
freq = fp.fft2(im_cor)
kernel = np.pad(kernel, (((M-k)//2,(M-k)//2+1), ((N-k)//2,(N-k)//2+1)), \
                                              mode='constant')
epsilon = 10e-3
im_res_pseudo, F_pseudo = pseudo_inverse_filter(im_cor, kernel, epsilon)
```

A couple of steps from the preceding code snippet demand more explanation:

1. **Creating the motion blur kernel**:

    a. A $k \times k$ matrix of zeros (**kernel = np.zeros((k, k))**) is created.

    b. The middle row of this matrix is filled with ones (**kernel[int((k-1)/2), :] = np.ones(k)**) to simulate **horizontal motion blur**.

    c. The kernel is normalized by dividing by k to ensure that the sum of all elements is 1, ensuring proper blurring.

2. **Blurring the image**:

    a. The image is blurred by convolving it with the motion blur kernel using **convolve2d()**. This simulates the motion blur effect on the image.

    b. In this case, no additional noise is added; the corrupted image **im_cor** is simply the blurred image.

If you run the preceding code snippet and plot the **motion-blurred** and the **deblurred** (restored) images in both the **spatial** and **frequency** domains, you should obtain a figure as follows:

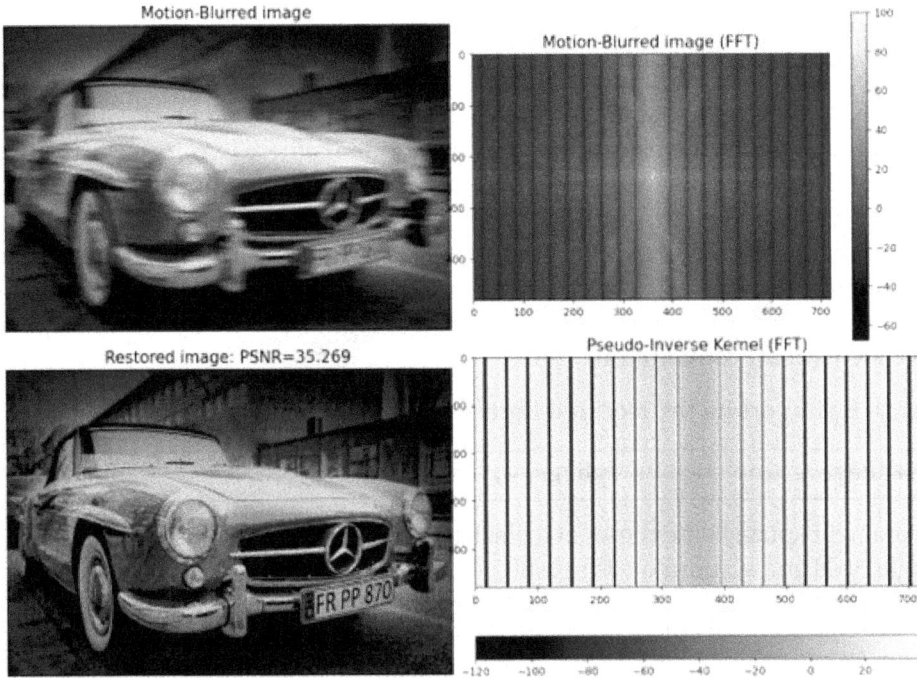

Figure 1.9: Restoration of a motion-blurred image with pseudo-inverse filter

If you plot the magnitude of frequency spectrums in 3D, you will obtain a figure as follows:

```
plot_freq_spec_3d(fp.fft2(im_cor))  plot_freq_spec_3d(fp.fft2(im_res_cutoff))  plot_freq_spec_3d(fp.fft2(im_blur))
```

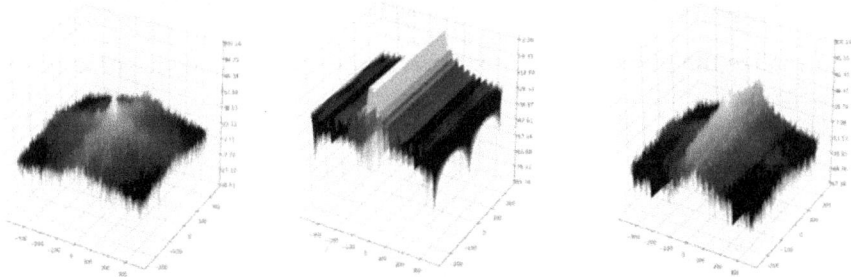

```
plot_freq_spec_3d(fp.fft2(im_res_pseudo))   plot_freq_spec_3d(F_pseudo)
```

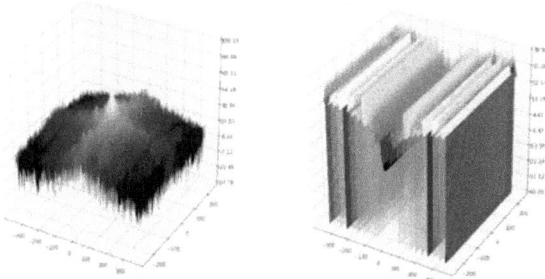

Figure 1.10: Frequency spectrum of the image, blur kernel, blurred and restored image

Simulating the bokeh blur

The **bokeh effect** is a pleasing visual artifact, and it often enhances the aesthetics of a photograph. Let us understand how the effect can be created. Light rays (from light sources) get reflected by the objects in the scene, and the camera lens focuses them onto the image plane. The points that appear in focus are the ones that fall inside a certain distance range, and the remaining ones appear out of focus (being too far / too close). Among these points, the bright spots (for example, light sources) create circles of confusion that are more visible than the ones created by darker points (by the contrast effect). This phenomenon is known as the bokeh effect. In this section, you will learn how to *simulate* this effect using Python code with 2D convolution.

Let us start by importing the required libraries using the next line of code:

```python
from skimage.color import rgb2gray, rgba2rgb
```

Consider a white pixel at the center of a black image. Let us shift this image in all directions by a single pixel and accumulate the results. It will smear the white pixel over its neighbors.

Let us implement the function **apply_bokeh_blur()** to simulate this effect. The function takes two arguments: an input image and a binary mask image (a small white star/ hexagon/circle at the bottom left corner in a black background) of the same shape. Start with a blank output image where the smearing effects will get accumulated.

For each white pixel $P(i, j)$ from the mask image, shift the input color image by (i, j), using the function **np.roll()**, strengthen the effect by using **func()** (for example, a cubic function), and multiply it by the mask pixel value, and add the result to the output image.

Finally, normalize the pixel values, as shown in the following code snippet:

```python
def func(x):
    return x**3

def apply_bokeh_blur(img, mask):
    h, w = mask.shape
    out = np.zeros(img.shape)
    total = 0
    for i in range(h):
        for j in range(w):
            if mask[i, j] != 0:
                out += mask[i, j] * func(np.roll(img, (i,j), (0,1)))
                total += mask[i, j]
    out /= total
    out /= out.max()
    return out
```

Read the input RGB color image of an X-mas tree. Let us use a black image with a small white star (mask) at the bottom left corner as the mask image. Invoke the function **apply_bokeh_blur()** with the input and the mask image to obtain the output image with the desired effect.

```
mask = rgb2gray(rgba2rgb(imread('images/xmask.png')))
img = cv2.resize(imread('images/xtree.png') / 255, mask.shape[::-1])
out = apply_bokeh_blur(img, mask)
```

Plot the input image and the output image using **bokeh blur**. Create visually interesting results by varying the shape of the mask (for example, use a hexagonal mask instead); you should get a figure as follows:

Figure 1.11: *Applying the bokeh blur to an image*

Wiener deconvolution with opencv-python

The inverse filter performs poorly when the noise level is high. Wiener filter is an improved version of the inverse filter, it works in the frequency domain and uses prior **regularization** (penalization of high-frequency terms which have a poor Signal-to-Noise Ratio). The regularization parameter generally needs to be hand-tuned. Refer to the following figure for an example of Wiener deconvolution:

$$G(u,v) = H(u,v)\, F(u,v) + N(u,v)$$

objective $\quad \min\limits_{W} E[\, (f - \hat{f})^2\,]$

$= \min\limits_{W} E[\, |F(u,v) - \hat{F}(u,v)|^2\,]$ by Parseval's Theorem

s.t. $\quad \hat{F}(u,v) = G(u,v) W(u,v)$

solution:

$$W(u,v) = \frac{H^*(u,v)}{|H(u,v)|^2 + \frac{|N(u,v)|^2}{|F(u,v)|^2}} = \frac{H^*(u,v)}{|H(u,v)|^2 + K}$$

$$= \frac{1}{H(u,v)} \cdot \frac{|H(u,v)|^2}{|H(u,v)|^2 + \frac{|N(u,v)|^2}{|F(u,v)|^2}}$$

inverse filter $\qquad$ 1/SNR

$$W(u,v) = \frac{H^*(u,v)}{|H(u,v)|^2 + \lambda|\Lambda_D|^2}$$

balance Freq. response of Laplacian

scikit-image restoration's wiener()

Figure 1.12: *Wiener deconvolution*

The frequency response of the Wiener filter can be expressed as:

$$W(u,v) = \frac{1}{H(u,v)} \frac{1}{1 + 1/(|H(u,v)|^2 SNR)}$$

Where **SNR**, or the **Signal-to-Noise Ratio**, is the ratio of the frequency responses of the original image (signal) to noise. Here is a brief explanation:

- First note that $\lim\limits_{N(u,v)\to\infty} SNR = 0$ and $\lim\limits_{N(u,v)\to 0} SNR = \infty$, for some frequency (u,v).
- When the noise is 0 (i.e. *SNR* is ∞), the Wiener filter simply reduces to an *inverse filter*, i.e., $\lim\limits_{N(u,v)\to 0} W(u,v) = \frac{1}{H(u,v)} \cdot \frac{1}{1+0} = \frac{1}{H(u,v)}$.
- With the increase of noise at certain frequencies, which results in a drop in the SNR ratio, the Wiener filter attenuates frequencies according to their filtered SNR ratio, since $\lim\limits_{N(u,v)\to\infty} W(u,v) = \frac{1}{H(u,v)} \cdot \frac{1}{\infty} = 0$.
- The λ parameter balances between the data and the regularization term.

In this section, we shall implement the **Wiener filter** to deblur a degraded image again, but this time using **opencv-python (cv2)** library functions. It shows how DFT can be used apply **Wiener deconvolution** to an image with a user-defined **PSF**.

Let us first implement the function **blur_edge()** to apply **Gaussian blur** on an image. Also, implement the functions **motion_kernel()** and **defocus_kernel()** to create the motion blur and defocus blur kernels, respectively. The function **deconvolve()** implements the Wiener deconvolution as follows:

```
def blur_edge(img, d=31):
    h, w  = img.shape[:2]
    img_pad = cv2.copyMakeBorder(img, d, d, d, d, cv2.BORDER_WRAP)
    img_blur = cv2.GaussianBlur(img_pad, (2*d+1, 2*d+1), -1)[d:-d,d:-d]
    y, x = np.indices((h, w))
    dist = np.dstack([x, w-x-1, y, h-y-1]).min(-1)
    w = np.minimum(np.float32(dist)/d, 1.0)
    return img*w + img_blur*(1-w)

def motion_kernel(angle, d, sz=63):
    kern = np.ones((1, d), np.float32)
    c, s = np.cos(angle), np.sin(angle)
    A = np.float32([[c, -s, 0], [s, c, 0]])
    sz2 = sz // 2
    A[:,2] = (sz2, sz2) - np.dot(A[:,:2], ((d-1)*0.5, 0))
    kern = cv2.warpAffine(kern, A, (sz, sz), flags=cv2.INTER_CUBIC)
    return kern

def defocus_kernel(d, sz=63):
    kern = np.zeros((sz, sz), np.uint8)
    cv2.circle(kern, (sz, sz), d, 255, -1, cv2.LINE_AA, shift=1)
    kern = np.float32(kern) / 255
    return kern

def deconvolve(img, kern):
    kern /= kern.sum()
    kern_pad = np.zeros_like(img)
    kh, kw = kern.shape
    kern_pad[:kh, :kw] = kern
    freq = cv2.dft(img, flags=cv2.DFT_COMPLEX_OUTPUT)
    kern_freq=cv2.dft(kern_pad,flags=cv2.DFT_COMPLEX_OUTPUT,nonzeroRows=kh)
    kern_freq2 = (kern_freq**2).sum(-1)
    kern_wiener = kern_freq / (kern_freq2 + noise)[...,np.newaxis]
    res = cv2.mulSpectrums(freq, kern_wiener, 0)
    res = cv2.idft(res, flags=cv2.DFT_SCALE | cv2.DFT_REAL_OUTPUT)
    res = np.roll(res, -kh//2, 0)
    res = np.roll(res, -kw//2, 1)
    return res
```

Read the input image as a gray-scale image and apply the **Gaussian blur** to the image as follows:

```
img = cv2.imread('images/barbara.jpg', cv2.IMREAD_GRAYSCALE)
img = np.float32(img) / 255
img = blur_edge(img)
angle, d, snr = np.deg2rad(135), 22, 25
noise = 10**(-0.1*snr)
```

Defocus the image by applying the **defocus blur** kernel and then restore the defocused image using the **deconvolve()** function defined as follows:

```
kern_defocus = defocus_kernel(d)
img_defocussed = cv2.filter2D(img,-1, kern_defocus) # apply defocus blur
res_defocussed = deconvolve(img_defocussed, kern_defocus)
```

Next, apply **motion blur** to the original image and then restore the defocused image using the **deconvolve()** function defined as follows:

```
kern_blur = motion_kernel(angle, d)
img_blur = cv2.filter2D(img,-1, kern_blur)   # apply motion blur
res_blur = deconvolve(img_blur, kern_blur)
```

Plot the original image, and the defocus and the motion blur kernels. You should obtain a figure as follows:

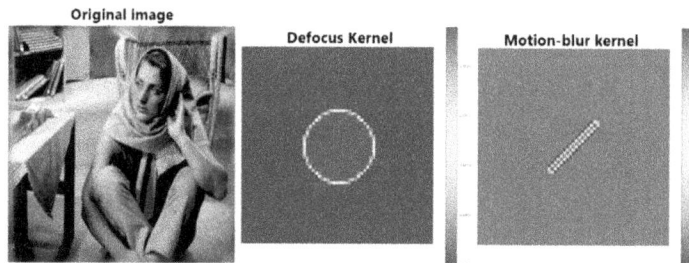

Figure 1.13: *Input (Barbara) image with the defocus and motion blur kernel*

Now, if you plot the defocused, blurred and restored images, you should obtain a figure as follows:

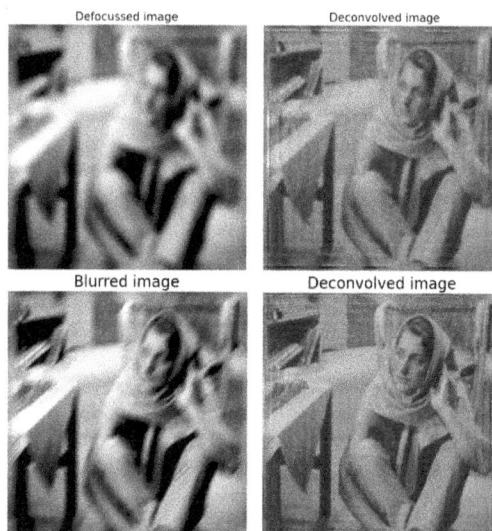

Figure 1.14: *Restoring defocused/motion/blurred images using deconvolution with the Wiener filter*

Deconvolution with unsupervised Weiner filter with scikit-image

The unsupervised Wiener algorithm uses a data learning algorithm (based on an iterative stochastic **Gibbs sampler**) to obtain self-tuned regularization parameters . The algorithm is fast since it is based on linear models but may not restore sharp edges like the non-linear methods (for example, **TV restoration**, we shall explore later in this chapter).

From the **Bayesian** perspective, the deconvolved (estimated) image can be defined as the posterior mean (defined by the sum of all possible images weighted by their probability). But the exact sum being intractable, the algorithm uses **Markov Chain Monte Carlo** (**MCMC**) simulation to draw images under posterior law (drawing highly probable images more often than the less probable images) and then computes the empirical mean of the samples.

In this section, we shall use **skimage.resoration** module's implementation of **unsupervised Wiener filter** to deconvolve and restore an image degraded with noise (we shall also **scipy.signal**'s implementation of the **Wiener filter**, we shall leave the comparison of the restored image qualities and parameter tuning for the Gibbs sampler for unsupervised Wiener as an exercise for the interested reader).

Let us start by importing all the required libraries as follows:

```
from skimage import color, restoration
from scipy.signal import convolve2d
```

Read the cameraman grayscale image and degrade with **box-blur** (for example, a 5×5 kernel of ones normalized by 25, to average each pixel with its 5×5 neighborhood), and Gaussian noise, using the next code snippet:

```
im = rgb2gray(imread('images/cameraman.jpg'))
noisy = im.copy()
psf = np.ones((5, 5)) / 25
noisy = convolve2d(noisy, psf, 'same')
noisy += 0.1 * im.std() * np.random.standard_normal(im.shape)
```

Use the **unsupervised_wiener()** function from **skimage.restoration** to apply the **unsupervised Wiener deconvolution** on the degraded image. The function accepts the following arguments:

- **image**: The degraded input image.
- **psf**: The impulse function, 5×5 average kernel is used here.
- **reg**: The regularization operator, the default of which is Laplacian.

The function returns the **deconvolved** image (**posterior mean**), and a dictionary with the keys **noise** and **prior** (we are not using them here).

Use `scipy.signal` module's `wiener()` function to apply the classic **Wiener deconvolution** to the degraded image, and compare the following output image with the previous one:

```
deconvolved_unsup, _ = restoration.unsupervised_wiener(noisy, psf)
deconvolved = scipy.signal.wiener(noisy, (5,5))
```

Figure 1.15: *Image restoration with scipy.signal implementation of Wiener filter and its unsupervised version*

Non-blind deconvolution with Richardson-Lucy algorithm

The Richardson–Lucy algorithm, also known as **Lucy–Richardson deconvolution** [9], is an iterative procedure for recovering an underlying image that has been blurred by a known point spread function. It is an iterative **Bayesian** algorithm for image restoration. The iterative updation step of the algorithm is shown in the following figure:

$$\underset{\substack{\text{restored}\\\text{iteration } i+1}}{f_{i+1}(x)} = \left\{ \left[\frac{\overset{\text{degraded}}{c(x)}}{\underset{\text{PSF}}{f_i(x) \otimes g(x)}} \right] \otimes g(-x) \right\} \underset{\substack{\text{restored}\\\text{iteration } i}}{f_i(x)}$$

Figure 1.16: *Iterative updation step of the Richardson-Lucy algorithm*

Since the **PSF** $g(x)$ is known, we can just focus on just finding the restored $f(x)$ by iterating over the preceding equation until convergence. An initial guess is required for the restored $f_0(x)$ to start the algorithm. In subsequent iterations, large deviations of the estimate from the true object are reduced rapidly during the early stages, while finer details are recovered more gradually in later iterations. Advantages of this algorithm include a nonnegativity constraint if the initial guess $f_0(x) \geq 0$, and the conservation of total energy as the iteration proceeds.

Now, let us deconvolve a degraded image using **Richardson-Lucy deconvolution** algorithm, using **skimage.restoration** module's implementation. The algorithm is based on a PSF, which is described as the impulse response of the optical system. The blurred image is progressively sharpened through a number of iterations, the number of which (**num_iter**) needs to be hand-tuned.

First, read the input **cameraman** image, convert it to grayscale. Then, convolve the image with a 5×5 box kernel to blur it and add random **Poisson noise** with a rate parameter λ, using the function **np.random.poisson()**, and obtain the degraded image, as shown in the following code snippet:

```
im = color.rgb2gray(imread('images/cameraman.jpg'))
im_noisy = im.copy()
psf = np.ones((5, 5)) / 25
im_noisy = convolve2d(im_noisy, psf, 'same')
im_noisy += (np.random.poisson(lam=25, size=im.shape) - 10) / 255.
```

Next, restore the image with the **Richardson-Lucy** algorithm (with the **non-blind** version and a known **PSF**), using the function **richardson_lucy()** from **scikit-image**'s restoration module, as shown in the next code snippet, try different number of iterations (for example, 20, 50 etc.).

The function accepts the following arguments, and the relevant ones are described as follows:

- **image**: The degraded input image.
- **psf**: The point spread function (blur kernel).
- **num_iter**: Specifies the number of iterations for the update process, acting as a regularization hyperparameter.

The function returns the deconvolved (restored) image as:

```
deconvolved_RL = restoration.richardson_lucy(im_noisy, psf, num_iter=20)
```

Plot the restored images at different iterations, along with the input and noisy image. You should get a figure as follows:

Figure 1.17: Restoring degraded cameraman image with (non-blind) Richardson-Lucy algorithm

Blind deconvolution with Richardson-Lucy algorithm

So far, we have discussed image restoration using **non-blind deconvolution** techniques, where the **PSF** is **known**. In such cases, image restoration reduces to an inverse filtering problem. However, in **blind deconvolution**, where the **PSF** is **unknown**, we need an iterative algorithm that simultaneously estimates the **PSF** and the latent (true) **image**. The **Richardson–Lucy (RL)** algorithm, initially developed for **Maximum Likelihood (ML) deconvolution** under a Poisson noise model, has been extended to handle the blind case through an iterative PSF estimation framework [10].

Mathematical foundation

In standard **non-blind Richardson–Lucy** deconvolution, the image is estimated iteratively by fixing the **known PSF**. For an observed degraded image $c(x)$, the image update is performed as:

$$f^{(k+1)}(x) = f^{(k)}(x) \cdot \left(\frac{c(x)}{(f^{(k)} * g)(x)} * g^\star(-x) \right) \tag{1}$$

Where we have:

- $f^{(k)}(x)$: estimate of the true image at iteration,

- $g(x)$: PSF,
- $*$: convolution operator,
- $g^{*}(-x)$: flipped PSF.

In **blind Richardson–Lucy**, both the true image $f(x)$ and PSF $g(x)$ are unknown and estimated by alternating steps:

- **Image Update**: Fix the PSF g, and update f using Equation (1).
- **PSF Update**: Fix the image f, and compute g using a similar update step:

$$g^{(i+1)}(x) = g^{(i)}(x) \cdot \left(\frac{c(x)}{(f*g^{(i)})(x)} * f^{*}(-x) \right) \qquad (2)$$

This alternation continues for a number of outer iterations. The iteration indices:

- k: image update iteration
- i: PSF update iteration

Algorithm overview

At the k-th outer iteration, assuming the current estimate of the image is f^k, the algorithm:

1. Uses the current PSF estimate g^k to update f^k using the RL formula.
2. Then, using the updated image f^k, updates the PSF g^{k+1}.
3. This alternation is repeated for a fixed number of iterations or until convergence.

Initial guesses are provided for both the image $f_0^0(x)$ and the PSF $g_0^0(x)$, and the aforementioned steps are repeated iteratively.

Code implementation

Let us now implement the **blind Richardson–Lucy deconvolution** using Python. Start by importing the required libraries, as always:

```
from skimage import color, io
from scipy.signal import gaussian, convolve2d
from skimage.metrics import peak_signal_noise_ratio as psnr
import numpy as np
import matplotlib.pyplot as plt
```

Define the function **richardson_lucy_blind()**, it performs **blind image deconvolution** using the **Richardson–Lucy (RL) algorithm**. In blind deconvolution, both the **latent (true) image** $f(x)$, and the **point spread function (PSF)** $g(x)$ are unknown and must be **estimated simultaneously** from a blurred and noisy observation $b(x)$.

The function alternates between:

- **Image update** (fix PSF g, update f).

- **PSF update** (fix image f, update g).

This is done over **n_psf_updates** outer iterations (i.e., blind updates), and within each outer iteration, the image is updated for **n_image_updates** inner iterations (assuming the current PSF is correct), as shown in the next code snippet. The next table summarizes the algorithm steps executed inside the function:

Step	Purpose	Equation
Image update	Refine latent image f using current PSF g	$f^{(k+1)} = f^{(k)} \cdot \left(\dfrac{b}{f * g} * g^{\star} \right)$
PSF update	Refine blur kernel g using current image f	$g^{(i+1)} = g^{(i)} \cdot \left(\dfrac{b}{f * g} * f^{\star} \right)$
Normalization	Ensure PSF validity	$\sum_x g(x) = 1, \; g(x) \geq 0$

Table 1.1: Algorithm steps executed inside the function

The function returns the restored image and estimated PSF, as shown in the following code snippet:

```python
def richardson_lucy_blind(b, f_init, g_init, \
                          n_psf_updates=10, n_image_updates=10):
    """
    Blind Richardson-Lucy deconvolution (corrected version).

    Parameters:
        b : 2D np.ndarray
            Blurred and noisy input image.
        f_init : 2D np.ndarray
            Initial guess for the true image.
        g_init : 2D np.ndarray
            Initial guess for the PSF (must be normalized).
        n_psf_updates : int
            Number of outer iterations (PSF updates).
        n_image_updates : int
            Number of inner iterations (image updates).
    Returns:
        f : 2D np.ndarray
            Restored image.
        g : 2D np.ndarray
            Estimated PSF.
    """

    eps = 1e-7  # Small constant to prevent division by zero
    f = f_init.copy()
    g = g_init.copy()

    for i in range(n_psf_updates):
```

```
        # --- Fix PSF and update image ---
        for k in range(n_image_updates):
            conv_fg = convolve2d(f, g, mode='same', boundary='wrap')
            relative_blur = b / (conv_fg + eps)
            correction = convolve2d(relative_blur, \
                              np.flip(np.flip(g, axis=0), axis=1), \
                              mode='same', boundary='wrap')
            f *= correction
        # --- Fix image and update PSF ---
        conv_fg = convolve2d(f, g, mode='same', boundary='wrap')
        relative_blur = b / (conv_fg + eps)
        g *= convolve2d(f, relative_blur, mode='valid', boundary='wrap')

        # Normalize PSF to maintain energy
        g = np.clip(g, 0, None)   # Ensure non-negative
        g /= np.sum(g)
    return f, g
```

Read the *Lena* grayscale image as input. Apply 5×5 Gaussian kernel (using the function **gaussian_kernel()**) to blur the image and add Gaussian noise (using the function **np.random.randn()**) to degrade the image, as shown in the following code snippet:

```
def gaussian_kernel(size=5, sigma=1):
    """Generates a 2D Gaussian kernel."""
    g1d = gaussian(size, std=sigma)
    kernel = np.outer(g1d, g1d)
    kernel /= np.sum(kernel)   # Normalize
    return kernel

im = io.imread('images/lena.jpg', True)
psf_true = gaussian_kernel(5, 5) #np.ones((5,5)) / 25
blurred = convolve2d(im, psf_true, 'same', boundary='wrap')
noisy = blurred + 0.25 * np.random.randn(*blurred.shape)
```

Initialize the image estimate (**f_init**) with the degraded image itself, and the PSF estimate (**g_init**) with a flat box kernel to start with. Invoke the function **richardson_lucy_blind()** to apply the blind deconvolution to the degraded image for simultaneous estimation of the blur kernel (**g_estimated**) and restoration of the image (**f_restored**), as shown in the following code snippet:

```
# Initial guesses
f_init = noisy.copy()
g_init = np.ones((5,5)) / 25   # flat guess
g_init = np.random.random((5, 5))
g_init /= np.sum(g_init)

# Perform blind deconvolution
f_restored, g_estimated = richardson_lucy_blind(noisy, f_init, g_init)
```

Plot the restored image along with the original and the degraded images (compute the PSNR values), and you should obtain a figure like the one shown as follows (note the increase in PSNR in the restored image):

Figure 1.18: Restoring degraded Lena image with (blind) Richardson-Lucy algorithm

Total variation denoising

TV denoising is a classical image processing technique that aims to restore images while preserving important features like edges. It is based on the idea that natural images typically have sparse gradients — meaning, they are mostly piecewise smooth with sharp transitions at edges. TV methods seek to exploit this property by minimizing the total variation norm, promoting solutions that are smooth in homogeneous regions while maintaining sharp discontinuities.

TV denoising methods assume that the high total variation in signals is caused by excessive/spurious detail. The goal is to remove unwanted but preserve important details (for example, edges) in the image by reducing the total variation of the (degraded) image so that it remains a close match to the original image. This is known as the **Rudin-Osher-Fatemi (ROF)** model [5]. The original TV regularization method targeted image denoising under Gaussian noise, nevertheless it has evolved into a more general technique for inverse problems.

In this section we shall use functions from `skimage.restoration` to implement TV denoising.

TV denoising with Rudin-Osher-Fatemi algorithm

TV regularization is a technique that was originally developed for **Additive White Gaussian Noise (AWGN)** image denoising by *Rudin, Osher,* and *Fatemi*. They proposed to estimate the denoised image u as the solution of the following minimization problem:

$$\underset{u \in BV(\Omega)}{min} \|u\|_{TV(\Omega)} + \frac{\lambda}{2} \int_{\Omega} (f(x) - u(x))^2 dx$$

where λ is a positive parameter, here the first term is for **regularization** and the second term represents the **data fidelity** term, which depends on the noise model. This L_2-*TV* the problem is referred to as the **ROF** problem.

Denoising is performed as an infinite-dimensional minimization problem, where the search space is all **Bounded Variation (BV)** images. $BV(\Omega)$ refers the family of functions (with bounded variation) over the domain Ω, $TV(\Omega)$ is the total variation over the domain, and λ is a penalty term. When u is smooth, the total variation is equivalent to the integral of the gradient magnitude:

$$\|u\|_{TV(\Omega)} = \int_{\Omega} \|\nabla u\| dx$$

Where $\|\cdot\|$ is the Euclidean norm. Then, the objective function of the minimization problem becomes:

$$\underset{u \in BV(\Omega)}{min} \int_{\Omega} \left[\|\nabla u\| + \frac{\lambda}{2}(f - u)^2 \right] dx$$

Using the **Euler-Lagrange equation** for minimization of the preceding functional [6] results in the following **Partial Differential Equation (PDE)**:

$$\begin{cases} \nabla.\left(\frac{\nabla u}{\|\nabla u\|}\right) + \lambda(f - u) = 0, & u \in \Omega \\ \frac{\partial u}{\partial n} = 0, & u \in \partial\Omega \end{cases}$$

Here is the time-dependent version of the ROF equation:

$$\frac{\partial u}{\partial t} = \nabla.\left(\frac{\nabla u}{\|\nabla u\|}\right) + \lambda(f - u)$$

In this section, you will learn how to denoise an image with **scikit-image** implementation of TV denoising, using the algorithm proposed by **Chambolle**, as shown in the following figure:

$$\text{TV}: \quad J(u) = \sum_{1 \leq i,j \leq N} |(\nabla u)_{i,j}|$$

$$\text{solve} \quad \underset{u \in X}{min} \frac{\|u - g\|^2}{2\lambda} + J(u)$$

$$\text{by} \quad u = g - \lambda \left(I + \frac{1}{\lambda}\partial J^*\right)^{-1} \left(\frac{g}{\lambda}\right)$$

$$\text{where} \quad J^*(v) = \sup \langle u, v \rangle_X - J(u)$$
$$\text{Legendre–Fenchel transform}$$

Figure 1.19: *TV denoising algorithm by Chambolle*

TV denoising tries to minimize the total variation of an image (which is roughly equivalent to the integral of the norm of image gradient) and often produces cartoon-like (piecewise-constant) images.

Let us start by importing the required libraries, using the following code snippet. Notice that the version of the **scikit-image** library must be ≥ 0.14.

```python
import skimage
print(skimage.__version__) # should be >= 0.14
from skimage.restoration import denoise_tv_chambolle
# 0.17.2
```

Read the image, convert it to a grayscale, and add Gaussian noise to the image using the function **np.random.normal()** as follows:

```python
im = 255*rgb2gray(imread('images/cameraman.jpg'))
noisy = im + np.random.normal(loc=0, scale=im.std() / 4, size=im.shape)
```

Use the function **denoise_tv_chambolle()** from **scikit-image restoration** module to implement **TV denoising**. The function accepts the following arguments:

- **image**: Input image to be denoised.

- **weight**: Denoising weight. Larger weight results in more denoising (at the cost of fidelity to the input image).

- **n_iter_max**: Maximum number of iteration steps to be run to optimize.

It returns the denoised image. The following code snippet shows how the function can be used to denoise the noisy **cameraman** grayscale image. The denoising strength is controlled by the weight parameter; higher values result in stronger smoothing. Different values of weight (10, 25, 50, and 100) are tested to observe the effect on image quality:

```python
for weight in [10, 25, 50, 100]:
    tv_denoised = denoise_tv_chambolle(noisy, weight=weight)
```

The following figure shows the original, noisy, and TV-denoised images with a couple of different weights:

Figure 1.20: TV denoising of the noisy cameraman image (with scikit-image's Chambolle implementation)

As shown in *Figure 1.20*, as we go on increasing the **weights**, we get more **denoising** effect, at the cost of **fidelity** to the input image (for example, **texture flattening**).

TV denoising with Chambolle vs. Bregman

In this section, we shall implement total-variation denoising with **split Bregman** optimization [5], using **skimage.restore** module functions. As discussed, TV denoising, also called TV regularization, seeks to recover a denoised image (u) from a noisy image (f) by minimizing the total variation energy (formulated by the **ROF** model)

$$\min_{u} \frac{1}{2} \| u - f \|_2^2 + \lambda \| \nabla u \|_1$$

- The first term $\frac{1}{2} \| u - f \|_2^2$ encourages similarity to the observed image.

- The second term $\| \nabla u \|_1$ penalizes large gradients, preserving edges while smoothing out noise.

- λ is a regularization parameter that controls the trade-off between the two.

Difficulty

The mix of the ℓ2 term (smooth, differentiable) and the ℓ1 term (non-smooth) makes direct optimization difficult.

How the Split Bregman method helps

The **Split Bregman** method reformulates the problem by introducing an auxiliary variable $d \approx \nabla u$, which splits the problem into more manageable subproblems:

$$\min_u \frac{1}{2} \parallel u - f \parallel_2^2 + \lambda \parallel \nabla u \parallel_1, \text{ subject to } d = \nabla u$$

This constraint is incorporated using **Bregman iteration**, leading to the following **iterative scheme** and the optimization problem is solved in an iterative fashion. The Split Bregman method breaks the problem into easier parts:

1. It introduces a new variable d to **split** the gradient from the image.

2. Then it solves the problem step by step, alternating between:

    a. Updating the image u (solving a smooth least-squares problem).

    b. Updating the gradient d (using a soft thresholding / shrinkage rule).

    c. Adjusting a helper variable b (**Bregman variable**) that guides convergence.

This results in **fast, stable optimization**—ideal for problems involving total variation and sparsity.

As described in the last section, **Chambolle**'s algorithm solves the **ROF TV denoising model**. But instead of introducing an auxiliary variable like Bregman, it directly **solves the dual problem**. The method uses **dual variable projection** to enforce the constraint, thereby avoiding the ℓ1-non-differentiability directly. It works well and is simple to implement for denoising tasks. The following table compares these two methods:

Feature	Chambolle's method	Split Bregman
Formulation	Dual (solves dual ROF problem)	Primal with variable splitting
Handles constraints?	Yes, via projection (dual norm ≤ 1)	Yes, via soft-thresholding + penalty
Auxiliary variables?	No	Yes (d, b variables)
Flexibility	Mostly for TV denoising	More general (inpainting, CS, etc.)
Update types	Gradient descent + projection	Alternating minimization (shrinkage + least squares)
Convergence	Fast and stable for basic TV	Fast, scalable to more complex problems

Table 1.2: Comparison of Chambolle's method and split Bregman

Now, let us use `skimage.restoration` module's implementation of the preceding algorithms to recover a degraded image. Let us start by importing the required libraries using the following line of code:

```
from skimage.restoration import denoise_tv_chambolle, denoise_tv_bregman
```

Read the image, convert it to grayscale, and add Gaussian noise to the image to create the degraded version, this time using the **random_noise()** function from **skimage.util** as follows:

```
img = img_as_float(imread('images/zelda.png'))
noisy = random_noise(img, var=0.02)
noisy = np.clip(noisy, 0, 1)
```

We shall use the function **denoise_tv_bregman()** from **scikit-image** restore module for **split-Bregman** method. This function accepts the following arguments:

- **image**: Degraded input image (converted to **float** with pixel values in [0,1] using **img_as_float**).

- **weight**: Denoising weight, the regularization parameter lambda is chosen as **2 * weight**.

- **isotropic**: False if anisotropic TV denoising.

- **channel_axis**: For color images, specify the color channel (for example, the last channel, i.e., -1), TV denoising is applied separately for each channel.

The function returns a denoised image.

The following code snippet shows how the function can be used to denoise the RGB color image of Zelda, for different weights and modes (**isotropic** vs. **anisotropic**), then compares it with the one obtained by denoising with TV **Chambolle**, and evaluates the quality of the restored images using **PSNR** values (with the function **peak_signal_noise_ratio()** from **skimage.metrics** module):

```
def plot_image(img, title):
    plt.imshow(img), plt.axis('off'), plt.title(title, size=20)

plt.figure(figsize=(20,22))
plt.subplot(331), plot_image(img, 'Original')
plt.subplot(332), plot_image(noisy, 'Noisy, PSNR: {}' \
                             .format(np.round(psnr(img, noisy),3)))
i = 3
for weight in [0.1, 0.25]:
    tvd_out = denoise_tv_chambolle(noisy, weight=weight, channel_axis=-1)
    plt.subplot(3,3,i)
    plot_image(tvd_out, 'TVD Chambolle (w={}), PSNR: {}' \
                        .format(weight, np.round(psnr(img, tvd_out),3)))
    i += 1

for weight in [10, 7]:
    for isotropic in [False, True]:
        tvd_out = denoise_tv_bregman(noisy, weight=weight, isotropic=isotropic, \
```

```
                                              channel_axis=-1)
plt.subplot(3,3,i)

plot_image(tvd_out, 'TVD Bregman (w={}), PSNR: {}, iso: {}'.format(weight,\
                np.round(psnr(img, tvd_out),3), str(isotropic)[0]))
        i += 1

plt.subplots_adjust(wspace=0.05, hspace=0.05, top=0.95, bottom=0, left=0, right=1)
plt.show()
```

If you run the preceding code snippet, you should obtain a figure as follows:

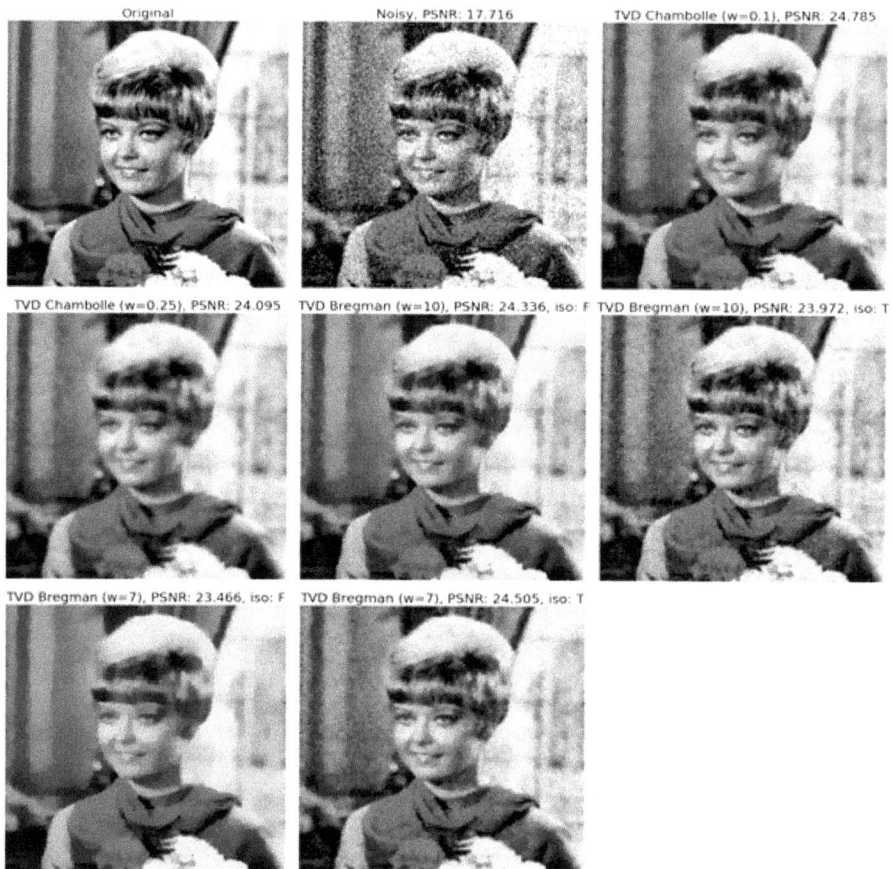

Figure 1.21: *TV denoising of the noisy Zelda image (with scikit-image's Chambolle vs. Bregman method)*

Image denoising with wavelets

Wavelets provide a powerful and general framework for representing and analyzing multiresolution images. An image can be reconstructed by summing over its Laplacian pyramid levels. Wavelets extend this idea by offering a **mathematically grounded basis** for such decomposition.

A **wavelet** is a localized wave-like oscillation with **zero mean** and **finite energy**, defined over a finite duration. Wavelets [17] represent the scale of features in an image, as well as their position. Unlike sinusoids in the **Fourier basis**, wavelets decay rapidly and are capable of capturing both **spatial** (or temporal) and **frequency** information. This makes them especially effective in representing abrupt transitions and localized features in signals and images.

Formally, wavelets form an **orthonormal basis** for $L^2(\mathbb{R})$, the space of square-integrable functions, allowing a function $f(t)$ to be expressed as: $f(t) = \sum_{j,k} c_{j,k}\psi_{j,k}(t)$, where $\psi_{j,k}(t) = 2^{j/2}\psi(2^j t - k)$ is the scaled and shifted version of the *mother wavelet* , with **scale** and **translation** k.

The key concepts in wavelets are:

- **Scaling (dilation)**: Controls the resolution. A wavelet scaled by a factor $s > 0$ is $\psi(t/s)$. Larger s captures coarse features (low frequency); smaller captures fine features (high frequency).

- **Shifting (translation)**: Moves the wavelet along the signal: $\psi(t - k)$, enabling localization in space or time.

- **Dyadic scales and shifts (powers of 2)**: We do not need continuous scale shifts— dyadic decomposition suffices: $\psi_{j,k}(x) = 2^{j/2}\psi(2^j x - k)$, $j, k \in Z$.

We do not need to calculate wavelet coefficients at every possible scale. We can choose scales based on powers of 2, i.e., 2^j and translation as $2^j x$, with $j, x \in \{1,2,3,...\}$ and get equivalent accuracy.

In **multiresolution analysis (MRA)**, which underpins the wavelet transform:

- The signal space is decomposed into nested subspaces Vj, each representing the signal at a particular resolution or scale.

- The **scaling function** ϕ(t) spans the **approximation space** Vj. It captures the **coarse** (low-frequency) components of the signal.

- The wavelet function ψ(t), on the other hand, spans the **detail space** Wj, capturing the **high-frequency** or **detail** components.

A discrete function $f(n)$ thus be approximated as a sum of scaled and translated wavelets $\psi(n)$, plus a coarse approximation $\phi(n)$, as shown in the following figure [8]:

$$f(n) = \frac{1}{\sqrt{M}}\sum_k W_\varphi(j_0,k)\varphi_{j_0,k}(n) + \frac{1}{\sqrt{M}}\sum_{j=j_0}^{\infty}\sum_k W_\psi(j,k)\psi_{j,k}(n)$$

"Approximation" coefficients	"Detail" coefficients
$W_\phi(j_0,k) = \frac{1}{\sqrt{M}}\sum_x f(x)\varphi_{j_0,k}(x)$	$W_\psi(j,k) = \frac{1}{\sqrt{M}}\sum_x f(x)\psi_{j,k}(x)$

Figure 1.22: Approximation of a function by wavelets

Here j_0 is an arbitrary starting scale, and $n = 0,1,2,\dots,M$. The preceding represents x the DWT for a 1-D signal x, an image being a 2D signal, we need a 2D DWT instead. The concept **extends naturally** to 2D signals such as images using **tensor products** of 1D wavelets.

The 2D DWT decomposes an image into four components at each scale:

- **LL**: Approximation ($\phi \otimes \phi$)
- **LH**: Horizontal detail ($\phi \otimes \psi$)
- **HL**: Vertical detail ($\psi \otimes \phi$)
- **HH**: Diagonal detail ($\psi \otimes \psi$)

This is done by applying the 1D DWT along **rows and then columns** of the image.

Mathematically, a 2D function $f(x, y)$ can be expressed as:

$$f(x,y) = \sum_{j,k,l} a_{j,k,l}\phi_{j,k}(x)\phi_{j,l}(y) + \sum_{j,k,l} d^H_{j,k,l}\phi_{j,k}(x)\psi_{j,l}(y) +$$

$$\sum_{j,k,l} d^V_{j,k,l}\psi_{j,k}(x)\phi_{j,l}(y) + \sum_{j,k,l} d^D_{j,k,l}\psi_{j,k}(x)\psi_{j,l}(y)$$

Where we have,

- $a_{j,k,l}$: Approximation coefficients (LL)
- $d^H_{j,k,l}, d^{HV}_{j,k,l}, d^D_{j,k,l}$: Horizontal, vertical, diagonal detail coefficients

Discrete wavelet transform

The basic ingredient in **discrete wavelet transform** (**DWT**) is the MRA. The main point is that the wavelet coefficients encode local information about the image in a way that makes it possible to discard all coefficients with absolute values below a given threshold and still be able to reconstruct the signal (image) with acceptable accuracy (allowing a sparse representation).

Again, an image, being a 2D function, can be represented by a sum of approximation plus details. The 2D DWT decomposes an image into approximation and details (for example, horizontal, vertical, and diagonal details) at different scales/levels (using downsampling at Nyquist rate) recursively.

Similarly, IDWT reconstructs the images from the approximate and detailed coefficients at different scales (using upsampling), as shown in the following figure:

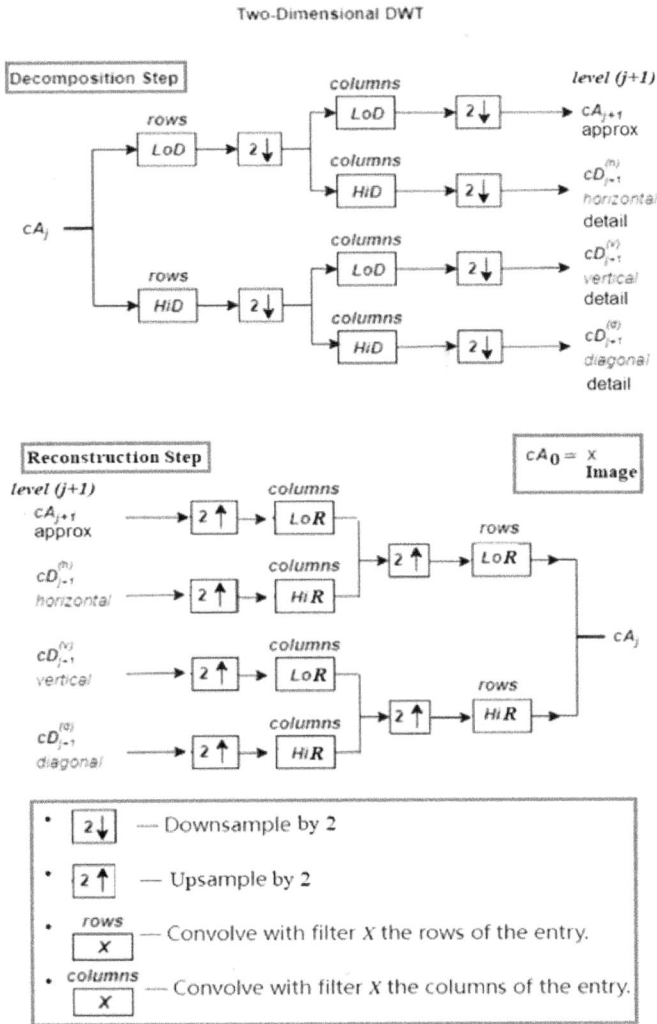

Figure 1.23: *Image reconstruction with 2D discrete wavelet transform and its inverse*

Thus, wavelet transforms enable sparse representation and are widely used in **denoising, compression, image fusion**, and **feature extraction**.

Summarizing, the general steps in wavelet-based image processing include:

- Compute the 2D **discrete wavelet transform (DWT)**.
- Modify the **transform coefficients** (for example, for denoising or compression).
- Compute the **inverse discrete wavelet transform (IDWT)** for reconstruction.

Wavelets come in different sizes and shapes; the following figure shows a few well-known families of wavelet basis functions (there are many others), they need to be chosen carefully based on the application:

Wavelet Family	Short Name	Mother Wavelet $\psi(t)$	Scaling Function $\phi(t)$	Key Properties	Typical Applications
Haar	`'haar'`	$\psi(t) = \begin{cases} 1 & 0 \le t < 0.5 \\ -1 & 0.5 \le t < 1 \\ 0 & \text{otherwise} \end{cases}$	$\phi(t) = \begin{cases} 1 & 0 \le t < 1 \\ 0 & \text{otherwise} \end{cases}$	Simple, orthogonal, compact support	Basic signal processing, image compression
Daubechies	`'dbN'`	Defined via recursion; no simple closed-form	Defined via recursion; no simple closed-form	Orthogonal, compact support, varying vanishing moments	Signal and image compression, denoising
Symlets	`'symN'`	Similar to Daubechies but more symmetric	Similar to Daubechies but more symmetric	Symmetric, orthogonal, compact	Image processing, denoising
Coiflets	`'coifN'`	Designed to have both $\psi(t)$ and $\phi(t)$ with vanishing moments	Designed to have both $\psi(t)$ and $\phi(t)$ with vanishing moments	Orthogonal, compact support, vanishing moments for both scaling and wavelet functions	Signal analysis, denoising
Biorthogonal	`'bior'`	Constructed to have linear phase and symmetry	Constructed to have linear phase and symmetry	Biorthogonal, symmetric, linear phase	Image compression (e.g., JPEG2000)

Figure 1.24: *Wavelet families*

The following figure shows how the function **wavedec2()** (which implements **2D DWT**) from the Python package **pywt** works (at *level = n*):

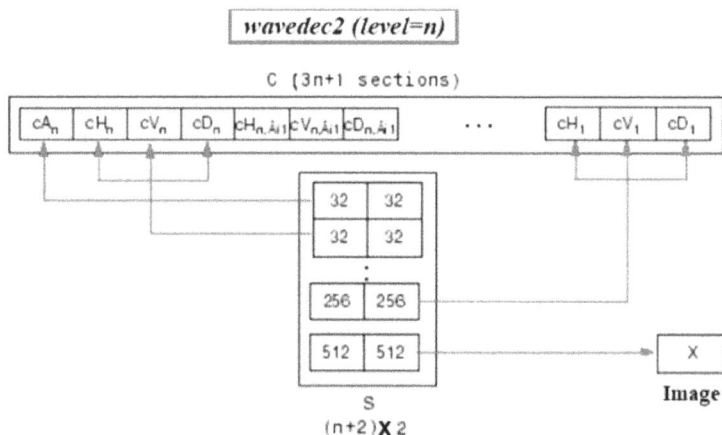

Figure 1.25: *The function wavedec2() from the python package pywt*

In this section, we will see how an image can be denoised and restored using wavelets (**DWT**), first using the DWT implementation from the library **pywt** and then using the corresponding implementation from **skimage.restoration**.

Wavelet-denoising with pywt

Thresholding is a nonlinear technique, yet it is very simple because it operates on one wavelet coefficient at a time. The key idea is to choose a threshold value (for example, **Donoho-Johnstone universal threshold**) and zero out the wavelet coefficients obtained from multilevel DWT below the threshold, in order to remove noise from the degraded input image.

In this section, you will learn how to use the functions from the library **pywt** to denoise an image using **thresholding** the **wavelet coefficients** of a degraded image. Wavelet denoising has the following steps:

1. Perform a **multilevel wavelet decomposition** (use **wavedecn()** from **pywt**).

2. Identify a **thresholding** technique (**soft** or **hard** thresholding **mode**).

3. Threshold (using the **threshold()** function from **pywt**) and reconstruct (use **waverecn()** from **pywt**).

Let us start by importing the **pywt** library:

```
import pywt
```

Read the grayscale input image of **beans** and degrade it by adding Gaussian noise with:

```
noise_sigma = 0.1
im = rgb2gray(imread('images/a.jpg'))
noisy = im + np.random.normal(0, noise_sigma, size=im.shape)
```

Let us perform multilevel wavelet decomposition using the function **wavedecn()**, which accepts the input image, the name of the wavelet family (**db1**) and number of levels (=2 here) of decomposition. This function provides a generalized implementation of DWT for n-dimensional data (including 2D, 3D, etc.), whereas **wavedec2()** performs 2D DWT on 2D data (for example, grayscale images), also **wavedecn()** returns more structured coefficient access.

Let us plot the **approximate** and **detailed** coefficients at different scales by using the function **coeffs_to_array()**, by arranging the wavelet coefficients list obtained from **wavedecn()** in a single array, using the next code snippet:

```
levels = 2
wavelet = 'db1'
coeffs = pywt.wavedecn(im, wavelet=wavelet, level=levels)
arr, _ = pywt.coeffs_to_array(coeffs)

plt.figure(figsize=(20,20))
plt.imshow(arr, cmap='gray')
plt.title('Discrete Wavelet Transform Coefficient for db1 Wavelet for level 3', \
          size=20)
plt.show()
```

If you run the preceding code snippet, you should obtain a figure like the following one:

Figure 1.26: Multilevel wavelet decomposition with db1 wavelet family

Implement **wavelet denoising** with **thresholding**: define the **denoise()** function that accepts the degraded image, the name of the **wavelet basis** to be used, the **noise standard deviation** σ, and the **mode** of **thresholding** (hard or soft).

Threshold the detail (i.e., high frequency) coefficients using a **Donoho-Johnstone universal threshold** $t_n = \sigma\sqrt{2\log n}$, here n refers to the number of elements in the detail coefficients.

Hard thresholding sets coefficients below the threshold to zero, while **soft thresholding** shrinks all coefficients toward zero by the threshold value. The following figure demonstrates the difference between soft and hard thresholding:

data values (x)	soft thresholding	hard thresholding
with absolute value < thresholding value (t)	replaced with substitute	replaced with substitute
with absolute value ≥ thresholding value (t)	shrunk toward zero	stay untouched

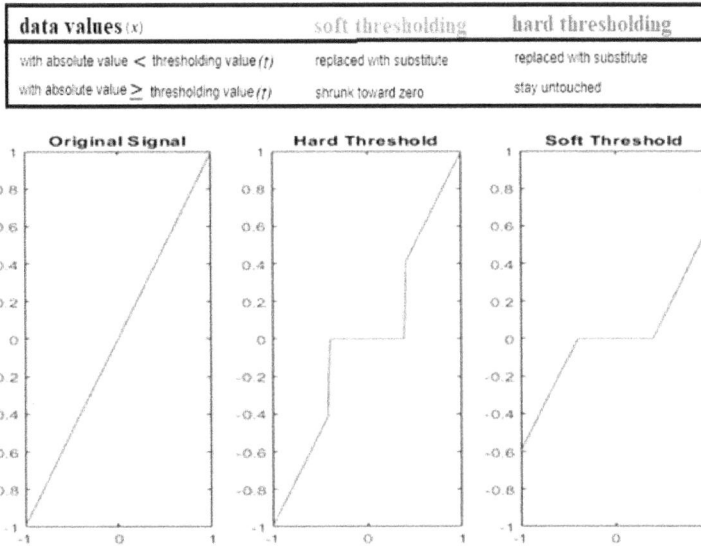

Figure 1.27: Soft vs. hard thresholding for a signal

In soft thresholding with threshold value (t), the data (x) is replaced by $sgn(x)(|x| - t)_+$, i.e., with python expression **data/np.abs(data) * np.maximum(np.abs(data) - value, 0)** [18].

Invoke the function **denoise()** with appropriate arguments to obtain a smoothed image with different types of wavelets, starting from the degraded **beans** image, using the following code snippet:

```python
def denoise(img, wavelet, noise_sigma, mode='soft'):
    levels = int(np.floor(np.log2(img.shape[0])))
    coeffs = pywt.wavedecn(img, wavelet, level=3) #levels)
    threshold = noise_sigma*np.sqrt(2*np.log2(img.size))
    denoised_detail = [{key: pywt.threshold(level[key], value=threshold, \
                mode=mode) for key in level} for level in coeffs[1:]]
    denoised_root = pywt.threshold(coeffs[0], value=threshold, mode=mode)
    denoised_coeffs = [denoised_root] + [d for d in denoised_detail]
    out = pywt.waverecn(denoised_coeffs, wavelet)
    return out

im = rgb2gray(imread('images/beans.jpg'))
noisy = im + np.random.normal(0, noise_sigma, size=im.shape)
im_denoised_haar = denoise(noisy, wavelet='haar', noise_sigma=noise_sigma)
im_denoised_haar_hard = denoise(noisy, wavelet='haar', noise_sigma=noise_sigma, \
                                                    mode='hard')
im_denoised_db6 = denoise(noisy, wavelet='db6', noise_sigma=noise_sigma)
```

Plot the restored image using different wavelet families of basis functions (for example, **haar, db6, bior2.8, coif2**) and different modes of thresholding (**hard** vs. **soft**), along with the original and the degraded images. You should obtain a figure like the following one:

Figure 1.28: Image denoising using different wavelet families with hard vs. soft thresholding

Wavelet-denoising with scikit-image

In this section, you will learn how to use wavelet-based denoising functions from **skimage. restoration** module. Similar to the frequency domain in DFT, the wavelet domain is yet another domain corresponding to a sparse representation of the image (with the majority of values zero and true random noise represented using many small values). For denoising, the usual approach is to set all values below a threshold (t) to 0. If the threshold used is large, it can additionally remove the finer details in the image. In a multichannel (3D) input image, wavelet denoising is performed on each color plane separately.

Let us start by importing the required functions from **scikit-image** library's **restoration** module:

```
from skimage.restoration import (denoise_wavelet, estimate_sigma)
```

Read the (RGB) color input image and degrade it with Gaussian noise, using the **random_ noise()** function, as shown in the next code snippet.

Use the function **estimate_sigma()** from **skimage.restoration** module to estimate noise standard deviation (it estimates by analyzing high-frequency components in the degraded image using a wavelet-based approach) for different color channels.

The estimated standard deviation is expected to a bit smaller than the specified , due to clipping in **random_noise()**.

Use the function **denoise_wavelet()** to apply the wavelet denoising on the degraded image. The following are few of the arguments it accepts:

- **image**: Input image to be denoised.

- **sigma**: The noise standard deviation. It is used to compute detail coefficient thresholds.

- **wavelet**: The algorithm (type of wavelet) to be used, **db1** being the default one.

- **mode**: Type of denoising, can be **soft** or **hard**. Soft thresholding finds the best approximation of the original image from the input noisy image, given the noise is additive.

- **convert2ycbcr**: Set to **True**, to perform wavelet denoising in **YCbCr** colorspace given multichannel (RGB color) input image, yielding better results often.

- **method**: Refers to the thresholding method to be used, which can be either of **BayesShrink** or **VisuShrink**.

The function **denoise_wavelet()** applies **BayesShrink** thresholding by default. Separate thresholds for each of wavelet sub-bands are computed in this adaptive thresholding method.

The **VisuShrink** thresholding, on the other hand, applies a single universal threshold to all of the wavelet detail coefficients. It removes all Gaussian noise with a given s.d. (σ) with high probability, but it is also prone to produce overly-smooth images.

Use different scale factors (for example, 2, 3, 4) with estimated σ (**sigma_est**) to decrease the threshold by these factors and observe the impact on the denoised image.

Compute **PSNR** as an indication of the denoised output image quality, given the input *noisy* image.

Plot the denoised images using different methods and thresholding modes, along with their **psnr** values as follows:

```
original = img_as_float(imread('images/cat.jpg'))
sigma = 0.12
noisy = random_noise(original, var=sigma**2)
sigma_est = estimate_sigma(noisy, average_sigmas=True, channel_axis=-1)
print(f'Estimated Gaussian noise standard deviation = {sigma_est}')
# Estimated Gaussian noise standard deviation = 0.1208983266753569

im_bayes = denoise_wavelet(noisy, convert2ycbcr=True, method='BayesShrink', \
                           mode='soft', rescale_sigma=True, channel_axis=-1)
psnr_noisy, psnr_bayes = psnr(original, noisy), psnr(original, im_bayes)
for sigma in [sigma_est/2, sigma_est/3, sigma_est/4]:
    im_visushrink = denoise_wavelet(noisy,convert2ycbcr=True,method='VisuShrink', \
                mode='soft', sigma=sigma, rescale_sigma=True, channel_axis=-1)
    psnr_visushrink = psnr(original, im_visushrink)
    # plot the denoised output images im_visushrink and psnr_visushrink here
    # TODO: your code here, by now you can write code to plot images.
```

If you plot the denoised output images, you should obtain a figure as follows:

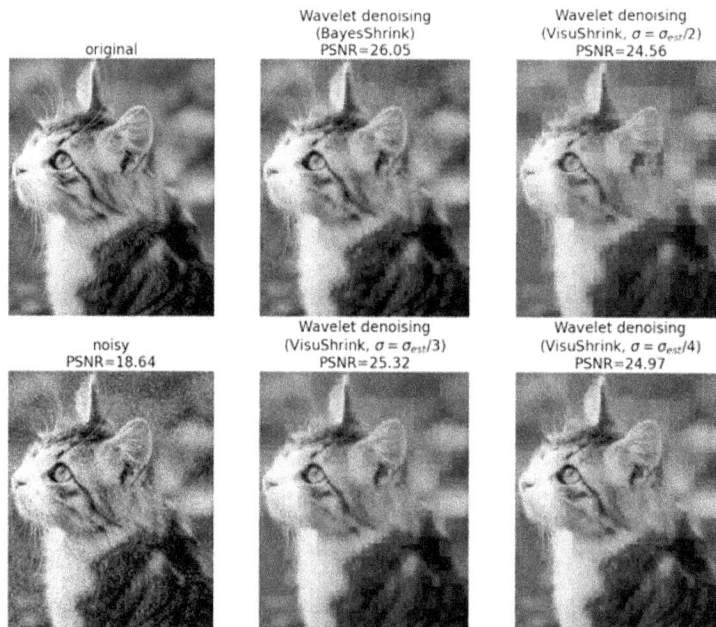

Figure 1.29: Wavelet denoising with BayesShrink vs. ViruShrink thresholding

scikit-image internally uses **pywavelets** for the implementation. The thresholding methods assume an orthogonal wavelet transform (for example, **Daubechies - db2**, **symmlet - sym2** families); they are desirable for the following reasons:

- They ensure the white noise in the input remains white noise in the subbands (as opposed to the **biorthogonal** wavelets that produce colored noise in the subbands).

- In **pywavelets**, the orthogonal wavelets are also orthonormal, and hence, the noise variance in the subbands remains the same as that of input.

Denoising using non-local means with opencv-python

The principle of the first denoising method suggests replacing the color of a pixel with an average of the colors of nearby (**local**) pixels. While simple local averaging reduces noise, it also tends to blur important image details. According to the **law of variance of the mean** in probability theory, averaging n **independent** and **identically distributed** (**i.i.d.**) random variables each with variance σ^2 results in a mean with variance $\frac{\sigma^2}{n}$, and thus a standard deviation of $\frac{\sigma}{\sqrt{n}}$. That is, averaging multiple independent noisy observations reduces the variance—for example, averaging nine independent pixels reduces the standard deviation of the noise by a factor of three.

However, in real images, the most similar pixels to a given pixel may not be spatially close to it. This insight is the foundation of the **non-local means (NLM)** denoising algorithm, which improves upon local methods by scanning a larger region of the image to find all patches that closely resemble the one centered around the target pixel. Denoising is then done by computing the average color of these most resembling pixels, weighted the similarity of these pixels to the target pixel. It reduces the loss of detail (blurring) in the denoised image (when compared to its local counterpart), at the cost of more computation time.

Formally, a denoising method D_h applied to a noisy image v can be defined as a decomposition $v = D_h v + n(D_h, v)$, where is a filtering parameter which usually depends on the the noise variance σ^2. Ideally, $D_h v$ is smoother than v and $n(D_h, v)$ (i.e., the noise guessed by the method, defined as the method noise) should look like the realization of a white noise [20].

Given a noisy image $v = \{v(i) | i \in I\}$, the estimated value $NL[v](i)$, for a pixel i, is computed as a weighted average: $NL[v](i) = \sum_{j \in I} w(i,j) v(j)$, where the family of weights $\{w(i,j)\}_j$ depend on the similarity between the neighborhoods (patches) N_i and N_j, centered at pixels i and j. These weights satisfy the usual conditions: $0 \leq w(i,j) \leq 1$ and $\sum_j w(i,j) = 1$. The similarity between two pixels i and j depends on the similarity of the intensity gray level vectors $v(N_i)$ and $v(N_j)$, where N_k denotes a square neighborhood (patch) of fixed size and centered at a pixel k.

The similarity is usually measured as the **Gaussian-weighted Euclidean distance** between the patches $v(N_i)$ and $v(N_j)$, and the weights are computed as:

$$w(i,j) = \frac{1}{Z(i)} exp\left(-\frac{\| v(N_i) - v(N_j) \|_2^2}{h^2}\right)$$

Where $Z(i)$ is a normalizing constant to ensure that weights sum to 1.

In summary, the **NLM** algorithm considers a patch around each pixel, searches for similar patches throughout a larger region, averages them using similarity-based weights, and replaces the central pixel accordingly. Unlike local methods, the residual noise in NLM tends to resemble white noise—making it less visually distracting.

In this section, we explore how to apply **OpenCV's cv2.fastNlMeansDenoisingColored()** function to perform such denoising in practice. The function first converts the image from RGB colorspace to CIELAB (**Commission Internationale de l'Éclairage Lab***, where **L*** represents lightness, and **a*** and **b*** represent color-opponent dimensions). It then denoises *L* and *AB* channels separately using the function **cv2.fastNlMeansDenoising()**. The function accepts the following arguments:

- **src**: The input image, here the *Zelda* RGB color image is used.
- **templateWindowSize**: The template **patch size** (in pixels) to be used to compute weights.

- **searchWindowSize**: Size of the window to be used to compute the weighted average for a given pixel (the larger the window, the slower the filter).

- **h**: Controls filter strength for *L* (luminance) channel. Larger *h* removes noise along with image details.

- **hColor**: Same as *h* for color components. For most images having $hColor = 10$ is enough to remove colored noise without color distortion.

The function returns the denoised image.

Let us now proceed to use the aforementioned function to denoise a noisy color input image. First load the RGB color image of *Zelda* and degrade it with Gaussian noise, using **cv2.randn()** as follows:

```
import cv2

img = cv2.imread('images/zelda.jpg')
noisy = img + cv2.randn(np.copy(img), (0,0,0),(10,10,10))
```

The following code snippet demonstrates the use of the function on the noisy color input image for different values of parameters **searchWindow** (for example, 15, 21) and **h** (for example, 7, 10, 15). Plot and compare the denoised output image's quality with *PSNR* and also compare the time taken to denoise, you should obtain a figure like *Figure 1.30*:

```
for sz in [15, 21]:
    for h in [7, 10, 15]:
        start = time()
        dst = cv2.fastNlMeansDenoisingColored(noisy, None, \
                    templateWindowSize=12, searchWindowSize=sz, h=h, hColor=10)
        end = time()
        # plot the denoised output image dst
        # TODO: your code here
```

If you run the preceding code snippet, and plot the original, noisy input and denoised output images, you should obtain a figure as follows:

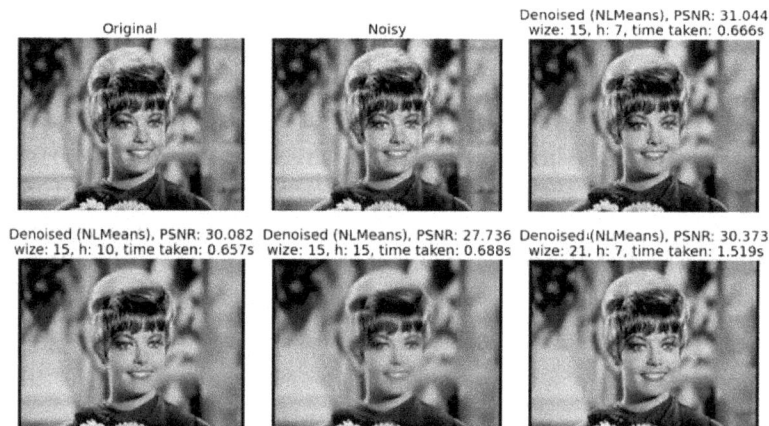

Figure 1.30: Denoising the Zelda color image with non-local means algorithm (opencv-python's implementation)

Denoising with bilateral filter

A bilateral filter is a non-linear edge-preserving and noise-reducing smoothing, commonly used in image denoising. Like traditional spatial filters (for example, the average or Gaussian filter), each pixel is replaced by a (weighted) average of its neighbors (where weights can come from a Gaussian distribution). However, unlike those filters, the bilateral filter assigns weights based not only on the **spatial proximity** of pixels but also on their **radiometric similarity** (for example, **intensity** or **color** difference), enabling it to preserve the sharp edges [19]. The filter relies on two key parameters:

- σ_s (`spatial parameter`): controls the influence of neighboring pixels based on their Euclidean distance.

- σ_r (`range parameter`): controls the influence of neighboring pixels based on their intensity difference

Formally, for a pixel located at (i, j), and one of its neighbors at (k, l), the weight assigned is:

$$w(i,j,k,l) = \exp\left(-\frac{(i-k)^2 + (j-l)^2}{2\sigma_s^2} - \frac{\|I(i,j) - I(k,l)\|^2}{2\sigma_r^2}\right),$$

Where we have:

- $I(i,j)$ and $I(k,l)$ are the intensity values at pixels (i,j) and (k,l),

- σ_s is the **spatial** standard deviation,

- σ_r is the **range** standard deviation.

After computing all weights, the **denoised pixel intensity** at (i,j) is computed as $I_D(i,j) = \frac{\sum_{k,l} I(k,l) w(i,j,k,l)}{\sum_{k,l} w(i,j,k,l)}$ where I_D is the denoised intensity of pixel (i,j).

The filter behavior depends on the values of σ_r and σ_s:

- As σ_r increases, at $\sigma_r \to \infty$, the filter approaches a standard **Gaussian blur**, losing edge-preservation.

- As σ_s increases, the spatial neighborhood grows, leading to smoother large-scale structures.

In this section, you will explore how to apply bilateral filtering from the libraries **SimpleITK** and **opencv-python** to denoise a corrupted image, while maintaining edge sharpness.

Using SimpleITK

SimpleITK library's **BilateralImageFilter()** uses bilateral filtering to blur an image using both **spatial** (also called **domain**) and **range** neighborhoods. As described, the pixels that are close to a pixel in the image domain and similar to a pixel in the image range are used to calculate the filtered value. Two Gaussian kernels (one in the image domain and one in the image range) are used to smooth the image.

The result is an image that is smoothed in homogeneous regions yet has edges preserved. The result is similar to **anisotropic diffusion** (refer to the one discussed in the book *Image Processing masterclass with python*), but the implementation is non-iterative. Another benefit to bilateral filtering is that any distance metric can be used for kernel smoothing the image range. Hence, color images can be smoothed as vector images, using the **CIE** distances between intensity values as the similarity metric (the Gaussian kernel for the image domain is evaluated using CIE distances).

Let us start by importing the required libraries, as usual:

```
import SimpleITK as sitk
```

Read the input **Zelda** image as a grayscale image, instantiate the **ShotNoiseFilter** object to degrade the image with **shot noise**. The shot noise follows a **Poisson** distribution, using the following code snippet:

```
img = sitk.ReadImage('images/zelda.jpg', sitk.sitkUInt8)
sf = sitk.ShotNoiseImageFilter()
noisy = sf.Execute(img)
```

Instantiate an object of the **BilaterImageFilter** class:

```
f = sitk.BilateralImageFilter()
```

Use the methods **SetDomainSigma()** and **SetRangeSigma()**, to set σ_d and σ_r parameters, respectively. **DomainSigma** is specified in the same units as the Image spacing. **RangeSigma** is specified in the units of intensity.

Use the member function **Execute()** to apply the filter on the noisy input image, to have the denoised output returned.

Use a few different values of σ_d (same as σ_s defined above) and σ_r, to observe the impact of these parameters on the denoised output.

Plot the images using the function **show_image()** the code snippet shown as follows:

```
def show_image(img, title=None):
    nda = sitk.GetArrayViewFromImage(img)
    plt.imshow(nda, cmap='gray'), plt.axis('off')
    if(title): plt.title(title, size=20)
plt.figure(figsize=(20,17))
plt.subplot(331), show_image(img, 'original')
plt.subplot(332), show_image(noisy, 'noisy')

i = 3
for σ_d in [5, 10]:
    for σ_r in [25, 50, 75]:
        f.SetDomainSigma(σ_d)
        f.SetRangeSigma(σ_r)
```

```
denoised = f.Execute(noisy)
plt.subplot(3,3,i), show_image(denoised, 'denoised (σ_d={}, σ_r={})' \
                                         .format(σ_d, σ_r))
        i += 1

plt.tight_layout()
plt.show()
```

If you run the given code snippet, you should obtain a figure as follows:

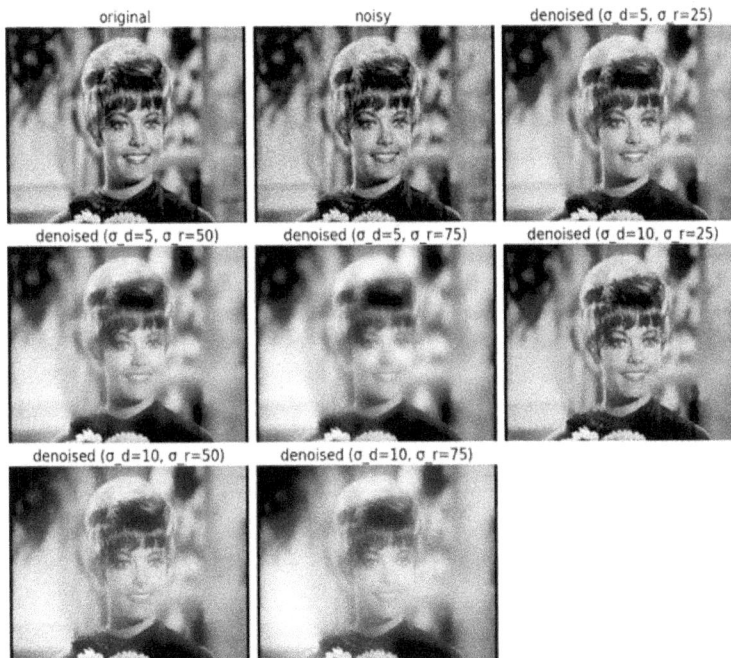

Figure 1.31: Denoising the grayscale Zelda image with bilateral filter (SimpleITK's implementation)

Using opencv-python

As explained, bilateral filtering operates both in the **range** and the **domain** of an image, unlike a traditional filter that operates only on the domain. Two pixels in an image can be close because of their spatial proximity or similarity in pixel values (i.e., in some perceptually meaningful manner), which is why bilateral filtering combines filtering in both the domain and range space.

In this section, you will explore how to use **opencv-python** implementation of a bilateral filter to clean a degraded image and preserve the edges simultaneously. However, bilateral filters are computationally expensive and can be slow.

Let us start by reading the RGB color image of **Zelda** and degrading the image by adding random Gaussian noise to the image using the **cv2.randn()** function, with standard deviation for each color channel, using the next couple of lines of code:

```
img = cv2.imread('images/zelda.jpg')
noisy = img + cv2.randn(np.copy(img), (0,0,0), (10,10,10))
```

Apply the bilateral filter using the function **cv2.bilateralFilter()** that accepts the following parameters:

- **src**: The (noisy) input image (can be grayscale or color).

- **d**: Diameter of pixel nbd (or the filter size). Large filters ($d > 5$) are very slow, let us use $d = 5$ for real-time applications.

- **sigmaColor**: σ_c (same as σ_r defined earlier), s.d. of the Gaussian in color space (larger value implies mixing of farther colors in the *nbd*, resulting in larger areas of semi-equal color).

- **sigmaSpace**: σ_s s.d. of the Gaussian in coordinate space (larger value indicates farther pixels influencing each other, provided their colors are close).

For simplicity, both the sigma parameters can be set to the same value. Small (for example, < 10) values will not have much effect, whereas large (for example, < 150) will have a strong effect (the output image will be *cartoonish*).

Use a few different values for the parameters **d** (for example, 9,15), **sigmaColor,** and **sigmaSpace** (for example, both in) to observe the impact on these parameters on bilateral denoising and plot the denoised output images:

```
for d in [9, 15]:
    for σ_c in [75, 180]:
        for σ_s in [75, 180]:
            dst = cv2.bilateralFilter(noisy,d=d,sigmaColor=σ_c,sigmaSpace=σ_s)
            # plot the denoised output image dst here
            # TODO: your code...
```

If you plot the denoised output images obtained using bilateral filtering with different combination of parameter values, by running the preceding code snippet, you should obtain a figure as follows:

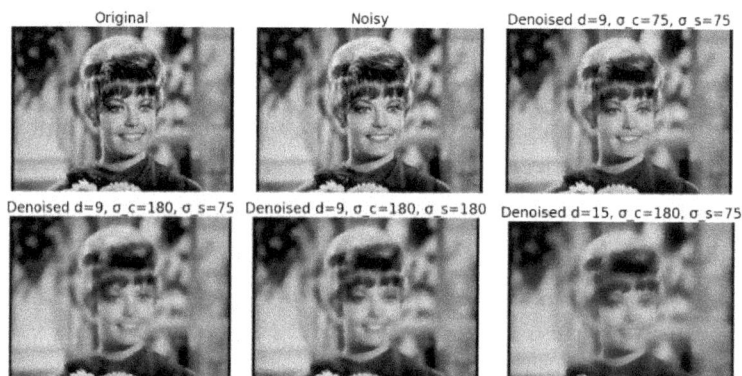

Figure 1.32: Denoising the Zelda color image with bilateral filter (opencv-python's implementation)

Denoising with MAP Bayesian with an MRF prior

In **Bayesian image denoising**, the goal is to estimate the **optimal** noiseless image X given an observed noisy image Y. The optimal noiseless image is defined as the one that maximizes the **posterior probability** given the observed noisy image, using **Bayes' theorem**:

$$P(X \mid Y) = \frac{P(Y)P(Y \mid X)}{P(X)}$$

The **Maximum A Posteriori** (**MAP**) estimate of the clean image $\hat{X}_{MAP}$ is given by:

$$\hat{X}_{MAP} = \underset{X}{\operatorname{argmax}} P(X \mid Y) = \underset{X}{\operatorname{argmax}} P(Y)P(Y \mid X)P(X)$$

Since P(Y) is constant with respect to X, this is equivalent to minimizing the **negative log-posterior**:

$$\hat{X}_{MAP} = \underset{X}{\operatorname{argmin}}(-logP(Y \mid X) - logP(X))$$

To compute the posterior probability and compute **MAP** estimation, we need to first define the following two key probabilistic terms:

- **Likelihood term** $P(Y \mid X)$: Represents the noise model; describes how the noisy how the noisy observation Y is generated from the underlying clean image X, typically modeled using a Gaussian distribution in the case of additive white noise.

- **Prior term** $P(X)$: Captures assumptions about the smoothness or structure of the clean image using a **Markov Random Field (MRF)**. A 4-neighborhood **MRF prior** is commonly used, which satisfies the **Markov property**—meaning each pixel's value depends only on its four immediate neighbors (up, down, left, right).

Assumptions and noise model

Let us first define the following variable to formally define the model:

- $Y = \{y_i\}$ be the observed noisy image,
- $X = \{x_i\}$ be the unknown true image,
- x_i is modelled as an **MRF**, with 4-neighborhood dependency,
- The noise is assumed to be **i.i.d. Gaussian** with variance σ^2.

Then the **likelihood model** becomes:

$$P(y_i \mid x_i) = N(y_i; x_i, \sigma^2) \Rightarrow -logP(y_i \mid x_i) \propto \sigma^2(y_i - x_i)^2$$

MRF prior: Image regularization

The MRF prior is defined using **pairwise potential functions** over neighboring pixels:

$$P(X) \propto exp\left(-\textstyle\sum_{(i,j)\in N} V(x_i, x_j)\right), \text{ with } V(x_i, x_j) = g(x_i - x_j)$$

Different choices of the function $g(u)$ lead to different smoothing characteristics:

- **Quadratic prior (used here)**: $g_1(u) = |u|^2$
- **Huber prior**: Handles small variations quadratically and large differences linearly (edge-preserving), here $g_2(u) = \begin{cases} \frac{1}{2}u^2, & if \ |u| \le \gamma \\ \gamma|u| - \frac{1}{2}\gamma^2, & if \ |u| > \gamma \end{cases}$
- **Discontinuity-adaptive log prior**: $g_3(u) = \gamma|u| - \gamma^2 log(1 + |u|/\gamma)$, good for sharp edges.

Combined MAP estimation objective

The **MAP** estimate is obtained by minimizing the negative log-posterior (obtained by combining the likelihood and the prior), which leads to minimization of the following energy (or cost) function:

$$\hat{X} = \underset{X}{\text{argmin}} \sum_i \alpha(y_i - x_i)^2 + \sum_{j \in N(i)} g(x_i - x_j)$$

Where $\alpha = \frac{1}{\sigma^2}$ is a parameter balancing **fidelity** (data) and **regularity** (smoothness).

Now, let us implement a **MAP** Bayesian denoising algorithm [22], that uses the aforementioned **noise model** coupled with the **MRF prior**.

Optimizing with gradient-based solver

Let us start by importing the required libraries as follows:

```
from scipy.optimize import minimize
```

Implement the gradient function **grad_g()** for the prior chosen and use the **L-BFGS-B** optimization method from **scipy**.

Define prior and gradient functions

The following code snippet defines the **quadratic MRF prior** function $g(u) = |u|^2$ and the corresponding gradient $\nabla g(u) = 2u$:

```
def g(u):
    return np.sum(u**2)
def grad_g(u):
    return 2*u
```

Define objective and gradient for optimization

For the chosen $g(.)$ function, minimize the following objective function (using the **minimize()** function from the **scipy.optimize** module) to get the denoised image:

$$\sum \alpha(y_i - x_i)^2 + g(x_i - x_{i1}) + g(x_i - x_{i2}) + g(x_i - x_{i3}) + g(x_i - x_{i4})$$

Where *i1, i2, i3, i4* are the 4 neighboring pixels at position *i*, and y_i, x_i denote the noisy and clean pixel intensities at position *i*, respectively.

Define the optimization objective (cost) function in **comp_obj_fun()**, which accepts the input noisy image *Y* and the output image *X*, along with a weight α.

The function $g(\cdot)$ is a **regularizer**; for example, $g(u) = u^2$ (quadratic prior) enforces smoothness. This decomposition reflects the Bayesian framework where the **data fidelity** term $(y_i - x_i)^2$ arises from the likelihood, and the neighborhood smoothness terms $g(x_i - x_{ij})$ arise from the **prior**.

The role of $g(.)$ is to promote edge preservation by encouraging neighboring pixel values to be similar—except at edges where large differences are permitted, while the term $(y_i - x_i)^2$ enforces fidelity to the observed noisy image and contributes to noise removal.

The constant α is to give weights to noise removal and edge preservation (controls the weighting between the **prior** and the **likelihood**).

Define the function **compute_grad()** to compute the gradient of cost, it uses the function **grad_g()** to compute $\nabla g(.)$, using the next code snippet:

```
def compute_grad(X,Y,alpha):
    X, Y = X.reshape(im_size), Y.reshape(im_size)
    X1, X2, X3, X4 = np.roll(X, -1, 0), np.roll(X, 1, 0), np.roll(X, -1, 1), \
                                                    np.roll(X, 1, 1)
    grad = alpha*grad_g(X-Y) + grad_g((X-X1) + (X-X2) + (X-X3) + (X-X4))
    return grad.ravel()
def compute_obj_fun(X,Y,alpha):
    X, Y = X.reshape(im_size), Y.reshape(im_size)
    X1, X2, X3, X4 = np.roll(X, -1, 0), np.roll(X, 1, 0), np.roll(X, -1, 1), \
                                                    np.roll(X, 1, 1)
    cost =  alpha*g(X-Y) + g(X-X1) + g(X-X2) + g(X-X3) + g(X-X4)
    return cost
```

Apply optimization to restore the noisy image

Read the input grayscale image of a ship and add salt and pepper noise to the image. Initialize the output image with zeros before starting the iterative optimization, using the following code snippet:

```
original = cv2.imread('images/ship.png', 0)
original = original / original.max()
noisy = random_noise(original, mode='s&p')
denoised = np.zeros_like(noisy)
im_size, alpha = original.shape, 1.5
```

If you plot the **original** and the **noisy** input images, along with the initialization for the **denoised** (black) zero output image and the difference image (computed as **noisy** - **denoised**) at the very outset, you will get a figure as follows:

Denoising with L-BFGS-B (Initialization)

Noisy, PSNR=18.4965   Denoised, PSNR=5.3426   Difference Image (Noise)   Original

Figure 1.33: Denoising image with iterative LFBGS-B optimization algorithm (starting with zero image)

Minimize using L-BFGS-B

The **minimize()** function from **scipy.optimize** module is an iterative solver that finds the minimum of a scalar function using optimization algorithms like **BFGS, CG** or **L-BFGS-B**, given an initial guess and optional gradient (jacobian). Here we shall use the **minimize()** function to minimize the objective function **compute_obj_fun** defined, and we shall pass the gradient function **compute_grad** as the *Jacobian* argument to the **minimize()** function). The **minimize()** function takes the following arguments, a few of the relevant ones are listed as follows:

- **func**: Objective function we want to minimize.

- **x_0**: The initial guess (of the clean image) to start with (we initialized with zeros).

- **jac**: Function to compute gradient.

- **args**: Extra arguments to be passed to objective function and its derivative.

- **method**: Solver to be used (for example, **L-BFGS-B**).

- **maxiter**: Sets the maximum number of iterations

- **gtol**: Specifies the gradient norm tolerance for convergence.

Let us use the maximum iteration (**maxiter**) as for the iterative solver and tolerance (**gtol**) as 0.1, as shown in the following code snippet:

```
res = minimize(func=compute_obj_fun, x0=denoised.ravel(), \
            jac=compute_grad, method='L-BFGS-B', args=(noisy.ravel(), alpha), \
            options={'maxiter':4, 'gtol':0.1, 'disp': True})
```

Retrieve final output

Retrieve the solution (**res**) obtained and reshape it back into the size of the original image, to obtain the denoised output image:

```
denoised = res.x.reshape(im_size)
```

Visual and quantitative evaluation

Plot the **denoised** output image along with the difference image and compute the **PSNR** to measure the quality of image. The final output should be the one, as shown in the next figure, note the increase in PSNR in the denoised image:

Denoising with L-BFGS-B (iteration=4)

Noisy, PSNR=18.4965   Denoised, PSNR=25.6125   Difference Image (Noise)   Original

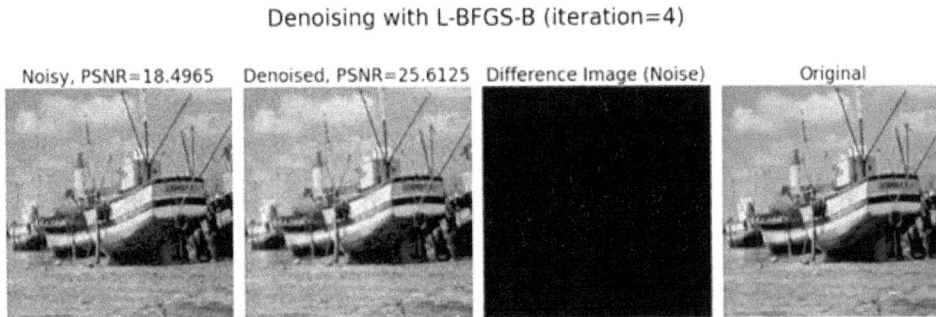

Figure 1.34: *Denoising image with iterative LFBGS-B optimization algorithm (denoised image after 4 iterations)*

To summarize, the aforementioned method uses a principled Bayesian approach with an MRF prior to denoise images:

- **Likelihood**: Captures how likely the observed image is given a denoised candidate.

- **MRF prior**: Encourages piecewise smoothness while allowing discontinuities (edges).

- **Optimization**: Uses gradient-based techniques to minimize the energy.

Denoising images with Kernel PCA

Kernel PCA (**kPCA**) is an extension of **Principal Component Analysis (PCA)**, a widely used linear dimension reduction technique. Unlike standard **PCA**, which is limited to linear mappings, **kPCA** introduces non-linearity through the use of **kernel** functions.

In kPCA we select a mapping function Φ that conceptually transforms the input data into a high-dimensional feature space. However, instead of explicitly computing this transformation, **kPCA** uses a **kernel** function $K = k(\mathbf{x}, \mathbf{y}) = \big(\Phi(\mathbf{x}), \Phi(\mathbf{y})\big) = \Phi(\mathbf{x})^T \Phi(\mathbf{y})$, which calculates the inner product in the feature space indirectly. This approach, known as the **kernel trick**, avoids the computational cost of operating in the high-dimensional (intractable) feature-space. [21].

Using the dual form, the kPCA never actually computes the eigenvectors (the principal components) and eigenvalues of the covariance matrix in the $\Phi(\mathbf{x})$-space. Instead, it uses the kernel trick to compute the projections of the data onto the principal components, as shown in the following figure:

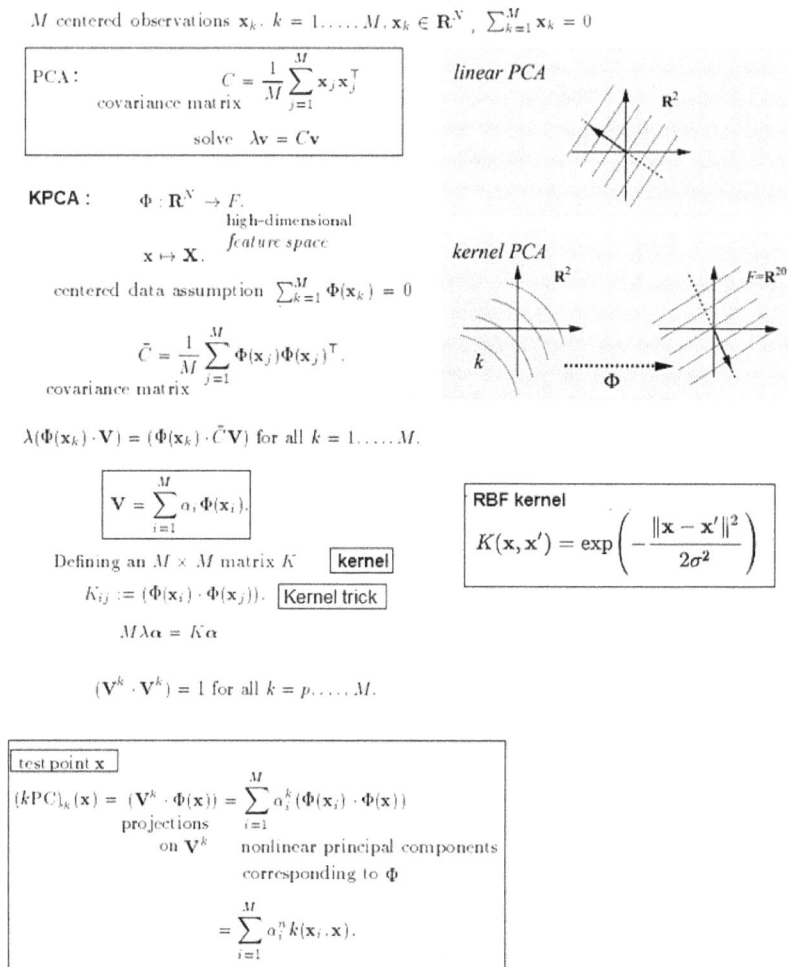

M centered observations $\mathbf{x}_k$, $k = 1, \ldots, M$, $\mathbf{x}_k \in \mathbf{R}^N$, $\sum_{k=1}^{M} \mathbf{x}_k = 0$

PCA: $$C = \frac{1}{M} \sum_{j=1}^{M} \mathbf{x}_j \mathbf{x}_j^\mathsf{T}$$
covariance matrix

solve $\lambda \mathbf{v} = C\mathbf{v}$

linear PCA

KPCA: $\Phi : \mathbf{R}^N \to F$.
high-dimensional
feature space
$\mathbf{x} \mapsto \mathbf{X}$.

centered data assumption $\sum_{k=1}^{M} \Phi(\mathbf{x}_k) = 0$

$$\bar{C} = \frac{1}{M} \sum_{j=1}^{M} \Phi(\mathbf{x}_j) \Phi(\mathbf{x}_j)^\mathsf{T}.$$
covariance matrix

kernel PCA

$\lambda(\Phi(\mathbf{x}_k) \cdot \mathbf{V}) = (\Phi(\mathbf{x}_k) \cdot \bar{C}\mathbf{V})$ for all $k = 1, \ldots, M$.

$$\mathbf{V} = \sum_{i=1}^{M} a_i \Phi(\mathbf{x}_i).$$

Defining an $M \times M$ matrix K ┌ **kernel** ┐

$K_{ij} := (\Phi(\mathbf{x}_i) \cdot \Phi(\mathbf{x}_j))$. ┌ **Kernel trick** ┐

$M\lambda\boldsymbol{\alpha} = K\boldsymbol{\alpha}$

RBF kernel
$$K(\mathbf{x}, \mathbf{x}') = \exp\left(-\frac{\|\mathbf{x} - \mathbf{x}'\|^2}{2\sigma^2}\right)$$

$(\mathbf{V}^k \cdot \mathbf{V}^k) = 1$ for all $k = p, \ldots, M$.

┌ **test point $\mathbf{x}$** ┐
$$(kPC)_k(\mathbf{x}) = (\mathbf{V}^k \cdot \Phi(\mathbf{x})) = \sum_{i=1}^{M} a_i^k (\Phi(\mathbf{x}_i) \cdot \Phi(\mathbf{x}))$$
projections
on $\mathbf{V}^k$ nonlinear principal components
corresponding to Φ

$$= \sum_{i=1}^{M} a_i^n k(\mathbf{x}_i, \mathbf{x}).$$

Figure 1.35: Image denoising with kPCA

While in standard PCA the number of **Principal Components** (**PC**) is bounded by the number of input features, in kPCA the number of components is bounded by the number of samples (since it works in the dual space). Many real-world datasets have large numbers of samples, and hence, often, finding all the components with a full kPCA is a waste of computation time, as data is mostly described by the first few components (for example, **n_components** ≤ 100).

In this section, you will explore how to use **sci-kit-learn's decomposition** module's **KernelPCA** implementation to denoise corrupted MNIST images (of handwritten digits). The idea will be to learn a PCA basis (with and without a kernel) on noisy images and then use these models to reconstruct clean images using these learned representations.

Let us start by importing the required libraries, modules and functions, using the following code snippet:

```
import numpy as np
import pandas as pd
from sklearn.preprocessing import MinMaxScaler
from sklearn.model_selection import train_test_split
from sklearn.decomposition import PCA, KernelPCA
```

Download the **mnist** train data from **Kaggle**: **https://www.kaggle.com/oddrationale/ mnist-in-csv** as a **.csv** file, where there are 60k rows, with each *row* having 785 columns: the last columns correspond to the pixel values of a 28×28 handwritten digit image and the first column represents the **label** (class) of the digit (0-9).

Read the **.csv** file using the function **read_csv()** from **pandas** and display the first few rows as follows:

```
df = pd.read_csv('images/mnist_train.csv')
df.head()
```

	label	1x1	1x2	1x3	1x4	1x5	1x6	1x7	1x8	1x9	...	28x19	28x20	28x21	28x22	28x23	28x24	28x25	28x26	28x27	28x28
0	5	0	0	0	0	0	0	0	0	0	...	0	0	0	0	0	0	0	0	0	0
1	0	0	0	0	0	0	0	0	0	0	...	0	0	0	0	0	0	0	0	0	0
2	4	0	0	0	0	0	0	0	0	0	...	0	0	0	0	0	0	0	0	0	0
3	1	0	0	0	0	0	0	0	0	0	...	0	0	0	0	0	0	0	0	0	0
4	9	0	0	0	0	0	0	0	0	0	...	0	0	0	0	0	0	0	0	0	0

5 rows × 785 columns

Figure 1.36: *MNIST digits – Pandas DataFrame with 784 columns (each row represents a 28 x 28 digit)*

Convert the images data to a **numpy** array and scale the pixel values in between - using the **MinMaxScaler()** from the module **sklearn.preprocessing**, using the next code snippet:

```
y = np.array(df.label.tolist())
X = df.drop(columns=['label']).values
X = MinMaxScaler().fit_transform(X)
X.shape, y.shape
# ((60000, 784), (60000,))
```

Use the function **train_test_split()** from **sklearn.model_selection** to split the dataset into a training and a test dataset, with 1000 and 100 randomly selected images, respectively. These images are noise-free, and we will use them to evaluate the accuracy of the denoising approaches.

In addition, let us create a copy of the original dataset and add Gaussian noise to create noisy version of the training, and test images separately, using the following code snippet:

```
X_train, X_test, y_train, y_test = train_test_split(X, y, stratify=y, \
                                    random_state=0, train_size=1_000, test_size=100)
rng = np.random.RandomState(0)
noise = rng.normal(scale=0.25, size=X_test.shape)
X_test_noisy = X_test + noise
noise = rng.normal(scale=0.25, size=X_train.shape)
X_train_noisy = X_train + noise
```

The goal here is to demonstrate that corrupted images can be denoised by learning a PCA basis from clean (uncorrupted) images. We will compare the denoising performances of PCA and **kernel PCA** (**kPCA**).

Instantiate objects of **PCA** and **KernelPCA** classes from **sklearn.decomposition** module to fit **PCA** and **kPCA** models on the training images, respectively.

The **KernelPCA** constructor accepts the following arguments, a few relevant ones are listed as follows:

- **n_components**: Number of components (we have chosen first 30 **PCs** for **PCA** and first 400 **PCs** for **kPCA**, out of 784 possible components).

- **kernel**: Kernel used for **kPCA** (here the **Radial Basis Function** (**rbf**) kernel is used, it is defined as $k(x, y) = e^{-\gamma \|x-y\|^2}$).

- **gamma**: Kernel coefficient γ for the **rbf** kernel.

- **alpha**: Hyperparameter of the **ridge-regression** that learns the inverse-transform (when **fit_inverse_transform=True**).

- **fit_inverse_transform**: Learn the inverse transform (used for reconstruction).

Use the **fit()** methods to fit the models on training images for both models as follows:

```
pca = PCA(n_components=30)
kernel_pca = KernelPCA(n_components=400, kernel="rbf", gamma=1e-3, \
                       fit_inverse_transform=True, alpha=5e-3)
pca.fit(X_train_noisy)
_ = kernel_pca.fit(X_train_noisy)
pca.n_features_in_, kernel_pca.n_features_in_
# (784, 784)
```

Now, let us project the noisy *test* images on the kernel space (with the function **transform()**) and then reconstruct (with **inverse_transform()**) the images (note that **KernelPCA** supports both **transform()** and **inverse_transform()**). Since the number of components used is less than the number of original features, it is not an exact but an approximate reconstruction, i.e., an approximation of the original test images will be obtained. By discarding the components that contribute the least to the overall variance in PCA (and similarly in kPCA), the aim is to suppress noise and retain the most significant structural information in the data.

For **kPCA**, a better reconstruction should happen since a non-linear kernel is used to learn the basis, and a **kernel ridge** is used to learn the mapping function as follows:

```
X_reconstructed_kernel_pca = kernel_pca.inverse_transform(kernel_pca.transform(\
                                      X_test_noisy))
X_reconstructed_pca = pca.inverse_transform(pca.transform(X_test_noisy))
```

Let us use the **mean squared error** (**MSE**) to quantitatively assess the image reconstruction (for example, compute MSE for **PCA** with **np.mean((X_test - X_reconstructed_pca) ** 2)),** and similarly compute for compute MSE for **kPCA**.

Plot the original (uncorrupted) and the reconstructed test digit images (obtained with **PCA** and **kPCA**) along with the **MSE** values, using the **plot_digits()** function. You should get a figure like the following one:

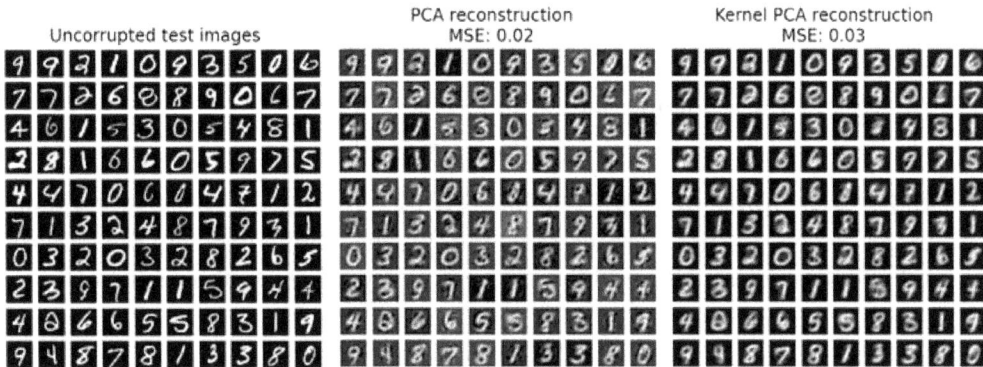

Figure 1.37: *PCA vs. kPCA reconstructions of noisy MNIST digits*

From the preceding output, although it can be seen that PCA has lower MSE than kPCA, observe that kPCA is able to remove background noise better and provide a smoother image.

Moreover, the results of the denoising with **kPCA** will depend on the hyperparameters **n_components**, **gamma**, and **alpha** (tune them and note the change in MSE).

Conclusion

In this chapter, we focused on solving quite a few problems in image restoration and inverse problems in image processing. By now, you should be able to apply non-linear filters such as median and weighted median filters to denoise an image, apply non-blind deconvolutions to restore degraded images using Inverse, Wiener filters, blind and non-blind deconvolution with RL algorithm, TV denoising with Chambolle and Bregman algorithms, Wavelet denoising, nonlocal and bilateral filters for image restoration, Bayesian MAP estimation and Kernel PCA for image denoising, using different Python libraries such as **scikit-image**, **scipy.ndimage**, **SimpleITK**, **opencv-python**, **pywt**, and **matplotlib**.

In the next chapter, we shall continue our discussion on solving more image restoration and image inpainting problems; we shall see how a few deep neural nets (such as AutoEncoders and GANs) can be applied to solve problems such as image deblurring and deraining.

Key terms

TV denoising, Richardson-Lucy, kernel PCA, Wiener, MAP Bayesian, Wavelet, Deconvolution, ROF, Chambolle, Bregman.

Questions

1. Prove that the solution to the optimization (minimization) problem with the loss function

$$loss_{Ridge} = (g - Af)^T(g - Af) + \alpha f^T f$$

   is given by the following normal equation:

$$f = (A^T A + \alpha I)^{-1} A^T g$$

2. Rather than using the normal equations to solve inverse problems, numerical analysis suggests that it is preferable to solve the augmented equations, as shown in the following equation, which can be done by a **least squares solver** (**lsqr**).

$$\begin{pmatrix} A \\ \sqrt{\alpha}.I \end{pmatrix} f = \begin{pmatrix} g \\ 0 \end{pmatrix}$$

   Compare the performance with the one you used in this chapter to solve normal equations, in terms of the number of iterations required to achieve convergence.

3. The sum of absolute deviations is minimum when it is taken from the median: Let us $S = \{X_1, X_2, ..., X_n\}$ be a set of numbers s.t., $X_1 \leq X_2 \leq \cdots \leq X_n$. Prove that $\sum_{k=1}^{n} |X_k - \theta|$ is minimum when $\theta = median(S)$.

4. Start with the noisy beans image; visualize how the **DWT** coefficients change when thresholded with different threshold values, along with plotting the change in **PSNR** of the denoised image, with hard vs. soft thresholding, and find the thresholds corresponding to the peak **PSNR** values; you should get a figure that looks like the one shown:

Figure 1.38: Denoising the beans grayscale image with DWT (hard vs. soft thresholding)

5. Use **Savitzky–Golay** filter (scipy.signal.savgol_filter) to denoise an image. Tune the *window-length* and *polynomial-degree* parameters to understand the impact on smoothing.

6. **Impact of noise on Inverse Filter**: Start with $G(u, v) = F(u, v)H(u, v) + N(u, v)$, where $N(u, v)$ is the frequency spectrum of the additive noise. Show that restoration with an inverse filter gets impacted badly as the additive noise gets stronger (demonstrate with an example). Can the Wiener filter resolve the problem?

7. Compare the restored image quality (for example, with **PSNR**) obtained with the Wiener deconvolution implementations from scipy.signal and those obtained using the **Wiener-Hunt deconvolution** and its unsupervised version's implementations from skimage.restoration.

8. Use denoise_nl_means() and denoise_bilateral() functions from skimage.restoration to apply non-local mean and bilateral denoising on a noisy image. Compare the results with those obtained using opencv-python.

9. Use the code for non-local means denoising implementation with opencv-python to visualize (in 3D) how the PSNR and the time taken to denoise varies with input parameters h and searchWindowSize, you should obtain a figure as follows:

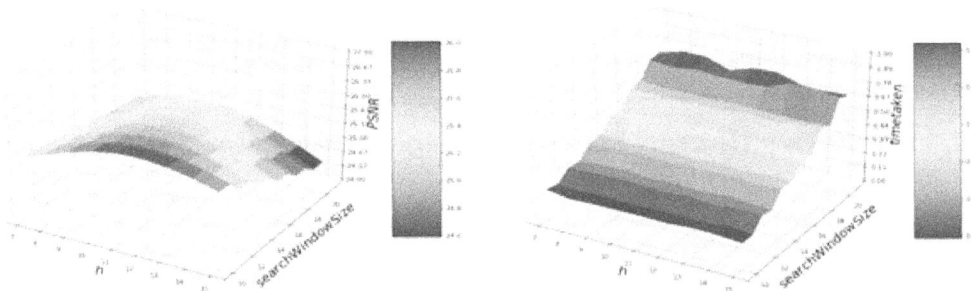

Figure 1.39: *3D plot of PSNR w.r.t. parameters h and searchWindowSize*

Try changing the value of the other parameters too, in roddr to observe the impact on the denoised image quality and the computational efficiency.

10. **Anisotropic diffusion**: Refer to the book *Image Processing Masterclass with Python* (Chapter 5) to implement the classic **Perona–Malik** algorithm to restore a degraded image and compare the output obtained with the other restoration methods.

11. **Deep Inverse problems in Python**: Implement deep image reconstruction with the Python package deepinpy, as explained in the following research paper **https://www1.icsi.berkeley.edu/~stellayu/publication/doc/2020deepInPyISMRM.pdf**.

References

1. **https://math.stackexchange.com/questions/113270/the-median-minimizes-the-sum-of-absolute-deviations-the-ell-1-norm/4281480#4281480**

2. **https://www.owlnet.rice.edu/~elec539/Projects99/BACH/proj2/intro.html**

3. **https://www.youtube.com/watch?v=WYtKSZcX944**

4. **http://www0.cs.ucl.ac.uk/staff/S.Arridge/teaching/optimisation/**

5. **https://www.ipol.im/pub/art/2012/g-tvd/article_lr.pdf**

6. **https://mathworld.wolfram.com/Euler-LagrangeDifferentialEquation.html**

7. https://sipi.usc.edu/database/database.php

8. http://leap.ee.iisc.ac.in/sriram/teaching/MLSP_16/refs/W24-Wavelets.pdf

9. https://courses.cs.duke.edu/cps258/fall06/references/Nonnegative-iteration/Richardson-alg.pdf

10. https://web.archive.org/web/20190110142859/https://pdfs.semanticscholar.org/9e3f/a71e22caf358dbe873e9649f08c205d0c0c0.pdf

11. https://www.amazon.com/Python-Image-Processing-Cookbook-processing-ebook/dp/B084ZN7Y5F/

12. https://www.amazon.com/Hands-Image-Processing-Python-interpretation-ebook/dp/B07J664F9S/

13. https://www.amazon.com/Image-Processing-Masterclass-Python-Techniques-ebook/dp/B08YK4CC7S/

14. https://www.scratchapixel.com/lessons/digital-imaging/simple-image-manipulations/bookeh-effect

15. https://arxiv.org/pdf/1004.5538.pdf

16. https://scikit-image.org/docs/dev/api/skimage.restoration.html

17. https://in.mathworks.com/videos/understanding-wavelets-part-1-what-are-wavelets-121279.html

18. https://web.stanford.edu/dept/statistics/cgi-bin/donoho/wp-content/uploads/2018/08/denoiserelease3.pdf

19. https://users.soe.ucsc.edu/~manduchi/Papers/ICCV 98.pdf

20. http://www.iro.umontreal.ca/~mignotte/IFT6150/Articles/Buades-NonLocal.pdf

21. https://citeseerx.ist.psu.edu/viewdoc/download;jsessionid=C2973F67552E7DD1D2FB5D592DFE9ACB?doi=10.1.1.100.3636&rep=rep1&type=pdf

22. https://github.com/wncc/CodeInQuarantine/blob/master/Week_3_ML/denoising-task/task.pdf

Join our Discord space

Join our Discord workspace for latest updates, offers, tech happenings around the world, new releases, and sessions with the authors:

https://discord.bpbonline.com

## CHAPTER 2

More Image Restoration and Image Inpainting

Introduction

Image restoration and inpainting are crucial tasks in image processing and computer vision, aimed at recovering degraded or missing parts of an image. Restoration techniques enhance image quality by removing noise, correcting blur, and reconstructing lost information, while inpainting focuses on filling in missing or damaged regions in a visually plausible manner.

In this chapter, we shall continue with image restoration, focusing on solving image inpainting problems, using both traditional and deep learning-based approaches. As explained in *Chapter 1, Image Restoration and Inverse Problems in Image Processing*, inpainting is a restoration process where damaged, missing, or corrupted parts of an image are filled/replaced. We shall learn how to use variational methods to solve image inpainting problems. However, our main focus in this chapter will be to use recent advanced deep learning models, such as autoencoders and GANs, to solve image denoising and inpainting problems.

Structure

In this chapter, we will go over the following topics:

- Denoising with autoencoders
- Blind deblurring with DeblurGAN

- Image inpainting
- Image denoising with anisotropic diffusion with opencv-python
- Simple deep image painting with keras
- Semantic image inpainting with DCGAN

Objectives

By the end of this chapter, the reader will have a deeper understanding of various image restoration and inpainting techniques to recover degraded images and reconstruct missing regions. You will explore denoising with autoencoders, blind deblurring using DeblurGAN, and different inpainting methods. Additionally, you will gain hands-on experience with anisotropic diffusion-based denoising in **opencv-python**, deep image inpainting with Keras, and semantic inpainting using **Deep Convolutional Generative Adversarial Network** (**DCGAN**). These techniques will equip you with the skills to effectively restore and enhance images for practical applications in computer vision.

Denoising with autoencoders

An autoencoder is a neural network that learns a representation of input data (using its hidden layers $h_{w,b}(x) \approx x$) in an unsupervised manner. In other words, it learns an approximation to the identity function so that the output $\hat{x}$ is similar to the input x (as shown in *Figure 2.1*). By placing constraints on the network, for example, by having a much smaller number of hidden units (than the input), we can discover interesting structures in the input data (for example, learn a compressed representation in the hidden units and then reconstruct the output). Refer to the following figure:

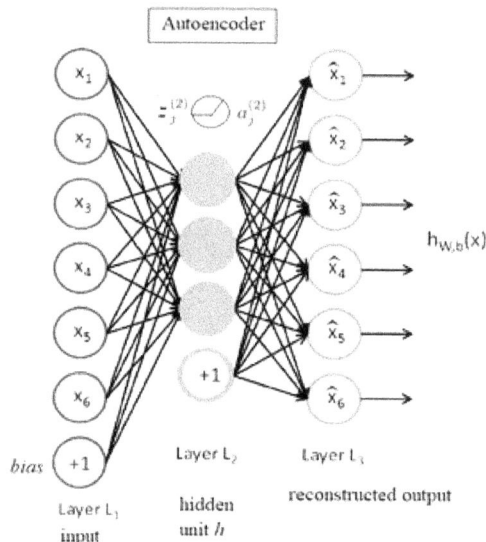

Figure 2.1: Basic architecture of an autoencoder

A **denoising autoencoder** is a stochastic version of an autoencoder that takes inputs corrupted by noise and then it is trained to recover the original inputs, to learn a good representation. We first train a denoising autoencoder to learn robust representations from a set of noisy & (ground-truth) clean (training) input images and then use it to generate denoised output images given noisy (test) input images.

Sparse denoising autoencoder

In sparse autoencoder, a **sparsity constraint** is imposed on the hidden units and the autoencoder is trained to discover interesting structure in the input. When the output value of a hidden neuron is close to 1, it can be considered to be active (firing). On the contrary, if its output value is close to 0, it is considered inactive. The constraint is to keep the hidden neurons inactive most of the time. Refer to the *Figure 2.1*: if $a_j^{(2)}(x)$ denotes the activation of the jth hidden unit (in the hidden layer, i.e., the layer 2), when the network is given a specific input x and the average activation of hidden unit j is denoted by $\hat{\rho}_j = \frac{1}{m}\sum_{i=1}^{m} a_j^{(2)} x^{(i)}$, then the constraint enforced is $\hat{\rho}_j = \rho$, where the hyperparameter ρ represents *sparsity*. It is typically assigned to a very small value close to 0 (for example, ρ = 0.05).

In order to satisfy the sparsity constraint, the majority of the hidden unit's activations must be around 0 and thus an extra penalty term is added to the optimization objective function that penalizes $\hat{\rho}_j$ deviating significantly from ρ. For example, the following **Kullback-Leibler (KL)** divergence term for each hidden unit j, is added as penalty term to the cost function:

$$KL(\rho||\hat{\rho}_j) = \rho log \frac{\rho}{\hat{\rho}_j} + (1-\rho)log \frac{1-\rho}{1-\hat{\rho}_j}$$

This penalty function has the property that $KL(\rho||\hat{\rho}_j) = 0$ minimum when $\hat{\rho}_j = \rho$. Otherwise, it increases monotonically as $\hat{\rho}_j$ diverges from ρ. Hence, when this penalty term is minimized, it will force $\hat{\rho}_j$ to be close to ρ. The overall cost function is:

$$J_{sparse}(W,b) = J(W,b) + \beta \sum_{j=1}^{s_2} KL(\rho||\hat{\rho}_j)$$

Here, s_2 is the size of the hidden layer L_2 (number of hidden units) and W, b represents the weights and bias parameters that are learned with back-propagation of the loss, with β being a hyperparameter controlling the penalty (sparsity) term's weight.

Now that we went through the basic concepts, we are ready implement a **sparse denoising autoencoder** with `tensorflow`. We shall start with a noisy version of **notMNIST** input images (of English alphabets) and train an autoencoder to reconstruct clean images from the input.

As usual, let us start by importing the required Python libraries. Note that we shall use the features of **tensorflow** v1 and disable the eager execution for v2:

```
import tensorflow as tf
print(tf.__version__)
# 2.6.0
tf.compat.v1.disable_eager_execution()
import math
import matplotlib.pyplot as plt
import os
import numpy as np
from cv2 import imread
```

Let us load the input notMNIST alphabet $(A - J)$ images from the corresponding folder using the following function **read_images()**. Note that it searches all the **png** image files inside each of the 10 subfolders (one for each alphabet), using **os.walk()** function, and stores the image and label (class) for each image found. Refer to the following code snippet:

```
def read_images(dataset_path = 'images/notmnist'):
    images = []
    labels = []
    label = 0
    classes = sorted(os.walk(dataset_path).__next__()[1])
    for c in classes:
        c_dir = os.path.join(dataset_path, c)
        walk = os.walk(c_dir).__next__()
        for sample in walk[2]:
            if sample.endswith('.png'):
                try:
                    image = imread(os.path.join(c_dir, sample), 0)
                    images.append(image.ravel())
                    labels.append(c)
                except:
                    None
        label += 1
    images = np.asarray(images, dtype=np.uint8)
    return images
```

The next function **kl_divergence()** implements the KL divergence function, the penalty term to be added to the optimization cost function to ensure sparsity:

```
def kl_divergence(p, p_hat):
    return p * tf.math.log(p) - p * tf.math.log(p_hat) + \
    (1 - p) * tf.math.log(1 - p) - (1 - p) * tf.math.log(1 - p_hat)
```

Now, let us normalize the pixel values in the input images between [0,1] and shuffle the images before starting training:

```
x_train = read_images()
x_train = x_train / x_train.max()
np.random.shuffle(x_train)
```

Let us set the hyperparameter values. Note that the number of hidden units in the single hidden layer L_2 is chosen to be 200 and each input image is 28×28. Hence, when flattened, the input dimension n becomes 784. Refer to the following code snippet:

```
p = 0.01
learning_rate = 1e-3
epochs = 40
batch_size = 100
reg_term_lambda = 2*1e-3
beta = 3
n = 784
n_hidden = 200
```

Let us now dive into the core of the implementation, follow the next steps, to define the model:

1. Let us define the **tensorflow** (v1) placeholders for the inputs (one for the original input x and another one for the corrupted version x_{noisy}) / reconstructed outputs ($\hat{x}$), and **tensorflow** variables to store the weight and bias parameters to be learned. Initialize the variables with **tf.random.normal()** function with appropriate arguments.

2. Note that we have a couple of sets of weight parameters (W_1, W_2), , the first one between the input and the hidden layer, and the other one between the hidden and the output layer. The same is true for the bias parameters.

3. Compute the forward propagation with matrix multiplications for both the hidden and output layers.

4. Compute the average activation of hidden units $\hat{\rho}$.

5. Compute the KL divergence penalty term $loss_{KL}$, to ensure the sparsity.

6. Define the squared loss function for reconstruction. Note that the loss function uses the reconstruction error of the original image x and not the noisy input, that is, $loss_{MSE} = (x - \hat{x})^2$

7. Add L_2 regularization on the weights (to prevent overfitting) $reg_{L_2}(W)$ with the cost function.

8. Add an additional penalty term as the KL divergence $loss_{KL}$.

9. The cost function is the sum of the above 3 functions: $loss = loss_{MSE} + reg_{L_2} + loss_{KL}$

10. During forward pass, you need to compute $\hat{\rho}$ values so that you can compute the penalty term for sparsity.

11. Note that we are using **Adam** (Adaptive Moment Estimation, uses adaptive learning rates and momentum for efficient stochastic gradient descent) optimizer here (for updating the parameters with backpropagation).

Refer to the following code snippet:

```python
x = tf.compat.v1.placeholder(tf.float32, [None, n])
x_noisy = tf.compat.v1.placeholder(tf.float32, [None, n])
xhat= tf.compat.v1.placeholder(tf.float32, [None, n])

W1 = tf.Variable(tf.random.normal([n, n_hidden], stddev=0.03), name='W1')
b1 = tf.Variable(tf.random.normal([n_hidden]), name='b1')

W2 = tf.Variable(tf.random.normal([n_hidden, n], stddev=0.03), name='W2')
b2 = tf.Variable(tf.random.normal([n]), name='b2')

linear_layer_one_output = tf.add(tf.matmul(x_noisy, W1), b1)
layer_one_output = tf.nn.sigmoid(linear_layer_one_output)

linear_layer_two_output = tf.add(tf.matmul(layer_one_output,W2),b2)
xhat = tf.nn.sigmoid(linear_layer_two_output)

mse_loss = (xhat - x)**2

p_hat = tf.reduce_mean(tf.clip_by_value( \
                       layer_one_output,1e-10,1.0),axis=0)
kl = kl_divergence(p, p_hat)

cost = tf.reduce_mean(tf.reduce_sum(mse_loss, axis=1)) + \
            reg_term_lambda*(tf.nn.l2_loss(W1) + tf.nn.l2_loss(W2)) + \
            beta*tf.reduce_sum(kl)
optimiser = tf.compat.v1.train.AdamOptimizer(learning_rate=learning_rate,\
            beta1=0.9, beta2=0.999, epsilon=1e-08).minimize(cost)
init_op = tf.compat.v1.global_variables_initializer()
```

Let us go over the following steps now, to learn the weight parameters of the model:

1. Train the model on the dataset. Let us run training **epochs** (for example, run for 40 **epochs**) inside a session created with **tf.compat.v1.Session()**, using the following code snippet.

2. The **session** allows the execution of graphs or part of graphs. It allocates resources for this purpose and holds the actual values of intermediate results and variables.

3. Iterate over the batches, and each time fetch **batch_size=100** images from the training dataset with **x_train[cur:cur+batch_size]**.

4. Add random Gaussian noise (with **np.random.normal()** function) to corrupt the input images (x) and the (current) batch with noise standard deviation 0.15 (try changing this), $x_{noisy} = x + noise$.

5. Note that you need to pass both x and x_{noisy} (in batches) to **tensorflow session. run()** graph computation's **feed_dict**, for the corresponding placeholders.

6. Compute the loss function value (averaged across the batches) for every epoch and store in in the list **losses**.

7. Obtain the weights learned so far, with **W1.eval(session)**.

8. Predict the **denoised** images ($\hat{x}$) with the model trained so far, with **xhat. eval(session)**.

Refer to the following code snippet:

```
losses = []
with tf.compat.v1.Session() as sess:
    sess.run(init_op)
    total_batch = int(len(y_train) / batch_size)
    cur = 0
    for epoch in range(epochs):
        mean_cost = 0
        for i in range(total_batch):
            batch_x = x_train[cur:cur+batch_size]
            noise = np.random.normal(0, 0.15, batch_x.shape)
            batch_x_noisy = batch_x + noise
            _, c = sess.run([optimiser, cost], \
                    feed_dict={x: batch_x, x_noisy: batch_x_noisy})
            mean_cost += c / total_batch
        losses.append(mean_cost)
        if((epoch + 1) % 10 == 0):
            input_images = batch_x
            noisy_image = batch_x_noisy
            weight_images = W1.eval(sess).transpose()
            output_images = xhat.eval(feed_dict={x: batch_x, \
                                x_noisy: batch_x_noisy}, session=sess)
            # TODO: plot images here
        cur += batch_size
```

As can be seen from the preceding code snippet, you can plot the training progress (expected decrease in **loss** function value) and visualize the original and denoised images (obtained with model prediction), the code for plotting is left as an exercise (fill-in the *TODO* section before), as follows:

1. Plot the **loss** function values to see the decay over **epochs** (left as an exercise, insert your code at the **TODO** section, inside the preceding code snippet. The following *Figure 2.2* shows the output that you could see after 40 **epochs**:

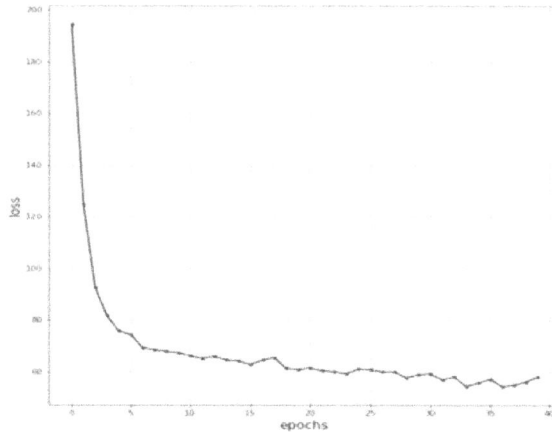

Figure 2.2: *Decay of the loss function value over epochs*

2.   Plot the original and noisy inputs, the weights learned, and the denoised output (for example, every 10 **epochs**). You should obtain a figure like the following one (after 40 epochs, for example):

Figure 2.3: *Denoising notMNIST images with sparse denoising autoencoder*

Denoising with convolution autoencoder with skip connection

In this section, you will learn to use a very deep fully convolutional **Residual Encoder-Decoder Neural Network** (**RED-Net**), for image denoising and restoration. The network is composed of multiple convolution and transposed-convolution layers, enabling it to learn end-to-end mappings from corrupted images (provided as input) to denoised original images (to be produced as output). The convolution layers eliminate corruptions by capturing the abstraction of image contents. Transposed-convolutional layers recover the image details by up-sampling the feature maps [1].

To avoid difficulty in training, convolutional and transposed-convolutional layers are symmetrically linked with skip-layer connections (as shown in the following *Figure 2.4*), to get the training process converge faster with better results:

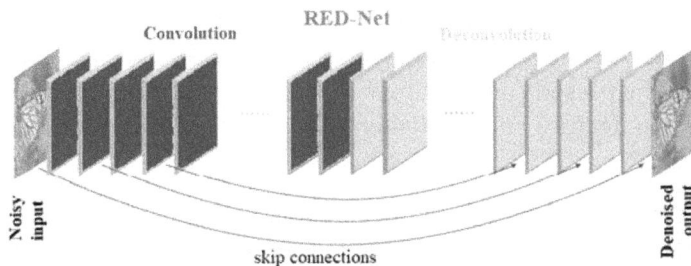

Figure 2.4: *RED-Net architecture*
Source: *https://arxiv.org/pdf/1606.08921.pdf*

The skip connections from convolutional layers to their mirrored corresponding transposed-convolutional layers exhibit the following couple of advantages:

- It handles the vanishing gradient problem while back-propagation.

- The skip connections pass image details from convolutional layers to transposed-convolutional layers, which is beneficial in recovering the clean image.

Again, we shall implement the deep learning model with **tensorflow**, and this time, we shall use the **keras** library functions. Let us start by importing the required libraries:

```
import tensorflow as tf
from keras import layers, models, initializers
import numpy as np
import cv2
import matplotlib.pyplot as plt
```

Let us go over the following, as a detailed guidance for a step-by-step implementation:

1. In general, there are the following layers in the network: convolution (**Conv2D**), transposed-convolution (**Conv2DTranspose**) and element-wise sum (**Add**). Each layer is followed by a **Rectified Linear Unit** (**ReLU**).

2. An additional layer **BatchNormalization** is added. It applies a transformation that maintains the mean output close to 0 and the output standard deviation close to 1. The layer will only normalize its inputs during inference after being trained on data with similar statistics to the inference data and tackles the **internal covariate shift** problem.

3. For the element-wise sum layer, the output is the element-wise sum of two inputs.

4. Learning the end-to-end mapping from corrupted images to clean images needs to estimate the weights Θ represented by the convolutional and transposed-convolutional kernels.

5. Convolution layers work as feature extraction units, preserving the image's details and eliminating the corruption. After a forward pass through the convolutional layers, the corrupted input gets converted into a clean one, although subtle details may be lost. The transposed-convolutional layers are then combined to recover the details, outputting the recovered clean version. Moreover, skip connections from a convolutional layer to its corresponding mirrored transposed-convolutional layer are added. The passed convolutional feature maps are summed to the transposed-convolutional feature maps element-wise and passed to the next layer after rectification.

6. Depth of the network used for image denoising varies from 20 and 30 layers. This is implemented with a for loop, by adding group of layers iteratively, as done in the next code snippet, with the **rednet()** function which returns a model of the specified depth, with the **depth** and the number of filters (**n_filters**), for the convolution/transposed-convolution layers (defaulting to 128), passed as input arguments.

7. Note that transposed-convolution is sometimes (wrongly) called deconvolution, since deconvolution implies removing the effect of convolution, which is not the goal here. It is also known as upsampled convolution, which is intuitive to the task it is used to perform, that is, upsample the input feature map.

Refer to the following code sample:

```python
def rednet(depth=20, n_filters=128, kernel_size=(3, 3), \
                              skip_step=2, n_channels=1):

    num_connections = np.ceil(depth / (2 * skip_step)) \
                                    if skip_step > 0 else 0
    x = layers.Input(shape=[None, None, n_channels], name="InputImage")
    y = x
    encoder_layers = []

    with tf.name_scope("REDNet"):

        for i in range(depth // 2):
```

```
                with tf.name_scope("EncoderLayer{}".format(i + 1)):
                    y = layers.Conv2D(n_filters, kernel_size=kernel_size, \
                        kernel_initializer=initializers.glorot_uniform(),\
                        padding="same", activation=None, use_bias=False,
                        name="Layer{}_Conv".format(i + 1))(y)
                    y = layers.BatchNormalization(name="Layer{}_BatchNorm" \
                                                .format(i + 1))(y)
                    y = layers.ReLU(name="Layer{}_Actv".format(i + 1))(y)
                    encoder_layers.append(y)

        j = int((num_connections - 1) * skip_step)   # Encoder Layers count
        k = int(depth-(num_connections-1)*skip_step) # Decoder Layers cnt

        for i in range(depth // 2 + 1, depth):
            with tf.name_scope("DecoderLayer{}".format(i + 1)):
                y = layers.Conv2DTranspose(n_filters, \
                    kernel_size=kernel_size, \
                    kernel_initializer=initializers.glorot_uniform(), \
                    padding="same", activation=None, use_bias=False, \
                    name="Layer{}_Conv".format(i))(y)
                y = layers.BatchNormalization(name="Layer{}_BatchNorm"\
                                            .format(i))(y)

                if i == k:
                    y = layers.Add(name="SkipConnect_Enc_{}_Dec_{}"\
                            .format(j, k))([encoder_layers[j - 1], y])
                    k += skip_step
                    j -= skip_step
                y = layers.ReLU(name="Layer{}_Actv".format(i))(y)

        with tf.name_scope("OutputLayer"):
            y = layers.Conv2DTranspose(1, kernel_size=kernel_size, \
                    kernel_initializer=initializers.glorot_uniform(), \
                    padding="same", activation=None, use_bias=False, \
                                    name="Output_Conv")(y)
            y = layers.BatchNormalization(name="Output_BatchNorm")(y)
            y = layers.Add(name="SkipConnect_Input_Output")([x, y])
            y = layers.ReLU(name="Output_Actv")(y)
    return models.Model(inputs=[x], outputs=[y])

rednet30 = rednet(30, n_channels=3)
```

Next, create a noisy input dataset by following the next steps:

1. Let us use the **CIFAR10** image dataset (available in **tf.keras.datasets**), add noise to the images (and later denoise it using **RED-Net**).

2. Load the training and test datasets using the **load_data()** function and normalize the pixel values, using the following code block:

```
(x_train, y_train), (x_test, y_test) = tf.keras.datasets.cifar10.load_data()
x_train = x_train / 255
x_test = x_test / 255
np.random.shuffle(x_train)
noise = np.zeros(x_train.shape)
for i in range(x_train.shape[-1]):
    noise[..., i] = np.random.normal(0, 0.1, size=x_train.shape[:-1])
x_train_noisy = x_train + noise
noise = np.zeros(x_test.shape)
for i in range(x_test.shape[-1]):
    noise[..., i] = np.random.normal(0, 0.1, size=x_test.shape[:-1])
x_test_noisy = x_test + noise
```

Now, compile the model and run training (using **fit()** on the noisy and clean training images) for 10 epochs. Train on a **GPU** (use Google Colab) for faster training, on CPU it will be slow. Refer to the following code snippet:

```
rednet30.compile(
    optimizer=tf.keras.optimizers.Adam(learning_rate=5*1e-6),
    loss=tf.keras.losses.binary_crossentropy
)

history = rednet30.fit(x_train_noisy, x_train, batch_size=64, epochs=10)
```

Plot the decaying **loss** from the history, using the following code snippet:

```
plt.plot(range(len(history.history['loss'])), history.history['loss'])
plt.grid()
plt.xlabel('Epochs', size=10)
plt.ylabel('Loss', size=10)
plt.show()
```

If you run the preceding code snippet, you should obtain a figure like the next one:

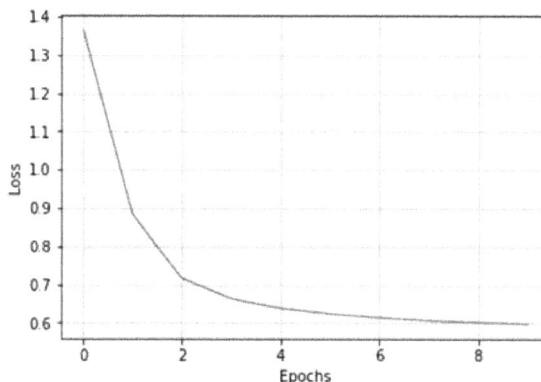

Figure 2.5: *Learning over epochs*

Predict to restore the clean images from the noisy test images:

```
x_test_p = rednet30.predict(x_test_noisy)
```

Choose a random sample of 10 noisy test images, denoise them with RED-Net. Plot the noisy along with the recovered images. You should obtain a figure as follows:

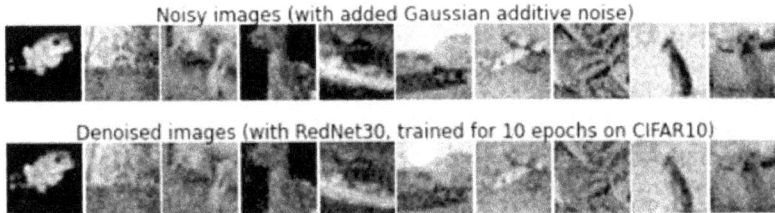

Figure 2.6: Denoising images from CIFRA10 dataset with RED-Net

Deraining with GCANet

In this problem, we shall focus on de-raining an image using *a pre-trained* deep learning model (**dehazing** network), that is, the input will be an image in a rainy environment and the output will be one without the rain-streak component. Given a hazy input image, the dehazing network tries to retrieve the uncorrupted content. Again, instead of using traditional handcrafted or low-level image priors as the constraints for handcrafted, the output haze-free image will be directly restored using an end-to-end deep neural net named **Gated Context Aggregation Network** (**GCANet**). In this network, the latest smoothed dilation technique is used to get rid of the gridding artifacts caused due to the dilated convolution, and a gated sub-network will be used to fuse the features from different levels. The following *Figure 2.7* shows the architecture of the deep neural net [3]:

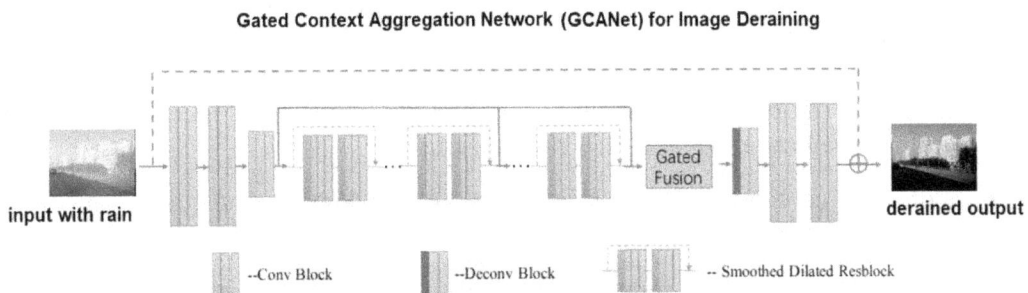

Figure 2.7: GCANet architecture
Source: https://arxiv.org/pdf/1811.08747.pdf

Let us understand how this model works:

- Using the encoder, a hazy input image is encoded into the feature maps. Next, more context information is aggregated, and features from different levels are fused (without down-sampling) to enhance the feature maps.

- Smoothed **dilated convolution** (implemented using dilated convolutional layer) and an extra gated sub-network are used.

- The target haze residue is computed after decoding the enhanced feature maps back to original image space. Next, the residue obtained is added to the hazy input image, and the final haze-free image is obtained.

- The feature maps from different levels F_l, F_m, F_h are extracted and fed into the gated fusion subnetwork. Three different importance weights, namely, $(M_l, M_m, M_h$) are output by the gated fusion sub-network (corresponding to the three feature levels, respectively). Finally, the regressed importance weights obtained are used to (linearly) combine these three feature maps from different levels.

Let us implement the model, this time using PyTorch. Start by importing the libraries needed:

```python
import torch
import torch.nn as nn
import torch.nn.functional as F
from torch.autograd import Variable
import numpy as np
from PIL import Image
import os
```

Let us deep dive into the core of the implementation using the following code snippet using the original **GCANet** implementation [8]:

- The class **SmoothDilatedResidualBlock** in the next code block implements the smooth dilated **ResBlock** (**Residual Block** is a key component in deep neural networks that helps in training very deep models by using **skip connections** to mitigate the **vanishing gradient** problem) by stacking smooth dilated convolution blocks using the **ShareSepConv** class, ordinary convolution blocks (**nn.Conv2d**), and instance normalization blocks (**nn.InstanceNorm2d**, which computes the mean and standard deviation across each individual channel for a single example and implements instant-specific normalization).

- Note that all the classes inherit from **torch.nn.Module** and they implement a couple of methods:

  o **__init__()**: The constructor called upon the instantiation of the object, it defines the structure of the network and initializes the member variables.

  o **forward()**: This method is called to run a forward pass on the layers in the block.

Refer to the following code snippet:

```python
class ShareSepConv(nn.Module):
    def __init__(self, kernel_size):
        super(ShareSepConv, self).__init__()
        assert kernel_size % 2 == 1, 'kernel size should be odd!'
        self.padding = (kernel_size - 1) // 2
        weight_tensor = torch.zeros(1, 1, kernel_size, kernel_size)
        weight_tensor[0, 0, (kernel_size - 1) // 2, \
                            (kernel_size - 1) // 2] = 1
        self.weight = nn.Parameter(weight_tensor)
        self.kernel_size = kernel_size

    def forward(self, x):

        inc = x.size(1)
        expand_weight = self.weight.expand(inc, 1, self.kernel_size, \
                                        self.kernel_size).contiguous()
        return F.conv2d(x, expand_weight, None, 1, self.padding, 1, inc)


class SmoothDilatedResidualBlock(nn.Module):
    def __init__(self, num_channels, dilation=1, groups=1):
        super(SmoothDilatedResidualBlock, self).__init__()
        self.pre_conv1 = ShareSepConv(dilation*2 - 1)
        self.conv1 = nn.Conv2d(num_channels, num_channels, 3, 1, \
            padding=dilation, dilation=dilation, groups=groups, bias=False)
        self.norm1 = nn.InstanceNorm2d(num_channels, affine=True)
        self.pre_conv2 = ShareSepConv(dilation*2 - 1)
        self.conv2 = nn.Conv2d(num_channels, num_channels, 3, 1, \
            padding=dilation, dilation=dilation, groups=groups, bias=False)
        self.norm2 = nn.InstanceNorm2d(num_channels, affine=True)

    def forward(self, x):
        y = F.relu(self.norm1(self.conv1(self.pre_conv1(x))))
        y = self.norm2(self.conv2(self.pre_conv2(y)))
        return F.relu(x+y)

class ResidualBlock(nn.Module):
    def __init__(self, num_channels, dilation=1, groups=1):
        super(ResidualBlock, self).__init__()
        self.conv1 = nn.Conv2d(num_channels, num_channels, 3, 1, \
                            padding=dilation, dilation=dilation, \
                            groups=groups, bias=False)
```

```
        self.norm1 = nn.InstanceNorm2d(num_channels, affine=True)
        self.conv2 = nn.Conv2d(num_channels, num_channels, 3, 1, \
                               padding=dilation, dilation=dilation, \
                               groups=groups, bias=False)
        self.norm2 = nn.InstanceNorm2d(num_channels, affine=True)

    def forward(self, x):
        y = F.relu(self.norm1(self.conv1(x)))
        y = self.norm2(self.conv2(y))
        return F.relu(x+y)
```

The class **GCANet** implements the **GCANet** architecture. As shown in *Figure 2.7*, the network first uses a bunch of convolution layers, followed by a bunch of **SmoothDilatedResidualBlock** layers, followed by a **ResidualBlock**, and finally a transposed convolution (**nn.ConvTranspose2d**) block, followed by a bunch of convolution blocks.

```
class GCANet(nn.Module):
    def __init__(self, in_c=4, out_c=3, only_residual=True):
        super(GCANet, self).__init__()
        self.conv1 = nn.Conv2d(in_c, 64, 3, 1, 1, bias=False)
        self.norm1 = nn.InstanceNorm2d(64, affine=True)
        self.conv2 = nn.Conv2d(64, 64, 3, 1, 1, bias=False)
        self.norm2 = nn.InstanceNorm2d(64, affine=True)
        self.conv3 = nn.Conv2d(64, 64, 3, 2, 1, bias=False)
        self.norm3 = nn.InstanceNorm2d(64, affine=True)

        self.res1 = SmoothDilatedResidualBlock(64, dilation=2)
        self.res2 = SmoothDilatedResidualBlock(64, dilation=2)
        self.res3 = SmoothDilatedResidualBlock(64, dilation=2)
        self.res4 = SmoothDilatedResidualBlock(64, dilation=4)
        self.res5 = SmoothDilatedResidualBlock(64, dilation=4)
        self.res6 = SmoothDilatedResidualBlock(64, dilation=4)
        self.res7 = ResidualBlock(64, dilation=1)

        self.gate = nn.Conv2d(64 * 3, 3, 3, 1, 1, bias=True)

        self.deconv3 = nn.ConvTranspose2d(64, 64, 4, 2, 1)
        self.norm4 = nn.InstanceNorm2d(64, affine=True)
        self.deconv2 = nn.Conv2d(64, 64, 3, 1, 1)
        self.norm5 = nn.InstanceNorm2d(64, affine=True)
        self.deconv1 = nn.Conv2d(64, out_c, 1)
        self.only_residual = only_residual

    def forward(self, x):
        y = F.relu(self.norm1(self.conv1(x)))
        y = F.relu(self.norm2(self.conv2(y)))
```

```
        y1 = F.relu(self.norm3(self.conv3(y)))
        y = self.res1(y1)
        y = self.res2(y)
        y = self.res3(y)
        y2 = self.res4(y)
        y = self.res5(y2)
        y = self.res6(y)
        y3 = self.res7(y)

        gates = self.gate(torch.cat((y1, y2, y3), dim=1))
        gated_y = y1 * gates[:,[0],:,:] + y2 * gates[:, [1], :, :] + \
                                          y3 * gates[:, [2], :, :]
        y = F.relu(self.norm4(self.deconv3(gated_y)))
        y = F.relu(self.norm5(self.deconv2(y)))
        if self.only_residual:
            y = self.deconv1(y)
        else:
            y = F.relu(self.deconv1(y))

        return y
```

Along with the input image, if the pre-calculated edges in the input image are fed as auxiliary information to the network, it often turns out to be very helpful to the network learning. For this purpose, the function **edge_compute()** pre-computes the edges from the image.

```
def edge_compute(x):
    x_diffx = torch.abs(x[:,:,1:] - x[:,:,:-1])
    x_diffy = torch.abs(x[:,1:,:] - x[:,:-1,:])
    y = x.new(x.size())
    y.fill_(0)
    y[:,:,1:] += x_diffx
    y[:,:,:-1] += x_diffx
    y[:,1:,:] += x_diffy
    y[:,:-1,:] += x_diffy
    y = torch.sum(y,0,keepdim=True)/3
    y /= 4
    return y
```

Let us understand how to instantiate the model class, load the pretrained weights and run inference on the model, with a step-by-step explanation of the next code snippet:

1. Instantiate the **GCANet** class into the variable **net** and load the pretrained model weights using the method **torch.load()**. Then set the network to evaluation mode with **net.eval()**, and it becomes ready for prediction.

2. Read the rainy input image (with **PIL**'s **Image.open()** method). The image size is assumed to be a multiple of 4. If it is not, it is resized accordingly.

3. Concatenate (using **torch.cat()**) the pre-calculated edges (using **edge_compute()**) with the hazy input image along the channel dimension to obtain the final input to the model.

4. Compute **numpy ndarray** to **pytorch tensor** (with **torch.from_numpy()**) and back (using the method **.numpy()**), as and when required.

5. **torch.no_grad()** deactivates autograd engine, by setting all of the **requires_grad** flags to **False** temporarily.

6. Run a forward pass on the neural net (using **net()**) to predict the derained output image.

7. Plot the input and output derained image using the following code snippet:

```python
model = 'models/wacv_gcanet_derain.pth'

net = GCANet(in_c=4, out_c=3, only_residual=False)
net.float()
net.load_state_dict(torch.load(model, map_location='cpu'))
net.eval()

img_path = 'images/bridge.jpg'
img = Image.open(img_path).convert('RGB')
im_w, im_h = img.size
if im_w % 4 != 0 or im_h % 4 != 0:
    img = img.resize((int(im_w // 4 * 4), int(im_h // 4 * 4)))
img = np.array(img).astype('float')

img_data = torch.from_numpy(img.transpose((2, 0, 1))).float()
edge_data = edge_compute(img_data)
in_data = torch.cat((img_data, edge_data), dim=0)\
                                        .unsqueeze(0) - 128
in_data = in_data.float()

with torch.no_grad():
    pred = net(Variable(in_data))
out_img_data = pred.data[0].cpu().float().round().clamp(0, 255)
out_img = Image.fromarray(out_img_data.numpy().astype(np.uint8)\
                                        .transpose(1, 2, 0))

plt.figure(figsize=(12,10))
plt.subplots_adjust(0,0,1,0.95,0.05,0.05)
plt.subplot(121), plt.imshow(img.astype(int)), plt.axis('off')
plt.title('original', size=20)
plt.subplot(122), plt.imshow(out_img), plt.axis('off')
plt.title('derained', size=20)
plt.show()
```

If you run the preceding code snippet, you should obtain a figure as follows:

Figure 2.8: Deraining with pretrained GCANet

Blind deblurring with DeblurGAN

In this section, we shall learn how to solve the blind motion-deblurring problem for a single photograph, using an end-to-end generative deep learning model called **DeblurGAN**. The learning is based on a conditional **Generative Adversarial Network (GAN)** and content loss. As described in *Chapter 1, Image Restoration and Inverse Problems in Image Processing,* the family of deblurring problems is divided into two types: **blind** and **non-blind** deblurring, without and with an assumption that the blur kernel is known, respectively. When the blur function is unknown, and blind deblurring algorithms estimate both latent sharp image and blur kernel (as **Richardson-Lucy** algorithm, implemented in *Chapter 1, Image Restoration and Inverse Problems in Image Processing*).

GAN, a form of unsupervised machine learning, trains two competing networks, namely, the discriminator and the generator simultaneously, as shown in *Figure 2.9*. Their roles are:

- The **generator** G receives noise as an input and generates a sample. The goal of the generator is to fool the discriminator by generating perceptually convincing samples that can not be distinguished from the real ones.

- The **discriminator** D receives a real and generated (fake) sample and tries to distinguish between them. The goal of the discriminator is to detect the fake image generated, it acts as a binary classifier, outputting 1 when the input is a real image and 0 in case of a fake one.

Refer to the following figure:

Generative Adversarial Network

$$Z \sim \mathcal{N}(\mu, \sigma)$$

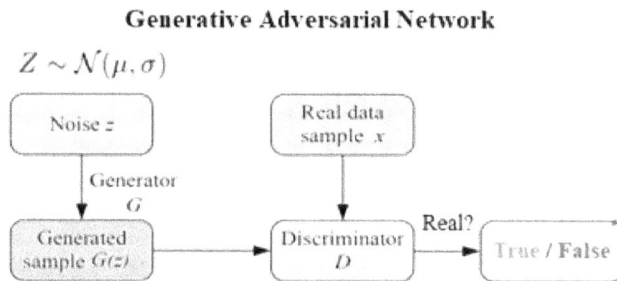

Figure 2.9: Schematic diagram of a generative adversarial network

If x be a real image and $\tilde{x}$ be a fake image generated by G (from noise z, by $\tilde{x} = G(z)$),

- The discriminator D tries to maximize $D(x)$ and minimize $D(\tilde{x})$ (or equivalently maximize $1 - D(\tilde{x})$) to detect *fake* images generated by G.

- The generator G tries to maximize $D(\tilde{x})$ (or equivalently minimize $1 - D(\tilde{x})$) to fool D.

Where we have:

- $D(x)$: The discriminator's estimate of the **probability** that (real) image x is **real** (i.e., from the true data distribution).

- $D(\tilde{x}) = D(G(z))$: The discriminator's estimate of the **probability** that a generated (fake) image $\tilde{x}$ is **real**.

Hence, the game between the generator and discriminator then can be formulated by the following minimax objective (in the space), also called **adversarial loss**:

$$\min_{G} \max_{D} E_{x \sim P_r}\left[log\left(D(x)\right)\right] + E_{\tilde{x} \sim P_g}\left[log\left(1 - D(\tilde{x})\right)\right]$$

Where, P_r is the data distribution and P_g is the model distribution, defined by $\tilde{x} = G(z)$. The input z is a sample from a simple noise distribution and $G(z)$ is the (fake) image output by the generator-given input z. GANs are known for their ability to generate samples of good perceptual quality.

Conditional GAN (cGAN) is an extension of the GAN framework. An additional conditional information is input to both discriminator and generator (as shown in *Figure 2.10*) that describes some aspect of the images (for example, if it is MNIST images, C could describe the digit class/label). This attribute information is inserted in both the generator and the discriminator. Hence, when the adversarial training is over, the generator can generate a digit of a specific class when asked. Unlike vanilla GAN, cGAN learns mapping from observed image x and random noise vector z to y, $G: x, z \rightarrow y$. Here we have:

- x: **Conditioning input** (for example, a label, an image, or some observed data)

- z: **Random noise vector** (used to introduce stochasticity/variety)

- y: Target output (for example, a label-specific image, deblurred image, translated image, and so on)

The goal of **DeblurGAN** (which is effectively a form of **Conditional GAN**) is to recover sharp image I_S given only a blurred image I_B as an input (which acts a the **conditioning input** to the **cGAN**), without any information about the blur kernel. Debluring is done by the trained CNN G_{θ_G}, which acts as the **generator**. For each I_B it estimates the corresponding I_S image. In addition, during the training phase, the critic network D_{θ_D} is introduced, and both networks are trained in an adversarial manner (i.e., the generator and critic compete, with the generator trying to fool the critic and the critic trying to distinguish real from fake).

DeblurGAN learns: $G(I_{blur}) \rightarrow I_{sharp}$, the next table maps the variables:

Symbol	Meaning in cGAN	Meaning in DeblurGAN
x	Conditioning input	Blurred image I_{blur}
z	Noise vector	Omitted ($z = 0$) or ignored
y	Target output	Sharp image I_{harp}

Table 2.1: Mapping the variables

DeblurGAN does not use a noise vector z during inference or training. It's **deterministic** — the generator maps directly from the blurred image to a sharp one (there's a *single correct* sharp image for a given blur).

The loss function is formulated as a combination of **content loss** (which is the perceptual difference between the generated deblurred image and the ground truth sharp image) and **adversarial loss**:

$$L = \underbrace{\underbrace{L_{GAN}}_{adversarial\ loss} + \lambda \underbrace{L_\chi}_{content\ loss}}_{total\ loss}$$

The following figure shows the architecture of the generator network G:

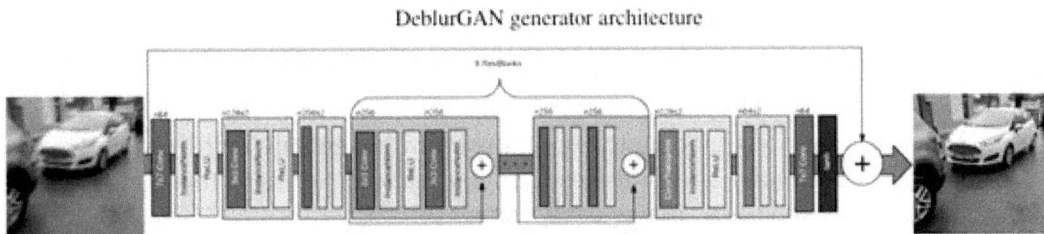

DeblurGAN generator architecture

Figure 2.10: Generator architecture in DeblurGAN
Source: https://arxiv.org/pdf/1711.07064

As can be seen from the preceding figure, it contains two *strided convolution blocks* with stride 1 or 2, nine residual blocks (**ResBlocks**) and two transposed convolution blocks. Each

ResBlock consists of a convolution layer, instance normalization layer, and **ReLU** activation. **Dropout** regularization with a probability of 0.5 is added after the first convolution layer in each **ResBlock**. In addition, a global **skip** connection, referred to as ResOut, is introduced CNN learns a residual correction I_R to the blurred image I_B, so $I_S = I_B + I_R$. It is found that such formulation makes training faster and resulting model generalizes better [2].

Let us start our implementation by importing all the required libraries, using the following code block:

```
import tensorflow as tf
from tensorflow.keras.layers import Input, Conv2D, Activation, Add, \
                            UpSampling2D, BatchNormalization, Dropout
from tensorflow.keras.layers import LeakyReLU, Conv2D, Dense, Flatten, \
                            Lambda, InputSpec, Layer
from tensorflow.keras.models import Model
import tensorflow.keras.utils as conv_utils
import tensorflow.keras.backend as K
from PIL import Image
import numpy as np
import matplotlib.pylab as plt
from glob import glob
```

Let us go through the following python implementation steps, accompanied by detailed explanation:

- Refer to the preceding network architecture. We are going to implement a slightly modified version of this network using **keras**.

- The function **res_block()** in the following code snippet instantiates a Keras Resnet block using **Keras functional API**. It accepts the following parameters: an input (tensor), number of filters, kernel size and shape of strides for the convolution, whether to use dropout or not and returns a **Keras** model. It uses couples of **ReflectionPadding2D** instances with an optional **Dropout** layer (to prevent overfitting) in the middle.

- The function **normalize_tuple()** transforms a single integer or iterable of integers into an integer tuple.

- Note that here we are going to expect the input image only in the **channels_last** image data format (modify the code if you want to support other data formats), which is the same as **K.image_data_format()**.

```
data_format = K.image_data_format()

def res_block(input, filters, kernel_size=(3, 3), strides=(1, 1), \
                                dropout=False):

    x = ReflectionPadding2D((1, 1))(input)
    x = Conv2D(filters=filters, kernel_size=kernel_size, \
                                strides=strides)(x)
    x = BatchNormalization()(x)
    x = Activation('relu')(x)

    if dropout:
        x = Dropout(0.5)(x)

    x = ReflectionPadding2D((1, 1))(x)
    x = Conv2D(filters=filters, kernel_size=kernel_size, \
                                strides=strides,)(x)
    x = BatchNormalization()(x)

    merged = Add()([input, x])
    return merged

def normalize_tuple(value, n):
   return (value,) * n if isinstance(value, int) else tuple(value)
def spatial_reflection_2d_padding(x, padding=((1, 1), (1, 1))):
    #assert len(padding)==2 & len(padding[0])==2 & len(padding[1])==2
    pattern = [[0, 0], list(padding[0]), list(padding[1]), [0, 0]]
    return tf.pad(x, pattern, "REFLECT")

class ReflectionPadding2D(Layer):

    def __init__(self, padding=(1, 1), **kwargs):
        super(ReflectionPadding2D, self).__init__(**kwargs)
        self.data_format = data_format
        if isinstance(padding, int):
            self.padding = ((padding, padding), (padding, padding))
        elif hasattr(padding, '__len__'):
            # assert len(padding) == 2:
            height_padding = normalize_tuple(padding[0], 2)
            width_padding = normalize_tuple(padding[1], 2)
            self.padding = (height_padding, width_padding)

        self.input_spec = InputSpec(ndim=4)

def compute_output_shape(self, input_shape):
        rows = input_shape[1] + self.padding[0][0] + self.padding[0][1] \
                                if input_shape[1] is not None else None
        cols = input_shape[2] + self.padding[1][0] + self.padding[1][1] \
                                if input_shape[2] is not None else None
        return (input_shape[0], rows, cols, input_shape[3])
```

```
    def call(self, inputs):
        return spatial_reflection_2d_padding(inputs, padding=self.padding)

    def get_config(self):
        config = {'padding': self.padding,
                  'data_format': self.data_format}
        base_config = super(ReflectionPadding2D, self).get_config()
        return dict(list(base_config.items()) + list(config.items()))
```

Let us proceed to the next part:

- Now implement the generator model, using the preceding **res_block**. Note that the input shape of the image used here is hard coded to (256,256,3), you may want to play with the size and observe the impact on the output.

- As shown in the model architecture diagram, the following implementation uses nine (**n_blocks_gen=9**) **res_blocks**.

- Note that the **res_blocks** use dropout (**use_dropout=True**) to prevent overfitting.

- It uses **BatchNormalization** layer though instead of instance normalization (to see the difference, we have to change the network to use instance normalization instead and observe the impact).

- It uses **UpSampling2D** layer instead of **Conv2DTranspose** (find out the difference, left as an exercise).

```
n_blocks_gen = 9

def generator_model():

    inputs = Input(shape=(256, 256, 3))

    x = ReflectionPadding2D((3, 3))(inputs)
    x = Conv2D(filters=ngf, kernel_size=(7, 7), padding='valid')(x)
    x = BatchNormalization()(x)
    x = Activation('relu')(x)

    n_downsampling = 2
    for i in range(n_downsampling):
        mult = 2**i
        x = Conv2D(filters=ngf*mult*2, kernel_size=(3, 3), strides=2, \
                                                padding='same')(x)
        x = BatchNormalization()(x)
        x = Activation('relu')(x)

    mult = 2**n_downsampling
    for i in range(n_blocks_gen):
        x = res_block(x, ngf*mult, use_dropout=True)
```

```
n_blocks_gen = 9

def generator_model():

    inputs = Input(shape=(256, 256, 3))

    x = ReflectionPadding2D((3, 3))(inputs)
    x = Conv2D(filters=ngf, kernel_size=(7, 7), padding='valid')(x)
    x = BatchNormalization()(x)
    x = Activation('relu')(x)

    n_downsampling = 2
    for i in range(n_downsampling):
        mult = 2**i
        x = Conv2D(filters=ngf*mult*2, kernel_size=(3, 3), strides=2, \
                                                 padding='same')(x)
        x = BatchNormalization()(x)
        x = Activation('relu')(x)

    mult = 2**n_downsampling
    for i in range(n_blocks_gen):
        x = res_block(x, ngf*mult, use_dropout=True)

    for i in range(n_downsampling):
        mult = 2**(n_downsampling - i)
        x = UpSampling2D()(x)
        x = Conv2D(filters=int(ngf * mult / 2), kernel_size=(3, 3), \
                                               padding='same')(x)
        x = BatchNormalization()(x)
        x = Activation('relu')(x)

    x = ReflectionPadding2D((3, 3))(x)
    x = Conv2D(filters=output_nc, kernel_size=(7, 7), padding='valid')(x)
    x = Activation('tanh')(x)

    outputs = Add()([x, inputs])
    outputs = Lambda(lambda z: z/2)(outputs)

    model = Model(inputs=inputs, outputs=outputs, name='Generator')
    return model
```

Let us go over the following points:

- Once the generator architecture is defined, we are ready to load the pretrained weights in the generator and run deblurring.

- The function **load_image()** in the following code snippet uses the PIL library method **Image.open()** to open load an image from disk, given its path.

- The function **preprocess_image()** normalizes the input image pixels (assuming that pixel values are in [0,255]).

- The function **deprocesss_image()** does the reverse operation: it converts normalized pixel values back into the range [0,255] and changes the image type back to an 8-bit unsigned integer (**np.uint8**).

- The function **deblur()** accepts a couple of input parameters, the first one being the blurred image to be sharpened and the second one being the pre-trained DeblurGAN model that will be used to deblur the image. The function preprocesses the blurred input image, loads the pre-trained weights in the generator model, and uses the generator to predict the generated (de-blurred) image, deprocesses it, and returns it.

- Finally, load the original input image and its blurred version (implement a custom blur kernel to simulate a motion-blurred version of the input image, refer to the questions at the end of the chapter). Invoke the **deblur()** function with the blurred image as an input argument to obtain the sharpened output in return.

```python
def load_image(path):
    img = Image.open(path)
    return img

def preprocess_image(img):
    img = img.resize((256,256))
    img = np.array(img)
    img = (img - 127.5) / 127.5
    return img

def deprocess_image(img):
    img = img * 127.5 + 127.5
    return img.astype('uint8')

def deblur(blurred, model_path):
    x_test_lst = [preprocess_image(blurred)]
    batch_size = len(x_test_lst)
    x_test = np.array(x_test_lst)
    g = generator_model()
    g.load_weights(model_path)
    generated_images = g.predict(x=x_test, batch_size=1)
    generated = np.array([deprocess_image(img) \
                          for img in generated_images])[0]
    return generated

blurred = load_image('images/parrot_blur.jpg')
deblurred = deblur(blurred, 'models/generator.h5')
```

If you plot the original, blurred, and deblurred (with DeblurGAN) images, you should get the following output figure:

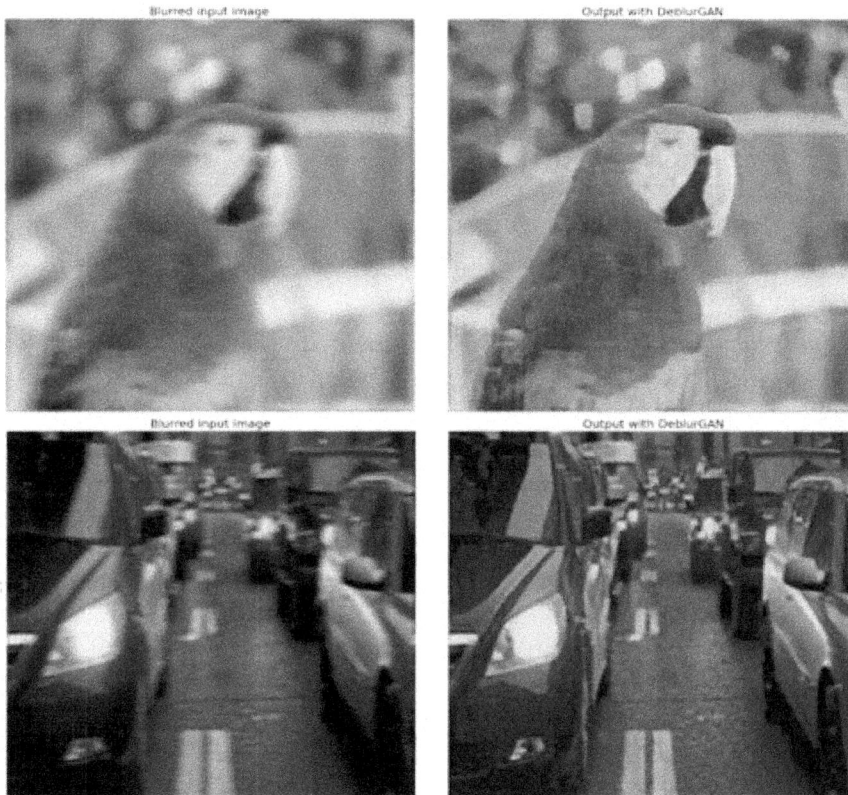

Figure 2.11: *Deblurring images with DebulrGAN*

Image inpainting

Image inpainting is a form of image restoration and conservation, and the technique is generally used to repair images with missing areas. Given an image and a (corrupted) region Ω inside it, the goal of an image inpainting method is to modify the pixel values inside Ω, so that this inpainted region does not stand out with respect to its neighboring regions (surroundings). The goal of inpainting is either to restore damaged portions or to remove unwanted elements present in an input image. The region Ω is provided by the user, with a binary mask (where the white/black pixels represent the damaged/ undamaged part of the image, respectively, or sometimes the other way around). In this section, we shall learn how to apply a few inpainting techniques to restore the damaged parts of an input image, first using a few variational methods with the library **opencv-python** and then using a machine learning based method using the **scikit-learn** library.

Inpainting with opencv-python

There are several algorithms out there for digital image inpainting, but OpenCV natively provides implementations for a few of them, namely:

- **INPAINT_TELEA**: This algorithm uses **Fast Marching Method** (**FMM**) for inpainting the corrupted region in an image. The algorithm starts from the boundary of the region to be inpainted and then proceeds gradually inside the region. It first fills everything in the boundary. A pixel (to be inpainted) is replaced by the (normalized) weighted sum of all known pixels in a small neighborhood around it (nearby pixels in the neighborhood/near the normal of the boundary/ on the boundary contours get more weightage). After the pixel gets inpainted, it goes to the next and nearest pixel to be inpainted, by using the FMM (by treating the region to be inpainted as level sets).

- **INPAINT_NS**: This algorithm is based on fluid dynamics and is called **Navier-Stokes** based inpainting. It is a heuristic-based algorithm, with couple of constraints:

  o   Preserve gradients

  o   Continue to propagate color information in smooth regions

  Partial differential equations (**PDE**) are used to update image intensities inside the region with the constraints. It travels from known to unknown regions along the edges first (to maintain the continuity of the edges). It propagates image smoothness information (estimated by the Laplacian) along the **isophotes** (contour line joining pixels with same intensity), at the same time, it matches the gradients at the boundary of region to be inpainted.

- **INPAINT_SHIFTMAP**: This algorithm searches for dominant correspondences (transformations) of image patches and tries to seamlessly fill-in the area to be inpainted using these transformations.

- **INPAINT_FSR**: This algorithm uses **Frequency Selective Reconstruction** (**FSR**), which is a high-quality signal extrapolation algorithm. Successively, the signal of a distorted block is extrapolated using known samples and already reconstructed pixels as support. An essential feature of FSR is the fact that the calculations are carried out in the Fourier domain, which leads to a fast implementation. This further has two quality profiles, one of the them needs to be chosen, depending on how fast we need the reconstruction, they are: **INPAINT_FSR_FAST** and **INPAINT_ FSR_BEST**.

In this section, we shall simply use the **opencv-python** implementations described, to inpaint an image distorted by adding a random pattern. We shall compare the quality of the inpainted outputs obtained with different algorithms using the following two metrics, namely,

- **PSNR**: PSNR between the original image f and reconstructed image $\hat{f}$ is expressed as:

$$PSNR(f,\hat{f}) = 10log_{10} \frac{\left(MAX(\hat{f})\right)^2}{MSE(f,\hat{f})}$$

Here, $MAX(\hat{f}) = 255$ is for a grayscale image of type uint8 and MSE is defined as:

$$MSE(f,\hat{f}) = \frac{\| f - \hat{f} \|_F^2}{s}$$

Where, F represents the **Frobenius norm** of the error image matrix $(f - \hat{f})$ and s is size of image f (s = number of pixels). PSNR is a representation of absolute error in dB.

- **Structural Similarity Index Method (SSIM)**: In this perception-based model, image degradation is apprehended as perception-change in structural-information. SSIM is defined by [9]:

$$SSIM(f,\hat{f}) = [l(f,\hat{f})]_\alpha \cdot [c(f,\hat{f})]_\beta \cdot [s(f,\hat{f})]_\gamma = \frac{(2\mu_f\mu_{\hat{f}} + M_1)(2cov(f,\hat{f}) + M_2)}{\left(\mu_f^2 + \mu_{\hat{f}}^2 + M_1\right)\left(\sigma_f^2 + \sigma_{\hat{f}}^2 + M_2\right)}$$

Here, μ, σ and cov respesent the mean, standard deviation and covariance of the images, $M_1 = (E_1F)^2$ and $M_2 = (E_2F)^2$, where the values $E_1 = 0.01$, $E_2 = 0.003$ and $F = 255$ are used for grayscale images.

Moreover, l refers to luminance (brightness), c refers to contrast (range of the pixel intensities, distance between the intensities of the darkest and the brightest regions) and s refers to structure (the local luminance pattern), where α, β and γ are +ve constants.

Let us dive into the following python implementation steps:

1. Let us start by importing the required libraries. Also, note the version of **opencv-python (cv2)** used.

```
import numpy as np
from matplotlib import pyplot as plt
import cv2
print(cv2.__version__)
# 4.5.5
```

2. Read the input color image and the mask image as a grayscale image (with the flag **cv2.IMREAD_GRAYSCALE** which is 0).

3. Create the binary mask for the region to be inpainted, by thresholding the mask image, by using a constant threshold (for example, 128).

4. Create the corrupted image **image_defect** by masking the same region in each color channel, as done in the next code block:

```python
image_orig = cv2.imread('images/house.jpg')
mask = cv2.imread('images/random_mask.jpg', 0)
thres = 128
mask[mask > thres] = 255
mask[mask <= thres] = 0
image_defect = image_orig.copy()
for layer in range(image_defect.shape[-1]):
    image_defect[np.where(mask)] = 0
```

5. Let us run the preceding algorithms one after another on the corrupted image and store the recovered images in a python dictionary **images_rec**, indexed by the algorithm names.

6. The algorithms **INPAINT_TELEA** and **INPAINT_NS** can be accessed by the function **cv2.inpaint()**, whereas, the **INPAINT_SHIFTMAP** and **INPAINT_FSR** can be accessed by the function **cv2.xphoto.inpaint()**.

7. The function **cv2.inpaint()** accepts the following arguments:

   a. **src**: The source image with corrupted/missing regions).

   b. **inpaintMask**: A binary mask indicating pixels to be inpainted.

   c. **inpaintRadius**: Specifies the radius of the circular neighborhood around a pixel used for inpainting. A value of 3 is commonly used, especially when the regions to be inpainted are narrow or thin, as smaller radii tend to produce sharper and less blurry results in such cases.

   d. **flags**: **INPAINT_NS** (Navier-Stokes based method) or **INPAINT_TELEA** (fast marching based method).

8. The function **cv2.xphoto.inpaint()** expects an additional argument **dst** to store the inpainted output image. These algorithms expect the mask to have black pixels corresponding to the region Ω to be inpainted. That is why we need to invert the mask since the original mask has white pixels corresponding to Ω.

```python
images_rec = {}
for algo_name, algo_id in zip(['TELEA', 'NS'], \
                              [cv2.INPAINT_TELEA, cv2.INPAINT_NS]):
    images_rec[algo_name] = cv2.inpaint(image_defect, mask, 3, \
                                                        algo_id)

inverse_mask = (255 - mask)
image_rec = np.zeros_like(image_defect, dtype=np.uint8)
for algo_name,algo_id in zip(['SHIFTMAP', 'FSR_FAST', 'FSR_BEST'], \
    [cv2.xphoto.INPAINT_SHIFTMAP, cv2.xphoto.INPAINT_FSR_FAST, \
                                cv2.xphoto.INPAINT_FSR_BEST]):
    cv2.xphoto.inpaint(src=image_defect, mask=inverse_mask, \
                    dst=image_rec, algorithmType=algo_id)
    images_rec[algo_name] = image_rec.copy()
```

9. Use the functions **peak_signal_noise_ratio()** and **structural_similarity()** from the library **skimage.metrics** to compute the PSNR and SSIM between the original and recovered images, for different algorithms.

10. Moreover, you can compute the time taken by different algorithms to produce the inpainted output (for example, use the **time** module).

11. Display the output inpainted image by running an algorithm, and plot the quality of inpainting reported by PSNR and SSIM values, using the **show_recovered_image()** function from the following code snippet.

12. Be sure to convert the image color space from **BGR** to **RGB** before displaying it with **matplotlib** (use **cv2.cvtColor()** function with **cv2.COLOR_BGR2RGB** argument), since the image is read with **cv2.imread()**, which reads the image in **BGR** color space by default.

```python
from skimage.metrics import peak_signal_noise_ratio as psnr, \
                            structural_similarity as ssim
def show_recovered_image(im_orig, im_rec, algo_name):
    plt.imshow(im_rec), plt.axis('off')
    plt.title('{} \n PSNR: {:.02f}, SSIM: {:.02f}'.format( \
        algo_name,  psnr(im_orig, im_rec), ssim(im_orig, im_rec,  \
        data_range=im_rec.max()-im_rec.min(), multichannel=True)), \
                                                        size=20)
```

Let us plot the original input image, binary mask, degraded image and all the recovered images obtained by running different inpainting algorithms (use the function **show_recovered_image()** defined previously). You should obtain a figure as shown in *Figure 2.12*. Notice that the inpainting algorithm **FSR_FAST** produces the best quality output in terms of **PSNR** and **SSIM** metrics:

Figure 2.12: Image inpainting with opencv-python

Inpainting with scikit-learn k-NN regression model

In this section, we shall formulate the image inpainting problem as a supervised machine learning regression problem. More specifically, we shall try to learn an approximate function $\hat{f}$ for the image function $f: x, y \rightarrow R$, by:

- Training a supervised machine learning model M_θ that learns the function $\hat{f}$ (by updating its parameters θ), by minimizing a loss function $L\left(f(x,y), \hat{f}(x,y)\right)$, for $(x,y) \in \Omega^-$, that is, for the region where the image is not corrupted (Ω^-). For example, for a model like linear regression, we can use the **Sum Squared Error** (**SSE**), also called the L_2 loss function defined by $\| f - \hat{f} \|_2^2$ or equivalently the MSE obtained by dividing SSE by image size.

- Using the model M_θ we just trained (and the function $\hat{f}$ we just learned), to predict the pixel values with $\hat{f}(x,y), \; \forall (x,y) \in \Omega$, for the region Ω to inpaint (that is, where the image pixels are corrupted).

Here, we shall use the **k-Nearest Neighbor** (**kNN**) regression model (`KNeighborsRegressor` from `scikit-learn` library's `neighbors` module) to learn the function $\hat{f}$. We can use any other regression model too (for example, try the ordinary least square linear regression with MSE loss function and the ensemble model random forest regression and compare the results).

First, let us follow the next steps to create a masked image, masking the corrupted pixels that need to be inpainted:

- First read the original input and the mask image as `np.uint8` arrays, using the following code snippet.

- Note that here we are assuming that the input is a grayscale image and thus reading both the input and mask images with `cv2.imread` with mode flag as 0 (that is, `cv2.IMREAD_GRAYSCALE`). We can extend the implementation to inpaint an RGB color input image simply by learning a model for each color channel (see exercise problem).

- Threshold the mask image (with a constant threshold 0.5, for example) to obtain a binary mask (here, the inpainting region Ω is defined by the white pixels in the mask), convert it to **boolean** array. Assuming that the white pixels in mask define the corrupted region, let us now create the degraded image (`image_defect`) by turning the corresponding pixels off:

```
image_orig = cv2.imread('images/lena.jpg', 0)
mask = cv2.imread('images/mask.jpg', 0)
mask = mask / mask.max()
thres = 0.5
mask[mask > thres] = 1
mask[mask <= thres] = 0
mask = mask.astype('bool')

image_defect = image_orig.copy()
for layer in range(image_defect.shape[-1]):
    image_defect[mask] = 0
```

Next, instantiate a kNN regression model with **scikit-learn**, fit it on the known pixels and predict the unknown (corrupted) pixels, following the next steps:

1. First, we need to preprocess the image, so that it is suitable to be used by the kNN regression model (need to separate out the feature and the target variables). The only feature variables (that we shall use here to predict a target pixel value) are the (x, y) coordinates of the pixel. Hence, let us generate all possible image coordinates in the grid that a pixel in the image can possibly have. This is exactly done by **np.meshgrid()** function, as shown in the next code snippet. Extract the pixel values for all pixels in the grid, note that the x, y coordinates are swapped, can you say why?

2. Next, let us divide the image into two parts, namely training and test dataset. The training dataset (**x_train, y_train, d_train**) will correspond to the uncorrupted region Ω in the image (from where the model will learn the association between the pixel value and the coordinates). In contrast, the test dataset (**x_test, y_test, d_test**) will correspond to the corrupted region (on these coordinates the trained model will predict pixel values). Here is where the Boolean **mask** will come in handy. Use the inverted mask and the mask, respectively, to obtain the training and the test dataset.

3. Instantiate a **KNeighborsRegressor** class (with default parameters) and train the model (with the method **fit()**) on the training dataset.

4. The kNN regression model uses the local interpolation of the *target* variable values from the kNN pixels from the training dataset, to predict the target variable value for a test datapoint.

5. The number of neighbors k to be used for prediction (**n_neighbors** argument in the **KNeighborsRegressor** class constructor) defaults to 5. Try changing this hyperparameter (for example, to 3,7,9) and observe the (**overfitting / underfitting**) impact on the inpainting result.

6. Finally, predict the corrupted pixels corresponding to the test dataset (with the method **predict()**). Use the binary **mask** array again to create an output image (**image_out**) with the known and the predicted pixels, this is the final inpainted image:

```
from sklearn.neighbors import KNeighborsRegressor

x, y = np.meshgrid(range(image_orig.shape[1]), \
                   range(image_orig.shape[0]))
d = image_orig[y, x]
x_train, y_train, d_train = x[~mask], y[~mask], d[~mask]
x_test, y_test, d_test = x[mask], y[mask], d[mask]

image_out = np.zeros_like(image_orig)
d_pred = np.zeros_like(d_test)
model = KNeighborsRegressor()
model.fit(np.vstack((x_train, y_train)).T, d_train)
d_pred = model.predict(np.vstack((x_test, y_test)).T)
image_out[~mask] = image_orig[~mask]
image_out[mask] = d_pred
```

Now, plot the original, corrupted, and the inpainted (recovered) image side by side. You should obtain a plot like the following figure. Note that the algorithm could successfully inpaint the damaged image.

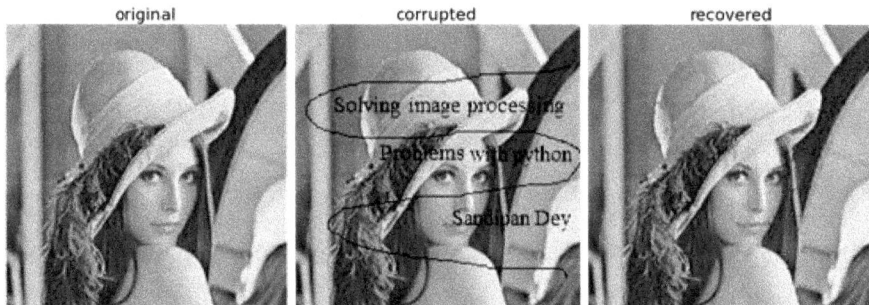

Figure 2.13: Inpainting a corrupted Lena image with scikit-learn kNN regressor

Image denoising with anisotropic diffusion with opencv-python

In this section, we shall learn how to use the anisotropic (heat) diffusion equation to denoise an image, preserving the edges using an extended image processing function from the library **opencv-python**. Isotropic diffusion is identical to applying a Gaussian filter, which blurs an image without preserving the edges in the image, as we have already seen. It refers to a uniform diffusion process where the smoothing is applied equally in all directions. This approach treats all regions of the image the same, typically leading to the even blurring of both edges and homogeneous regions.

Anisotropic diffusion, on the other hand, is direction-dependent and allows for selective smoothing. It preserves edge details by reducing the diffusion (or smoothing) across edges while allowing diffusion within homogeneous regions. This approach helps in enhancing important features like edges in images while reducing noise. The features of anisotropic diffusion are listed as follows:

- It can be used to smooth (denoise) an image by keeping the edges mostly unchanged (even sharpened).

- It is **anisotropic** in the sense that the diffusion happens in different neighboring direction at different rates (depending on the presence of an edge or not). This is implemented by the **PDE** shown in *Figure 2.14*, where the **conductivity** term uses an edge stopping function (kernel) $g(.)$ to stop diffusion along sharp edges in the input.

- The anisotropic diffusion process is an iterative process, the Gaussian kernel or an inverse-square kernel function $g(.)$ used as a conductivity function (c), according to **Perona-Malik** *equation 1* or *equation 2* [6, 7], respectively, as shown in the following figure:

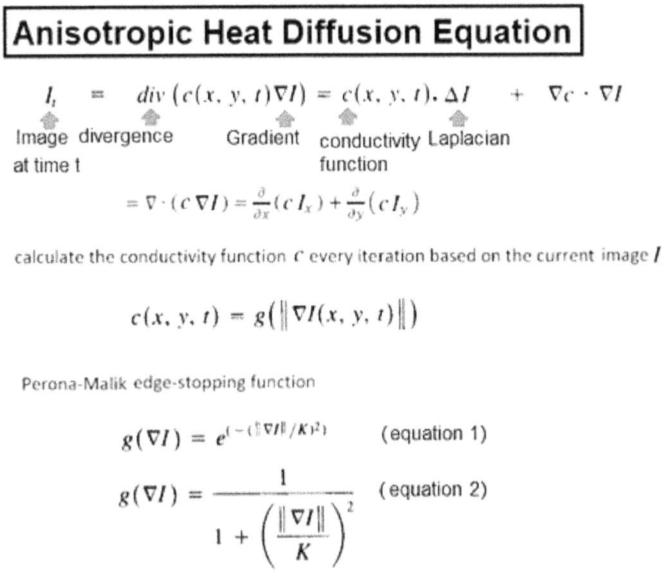

Anisotropic Heat Diffusion Equation

$$I_t \;=\; div\,(c(x,\,y,\,t)\nabla I) \;=\; c(x,\,y,\,t).\,\Delta I \;\;+\;\; \nabla c \cdot \nabla I$$

Image divergence   Gradient   conductivity   Laplacian
at time t   function

$$= \nabla \cdot (c\,\nabla I) = \frac{\partial}{\partial x}(c\,I_x) + \frac{\partial}{\partial y}(c\,I_y)$$

calculate the conductivity function c every iteration based on the current image I

$$c(x,\,y,\,t) \;=\; g\big(\|\nabla I(x,\,y,\,t)\|\big)$$

Perona-Malik edge-stopping function

$$g(\nabla I) \;=\; e^{(-(\|\nabla I\|/K)^2)} \qquad \text{(equation 1)}$$

$$g(\nabla I) \;=\; \frac{1}{1 + \left(\dfrac{\|\nabla I\|}{K}\right)^2} \qquad \text{(equation 2)}$$

Figure 2.14: *Anisotropic diffusion equation*
Source: *http://image.diku.dk/imagecanon/material/PeronaMalik1990.pdf*

Let us start the implementation by importing the required libraries, modules and functions, using the following code snippet:

```python
import numpy as np
import matplotlib.pylab as plt
import cv2
print(cv2.__version__)
from skimage.io import imread
from skimage.util import random_noise
# 4.5.5
```

Follow the next steps for implementation with **opencv-python**:

1. First, read the input RGB color image from disk and add random Gaussian noise (with a variance of 0.05) to it, using **scikit-image** library's **util.random_noise()** function, to obtain the noisy degraded image.

2. Apply the **Gaussian blur** (also can be thought of as **isotropic diffusion**) to the image to remove noise, using **cv2.GaussianBlur()** function, with the input noisy image and a tuple representing the blur kernel size (11×11) as first two input arguments. Set the third argument to the function to 0 (**OpenCV** is instructed to automatically compute the variance of the Gaussian blur based on the kernel size).

3. Now let us compare the denoised output with one obtained using anisotropic diffusion performed with the function **cv2.ximgproc.anisotropicDiffusion()**.

4. The function **cv2.ximgproc.anisotropicDiffusion()** applies Perona-Malik anisotropic diffusion to the noisy input image. The function accepts the following parameters:

    a. **src**: The 3-channel input (in our case, it will be the noisy RGB color image **noisy**).

    b. **alpha**: Time delta forwarded per iteration (typically has values in [0,1]).

    c. **K**: Sensitivity to edges in the image.

    d. **niters**: Number of iterations to run.

5. Use **aplha=0.05** and **K=30** for two different numbers of iterations, namely, 5 and 10 (to see how the convergence takes place at successive iterations). Play with the values of the parameters, plot the output denoised images, and observe the impact on the quality of the denoised output image (in terms of edges preserved, blurring, PSNR, SSIM) as follows:

```python
im = imread('images/building.jpeg')
noisy = (255*random_noise(im, var=0.05)).astype(np.uint8)

plt.figure(figsize=(12,13))
plt.subplots_adjust(0,0,1,0.95,0.05,0.05)
plt.gray()
plt.subplot(221), plt.imshow(noisy), plt.axis('off')
plt.title('Noisy Image', size=20)
output_blur = cv2.GaussianBlur(noisy, (11,11), 0)
plt.subplot(222)
show_recovered_image(im, output_blur, \
                                    'gaussian blur: kernel=(11,11)')
niters = [5, 10]
for i in range(2):
    plt.subplot(2,2,i+3)
```

```
output_aniso = cv2.ximgproc.anisotropicDiffusion(noisy, \
                            alpha=0.05, K=30, niters=niters[i])
show_recovered_image(im, output_aniso, \
            'anisotropic diffusion: #iter=' + str(niters[i]))
plt.show()
```

If you run the preceding code snippet, you should obtain a figure like the next one:

Figure 2.15: *Denoising image with anisotropic diffusion with opencv-python*

As can be seen from the preceding figure, the denoised images with anisotropic diffusion preserve edges better.

Sketch with anisotropic diffusion

Anisotropic diffusion can produce sketches from an image by subtracting the diffused image from the original image (with different iterations and varying parameter values we can get edges at different scale-space). The following code provides a simple implementation. Let us understand the implementation step-by-step:

1. This time we shall use the anisotropic diffusion implementation **medpy.filter. smoothing.anisotropic_diffusion()** from the library **medpy** (install the library first, if you have not already done so).

2. Note that the input image used is a 4-channel **.png** image (with an additional channel for transparency). So, we need to first convert it to a 3 channel image using the function **rgba2rgb()** from **scikit-image**'s **color** module and then convert it to a grayscale image (expected input for the function **anisotropic_diffusion()**).

3. The function **edges_with_anisotropic_diffusion()** computes the edges as a difference between the original and diffused image.

4. The function **sketch()** makes the edges more prominent (by elementwise multiplication of edges image with original image) to produce the output sketch.

Refer to the following Python code snippet:

```python
import warnings
warnings.filterwarnings('ignore')
# ! pip install medpy
from medpy.filter.smoothing import anisotropic_diffusion
from skimage.io import imread
from skimage.color import rgb2gray, rgba2rgb
from skimage.filters import gaussian

def sketch(img, edges):
    output = np.multiply(img, edges)
    output[output > 1] = 1
    output[edges == 1] = 1
    return output

def edges_with_anisotropic_diffusion(img, niter=100, \
                                      kappa=50, gamma=0.2):
    img = gaussian(img, sigma=0.5)
    output = img - anisotropic_diffusion(img, niter=niter,\
        kappa=kappa, gamma=gamma, voxelspacing=None, option=1)
    output[output > 0] = 1
    output[output < 0] = 0
    return output
im = rgb2gray(rgba2rgb(imread('images/umbc.png')))
output_aniso = sketch(im, edges_with_anisotropic_diffusion(im))
```

Plot the input and output images side by side, and you should obtain a figure like the following one:

Figure 2.16: *Sketching with anisotropic diffusion*

Simple deep image painting with keras

In this section, we shall use the same idea that we used in image inpainting with supervised machine learning, but this time using deep neural network with **keras**. We shall reconstruct RGB values for an entire image as a function of the pixel coordinates only, $f: R^2 \to R^3$ and approximate the vector-valued function $f([x \, y]) = [R \, G \, B]$ using a function $\hat{f}$ which will be learned from the image data with the deep neural net, using the squared-loss function, given by $\| f - \hat{f} \|_2^2$. The reconstruction will be done by prediction with this model and we shall call this process as **painting** the image, since it will reproduce a smooth approximation of the image, as we shall see.

Let us start by importing the libraries and modules required:

```
import tensorflow as tf
from tensorflow.keras.models import Sequential
from tensorflow.keras.layers import Dense
from tensorflow.keras import backend as K
from keras.utils.vis_utils import plot_model
from PIL import Image
import numpy as np
import matplotlib.pylab as plt
```

Now, let us go through the following step-by-step implementation:

1. The function **get_data()** in the following code snippet extracts the feature variables $x \in R^2$ (pixel coordinates) and target variable $y \in R^3$ (RGB pixel values), to get the data ready for training.

2. The function accepts a **PIL** image as input, and the image data can be extracted with the method **Image.getdata()**, as shown in the following code snippet.

3. Extract the **r, g, b** values.

```
def get_data(img):
    width, height = img.size
    pixels = img.getdata()
    x_data, y_data = [],[]
    for y in range(height):
        for x in range(width):
            idx = x + y * width
            r, g, b = pixels[idx]
            x_data.append([x / width, y / height])
            y_data.append([r, g, b])
    x_data = np.array(x_data)
    y_data = np.array(y_data)
    return x_data, y_data

im = Image.open("images/me.jpg")
x, y = get_data(im)
```

4. The function **create_model()** in the following code snippet uses **keras** Sequential API to define the deep neural net model.

5. The network consists of a few fully connected (**Dense**) layers, with nonlinear **Relu** activation.

6. The input of the model is of dimension (**input_shape**) 2 (namely, the x, y coordinates of a pixel).

7. The output of the model has dimension 3 (**Dense(3)**) (namely, the R, G, B pixel values).

8. The loss function used is MSE (**mean_squared_error**), with **Adam** optimizer, which is defined by the **model.compile()** method.

9. The function **generate_image()** accepts the trained model as an input argument and reconstructs the same image (by predicting the pixel values with the model) of given **width** and **height** and the pixel coordinates x. This nested **for** loop populates the output image pixel-by-pixel using RGB values predicted by the model, reconstructing a full-color image from the model's output.

   o **idx = x + y * width** converts the 2D coordinates (x, y) into a flat index **idx**, assuming **y_pred** is a flattened list/array of pixel RGB values.

   o **r, g, b = y_pred[idx]** retrieves the predicted RGB values for the pixel at position (x, y).

Now, refer to the next code snippet:

```
def create_model():
    model = Sequential()
    model.add(Dense(2, activation='relu', input_shape=(2,)))
    model.add(Dense(20, activation='relu'))
    model.add(Dense(20, activation='relu'))
    model.add(Dense(20, activation='relu'))
    model.add(Dense(20, activation='relu'))
    model.add(Dense(20, activation='relu'))
    model.add(Dense(20, activation='relu'))
    model.add(Dense(20, activation='relu'))
    model.add(Dense(3))
    model.compile(loss='mean_squared_error', optimizer='adam')
    return model

def generate_image(model, x, width, height):
    img = Image.new("RGB", [width, height])
    pixels = img.load()
    y_pred = model.predict(x)
    for y in range(height):
        for x in range(width):
            idx = x + y * width
            r, g, b = y_pred[idx]
            pixels[x, y] = (int(r), int(g), int(b))
    return img
```

10. Create the model and plot the model architecture using the **plot_model()** function from **keras.utils.vis_utils** module, as shown in the following figure:

```
m = create_model()
plot_model(m, to_file='images/model_arch.png', show_shapes=True, \
                                               show_layer_names=True)
```

Refer to the following figure:

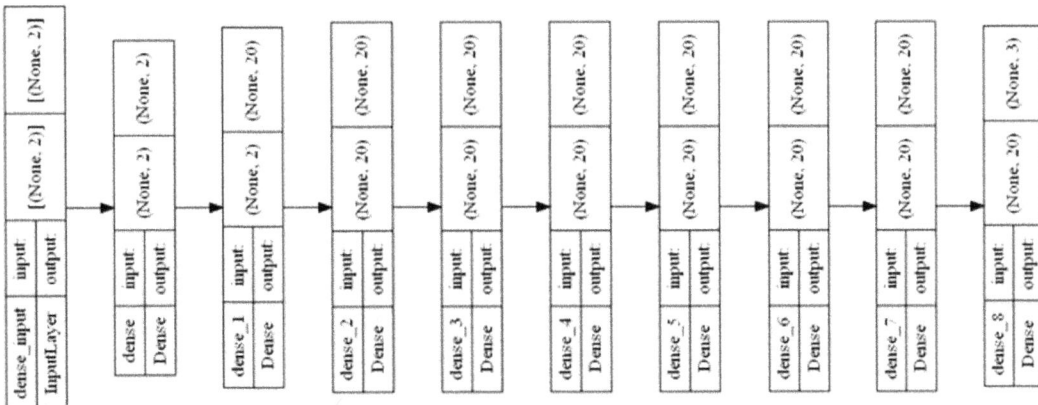

Figure 2.17: Keras model architecture

11. Train the model on the dataset created (using the **fit()** method), for 10 **epochs** and with **batch_size** 5.

12. Use the model to predict the pixel RGB values for the given coordinates. It returns the reconstructed (painted) image.

13. Plot the original input and the reconstructed output image as follows:

```
m.fit(x, y, batch_size=5, epochs=10, verbose=1, \
                                      validation_data=(x, y))
out = generate_image(m, x, im.width, im.height)

plt.figure(figsize=(10,10))
plt.subplot(121), plt.imshow(im), plt.axis('off') plt.
title('Original', size=20)
plt.subplot(122), plt.imshow(out), plt.axis('off')
plt.title('Neural Net Painted', size=20)
plt.show()

# Epoch 1/10
# 61440/61440 [==============================] - 125s 2ms/step -
loss: # 1449.2676 - val_loss: 1249.4037
# Epoch 2/10
# 61440/61440 [==============================] - 120s 2ms/step -
loss: # 1041.2477 - val_loss: 647.8983
# Epoch 3/10
# 61440/61440 [==============================] - 134s 2ms/step -
loss: # 539.8658 - val_loss: 321.4036
# Epoch 4/10
# 61440/61440 [==============================] - 145s 2ms/step -
loss: # 361.0727 - val_loss: 332.0901
# Epoch 5/10
# 61440/61440 [==============================] - 120s 2ms/step -
loss: # 319.6828 - val_loss: 258.9804
# Epoch 6/10
# 61440/61440 [==============================] - 121s 2ms/step -
loss: # 299.9219 - val_loss: 260.5214
# Epoch 7/10
# 61440/61440 [==============================] - 140s 2ms/step -
loss: # 287.6617 - val_loss: 237.3738
# Epoch 8/10
# 61440/61440 [==============================] - 129s 2ms/step -
loss: # 275.5465 - val_loss: 272.4277
# Epoch 9/10
# 61440/61440 [==============================] - 142s 2ms/step -
loss: # 269.4614 - val_loss: 253.6740
# Epoch 10/10
# 61440/61440 [==============================] - 129s 2ms/step -
loss: # 258.9236 - val_loss: 259.6959
```

If you run the preceding code snippet, you should obtain a figure like the next one:

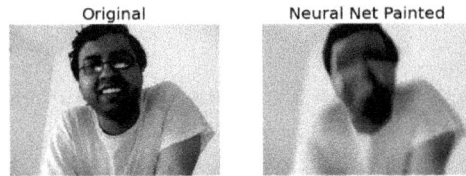

Figure 2.18: *Neural painting with Keras*

Semantic image inpainting with DCGAN

DCGAN introduces certain architectural constraints in implementing an ordinary GAN and yields better results with stronger representation learning. It eliminates the fully connected layers (and also the **global average pooling**, which hurts the convergence speed), turning it into an **all-convolutional** net, replaces deterministic spatial pooling functions (such as max-pooling) with **strided convolutions**, allowing the discriminator and the generator to learn their own spatial downsampling and spatial upsampling, respectively.

Here are the architecture guidelines for stable **DCGAN** [4]:

- Use **strided convolutions** and **fractional-strided convolutions** instead of the pooling layers, for the discriminator and the generator, respectively.

- Use **batch-normalization** in generator and discriminator (except for the layers generator output and the discriminator input).

- For deeper architectures, get rid of fully connected hidden layers.

- For all layers in the generator, use the **ReLU** activation (except for the output, for which, use **Tanh** activation).

- For all layers in the discriminator, use the **LeakyReLU** activation.

The following figure shows the DCGAN generator architecture:

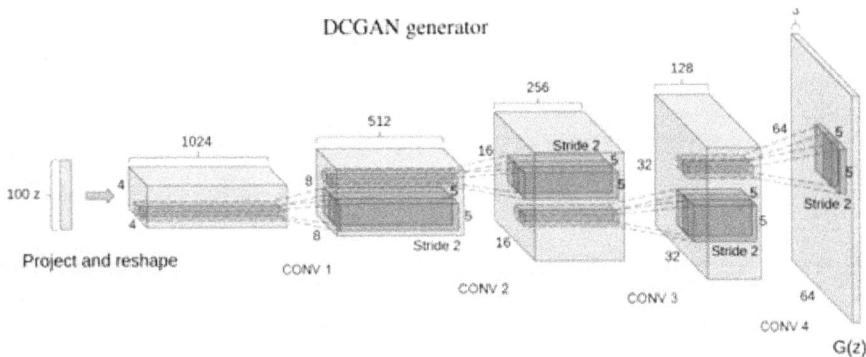

Figure 2.19: *DCGAN generator architecture*
Source: *https://arxiv.org/pdf/1511.06434.pdf*

In this section, we shall learn how to use DCGAN for image completion, given a partially corrupted image. Let us understand how we can implement it with semantic image inpainting using DCGAN:

- Semantic image inpainting is a challenging task where large missing regions have to be filled based on the available visual data.

- Unlike traditional inpainting (which relies on low-level features like edges or textures), **semantic inpainting** uses **high-level understanding** of **objects** and **scenes** to plausibly reconstruct what is missing. For example:

  o If part of a face is missing, a semantic inpainting model can infer and generate eyes, nose, or mouth using prior knowledge of how faces typically look.

  o It doesn't just fill in similar colors or textures — it fills in the correct object parts, based on learned context.

- Given a trained generative model, the closest encoding of the corrupted image is searched in the latent image manifold using the **context** and **prior losses**. This encoding is then passed through the generative model to infer the missing content.

- The inference is possible irrespective of how the missing content is structured.

- Back-propagation to the input data is employed to find the encoding close to the provided corrupted image.

- To fill large missing regions in images, our method for image inpainting utilizes the **generator** G and the **discriminator** D, both of which are trained with uncorrupted data. The encoding $\hat{z}$ closest to the corrupted image is recovered while being constrained to the manifold, as shown in the following figure. After $\hat{z}$ is obtained, the missing content can be generated by using the trained generator [5].

Refer to the following figure:

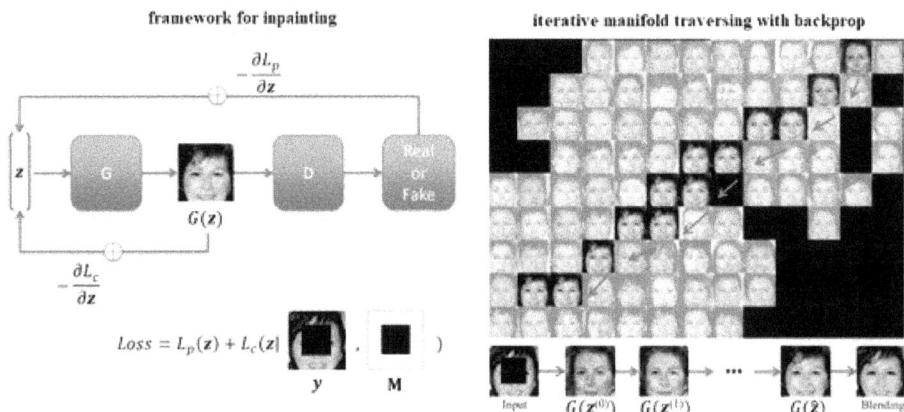

Figure 2.20: Semantic image inpainting with DCGAN
Source: https://arxiv.org/pdf/1607.07539.pdf

- The process of finding $\hat{z}$ can be formulated as an **optimization problem**. Let y be the corrupted image and M be the binary mask with a size equal to the image to indicate the missing parts. The *closest* encoding $\hat{z}$ is defined as:

$$\hat{z} = \arg\min_{z} \{ \underbrace{\mathcal{L}_c(z|y, M)}_{\text{context loss}} + \underbrace{\mathcal{L}_p(z)}_{\text{prior loss}} \}$$

- The **context loss** constrains the generated image z given the input corrupted image y and the hole mask M, whereas the **prior loss** penalizes **unrealistic** images.

- **Weighted context loss**: To fill large missing regions, we need to take advantage of the remaining available data. The context loss is designed to capture such information. A convenient choice for the context loss is simply the l_2 norm between the generated sample $G(z)$ and the uncorrupted portion of the input image y, but such a loss treats each pixel equally, which is not desired.

- A context loss is to be defined with the hypothesis that the importance of an uncorrupted pixel is positively correlated with the number of corrupted pixels surrounding it. A pixel that is very far away from any holes plays very little role in the inpainting process. This intuition is captured with the importance weighting term, W defined as follows:

$$\underset{\substack{\text{pixel location} \\ \text{importance weight}}}{\mathbf{W}_i} = \begin{cases} \underset{j \in N(i)}{\sum} \dfrac{(1 - \mathbf{M}_j)}{|N(i)|} & \text{if } \mathbf{M}_i \neq 0 \\ \underset{\text{neighbors}}{0} & \text{if } \mathbf{M}_i = 0 \end{cases},$$

$$\underset{\text{context loss}}{\mathcal{L}_c(z|y, M)} = \| \mathbf{W} \odot (\overset{\text{recovered image}}{G(z)} - \underset{\text{uncorrupted portion}}{y}) \|_1.$$

$\underset{}{\ell_1\text{-norm}}$

$\odot$ *element-wise multiplication*

$$\underset{\text{perceptual loss}}{L_p(z)} = \lambda \, log(1 - D(G(z)))$$

$$\underset{\text{total loss}}{L(z)} = L_c(z) + \lambda L_p(z)$$

$$\hat{z} = \arg\min_{\lambda} L(z)$$

- After generating $G(\hat{z})$, the inpainting result can be obtained by overlaying the uncorrupted pixels from the input. However, the predicted pixels may not exactly preserve the same intensities of the surrounding pixels, which is corrected using **Poisson blending** (by keeping the gradients of $G(\hat{z})$ to preserve image details while shifting the color to match the color in the input image y). The final solution, the recovered image $\hat{x}$, can be obtained by:

$$\hat{\mathbf{x}} = \arg\min_{\mathbf{x}} \|\nabla \mathbf{x} - \nabla G(\hat{\mathbf{z}})\|_2^2,$$

$$\text{s.t. } \mathbf{x}_i = \mathbf{y}_i \text{ for } \mathbf{M}_i = 1$$

In this section, we shall use a pretrained **DCGAN** model with **tensorflow** (v1), trained on celebrity faces (**celebA** dataset). Let us dive into python implementation, follow the next steps:

1. Let us start by importing the required libraries, with the following code snippet:

```python
import tensorflow.compat.v1 as tf
import numpy as np
import matplotlib.pylab as plt
from glob import glob
from skimage.io import imread
from scipy.signal import convolve2d
```

2. Read the input face images and cast to **uint8**.

3. Generate square masks at the center of the images using the function **gen_mask()**. The default input image size is 64×64 and the **scale** is 0.25, which determines the size of the mask.

4. Corrupt the input images by removing the central square part from the image using the masks created, by using logical AND (**&**) operation as:

```python
def gen_mask(img_sz = 64, scale = 0.25):
    image_shape = [img_sz, img_sz]
    mask = np.ones(image_shape)
    #assert(scale <= 0.5)
    mask = np.ones(image_shape)
    l = int(img_sz*scale)
    u = int(img_sz*(1.0-scale))
    mask[l:u, l:u] = 0.0
    return mask

imgfilenames = sorted(glob('images/faces' + '/*.png'))
images = np.array([imread(f, pilmode='RGB').astype('float') \
                    for f in imgfilenames]).astype(np.uint8)

masked_images = images.copy()
mask = gen_mask()
mask = (255*mask).astype(np.uint8)
for i in range(len(images)):
    masked_images[i,...] = masked_images[i,...] & \
                            np.expand_dims(mask,2)
masked_images = masked_images.astype(np.float64)
mask = (mask / 255).astype(np.float64)
```

5. Load the pretrained **graph** from ProtoBuf file with the function **loadpb()**. It accepts a couple of arguments: **filename** (path to ProtoBuf graph definition) and **model_name** (prefix to assign to loaded graph node names). The function returns **graph** and **graph_def**, as per TensorFlow definitions.

6. Use the function **tf.get_tensor_by_name()** to access the tensors corresponding to input, output and loss in the **graph** object as:

```python
def loadpb(filename, model_name='dcgan'):

    with tf.io.gfile.GFile(filename, 'rb') as f:
        graph_def = tf.GraphDef()
        graph_def.ParseFromString(f.read())

    with tf.Graph().as_default() as graph:
        tf.import_graph_def(graph_def,
                            input_map=None,
                             return_elements=None,
                             op_dict=None,
                             producer_op_list=None,
                             name=model_name)
    return graph, graph_def

model_name = 'dcgan'
gen_input, gen_output, gen_loss = 'z:0', 'Tanh:0', 'Mean_2:0'
graph, graph_def = loadpb('models/dcgan-100.pb', model_name)

gi = graph.get_tensor_by_name(model_name+'/' + gen_input)
go = graph.get_tensor_by_name(model_name+'/' + gen_output)
gl = graph.get_tensor_by_name(model_name+'/' + gen_loss)
image_shape = go.shape[1:].as_list()
```

7. The function **create_weighted_mask()** computes the importance weight mask, as defined.

8. The function **create_3_channel_mask()** creates a 3 channel mask by repeating the single channel and the function **binarize_mask** computes binary mask given a non-binary one.

9. The function **build_restore_graph()** creates the placeholders for masks and images and builds the computation graph for the context/perceptual loss and gradients. Note that since *eager execution* is not enabled in **tensorflow v1**, the execution will only happen when a **session** is created.

10. The function **preprocess()** transforms the images and the masks prior to passing them to the model in the appropriate format.

11. The function **postprocess()** extracts the inpainted image from the output **tensor** after the execution happens as:

```python
def create_weighted_mask(mask, nsize=7):
    ker = np.ones((nsize,nsize), dtype=np.float32)
    ker = ker/np.sum(ker)
    wmask = mask * convolve2d(1-mask, ker, mode='same', \
                              boundary='symm')
    return wmask

def binarize_mask(mask, dtype=np.float32):
    assert(np.dtype(dtype) == np.float32 or \
                  np.dtype(dtype) == np.uint8)
    bmask = np.array(mask, dtype=np.float32)
    bmask[bmask>0] = 1.0
    bmask[bmask<=0] = 0
    if dtype == np.uint8:
        bmask = np.array(bmask*255, dtype=np.uint8)
    return bmask

def create_3_channel_mask(mask):
    return np.repeat(mask[:,:,np.newaxis], 3, axis=2)

def build_restore_graph(graph):
    image_shape = go.shape[1:].as_list()
    with graph.as_default():
        masks = tf.placeholder(tf.float32, [None] + image_shape, \
                          name='mask')
        images = tf.placeholder(tf.float32, [None] + image_shape, \
                          name='images')
        x = tf.abs(tf.multiply(masks, go) - tf.multiply(masks, images))
        context_loss = tf.reduce_sum(tf.reshape(x, \
                                  (tf.shape(x)[0], -1)), 1)
        perceptual_loss = gl
        inpaint_loss = context_loss + l*perceptual_loss
        inpaint_grad = tf.gradients(inpaint_loss, gi)
    return inpaint_loss, inpaint_grad, masks, images

def preprocess(images, imask, useWeightedMask=True, \
                  batch_size=64, nsize=15):
    images = images / 127.5-1
    mask = create_3_channel_mask(create_weighted_mask(imask, nsize))
    bin_mask = create_3_channel_mask(binarize_mask(imask, \
                                  dtype='uint8'))
    masks_data = np.repeat(mask[np.newaxis, :, :, :], \
                        batch_size, axis=0)
    num_images = images.shape[0]
```

```
        images_data = np.repeat(images[np.newaxis, 0, :, :, :], \
                            batch_size, axis=0)
    ncpy = min(num_images, batch_size)
    images_data[:ncpy, :, :, :] = images[:ncpy, :, :, :].copy()
    return masks_data, images_data
def postprocess(g_out, images_data, masks_data):
    images_out = (np.array(g_out) + 1.0) / 2.0
    images_in = (np.array(images_data) + 1.0) / 2.0
    images_out = np.multiply(images_out, 1-masks_data) + \
                np.multiply(images_in, masks_data)
    return images_out
```

12. The function **backprop_to_input()** is the key function that performs the actual execution (**sess.run()**) on the session **sess** passed as an argument.

13. The function accepts the **tensorflow** placeholders (**images, masks**) and the data (**images_data, masks_data**) for the corrupted input images and masks.

14. The input corrupted images and masks need to be passed to the **feed_dict** for the placeholders.

15. The function accepts total **batch_size** (initialized to 64) number of random input noise vectors **z**, each of dimension **z_dim** (100). It iteratively performs back-propagation through the latent manifold (runs for **niter** =200 by default) and returns the reconstructed output image **imout**.

16. The function **restore_image()** combines all using the functions defined: it first preprocesses the input image/mask batch, then builds the **tf graph** for computation, then performs back-prop to obtain the output batch, and finally postprocesses the output to transform it to inpainted image batch, as shown in *Figure 2.21:*

```
def backprop_to_input(sess, inpaint_loss, inpaint_grad,
                    masks, images, masks_data, images_data, z,
                    niter=200, verbose=True):
    momentum, lr = 0.9, 0.01
    v = 0
    for i in range(niter):
        out_vars = [inpaint_loss, inpaint_grad, go]
        in_dict = {masks: masks_data, gi: z, images: images_data}
        loss, grad, imout = sess.run(out_vars, feed_dict=in_dict)
        v_prev = np.copy(v)
        v = momentum*v - lr*grad[0]
        z += (-momentum * v_prev + (1 + momentum) * v)
        z = np.clip(z, -1, 1)
        if verbose:
```

```
            if i % 10 == 0:
                print('Iteration {}: {}'.format(i, np.mean(loss)))
    return imout

def restore_image(images, masks, graph, sess):
    masks_data, images_data = preprocess(images, masks)
    inpaint_loss, inpaint_grad, masks, images = \
                                build_restore_graph(graph)

    imout = backprop_to_input(sess, inpaint_loss, inpaint_grad, \
                        masks, images, masks_data, images_data, z)
    return postprocess(imout, images_data, masks_data), \
                                            images_data, imout

batch_size, z_dim = 64, 100
z = np.random.randn(batch_size, z_dim)
sess = tf.Session(graph=graph)
inpaint_out, images_data, imout = restore_image(masked_images, \
                                        mask, graph, sess)

# Iteration 0: 221.28106689453125
# Iteration 10: 137.1205291748047
# Iteration 20: 120.86093139648438
# Iteration 30: 120.55803680419922
# Iteration 40: 118.15397644042969
# Iteration 50: 111.87590026855469
# Iteration 60: 111.30235290527344
# Iteration 70: 109.60200500488281
# Iteration 80: 112.72096252441406
# Iteration 90: 108.38629150390625
# Iteration 100: 106.88809204101562
# Iteration 110: 106.95480346679688
# Iteration 120: 106.71363830566406
# Iteration 130: 105.97818756103516
# Iteration 140: 103.75382995605469
# Iteration 150: 101.30975341796875
# Iteration 160: 104.94699096679688
# Iteration 170: 101.54997253417969
# Iteration 180: 107.21031951904297
# Iteration 190: 103.7147445678711
```

As can be seen from the preceding output, the loss has a decreasing trend with iterations, which means we will likely find better reconstructions for the corrupted images. Plot the original, masked (corrupted) input and the inpainted output images with the DCGAN. You should obtain a figure as shown:

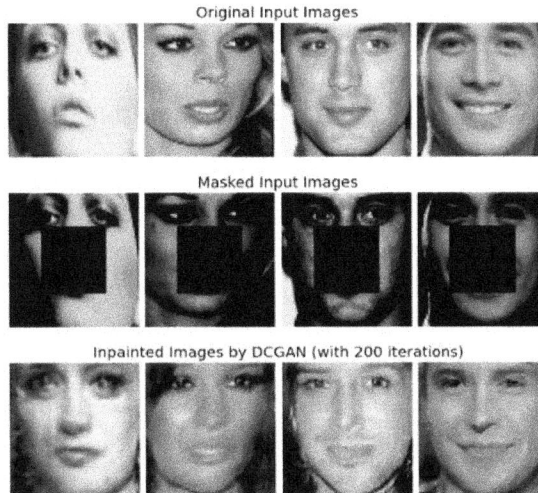

Figure 2.21: Image inpainting with DCGAN

Conclusion

In this chapter, we learnt a few more advanced techniques for image restoration, denoising, deblurring and image inpainting. Although we learned how to use a few variational method implementations (for example, diffusion) and a machine learning model (kNN) for image restoration, the majority of the methods we learnt to implement were based on very recent deep learning models, such as different flavors of autoencoders (sparse, variational) and GANs (DCGAN, CGAN). By now, you should be able to solve image restoration problems using deep learning pre-trained models and also write **python** code train models from scratch, using both the libraries **pytorch** and **tensoflow/keras**. In the next chapter, we shall start with a new and a very important topic in image processing, namely image segmentation.

Note: Throughout the chapter, we used the term parameters in a couple of contexts:

- The first one is in the programming context: parameters (arguments) to a Python function.

- The second one is in the AI/ML context: learnable parameters (for example, weights and biases) for a machine learning model.

Key terms

Inpainting, anisotropic diffusion, DeblurGAN, DCGAN, conditional GAN, stacked autoencoder, sparse autoencoder, kNN regression, Navier-Stokes, Fast Marching

Questions

1. A very simple Blur function: Implement a python function get_custom_blurkernel() to simulate a custom motion motion-blur kernel. Implement another function gen_blurred_image() that accepts an input and an output image file and your custom blur function, reads the input image file, applies the blur kernel (by invoking the blur function passed as argument) to the input image and saves the output in the output image file. Plot the input image, the generated kernel and the blurred output image.

    a. For example, if you want to generate your blur-kernel with a cubic spline (for example, blurred input images for **DeblurGAN** were created using it), you just need to call the function gen_blurred_image() with the function get_custom_blurkernel() which returns the desired kernel:

    ```
    gen_blurred_image(path_to_input_img, path_to_save_blurred_img, \
                        get_custom_blurkernel)
    ```

    And the output will look like the one shown in the following figure:

    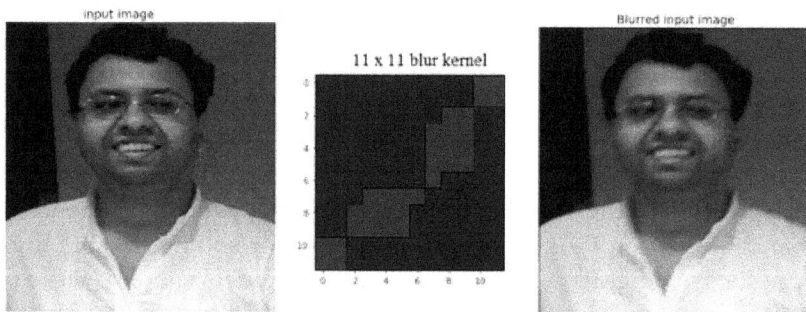

    Figure 2.22: *Blurring an image with custom blur kernel*

    b. Now, implement the motion blur kernel generation algorithm from the paper **https://arxiv.org/pdf/1711.07064.pdf.** Blur an image with the function you implemented and apply **DeblurGAN** to obtain the sharpened version of the image.

2. In this chapter, we used available pre-trained weights **GCANet** and **DeblurGAN** deep learning models. Now let us train the models on custom annotated images (you will need hazy/blurred and clean version of every image in the training dataset) to be used for dehazing and deblurring, respectively. Note that you can train a deep neural net model:

    a. Partially (using **transfer learning**), by training the weights of last few layers only (preferably when you have smaller number of annotated training images).

    b. Fully (from scratch), when you have a whole lot of annotated images.

In any case, or training a very deep learning model, you will need a *GPU* for faster training (use **Google Colab**).

3. Use opencv-python's **bm3d** implementation (cv2.xphoto.bm3dDenoising()) for denoising (note that the algorithm is patented, you need to build OpenCV with an appropriate flag). You should obtain a figure like the following one:

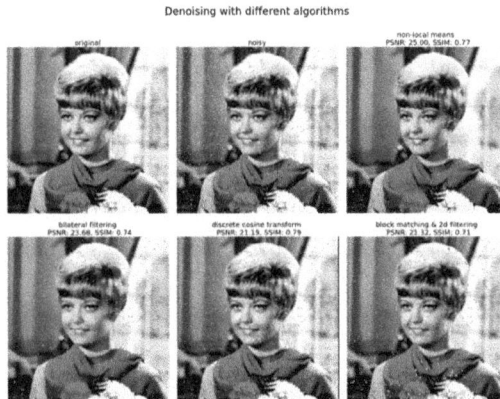

Figure 2.23: Image denoising with different filtering algorithms

4. Use **kNN regressor** to inpaint the following RGB color image with the given binary mask. You should obtain a figure like the following one:

Figure 2.24: Image inpainting with knn regressor

References

1. **https://arxiv.org/pdf/1606.08921.pdf**

2. **https://arxiv.org/pdf/1711.07064.pdf**

3. **https://arxiv.org/pdf/1811.08747.pdf**

4. **https://arxiv.org/pdf/1511.06434.pdf**

5. **https://arxiv.org/pdf/1607.07539.pdf**

6. https://authors.library.caltech.edu/6498/1/PERieeetpami90.pdf

7. https://aip.scitation.org/doi/pdf/10.1063/1.4887563

8. https://github.com/cddlyf/GCANet

9. https://github.com/aizvorski/video-quality/blob/d16674a14c66d9014ac82fcb7925dbc86e568d7e/ssim.py

10. https://www.youtube.com/watch?v=XOcCXvksbTI

Join our Discord space

Join our Discord workspace for latest updates, offers, tech happenings around the world, new releases, and sessions with the authors:

https://discord.bpbonline.com

## CHAPTER 3

Image Segmentation

Introduction

Image segmentation is a task in image processing and computer vision that involves partitioning an image into multiple segments or regions. The goal is to group together pixels that share similar characteristics, such as color, intensity, texture, or other visual properties. The purpose of image segmentation is to simplify the representation of an image or to make it more meaningful for further analysis.

Mathematically, image segmentation can be defined as the process of assigning a label or identifier to each pixel in an image based on certain criteria. Let us denote an input image as I, and the goal is to partition it into N segments. The task segmentation can be represented as a function (x, y) that maps each pixel in the image to a segment label:

$$S: (x, y) \rightarrow \{1, 2, \ldots, N\}$$

Here, N is the total number of segments, and $s = S(x, y) \in \{1, 2, \ldots, N\}$ represents the segment label assigned to the pixel (x, y). The segmentation function S is typically determined by analyzing the properties of the pixels in the image, and it aims to group pixels with similar characteristics into the same segment.

There are various approaches to image segmentation, ranging from traditional methods to deep learning techniques. Some common and popular methods include thresholding, region-based segmentation, edge-based segmentation and, more recently, deep learning **convolutional neural networks** (**CNN**) for semantic segmentation.

These methods vary in complexity and suitability for different types of images and applications. In this chapter and the next one, we will discuss a few different algorithms for segmentation with aforementioned approaches and learn how to use functions from Python libraries `scikit-image`, `opencv-python`, `scipy.ndimage`, `SimpleITK, tensorflow`, `keras` and `pytorch`.

Structure

This chapter will explore the following topics:

- Gray level and bitplane slicing

- Binarizing an image with thresholding

- Segmentation using clustering

- MeanShift segmentation with opencv-python and scikit-learn

- Watershed segmentation with opencv-python and SimpleITK

- GrabCut segmentation with opencv-python

- RandomWalk segmentation with scikit-image

- Segmentation using SLIC/NCut algorithms with scikit-image

Objectives

By the end of this chapter, you will learn various image segmentation techniques, ranging from basic to advanced methods. You will explore fundamental approaches such as graylevel and bitplane slicing, thresholding, and clustering-based segmentation. Additionally, you will gain hands-on experience with advanced techniques, including **MeanShift**, **watershed**, **GrabCut**, **RandomWalk**, and **fast marching** segmentation, using Python libraries like `opencv-python`, `scikit-image`, and `SimpleITK`. You will also learn how to apply segmentation using **Simple Linear Iterative Clustering** (**SLIC**) and **NCut** algorithms. These methods will equip you with the skills needed to effectively segment images for diverse image processing and computer vision applications.

Gray level and bitplane slicing

These operations apply piecewise linear transformation functions to an image. **Gray level slicing** is a technique used in image processing where specific intensity levels or ranges of pixel values are selected and highlighted in the output image while the rest of the intensity levels are either ignored or suppressed. This process is often applied to enhance certain features or details in an image. **Bitplane slicing** is a technique used to decompose an image into its bitplane components.

Gray level slicing

As described earlier, this technique is used for highlighting a specific range of intensities in an image. There can be following two approaches for gray level (intensity level) slicing:

- **Without background**: Display in one value (e.g., white) all the values in the range of interest, and in another (e.g., black, i.e., 0) all other intensities (as shown in the following figure).

- **With background**: Brightens or darkens the desired range of intensities but leaves all other intensity levels in the image unchanged.

As shown in the *Figure 3.1* (for an 8-bit grayscale image we have $L = 256$), the source and target image gray levels being denoted by r and s, respectively. The point transformation T (gray-level slicing) is applied to obtain the target image's gray level $s = T(r)$.

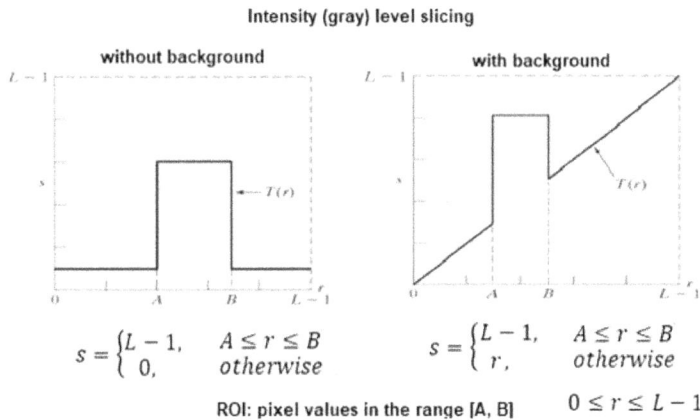

$$s = \begin{cases} L - 1, & A \leq r \leq B \\ 0, & otherwise \end{cases}$$

ROI: pixel values in the range [A, B]

$$s = \begin{cases} L - 1, & A \leq r \leq B \\ r, & otherwise \end{cases}$$

$$0 \leq r \leq L - 1$$

Figure 3.1: *Gray level slicing*

Let us implement gray level slicing and import the required Python libraries and functions to start with:

```
%matplotlib inline
from skimage.io import imread
from skimage.color import rgb2gray
import numpy as np
import matplotlib.pylab as plt
import warnings
warnings.filterwarnings('ignore')
```

The function **gray_level_slice()** accepts an input grayscale image, along with a minimum and a maximum pixel value as input arguments. It applies intensity level slicing with/without background, as described earlier, as specified by the value of the boolean argument **with_background**, to be set to **True**/**False**, respectively, with the value defaulting to **False**, as shown in the following code snippet. The function returns the gray level sliced image and the mask created by filtering out the pixels outside the pixel range (provided as input).

The function **plot_images()** accepts a list of images (as NumPy arrays) and the corresponding titles and uses **matplotlib.pylab** to plot them with those titles:

```python
def gray_level_slice(im, min_pixel, max_pixel, with_background=False):
    im_sliced = im.copy()
    im_mask = (im >= min_pixel) & (im <= max_pixel)
    im_sliced[im_mask] = 255
    if not with_background:
        im_sliced[~im_mask] = 0
    return im_sliced, im_mask

def plot_images(ims, titles, suptitle = None):
    n = len(ims)
    plt.figure(figsize=(15,7))
    plt.gray()
    plt.subplots_adjust(0,0,1,0.95,0.05,0.05)
    for i in range(n):
        plt.subplot(1,n,i+1), plt.imshow(ims[i]), plt.axis('off')
        plt.title(titles[i], size=20)
    if suptitle:
        plt.suptitle(suptitle, size=25)
    plt.show()
```

Let us first read the image **coins.png**. Plot the image gray level histogram to identify the range of grey levels within the coins, using the next lines of code:

```python
im = rgb2gray(imread('images/coins.png'))
im = (255 * im / im.max()).astype(np.uint8)

plt.figure(figsize=(5,3))
plt.hist(im.flatten(), bins=100), plt.grid()
plt.title('hisogram of gray levels', size=20)
plt.show()
```

If you run the following code snippet, you should obtain a figure as follows. As shown in the following figure, most pixels are between 100 and 240:

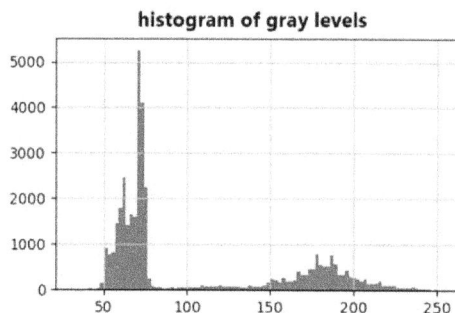

Figure 3.2: Bimodal histogram of gray levels

Now, let us find all the coins based on pixel range (**min_pixel=90** and **max_pixel=255**), with gray level slicing, using the function **gray_level_slice()** implemented earlier, and set pixels inside the coin to white.

For slicing with background set **with_background=True** specifically, otherwise the rest of the pixels outside the pixel range provided are set to black:

```
min_pixel, max_pixel = 90, 255
# to improve use median filter on background to remove light gray pixels
# initialise your output images
im_sliced_without_bg, im_mask = gray_level_slice(im, min_pixel, max_pixel)
im_sliced_with_bg, im_mask = gray_level_slice(im, min_pixel, max_pixel, True)

plot_images([im, im_sliced_without_bg, im_sliced_with_bg],
            ['original image', 'without background', 'with background'],
            suptitle = 'gray level slicing with and without background')
```

If you run the following code snippet, you should obtain a figure as follows:

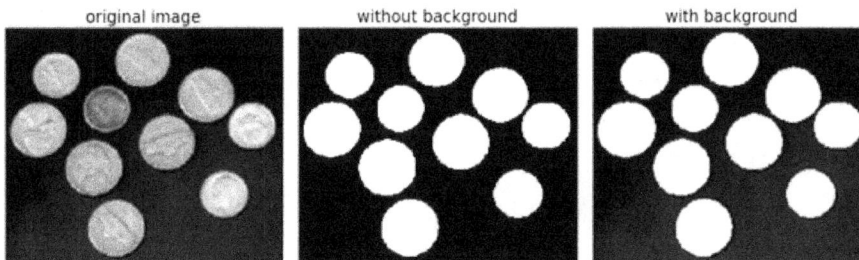

Figure 3.3: Gray level slicing

Increasing contrast within ROI

Gray level slicing is used to emphasize specific regions in an image by isolating the pixel values corresponding to those regions. Let us use the aforementioned implementation on the **region of interest** (**ROI**) of the coin's image (e.g., the coins) and increase the contrast within the coins using the following code snippet.

The function **enhance_image()**, as defined in the following code snippet, takes the original image along with the ROI mask created (using the gray level slicing) as input and enhances the image only in the ROI. It uses a non-linear transformation on the ROI to improve the contrast of the coins (and clamps the pixel values in [0,255] with **np.clip()**). Finally, it sets the background (outside mask) to another gray level (note that having a single grey level as background may not feel right for human vision).

```
def enhance_image(im, im_mask, min_pixel):
    im_enhanced = 0 * im
    im_enhanced[im_mask] = np.clip(np.round((im[im_mask] - min_pixel)**1.1), \
                                                                    0, 255)

    im_enhanced[~im_mask] = 25 # could be any value or another transform
    return im_enhanced
im_enhanced = enhance_image(im, im_mask, min_pixel)
plot_images([im, im_sliced_without_bg, im_enhanced], \
            ['original image', 'gray level slicing mask', 'image enhanced'])
```

If you run the aforementioned code snippet, you should obtain a figure as follows:

Figure 3.4: Increasing contrast within ROI (mask)

Bitplane slicing

In digital image processing, each pixel in an image is represented by a binary number (composed of bits), and bitplane slicing involves extracting the bit values at a specific bit position across all pixels. For an 8-bit image, there are 8 bitplanes (from the **most significant bit** (**MSB**), to the **least significant bit** (**LSB**)), as shown in the following figure. Each bitplane represents a different level of image detail. Instead of highlighting the gray level range, we could highlight the contribution made by each bit. This method can be used in (lossy) image compression (by prioritizing and encoding higher-order bitplanes, which contain most of the image's visual information, while discarding or compressing lower-order planes to reduce data size).

Higher-order (the most significant) bits contain the majority of visually significant data. Lower-order bits contain subtle details. Often, by isolating particular bits of the pixel values in an image, we can highlight interesting aspects of that image. The following figure shows a schematic diagram for bitplance slicing:

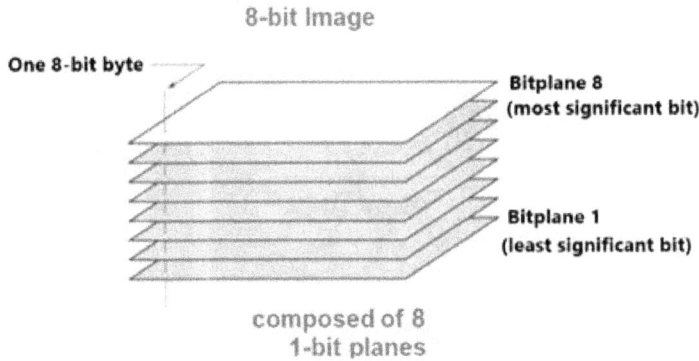

Figure 3.5: *Bitplane slicing*

The following code snippet reads a grayscale image and performs bitplane slicing (extracts the bits from different bitplances using the function **np.unpackbits()**). As shown in the following code, the higher bitplanes contain the most visual information:

```python
im = (255*rgb2gray(imread('images/pattern.jpg'))).astype(np.uint8)
h, w = im.shape
bitplanes = np.unpackbits([im.flatten()], axis=0)

plt.figure(figsize=(15,12))
plt.subplots_adjust(0,0,1,0.95,0.05,0.05)
plt.gray()
plt.subplot(3,3,1), plt.imshow(im), plt.axis('off')
plt.title('original', size=15)
for i in range(8):
    plt.subplot(3,3,i+2)
    plt.imshow(bitplanes[i,:].reshape(h,w)), plt.axis('off')
    plt.title('bitplane {}'.format(8-i-1))
plt.show()
```

If you run the aforementioned code snippet, you should obtain a figure as follows:

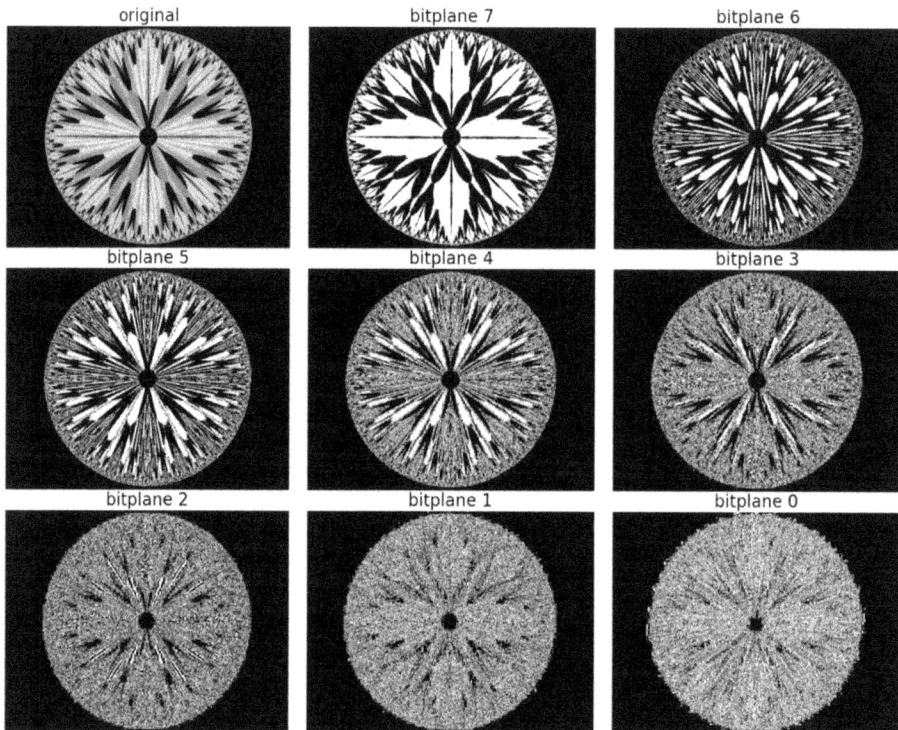

Figure 3.6: Original image and the bitplane images

Binarizing an image with thresholding

Image thresholding is a technique used in image processing to separate objects or regions in an image by dividing it into two parts: **foreground** and **background**. This separation is based on a **threshold** value, where pixels with intensities above the threshold are assigned to one class (often known as foreground), and those below the threshold are assigned to another (often called background). The result is a binary image where pixels are either black or white.

Thresholding with scikit-image

The library `scikit-image` provides a variety of thresholding methods. Here, you will learn how to use different global image thresholding algorithms to binarize an image.

Global thresholding

Global image thresholding involves applying a single threshold value to the entire image. This threshold value is determined based on the characteristics of the entire image, and it is used to separate the image into two regions: one above the threshold and one below the threshold. The result is a binary image with pixels classified into foreground or background.

Let us start the implementation by importing the required libraries, as usual, as shown:

```
from skimage.io import imread
from skimage.color import rgb2gray
import matplotlib.pylab as plt
from skimage.filters import try_all_threshold, threshold_otsu, rank
```

The function **try_all_threshold()** from **skiamge.filters** is a useful tool for comparing different global and local thresholding methods. It generates a visual comparison of various thresholding methods, making it easier to choose an appropriate method for a specific image.

The following is an overview of a few global image thresholding algorithms that we shall use:

- **ISODATA**: This **Iterative Self-Organizing Data Analysis (ISODATA)** method calculates the threshold as the mean between the average of the pixels below the threshold and the pixels above it. It continues this process until convergence.

- **Mean**: This method calculates the threshold value as the mean intensity of the entire image. Pixels with intensity values above the mean are assigned to one class, while those below are assigned to another.

- **Li/Yen**: These are minimum cross-entropy thresholding methods that seek a threshold that minimizes the cross-entropy between the original and binarized images.

- **Minimum**: The histogram of the input image is computed and smoothed until there are only two maxima. The minimum in between is returned as the threshold value.

- **Otsu**: This method finds the (**optimal**) threshold that minimizes the intra-class variance (or maximizes inter-class variance) of pixel intensities in an image. The algorithm works well for images with bimodal histograms, where there are two distinct intensity peaks corresponding to the foreground and background.

The following are the steps to apply binary segmentation on an image, using the thresholding algorithms:

1. Load a sample image and convert it to a grayscale.

2. Use the **try_all_threshold()** function to generate a visual comparison of different global thresholding methods.

3. Display the binary images produced using different algorithms.

```
img = rgb2gray(imread('images/tagore.jpg'))
img = (255* img / img.max()).astype(np.uint8)
# Here, we specify a radius for local thresholding algorithms.
# If it is not specified, only global algorithms are called.
fig, ax = try_all_threshold(img, figsize=(12, 18), verbose=False)
plt.show()
```

If you run the aforementioned code snippet, you should obtain a figure as follows:

Figure 3.7: Binary thresholding with different algorithms

It seems the **triangle,** and the **Yen** methods outperform the others for this particular input image.

Local thresholding

As discussed earlier, global image thresholding involves applying a single threshold value to the entire image. Local image thresholding, on the other hand, determines different threshold values for different regions of the image. Each pixel's threshold is computed based on the local characteristics of its neighborhood. This approach is useful when the image exhibits variations in intensity or contrast across different regions.

To simulate local intensity variation, we shall add a small multiplicative (horizontal ramp) noise to the image, using the **add_mult_noise()** function defined, using the following code snippet:

```python
from skimage.morphology import disk
def add_mult_noise(img):
    ramp = np.clip(np.tile(np.linspace(0, 1, img.shape[1]), \
                           (img.shape[0],1)), 0, 255)
    return (img * ramp).astype(np.uint8)
noisy_img = add_mult_noise(img)
```

Here we shall discuss how to use the **local** and the **global** version of **Otsu's** thresholding algorithm to binarize an image.

To obtain local thresholds, first, create a neighborhood disk of **radius=30** (change the radius to see the impact on the binary output image) using the function **disk()** from **skimage.morphology** and the function **rank.otsu()**, along with the input image and neighborhood disk. Use the local thresholds array to obtain the binary image **local_otsu**.

To obtain a global threshold value (**global_thresh**) using Otsu's method use the function **threshold_otsu()** from **skimage.filters** module and use the threshold value to create the binary image **global_otsu**.

Finally display the input and output images, notice that local **otsu** produces a much better binary output image, whereas the one obtained with the global version loses much information:

```python
radius = 30
footprint = disk(radius)
local_thresh = rank.otsu(noisy_img, footprint)
local_otsu = noisy_img > local_thresh

global_thresh = threshold_otsu(noisy_img)
print(global_thresh)
# 78
global_otsu = noisy_img > global_thresh

fig, axes = plt.subplots(nrows=2, ncols=2, figsize=(12, 12))
ax = axes.ravel()
```

```
ax[0].imshow(noisy_img, cmap=plt.cm.gray, aspect='auto')
ax[0].set_title('input', size=20), ax[0].axis('off')
ax[1].imshow(local_otsu, cmap=plt.cm.gray, aspect='auto')
ax[1].set_title('local Otsu', size=20), ax[1].axis('off')
ax[2].hist(noisy_img.ravel(), bins=256)
ax[2].set_title('Histogram', size=20)
ax[2].axvline(global_thresh, color='r')
ax[3].imshow(global_otsu, cmap=plt.cm.gray, aspect='auto')
ax[3].set_title('global Otsu', size=20), ax[3].axis('off')
plt.tight_layout()
plt.show()
```

If you run the aforementioned code snippet, you should obtain a figure as follows:

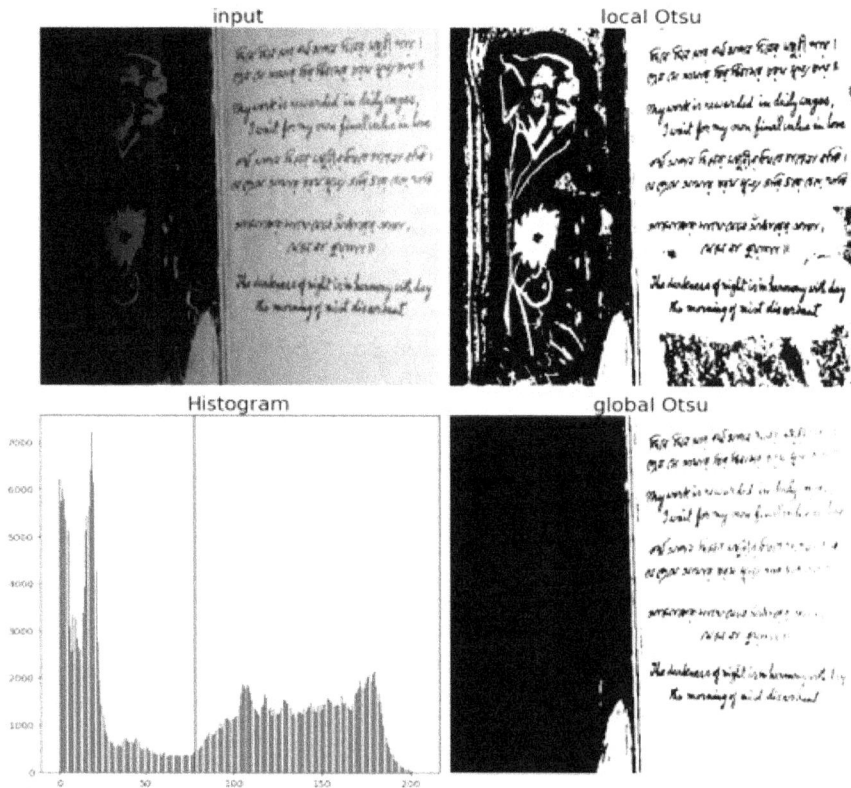

Figure 3.8: Optimal thresholding with Otsu's algorithm (local vs. global)

Max-entropy thresholding with SimpleITK

Now, let us see how we can use the **SimpleITK** library's implementation of an entropy-based thresholding algorithm. **MaximumEntropyThresholdImageFilter** in **SimpleITK** is an implementation of an automatic thresholding algorithm based on maximum entropy. The goal of the algorithm is to find a threshold that maximizes the entropy of the resulting binary image. Entropy is a measure of uncertainty or disorder, and in the context of image thresholding, it reflects the amount of information carried by the pixel intensity values.

The idea behind using **maximum entropy** as a criterion is to find a threshold that maximizes the information gained when going from a grayscale image to a binary image. The method tends to work well when the image has a bimodal histogram with distinct foreground and background intensities. The algorithm first computes the normalized intensity histogram for the input image, then computes the **cumulative distribution function** (**CDF**), computes the entropy of the output binary image for each possible threshold, and finds the optimal threshold that maximizes the entropy.

The following code snippet first reads the image with **sitk.ReadImage()** function scales the intensity values in the range [0,1] using the **RescaleIntensityImageFilter()** and then applies the **MaximumEntropyThresholdImageFilter()** to the rescaled image to obtain the output image using the **Execute()** function. Next, it plots the input and output images.

```python
import SimpleITK as sitk

input_image = sitk.ReadImage('images/tagore.jpg', sitk.sitkFloat32)
rescale = sitk.RescaleIntensityImageFilter()
rescale.SetOutputMaximum(1.0)
input_image = rescale.Execute(input_image)

filter = sitk.MaximumEntropyThresholdImageFilter()
filter.SetOutsideValue(1)
filter.SetInsideValue(0)
output_image = filter.Execute(input_image)
print(filter.GetThreshold())
# 0.6269776821136475
plt.figure(figsize=(20,15))
plt.gray()
plt.subplot(121), plt.imshow(sitk.GetArrayFromImage(input_image))
plt.axis('off'), plt.title('input', size=20)
plt.subplot(122), plt.imshow(sitk.GetArrayFromImage(output_image))
plt.axis('off'), plt.title('thresholded', size=20)
plt.tight_layout()
plt.show()
```

If you run the aforementioned code snippet, you should obtain a figure as follows:

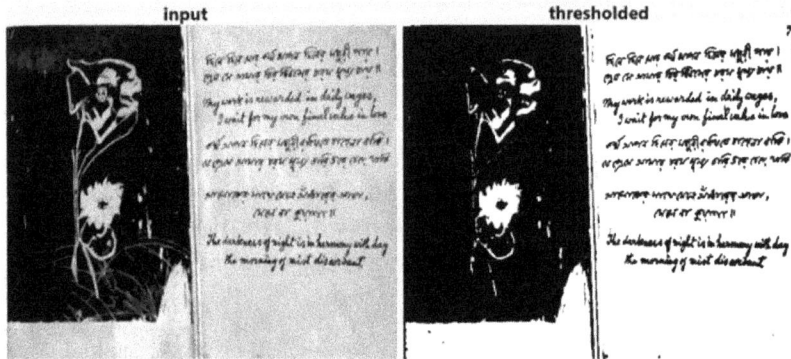

Figure 3.9: *Grayscale to binary image conversion with max-entropy thresholding*

Adaptive thresholding with opencv-python

Adaptive image thresholding is a specific implementation of local image thresholding where the threshold values adapt to local variations in the image. Again, the threshold for each pixel is computed based on the local neighborhood around it.

Now, let us understand how to use the function **cv2.adaptiveThreshold()** from **opencv-python** to perform adaptive thresholding. The function **cv2.adaptiveThreshold()** takes an input image, a **maxValue** (value given to pixels exceeding the threshold), an adaptive method (to be used to compute the adaptive threshold), **thresholdType** (type of thresholding applied), **blockSize** (size of the neighborhood area), and **C** (a constant subtracted from the mean or weighted mean). The adaptive methods can be selected from the following ones:

- **cv2.ADAPTIVE_THRESH_GAUSSIAN_C:** specifies that the adaptive threshold is computed as the weighted sum of the neighborhood values, where weights are given by a Gaussian window.

- **cv2.ADAPTIVE_THRESH_MEAN_C:** the method calculates the threshold for each pixel as the mean of the pixel values in its local neighborhood.

- **cv2.THRESH_BINARY:** specifies that pixels with values above the threshold are set to **maxValue (255)**, and others are set to 0.

Experiment with different values for **blockSize** and **C** to see how they affect the adaptive thresholding result based on the characteristics of the input image.

The following code snippet implements adaptive thresholding using the mean and Gaussian adaptive threshold methods and plots the output binary images along with the input image:

```
import cv2
import numpy as np
import matplotlib.pylab as plt

im = cv2.imread('images/tagore.jpg', 0)

thresh1 = cv2.adaptiveThreshold(im, 255, cv2.ADAPTIVE_THRESH_MEAN_C,
                                cv2.THRESH_BINARY_INV, 21, 10)
thresh2 = cv2.adaptiveThreshold(im, 255, cv2.ADAPTIVE_THRESH_GAUSSIAN_C,
                                cv2.THRESH_BINARY_INV, 21, 4)

plt.figure(figsize=(20,12))
plt.gray()
plt.subplot(131), plt.imshow(im), plt.axis('off')
plt.title('input', size=20)
plt.subplot(132), plt.imshow(thresh1), plt.axis('off')
plt.title('adaptive thresholded (mean)', size=20)
plt.subplot(133), plt.imshow(thresh2), plt.axis('off')
plt.title('adaptive thresholded (gaussian)', size=20)
plt.tight_layout()
plt.show()
```

If you run the aforementioned code snippet, you should obtain a figure as follows:

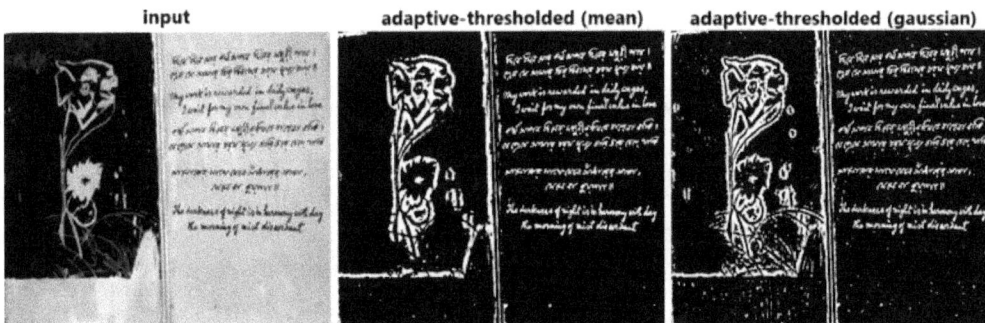

Figure 3.10: Adaptive thresholding with opencv-python

Segmentation using clustering

Clustering is an **unsupervised** technique in machine learning and data analysis where data points are grouped together based on similarity or some inherent structure in the data. The goal of clustering is to partition a dataset into groups, or clusters, such that data points within the same cluster are more similar to each other than to those in other clusters.

Mathematically, clustering can be defined as follows. Let $X = \{x_1, x_2, ..., x_n\}$ be a set of n data points in a feature space. The objective of clustering is to find a partition of X into K clusters $C = \{C_1, C_2, ..., C_K\}$, where each C_k represents a cluster.

The partition should satisfy the following criteria:

- **Homogeneity within clusters**: Data points within the same cluster are more similar to each other.

- **Heterogeneity between clusters**: Data points from different clusters are dissimilar.

Now, regarding image segmentation, clustering techniques can be employed to group pixels with similar characteristics into segments. Each pixel is treated as a data point, and the features extracted from the pixels (such as color, intensity, and texture) serve as dimensions in the feature space.

The steps for using clustering for image segmentation includes:

- **Feature extraction**: Extract relevant features from each pixel in the image.

- **Clustering**: Apply a clustering algorithm (e.g., k-means) to group similar pixels based on their feature vectors.

- **Segmentation**: Assign each pixel to the cluster it belongs to and consider each cluster as a segment in the segmented image.

In this section, you will learn how to:

- Implement image segmentation with clustering using **scikit-learn** and **scipy** library functions

- Cluster similar images into groups.

Clustering with Mahalanobis distance

Mahalanobis distance is a measure used to quantify the distance between a point and a distribution. It is a generalized form of the **Euclidean distance,** but it also takes into account the correlations between different features. This distance metric is particularly useful when dealing with multivariate data where the features are correlated.

The **Mahalanobis distance** (D_M) between a point x and a distribution with mean μ and covariance matrix Σ is calculated as follows:

$$D_M(x) = (x - \mu)^T \Sigma^{-1}(x - \mu)$$

In the context of image segmentation, Mahalanobis distance can be applied to cluster pixels based on their feature vectors.

The following is a general outline of how you can use Mahalanobis distance for image segmentation:

- **Feature extraction**: Extract relevant features from each pixel in the image. Here, we shall use RGB colors as features. Hence, the feature space will consist of 3D vectors. Each pixel is represented as a feature vector.

- **Compute mean and covariance**: Compute the mean (μ) and covariance matrix (Σ) of the feature vectors in the entire image or in predefined regions.

- **Calculate Mahalanobis distance**: For each pixel's feature vector, calculate its Mahalanobis distance from the mean using the formula mentioned earlier.

- **Segmentation**: Assign pixels to different segments or clusters based on their Mahalanobis distances. Pixels with smaller distances are more likely to belong to the same cluster.

- **Thresholding or clustering**: Apply a threshold or use clustering techniques (e.g., k-means clustering) to group pixels into distinct segments based on their Mahalanobis distances.

Let us start the implementation by importing the required libraries and modules:

```
import numpy as np
import scipy
from skimage.io import imread
from skimage.util import crop
import matplotlib.pylab as plt
cdist = scipy.spatial.distance.cdist
```

Now, let us aim to segment the RGB color pepper image into two regions ($K = 2$), for example, one containing the red vegetables and the other containing the green vegetables. This is done in the function **cluster_rgb_mahalanobis()** defined in the following code snippet.

We need to start with two predefined sub-regions by cropping small subsets of pixels from the original image, each one acting as a reference for the corresponding segment.

Use **skimage.util.crop()** function to crop the reference image patches from the original image by specifying the starting and ending indices along each axis, given by **cluster_sample_locs**, passed as an argument to the function **cluster_rgb_mahalanobis()**.

The function **cluster_rgb_mahalanobis()**, in turn, uses the function **compute_mahalanobis()**, which accepts the original image **I** and the predefined reference image patches **S** and computes the **Mahalanobis distance** between each pixel and the predefined (reference patches). For a $m \times n$ image, we need to store (mn, 2) distance values (for each of the mn pixels we need to store the Mahalanobis distances to predefined patches).

The function **compute_mahalanobis()**, in turn, uses the function **mahalanobis()** to first compute μ, Σ for the reference patches x and then compute the **Mahalanobis distance** between a pixel RGB vector y and the predefined pixel subsets (clusters).

Assign each pixel to its **nearest cluster** using the **minimum** of the **Mahalanobis** distances computed, as shown in the following code block:

```python
def mahalanobis(y, x):
    cov_x_inv = np.linalg.inv(np.cov(x,rowvar=False))
    return cdist(y, np.reshape(np.mean(x, axis=0), (1, -1)),
                        'mahalanobis', VI=cov_x_inv)

def compute_mahalanobis(I, S):
    R, G, B = I[:,:,0], I[:,:,1], I[:,:,2] #color components
    subset_R, subset_G, subset_B = S[:,:,0], S[:,:,1], S[:,:,2]
    x = np.hstack((subset_R.reshape(-1,1), subset_G.reshape(-1,1),
                                        subset_B.reshape(-1,1)))
    y = np.hstack((R.reshape(-1,1), G.reshape(-1,1), B.reshape(-1,1)))
    return mahalanobis(y, x).ravel()

def cluster_rgb_mahalanobis(im, cluster_sample_locs):
    mahal_dist   = np.zeros((np.prod(im.shape[:2]), \
                            len(cluster_sample_locs)))
    for i in range(len(cluster_sample_locs)):
        im_patch = crop(im, cluster_sample_locs[i], copy=False)
        mahal_dist[:,i] = compute_mahalanobis(im, im_patch)
    ind = np.argmin(mahal_dist, axis=1)
    ind = ind.reshape(im.shape[:2])
    mask = np.zeros(im.shape[:2])
    for k in range(mahal_dist.shape[1]):
        mask[ind == k] = k
    return mask
```

Now, let us read the pepper image from disk.

Define the locations of the small red and green patches (to be cropped from the original image and used for reference) as **cluster_sample_locs**.

Use the function **cluster_rgb_mahalanobis()** defined earlier to segment the image using **Mahalanobis** distance.

The function **cluster_rgb_mahalanobis()** accepts the input image along with the predefined reference pixels for the segments, as shown in the following code snippet. The function returns the segmentation mask. Display the segmentation mask, along with the original RGB image.

```
im = imread('images/pepper.png')
cluster_sample_locs = [
                        ((36, 150), (115, 90), (0,0)),
                        ((127, 70), (143, 60), (0,0))
                      ]
mask = cluster_rgb_mahalanobis(im, cluster_sample_locs)

plt.figure(figsize=(12,6))
plt.subplots_adjust(0,0,1,0.95,0.05,0.05)
plt.subplot(121), plt.imshow(im, aspect='auto'), plt.title('RGB IMAGE')
plt.axis('off')
plt.subplot(122), plt.imshow(mask, cmap='jet', aspect='auto')
plt.colorbar(), plt.title('CLUSTERS'), plt.axis('off')
plt.show()
```

If you run the aforementioned code snippet, you should obtain a figure as follows:

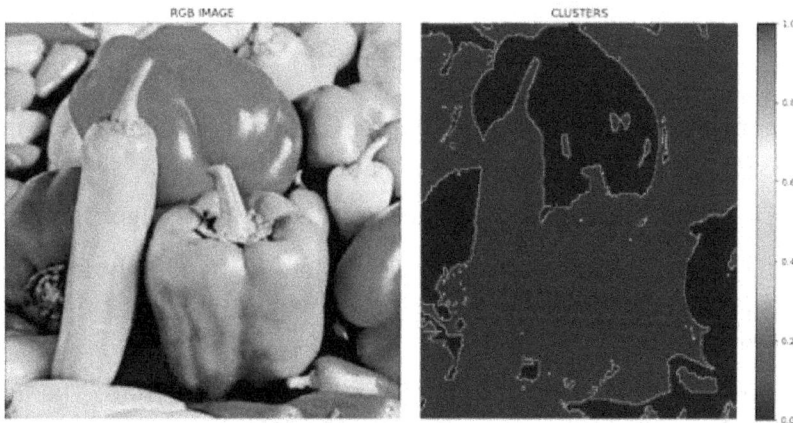

Figure 3.11: *Clustering with Mahalanobis distance*

Now, display the segments separately, as shown in the following figure (the code is left as an exercise to the reader):

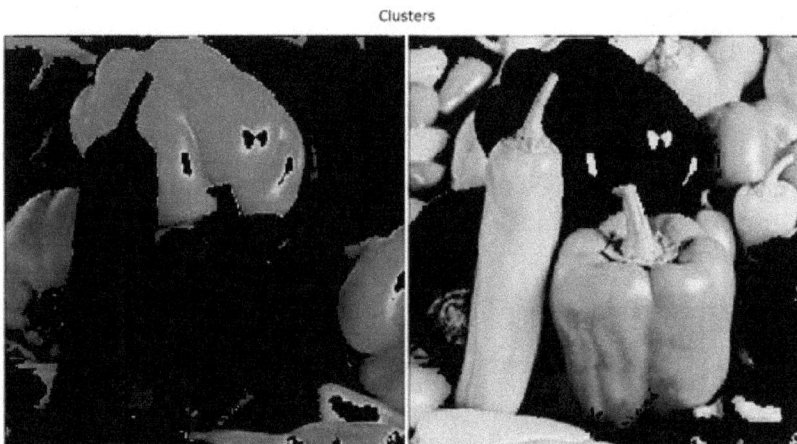

Figure 3.12: *Two clusters obtained with Mahalanobis distance based clustering*

K-means vs. spectral clustering

K-means clustering is a popular unsupervised machine learning algorithm used for partitioning a dataset into K distinct, non-overlapping subsets (clusters). The goal of the k-means algorithm is to assign each data point to one of the K clusters in a way that minimizes the sum of squared distances within each cluster. It is widely used for clustering analysis in various domains, including image processing, data analysis, and machine learning.

A common mathematical formulation for **k-means clustering** involves defining an **objective function** that quantifies the similarity within clusters and dissimilarity between clusters as follows:

$$\text{Minimize} \quad \sum_{k=1}^{K} \sum_{x \in C_k} \| x - \mu_k \|^2$$

Here, μ_k is the mean of the data points in cluster C_k. The algorithm aims to minimize the objective function (i.e., the sum of squared distances within each of the K clusters).

The following is a brief overview of how the k-means clustering algorithm works:

- **Initialization**: Choose the number of clusters K. Randomly initialize K cluster centroids in the feature space (You can use better initialization methods such as **KMeans++**).

- **Assignment**: Assign each data point to the nearest centroid. The assignment is based on the Euclidean distance between the data point and each centroid.

- **Update centroids**: Recalculate the centroids of the clusters as the mean of all data points assigned to each cluster.

- **Repeat**: Repeat steps 2 and 3 until convergence. Convergence occurs when the centroids no longer change significantly or when a predefined number of iterations is reached.

The number of clusters (K) needs to be specified in advance, and the algorithm's performance can be sensitive to this choice and initialization of the clusters.

Performing image segmentation using k-means clustering involves applying the k-means algorithm to group pixels in an image based on their color or intensity values. Each cluster represents a segment in the image.

Here, we shall use the `scikit-learn` library's k-means clustering implementation.

Let us start by importing the required libraries as follows:

```
from sklearn import cluster
from skimage.io import imread
from skimage.color import rgb2gray
from skimage.transform import resize as imresize
from sklearn.utils import shuffle
from sklearn.feature_extraction import img_to_graph
import numpy as np
import matplotlib.pylab as plt
import warnings
warnings.filterwarnings('ignore')
```

Here is a step-by-step guide to perform segmentation using k-means clustering, as shown in the following code snippet:

1. Load the image using the **skimage.io.imread()** function, and we shall use three color channels as features.

2. Reshape the 3D image array into a 2D array of pixels using **np.reshape()**.

3. **Reduce the number of colors**: To improve the algorithm's performance, randomly sample a subset of pixels (e.g., 1000 pixels) from the image using the function **sklearn.utils.shuffle()**.

4. **Apply k-means clustering**: Create an instance (object) of the **KMeans** class from **scikit-learn** to perform k-means clustering. Fit the model to the sampled pixels using the function **fit()**.

5. Predict the cluster labels for all pixels in the image using the function **predict()**.

6. **Generate segmented image**: Replace each pixel in the original image with the color of its assigned cluster centroid as follows:

```
im = imread('images/horses.png')[...,:3]

X = np.reshape(im, (-1, im.shape[-1]))
X_sample = shuffle(X, random_state=0)[:1000]

k = 2
kmeans = cluster.KMeans(n_clusters=k, random_state=10)
kmeans.fit(X_sample)
y_pred = kmeans.predict(X).astype(np.uint8)
labels_kmeans = np.reshape(y_pred, im.shape[:2])
```

Spectral Clustering is a graph-based clustering algorithm that uses the spectral decomposition of the affinity matrix of the data points. It is particularly effective for clustering datasets that exhibit complex structures, including non-convex shapes and clusters of varying shapes and sizes.

The following is an overview of how **Spectral Clustering** works, along with the concepts that we need to understand:

- **Affinity matrix**: Given a dataset with data points, the first step is to construct an affinity matrix , which measures the similarity between data points. Common choices for affinity include the Gaussian **Radial Basis Function** (**RBF**) kernel or the nearest neighbor's graph.

  For example, with RBF, we have, $A_{ij} = e^{-\frac{\|x_i - x_j\|^2}{2\sigma^2}}$ and $A_{ii} = 0$.

- **Degree matrix**: Form a diagonal matrix D, where $D_{ii} = \sum_j A_{ij}$, each element D_{ii} is the sum of the elements in the corresponding row of the affinity matrix A.

- **Laplacian matrix**: The unnormalized Laplacian matrix can be computed as $L = D - A$, and the normalized versions can be computed as $L_{sym} = I - D^{-1/2}AD^{-1/2}$.

- **Spectral decomposition**: Compute the eigenvectors and eigenvalues of the (unnormalized) Laplacian matrix. Stack the k eigenvectors corresponding to the k smallest eigenvalues as columns of a matrix $U \in R^{n \times k}$, with n as the number of data points and k as the number of clusters.

- **Clustering**: Treat each row vector of U (i.e., each data point's representation in the new spectral space) as a point in R^k. Apply k-means (or other clustering algorithms) on these rows to group them into k clusters. This way, the original data is clustered based on their low-dimensional spectral embeddings that capture the structure of the graph.

The key idea behind spectral clustering is that the eigenvectors capture the underlying structure of the data, and clustering in the spectral space can reveal complex structures that may be hard to capture in the original feature space.

To use spectral clustering for image segmentation, you can treat the pixels in the image as data points and apply the spectral clustering algorithm to group them into clusters based on their similarity.

The algorithm is configured to use the nearest neighbors' graph as the affinity measure (with a number of neighbors, **n_neighbors= 25**) in the following code snippet, which uses the **SpectralClustering** class from **scikit-learn**. The method **fit_predict()** is used to fit the model and then predict the labels of the pixels in the image.

The image is reduced to a smaller size for faster execution speed as follows:

```
h, w, _ = im.shape
im_small = imresize(im, (h//4, w//4))
X = np.reshape(im_small, (-1, im.shape[-1]))
spectral = cluster.SpectralClustering(n_clusters=k, eigen_solver='arpack',
                                      affinity="nearest_neighbors",
                                      n_neighbors=25,
                                      assign_labels = 'discretize',
                                      random_state=10)
y_pred = spectral.fit_predict(X).astype(np.uint8)
labels_spectral = np.reshape(y_pred, im_small.shape[:2])
```

Visualize the binary segmentation mask and segmented original image side by side for both the clustering algorithms as follows:

```
plt.figure(figsize=(20,12))
plt.gray()
plt.subplots_adjust(0,0,1,0.96,0.05,0.05)
plt.subplot(221), plt.imshow(labels_kmeans)
plt.title('k-means segmentation (k=2)', size=30), plt.axis('off')
plt.subplot(222), plt.imshow(im.copy()), plt.axis('off')
for l in range(k):
    plt.contour(labels_kmeans == l, colors='r', linewidths=5)
plt.title('k-means contour (k=2)', size=30)
plt.subplot(223), plt.imshow(labels_spectral)
plt.title('spectral segmentation (k=2)', size=30), plt.axis('off')
plt.subplot(224), plt.imshow(im_small.copy()), plt.axis('off')
for l in range(k):
    plt.contour(labels_spectral == l, colors='r', linewidths=5)
plt.title('spectral contour (k=2)', size=30)
plt.show()
```

If you run the preceding code snippet, you should obtain a figure as follows:

Figure 3.13: Image segmentation with k-means vs. spectral clustering

MeanShift segmentation with opencv-python and scikit-learn

MeanShift segmentation is a **region-based** image segmentation that involves grouping similar pixels into regions. The basic idea behind MeanShift is to iteratively shift data points towards the mode (peak) of the data distribution, allowing the points to converge to local maxima. In the context of image segmentation, this means grouping together pixels with similar color or intensity values. This algorithm is used for **non-parametric clustering** and is particularly effective for situations where the number of clusters is not known beforehand (as opposed to **k-means**, where we must specify the number of clusters beforehand). In this section, we will learn how to implement MeanShift segmentation with `opencv-python` and `scikit-learn` library functions.

MeanShift filtering with opencv-python

As explained, MeanShift algorithm can be applied to group similar pixels into regions, effectively segmenting the image. The algorithm works by iteratively shifting each pixel towards the mean of the pixels within a local spatial and color range until convergence. In **opencv-python** this algorithm can be implemented using MeanShift filtering function `cv2.pyrMeanShiftFiltering()`.

The function `cv2.pyrMeanShiftFiltering()` operates on an image pyramid. This function is designed to perform more efficient and multi-scale MeanShift segmentation by working on different levels or scales of the image.

The function implements the filtering stage of the algorithm, i.e., it outputs a filtered *posterized* image with flattened color gradients and fine-grain texture.

At each pixel (X, Y) of the input image, the neighborhood of the pixel in the joint space-color (sp, sr) hyperspace is considered:

$$(x, y): X - sp \leq x \leq X + sp, \quad Y - sp \leq y \leq Y + sp, \quad \| (R, G, B) - (r, g, b) \| \leq sr$$

Where (R,G,B) and (r,g,b) are color component vectors at (X,Y) and (x,y), respectively. The average spatial value (X', Y') and average color vector (R', G', B') are computed over the neighborhood and they become the neighborhood centers on the next iteration.

When the algorithm converges, the color components of the initial pixel are set to the final value (average color at the last iteration):

$$I(X, Y) \leftarrow (R^*, G^*, B^*)$$

The function `cv2.pyrMeanShiftFiltering()` accepts the following parameters as input:

- **src**: The source image.
- **sp**: The spatial window radius (the spatial neighborhood).
- **sr**: The color window radius (the color neighborhood).
- **maxLevel**: The maximum level of the image pyramid for the segmentation. It determines how many levels of the pyramid will be used. Higher levels represent lower resolutions of the image. This is an optional parameter with default value = 1. When maxLevel > 0, the **Gaussian pyramid** of `maxLevel` +1 levels is built, and

the aforementioned procedure is run on the smallest layer first. Next, the results are propagated to the larger layer, and the iterations are run again only on those pixels for which the layer colors differ by more than **sr** from the lower-resolution layer of the pyramid. It helps creating color sharper regions boundaries.

- **termcrit**: Termination criteria for the iterative procedure, an optional parameter, often specified as a tuple (**epsilon**, **max_iterations**), indicating the desired accuracy and the maximum number of iterations, respectively.

The function **cv2.meanShift()** is often confused with the **cv2.pyrMeanShiftFiltering()** function, but it is not specifically designed for image segmentation using the traditional MeanShift segmentation algorithm. Instead, it is often used for object tracking.

Let us demonstrate how the function **cv2.pyrMeanShiftFiltering()** can be used for image segmentation using the following code snippet. As usual, let us start by importing the required libraries, along with **opencv-python (cv2)**.

Load an image of flowers and perform pyramid mean shift filtering with **cv2. pyrMeanShiftFiltering()**, using $sp = 20$ and $sr = 50$.

```python
import cv2
import numpy as np
import matplotlib.pylab as plt

image = cv2.imread('images/coins.jpg')
original = np.copy(image)
shifted = cv2.pyrMeanShiftFiltering(image, 20, 50)
```

Convert the mean shift image to grayscale, then apply **Otsu**'s thresholding with the function **cv2.threshold()**.

Find contours in the thresholded image using the function **cv2.findContours()**, loop over the contours, and draw the contours using the following code snippet:

```python
gray = cv2.cvtColor(shifted, cv2.COLOR_BGR2GRAY)
mask = np.invert(cv2.threshold(gray, 0, 255, cv2.THRESH_BINARY | \
                               cv2.THRESH_OTSU)[1])
cnts, _ = cv2.findContours(mask.copy(), cv2.RETR_EXTERNAL, \
                           cv2.CHAIN_APPROX_SIMPLE)
print("{} unique contours found".format(len(cnts)))
# 2 unique contours found

for (i, c) in enumerate(cnts):
    ((x, y), _) = cv2.minEnclosingCircle(c)
    cv2.putText(image, "#{}".format(i + 1), (int(x) - 10, int(y)), \
                cv2.FONT_HERSHEY_SIMPLEX, 0.6, (0, 0, 255), 2)
    cv2.drawContours(image, [c], -1, (0, 255, 0), 2)
```

Plot the original image, MeanShift segmentation output, the binary mask obtained, and the contours overlayed on the original image, side-by-side, using the following code snippet:

```
plt.figure(figsize=(20,15))
plt.subplot(221), plt.imshow(cv2.cvtColor(original, cv2.COLOR_BGR2RGB))
plt.axis('off'), plt.title('Original image', size=20)
plt.subplot(222), plt.imshow(cv2.cvtColor(shifted, cv2.COLOR_BGR2RGB))
plt.axis('off'), plt.title('With MeanShift', size=20)
plt.subplot(223), plt.imshow(mask, cmap='gray'), plt.axis('off')
plt.title('With MeanShift + Otsu', size=20)
plt.subplot(224), plt.imshow(image), plt.axis('off')
plt.title('With Contours', size=20)
plt.show()
```

If you run the preceding code snippet, you should obtain the following figure:

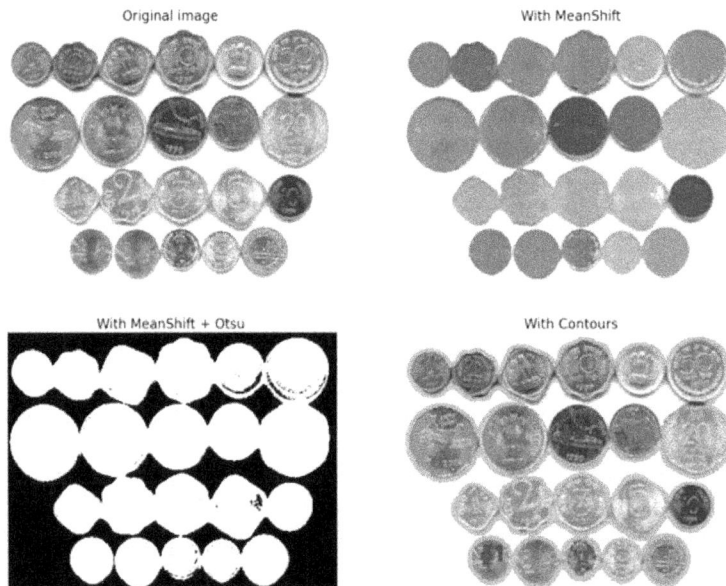

Figure 3.14: *MeanShift filtering with opencv-python*

Segmentation with MeanShift clustering in lab space with scikit-learn

Let us now demonstrate how we can use **scikit-learn.cluster** module's implementation of MeanShift clustering. Last time, we used RGB color space but this time, we shall work on the **Lab** color space (**L**: Lightness, **a**: Green-Red, and **b**: Blue-Yellow channel) for the input image.

The following are the steps to be followed:

1. Load the input image and flatten it, so that $m \times n \times 3$ image becomes $mn \times 3$ ndarray.

2. Use the function **sklearn.cluster.estimate_bandwidth()** to estimate the bandwidth parameter for MeanShift clustering. The **bandwidth** is a crucial parameter in the MeanShift algorithm as it determines the size of the region for which points are considered similar during the mean shift process. The **quantile** parameter controls the proportion (fraction) of sample data points to be used in the **KDE** (kernel density estimation): the default value is 0.3, meaning that the bandwidth will be chosen to include 30% of the samples, whereas the **n_samples** parameter indicates the number of samples to use for the estimation (if **None**, all samples are used)

3. Given the estimated bandwidth, the MeanShift algorithm is applied (using the function **sklearn.cluster.MeanShift()**) to cluster the data points (pixels). For each data point, a mean shift vector is computed, pointing towards the mode of the data distribution within the specified bandwidth. The point is then shifted in the direction of this vector, as shown in the following code snippet.

4. The process of computing MeanShift vectors and shifting points is repeated until convergence. Convergence occurs when the MeanShift vectors become very small or when the maximum number of iterations is reached.

5. After convergence, the algorithm assigns each data point to the cluster to which it converged. Points that converge to the same mode are considered part of the same cluster.

6. Finally, plot the original and the segmented image, along with the scatterplot with the **a-b** channels for the **Lab** color space, to visualize how the MeanShift algorithm groups the pixels of the same colors together, as shown in the following code snippet:

```python
import numpy as np
from sklearn.cluster import MeanShift, estimate_bandwidth
import matplotlib.pyplot as plt
from skimage.io import imread
from skimage.color import rgb2lab, label2rgb

image = imread('images/flowers.jpg')
flattened_image = np.reshape(rgb2lab(image), [-1, 3])

# estimate bandwidth
bandwidth = estimate_bandwidth(flattened_image[:, 1:], quantile=.2,
                                                    n_samples=5000)
ms = MeanShift(bandwidth=bandwidth, bin_seeding=True)
ms.fit(flattened_image)
labels = ms.labels_
print(len(np.unique(labels)))
# 7
```

```
labels2 = np.reshape(labels, image.shape[:2])
plt.figure(figsize=(15,15))
plt.subplot(221), plt.imshow(image), plt.axis('off')
plt.title('original image', size=20)
plt.subplot(222)
plt.scatter(flattened_image[:,1],flattened_image[:,2],
            color=np.reshape(image, [-1, 3])/255)
plt.xlabel('a'), plt.ylabel('b'), plt.grid()
plt.title('scattering with a-b', size=20)
plt.subplot(223)
plt.scatter(flattened_image[:,1],flattened_image[:,2],
            color=np.reshape(label2rgb(labels2, image, kind='avg'),
            [-1,3])/255, cmap='jet')
plt.xlabel('a'), plt.ylabel('b'), plt.grid()
plt.title('segmenting with a-b', size=20)
plt.subplot(224), plt.imshow(label2rgb(labels2, image, kind='avg'))
plt.axis('off'), plt.title('segmented image with Meanshift', size=20)
plt.show()
```

If you run the aforementioned code snippet, you should obtain a figure as follows:

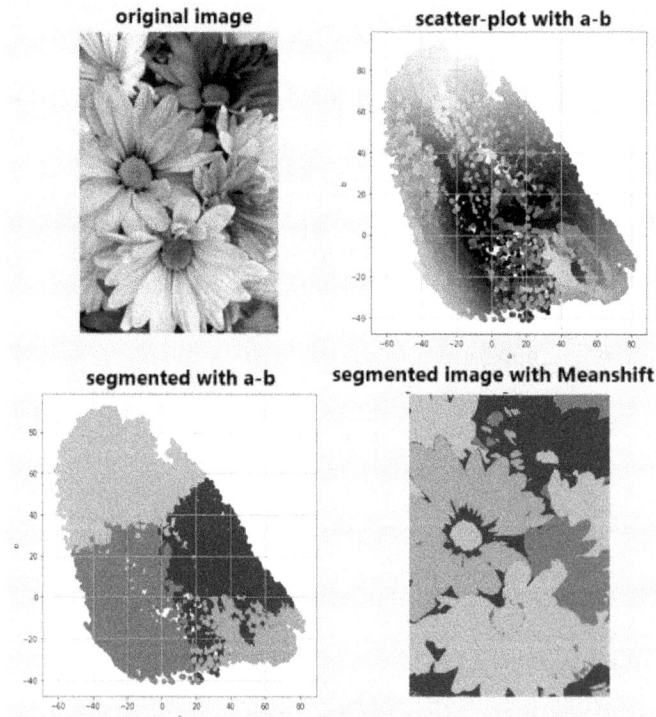

Figure 3.15: MeanShift segmentation in Lab color space with scikit-learn

Watershed segmentation with opencv-python and SimpleITK

Watershed segmentation is a digital image processing technique used for segmentation, which is the process of dividing an image into different regions or segments. The watershed algorithm is primarily considered a region-based segmentation algorithm. The term **watershed** is borrowed from hydrology, where it refers to the boundary line separating two adjacent drainage basins. In image processing, the concept is applied to separate different objects or regions based on the **topological** features of the image.

The following is a simplified explanation of how watershed segmentation works:

- **Gradient computation**: The first step involves computing the gradient of the image. The gradient represents the intensity change in the image, highlighting regions where the intensity varies significantly.

- **Intensity marking**: Local minima in the gradient image are identified as **markers**. These markers serve as **seeds** for the segmentation process. Each marker is associated with a specific region in the image.

- **Label propagation**: Starting from the markers, labels are propagated outward to neighboring pixels. The goal is to flood the image with labels, simulating the filling of basins in a topographical map.

- **Catchment basins**: As the labels propagate, they eventually meet at certain points, forming boundaries between different catchment basins. These boundaries correspond to the desired segmentation.

- **Segmentation result**: The final result of watershed segmentation is a partitioning of the image into regions separated by the boundaries identified in the process.

Watershed segmentation can be applied to grayscale or color images. It is particularly useful in scenarios where objects in an image have poorly defined boundaries or when there are significant intensity variations. However, watershed segmentation can lead to over-segmentation, where small details are treated as separate regions. To address this, techniques such as marker-controlled watershed segmentation are used, allowing users to guide the segmentation process by specifying markers for certain regions of interest.

In this section you will learn how to segment an image using a couple of different implementations of the watershed segmentation algorithm, with libraries such as **opencv-python** and **SimpleITK**.

Watershed with opencv-python

You can perform watershed segmentation using the **cv2.watershed()** function from the library **opencv-python**. Here we shall use the algorithm to separate the foreground object from the background (i.e., obtain a binary segmentation) in the coins image. Let us start the implementation by importing the required libraries and modules as:

```
import cv2
import numpy as np
import matplotlib.pyplot as plt
```

Let us implement the function **run_watershed()** as shown in the following code snippet. The function accepts the input image (to be segmented) as the input argument and performs the following operations step by step:

1. Converts the input image from BGR to grayscale using the function **cv2.cvtColor()** with the flag **cv2.COLOR_BGR2GRAY**.

2. Applies thresholding with **cv2.threshold()** (using **Otsu**'s method **cv2.THRESH_OTSU**) to create a binary image. Performs **morphological opening** with **cv2.morphologyEx()** and **cv2.MORPH_OPEN** (using a 3 × 3 square structural element) to remove noise and small objects.

3. **Dilates** (using the function **cv2.dilate()**) the binary image to obtain a sure background. Calculates the distance transform in the binary image (with the function **cv2.distanceTransform()**) to find the sure foreground by thresholding. The distance transform calculates the distance from each pixel to the nearest zero (**background**) pixel. This function is particularly useful for finding the distance to the closest boundary or object in a binary image.

4. Converts the binary image (with sure foreground locations) to an 8-bit image and finds the unknown regions by subtracting (using **cv2.subtract()**) the sure foreground from the sure background.

5. Labels the sure foreground regions using the **connected components** algorithm (using the function **cv2.connectedComponents()**). Add 1 to all labels and **mark** the **unknown** regions with 0.

6. Applies the **watershed** algorithm with the **markers**, using the function **cv2.watershed()**, as demonstrated in the following code snippet.

7. Marks the watershed boundaries in green and uses the function **cv2.findContours()** to find contours in the binary masks obtained through thresholding. The contours are then drawn on the original image using **cv2.drawContours()**. Note that here we are interested to draw the innermost contours, hence we have used the hierarchy information (using **mode = cv2.RETR_TREE**) obtained from **cv2.findContours()**, hence we have looped through the contours and considered only those contours whose **hierarchy[contour_index][3] (parent)** is not -1.

The function **run_watershed()** returns the **dist_transform**, the **markers** and the final **image** with the contours drawn on top, as demonstrated in the following code snippet. Finally, load the input coins image and segment it with watershed algorithm using the function **run_watershed()**.

```python
def run_watershed(image):

    gray = cv2.cvtColor(image, cv2.COLOR_BGR2GRAY)
    # threshold to obtain binary image
    ret, thresh = cv2.threshold(gray,0,255,cv2.THRESH_BINARY_INV + \
                                          cv2.THRESH_OTSU)

    # noise removal
    kernel = np.ones((3,3),np.uint8)
    opening = cv2.morphologyEx(thresh,cv2.MORPH_OPEN,kernel, iterations = 1)
    # sure background area
    sure_bg = cv2.dilate(opening,kernel,iterations=3)
    # Finding sure foreground area
    dist_transform = cv2.distanceTransform(opening, cv2.DIST_L2, 5)
    ret, sure_fg = cv2.threshold(dist_transform,0.0001*dist_transform.max(),\
                                                      255,0)

    # Finding unknown region
    sure_fg = np.uint8(sure_fg)
    unknown = cv2.subtract(sure_bg, sure_fg)

    # Marker Labelling
    ret, markers = cv2.connectedComponents(sure_fg)
    # Add one to all labels so that sure background is not 0, but 1
    markers = markers+1
    # Now, mark the region of unknown with zero
    markers[unknown==255] = 0

    markers = cv2.watershed(image,markers)
    image[markers == -1] = [255,0,0]

    # loop over the unique labels returned by the Watershed algorithm
    for label in np.unique(markers):
        # if the label is zero, it's 'background', so simply ignore it
        if label == 0:
            continue

        # otherwise, allocate memory for label region and draw it on the mask
        mask = np.zeros(gray.shape, dtype="uint8")
        mask[markers == label] = 255

        # detect contours in the mask and grab the largest one
        contours, hierarchy = cv2.findContours(mask.copy(), cv2.RETR_TREE, \
                                               cv2.CHAIN_APPROX_SIMPLE)
        for i in range(len(contours)):
            # Check if the contour has a parent (not the outermost contour)
            if hierarchy[0][i][3] != -1:
                color = (0, 255, 0)  # Green color
                cv2.drawContours(image, contours, i, color, 2, cv2.LINE_8, \
                                                      hierarchy, 0)
```

```
    return dist_transform, markers, image
# Load the image
image = cv2.imread('images/coins.jpg')
original = image.copy()
dist_transform, markers, image = run_watershed(image)
```

Plot the input coins image along with the segmented image and draw the contours of the objects with **matplotlib.pylab**:

```
plt.figure(figsize=(12,8))
plt.subplot(221), plt.imshow(cv2.cvtColor(original, cv2.COLOR_BGR2RGB))
plt.axis('off'), plt.title('Original image', size=20)
plt.subplot(222), plt.imshow(dist_transform, cmap='Spectral') plt.
axis('off')plt.title('Distance', size=20)
plt.subplot(223), plt.imshow(markers, cmap='coolwarm'), plt.axis('off')
plt.title('Segmentation Labels', size=20)
plt.subplot(224), plt.imshow(image), plt.axis('off')
plt.title('With Contours', size=20)
plt.tight_layout()
plt.show()
```

If you run the aforementioned code snippet, you should obtain a figure as follows:

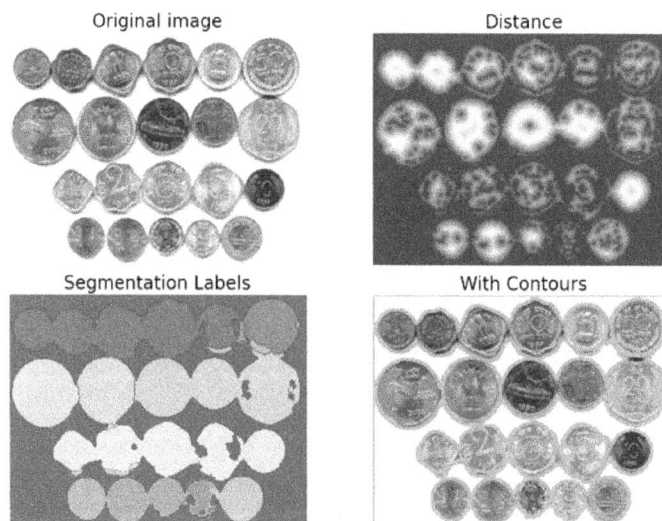

Figure 3.16: Watershed segmentation with opencv-python

Morphological watershed with SimpleITK

The **morphological watershed** algorithm is an extension or modification of the basic watershed algorithm. It often involves combining **morphological operations** (image processing techniques that probe and transform the structure of an image using a predefined shape called a **structuring element**) with the **watershed** algorithm to improve segmentation results (note that in the last section, we used a few morphological operations such as **opening, dilation** explicitly and separately as **preprocessing** steps for watershed segmentation). It is again based on the concept of flooding and watershed lines, like how water flows in terrain and collects in basins. In image processing, the grayscale intensity values are considered as terrain, and the watershed algorithm is applied to segment different regions based on intensity.

Now, let us implement morphological watershed segmentation using **SimpleITK** in Python:

- Import the **SimpleITK** library and alias it as **sitk** for convenience, along with other required libraries.

- Read the input image of a whale as a grayscale image, we shall again perform a binary segmentation on this image, but this time using **SimpleITK**'s watershed implementation.

- Rescale the intensity values of the input image using **RescaleIntensityImageFilter()**, apply this filter to normalize or adjust range of pixel intensities of the input image, to be in the range , as shown in the following code snippet:

```
import SimpleITK as sitk
import numpy as np
import matplotlib.pylab as plt

img = sitk.ReadImage('images/whale.jpg', sitk.sitkFloat64)
rescale = sitk.RescaleIntensityImageFilter()
rescale.SetOutputMaximum(1.0)
img = rescale.Execute(img)
```

- Compute the gradient magnitude of the input image as **feature_img**, using the function **GradientMagnitude()**. The gradient magnitude highlights regions where intensity changes.

- Generate markers based on the gradient magnitude. In this example, connected components are identified where the gradient magnitude is greater than the mean value.

- Use regional minima (with **RegionalMinima()**) as markers in subsequent watershed segmentation to define the initial flooding points.

- Use the function **ConnectedComponent()** to identify and label individual regions connected to the detected regional minima.

- We shall use 3 additional points as hints (plotted as magenta pixels on top the input image), a couple of them belong to background and the remaining one on the foreground object, let us specify the labels of the corresponding pixels in the marker image (with values 1 and 2, respectively), as shown in the following code snippet.

- Apply morphological watershed segmentation using the gradient magnitude and markers, using the function **MorphologicalWatershedFromMarkers()**, which accepts the gradient and the marker images as input.

- Use the function **LabelToRGB()** to obtain the binary segmentation mask image.

- Overlay the mask on top of the input image using the function **LabelOverlay()** with a given **opacity**.

```python
feature_img = sitk.GradientMagnitude(img)
min_img = sitk.RegionalMinima(feature_img, backgroundValue=0,
                foregroundValue=1.0, fullyConnected=False,
                flatIsMinima=True)
marker_img = sitk.ConnectedComponent(min_img)
marker_img *= 0
marker_pts = {(10,10):1, (350,200):2, (500,300):1}
for pt, label in marker_pts.items():
    marker_img[pt] = label
ws = sitk.MorphologicalWatershedFromMarkers(feature_img, marker_img,
                    markWatershedLine=True, fullyConnected=False)
labels = sitk.LabelToRGB(ws)
overlay = sitk.LabelOverlay(img, ws, opacity=0.001)
labels = rescale.Execute(labels)
overlay = rescale.Execute(overlay)
```

- Plot the images obtained. The following figure shows the segmented output image, along with the input image.

```python
plt.figure(figsize=(20,10))
plt.subplot(131), plt.imshow(sitk.GetArrayFromImage(img), cmap='gray')
plt.axis('off')
for pt, label in marker_pts.items():
    plt.scatter(pt[0], pt[1], c=label, s=100, cmap='Spectral')
plt.title('input (with markers)', size=20)
plt.subplot(132), plt.imshow(255*sitk.GetArrayFromImage(labels))
plt.axis('off'), plt.title('segmented', size=20)
plt.subplot(133), plt.imshow(sitk.GetArrayFromImage(overlay))
plt.axis('off'), plt.title('overlayed', size=20)
plt.tight_layout()
plt.show()
```

If you run the preceding code snippet, you should obtain a figure as follows:

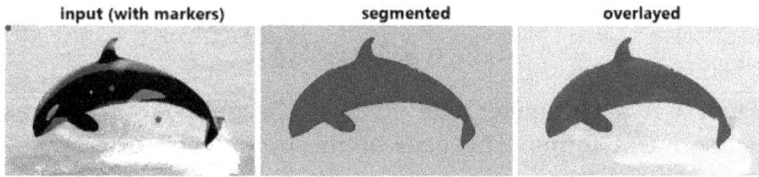

Figure 3.17: *Morphological watershed segmentation with SimpleITK*

GrabCut segmentation with opencv-python

GrabCut is an image segmentation algorithm that that combines image clustering and **graph cuts** to achieve image segmentation. It is designed to automatically segment an image into foreground and background regions. GrabCut is an improvement over basic **graph cut segmentation**, as it combines both data-driven and user-provided information to achieve better segmentation results.

The following is a brief overview of these segmentation techniques:

* **Graph cut segmentation**: Basic **graph cut segmentation** is basically an optimization technique that formulates image segmentation as an **energy-minimization** problem. It constructs a graph where pixels are nodes, and edges represent the relationships between neighboring pixels. The goal is to find a cut in the graph that minimizes the energy, separating the image into segments. The **energy function** typically consists of two main terms: the **data term** and the **smoothness term**.

  o The **data term** measures the cost or likelihood of assigning a particular label (foreground or background) to each pixel in the image. Mathematically, the data term can be represented as:

  $$D(X) = \sum_i D_i(X_i)$$

  Here, X_i is the label assigned to pixel i, and $D_i(X_i)$ is the data cost associated with assigning label X_i to pixel i.

  o The **smoothness term** (pairwise term) encourages neighboring pixels to have similar labels, promoting spatial coherence in the segmentation. It penalizes abrupt changes in labels between neighboring pixels. This term helps to smooth-out the segmentation boundaries. Mathematically, the smoothness term can be represented as:

  $$S(X) = \sum_{(i,j) \in \text{Nbd}} S_{ij}(X_i, X_j)$$

  Here, $S_{ij}(X_i, X_j)$ is the smoothness cost associated with the labels of neighboring pixels i and j.

o The **overall energy function** for the image segmentation problem with graph cuts is a combination of the **data term** and the **smoothness term**:

$$E(X) = D(X) + \lambda S(X)$$

o Here λ is a parameter that controls the trade-off between the data and smoothness terms. The goal of the optimization process is to find the labeling X that minimizes this energy function. Graph cut algorithms, such as the **max-flow / min-cut** algorithm, are then applied to efficiently find the optimal partition or labeling that **minimizes** the **energy**.

- **GrabCut segmentation**: GrabCut is an interactive segmentation algorithm that combines user input with an iterative optimization process. The user provides a bounding box around the object of interest, and GrabCut iteratively refines the segmentation based on user input and image data. It employs a graphical model with a graph structure to represent the relationships between pixels and incorporates user scribbles to guide the segmentation.

  o Initially, pixels are classified into:

    ▪ Definite foreground (marked by user)

    ▪ Definite background (marked by user)

    ▪ Possible foreground

    ▪ Possible background

  Constraints for the definite pixels are incorporated into the minimization problem to fix their labels, ensuring they cannot be reassigned during optimization.

  o **Gaussian Mixture Model** (**GMM**) is used to model the foreground and background. Using the input scribbles (hints), GMM learns to estimate the **class-conditional distributions** for the **foreground** and **background**, i.e., it estimates $P(x \mid foreground)$ and $P(x \mid background)$, where x is the color vector (e.g., RGB values) of a pixel.

  o A graph isconstructed, where:

    ▪ Nodes represent pixels.

    ▪ Additional two nodes are added, **source** node and **sink** node. Every **foreground** pixel is connected to **source** node and every **background** pixel is connected to **sink** node.

    ▪ The **data term** in the **energy function** corresponds to the **negative log-likelihood** of a pixel's **color** given its **class** (**foreground** or **background**).

- The **smoothness term** corresponds to a prior that encourages spatial coherence by favoring similar labels for neighboring pixels with similar colors.

o   The **weights** of edges connecting pixels to source/sink node are defined by the (posterior) probability of a pixel being foreground/background. The weights between the pixel nodes are defined by the edge information or pixel similarity. If there is a large difference in pixel color, the edge between them will get a low weight.

o   A **max-flow / min-cut** (**minimum cut**) algorithm is used to segment the graph. It cuts the graph into two partitions, separating source node and sink node, it finds the cut with minimum value of the cost function. The cost function is the sum of all weights of the edges that are cut. After the cut, all the pixels connected to **source** node become the **foreground** and those connected to the **sink** node become the **background**.

o   This approach allows **interactive refinement**—modifying scribbles iteratively improves the accuracy of segmentation.

Let us start with an image to segment (for example, a flower from the **Berkely segmentation dataset**) and a rectangle around the object of interest (**rect**), providing the **foreground** hint. The **GrabCut** algorithm will then iteratively refine the segmentation based on this user input. The resulting segmented image is displayed using the **imshow()** function from **matplotlib.pylab**.

Now, let us demonstrate how to use **cv2.grabCut()** function to implement binary segmentation using the **Grabcut** algorithm. The function in **opencv-python** has several arguments that control the behavior of the algorithm. Here is an overview of the main arguments:

- **img**: Input image (to be segmented).

- **mask**: A mask image used to initialize and store the segmentation. It should be a 2D array with the same height and width as the input image. The mask is typically initialized with zeros, and the user provides **seed** points (rectangles or points) to indicate the initial estimate of the foreground and background.

- **rect**: A rectangle, a tuple specifying the rectangle that encloses the object of interest. The tuple format is **(x, y, width, height)**. This rectangle is used as an initial estimate for the **foreground**.

- **bgdModel and fgModel**: Background and foreground model. These are arrays used by the algorithm internally; they are updated by the function during the iterative optimization process.

- **iterCount**: The number of iterations the GrabCut algorithm will run to refine the segmentation. A larger number of iterations may lead to a more accurate segmentation (set to in the following code snippet).

- **mode**: An optional parameter that specifies the operation mode. It can take one of the following values:

  o **cv2.GC_INIT_WITH_RECT**: The rectangle provided (**rect**) is used as the initial segmentation.

  o **cv2.GC_INIT_WITH_MASK**: The mask provided (**mask**) is used as the initial segmentation.

  o If **None**, the function starts with an internally computed segmentation (may not be accurate).

```python
import numpy as np
import cv2
from matplotlib import pyplot as plt

orig = cv2.imread('images/gerbara.png')
img = np.copy(orig)
mask = np.zeros(img.shape[:2],np.uint8)

# specify rectangle around object of interest (x, y, width, height)
rect = (25,20,400,280)
cv2.grabCut(img, mask, rect, None, None, 5, cv2.GC_INIT_WITH_RECT)

# Modify the mask to get the binary segmentation result
mask = np.where((mask==2)|(mask==0),0,1).astype('uint8')
# Apply the mask to the original image
img = img * mask[:,:,np.newaxis]

fig, (ax1, ax2) = plt.subplots(1, 2, figsize=(12, 7), \
                                    sharex=True, sharey=True)
cv2.rectangle(orig, (rect[0], rect[1]), (rect[2], rect[3]),
(255,0,0), 2)
ax1.imshow(cv2.cvtColor(orig, cv2.COLOR_BGR2RGB)), ax1.axis('off')
ax1.set_title('Original Image (with Object hint rectangle)',
size=15)
ax2.imshow(cv2.cvtColor(img, cv2.COLOR_BGR2RGB)), ax2.axis('off')
ax2.set_title('Segmented Object with GrabCut', size=15) #,plt.
colorbar()
plt.tight_layout()
plt.show()
```

If you run the preceding code snippet, you should obtain a figure as follows:

Figure 3.18: *Interactive GrabCut segmentation with opencv-python*

RandomWalk segmentation with scikit-image

RandomWalk image segmentation uses the concept of a random walk on a graph to partition an image into different regions. In this method, each pixel in the image is treated as a node in a graph, and the intensity values or features of the pixels determine the weights of the edges between the nodes. The random walk algorithm then simulates a random walker moving on the graph, and the segmentation is obtained based on the probabilities of the walker reaching different regions.

Now, let us demonstrate **scikit-image**'s implementation of the random walker segmentation algorithm. Start by importing the required Python libraries, modules and functions as:

```
from skimage.segmentation import random_walker
from skimage.io import imread
import numpy as np
import matplotlib.pyplot as plt
from mpl_toolkits.axes_grid1 import make_axes_locatable
```

The **random_walker** function in **scikit-image** is part of the **skimage.segmentation** module. We shall use this function for random walker image segmentation. Here is an overview of the key arguments of the function:

- **data**: The input image (a 2D grayscale or a 3D multichannel image) to be segmented.

- **markers**: An array of the same shape as data where markers indicate the segmentation regions. It should be an array of integers, where different integers represent different regions. Typically, you would set certain pixels as markers (e.g., background and foreground markers) to guide the segmentation.

- **beta**: A parameter that controls the influence of the smoothness term. Higher values of beta result in smoother segmentations. Adjust this parameter based on the characteristics of your images.

- **mode**: Specifies the update rule, default is **'bf'** (backward / forward) and often more stable than other update rules.

- **channel_axis**: Specifies the channel axis for a multichannel image, i.e., -1 indicates that the last dimension is the channel dimension.

Let us use a white horse image as the input image, and we aim to segment the horse (foreground object) from the background:

- The horse image is annotated (scribbled), red and green scribbles denote the background and foreground regions, respectively. The **marker** image is created, by starting from blank image and then marking the corresponding pixels by different integers (e.g., 1 and 2), as shown in the following code snippet.

- Use the **random_walker()** function to get the labels for the segmented image, along with the probability of **foreground** and **background** predicted by the function, for each pixel in the image, obtained by setting the argument **return_full_prob=True**.

```python
img = imread('images/horse.png')[...,:3]
mask = imread('images/mask_horse.png')
markers = np.zeros(img.shape[:2], dtype=np.uint8)
markers[(mask[...,0] >= 200)&(mask[...,1] <= 20)&(mask[...,2] <= 20)] = 1
markers[(mask[...,0] <= 20)&(mask[...,1] >= 200)&(mask[...,2] <= 20)] = 2

# Run random walker algorithm
labels = random_walker(img, markers, beta=1, mode='bf', channel_axis=-1)
labels_prob = random_walker(img, markers, beta=9, mode='bf', \
                      channel_axis=-1, return_full_prob = True)
```

- Plot the original image, segmentation contour, binary segmentation mask, and the probability of foreground pixels using the following code snippet. You should obtain an output as shown in the following figure:

```python
fig, ((ax1, ax2), (ax3, ax4)) = plt.subplots(2, 2, figsize=(20, 15), \
                                        sharex=True, sharey=True)
ax1.imshow(mask, interpolation='nearest'), ax1.axis('off')
ax1.set_title('Original Image with Markers', size=30)
ax2.imshow(img, interpolation='nearest')
ax2.contour(labels, linewidths=5, colors='y'), ax2.axis('off')
ax2.set_title('Segmentation Contour', size=30)
ax3.imshow(labels,cmap='gray',interpolation='nearest'),
ax3.axis('off')
```

```
ax3.set_title('Segmentation', size=30)
prob = ax4.imshow(labels_prob[1,...], cmap='Spectral', \
                                    interpolation='nearest')
ax4.axis('off'), ax4.set_title('Segmentation Probabilities', size=30)
divider = make_axes_locatable(ax4)
cax = divider.new_vertical(size="5%", pad=0.5, pack_start=True)
fig.add_axes(cax)
fig.colorbar(prob, cax=cax, orientation="horizontal")
fig.tight_layout()
plt.show()
```

If you run the aforementioned code snippet, you should obtain a figure as follows:

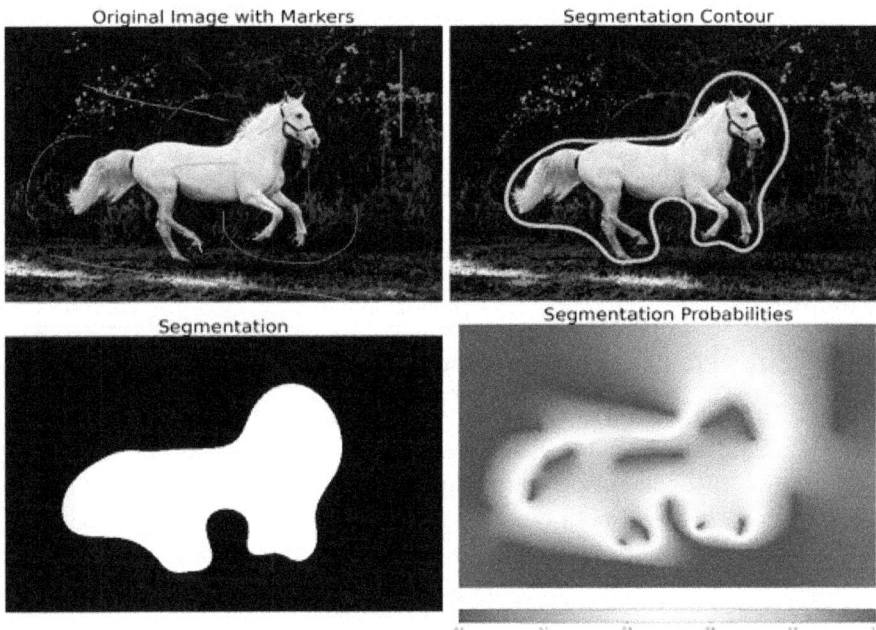

Figure 3.19: Random walk segmentation with scikit-image

Fast marching segmentation with SimpleITK

Fast marching image segmentation is a method that evolves contours based on speed functions to segment object boundaries efficiently. It is based on the **Fast Marching Method** (**FMM**), which is a numerical technique for solving the **Eikonal equation**. The Eikonal equation describes the evolution of a front or wavefront in a way that is dependent on the local speed at each point. Mathematically, the Eikonal equation is given by:

$$| \nabla T | = F$$

Where T is the arrival time (the time it takes for the front to reach a certain point), $|\nabla T|$ is the magnitude of the gradient of T and F is the speed function.

In the context of image segmentation using the FMM, the speed function represents the likelihood or confidence of a pixel belonging to a particular segment or region. It guides the evolution of the front, with regions of higher speed being reached earlier by the front. FMM evolves a front through the image, assigning labels to pixels based on the information obtained from the speed function.

Now, let us apply the fast-marching segmentation on an image, using SimpleITK's implementation of the algorithm.

The following are the steps you need to follow:

1. Let us start by importing the required libraries and defining the parameter values for the functions to be used, using the following code snippet:

```
import SimpleITK as sitk
import numpy as np
import matplotlib.pylab as plt

seed_position = (70, 170)
sigma = 0.25
alpha = -3.0
beta = 10.0
stopping_time = 100
```

2. Read the input grayscale image using the **ReadImage()** function from **SimpleITK**.

3. Let us first apply the filter function **CurvatureAnisotropicDiffusionImageFilter()** to the image, this filter is used for image smoothing or denoising. It applies an anisotropic diffusion process that is guided by the local image structure, helping to preserve edges and boundaries while reducing noise. This filter is particularly useful for enhancing the visibility of structures in images. The method **Execute()** applies the filter to the input image to obtain the smoothed image **smoothing_output**, as shown in the following code snippet.

4. Next, apply the filter function **GradientMagnitudeRecursiveGaussianImageFilter()** to the smoother image. This filter calculates the gradient magnitude of an image using a recursive Gaussian filter. This filter is commonly used to emphasize edges and highlight transitions between different intensity levels.

5. Apply **SigmoidImageFilter()** to the gradient magnitude image for contrast adjustment or to enhance specific intensity range.

6. Finally, apply **FastMarchingImageFilter()** function to the image. The **FastMarchingImageFilter** in **SimpleITK** is part of the toolkit's segmentation module and is designed to perform image segmentation using the **FMM**. You need to provide the filter with the seed points (using the function **SetTrialPoints()**).

These are the initial points from which the front will start to evolve. The filter will set these points as known and then iteratively update the arrival times around them.

You can set additional parameters, such as the stopping value (with the method **SetStoppingValue()**), determining when the front evolution should stop. You can subsequently apply the **BinaryThresholdImageFilter()** for thresholding the output image to create a binary image, as shown in the figure. Display all the images using the **plot_image()** function, as shown in the following code snippet:

```python
def plot_image(img, title, img_type=np.float32):
    im = sitk.GetArrayViewFromImage(img).astype(img_type)
    im = im / im.max()
    plt.imshow(im), plt.axis('off'), plt.title(title, size=20)

input_image = sitk.ReadImage('images/Img_03_09.png', sitk.sitkFloat32)

smoothing = sitk.CurvatureAnisotropicDiffusionImageFilter()
smoothing.SetTimeStep(0.125)
smoothing.SetNumberOfIterations(5)
smoothing.SetConductanceParameter(9.0)
smoothing_output = smoothing.Execute(input_image)

gradient_magnitude = sitk.GradientMagnitudeRecursiveGaussianImageFilter()
gradient_magnitude.SetSigma(sigma)
gradient_magnitude_output = gradient_magnitude.Execute(smoothing_output)
rescale = sitk.RescaleIntensityImageFilter()
gradient_magnitude_output = rescale.Execute(gradient_magnitude_output)

sigmoid = sitk.SigmoidImageFilter()
sigmoid.SetOutputMinimum(0.0)
sigmoid.SetOutputMaximum(255)
sigmoid.SetAlpha(alpha)
sigmoid.SetBeta(beta)
sigmoid_output = sigmoid.Execute(gradient_magnitude_output)

seed_value = 0
fast_marching = sitk.FastMarchingImageFilter()
trialPoint = (seed_position[0], seed_position[1], seed_value)
fast_marching.AddTrialPoint(trialPoint)
fast_marching.SetStoppingValue(stopping_time)
fast_marching_output = fast_marching.Execute(sigmoid_output)

thresholder = sitk.BinaryThresholdImageFilter()
thresholder.SetLowerThreshold(0)
thresholder.SetUpperThreshold(255)
thresholder.SetOutsideValue(0)
thresholder.SetInsideValue(1)
output_image = thresholder.Execute(fast_marching_output)
```

```
plt.figure(figsize=(20,15))
plt.gray()
plt.subplots_adjust(0,0,1,0.95,0.05,0.05)
plt.subplot(231), plot_image(input_image, 'input')
plt.subplot(232), plot_image(smoothing_output, 'smoothed')
plt.subplot(233)
plot_image(gradient_magnitude_output, 'gradient', np.uint8)
plt.subplot(234), plot_image(sigmoid_output, 'sigmoid output')
plt.subplot(235)
plot_image(fast_marching_output, 'segmented (FastMarching)')
plt.subplot(236), plot_image(output_image, 'segmentred (binarized)')
plt.show()
```

If you run the aforementioned code snippet, you should obtain a figure as follows:

Figure 3.20: *Fast marching image segmentation with SimpleITK*

Segmentation using SLIC/NCut with scikit-image

In this section, you will learn a few more segmentation algorithms, e.g., **superpixel-based (SLIC)** and **normalized cut (NCut)** based algorithms. We shall demonstrate how to segment an image with these algorithms using **skimage.segmentation** and **skimage.graph** module functions, respectively.

SLIC segmentation

SLIC is a **superpixel segmentation** algorithm used in computer vision and image processing. The goal of SLIC is to group pixels into perceptually meaningful and spatially compact regions called **superpixels**. Superpixels are essentially sets of contiguous pixels that share similar color and texture characteristics. SLIC is particularly useful for segmenting images into regions with similar color and texture. It is an extension of k-means clustering applied in a spatially localized manner.

The following is a brief overview of how SLIC segmentation works:

- **Initialization**: The algorithm starts by sampling a set of initial cluster centers, which are distributed regularly throughout the image. These initial cluster centers are determined based on a combination of image intensity and spatial proximity.

- **Assignment of pixels to super pixels**: Each pixel is then assigned to the nearest cluster center in a 5D space, consisting of color information (usually in the RGB or LAB color space) and spatial information (x, y coordinates). This assignment is done by considering both the color similarity and the spatial proximity of pixels to the cluster centers.

- **Update of cluster centers**: After the initial assignment, the cluster centers are updated by computing the mean color and position of all pixels assigned to each cluster. This step helps to refine the superpixel boundaries.

- **Iteration**: Steps 2 and 3 are iteratively repeated until convergence. The process converges when the cluster centers and assignments do not change significantly between iterations.

- **Compactness constraint**: SLIC includes a compactness constraint to ensure that the resulting superpixels are spatially compact. This is achieved by penalizing the distance between pixels and their assigned cluster centers based on the Euclidean distance in the 5D space.

The algorithm's parameters include the number of desired super pixels and a weighting factor that controls the trade-off between color similarity and spatial proximity in the assignment step. By adjusting these parameters, users can control the size and regularity of the superpixels generated by SLIC. The SLIC method is known for its efficiency and effectiveness in producing visually meaningful superpixels.

Normalized cut

Image segmentation with **NCut** is a technique that aims to partition an image into coherent regions based on the similarities between pixels. **Normalized cut** is a graph-based method that considers both the similarities within the same segments and the dissimilarities between the different segments.

The objective function to be minimized in Ncut segmentation is defined to balance the desire for high similarity within clusters and low similarity between clusters. The goal is to find a partition of the graph (representing an image or data) that minimizes the normalized cut value.

The **objective** function for **Ncut** segmentation is typically expressed as follows:

$$NCut(A,B) = \frac{assoc(A,V)}{cut(A,B)} + \frac{assoc(B,V)}{cut(A,B)}$$

Where we have:

- $cut(A,B)$: The cut between clusters A and B, representing the sum of weights of edges connecting nodes in A to nodes in B.

- $assoc(A,V)$: The association of cluster A with all vertices V, representing the sum of weights of edges connected to nodes in A.

- V: The set of all vertices in the graph.

The goal is to partition the graph into non-overlapping clusters A and B in such a way that the cut between them is minimized while considering the sizes of the clusters. The division by the association terms normalizes the cut values, making it independent of the sizes of the clusters.

The overall objective is to find clusters that have high internal similarity and low external similarity. The segmentation algorithm achieves this by solving an optimization problem that minimizes the normalized cut value. In practice, this is often achieved using spectral methods, where the eigenvectors of a certain matrix (usually the **graph Laplacian**) are used to represent the clusters. The algorithm seeks to find an optimal partition that satisfies these constraints while minimizing the normalized cut value, resulting in a meaningful segmentation of the image. It also penalizes unbalanced partitions, discouraging solutions where one segment is significantly smaller than the other.

Now, let us demonstrate how an input image containing apples and oranges can be segmented using the **scikit-image** implementations of the aforementioned algorithms:

- We shall use the function `segmentation.slic()` to segment the input image using **SLIC**. The argument `n_segments` to the function determines the approximate number of segments to create, whereas **compactness** controls the balance between color similarity and spatial proximity in the segmentation.

- The function `graph.rag_mean_color()` function is part of the **Region Adjacency Graph** (**RAG**) analysis for image segmentation. The RAG is a graph representation where nodes correspond to image regions (superpixels or segments), and edges connect neighboring regions. The `rag_mean_color()` function specifically computes the mean color of each region in the RAG. The function returns a dictionary where keys are the region labels and values are the mean colors.

- Use the function `graph.cut_normalized()` to segment the image using **NCut** algorithm.

- Let us plot the original input image along with the segmented images, using the following code snippet:

```
import skimage
print(skimage.__version__)
# 0.21.0

from skimage import graph, segmentation, color
from skimage.io import imread
from matplotlib import pyplot as plt

img = imread('images/apples_oranges.png')[...,:3]

labels_slic = segmentation.slic(img, compactness=30, n_segments=400)
out_slic = color.label2rgb(labels_slic, img, kind='avg')

g = graph.rag_mean_color(img, labels_slic, mode='similarity')
labels_ncut = graph.cut_normalized(labels_slic, g)
out_ncut = color.label2rgb(labels_ncut, img, kind='avg')

fig, ax = plt.subplots(nrows=2, ncols=2, sharex=True, sharey=True, \
                                               figsize=(20, 15))
ax[0,0].imshow(img), ax[0,0].set_title('Original image', size=20)
ax[0,0].set_axis_off()
ax[0,1].imshow(out_slic)
ax[0,1].set_title('With SLIC superpixelation', size=20)
ax[1,0].set_axis_off(), ax[1,0].imshow(out_ncut)
ax[1,0].set_title('With Normalized-Cut', size=20)
ax[0,1].set_axis_off(), ax[1,1].set_axis_off()
plt.tight_layout()
plt.show()
```

If you run the aforementioned code snippet, you should obtain a figure as follows:

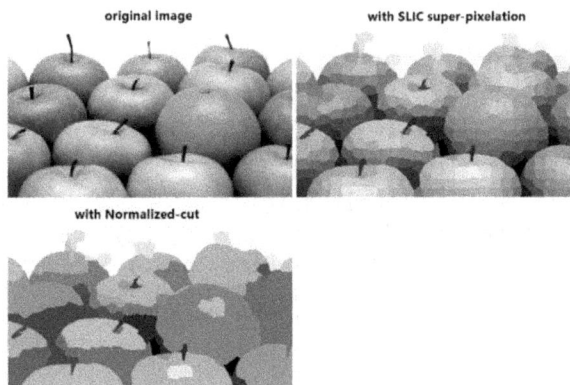

Figure 3.21: *SLIC/NCut segmentation with scikit-image*

RAG merging

RAG merging is a technique used in image segmentation, where the goal is to partition an image into meaningful regions. RAG merging involves the construction of a graph representation of an image, where nodes correspond to image regions, and edges represent the adjacency relationships between regions. The merging process is then applied to iteratively combine similar regions based on certain criteria. The following is a basic outline of the steps involved in RAG merging:

- **Region growing**: Start with an initial over-segmentation of the image. This can be achieved using techniques like region-growing or superpixel algorithms. Assign a unique label to each pixel or region.

- **Construct region adjacency graph**: Create a graph where each node corresponds to a region and edges connect adjacent regions. The weight of the edges can be defined based on a similarity metric between regions. This metric can consider color, texture, or other features.

- **Iterative merging**: Iterate through the edges of the RAG and merge regions that meet certain criteria. The merging criteria can be defined based on the similarity metric and a threshold. For example, merge adjacent regions if their color similarity is above a certain threshold.

- **Update RAG**: After merging, update the RAG by removing the edges between the merged regions and adding new edges to the merged region.

- **Repeat merging**: Repeat the merging process until no more merging is possible or until a predefined condition is met.

The following code snippet uses the function **`graph.cut_threshold()`** to combine regions separated by weight less than threshold (e.g., 50 in the following code snippet). Given an image's labels and its RAG, the function outputs new labels by combining regions whose nodes are separated by a weight less than the given threshold, as shown in the following code snippet:

```python
img = io.imread('images/bird.png')[...,:3]

labels_slic = segmentation.slic(img, compactness=30, n_segments=400)
out_slic = color.label2rgb(labels_slic, img, kind='avg')

g = graph.rag_mean_color(img, labels_slic)
labels_rag = graph.cut_threshold(labels_slic, g, 50)
out_rag = color.label2rgb(labels2, img, kind='avg')

fig, ax = plt.subplots(nrows=2, ncols=2, sharex=True, sharey=True, \
                                            figsize=(15, 12))
fig.subplots_adjust(0,0,1,0.95,0.05,0.05)
ax = ax.ravel()
ax[0].imshow(img), ax[0].set_title('Original image', size=20)
ax[1].imshow(segmentation.mark_boundaries(img, labels_slic,color=(0,0,0)))
ax[1].set_title('With SLIC (boundaries marked)', size=20)
ax[2].imshow(out_slic), ax[2].set_title('With SLIC', size=20)
ax[3].imshow(segmentation.mark_boundaries(out_rag, labels_rag, \
                                            color=(0,0,0)))
```

```
ax[3].set_title('With SLIC + RAG merging', size=20)
for a in ax:
    a.axis('off')
plt.show()
```

If you run the preceding code snippet, you should obtain a figure as follows:

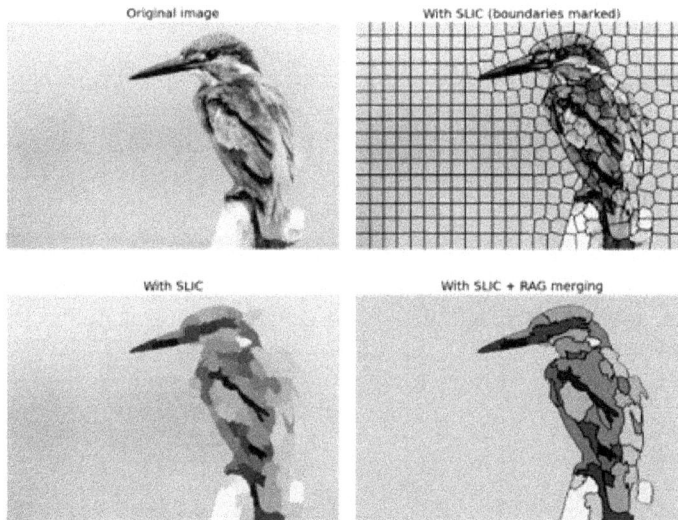

Figure 3.22: *SLIC segmentation/RAG merging with scikit-image*

Conclusion

In this chapter, we explored a wide range of image segmentation techniques, delving into the intricacies of image processing. We have already seen edge detection algorithms such as Canny and LoG, these algorithms can be used for edge-based segmentation. Our primary focus was on the region-based and machine learning-based segmentation techniques.

We understood the foundational concepts of graylevel and bitplane slicing, shedding light on the significance of intensity levels within an image. Gray level slicing emerged as a powerful tool, particularly when applied to regions of interest for contrast enhancement.

Moving forward, we demonstrated image binarization, employing thresholding techniques with python libraries scikit-image, SimpleITK, and opencv-python. Global and local thresholding methods were explored, alongside advanced approaches such as max-entropy and adaptive thresholding. The chapter further covered a comprehensive exploration of segmentation techniques, including Mahalanobis distance-based clustering, k-means vs. spectral clustering, MeanShift segmentation, watershed segmentation, GrabCut segmentation, RandomWalk segmentation, and fast marching image segmentation.

Our journey into segmentation continued with SLIC, NCut algorithms, and RAG merging. The diverse spectrum of techniques covered in this chapter provides readers with a comprehensive toolkit for image segmentation and enhancement, paving the way for innovative applications across various domains.

In the next chapter, we will understand a few advanced applications of deep learning models, introducing semantic / panoptic segmentation with Detectron2, background manipulation using DeeplabV3, and outlier detection employing autoencoder with H2O.

Key terms

Autoencoder, MeanShift, watershed, active contour, thresholding, Mahalanobis distance, GMM

Questions

1. Use the function threshold_local() from skimage.filters module to obtain a local binary thresholded image (based on local pixel neighborhood) using a few different algorithms (e.g., **mean**, **median**, **niblack**, etc.) with **camerman** input image from skimage.data. You should obtain a figure like the following one (with block size 25, e.g.):

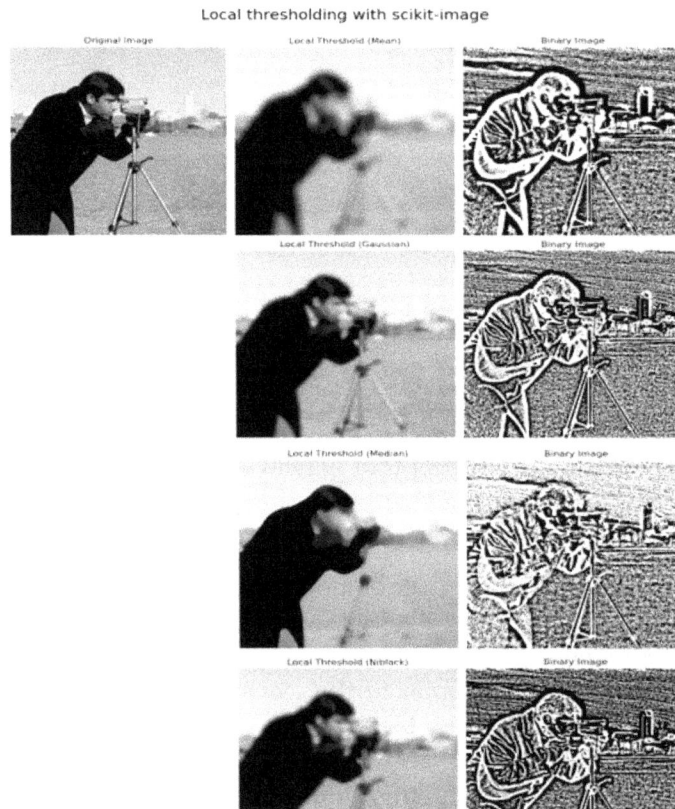

Figure 3.23: Local thresholding with scikit-image

Vary the block size to see the impact on the output binary image obtained.

2. **Segmentation** using **active contours** with SimpleITK: Active Contour Model, also known as **snake**, is a popular method for image segmentation. The basic idea is to evolve a curve within an image to find boundaries that separate different regions of interest. Use the function GeodesicActiveContourLevelSetImageFilter() from SimpleITK to implement active contour. For example, with the following input rose image you should obtain a segmented output like the following figure:

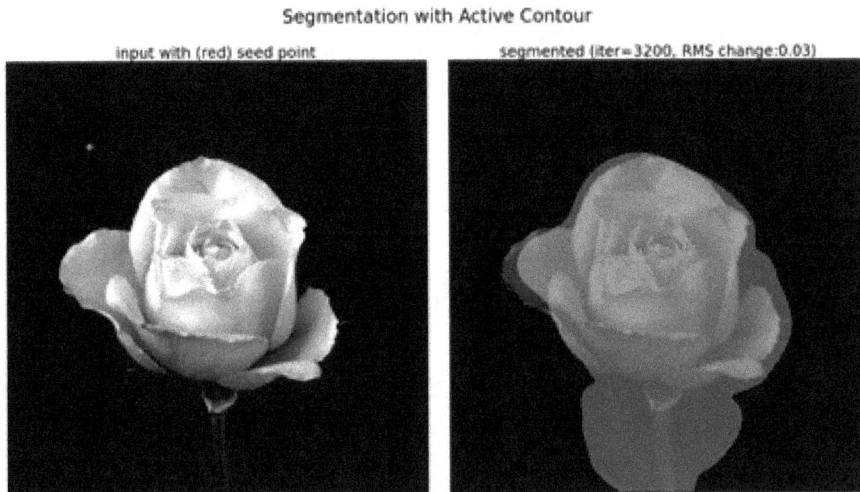

Figure 3.24: Segmentation with active contour

References

1. https://www.csd.uoc.gr/~tziritas/papers/segmentSpringer.pdf

2. https://www.iro.umontreal.ca/~mignotte/IFT6150/Articles/SLIC_Superpixels.pdf

3. https://dl.acm.org/doi/pdf/10.1145/1015706.1015720

4. https://people.eecs.berkeley.edu/~malik/papers/SM-ncut.pdf

5. http://vision.cse.psu.edu/people/chenpingY/paper/grady2006random.pdf

6. https://arxiv.org/pdf/1706.05587v3.pdf

7. https://www.youtube.com/watch?v=_HMyj_BIMoI

8. https://www.youtube.com/watch?v=DIODZIwwTK8

9. https://www.youtube.com/watch?v=seJ2jFvVGis

10. https://www.youtube.com/watch?v=PdAXkJObKGA

11. https://github.com/luiscarlosgph/grabcut

Join our Discord space

Join our Discord workspace for latest updates, offers, tech happenings around the world, new releases, and sessions with the authors:

https://discord.bpbonline.com

CHAPTER 4

More Image Segmentation

Introduction

As discussed in *Chapter 3, Image Segmentation*, image segmentation is a fundamental task in image processing and computer vision that involves partitioning an image into meaningful regions or segments, often to simplify analysis or extract specific objects of interest. The significance of segmentation lies in its ability to enable deeper understanding and interaction with visual data, forming the foundation for numerous applications, ranging from medical imaging to autonomous driving. With the growing accessibility of **Machine learning** (**ML**) and **deep learning** (**DL**) tools, image segmentation has evolved from simple rule-based methods to highly sophisticated, data-driven approaches capable of achieving human-like accuracy.

This chapter explores a variety of image segmentation techniques, showcasing their practical implementations using modern ML and DL frameworks. It begins with traditional methods such as **binary classification** for skin segmentation using scikit-learn and **connected component labeling** with scikit-image, demonstrating how foundational techniques can be applied to simpler segmentation problems. Next, it delves into dynamic **foreground-background separation** in videos using **GMM** with opencv-python, illustrating a probabilistic approach to temporal segmentation.

The chapter then transitions to more advanced DL-based methods, starting with **semantic segmentation**, which assigns class labels to every pixel in an image. Two powerful frameworks are explored: tensorflow with a pre-trained **DeepLabV3+ XCeptionNet** model and opencv-python paired with a pre-trained caffe **Efficient Neural Network** (**ENet**) model. Building on this, **panoptic segmentation**—a comprehensive approach that combines semantic and instance segmentation—is demonstrated using *Facebook*'s **Detectron2** framework.

Beyond segmentation, practical applications are highlighted, such as **blurring and altering backgrounds** in images and videos using **DeepLabV3+** models, and **outlier detection** for identifying anomalous images using autoencoders with H2O. Each section is designed to guide readers through implementation while emphasizing the practical trade-offs and use cases of the presented methods.

Structure

This chapter covers the following topics:

- Human skin segmentation with binary classifiers with scikit-learn
- Segmentation by labelling connected components with scikit-image
- Foreground-background separation in a video using GMM with opencv-python
- Semantic segmentation with DeepLabV3+ and ENet
- Panoptic segmentation with the deep learning model Detectron2
- Blurring and changing background in image and video using DeepLabV3
- Outlier detection using autoencoder with H2O

Objectives

By the end of this chapter, the reader will have a deeper understanding of both traditional machine learning and deep learning-based segmentation techniques and be equipped with the knowledge to tackle diverse segmentation challenges in real-world scenarios. You will learn to implement image segmentation using binary classifier with `scikit-learn`, by labeling connected components with `scikit-image`, and separate foreground/background with `opencv-python`. The reader will also learn **semantic/panoptic** segmentation using the pre-trained deep learning models with `tensorflow/caffe` with `opencv-python`, background modification in images, and anomalous image detection using the library **H2O**.

Human skin segmentation with binary classifiers with scikit-learn

In this section, our goal will be to segment human skins as foreground objects from an image, using a **supervised machine learning** model, namely, a **binary classifier**, which is trained to distinguish between two categories (classes): **skin** and **non-skin**. This could be useful in various applications, such as identifying skin diseases, detecting anomalies, evaluating the effectiveness of skincare products, or assisting in content moderation tasks like pornography detection. Here are the steps that you need to follow to build a skin-detector classifier:

1. **Prepare training dataset**: Start with a skin segmentation dataset from the **UCI Machine Learning Repository** (**https://archive.ics.uci.edu/dataset/229/skin+segmentation**). The dataset contains **positive** and **negative** examples (that is, a set of RGB pixel values and their labels indicating whether they correspond to **human skin** or **not**).

2. This dataset is collected by randomly sampling R, G, and B values from images of the faces of different age groups (young, middle-aged, old), regions, and genders. This dataset has the dimensions of 245057 x 4, the first three columns are B, G, R values (corresponding to the variables x1, x2, and x3, respectively) and the fourth column is the class label (**decision variable** y, where $y = 1$ is a positive, that is, a **skin** example, and $y = 2$ is a **nonskin** example). The following *Table 4.1* shows the size of the samples in the dataset:

Total learning sample size	Skin sample size	Non-skin sample size
245057	50859	194198

Table 4.1: Size of samples in the dataset

3. We shall use the **YCbCr** color space instead of RGB, since it separates the **luminance** (brightness) from **chrominance** (color information) in RGB values using a linear transform (thereby reducing the impact of lighting variations). Then, we will train a few binary classifiers on the given dataset, but only using the chrominance channels.

4. Let us start by importing the required libraries and the python classes corresponding to binary classifier models from the library **scikit-learn**. Next, load the dataset and convert it from **RGB** to **YCbCr** color space. We shall only use **Cb** and **Cr** channels as features to predict the label **skin**; hence, drop all other columns, as shown in the following code snippet. This dataset will act as training dataset for the classifier models to be trained:

```python
import numpy as np
import matplotlib.pyplot as plt
import pandas as pd
from sklearn.tree import DecisionTreeClassifier
from sklearn.naive_bayes import GaussianNB
from sklearn.ensemble import GradientBoostingClassifier
from sklearn.neighbors import KNeighborsClassifier
from skimage.io import imread
from skimage.color import rgb2ycbcr, gray2rgb
```

```
df = pd.read_csv('images/Skin_NonSkin.txt', header=None, \
                                            delim_whitespace=True)
df.columns = ['B', 'G', 'R', 'skin']
df.skin[df.skin == 2] = 0
df['Cb'] = np.round(128 -.168736*df.R -.331364*df.G + .5*df.B) \
                                                    .astype(int)
df['Cr'] = np.round(128 +.5*df.R - .418688*df.G -.081312*df.B) \
                                                    .astype(int)

df.drop(['B','G','R'], axis=1, inplace=True)
df.drop_duplicates(inplace=True)
df.head()
```

Refer to the following figure, showing first few pixel values (after RGB-YCbCr color-space transformation) corresponding to **skin**:

	skin	Cb	Cr
0	1	116	148
14	1	117	149
45	1	116	149
47	1	115	149
61	1	114	149

Figure 4.1: Skin color pixels in YCbCr color space

5. We shall use the following supervised machine learning models as binary classifiers. Here is a brief description of the models:

    a. **Gradient boosting**: An **ensemble learning** model that combines the predictions of several weak learners (typically decision trees) to create a strong learner. It builds trees sequentially, with each tree correcting the errors of the previous one.

    b. **Decision tree**: A type of supervised machine learning model used for both classification and regression tasks. It works by recursively splitting the dataset based on features, creating a tree-like structure. Each internal node represents a decision based on a feature, and each leaf node represents the output or class label. Decision trees are interpretable and can handle both numerical and categorical data.

    c. **Gaussian Naive Bayes**: A probabilistic (generative) classification model based on Bayes' theorem. It (naively) assumes that the features are **conditionally independent** given the **class** label and that the distribution of each feature is Gaussian (normal). Despite its simplicity and the naive assumption, it often performs well in practice, especially with continuous data.

d. **k-nearest neighbors (kNN)**: a simple and intuitive **instance-based learning** model used for classification and regression. In kNN, an object is classified by the majority class of its k nearest neighbors, where is a user-defined parameter. It works on the principle that similar instances in the feature space should have similar output values. The choice of affects the **trade-off** between **bias** and **variance** in the model.

6. Use `scikit-learn`'s implementation of the binary classifier models. Instantiate the objects corresponding to each of the model classes and train each model on the training dataset using the `fit()` method, as shown in the following code snippet:

```
Xy = df.values
X = Xy[:, 1:]
y = Xy[:, 0]

models = (GradientBoostingClassifier(n_estimators=1000, \
                    max_leaf_nodes=4, max_depth=None,
                    random_state=2, min_samples_split=5),
          DecisionTreeClassifier(random_state=0),
          GaussianNB(),
          KNeighborsClassifier(5))
models = [clf.fit(X, y) for clf in models]
```

7. Once trained, our models are ready to be used for prediction. To predict whether a pixel from an image is a skin pixel or a non-skin pixel, for each of the aforementioned models:

   a. We need to convert pixel **RGB** value to **YCbCr**.

   b. Pass the YCbCr value of the pixel as input to the model.

   c. The model will predict the class label (using the method `predict()`, as invoked from the function `plot_contours()` in the next code snippet).

8. Create a `meshgrid` of values for **Cb**, **Cr** and scatterplot the predicted value of a pixel with the given values of Cb, Cr as **skin** or **non-skin**, for each pixel. Scatterplot the training datapoints on top. As can be seen from *Figure 4.2*, the small red region indicates the pixels predicted as **skin**, also observe that the prediction by different classifier disagree at many pixels.

```python
def make_meshgrid(x, y, h=.02):
    x_min, x_max = x.min() - 1, x.max() + 1
    y_min, y_max = y.min() - 1, y.max() + 1
    xx, yy = np.meshgrid(np.arange(x_min, x_max, h),
                         np.arange(y_min, y_max, h))
    return xx, yy

def plot_contours(ax, clf, xx, yy, **params):
    Z = clf.predict(np.c_[xx.ravel(), yy.ravel()])
    Z = Z.reshape(xx.shape)
    out = ax.contourf(xx, yy, Z, **params)
    return out

# Set-up 2x2 grid for plotting.
fig, sub = plt.subplots(2, 2, figsize=(20,20))
plt.subplots_adjust(left=0, right=1, bottom=0, top=0.9, \
                                    wspace=0.05, hspace=0.08)

X0, X1 = X[:, 0], X[:, 1]
xx, yy = make_meshgrid(X0, X1, h=1)

# title for the plots
titles = ('GradientBoosting',
          'DecisionTree',
          'Gaussian Naive Bayes',
          'kNearestNeighbor')

for clf, title, ax in zip(models, titles, sub.flatten()):
    ax.scatter(X0, X1, c=y, cmap=plt.cm.coolwarm, s=5
    plot_contours(ax, clf, xx, yy, cmap=plt.cm.coolwarm, alpha=0.8)
    ax.set_xlim(xx.min(), xx.max())
    ax.set_ylim(yy.min(), yy.max())
    ax.set_xlabel('Cb', size=20)
    ax.set_ylabel('Cr', size=20)
    ax.set_xticks(())
    ax.set_yticks(())
    ax.set_title(title, size=20)

plt.suptitle('Decision Boundaries with different Classifiers', \
                                    size=30)
plt.show()
```

If you run the preceding code snippet, you should obtain a figure as follows:

Decision Boundaries with different Classifiers

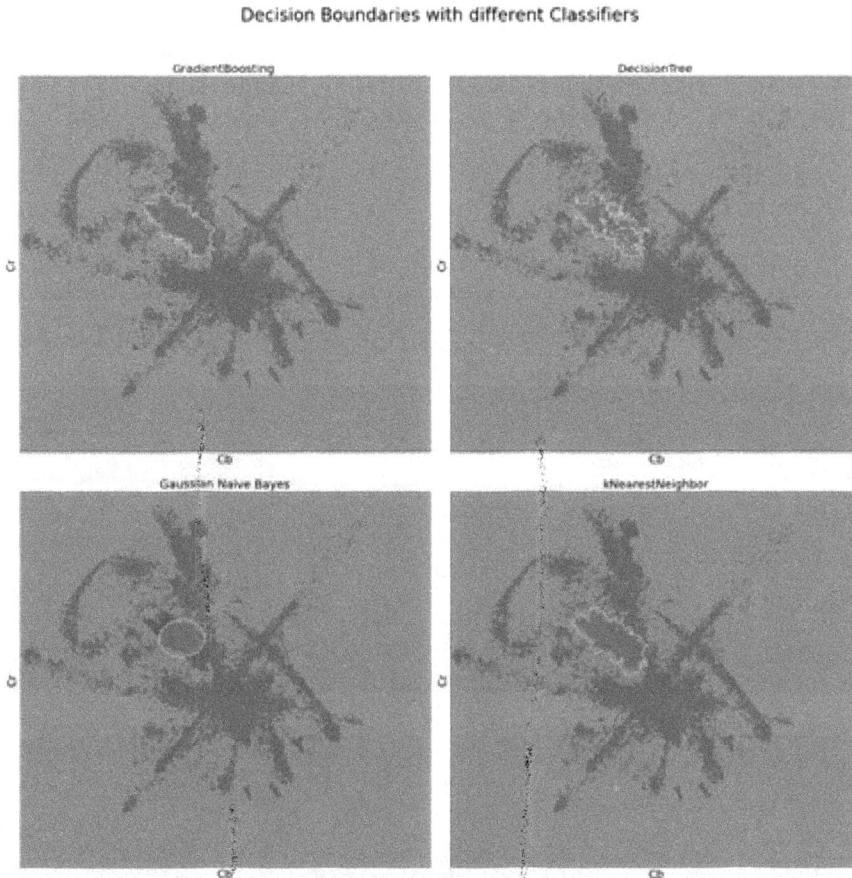

Figure 4.2: *Visualizing the decision boundaries for the binary classifiers to predict skin/non-skin pixels*

9. Next, load the input image that you want to segment (containing human faces/ skins), convert it to the YCbCr color space, and predict the label of the pixel as **skin** (1) or **non-skin** (0).

10. **Mask** out the pixels where the prediction is **nonskin**, and obtain the final segmentation result, for each of the binary classifiers, as demonstrated in the following code snippet:

```python
image = imread('images/players.png')[...,:3]
proc_image = np.reshape(rgb2ycbcr(image), (-1, 3))

fig, sub = plt.subplots(2, 2, figsize=(20,15))
plt.subplots_adjust(left=0, right=1, bottom=0, top=0.95, \
                                    wspace=0.05, hspace=0.08)

for clf, title, ax in zip(models, titles, sub.flatten()):
    print(title)
```

```
# GradientBoosting/DecisionTree/GaussianNB/kNearestNeighbor
skin = clf.predict(proc_image[...,1:])
skin = skin.reshape(image.shape[0], image.shape[1])
result = np.bitwise_and(gray2rgb(255*skin).astype(np.uint8), \
                                                    image)

ax.imshow(result), ax.axis('off')
ax.set_title('Skin Detected and Segmented with ' + title, \
                                                    size=20)

plt.show()
```

If you run the preceding code snippet, you should obtain a figure as follows:

Figure 4.3: *Human skin detection in image with binary classifiers*

Segmentation by labelling connected components with scikit-image

In this section, we will learn how to segment an image by finding the **connected components** in the **thresholded** binary image. A connected component is a set of connected pixels with the same label or intensity value. Various algorithms can be used for connected component labeling, such as:

- **Two-pass algorithm**: In the first pass, assign temporary labels to connected components. In the second pass, resolve label equivalences and assign final labels.

- **Union-Find algorithm**: Also known as disjoint-set data structure, it efficiently keeps track of connected components and merges equivalent labels.

Let us segment an image with connected component labeling algorithm with **scikit-image.measure** module's **label()** function. Start by importing the required libraries and functions. Here are the steps to be followed:

1. Read a land image (from satellite) as input and convert it to grayscale using **skimage.color.rgb2gray()** function.

2. Apply **Otsu** thresholding to obtain the binary image. Use **morphological closing** operation (using the function **skimage.morphology.closing()**) to close small holes or gaps in regions, smooth the boundaries of objects, and connect nearby regions that have small separations, if any. It is particularly useful for preprocessing binary images and improving the segmentation of objects.

3. Remove artifacts connected to image border with the function **clear_border()**.

4. Label image regions with the function **skimage.measure.label()**, which is specifically designed for connected component labeling in binary images. It assigns a unique label to each connected component in the input binary image. The **label()** function takes a binary image as input, where pixels are classified as either **foreground** (1) or **background** (0). The **connectivity** parameter defines which pixel neighbors should be considered (for example, use the value 2 for **8-connectivity** and the value 1 for **4-connectivity**).

5. As can be seen from the following code snippet, it finds 1482 regions. Plot the input image, overlay the labels on top of the image using the function **skimage.color.label2rgb()**.

6. Use **skimage.measure.regionprops()** function to loop through the regions found and draw a rectangle around large enough regions (for example., with **region.area >= 100**).

```python
from skimage.filters import threshold_otsu
from skimage.segmentation import clear_border
from skimage.measure import label, regionprops
from skimage.morphology import closing, square
from skimage.color import label2rgb, rgb2gray
import numpy as np
import matplotlib.pyplot as plt
import matplotlib.patches as mpatches

image = (255*rgb2gray(imread('images/land.png')[...,:3])) \
                                        .astype(np.uint8)

thresh = threshold_otsu(image)
bw = closing(image > thresh, square(3))
cleared = clear_border(bw)
```

```python
label_image = label(cleared, connectivity=2)
image_label_overlay = label2rgb(label_image, image=image)
print(np.max(label_image))
# 1482

fig, ax = plt.subplots(figsize=(20, 10))
ax.imshow(image_label_overlay, cmap='jet')

for region in regionprops(label_image):
    # take regions with large enough areas
    if region.area >= 100: # and region.area <= 80000:
        # draw rectangle around segmented regions
        minr, minc, maxr, maxc = region.bbox
        rect = mpatches.Rectangle((minc, minr), maxc-minc, maxr-minr,
                                  fill=False, edgecolor='yellow',
                                  linewidth=2)
        ax.add_patch(rect)
ax.set_axis_off()
plt.tight_layout()
plt.show()
```

If you run the preceding code snippet, you should obtain a figure as follows:

Figure 4.4: Segmentation by labeling connected components

7. By default, 0-valued pixels in the binary image are considered as **background** pixels by the **skimage.measure.label()** function. You can override this default behavior by passing a value in the **background** argument (for example, **background=1** will consider the 1-valued pixels as background).

8. Use the input image of the school building and obtain different segmentation results by varying the **threshold** for binarization, **background** value and color map (**cmap**) for **matplotlib.pylab.imshow()**. You should obtain a figure as the following one:

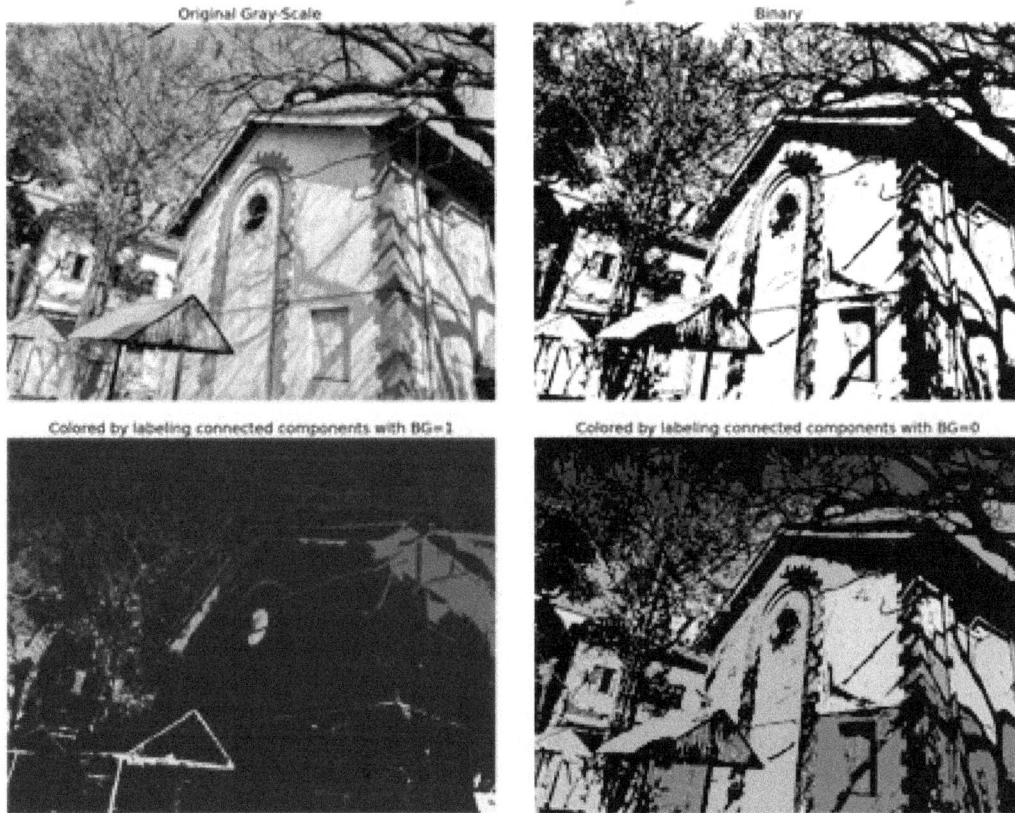

Figure 4.5: Coloring the segmented regions obtained by labelling with connected components

Foreground-background separation in a video using GMM with opencv-python

Background subtraction is a technique used in computer vision to separate the **foreground** (moving objects) from the **background** in a video stream or sequence of images. **OpenCV** provides several algorithms for background subtraction, and one commonly used method is the function **createBackgroundSubtractorMOG2()**, which implements a Gaussian Mixture based background/foreground segmentation algorithm. **GMM** is a probabilistic model used for representing a mixture of multiple Gaussian distributions.

In this section we shall demonstrate background subtraction in video frames, using the **opencv-python** function **createBackgroundSubtractorMOG2()**. Here are the steps to be followed:

1. Let us start the implementation by importing the required libraries.

2. Read the input video stream (here, we shall use a video of students walking in the corridor towards the camera) using **cv2.VideoCapture()**.

3. Instantiate a **GMM** background subtractor object with the function **cv2. createBackgroundSubtractorMOG2()**. The function accepts the following arguments:

   a. **history**: The number of previous frames used to build the background model. A higher value gives the algorithm an extended memory but it may be slower to adapt to changes. Default is 500.

   b. **varThreshold**: A threshold on the squared **Mahalanobis** distance between the pixel and the model to decide whether a pixel is well-described by the background model. A lower value makes the algorithm more sensitive to changes. Default is 16 (the following code snippet uses the value 32, and experiments with different values of this parameter).

   c. **detectShadows**: If **True**, the algorithm detects shadows and marks them in the foreground mask. Default value is **True**.

4. The background subtractor maintains an internal model of the background, and for each incoming frame, it compares the pixel values with this model. Pixels that deviate significantly from the background model are considered as foreground. The **detectShadows** parameter helps distinguish shadows from actual foreground objects.

5. Process each frame or image in a loop, applying the **GMM** background subtractor (with the method **apply()**), to obtain the **foreground mask**. *Figure 4.6* shows the foreground mask computed for a few different frames from the video. Refer to the following code snippet:

```python
import numpy as np
import cv2
import matplotlib.pylab as plt

cap = cv2.VideoCapture('images/Vid_03_01.mp4')
foreground_background = cv2.createBackgroundSubtractorMOG2(
                        history=500, varThreshold=32,
                        detectShadows=False)
count = 1
while True:
    _, frame = cap.read()
    if frame is None:
        break
    frame = frame.astype(np.uint8)
    foreground_mask = foreground_background.apply(frame)\
                                        .astype(np.uint8)

    if count in [50, 100, 170]:
        plt.subplot(121)
        plt.imshow(cv2.cvtColor(frame, cv2.COLOR_BGR2RGB))
        plt.axis('off'), plt.title('Original image', size=20)
        plt.subplot(122), plt.imshow(foreground_mask), plt.
        axis('off')
```

```
            plt.title('Motion-based Segmentation with MOG Background'
                                        'Subtraction', size=20)
            plt.suptitle('Frame: ' + str(count), size=30)
            plt.tight_layout()
            plt.show()
        count += 1

cap.release()
```

If you run the preceding code snippet, you should obtain a figure as follows:

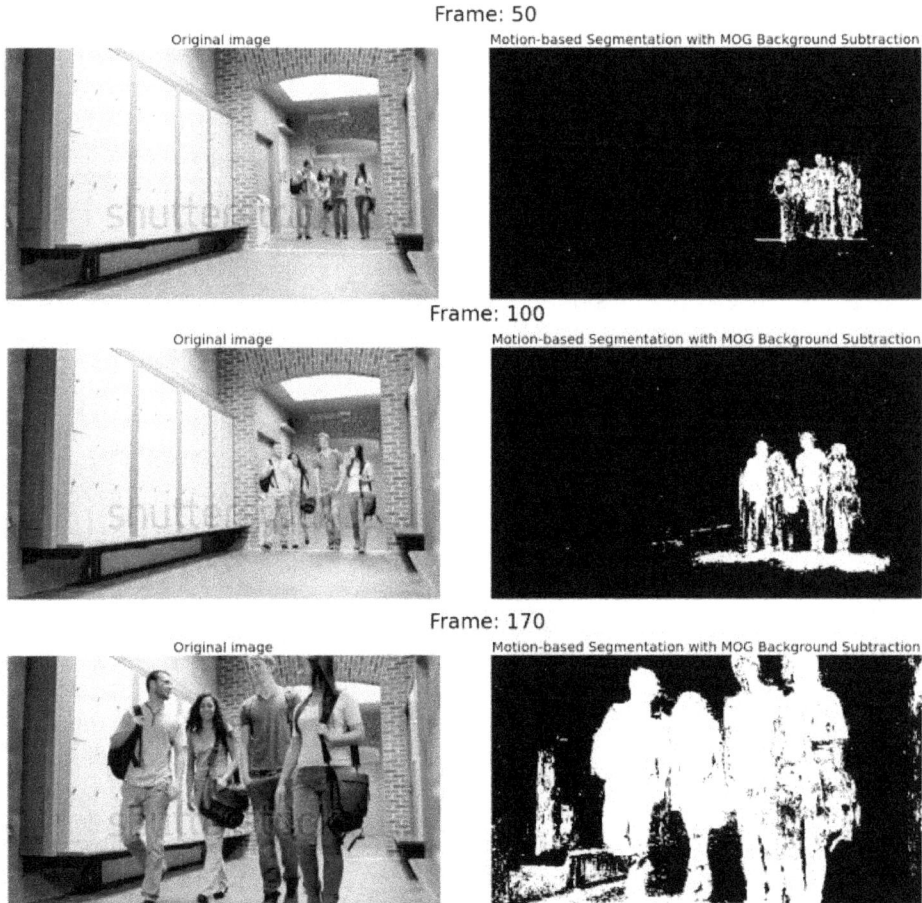

Figure 4.6: Foreground-background separation in video with opencv-python

Semantic segmentation with DeepLabV3+ and ENet

Semantic segmentation is a computer vision task that aims to classify each pixel in an image into **predefined classes**, such as **road**, **person**, **car**, and so on. It is called **semantic** because it assigns meaning (i.e., class labels) to every pixel based on what object it represents. Unlike object detection, which detects and localizes objects in an image, **semantic segmentation** provides a more detailed understanding of the scene by assigning a class label to every pixel. In this section, you will learn how to use a couple of popular **pre-trained** neural net models (namely **XCepionNet** and **ENet**) to perform semantic segmentation of an image.

Using pretrained DeepLabV3+ XCeptionNet model with TensorFlow

DeepLabV3+ with **XceptionNet** is a semantic segmentation model that combines the DeepLabV3+ architecture with the XceptionNet backbone. This model is designed for pixel-level segmentation tasks, where the goal is to classify each pixel in an image into specific object classes. DeepLabV3+ is an extension of the DeepLabV3 model, and the incorporation of the XceptionNet backbone enhances its performance.

Here is a breakdown of the key components:

- **DeepLabV3+ architecture**: DeepLabV3+ is an evolution of the DeepLab architecture developed by Google for semantic segmentation tasks. It incorporates several key features, including **atrous** (dilated) convolutions, **Atrous Spatial Pyramid Pooling (ASPP)**, and decoder modules. These features help capture multi-scale contextual information and improve the model's ability to segment objects in images.

- **XceptionNet backbone**: XCeptionNet is a deep neural network architecture based on depth-wise separable convolutions. It is known for its efficiency and has been used as a backbone in various computer vision tasks. In the context of DeepLabV3+, XceptionNet serves as the feature extractor to capture hierarchical features from the input image.

- **Atrous convolution and ASPP**: Atrous convolutions, also known as dilated convolutions, are used in DeepLabV3+ to capture multi-scale information without down-sampling the spatial resolution. The ASPP module further enhances this capability by using multiple atrous convolution rates in parallel to capture information at different spatial scales.

- **Decoder module**: The decoder module in DeepLabV3+ is responsible for refining the segmentation output. It up-samples the features to the original image resolution and combines them with features from earlier layers to improve localization accuracy.

XceptionNet, short for **Extreme Inception**, is a deep neural network architecture that was proposed by the creator of the **Keras** deep learning library. XceptionNet is a deep **convolutional neural network** (**CNN**) architecture that is often used for computer vision and image processing tasks, including semantic segmentation. The following figure shows the schematic diagram (taken from the corresponding paper) for the architecture of XCeptionNet:

XCeptionNet architecture

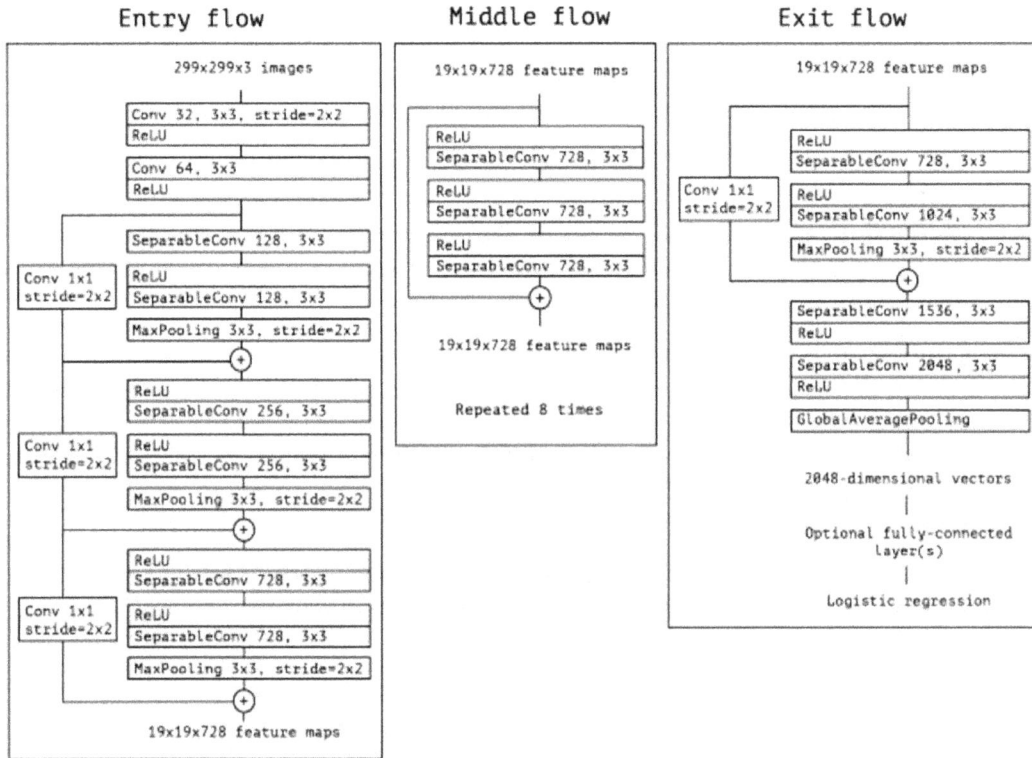

Figure 4.7: *XceptionNet architecture*
Source: *https://arxiv.org/pdf/1610.02357.pdf*

As can be seen in *Figure 4.7*, here are the key components of the XceptionNet architecture:

- **Entry flow**: The network begins with a standard convolutional layer followed by a series of convolutional blocks. Each block consists of a **depth-wise separable convolution**, **batch normalization**, and a **Rectified Linear Unit (ReLU)** activation. The entry flow is responsible for capturing low-level features.

- **Middle flow**: The middle flow is composed of several identical residual blocks. Each residual block consists of three separable convolutional layers. The middle flow helps the network capture more complex features by stacking these residual blocks.

- **Exit flow**: The exit flow is responsible for producing the final output of the network. It consists of a combination of separable convolutional layers, **global average pooling**, fully connected layers, and a **softmax** activation for classification, in case of image classification tasks. The global average pooling is used to reduce spatial dimensions and create a fixed-size representation regardless of the input size.

- **Depthwise separable convolutions**: The core building block of XceptionNet is the depth-wise separable convolution. Unlike traditional convolutions that operate on all input channels at once, depth-wise separable convolutions perform spatial convolutions independently for each input channel, followed by a 1x1 pointwise convolution to mix information between channels. This factorization reduces the number of parameters and computations, making the network more efficient.

- **Skip connections**: XceptionNet uses skip connections (**residual** connections) in both entry flow and middle flow. These connections help mitigate the **vanishing gradient** problem (which occurs when gradients become too small during **backpropagation**, causing neural networks to learn very slowly or stop learning altogether), allowing for easier training of very deep networks.

The XceptionNet architecture is known for its efficiency and strong performance on various computer vision tasks. It has fewer parameters compared to traditional architectures such as **InceptionV3** while achieving competitive or even superior results. The depthwise separable convolutions contribute to the model's ability to capture hierarchical features efficiently, making it well-suited for tasks such as image classification, object detection, and semantic segmentation.

Here we shall use a pretrained **DeepLabV3+** model with **XceptionNet** backbone (already trained on the **cityscapes** dataset) to perform **semantic segmentation** of an input image of a road with traffics.

Cityscapes is a widely used dataset for semantic understanding of urban street scenes. It is specifically designed for training and evaluating computer vision models, especially those aimed at tasks like semantic segmentation and object detection in urban environments.

Here are key details about the Cityscapes dataset:

- **Content**: The dataset consists of high-quality images captured in various cities, and each image is densely annotated for pixel-level semantic segmentation. This means that each pixel in an image is labeled with a specific class, indicating whether it belongs to a road, sidewalk, building, person, car, and so on.

- **Labels**: Cityscapes provides fine-grained annotations with 20-30 different classes, covering a wide range of urban scene elements. Some of the classes include `road`, `sidewalk`, `building`, `person`, `car`, `bus`, `traffic light`, and `vegetation`, among others. Each pixel in the images is assigned one of these class labels.

- **Image types**: The dataset includes a variety of image types, such as high-resolution images, stereo images, and images captured in different weather conditions (for example, sunny, rainy). This diversity is valuable for training models that can generalize well to different urban scenarios.

- **Usage for training**: Researchers and practitioners use the Cityscapes dataset to train and evaluate semantic segmentation models. Training involves feeding the images and corresponding pixel-level annotations into a deep learning model (such as **ENet, U-Net,** or **DeepLab**) to learn the mapping between pixels and semantic classes. The trained model can then be used to predict semantic segmentation masks for new images.

- **Benchmarking**: Cityscapes is also commonly used as a benchmark for evaluating the performance of different computer vision models. Researchers can compare the accuracy of their models on the Cityscapes test set, which consists of images not seen during training.

Let us now learn how to apply semantic segmentation to an image, using a pretrained model. Here are the steps you need to follow:

1. Load all the required libraries along with **tensorflow**. Note that we need tensorflow version 1 here (even though we have version 2 installed). Hence, use **tf.compat.v1** to maintain compatibility.

2. Define the functions **label_to_color_image()** to convert a **label** to a color using a **colormap**, and **visualize_segmentation()** to display an input image, along with the segmentation map passed as arguments, as shown in the following code snippet. Define the **label_names** corresponding to the **labels** output (map the label ids to class names) by the semantic segmentation model.

```python
from PIL import Image
import cv2
import numpy as np
import matplotlib.pylab as plt
from matplotlib import gridspec
import tensorflow
tensorflow.__version__
# 2.13.0
import tensorflow.compat.v1 as tf
from tensorflow.io.gfile import GFile

def label_to_color_image(label):

    if label.ndim != 2:
        raise ValueError('Expected 2-D input label')

    colormap = np.array([
        [128,  64, 128],
        [244,  35, 232],
        [ 70,  70,  70],
        [102, 102, 156],
        [190, 153, 153],
        [153, 153, 153],
        [250, 170,  30],
        [220, 220,   0],
        [107, 142,  35],
        [152, 251, 152],
        [ 70, 130, 180],
```

```
                [220,  20,  60],
                [255,   0,   0],
                [  0,   0, 142],

                [  0,   0,  70],
                [  0,  60, 100],
                [  0,  80, 100],
                [  0,   0, 230],
                [119,  11,  32],
                [  0,   0,   0]], dtype=np.uint8)

    if np.max(label) >= len(colormap):
        raise ValueError('label value too large.')

    return colormap[label]

label_names = np.asarray([
    'road', 'sidewalk', 'building', 'wall', 'fence', 'pole',
    'traffic light', 'traffic sign', 'vegetation', 'terrain', 'sky',
    'person', 'rider', 'car', 'truck', 'bus', 'train', 'motorcycle',
    'bicycle', 'void'])

full_label_map = np.arange(len(label_names))\
                                  .reshape(len(label_names), 1)
full_color_map = label_to_color_image(full_label_map)

def visualize_segmentation(image, seg_map):
  plt.figure(figsize=(20, 15))
  plt.subplots_adjust(left=0, right=1, bottom=0, top=0.95, \
                                  wspace=0.05, hspace=0.05)
  plt.subplot(221), plt.imshow(image), plt.axis('off')
  plt.title('input image', size=20)
  plt.subplot(222)
  seg_image = label_to_color_image(seg_map).astype(np.uint8)
  plt.imshow(seg_image), plt.axis('off')
  plt.title('segmentation map', size=20)
  plt.subplot(223), plt.imshow(image)
  plt.imshow(seg_image, alpha=0.7)
  plt.axis('off'), plt.title('segmentation overlay', size=20)
  unique_labels = np.unique(seg_map)
  ax = plt.subplot(224)
  plt.imshow(full_color_map[unique_labels].astype(np.uint8), \
                                  interpolation='nearest')
  ax.yaxis.tick_right()
  plt.yticks(range(len(unique_labels)), label_names[unique_labels])
  plt.xticks([], [])
  ax.tick_params(width=0.0, labelsize=20), plt.grid('off')
  plt.show()
```

3. **Load the pretrained XceptionNet model**: Load pre-trained **XceptionNet** model (trained on the cityscapes dataset). You can download the compressed model from the link **http://download.tensorflow.org/models/deeplabv3_cityscapes_**

train_2018_02_06.tar.gz. Unzip the compressed file and place the file **frozen_inference_graph.pb** inside the **models** folder.

4. Define a function **run_semantic_segmentation()** that takes two parameters: **image** (input image) and **model_path** (path to a pre-trained model). This function will perform semantic segmentation on an input **image** using the pre-trained model (it accepts **model_path** as an argument, which will be the path to the **frozen inference graph**).

5. **Load the tensorflow graph**: Create a new tensorflow graph and load the pre-trained model into the graph using the provided **model_path**. The model file is assumed to be in a binary format, and its content is read into **graph_def**. Check if the graph was successfully loaded. If not, raise a **RuntimeError()** indicating that the inference graph could not be found in the provided tar archive.

6. Import graph into a tensorflow **session** and set this graph as the default graph within the context, i.e., Create a tensorflow **session** (with **tf.Session()**) using the loaded graph.

7. Obtain the width and height of the input image. Resize the image to the specified **target_size** (2049, 1025) using the nearest-neighbor interpolation.

8. Run semantic segmentation **inference** on the preprocessed image. The output is stored in **batch_seg_map**. The output tensor name is assumed to be **SemanticPredictions:0**, and the input tensor name is **ImageTensor:0**.

9. **Post-process segmentation map**: Extract the segmentation map from the batch output. If the segmentation map has only two dimensions, add an extra dimension for later resizing. Resize the segmentation map back to the original image size using the nearest-neighbor interpolation. Return the final segmentation map, as demonstrated in the following code snippet.

10. Visualize the segmentation map along with the overlayed segmentation, using the function **visualize_segmentation()**. It also displays the labels as **legend**. If you run the next code snippet, you will obtain a figure like the one shown in *Figure 4.8*:

```
def run_semantic_segmentation(image, model_path):
    graph = tf.Graph()
    graph_def = None
    with GFile(model_path, 'rb') as f:
        graph_def = tf.GraphDef()
        graph_def.ParseFromString(f.read())
    if graph_def is None:
        raise RuntimeError('Cannot find inference graph.')
    with graph.as_default():
        tf.import_graph_def(graph_def, name='')
    sess = tf.Session(graph=graph)
```

```
    width, height = image.size
    target_size = (2049,1025)  # size of Cityscapes images
    resized_image = image.convert('RGB').resize(target_size, \
                                        Image.ANTIALIAS)
    batch_seg_map = sess.run('SemanticPredictions:0',
        feed_dict={'ImageTensor:0': [np.asarray(resized_image)]})
    seg_map = batch_seg_map[0]  # expected batch size = 1
    if len(seg_map.shape) == 2:
        seg_map = np.expand_dims(seg_map,-1)  # extra dim for resize
    seg_map = cv2.resize(seg_map, (width,height), \
                            interpolation=cv2.INTER_NEAREST)
    return seg_map
model = 'models/frozen_inference_graph.pb'
image = 'images/road.png'
image = Image.open(image)
seg_map = run_semantic_segmentation(image, model)
visualize_segmentation(image, seg_map)
```

If you run the preceding code snippet, you should obtain a figure as follows:

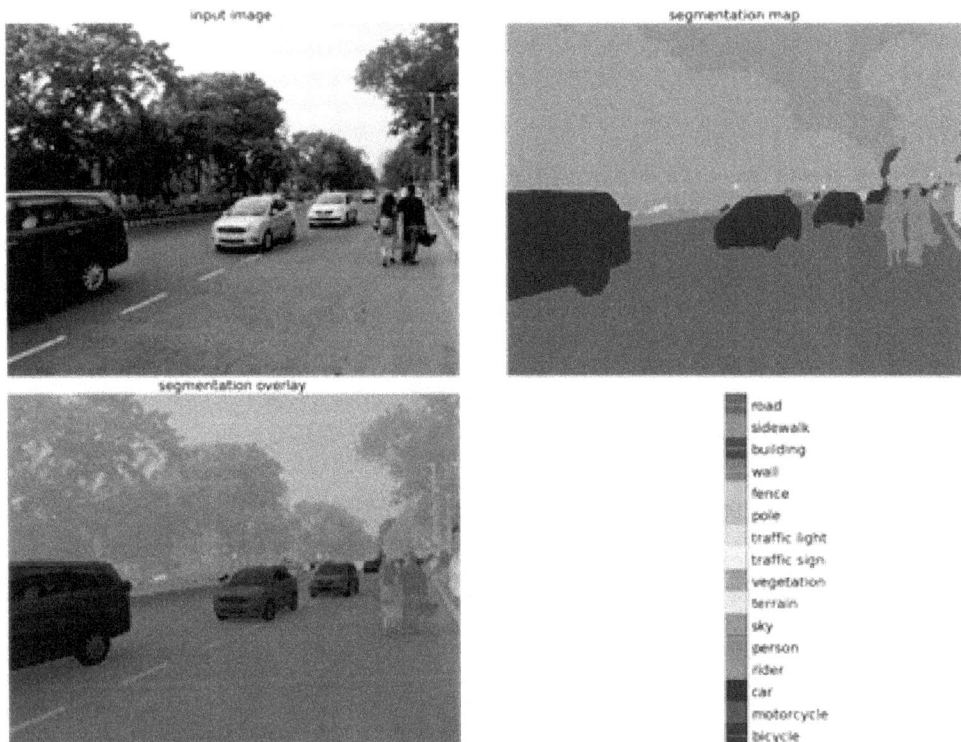

Figure 4.8: Semantic segmentation with DeepLabV3+/XceptionNet

With opencv-python and pretrained Caffe ENet model

The **Efficient Neural Network (ENet)** model is a lightweight and efficient neural network architecture designed for semantic segmentation. ENet was developed with a focus on achieving real-time performance with high accuracy, making it suitable for applications such as autonomous vehicles, robotics, and augmented reality. Here are some key features and aspects of ENet:

- **Architecture**: ENet is a CNN architecture that utilizes a combination of different layers, including convolutional layers, pooling layers, and skip connections. It has a symmetric **encoder-decoder** structure.

- **Efficiency**: One of the main goals of ENet is to be computationally efficient while maintaining good segmentation performance. It achieves this through various design choices, such as **factorized convolutions**, which decompose standard convolutions into a series of smaller convolutions to reduce computational complexity. The model is known for its speed and effectiveness in semantic segmentation tasks while having a relatively small number of parameters compared to some other deep neural networks.

- **Skip connections**: ENet employs skip connections between the **encoder** and **decoder** parts of the network. These connections help preserve spatial information and enable the network to capture both local and global context.

- **PReLU activation: Parametric Rectified Linear Unit** (PReLU) activations are used in ENet, which can help the model learn better representations by allowing negative values during training.

- **Spatial dropout**: ENet uses a spatial dropout technique, which involves randomly dropping entire channels of feature maps during training. This helps prevent overfitting and improves the robustness of the model.

- **Multi-scale processing**: ENet processes the input at multiple scales, capturing both fine and coarse details in the image. This is achieved through parallel processing at different resolutions.

Once trained, ENet can be used for **real-time semantic segmentation** of images or video frames, providing a pixel-wise classification of the visual content. Refer to the following figure:

ENet Architecture

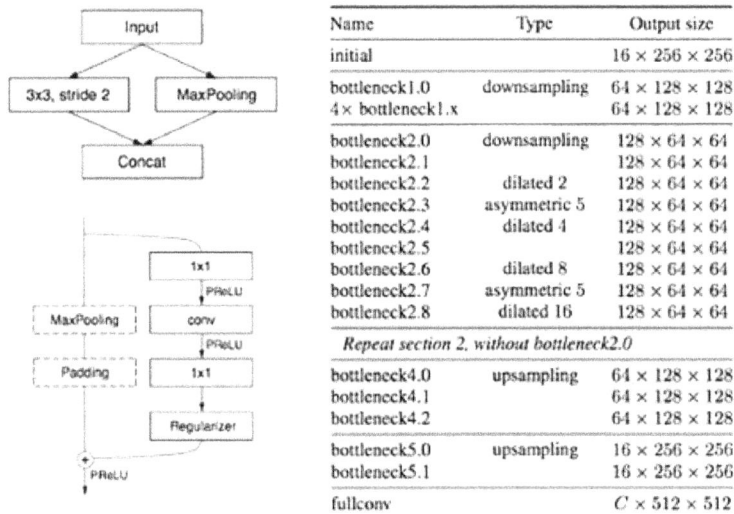

Name	Type	Output size
initial		$16 \times 256 \times 256$
bottleneck1.0	downsampling	$64 \times 128 \times 128$
$4\times$ bottleneck1.x		$64 \times 128 \times 128$
bottleneck2.0	downsampling	$128 \times 64 \times 64$
bottleneck2.1		$128 \times 64 \times 64$
bottleneck2.2	dilated 2	$128 \times 64 \times 64$
bottleneck2.3	asymmetric 5	$128 \times 64 \times 64$
bottleneck2.4	dilated 4	$128 \times 64 \times 64$
bottleneck2.5		$128 \times 64 \times 64$
bottleneck2.6	dilated 8	$128 \times 64 \times 64$
bottleneck2.7	asymmetric 5	$128 \times 64 \times 64$
bottleneck2.8	dilated 16	$128 \times 64 \times 64$
Repeat section 2, without bottleneck2.0		
bottleneck4.0	upsampling	$64 \times 128 \times 128$
bottleneck4.1		$64 \times 128 \times 128$
bottleneck4.2		$64 \times 128 \times 128$
bottleneck5.0	upsampling	$16 \times 256 \times 256$
bottleneck5.1		$16 \times 256 \times 256$
fullconv		$C \times 512 \times 512$

Figure 4.9: *ENet architecture*
Source: https://sh-tsang.medium.com/reading-enet-real-time-semantic-segmentation-semantic-segmentation-41f26b85468

To use a pretrained ENet model (trained on the cityscapes dataset) for semantic segmentation using **opencv-python**, follow these steps:

1. As usual, start by importing the necessary libraries/packages.

2. Download the pretrained ENet model (**enet-model.net**), cityscape class names (**enet-classes.txt**) and the RGB color values for the classes (**enet-colors.txt**) from the following link: **https://github.com/simogasp/opencv-semantic-segmentation/tree/master/enet-cityscapes** and save them in the **models** folder.

3. Load the class label names and label colors as follows:

```python
# import the necessary packages
import numpy as np
import imutils
import time
import cv2
import matplotlib.pylab as plt

classes = open('images/enet-classes.txt').read().strip().split("\n")
colors = open('images/enet-colors.txt').read().strip().split("\n")
colors = [np.array(c.split(",")).astype("int") for c in colors]
colors = np.array(colors, dtype="uint8")
```

4. Initialize the **legend** visualization. Loop over the class names and colors, draw the class name + color on the legend, using the following code snippet:

```
legend = np.zeros((((len(classes) * 25) + 25, 300, 3), dtype="uint8")
for (i, (className, color)) in enumerate(zip(classes, colors)):
    color = [int(c) for c in color]
    cv2.putText(legend, className, (5, (i * 25) + 17),
                    cv2.FONT_HERSHEY_SIMPLEX, 0.5, (0, 0, 255), 2)
    cv2.rectangle(legend, (100, (i * 25)), (300, (i * 25) + 25),
                                        tuple(color), -1)
```

5. Load the serialized model from disk, with the function **cv2.dnn.readNet()**.

6. Load the input image, resize it, and construct a **blob** from it, using the function **cv2.dnn.blobFromImage()**. This function will be used to preprocess an image before feeding it into a **deep neural network** (**DNN**) for running semantic segmentation. The function takes the input image and performs necessary transformations to create a 4-dimensional **blob** that can be used as input to the neural network.

   a. The function **cv2.dnn.blobFromImage()** accepts the following arguments:

      i. The input **image** to be segmented.

      ii. The **scalefactor**, used to scale the pixel values. Here we have used 1/255 to have pixel values in the range [0,1].

      iii. The spatial **size** to which the input image should be resized (keep in mind that the original input image dimensions ENet was trained on was 1024x512, and that is why we need to resize the input image.)

      iv. **swapRB: OpenCV** loads images in **BGR** order. While many pre-trained neural networks expect input images in **RGB** order, we need to set **swapRB=True** to automatically swap the channels.

      v. **crop** indicates whether to crop the image after resizing.

7. Set the image as input to the model and perform a **forward pass** on the ENet neural network model, using the function **net.forward()** and obtain the **output**.

8. Infer the total number of classes along with the spatial dimensions of the mask image via the shape of the **output** array.

9. Our output class ID map will be *num_classes* x *height* x *width* in size. So, let us use the **argmax()** function to find the class label with the largest probability for each and every (*x,y*)-coordinate in the image.

10. Given the class ID map, let us map each of the class IDs to its corresponding color.

11. Resize the mask and class map such that its dimensions match the original size of the input image.

12. Compute a weighted combination of the input image with the segmentation mask to obtain an overlay image, as shown in the following code snippet:

```python
net = cv2.dnn.readNet('models/enet-model.net')
image = cv2.imread('images/traffic.jpg')
image = cv2.cvtColor(image, cv2.COLOR_BGR2RGB)
image = imutils.resize(image, width=500)
blob = cv2.dnn.blobFromImage(image, 1 / 255.0, (1024, 512), 0, \
                             swapRB=True, crop=False)

net.setInput(blob)
start = time.time()
output = net.forward()
end = time.time()

(numClasses, height, width) = output.shape[1:4]
classMap = np.argmax(output[0], axis=0)
mask = colors[classMap]

mask = cv2.resize(mask, (image.shape[1], image.shape[0]), \
                                interpolation=cv2.INTER_NEAREST)
classMap = cv2.resize(classMap, (image.shape[1], image.shape[0]), \
                                interpolation=cv2.INTER_NEAREST)
output = ((0.4 * image) + (0.6 * mask)).astype("uint8")
```

13. Finally, visualize the overlayed image along with the segmentation mask output and the input image. Display the class names as **legends**, as shown in the following code snippet. You should obtain a figure as shown in *Figure 4.10*.

```python
plt.figure(figsize=(20,25))
plt.subplot(311), plt.imshow(image), plt.axis('off')
plt.title('Original Image', size=20)
plt.subplot(312), plt.imshow(output), plt.axis('off')
plt.title('Segmented Image', size=20)
plt.subplot(313), plt.imshow(legend), plt.axis('off')
plt.title('legends', size=20)
plt.tight_layout()
plt.show()
```

If you run the preceding code snippet, you should obtain a figure like the next one:

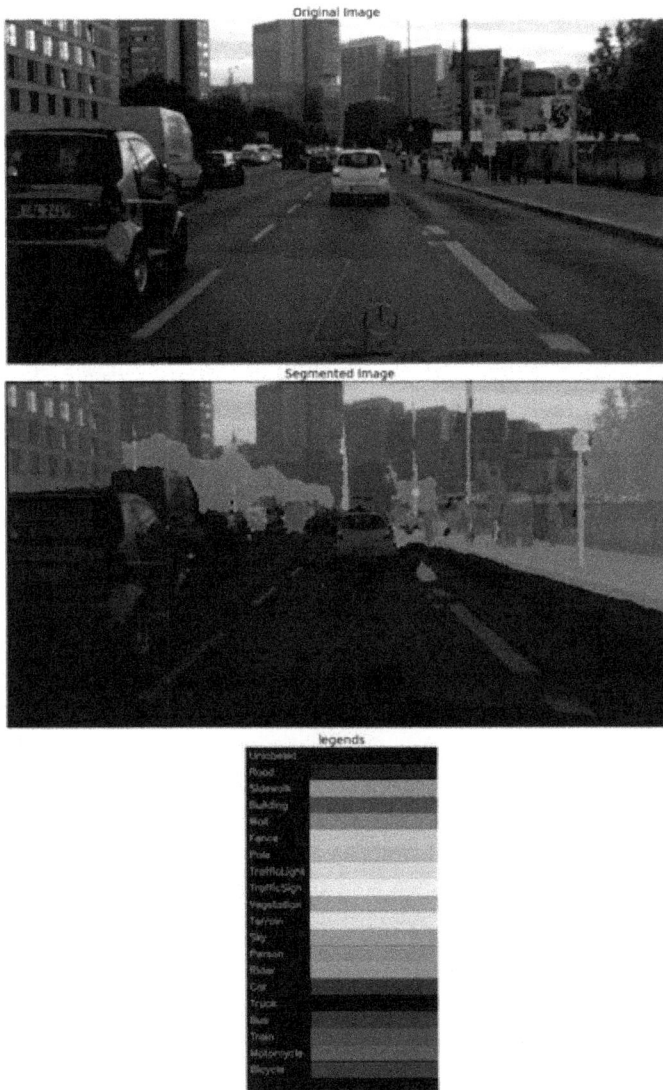

Figure 4.10: *Semantic segmentation with pretrained ENet model (Caffe)*

Panoptic segmentation with the deep learning model Detectron2

Panoptic segmentation is an image processing/computer vision task that combines instance segmentation and semantic segmentation. In panoptic segmentation, the goal is to assign a unique label to each pixel in an image, differentiating between stuff (such as, roads, sky) and things (for example, objects, people). This task unifies the outputs of semantic and instance segmentation, providing a comprehensive understanding of the scene. Let us first try to understand the differences between different types of deep-learning-based segmentation models we can have:

- **Semantic segmentation**: The goal of semantic segmentation is to classify each pixel in an image into predefined classes or categories without distinguishing between different instances of the same class. The output is a pixel-wise labeling map, where each pixel is assigned a class label (for example, road, car, person).

- **Instance segmentation**: The goal of instance segmentation is to identify and distinguish individual **instances** of objects within the same class. It involves not only classifying pixels but also assigning a **unique identifier** to each instance of an object. The output includes both the pixel-wise class labels and instance-specific masks, which differentiate between different instances of the same class.

- **Panoptic segmentation**: As mentioned previously, panoptic segmentation is a combination of **semantic** and **instance** segmentation. It aims to provide a unified understanding of an image by assigning a unique label to each pixel, differentiating between stuff (for example, background, roads) and things (such as, objects, people). The output consists of both semantic segmentation masks for stuff classes as well as instance segmentation masks for things classes. It unifies the outputs of semantic and instance segmentation into a single map.

In this problem, you will learn how to implement panoptic segmentation using the library **detectron2**, which is a popular open-source deep learning library developed by **Facebook AI Research** (**FAIR**) for object detection and instance segmentation tasks. While **Detectron2** is primarily designed for instance segmentation (and you will use the pretrained models for instance segmentation in the exercise), you can use it for panoptic segmentation by combining its instance segmentation outputs with a separate semantic segmentation model.

Let us demonstrate how the library can be used to perform panoptic segmentation. We will install the library (refer to the following link: **https://github.com/facebookresearch/ detectron2/blob/main/INSTALL.md**). Run the following code snippets with a GPU / TPU (for example, on Google Colab) for faster execution:

```
# must be run in colab with runtime type GPU / TPU
!python -m pip install 'git+https://github.com/facebookresearch/
detectron2.git'
```

Import the library **detectron2**, along with the modules and functions needed, using the following code snippet:

```
# Setup detectron2 logger
import detectron2
from detectron2.utils.logger import setup_logger
setup_logger()

import torch
```

```
TORCH_VERSION = ".".join(torch.__version__.split(".")[:2])
CUDA_VERSION = torch.__version__.split("+")[-1]
print("torch: ", TORCH_VERSION, "; cuda: ", CUDA_VERSION)
# torch: 2.6; cuda: cu124

# import some common libraries
import numpy as np
import matplotlib.pylab as plt
import os, json, cv2, random

# import some common detectron2 utilities
from detectron2 import model_zoo
from detectron2.engine import DefaultPredictor
from detectron2.config import get_cfg
from detectron2.utils.visualizer import Visualizer
from detectron2.data import MetadataCatalog, DatasetCatalog
```

Initialize the configuration, load the model weights for the pretrained model and instantiate the **predictor** (**DefaultPredictor**), with the next few lines of code:

```
cfg = get_cfg()
cfg.merge_from_file(model_zoo.get_config_file(
                "COCO-PanopticSegmentation/panoptic_fpn_R_101_3x.yaml"))
cfg.MODEL.WEIGHTS = model_zoo.get_checkpoint_url(
                "COCO-PanopticSegmentation/panoptic_fpn_R_101_3x.yaml")
predictor = DefaultPredictor(cfg)
```

Read the input image (of cats and dogs), run **inference** by invoking the function **predictor()** and use the **Visualizer** to overlay the segmentation labels using the following code snippet and plot the results obtained:

```
im = cv2.imread(cats_dogs.jpg')
panoptic_seg, segments_info = predictor(im)["panoptic_seg"]
v = Visualizer(im[:, :,::-1], MetadataCatalog.get(cfg.DATASETS.TRAIN[0]),\
                                                            scale=0.9)
out = v.draw_panoptic_seg_predictions(panoptic_seg.to("cpu"), \
                                                    segments_info)


im = im[:, :, ::-1]
out = out.get_image()[:, :, ::-1]
plt.figure(figsize=(20,10))
plt.subplot(121), plt.imshow(im), plt.axis('off')
plt.title('input image', size=20)
plt.subplot(122), plt.imshow(out), plt.axis('off')
plt.title('Panoptic Segmented + overlayed', size=20)
plt.tight_layout()
plt.show()
```

If you run the preceding code snippet, you should obtain a figure as follows:

Figure 4.11: *Panoptic segmentation with Detectron2*

Blurring and changing background in image and video using DeepLabV3

DeepLabV3 is a deep learning model designed for semantic image segmentation. In this section, we shall use this model to implement background-blurring in an image (or video). Background-blurring in video calls, such as Zoom meetings, enhances privacy and reduces distractions by keeping the focus on the speaker. Here is a general outline of how you can approach this task:

- **Object segmentation**: Use **DeepLabV3** to perform semantic segmentation on each frame of the video. This will give you a mask indicating the different objects present in the scene.

- **Identify background and foreground**: Once you have the segmentation masks, identify the regions corresponding to the background and foreground. You may need to set a threshold or use some post-processing techniques to refine the masks.

- **Apply blurring**: Apply a blur effect to the background while keeping the foreground (person or main subject) sharp. You can use traditional image processing techniques or other deep learning models designed for image manipulation.

- **Combine frames**: Combine the modified frames to create the final video with the blurred background.

Let us now implement the preceding steps, import the required libraries and modules to start with. Here we shall use the library **pytorch** to load and predict using a pretrained **DeepLabV3** model.

```python
import cv2
import numpy as np
import matplotlib.pyplot as plt
import torch
import torchvision
```

Now follow the next steps, as shown in the following code snippet:

1. The function **load_model()** can be used to load the pretrained **DeepLabV3** model with a **ResNet101** backbone (download it in your local machine from the **pytorch** model hub for the first time, using the function **torch.hub.load()**).

2. The function **get_pred()** can be used to obtain the semantically segmented output image, using the following steps:

   a. First check if the **GPU** is available **torch.cuda.is_available()**. If yes, use it for much faster execution.

   b. Apply the standard preprocessing transforms (using the function **torchvision.transforms.Normalize()**) that need to be done before running inference.

   c. Run the model with the preprocessed input image to obtain the segmentation labels and return the labels.

```python
def load_model():
    device = "cuda" if torch.cuda.is_available() else "cpu"
    model = torch.hub.load('pytorch/vision:v0.6.0', \
                        'deeplabv3_resnet101', pretrained=True)
    model.to(device).eval()
    return model

def get_pred(img, model):
    device = "cuda" if torch.cuda.is_available() else "cpu"
    imagenet_stats = [[0.485,0.456,0.406], [0.485,0.456,0.406]]
    preprocess =  torchvision.transforms.Compose( \
        [torchvision.transforms.ToTensor(),
         torchvision.transforms.Normalize(mean = imagenet_stats[0],
         std  = imagenet_stats[1])])
    input_tensor = preprocess(img).unsqueeze(0)
    input_tensor = input_tensor.to(device)
    with torch.no_grad():
        output = model(input_tensor)["out"][0]
        output = output.argmax(0)

    return output.cpu().numpy()
```

Now let us follow the steps listed, as shown in the next code snippet:

1. Load the pretrained **DeepLabV3** model to memory using the function **load_model()**.

2. Read (with **cv2.imread()**) the original input and the new background image (to replace original image's background). Use **cv2.cvtColor()** function to convert

from BGR to RGB mode. If you want to apply the background blur to a video, first extract the frames from the video and for each **frame** image apply the following operations.

3. Obtain the segmented input image using the function **get_pred()**. The specific labels and their meanings in the segmented image depend on the dataset that the model was trained on. In the case of DeepLabV3, it is often trained and evaluated on datasets such as **PASCAL VOC** or **COCO**, which have predefined class labels.

4. The **PASCAL VOC** dataset has 20 categories, in which our categories of interest are:

    a. **0**: Background

    b. **15**: Person

   Hence, wherever the class **person** is predicted, the label returned will be 15.

5. Create a binary mask for the background pixels and select the background with the mask.

6. Define a kernel size (for example, 15×15, as shown in the next code snippet) for **opencv-python**'s Gaussian blur (using the function **cv2.GaussianBlur()**).

7. Apply the Gaussian blur to the background pixels and obtain the image with the blurred background. Subsequently repeat the mask across RGB channels.

8. In order to change the background, crate a binary mask again, select all the pixels from the input except the ones identified as **person** (that is, has label 15). Resize the new background image to the input image (frame) size. Replace the background pixels from the input image with the corresponding ones from the background image, using the **mask**, as shown in the next code snippet.

9. Plot the input image, segmentation mask, the background-blurred image and the image with the background replaced, using the next code snippet:

```python
model = load_model()
orig = cv2.cvtColor(cv2.imread('images/me.png'), \
                                    cv2.COLOR_BGR2RGB)
frame = orig.copy()
width, height, channels = frame.shape

bg_image = cv2.imread('images/beach.jpg')
bg_image = cv2.cvtColor(bg_image, cv2.COLOR_BGR2RGB)

labels = get_pred(frame, model)

mask = labels == 0 # background
mask = np.repeat(mask[:, :, np.newaxis], channels, axis = 2)
blur_value = (51, 51)
```

```
blur = cv2.GaussianBlur(frame, blur_value, 0)
frame[mask] = blur[mask]

mask = labels == 15 # person
mask = np.repeat(mask[:, :, np.newaxis], 3, axis = 2)
bg = cv2.resize(bg_image, (height, width))
bg[mask] = frame[mask]
out_frame = bg

plt.figure(figsize=(15,15))
plt.subplots_adjust(0,0,1,0.95,0.05,0.05)
plt.subplot(221), plt.imshow(orig), plt.axis('off')
plt.title('original', size=20)
plt.subplot(223), plt.imshow(frame), plt.axis('off')
plt.title('blurred background', size=20)
plt.subplot(222), plt.imshow(labels, cmap='gray'), plt.axis('off')
plt.title('mask (from DeepLabV3)', size=20)
plt.subplot(224), plt.imshow(out_frame), plt.axis('off')
plt.title('changed background', size=20)
plt.show()
```

If you run the preceding code snippet, you should obtain a figure as follows:

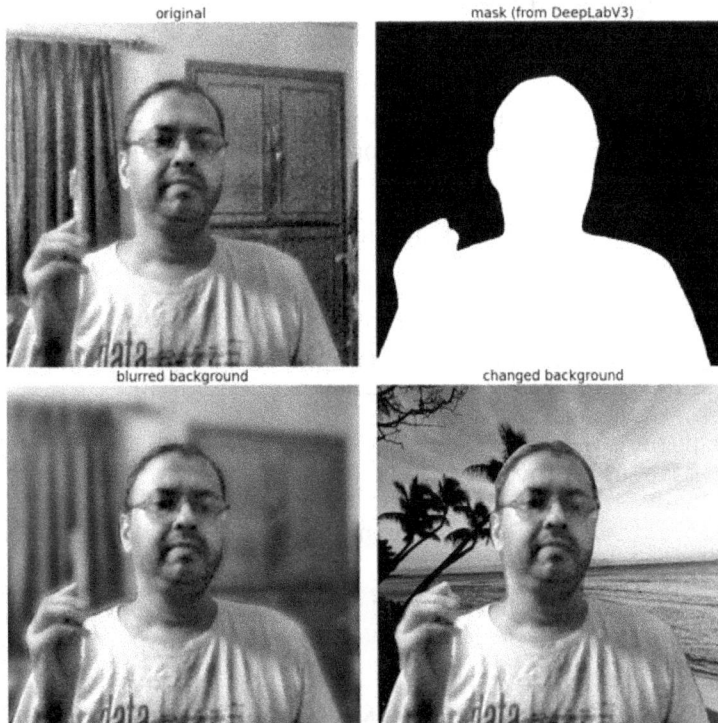

Figure 4.12: *Automatically changing background with DeepLabV3+*

Outlier detection using autoencoder with H2O

As we have seen in the earlier chapters, **autoencoder** is a type of artificial neural network used for **unsupervised** learning. It is often designed to encode the input data into a lower-dimensional representation and then reconstruct the input data from this representation. The network is divided into an **encoder** and a **decoder**:

- **Encoder**: This part of the network compresses the input data into a lower-dimensional representation, often referred to as the encoding or **latent** space.

- **Decoder**: This part of the network reconstructs the input data from the encoded representation. The goal is to generate an output that closely matches the input.

- The autoencoder is trained to **minimize** the **difference** between the **input** and the **reconstructed output**.

- Anomalous image detection using autoencoders involves training the neural network to learn a compressed representation of the **normal** images and then using it to reconstruct new data. The intuition is that the autoencoder is effective at reconstructing normal patterns but will struggle to accurately reconstruct anomalous patterns. Therefore, **anomalies** will have **higher reconstruction errors**. Anomalies can be detected by measuring the difference between the input and the reconstructed output.

In this problem, we shall use the Python library **H2O**, which is also an open-source machine learning platform. It supports autoencoders for anomaly detection. Here is a general outline of how you can perform anomalous image detection using autoencoders with H2O:

1. Make sure you have H2O installed in your Python environment (if not, install it with **pip**).

2. Import **h2o**, along with the other required packages. Start an **H2O cluster** by running the following code (with **h2o.init()**):

```
# pip install h2o
import numpy as np
import matplotlib.pylab as plt
import h2o
from h2o.estimators.deeplearning import H2OAutoEncoderEstimator

h2o.init()
# Checking whether there is an H2O instance running at
# http://localhost:54321 ..... not found.
# Attempting to start a local H2O server...
```

3. Load the handwritten images (**MNIST** dataset) image data (**train** and **test** partitions) into H2O (with **h2o.import_file()** as shown in the next code snippet).

Each row in the dataset contains a 28x28 digit image flattened to 784 dimensions. Get rid of the labels header (with **pop()**) since we shall go unsupervised.

```
resp = 784
train = h2o.import_file("https://s3.amazonaws.com/h2o-public-test-
data/bigdata/laptop/mnist/train.csv.gz")
test = h2o.import_file("https://s3.amazonaws.com/h2o-public-test-
data/bigdata/Laptop/mnist/test.csv.gz")
train.pop(resp)
test.pop(resp)
```

4. Define and train an autoencoder model using H2O (instantiate a **H2OAutoEncoderEstimator** object). Specify the encoding layer to have fewer neurons than the input layer, forcing the model to learn a compressed representation (for example, our model has the following dimensions: 784 64 32 64 784, with the **bottleneck layer** having dimensions). With the **hidden** parameter, you can adjust the number of neurons.

5. Use the **train()** function to train the model on the training images, for 25 epochs, for example, using the next code snippet. Print the model **MSE (Mean Squared Error** for image reconstruction, which measures the average squared difference between original and reconstructed image pixels, it is computed as shown:

$$MSE = \frac{1}{MN} \sum_{x=0}^{M-1} \sum_{y=0}^{N-1} \left(I_{original}(x, y) - I_{reconstructed}(x, y) \right)^2$$

Where M, N are image dimensions.

```
ae_model = H2OAutoEncoderEstimator(activation="Tanh",
                                   hidden=[64,32,64],
                                   model_id="ae_model",
                                   epochs=25,
                                   ignore_const_cols=False,
                                   reproducible=True,
                                   seed=1234)
ae_model.train(list(range(resp)), training_frame=train)
ae_model.mse()
# 0.016211654087278905
```

6. Use the trained autoencoder **ae_model** to reconstruct the test images (using the **predict()** method) and measure the reconstruction error. Sort the images in descending order of reconstruction error since anomalies will have higher reconstruction errors.

```
pred = ae_model.predict(test)
test_rec_error = ae_model.anomaly(test)
test_rec_error = test_rec_error.as_data_frame().values
test_rec_error = test_rec_error.ravel()
indices = np.argsort(test_rec_error)[::-1]
```

7. Finally, visualize top *k* (for example, *k* = 8) outliers, plot the original images and their reconstructions to gain insights into detected anomalies using the following code snippet:

```python
# Top k outliers
k = 8 #100
test_images = test.as_data_frame().values
pred_images = pred.as_data_frame().values
for i in range(k):
    idx = indices[i]
    k += 1
    plt.figure(figsize=(10,7))
    plt.gray()
    plt.subplot(121), plt.imshow(test_images[idx].reshape(28,28))
    plt.axis('off'), plt.title('original', size=10)
    plt.subplot(122), plt.imshow(pred_images[idx].reshape(28,28))
    plt.axis('off')
    plt.title('reconstructed, loss:{:.03f}' \
                            .format(test_rec_error[idx]), size=10)
    plt.tight_layout()
    plt.show()
```

You will get a figure as shown in the following *Figure 4.13* displaying the top outliers:

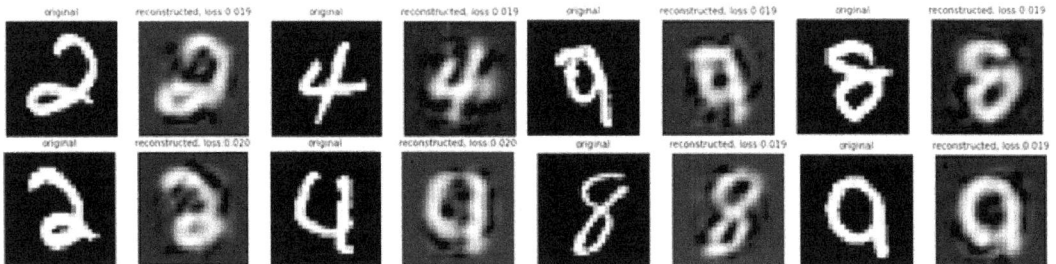

Figure 4.13: Top outliers detected with the autoencoder (with high reconstruction errors)

You can also visualize the images that are reconstructed properly (have low outlier scores) as shown in *Figure 4.14*:

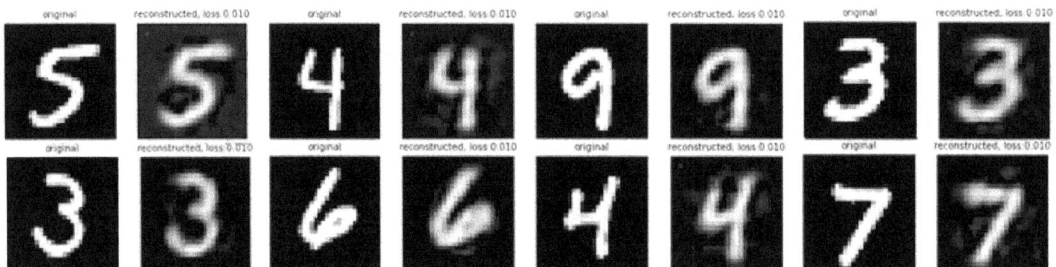

Figure 4.14: Images with less reconstruction error (low outlier scores) with the autoencoder

Conclusion

This chapter provided a comprehensive overview of image segmentation techniques, showcasing the application of both traditional machine learning and advanced deep learning approaches. Starting with fundamental methods, binary classification with scikit-learn was used for human skin segmentation, followed by connected component labeling with scikit-image for isolating regions in images. Foreground-background separation in videos was demonstrated using GMM with opencv-python, highlighting temporal segmentation.

Transitioning to deep learning, semantic segmentation was explored using two powerful frameworks: TensorFlow with a pretrained DeepLabV3+ XCeptionNet model and OpenCV-python paired with a pretrained Caffe ENet model. Advanced panoptic segmentation, which combines semantic and instance segmentation, was implemented using the Detectron2 framework. Practical applications were also discussed, including blurring and changing backgrounds in images and videos with DeepLabV3, and outlier detection (as a preprocessing step in any image processing task) using autoencoders with H2O.

By combining theoretical insights with practical implementations, this chapter equipped readers with the tools and techniques to apply both traditional and deep learning-based segmentation methods to a variety of real-world scenarios.

Key terms

Semantic segmentation, panoptic segmentation, outlier detection, autoencoder, U-Net, XCeptionNet, DeepLabV3, GMM

Questions

1. Use k-means clustering to group face images from **Labeled Faces in the Wild** (**LFW**) face dataset (from scikit-learn datasets). If the face dataset contains faces of 7 people, use $k = 7$ clusters for k-means. This time, you need to treat each image as a vector and cluster them based on their feature representations. The following *Figure 4.15* shows a few face samples from the face dataset:

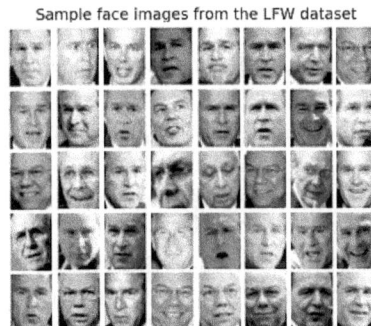

Sample face images from the LFW dataset

Figure 4.15: Few face samples from the LFW dataset

Use different algorithms to initialize the centroids for k-means (for example, set init argument of the function sklearn.KMeans() to **random**, **k-means++**, pca. components_ and so on) and observe how the metrics evaluating the cluster-quality varies. You should obtain a benchmarking result as shown in the following figure:

```
n_persons: 7,    n_samples 1288,         n_features 1850

init           time   inertia hono    compl   v-meas  ARI     AMI     silhouette
k-means++      2.38s  1615542 0.052    0.045   0.048   0.031   0.041   0.073
random         1.36s  1615251 0.049    0.043   0.046   0.029   0.038   0.076
PCA-based      0.15s  1618526 0.050    0.044   0.047   0.028   0.039   0.066
```

Figure 4.16: *Benchmarking results*

Finally, use a dimension reduction technique (for example, **PCA**) to visualize the clusters in 2D. You should obtain a figure like *Figure 4.17* (for example, plot the images at the location given by the 2D coordinates corresponding to their low dimensional representation):

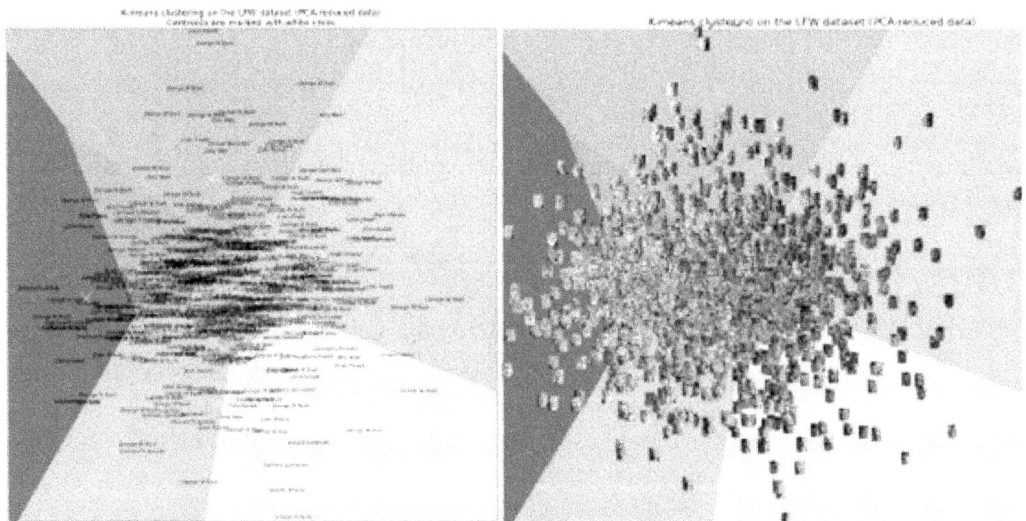

Figure 4.17: *Visualizing clusters obtained with k-means in 2D with PCA*

Compare the (unsupervised) cluster labels with the ground-truths. How can we improve the quality of the clusters?

2. Use **SLIC** and **NCut** algorithms to segment the same apples and oranges image. However, this time, vary the input parameters to the function skimage. segmentation.slic() and observe the impact on the segmented image. What values of the parameters will produce the following segmented images? Refer to the following figure:

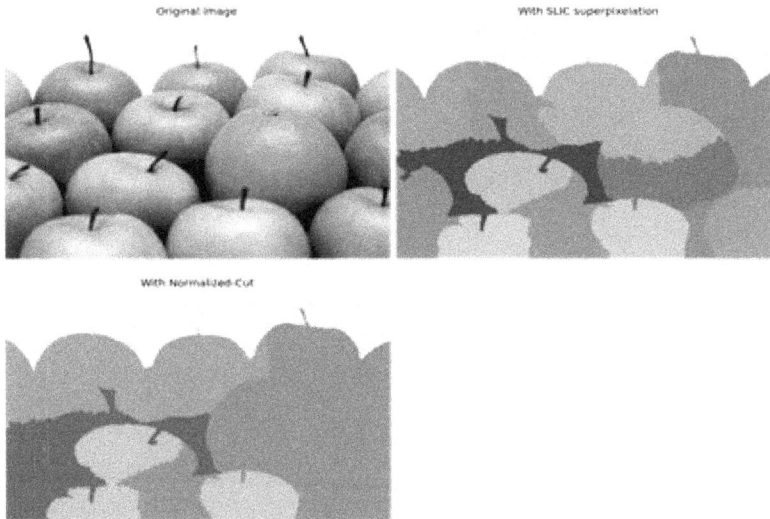

Figure 4.18: *Segmentation with SLIC/NCut*

3. Use scipy.ndimage to segment an image with connected component labeling (hint: use the function label()). Compute the area of the regions (for example, use the function np.bincount()). Plot the regions obtained. For the given original input image (as shown in the next figure), you should obtain a figure as follows:

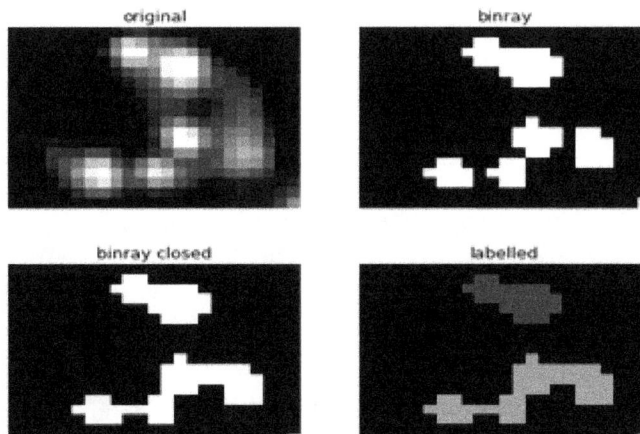

Figure 4.19: *Segmentation with connected component labelling with scipy.ndimage*

Now, use opencv-python's implementation for the same algorithm (for example, use the function cv2.connectedComponentsWithStats()). Compare the results obtained from a different library's implementations.

4. **Training a U-Net model on self-driving cars dataset**: The U-Net architecture is a CNN designed for semantic segmentation tasks in computer vision. It is characterized by its U-shaped structure, which consists of a contracting path

(**encoder**) followed by an expansive path (**decoder**). Build a **U-Net** architecture unet_model (hint: understand the building blocks and use the following code), by reusing conv_block and upsampling_block components, define with keras functional API.

```python
def unet_model(input_size=(96, 128, 3), n_filters=32, \
                                        n_classes=23):

    inputs = Input(input_size)
    #contracting path
    cblock1 = conv_block(inputs, n_filters)
    cblock2 = conv_block(cblock1[0], 2*n_filters)
    cblock3 = conv_block(cblock2[0], 4*n_filters)
    cblock4 = conv_block(cblock3[0], 8*n_filters, \
                                        dropout_prob=0.3)
    cblock5 = conv_block(cblock4[0],16*n_filters, \
            dropout_prob=0.3, max_pooling=None)

    #expanding path
    ublock6 = upsampling_block(cblock5[0], cblock4[1], \
                                        8 * n_filters)
    ublock7 = upsampling_block(ublock6, cblock3[1],  n_filters*4)
    ublock8 = upsampling_block(ublock7,cblock2[1] , n_filters*2)
    ublock9 = upsampling_block(ublock8,cblock1[1],  n_filters)
    conv9 = Conv2D(n_filters,
                    3,
                    activation='relu',
                    padding='same',
                    kernel_initializer='he_normal')(ublock9)

    conv10 = Conv2D(n_classes, kernel_size=1, \
                            padding='same')(conv9)
    model = tf.keras.Model(inputs=inputs, outputs=conv10)

    return model

def conv_block(inputs=None, n_filters=32, dropout_prob=0, \
                                        max_pooling=True):

    conv = Conv2D(n_filters,
                    kernel_size = 3,
                    activation='relu',
                    padding='same',
                    kernel_initializer = \
                        tf.keras.initializers.HeNormal())(inputs)
```

```
    conv = Conv2D(n_filters,
                  kernel_size = 3,
                  activation='relu',
                  padding='same', \
                  kernel_initializer = \
                     tf.keras.initializers.HeNormal())(conv)

    if dropout_prob > 0:
        conv = Dropout(dropout_prob)(conv)
    if max_pooling:
        next_layer = MaxPooling2D(pool_size=(2,2))(conv)
    else:
        next_layer = conv

    skip_connection = conv

    return next_layer, skip_connection
def upsampling_block(expansive_input, contractive_input, \
                                     n_filters=32):

    up = Conv2DTranspose(
                  n_filters,
                  kernel_size = 3,
                  strides=(2,2),
                  padding='same')(expansive_input)
    merge = concatenate([up, contractive_input], axis=3)
    conv = Conv2D(n_filters,
                  kernel_size = 3,
                  activation='relu',
                  padding='same', \
                  kernel_initializer = \
                     tf.keras.initializers.HeNormal())(merge)
    conv = Conv2D(n_filters,
                  kernel_size = 3,
                  activation='relu',
                  padding='same', \
                  kernel_initializer = \
                     tf.keras.initializers.HeNormal())(conv)

    return conv
```

Use the **CameraRGB** dataset from **lyft-udacity-challenge** (self-driving cars dataset) to train the **U-Net** model (which contains training images along with annotated ground-truth segmentation labels). Finally, run inference on the model to segment the test images. You should obtain better quality segmentation with higher epochs, as shown for a few sample test images. Refer to the following figure:

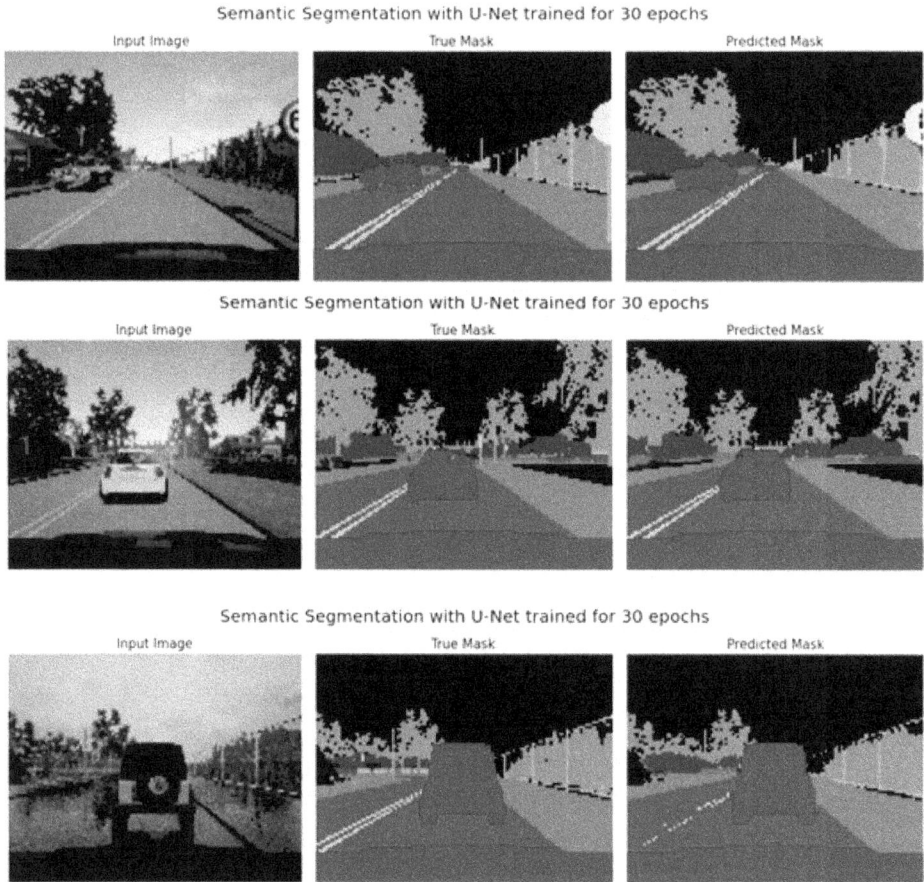

Figure 4.20: *Semantic segmentation with U-Net*

5. Use the Detectron2 pre-trained model to run instance segmentation and compare **instance** vs. **panoptic** segmentation using the input image used earlier. You should obtain a figure like the following one:

Instance Segmentation

Panoptic Segmentation

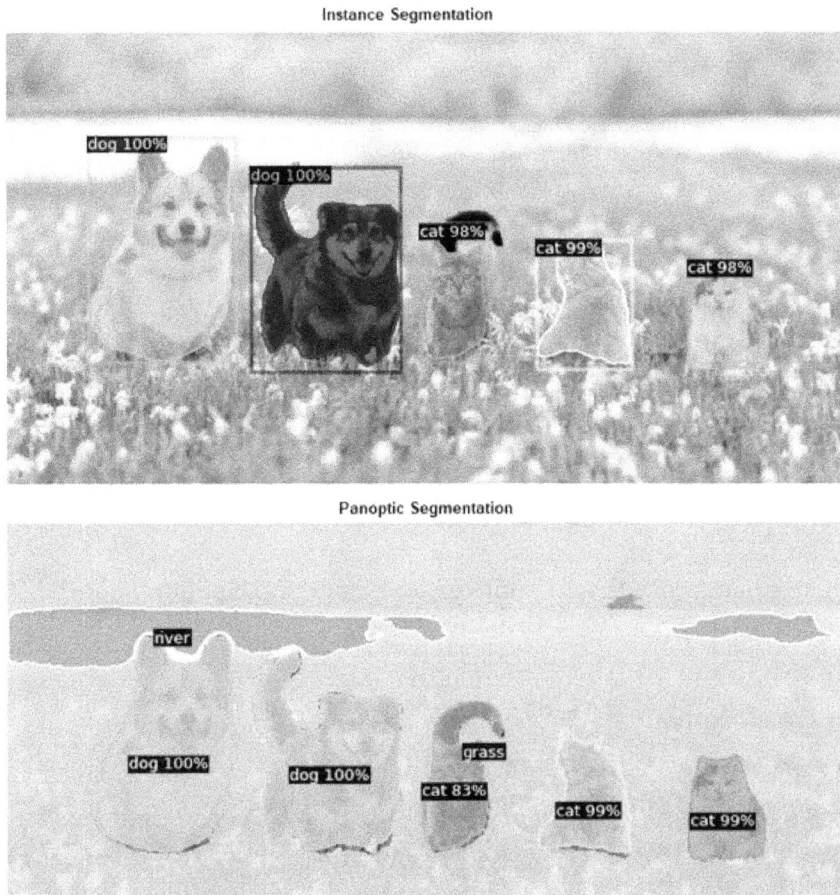

Figure 4.21: *Instance segmentation with Detectron2*

Now, train the model on a custom dataset and run inference to obtain segmented output.

6. torch.hub is a centralized repository where you can find and download pre-trained models without having to search and download from various external sources. Use **DeepLabV3 ResNet50** pretrained model from torch.hub (use the function torch.hub.load()) to perform semantic segmentation for the same image to get the output segmented image like *Figure 4.21*:

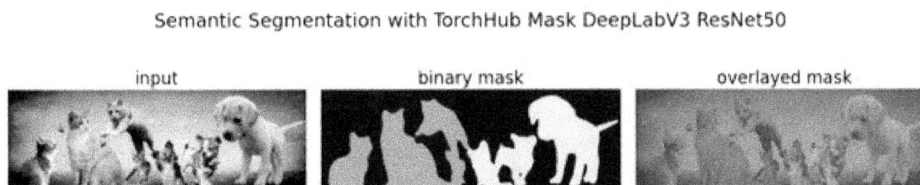

Semantic Segmentation with TorchHub Mask DeepLabV3 ResNet50

input   binary mask   overlayed mask

Figure 4.22: *Semantic segmentation with DeepLabV3/ResNet50 from torch.hub*

Use **Mask R-CNN ResNet50** pretrained model (use torch.hub.load()) to perform instance segmentation for the following image to get the output segmented image like the following one:

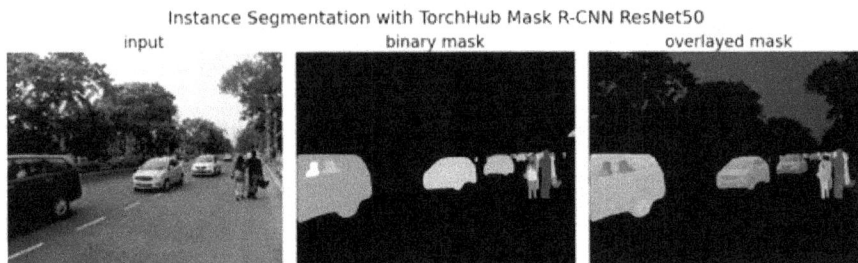

Figure 4.23: *Instance segmentation with DeepLabV3/ResNet50 from torchhub*

References

1. **https://openaccess.thecvf.com/content_cvpr_2017/papers/Chollet_Xception_Deep_Learning_CVPR_2017_paper.pdf**

2. **https://arxiv.org/pdf/1706.05587v3.pdf**

3. **https://arxiv.org/pdf/1610.02357.pdf**

4. **https://arxiv.org/abs/1606.02147**

5. **https://github.com/simogasp/opencv-semantic-segmentation/tree/master/enet-cityscapes**

Join our Discord space

Join our Discord workspace for latest updates, offers, tech happenings around the world, new releases, and sessions with the authors:

https://discord.bpbonline.com

## CHAPTER 5

Image Feature Extraction and Its Applications: Image Registration

Introduction

Feature detection in image processing and computer vision involves identifying key structures, such as points, edges, or regions, within an image to extract relevant information for further analysis. This process simplifies the image by reducing its high-dimensional, often redundant, pixel data into a compact set of features, making it easier for algorithms to process efficiently.

Feature detection is a foundational step in a variety of tasks, including object recognition, 3D reconstruction, image registration, and machine learning, where the extracted features are help improve accuracy and reduce computational complexity. It plays a critical role in many applications, such as robotics, autonomous navigation, medical imaging, and scene understanding, by focusing on the most important details within the visual data.

Feature extraction refers to the process of converting the input image into a structured set of feature vectors. By carefully selecting the right features, the goal is to capture the most relevant information from the image needed for a specific task, such as image matching, alignment, and registration—without relying on the full image content. This reduced representation enables faster, more robust, and scalable processing.

Structure

This chapter will cover the following topics:

- Different types of feature detectors and descriptors
- Corner detectors with opencv-python
- Image alignment/matching: Image registration
- Image color channel alignment using image registration with pystackreg
- Deformable image registration with pyelastix
- Image registration with SimpleITK
- Deep deformable image registration with VoxelMorph with tensorflow/keras

Objectives

In this chapter and the next one, we will explore how to extract the most relevant features from images, specifically key points of interest that carry significant visual information. **Feature detection** involves identifying these keypoints, and once detected, a **descriptor** is computed for each one of them. A local descriptor provides a compact representation of the area surrounding a keypoint, focusing on its shape and appearance in that specific region. Unlike global descriptors, which provide feature representations that describe an entire content of an image (as a single, unified vector or set of values), the local descriptors are better suited for tasks like matching due to their focus on localized details. We will learn how to compute both feature detectors and descriptors, and explore the different applications of these techniques in image processing. Additionally, we will cover widely used feature detectors, including **Harris Corner**, **Scale-Invariant Feature Transform** (**SIFT**), **Histogram of Oriented Gradients** (**HOG**), and **HAAR**, and apply them to key tasks like image matching, alignment, and object detection using `scikit-image` and `opencv-python` (`cv2`) libraries in Python. Again, taking a problem-oriented approach, the focus will be on understanding the core concepts, algorithms, and their real-world applications.

Different types of feature detectors and descriptors

Before diving deeper, let us clarify the distinction between **feature detectors** and **feature descriptors**, two foundational concepts that will be referenced throughout this chapter:

- **Feature detectors**: Feature detection is the process of identifying distinctive points or regions in an image that exhibit unique characteristics. These points, often referred to as **keypoints**, are selected based on their uniqueness and stability under transformations like rotation, scaling, and changes in viewpoint. A few popular feature detection methods include corner detectors (for example, **Harris** Corner detector) and blob detectors (such as, **Difference of Gaussians (DoG)**). The output of feature detection is a set of keypoints that represent salient points in the image.

- **Feature descriptors**: Feature description involves computing a compact and distinctive **representation** for each detected **keypoint**, typically based on the local image region surrounding the keypoint. These descriptors encode information such as texture, intensity, or gradient patterns, and are designed to be distinctive, robust to variations in scale, orientation, and lighting. A few popular feature description methods include **Oriented FAST and Rotated BRIEF (ORB)**, **Binary Robust Independent Elementary Features (BRIEF)**, **Speeded-Up Robust Features (SURF)** and SIFT. The output of feature description is a set of feature vectors or matrices corresponding to the keypoints, capturing their local context.

In summary, **feature detection** is the process of finding keypoints in an image, while **feature description** involves computing feature vectors for these keypoints. Together, feature detection and description enable robust and efficient extraction of meaningful information from images, which can be used for tasks such as image matching, object recognition, and a wide range of other computer vision applications.

Feature detectors and descriptors can be broadly be categorized into two types, namely:

- **Local feature detectors and descriptors**: These methods focus on extracting features from specific, distinctive regions of an image. They are designed to be robust to geometric transformations (e.g., rotation, scale, and changes in viewpoint). They are often designed to find keypoints, such as corners or blobs, where local image structures exhibit significant variations. Examples include Harris Corner detector, **Features from Accelerated Segment Test (FAST)**, **ORB** and **SURF**. Once these keypoints are located, local descriptors encode the surrounding image information into compact, distinctive representations, often using gradient or intensity-based statistics. Local features are especially useful in scenarios involving partial occlusion, varying viewpoints, change in illumination or non-uniform lighting—making them ideal for applications like object tracking, matching, and image registration.

- **Global feature descriptors**: These descriptors aim to capture information about the entire image, providing a holistic representation of its contents. They consider the entire image and encode information such as color histograms, texture statistics, or deep feature embeddings. Examples include color histograms, **Generalized Search Trees (GiST)**, **Bag of Visual Words (BoVW)**, and global deep features extracted from pre-trained neural networks. Global features are beneficial when the overall content or scene context is more important than specific local details. They are suitable for tasks such as image categorization, scene recognition, and large-scale image retrieval.

In this chapter, we will focus primarily on **local feature detectors and descriptors**, as they offer finer control and greater robustness for many real-world image processing tasks, particularly those involving image registration and matching. The following table provides a comparative overview of the key local feature detectors and descriptors discussed in this chapter, highlighting their advantages, limitations, and typical use cases to guide the selection of appropriate methods for various image processing and computer vision applications:

Feature method	Type	Invariance	Advantages	Disadvantages	Typical usage
Harris Corner	Detector	Not scale or rotation invariant	Simple and fast; good for detecting corners in well-defined structures	Sensitive to rotation and scale changes; not ideal for complex scenes	Basic corner detection, subpixel refinement
Features from Accelerated Segment Test (FAST)	Detector	Not scale or affine invariant	Very fast; well-suited for real-time applications	May detect too many corners; not rotation or scale invariant	Real-time corner detection, SLAM (Simultaneous Localization and Mapping)
Scale-Invariant Feature Transform (SIFT)	Detector + Descriptor	Invariant to scale, rotation, and partially affine transforms	Robust and highly distinctive; good matching performance	Computationally expensive; patent restrictions (now expired)	Image matching, panorama stitching, 3D reconstruction
Speeded Up Robust Features (SURF)	Detector + Descriptor	Invariant to scale and rotation	Faster than SIFT; robust to noise and transformations	Still relatively slow; less distinctive than SIFT	Object recognition, image registration
Oriented FAST and Rotated BRIEF (ORB)	Detector + Descriptor	Invariant to rotation; partially to scale	Very fast; open-source; combines FAST + BRIEF	Not as robust as SIFT/SURF for wide baseline matching	Real-time applications, mobile vision systems
Binary Robust Independent Elementary Features (BRIEF)	Descriptor	Not scale or rotation invariant	Compact binary descriptor; fast matching	Requires rotation-invariant detector; not robust to scale/rotation	Descriptor component in ORB and others
Histogram of Oriented Gradients (HOG)	Descriptor	Partial invariance (to small deformations and illumination)	Excellent for detecting objects like pedestrians	Not rotation or scale invariant; not a keypoint detector	Object detection, especially humans
HAAR features	Descriptor (used with cascades)	Not invariant to scale/rotation	Fast detection using cascades; good for faces	Requires extensive training; not general-purpose	Face detection (e.g., Viola-Jones algorithm)

Table 5.1: Comparative overview of the key local feature detectors and descriptors

Corner detectors with opencv-python

In this section, you will learn how to detect corner features using two classical algorithms, namely **Harris Corner detector** and **Shi-Tomasi Corner detector**. These methods are foundational in computer vision and widely used in applications such as image registration, motion tracking, and object recognition.

> **Note: Both Harris and Shi-Tomasi corner detectors are not invariant to scale or rotation. They perform best on images without significant scaling or rotation transformations.**

Harris Corner detector

The **Harris Corner detector** identifies regions in an image where the intensity changes significantly in multiple directions. This behavior is characteristic of **corners**, as opposed to edges or flat regions where intensity change is unidirectional or minimal.

The algorithm examines how the intensity of pixel values changes within a small window as it shifts across different locations in an image. While edges exhibit sharp intensity changes in just one direction, corners experience significant changes in intensity in multiple directions. The algorithm calculates the intensity variation for small shifts in different directions (denoted as u and v). This is expressed as:

$$E(u,v) = \sum_{x,y} \underbrace{w(x,y)}_{\text{window function}} \left[\underbrace{I(x+u, y+v)}_{\text{shifted intensity}} - \underbrace{I(x,y)}_{\text{intensity}} \right]^2$$

Where we have:

- $I(x,y)$: Image intensity at point (x, y)
- $w(x,y)$: A window function (e.g., Gaussian) giving more weight to central pixels
- u, v: Window shifts in x- and y-directions

At **edges**, this function increases significantly in only one direction. At **corners**, $E(u,v)$ increases in **all** directions, hence shifting the window in any direction leads to a large intensity change, which is a key characteristic exploited by the Harris Corner detector for identifying corners with good localization with high precision.

Applying first order Taylor expansion, $I(x+u, y+v) \approx I(x,y) + I_x u + I_y v$ to the preceding equation and with a few algebraic steps, we obtain the following:

$$E(u,v) \approx \begin{bmatrix} u & v \end{bmatrix} \left(\sum_{x,y} \underbrace{w(x,y)}_{\text{window function}} \begin{bmatrix} I_x^2 & I_x I_y \\ I_x I_y & I_y^2 \end{bmatrix} \right) \begin{bmatrix} u \\ v \end{bmatrix} \equiv \begin{bmatrix} u & v \end{bmatrix} M \begin{bmatrix} u \\ v \end{bmatrix}$$

Where the **structure tensor** matrix

$$M = \sum_{x,y} w\,(x,y) \begin{bmatrix} I_x I_x & I_x I_y \\ I_x I_y & I_y I_y \end{bmatrix}$$

Here, I_x and I_y represent the partial derivatives of the image in the x- and y-directions, respectively, and you can compute them with the function **cv2.Sobel()**).

To determine the likelihood of a corner (i.e., whether a window contains a Corner), compute the **Harris response** (a score R) as:

$$R = \det(M) - k\big(\text{trace}(M)\big)^2$$

Where we have:

- $det(M) = \lambda_1 \lambda_2$
- $trace(M) = \lambda_1 + \lambda_2$
- λ_1 and λ_2 are eigenvalues of the matrix M
- k is a tunable sensitivity parameter, typically $0.04 \le k \le 0.06$

Interpretation:

The eigenvalue magnitudes are used as follows to determine whether a region is a corner, an edge, or flat:

- If both λ_1 and λ_2 are small, then $|R|$ is small, and the region is **flat**.

- If one eigenvalue is large and the other small, e.g., if $\lambda_1 \gg \lambda_2$ or $\lambda_2 \gg \lambda_1$, then $R < 0$, and the region is **edge**.

- If both λ_1 and λ_2 are large and $\lambda_1 \sim \lambda_2$, then R is large, and the region is a **corner** (as shown in *Figure 5.1*):

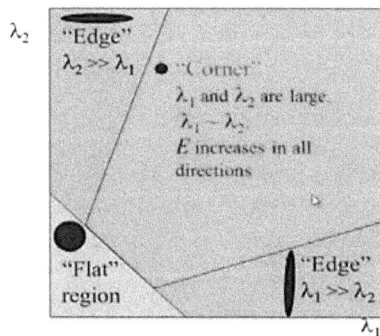

Figure 5.1: Harris Corner detection using eigenvalues of M

The Harris Corner detection algorithm outputs a grayscale image with the corner scores for each pixel. In order to obtain the corners in the image, we need to apply thresholding on the output with a suitable threshold value on the output scores.

Now, it is time for implementation. Let us start by importing the required libraries:

```
import numpy as np
import cv2
import matplotlib.pylab as plt
```

With **opencv-python** (**cv2**), the Harris Corner points can be detected using the **cornerHarris()** function, demonstrated in the next code snippet. This function is a practical implementation of the Harris corner detection algorithm and is used to identify points in an image where the pixel intensity exhibits significant changes in multiple directions—a characteristic trait of corners. The function accepts the following arguments:

- **img**: Input image. It should be grayscale and **float32** data type. This format is essential because the algorithm involves differentiation and matrix operations that require floating-point precision.

- **blockSize**: It is the size of neighborhood (or window) around each pixel that is considered for computing the covariance matrix **M** (refer to the aforementioned equations). A typical value might be 2 or 3. It determines how many surrounding pixels are used to compute the gradient structure tensor. n.

- **ksize**: Aperture parameter of the Sobel operator, which is used to compute the image gradients I_x and I_y (the partial derivatives of the image). A larger **ksize** results in a smoother gradient estimate but may reduce sensitivity to fine details.

- **k**: This is the empirical constant used in the Harris response equation.

The function returns a **corner response image** where each pixel contains the corresponding **corner score** R.

To detect corners, a threshold is applied to this response image to select the most prominent corners. For example, in the following code snippet, **img[dst > 0.075 * dst.max()] = [0, 255, 0]** highlights strong corners—those with a **Harris response** above 7.5% of the maximum—by coloring them green in the original image:

```
orig_img = cv2.imread('images/cube.png')
img = orig_img.copy()
gray = cv2.cvtColor(img,cv2.COLOR_BGR2GRAY)
gray = np.float32(gray)
dst = cv2.cornerHarris(gray,2,3,0.04)
# dilate to mark the corners
dst = cv2.dilate(dst,None)
# Threshold for an optimal value, it may vary depending on the image.
img[dst>0.075*dst.max()]=[0,255,0]
plt.figure(figsize=(10,8))
plt.imshow(cv2.cvtColor(img, cv2.COLOR_BGR2RGB)), plt.axis('off')
plt.show()
```

If you run the preceding code snippet, you should obtain a figure as follows:

Figure 5.2: *Corners detected with Harris Corner detector*

Corner with subpixel accuracy

The **cv2.cornerSubPix()** function refines detected corners to achieve subpixel accuracy. Here is how it works in the following code example:

1. First, we detect corners using the Harris method. Then, the centroids of these corners are passed to the **cornerSubPix()** function for further refinement. In the output, the original Harris Corners are shown in red, while the refined, more accurate corners are displayed in green.

2. To use this function, we must define criteria for stopping the iteration: either after a specified number of iterations or when the desired level of accuracy is reached. Additionally, the size of the neighbourhood (for example, a 5x5 area) around each corner must be specified, where the search for more accurate corner positions will be conducted, as shown in the following code snippet:

```python
# find Harris Corners
orig_img = cv2.imread('images/rcube_cropped.png')
img = orig_img.copy()
gray = cv2.cvtColor(img, cv2.COLOR_BGR2GRAY)
dst = cv2.cornerHarris(gray,2,3,0.04)
dst = cv2.dilate(dst, None)
ret, dst = cv2.threshold(dst,0.01*dst.max(),255,0)
dst = np.uint8(dst)
# find centroids
ret, labels, stats, centroids = \
                              cv2.connectedComponentsWithStats(dst)
# define the criteria to stop and refine the corners
criteria = (cv2.TERM_CRITERIA_EPS + cv2.TERM_CRITERIA_MAX_ITER, \
                                           100, 0.001)
corners = cv2.cornerSubPix(gray,np.float32(centroids), (5,5), \
                                           (-1,-1), criteria)
# Now draw them
res = np.hstack((centroids,corners))
res = np.int0(res)
img[res[:,1],res[:,0]]=[0,0,255]
img[np.minimum(res[:,3], img.shape[0]-1), np.minimum(res[:,2], \
                       img.shape[1]-1)] = [0,255,0]
```

```
plt.figure(figsize=(10,8))
plt.imshow(cv2.cvtColor(img, cv2.COLOR_BGR2RGB)), plt.axis('off')
plt.show()
```

If you run the preceding code snippet, you should obtain a figure as follows:

Figure 5.3: *Harris Corner detection with subpixel accuracy*

Shi-Tomasi Corner detector

Shi and *Tomasi* introduced an improvement to the Harris Corner detector in their paper *Good Features to Track*. Instead of using the Harris Corner scoring function, they proposed a simpler criterion (the minimum eigenvalue of the **structure tensor** matrix M):

$$R = \min(\lambda_1, \lambda_2)$$

If R exceeds a given threshold, the point is classified as a corner. In this method, a point is considered a corner only if both eigenvalues (λ_1 and λ_2) are above a minimum threshold λ_{min}, as shown in the green region of the plot in $\lambda_1 - \lambda_2$ space in the following figure:

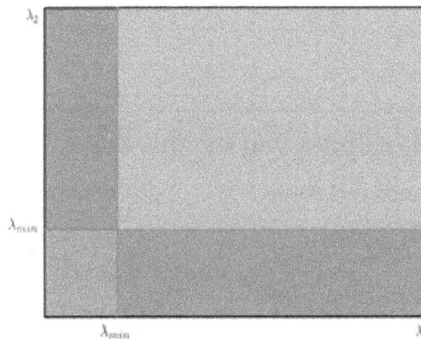

Figure 5.4: *Shi-Tomasi Corner detection with eigenvalue thresholding*

This method tends to **exclude edge points** more effectively and yields better feature quality for tracking. The **OpenCV** function **cv2.goodFeaturesToTrack()** is used to detect the strongest N corners in an image using either the Shi-Tomasi or Harris method (specified by the Boolean flag **useHarrisDetector**). The input image must be in grayscale.

Key parameters for this function include:

- **Number of corners (maxCorners)**: Specifies how many corners you want to detect (for example, 25).
- **Quality level (qualityLevel)**: A value between 0 and 1 that sets the minimum quality for a point to be considered a corner.

- **Minimum distance (`minDistance`)**: The minimum Euclidean distance between detected corners.

The function first filters out corners that fall below the specified quality level. The remaining corners are then sorted in descending order based on their quality. Starting with the strongest corner, the function eliminates any nearby corners within the specified minimum distance. Finally, it selects and returns the top **maxCorners** strongest corners.

The next code snippet shows how to find best corners, both using **Shi-Tomasi** and **Harris Corner detectors**:

```python
plt.figure(figsize=(10,8))

for useHarrisDetector in [True, False]:
    img = orig_img.copy()
    corners = cv2.goodFeaturesToTrack(gray,25,0.01,10, \
                          useHarrisDetector = useHarrisDetector)
    corners = np.int0(corners)
    for i in corners:
        x,y = i.ravel()
        cv2.circle(img,(x,y),3,(0,0,255),-1)
    plt.subplot(1,2,useHarrisDetector+1)
    plt.imshow(cv2.cvtColor(img, cv2.COLOR_BGR2RGB)), plt.axis('off')
    plt.title(f'useHarrisDetector={useHarrisDetector}', size=20)

plt.tight_layout()
plt.show()
```

If you run the preceding code snippet, you should obtain a figure as follows:

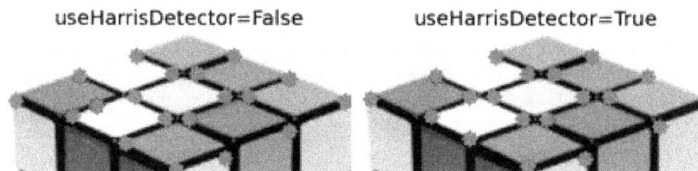

Figure 5.5: Shi-Tomasi vs. Harris Corner detection output with opencv-python

Image alignment/matching: Image registration

The goal of image registration in image processing is to align a target image with a source image by determining the spatial transformation that maps points in one image to their corresponding points in the other. This process, commonly referred to as alignment, involves estimating the transformation, while applying this transformation to warp the image is known as registration. There are three main approaches to image alignment:

- **Intensity based**: Directly compares pixel values between images, such as using mutual information.

- **Segmentation based**: Registers the binary segmentation of objects within the images.

- **Landmark (or feature) based**: Identifies key points in both images and computes a transformation that aligns corresponding landmarks.

The transformations that we will estimate (to register the images) may be any of the following types:

- **Rigid** (rotate, translate)

- **Affine** (rigid + scale and shear/skew)

- **Deformable** (free-form = affine + vector field)

Many other types of transformations are also possible.

In this section, we shall concentrate on intensity and feature-based image registration techniques and their applications.

Feature or landmark based image alignment

We shall now explore how to extract features using a few popular feature detection (and descriptor extraction) algorithms, such as **Oriented FAST and Rotated BRIEF (ORB)**, **Speeded-Up Robust Features (SURF)**, and **DIScrete Keypoints (DISK)**, and use them to align one image with another. A key advantage of the detectors like **ORB**, **Binary Robust Invariant Scalable Keypoints (BRISK)**, **SURF**, and **SIFT (Scale-Invariant Feature Transform)** is their **invariance to scale and rotation**, meaning they can reliably detect and match features even when the object appears at different sizes or orientations across images. This robustness is crucial in real-world computer vision applications such as Simultaneous Localization and Mapping (SLAM), 3D reconstruction, and augmented reality.

With ORB features with opencv-python

ORB is a fusion of two efficient algorithms:

- **FAST** is used as the **keypoint locator**, identifying stable and repeatable points in the image.

- **BRIEF** is used as the **descriptor**, providing a binary string that characterizes the neighborhood around each keypoint. ORB enhances BRIEF by adding orientation compensation and using a learning-based approach to improve performance, making it both **fast and rotation-invariant**.

In **ORB**, these two components work together as follows:

Component	Role in ORB
Locator	Uses FAST to detect keypoints based on corner-like patterns, which are robust under translation, rotation, and minor scale variations.
Descriptor	Uses an orientation-adjusted BRIEF descriptor (BRISK variant) to capture the visual context of the keypoint as a binary vector.

Table 5.2: Working of locator and descriptor

Here we shall demonstrate how to align a couple of (**moving**) images with a reference (**fixed**) image of *Tom & Jerry* (using **ORB** features). Let us start with the original image (as fixed reference image) and create (simulate) a couple of moving images by applying perspective and affine transformations, with the functions `cv2.warpPerspective()` and `cv2.warpAffine()` respectively (along with appropriate transformation matrices), to the fixed image and subsequently saving them to disk, using the next code snippet. These transformed images will later be aligned back to the reference image using ORB features.

```python
im1 = plt.imread('images/tom_jerry.jpg')
# slope of the perspective transform
h, w, _ = im.shape
slope = np.tan(np.radians(30))
perspective_matrix = np.linalg.inv(np.array([[1, 0, 0], \
                        [-slope/3, 1, slope * h / 3], \
                        [-slope/w, 0, 1 + slope/2]]))

im2 = cv2.warpPerspective(im, perspective_matrix, (w,h))
plt.imsave('images/tom_jerry_persp.jpg', im2)

rot = np.array([[np.cos(0.5), -np.sin(0.5), 0],\
                [np.sin(0.5), np.cos(0.5), 0], \
                [0,0,1]])
tr = np.array([[1,0, 50],[0, 1, -50], [0,0,1]])
sc = np.array([[1.1,0, 0],[0, 1.1, 0], [0,0,1]])

affine_mat = np.linalg.inv(rot @ tr @ sc)
im3 = cv2.warpAffine(im, affine_mat[:2,:], (w,h))
plt.imsave('images/tom_jerry_affine.jpg', im3)

plt.figure(figsize=(15,7))
plt.imshow(np.hstack((im1, im2, im3))), plt.axis('off')
plt.title('original (fixed) and moving images (created with perspective
& affine transformation respectively)', size=20)
plt.tight_layout()
plt.show()
```

If you run the preceding code snippet, you should obtain a figure as follows:

Figure 5.6: *Applying perspective and affine transformation to an image with opencv-python*

The preceding figure (*Figure 5.6*) shows the original (fixed) and the moving images created from it, the ones that are to be aligned with fixed image using ORB features.

To align two images using feature-based methods, we follow a series of systematic steps that involve detecting and matching distinctive keypoints. Here, we demonstrate this process using the **ORB** algorithm from **opencv-python**.

The steps in feature-based image alignment are as follows:

1. **Load and preprocess images**: Read the reference image (also called the **fixed** or the template image) and the images we want to align (also called the **moving** images) to this template. Convert the images to grayscale, as feature detectors typically operate on single-channel images.

2. **Feature detection and description:** Instantiate the ORB detector using **cv2.ORB_create()** with a maximum number of features (for example., **MAX_FEATURES = 500**). Then use **detectAndCompute()** to find keypoints and compute descriptors in both images.

3. **Feature matching:** Find the matching features (keypoints) in between the images. First instantiate a **matcher** object using the function **cv2.DescriptorMatcher_create()** with **BRUTEFORCE_HAMMING** metric. That is, use a brute-force matcher with the hamming distance as a measure of similarity between two feature descriptors. Then use the **match()** method to compare the descriptors from moving and fixed images, to find the best matches.

4. **Filter matches:** Subsequently sort the matches (keypoints) by goodness of match and retain only a top percentage of the best matches (for example, **GOOD_MATCH_PERCENT**). This helps reduce false matches and improves the robustness of alignment.

5. **Visualize matches:** Draw and display the good matches on the images, using the function **cv2.drawMatches()**. The matched features are shown in *Figure 5.7* by drawing lines connecting them, which visually confirms whether correct correspondences were found.

6. **Compute alignment using homography:** Define the function `compute_alignment()` to align a moving image to a fixed image, using matched keypoints between them.

   a. It first extracts matched keypoint coordinates from both images and uses them to estimate the homography matrix with `cv2.findHomography()`(with `cv2.RANSAC` to make the estimation robust to outliers).

   b. Then it applies the transformation (warp) to the moving image with the function `cv2.warpPerspective()`.

Invoke this function to align the simulated images with the original (fixed) image, as shown in the next code snippet:

```python
MAX_FEATURES = 500
GOOD_MATCH_PERCENT = 0.15

# reference image
im_ref = cv2.imread('images/tom_jerry .jpg')
# images to be aligned
im1 = cv2.imread('images/ tom_jerry_persp.jpg')
im2 = cv2.imread('images/ tom_jerry_affine.jpg')

# Convert images to grayscale
im_ref_g = cv2.cvtColor(im_ref, cv2.COLOR_RGB2GRAY)
im1_g, im2_g = cv2.cvtColor(im1, cv2.COLOR_RGB2GRAY), \
               cv2.cvtColor(im2, cv2.COLOR_RGB2GRAY)

# Detect ORB features and compute descriptors.
orb = cv2.ORB_create(MAX_FEATURES)
keypoints1, descriptors1 = orb.detectAndCompute(im1_g, None)
keypoints2, descriptors2 = orb.detectAndCompute(im2_g, None)
keypoints_ref, descriptors_ref = orb.detectAndCompute(im_ref_g, None)

# Match features.
matcher = cv2.DescriptorMatcher_create(\
                 cv2.DESCRIPTOR_MATCHER_BRUTEFORCE_HAMMING)
matches1 = matcher.match(descriptors1, descriptors_ref, None)
matches2 = matcher.match(descriptors2, descriptors_ref, None)

# Sort matches by score
matches1.sort(key=lambda x: x.distance, reverse=False)
matches2.sort(key=lambda x: x.distance, reverse=False)
# Remove not so good matches
num_good_matches = int(len(matches1) * GOOD_MATCH_PERCENT)
matches1 = matches1[:num_good_matches]
num_good_matches = int(len(matches2) * GOOD_MATCH_PERCENT)
matches2 = matches2[:num_good_matches]

# Draw top matches
plt.figure(figsize=(20,15))
im_matches = cv2.drawMatches(im1, keypoints1, im_ref, keypoints_ref, \
                                          matches1, None)
```

```python
plt.subplot(211)
plt.imshow(cv2.cvtColor(im_matches,cv2.COLOR_BGR2RGB)), plt.axis('off')
plt.title('Original vs. Perspective-Transformed Image', size=20)
im_matches = cv2.drawMatches(im2, keypoints2, im_ref, keypoints_ref, \
                                                    matches2, None)
plt.subplot(212)
plt.imshow(cv2.cvtColor(im_matches,cv2.COLOR_BGR2RGB)), plt.axis('off')
plt.title('Original vs. Affine-Transformed Image', size=20)
plt.show()

def compute_alignment(matches, im, keypoints, keypoints_ref):
    # Extract location of good matches
    points = np.zeros((len(matches), 2), dtype=np.float32)
    points_ref = np.zeros((len(matches), 2), dtype=np.float32)
    for i, match in enumerate(matches):
        points[i, :] = keypoints[match.queryIdx].pt
        points_ref[i, :] = keypoints_ref[match.trainIdx].pt
    # Find homography
    h, mask = cv2.findHomography(points, points_ref, cv2.RANSAC)
    # Use homography
    height, width, channels = im.shape
    im_ref_reg = cv2.warpPerspective(im, h, (width, height))
    # Print estimated homography
    print("\n Estimated homography : \n",  h)
    return im_ref_reg

im1_reg = compute_alignment(matches1, im1, keypoints1, keypoints_ref)
# Estimated homography:
# [[ 8.21788026e-01   1.61971819e-03 -2.40068712e+00]
# [-1.34251105e-01   8.00578888e-01   2.75024081e+01]
# [-1.52078398e-03   1.31085142e-05   1.00000000e+00]]

im2_reg = compute_alignment(matches2, im2, keypoints2, keypoints_ref)
# Estimated homography:
# [[ 9.83624364e-01 -5.34196484e-01   6.76430982e+01]
# [ 5.43767499e-01   9.74305147e-01 -2.11468782e+01]
# [ 1.15192040e-04 -3.90720842e-05   1.00000000e+00]]

plt.figure(figsize=(30,15))
plt.subplot(231), plt.imshow(cv2.cvtColor(im_ref, cv2.COLOR_BGR2RGB))
plt.axis('off'), plt.title('Original Image', size=20)
plt.subplot(232), plt.imshow(cv2.cvtColor(im1, cv2.COLOR_BGR2RGB))
plt.axis('off'), plt.title('Image to be aligned', size=20)
plt.subplot(233), plt.imshow(cv2.cvtColor(im1_reg, cv2.COLOR_BGR2RGB))
plt.axis('off'), plt.title('Aligned Image', size=20)
plt.subplot(234), plt.imshow(cv2.cvtColor(im_ref, cv2.COLOR_BGR2RGB))
plt.axis('off'), plt.title('Original Image', size=20)
plt.subplot(235), plt.imshow(cv2.cvtColor(im2, cv2.COLOR_BGR2RGB))
plt.axis('off'), plt.title('Image to be aligned', size=20)
plt.subplot(236), plt.imshow(cv2.cvtColor(im2_reg, cv2.COLOR_BGR2RGB))
plt.axis('off'), plt.title('Aligned Image', size=20)
plt.show()
```

If you run the preceding code snippet, you should obtain a figure as follows:

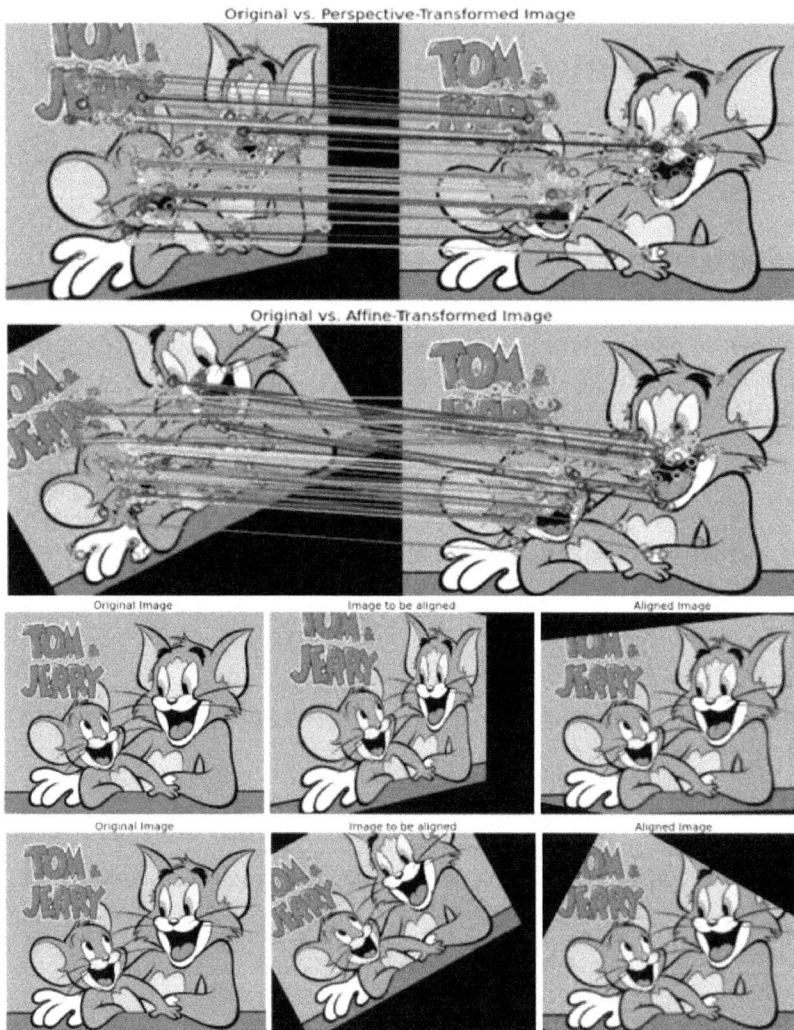

Figure 5.7: *Aligning images with ORB feature matching with opencv-python*

The preceding figure shows how the simulated moving images are aligned with a fixed image (of Tom & Jerry). It shows the fixed and moving images, along with the matched ORB keypoints, and the aligned output images obtained by applying the transformations with the estimated homography matrices.

> **Note: We may have many incorrect matches (false positives) and hence we need to use a robust method to calculate homography, for example, using the famous algorithm Random Sample Consensus (RANSAC), it identifies inliers among matched feature points by iteratively selecting random subsets and computing the best-fitting transformation while rejecting outliers.**

With ORB features using scikit-image

Now let us demonstrate image matching using the ORB features again, but this time the detection and binary descriptor computation algorithm comes from the **feature** module's functions from the library **scikit-image** (for example, the method **detect_and_extract()** from the class **ORB** and the function **match_descriptors()**, as shown in the next code snippet, most of which is self-explanatory). Compared to BRIEF features, ORB offers better scale and rotation invariance and uses the Hamming distance for efficient matching, making it a more suitable choice for real-time applications.

```python
import numpy as np
import matplotlib.pyplot as plt
from skimage.feature import (match_descriptors, ORB, plot_matches)
from skimage.io import imread, imsave
from skimage.color import rgb2gray

im1 = imread('images/ tom_jerry .jpg')
im2 = imread('images/ tom_jerry_persp.jpg')
im3 = imread('images/ tom_jerry_affine.jpg')

im1_g, im2_g, im3_g = rgb2gray(im1), rgb2gray(im2), rgb2gray(im3)
descriptor_extractor = ORB(n_keypoints=100)
descriptor_extractor.detect_and_extract(im1_g)
keypoints1, descriptors1 = descriptor_extractor.keypoints, \
                        descriptor_extractor.descriptors
descriptor_extractor.detect_and_extract(im2_g)
keypoints2, descriptors2 = descriptor_extractor.keypoints, \
                        descriptor_extractor.descriptors
matches12 = match_descriptors(descriptors1, descriptors2, \
                        cross_check=True)
descriptor_extractor.detect_and_extract(im3_g)
keypoints3, descriptors3 = descriptor_extractor.keypoints, \
                        descriptor_extractor.descriptors
matches13 = match_descriptors(descriptors1, descriptors3, \
                        cross_check=True)

fig, axes = plt.subplots(nrows=2, ncols=1, figsize=(20,10))
plt.gray()
plot_matches(axes[0], im1, im2, keypoints1, keypoints2, matches12)
axes[0].axis('off')
axes[0].set_title("Image matching with ORB features: Original Image vs. "
                "Perspective-Transformed Image", size=20)
plot_matches(axes[1], im1, im3, keypoints1, keypoints2, matches13)
axes[1].axis('off')
axes[1].set_title("Image matching with ORB features: Original Image vs. "
                "Affine-Transformed Image", size=20)
plt.show()
```

If you run the preceding code snippet, you should obtain a figure as follows:

Figure 5.8: *Aligning images with ORB feature matching with scikit-image*

With SURF features with opencv-python

The SURF algorithm is a widely used method for detecting and describing local features in images. It is particularly effective due to its scale and rotation invariance, making it suitable for robust matching across different viewpoints. In **OpenCV**, the SURF features can be extracted using the function **cv2.xfeatures2d.SURF_create()**, which requires OpenCV versions prior to 3.4.2.17 or a custom-built version, as the algorithm is patented and excluded from later versions.

The **SURF_create()** includes several configurable parameters that control the behavior and sensitivity of the detector:

- **hessianThreshold**: This threshold determines the minimum value for the Hessian matrix at each keypoint location. A higher value results in fewer keypoints being detected. Typical values vary between 300 and 500 (depends on image contrast). In this example, the threshold value used is 400.

- **nOctaves**: Specifies the number of octaves in the **Gaussian pyramid**, controlling the scale of detected features. Increasing this value detects larger scale features, while decreasing it focuses on smaller ones (finer details). The default value is 4.

- **nOctaveLayers**: Determines how many intermediate images are generated per octave in the pyramid. By default, it is set to 2.

- **extended**: A boolean that specifies whether to compute the basic (64-element) or extended (128-element) descriptors. The default is 0 (basic).

- **upright**: Another Boolean that decides whether to compute the orientation of each feature. Setting this to 1 disables orientation computation, which speeds up processing significantly, especially for stereo matching or image stitching where similar orientations can be assumed.

Keypoint detection and matching

The function **detectAndCompute()** can be used to locate keypoints and generate their descriptors from a grayscale input image. Once the descriptors are obtained, matching between feature sets can be performed using **cv2.BFMatcher()**, which is a brute-force matcher that compares the descriptors and finds the closest match for each one. For improved accuracy, especially in filtering ambiguous matches, **knnMatch()** retrieves the k-best matches, ordered by increasing distance. This process enables the alignment of images through homography estimation and transformation warping, just as with other feature detection methods like ORB or SIFT.

The subsequent code demonstrates aligning two images of the **Konark Temple** using **SURF** keypoints and descriptors. The next code snippet illustrates the practical application of SURF in image registration tasks, especially when handling scale and rotation variations:

```python
import numpy as np
# pip install opencv-python==3.4.2.17 opencv-contrib-python==3.4.2.17
import cv2
print(cv2.__version__)
# 3.4.2

from matplotlib import pyplot as plt

img1 = cv2.imread('images/konark_big.jpg') # queryImage
img2 = cv2.imread('images/konark_small.jpg') # trainImage

img1_gray = cv2.cvtColor(img1, cv2.COLOR_BGR2GRAY)
img2_gray = cv2.cvtColor(img2, cv2.COLOR_BGR2GRAY)

# Create a SURF detector object
surf = cv2.xfeatures2d.SURF_create(400)

# find the keypoints and descriptors with SURF
kp1, des1 = surf.detectAndCompute(img1_gray,None)
kp2, des2 = surf.detectAndCompute(img2_gray,None)

# BFMatcher with default params
bf = cv2.BFMatcher()
matches = bf.knnMatch(des1,des2, k=2)

# Apply ratio test
good = []
for m,n in matches:
    if m.distance < 0.75*n.distance:
        good.append([m])

# cv2.drawMatchesKnn expects list of lists as matches.
img3 = cv2.drawMatchesKnn(img1,kp1,img2,kp2,good,None,flags=2)
```

```
plt.figure(figsize=(20,10))
plt.imshow(cv2.cvtColor(img3, cv2.COLOR_BGR2RGB)), plt.axis('off')
plt.title('Image matching with SURF features', size=20)
plt.show()
```

If you run the preceding code snippet, you should obtain a figure as follows:

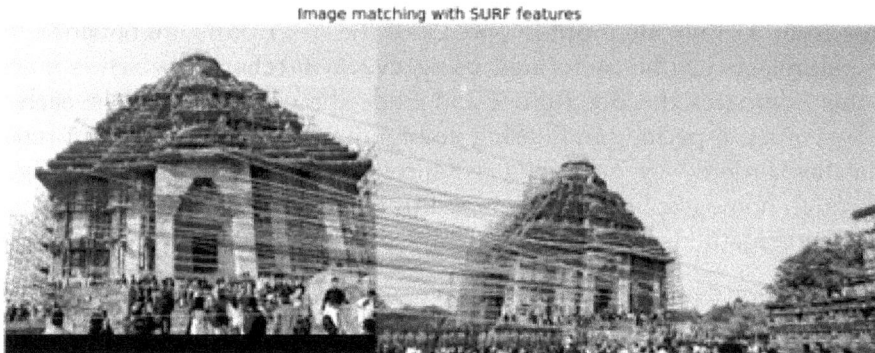

Figure 5.9: *Aligning images with SURF feature matching*

With DISK features with kornia

DISK (DIScrete Keypoints) is a learned local feature extraction method that jointly detects keypoints and computes descriptors using a deep neural network, trained with a **reinforcement learning** approach based on **policy gradients**. Unlike handcrafted methods such as **SIFT** or **ORB**, **DISK** is trained end-to-end to maximize downstream matching performance, making it highly effective and robust across a variety of tasks such as image matching and localization. The DISK pipeline operates as follows:

- **Keypoint detection and description**: A neural network predicts keypoints and corresponding descriptors jointly from input images. The keypoints are selected discretely through a learned sampling policy, and descriptors are extracted from local patches.

- **Reinforcement learning training**: The network is trained using policy gradients to directly optimize a reward based on successful matching outcomes, rather than heuristics or surrogate losses.

- **Robust matching**: The descriptors and keypoints are optimized for robustness and discriminative power, making them suitable for challenging real-world image alignment scenarios.

In this section, we shall use the library **kornia** for DISK feature extraction and matching. Let us first install **korina** with **pip**, if not already installed. Import all the libraries required, including **korina** and opencv-python. Run the following code on a GPU (for example, Google Colab), for faster execution:

```
# run in colab
# install libraries if not already installed by uncommenting the next two lines
# !pip install kornia
# !pip install kornia_moons --no-deps
import cv2
import kornia as K
import kornia.feature as KF
import matplotlib.pyplot as plt
import numpy as np
import torch
from kornia.feature.adalam import AdalamFilter
from kornia_moons.viz import *

device = K.utils.get_cuda_or_mps_device_if_available()
print(device)
# cuda:0
```

Now, let us understand the following step-by-step python implementation:

1. First load the images to be matched using **kornia.io.load_image()** function.

2. Load a pretrained model (trained end-to-end with depth-map supervision) using the function **KF.DISK.from_pretrained()**.

3. Concatenate the input images and extract the DISK features, by running a forward pass on the model (here we have used **num_features=2048** to detect a maximum of 2048 features).

4. Use the function **laf_from_center_scale_ori()** to create **kornia local affine frame** (**LAF**) from keypoint center, scale and orientations. An LAF represents a local coordinate system associated with an image region, particularly used for local feature extraction and matching and it is defined by a center, a scale, and an orientation. It provides a geometric description of a local image patch, allowing for robust feature matching across different images, scales, and orientations.

5. Finally, use the **kornia.feature.match_adalam()** function to compute descriptor matching, and then apply **Adaptive Locally-Affine Matching** (**AdaLAM**) filtering. The **AdaLAM** algorithm is an outlier rejection approach for local feature matching, designed to efficiently filter out outliers in matches obtained from descriptors. The parameters the function accepts are:

    a. **desc1 and desc2**: Tensors, the image descriptors

    b. **lafs1 and lafs2**: Tensors, corresponding **LAF**s

    c. **config (optional)**: Dictionary with **AdaLAM** config, defaults to **None**

    d. **dm (optional)**: Holds the distances between each descriptor in **desc1** and every descriptor in **desc2**. If a distance matrix (**dm**) is not supplied, the **torch.cdist()** function is used to calculate it.

6. The function returns the distance between the matching descriptors, along with the indices (here it finds tentative matches, as shown in the next code snippet):

```python
img1 = K.io.load_image("images/tom_jerry.jpg", \
                K.io.ImageLoadType.RGB32, device=device)[None, ...]
img2 = K.io.load_image("images/tom_jerry_affine.jpg", \
                K.io.ImageLoadType.RGB32, device=device)[None, ...]

disk = KF.DISK.from_pretrained("depth").to(device)

hw1 = torch.tensor(img1.shape[2:], device=device)
hw2 = torch.tensor(img2.shape[2:], device=device)

adalam_config = KF.adalam.get_adalam_default_config()
adalam_config["force_seed_mnn"] = False
adalam_config["search_expansion"] = 16
adalam_config["ransac_iters"] = 256

num_features = 2048

with torch.inference_mode():
    inp = torch.cat([img1, img2], dim=0)
    features1, features2 = disk(inp, num_features, \
                            pad_if_not_divisible=True)
    kps1, descs1 = features1.keypoints, features1.descriptors
    kps2, descs2 = features2.keypoints, features2.descriptors
    lafs1 = KF.laf_from_center_scale_ori(kps1[None], \
            96 * torch.ones(1, len(kps1), 1, 1, device=device))
    lafs2 = KF.laf_from_center_scale_ori(kps2[None], \
            96 * torch.ones(1, len(kps2), 1, 1, device=device))
    dists, idxs = KF.match_adalam(descs1, descs2, lafs1, lafs2,
                    hw1 = hw1, hw2 = hw2, config = adalam_config)

print(f"{idxs.shape[0]} tentative matches with DISK AdaLAM")
# 198 tentative matches with DISK AdaLAM
```

7. Use the function **get_matching_keypoints()** to extract the matched keypoints using the indices returned.

8. Use the function **cv2.findFundamentalMat()** to find the inliers from the matching points. It also computes the **fundamental matrix** (which represents the intrinsic relationship between corresponding points in two stereo images, encoding the **epipolar geometry** that governs their correspondence) from corresponding points in two images. The function takes several input parameters, here are the important ones:

    a. **points1**: Numpy array of points in the first image.

    b. **points2**: Numpy array of corresponding points in the second image.

c. **method**: algorithm used to compute the fundamental matrix, available algorithms are:

   i. **cv2.FM_8POINT**: Uses 8-point algorithm. This method requires at least 8 corresponding points.

   ii. **cv2.FM_RANSAC**: Uses **RANSAC** algorithm. This method is more robust to outliers.

   iii. **cv2.USAC_MAGSAC**: Uses **M-estimator Randomized Sample Consensus** (**MAGSAC**) algorithm, an extension of RANSAC that incorporates M-estimators, which are robust estimators of the error distribution of the data. M-estimators, in general, provide more robustness against outliers than simple least squares methods.

d. **ransacReprojThreshold**: Reprojection threshold used in RANSAC. This is the maximum allowed reprojection error to treat a point-pair as **inlier** during the **RANSAC** algorithm. Typical values: 0.5 to 3.0 (here we have used the value , change the value to see the impact on the matches obtained).

e. **confidence**: (Optional) Confidence level, between 0 and 1, for the RANSAC algorithm (Default: 0.99 or 0.999). It is the probability that the algorithm produces a useful result.

The function returns:

- **F**: The Fundamental matrix (3×3).

- **Mask**: The **inlier mask**, where **1 = inlier, 0 = outlier**.

The inlier matches can be identified using the binary mask that the function returns, with 1 indicating an inlier, and 0 otherwise (outlier). As can be seen from the next code snippet, out of the 198 tentaive matches, only 71 were considered to be **inliers**.

Now, refer to the next code snippet:

```
def get_matching_keypoints(kp1, kp2, idxs):
    mkpts1 = kp1[idxs[:, 0]]
    mkpts2 = kp2[idxs[:, 1]]
    return mkpts1, mkpts2

mkpts1, mkpts2 = get_matching_keypoints(kps1, kps2, idxs)

Fm, inliers = cv2.findFundamentalMat( \
    mkpts1.detach().cpu().numpy(), mkpts2.detach().cpu().numpy(), \
    cv2.USAC_MAGSAC, 0.5, 0.999, 100000) # 1.0
inliers = inliers > 0
print(f"{inliers.sum()} inliers with DISK")
# 71 inliers with DISK
```

9. Finally, draw the matches between the keypoints detected, using the function **draw_LAF_matches()**, as shown in the next code snippet:

```
draw_LAF_matches(
    KF.laf_from_center_scale_ori(kps1[None].cpu()),
    KF.laf_from_center_scale_ori(kps2[None].cpu()),
    idxs.cpu(),
    K.tensor_to_image(img1.cpu()),
    K.tensor_to_image(img2.cpu()),
    inliers,
    draw_dict={"inlier_color": (0.2, 1, 0.2),
               "tentative_color": (1, 1, 0.2, 0.3),
               "feature_color": None, "vertical": False},
)
```

If you run the preceding code snippet, you should obtain a figure as follows:

Figure 5.10*: Aligning images with DISK features with kornia*

Image color channel alignment using image registration with pystackreg

In this section, we shall explore how to align misaligned color channel images using image registration, leveraging the library **pystackreg**. As input, we shall use images from **Prokudin-Gorskii** collection, where the red, green, and blue channels were captured separately and often exhibit noticeable misalignment. Here the library **pystackreg** will be used to align (register) green and blue color channels of an RGB image to a common reference channel - typically the red channel - using rigid (translational) transformations. Here are the steps for color-channel alignment:

1. Install **pystackreg**, if not already installed with **pip**. Import the required libraries and modules.

2. Read the RGB image of birds (with misaligned color channels) using the function **skimage.io.imread()**. Split the RGB image into its individual channels.

3. Assuming that the color channels are misaligned due to translation only, let us use translational transformation (instantiate a **StackReg** object with translation type **StackReg.TRANSLATION**, to apply translational alignment).

4. Use the method **register_transform()** to align the color channels. The first argument to be passed to it is the fixed / reference image (here, the red channel) and the second argument is the moving image (here, the green and blue channels, respectively).

5. Merge the aligned (registered) green and blue channel with the reference red channel to obtain the color-channel-aligned image, crop the image (with **skimage. util.crop()** function, which accepts a tuple argument representing how many pixels to crop from the left and right sides for each axis of the input **numpy ndarray**) to get rid of unpleasant borders (remove alignment artifacts).

Refer to the following python code snippet:

```python
from pystackreg import StackReg
from skimage import io
from skimage.util import crop

im = io.imread('images/birds.jpg')
r, g, b = im[...,0], im[...,1], im[...,2]

# Load reference and "moved" image
# Translational transformation
sr = StackReg(StackReg.TRANSLATION)
g_ = sr.register_transform(r, g)
b_ = sr.register_transform(r, b)

im_rec = im.copy()
im_rec[...,1], im_rec[...,2] = g_, b_

im_rec = crop(im_rec, ((50, 50), (20, 20), (0,0)), copy=False)
plt.figure(figsize=(18,7))
plt.gray()
plt.imshow(np.hstack((r, g, g_, b, b_))), plt.axis('off')
plt.show()
plt.figure(figsize=(15,8))
plt.subplots_adjust(0,0,1,0.95,0.02,0.02)
plt.subplot(121), plt.imshow(im, aspect='auto'), plt.axis('off')
plt.title('original image', size=20)
plt.subplot(122), plt.imshow(im_rec, aspect='auto'), plt.axis('off')
plt.title('color-corrected image', size=20)
plt.show()
```

If you run the preceding code snippet, you should obtain a figure as follows:

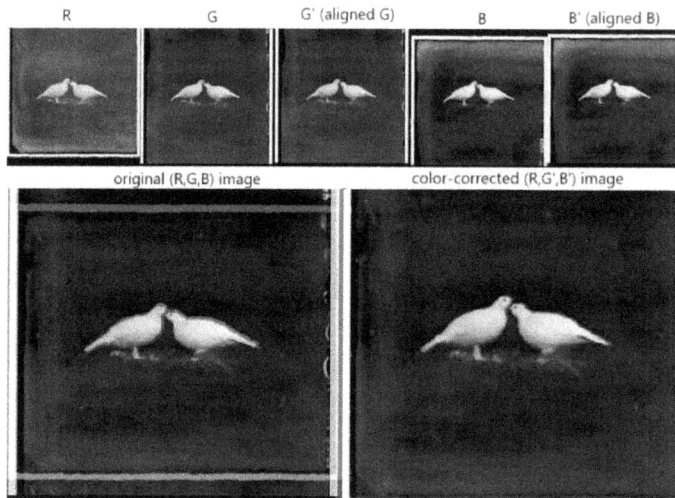

Figure 5.11: *Correcting an RGB image by aligning the color channels*

The preceding *Figure 5.11* shows the original image with color-channel misalignment, the aligned green and blue channels, and the cropped color- channel-aligned (color-corrected) output image. As can be seen, the color channels are much better aligned now, and the output image looks much less blurry that the original input.

Deformable image registration with pyelastix

PyElastix is a Python wrapper (interface) for the **Elastix** non-rigid image registration toolkit. It requires the Elastix command line to be installed and accessible in your system's environment, for proper functionality. You can download Elastix from the following link: **https://github.com/SuperElastix/elastix/releases/tag/5.1.0**. (Choose the correct ZIP file, based on your operating system and unzip it. Then, add the path to the executable to the environment variable **PATH** by appending the path string **os.environ["PATH"]**. Next, install **pyelastix** with **pip**, if not already installed. In this example, we shall use two palm images (one as the fixed/reference image and the other as the moving image) and align the moving image with the fixed one using nonrigid (deformable) image registration. Here are the steps:

1. Read the fixed (reference) and moving input images (with the function **imageio. imread()**) and convert them to grayscale images.

2. Use the function **pyelastix.register()** which accepts moving image and fixed image as arguments, along with the argument **parameters**. We shall use the default registration parameters obtained using **pyelastix.get_default_params()** and

set the **NumberOfResolutions** to 3 (to control multi-resolution registration levels). The function returns the registered moving image to fixed image, along with the displacement fields (in the x and y directions).

3. Plot the input fixed and moving images (overlayed), output registered image and displacement fields, as shown in the following code snippet:

```python
# ! pip install pyelastix
import pyelastix
import os
from skimage.color import rgb2gray
import imageio
import numpy as np
import matplotlib.pylab as plt

os.environ["PATH"] += os.pathsep + 'elastix-5.1.0-win64'

im_fixed = imageio.imread('images/hands1.jpg')
im_moving = imageio.imread('images/hands2.jpg')

im_fixed, im_moving = rgb2gray(im_fixed), rgb2gray(im_moving)

# Get default params and adjust
params = pyelastix.get_default_params()
params.NumberOfResolutions = 3
print(params)
# <10 parameters>
#                          Metric: 'AdvancedMattesMutualInformation'
#              NumberOfHistogramBins: 32
#                        ImageSampler: 'RandomCoordinate'
#              NumberOfSpatialSamples: 2048
#           NewSamplesEveryIteration: True
#              NumberOfResolutions: 3
#                          Transform: 'BSplineTransform'
#     FinalGridSpacingInPhysicalUnits: 16
#                      Optimizer: #'AdaptiveStochasticGradientDescent'
#          MaximumNumberOfIterations: 500
# Found elastix version: 4.900 in 'elastix.exe'
# Register!
im_reg, field = pyelastix.register(im_moving, im_fixed, params, \
                                   verbose=0)

# Visualize the result
fig = plt.figure(figsize=(15,8));
plt.gray()
plt.clf()
plt.subplot(231); plt.imshow(im_fixed), plt.axis('off')
plt.title('fixed image', size=20)
plt.subplot(232); plt.imshow(im_moving), plt.axis('off')
plt.title('moving image', size=20)
```

```
plt.subplot(233); plt.imshow(im_reg), plt.axis('off')
plt.title('registered image', size=20)
plt.subplot(234)
plt.imshow(np.dstack((im_fixed, im_moving, im_reg)))
plt.axis('off'), plt.title('comparing fixed, moving, reg', size=20)
plt.subplot(235); plt.imshow(field[0]), plt.axis('off')
plt.title('field-X', size=20)
plt.subplot(236); plt.imshow(field[1]), plt.axis('off')
plt.title('field-Y', size=20)
plt.tight_layout()
plt.show()
```

If you run the preceding code snippet, you should obtain a figure as follows:

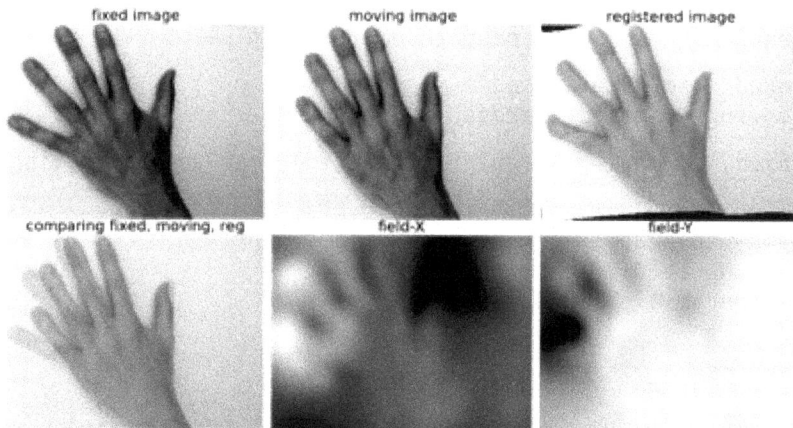

Figure 5.12: *Deformable image registration with pyelastix*

Note: The function `pyelastix.get_default_params()` provides a dictionary of default parameters tailored for nonrigid image registration using B-spline transformations. These parameters are designed to offer a robust starting point for general deformable registration tasks. We can customize various aspects of the registration process, such as the optimizer, similarity metric, and interpolation method, by modifying the returned dictionary. This flexibility allows adaptation to specific registration needs, including applications involving anatomical variability, such as aligning medical scans, or scenarios requiring nonrigid alignment due to local deformations.

Image registration with SimpleITK

In this section, we shall use the library **SimpleITK** to perform non-rigid registration. **SimpleITK** provides two flavors of non-rigid registration:

- **ITKv4-based registration framework**: Supports free-form deformation, **B-Spline** based, and **Demons** algorithms.

- **Standalone Demons filters**: A set of Demons filters that are independent of the registration framework (includes `DemonsRegistrationFilter`, `Diffeomorphic-DemonsRegistrationFilter`, `FastSymmetricForcesDemonsRegistrationFilter` and `SymmetricForcesDemonsRegistrationFilter`).

We shall demonstrate how to implement nonrigid registration methods, one from each flavor.

With B-Splines

B-Splines are popular for modeling local deformations in medical and natural images. However, they involve a large number of parameters, making the optimization of the deformation more complex and time-consuming. To address this, a **multi-resolution B-Spline** approach is employed, which starts the registration process at a lower resolution with fewer parameters.

At the initial stage, the transformation uses a coarser grid, and as the registration progresses, the B-Spline control points are resampled at progressively higher resolutions. This adaptive strategy, combined with the multi-level feature of the image registration process, allows for efficient solving of a wide range of registration problems.

The multi-level registration technique enables adjustments to various parameters at each level, including shrink factors, smoothing sigmas, sampling percentages, and the B-Spline resolution itself. The process begins with a low-resolution B-Spline transform, and the resolution increases at each level, typically doubling with each step. For instance, if the final resolution level is set to 5, the resolution scaling factors for each level might progress from 1 to 2, 4, and so on.

It is crucial to monitor the transformation at every stage of the registration. When the `inPlace=True` option in `SetInitialTransformAsBSpline()` is activated, the transformation is updated continuously during the registration process, making it possible to observe the current transform and apply it in event commands if needed.

Using consistent pixel types for all images in the process ensures compatibility when applying filters like the compose filter, which is often required when combining images or performing multi-stage transformations.

This adaptive B-Spline method helps efficiently manage complex image deformation tasks, making the registration process more scalable and flexible.

The next code snippet uses **BSplineTransform** from **SimpleITK** for image registration. The floor division operator (**//**) needs to be used to ensure that all the three images have the same pixel type, as required by the compose filter (**sitk.Compose()**).

```python
import SimpleITK as sitk
import sys, os

fixed = sitk.ReadImage('images/hands1.jpg', sitk.sitkFloat32)
moving = sitk.ReadImage('images/hands2.jpg', sitk.sitkFloat32)

transform_domain_mesh_size = [2] * fixed.GetDimension()
tx = sitk.BSplineTransformInitializer(fixed, transform_domain_mesh_size)
print(f"Initial Number of Parameters: {tx.GetNumberOfParameters()}")
# Initial Number of Parameters: 50

registration_method = sitk.ImageRegistrationMethod()
registration_method.SetMetricAsJointHistogramMutualInformation()
registration_method.SetOptimizerAsGradientDescentLineSearch(5.0, 100, \
                convergenceMinimumValue=1e-4, convergenceWindowSize=5)
registration_method.SetInterpolator(sitk.sitkLinear)
registration_method.SetInitialTransformAsBSpline(tx, inPlace=True, \
                                        scaleFactors=[1, 2, 5])
registration_method.SetShrinkFactorsPerLevel([4, 2, 1])
registration_method.SetSmoothingSigmasPerLevel([4, 2, 1])

outTx = registration_method.Execute(fixed, moving)

resampler = sitk.ResampleImageFilter()
resampler.SetReferenceImage(fixed)

resampler.SetInterpolator(sitk.sitkLinear)
resampler.SetDefaultPixelValue(100)
resampler.SetTransform(outTx)

out = resampler.Execute(moving)

simg1 = sitk.Cast(sitk.RescaleIntensity(fixed), sitk.sitkUInt8)
simg2 = sitk.Cast(sitk.RescaleIntensity(moving), sitk.sitkUInt8)
simg3 = sitk.Cast(sitk.RescaleIntensity(out), sitk.sitkUInt8)

# Visualize the result
fig = plt.figure(figsize=(15,6))
plt.gray()
plt.clf()
plt.subplot(131)
plt.imshow(sitk.GetArrayFromImage(sitk.Compose(simg1, simg2, \
                                    simg1 // 2.0 + simg2 // 2.0)))
plt.axis('off'), plt.title('fixed and moving image', size=20)
plt.subplot(132); plt.imshow(sitk.GetArrayFromImage(out)), plt.axis('off')
plt.title('registered image', size=20)
plt.subplot(133)
plt.imshow(sitk.GetArrayFromImage(sitk.Compose(simg1, simg3, \

                                    simg1 // 2.0 + simg3 // 2.0)))
plt.axis('off'), plt.title('fixed and registered image', size=20)
plt.suptitle('Image Regsitration with SimpleItk BSpline', size=22)
plt.tight_layout()
plt.show()
```

If you run the preceding code snippet, you should obtain a figure as follows:

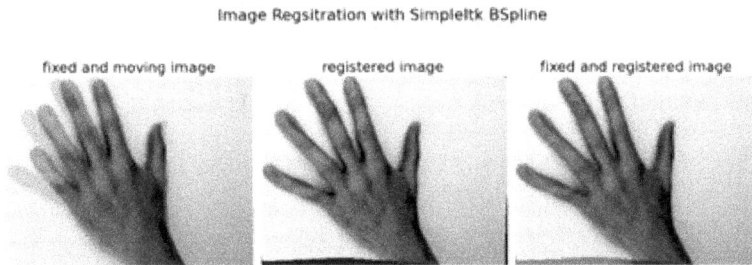

Figure 5.13: *Image registration using B-Spline with SimpleITK*

The preceding figure shows the moving image overlayed on the fixed image before and after registration – observe the alignment of the registered image is way better than the initial moving image.

With Demons

In this section, we will explore how to apply the Fast Symmetric Forces Demons algorithm for deformable image registration using **FastSymmetricForcesDemonsRegistrationFilter()** from **SimpleITK**. Unlike traditional algorithms, this method uses symmetric forces, instead of asymmetric displacement assumptions.

The algorithm's key parameters include the number of iterations, configured using the **SetNumberOfIterations()** method, and the Gaussian smoothing standard deviations for the total displacement field, set with **SetStandardDeviations()**. Additional controls allow for fine-tuning regularization, as well as smoothing the total field for the elastic model or the update field for the viscous model.

The core assumption of the Demons algorithm is that its intensities at corresponding points in the images are equal. To address this assumption, histogram matching (**HistogramMatchingImageFilter()**) is applied to make the images more comparable before registration. This approach is particularly useful when the intensity similarity assumption does not hold. Furthermore, the command design pattern can be employed to track the progress of the registration process.

The fixed image input used in the next code snippet is the **Lena** image and the moving image is a distorted version of the image. Use the **demons** algorithm to register the moving image with the fixed image. Display the registered image, along with the fixed and moving images.

Now let us dive into the implementation, using the following code snippet:

```python
import SimpleITK as sitk
import sys, os

fixed = sitk.ReadImage('images/lenag2.png', sitk.sitkFloat32)
moving = sitk.ReadImage('images/lenag1.png', sitk.sitkFloat32)

matcher = sitk.HistogramMatchingImageFilter()
matcher.SetNumberOfHistogramLevels(1024)
matcher.SetNumberOfMatchPoints(7)
matcher.ThresholdAtMeanIntensityOn()
moving = matcher.Execute(moving, fixed)

transformDomainMeshSize = [2] * fixed.GetDimension()
tx = sitk.BSplineTransformInitializer(fixed, transformDomainMeshSize)

print(f"Initial Number of Parameters: {tx.GetNumberOfParameters()}")
# Initial Number of Parameters: 50

# The basic Demons Registration Filter
# Note there is a family of Demons Registration algorithms in
# SimpleITK
demons = sitk.FastSymmetricForcesDemonsRegistrationFilter()
demons.SetNumberOfIterations(200)
# Standard deviation for Gaussian smoothing of displacement field
demons.SetStandardDeviations(1.0)

displacement_field = demons.Execute(fixed, moving)

print(f"Number Of Iterations: {demons.GetElapsedIterations()}")
print(f" RMS: {demons.GetRMSChange()}")
# Number Of Iterations: 200
# RMS: 0.2871094570605489

outTx = sitk.displacement_fieldTransform(displacement_field)

resampler = sitk.ResampleImageFilter()
resampler.SetReferenceImage(fixed)
resampler.SetInterpolator(sitk.sitkLinear)
resampler.SetDefaultPixelValue(100)
resampler.SetTransform(outTx)

out = resampler.Execute(moving)
simg1 = sitk.Cast(sitk.RescaleIntensity(fixed), sitk.sitkUInt8)
simg2 = sitk.Cast(sitk.RescaleIntensity(moving), sitk.sitkUInt8)
simg3 = sitk.Cast(sitk.RescaleIntensity(out), sitk.sitkUInt8)

# Visualize the result
fig = plt.figure(figsize=(15,9))
plt.gray()
```

```
plt.clf()
plt.subplot(231); plt.imshow(sitk.GetArrayFromImage(fixed))
plt.axis('off')
plt.title('fixed image', size=20)
plt.subplot(232); plt.imshow(sitk.GetArrayFromImage(moving))
plt.axis('off'), plt.title('moving image', size=20)
plt.subplot(233)
plt.imshow(sitk.GetArrayFromImage(sitk.Compose(simg1, simg2, \
                                    simg1 // 2.0 + simg2 // 2.0)))
plt.axis('off'), plt.title('fixed and moving image', size=20)
plt.subplot(234); plt.imshow(sitk.GetArrayFromImage(out)), plt.axis('off')
plt.title('registered image', size=20)
plt.subplot(235)
plt.imshow(sitk.GetArrayFromImage(sitk.Compose(simg1, simg3, \
                                    simg1 // 2.0 + simg3 // 2.0)))
plt.axis('off'), plt.title('fixed and registered image', size=20)
plt.suptitle('Image Regsitration with SimpleItk Demon', size=22)
plt.tight_layout()
plt.show()
```

If you run the preceding code snippet, you should obtain a figure as follows:

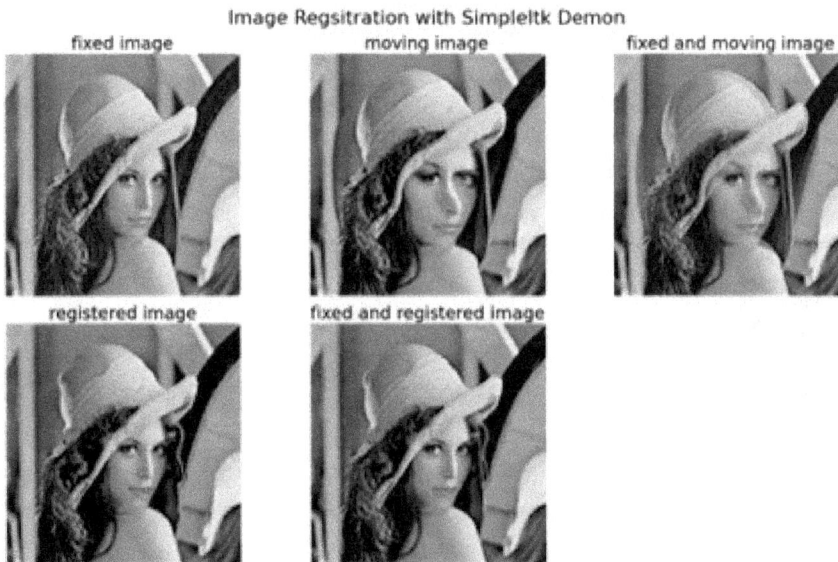

Figure 5.14: *Image registration with SimpleITK Demon*

Deep deformable image registration with VoxelMorph with tensorflow/keras

Image registration involves aligning different datasets into a common coordinate system. These alignments can range from simple rigid transformations, such as translations and rotations, to more complex transformations, such as affine (shear) or homography transforms, and even deformable models. The goal of deformable registration is to compute a pixel-wise displacement field between a source image and a target image. When applied to the source image, this displacement field ensures that the source and target images match as closely as possible, as shown in the following figure:

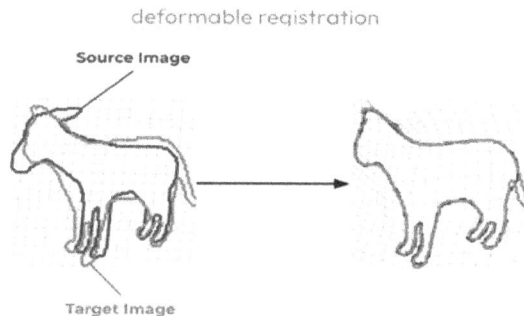

Figure 5.15: *Schematic for deformable registration*

In this section, we shall explore a state-of-the-art technique for deformable image registration using **deep learning**. The following figure illustrates a schematic of the training process for a deep learning-based pipeline designed for deformable image registration:

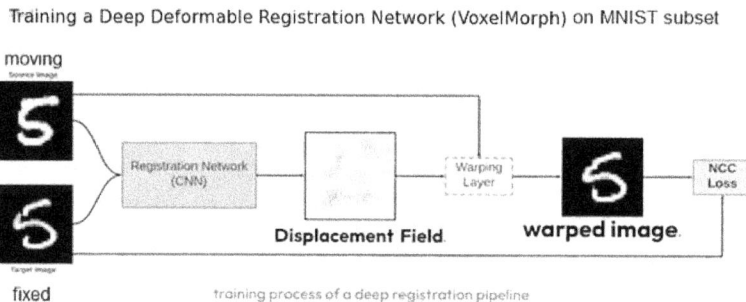

Computing Similarity Warped ↔ Target

Loss $MSE = ||I - J||^2$

(update wts with backprop)

$$NCC = \frac{1}{|\Omega|} \sum_{u \in \Omega} \left(\sqrt{\frac{(IJ \circledast W - (I \circledast W)(J \circledast W))^2}{(I^2 \circledast W - (I \circledast W)^2)(J^2 \circledast W - (J \circledast W)^2)}} \right) [u]$$

Figure 5.16: *Training VoxelMorph on MNIST*
Source: *https://www.sicara.fr/blog-technique/deformable-image-registration*

Training a CNN for registration

Let us first understand of how to train a deep CNN to perform image registration:

1. To perform image registration, a pair of images—a source (moving image) and a target (fixed image)—are provided as input to a registration network, typically a **convolutional neural network** (**CNN**) such as a **U-Net**. This network processes the input pair and generates a **Displacement Field**, which is a tensor mapping each pixel (x, y) from source image to $(\Delta x, \Delta y)$, a displacement vector.

2. Using the displacement field, the source image can be transformed by computing new pixel coordinates $(x', y') = (x + \Delta x, y + \Delta y)$, for each pixel. The source image is then sampled at these new coordinates to produce the warped image. This transformation is performed in the warping layer (shown in *Figure 5.16*).

3. To evaluate the quality of the registration and provide an optimization objective for the network, a **loss** function is employed. Two common loss functions used for image registration are as follows (also shown in *Figure 5.16*):

    a. The **mean squared error** (**MSE**) is a pixel-wise loss metric that metric compares two images pixel by pixel, and quantifies the average of the squares of the differences between corresponding pixel intensities of two images. A perfect match results in an MSE of 0.

    b. The **normalized cross correlation** (**NCC**) is a similarity measure that evaluates how well two image patches or signals align as one is shifted over the other as a function of their relative displacement, similar to the concept of convolution between two functions.

4. These **loss** functions guide the network during training to improve the alignment of the source and target images, by updating the weights of the CNN with **backpropagation**.

5. To train the deformable image registration network, loop over the training dataset and execute steps 1-4 for each source, target image pair.

Prediction with the trained CNN

Given a pair of (moving, fixed) test images, the trained network predicts the registered (output) image and the displacement field.

Let us instantiate **VoxelMorph**, which is a **CNN** (convolution neural network) for deep deformable image registration, using the library **voxelmorph** (install it with **pip**, if not already installed). Follow the next steps to run training and inference on the network:

1. We need **tensorflow 2.0** (or later) for the implementation. Handwritten digits dataset **MNIST** (with each digit image having size 28×28) will be used as input

dataset. We shall use a subset (for example, use only the images with label , as shown in the next code snippet) to train the network.

2. The next code snippet creates the training / test splits from the dataset and pads the images to have the size of the nearest power of 2, that is, 32×32:

```python
# install voxelmorph, it will install dependencies: neurite and pystrum
# !pip install voxelmorph
import os, sys

# third party imports
import numpy as np
import tensorflow as tf
assert tf.__version__.startswith('2.'), 'We need Tensorflow 2.0+'

# local imports
import voxelmorph as vxm
import neurite as ne

from tensorflow.keras.datasets import mnist

# Load MNIST data.
# Split the data into train and test.
(x_train_load, y_train_load), (x_test_load, y_test_load) = \
                                            mnist.load_data()

x_train_load = x_train_load / x_train_load.max()
x_test_load = x_test_load / x_test_load.max()

digit_sel = 8

# extract only instances of the digit 8
x_train = x_train_load[y_train_load==digit_sel, ...]
y_train = y_train_load[y_train_load==digit_sel]
x_test = x_test_load[y_test_load==digit_sel, ...]
y_test = y_test_load[y_test_load==digit_sel]

# Let's get some shapes to understand what we loaded.
print('shape of x_train: {}, y_train: {}'.format(x_train.shape, \
                                            y_train.shape))
# shape of x_train: (5851, 28, 28), y_train: (5851,)

nb_val = 1000   # keep 1,000 subjects for validation
x_val = x_train[-nb_val:, ...]    # this indexing means "the last nb_val
                                  # entries" of the zeroth axis
y_val = y_train[-nb_val:]
x_train = x_train[:-nb_val, ...]
y_train = y_train[:-nb_val]

pad_amount = ((0, 0), (2,2), (2,2))
```

```
# fix data
x_train = np.pad(x_train, pad_amount, 'constant')
x_val = np.pad(x_val, pad_amount, 'constant')
x_test = np.pad(x_test, pad_amount, 'constant')

# verify
print('shape of training data', x_train.shape)
# shape of training data (4851, 32, 32)
```

3. Let us create a **U-Net** framework (using the function **voxelmorph.networks. VxmDense()** with the input shape and **nbfeatures** specifying the layers in the encoder and decoder networks).

4. The loss functions to be used are **voxelmorph.losses.MSE()** along with **voxelmorph.losses.Grad('l2')**, to compute the loss, and the optimizer to be used is **Adam**.

5. Let us plot the network architecture using **tf.keras.utils.plot_model()** function, using the next code snippet:

```
# configure unet input shape (concatenation of moving and fixed images)
ndim = 2
unet_input_features = 2
inshape = (*x_train.shape[1:], unet_input_features)

# configure unet features
nb_features = [
    [32, 32, 32, 32],          # encoder features
    [32, 32, 32, 32, 32, 16]   # decoder features
]

# build model using VxmDense
inshape = x_train.shape[1:]
vxm_model = vxm.networks.VxmDense(inshape, nb_features, int_steps=0)

# voxelmorph has a variety of custom loss classes
losses = [vxm.losses.MSE().loss, vxm.losses.Grad('l2').loss]

# usually, we have to balance the two losses by a hyper-parameter
lambda_param = 0.05
loss_weights = [1, lambda_param]

vxm_model.compile(optimizer='Adam', loss=losses, \
                                    loss_weights=loss_weights)

tf.keras.utils.plot_model(vxm_model, to_file='model.png', \
                                    show_shapes=True)
```

Refer to the following figure, for the architecture of the deep neural net (U-Net) framework:

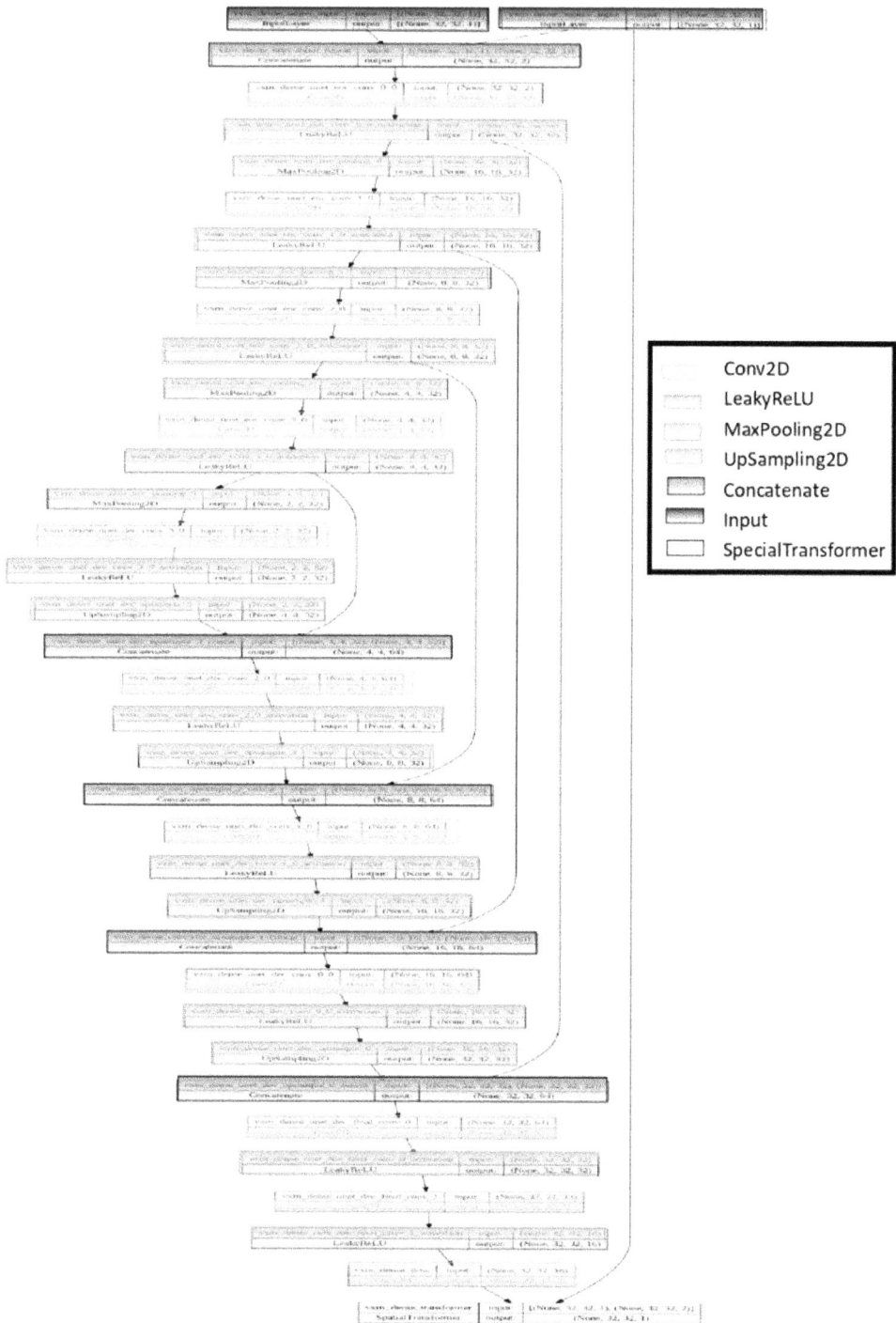

Figure 5.17: U-Net architecture

6. The function **plot_history()** shown in the next code block can be used to visualize the loss decreasing over epochs (training history).

7. The function **vxm_data_generator()** is a python generator (that yields values lazily using the **yield** keyword, allowing efficient memory usage by producing values one at a time instead of storing them all in memory), it will be used to generate **train** data (inputs and outputs for the CNN) now and **validation** data later. It takes in data of size [*N,H,W*], and yields data for our custom **voxelmorph** model. Note that we need to provide **numpy** data for each input, and each output.

8. The function yields the tuple (**inputs, outputs**) where:

   a. The variable **inputs** is assigned the tuple (**moving, fixed**) images of sizes **[batch_size, H, W, 1]** and **[batch_size, H, W, 1]**), respectively. It acts as input pair of images for the CNN (here *H* = *W* = *32* and **batch_size=32** by default).

   b. The variable **outputs** is assigned the tuple (**moved** image, zero-gradient **displacement** field) of sizes **[batch_size, H, W, 1]** and **[batch_size, H, W, 2]** respectively, to be used as the corresponding output pair of images for the CNN.

9. The output of the U-Net will be (**fixed**, ϕ), where ϕ is the **displacement field** (in *x* and *y* directions). The first term in the output tuple refers to the registered image and we want it to be close to the **fixed** image.

10. The displacement field is initialized with zero. Plot the **moving** (to be aligned), **fixed** (the reference), target (registered/aligned) ground-truth images and the displacement field (for example, in the *x* direction), using the function **ne.plot. slices()**, prior to the start of the training process.

```
def plot_history(hist, loss_name='loss'):
    plt.figure()
    plt.plot(hist.epoch, hist.history[loss_name], '.-')
    plt.ylabel('loss', size=20)
    plt.xlabel('epoch', size=20)
    plt.grid()
    plt.show()

def vxm_data_generator(x_data, batch_size=32):

    # preliminary sizing
    vol_shape = x_data.shape[1:] # extract data shape
    ndims = len(vol_shape)

    # prepare a zero array the size of the deformation
    zero_phi = np.zeros([batch_size, *vol_shape, ndims])
```

```
        while True:
            #prepare inputs: images need to be of sz [batch_size, H, W, 1]
            idx1 = np.random.randint(0, x_data.shape[0], size=batch_size)
            moving_images = x_data[idx1, ..., np.newaxis]
            idx2 = np.random.randint(0, x_data.shape[0], size=batch_size)
            fixed_images = x_data[idx2, ..., np.newaxis]
            inputs = [moving_images, fixed_images]

            # prepare outputs (the 'true' moved image):
            # of course, we don't have this, but we know we want to compare
            # the resulting moved image with the fixed image.
            # we also wish to penalize the deformation field.
            outputs = [fixed_images, zero_phi]

            yield (inputs, outputs)

# Let's test it
train_generator = vxm_data_generator(x_train)
in_sample, out_sample = next(train_generator)

print(len(in_sample), in_sample[0].shape)
# 2 (32, 32, 32, 1)

# visualize
images = [img[0, :, :, 0] for img in in_sample + out_sample]
titles = ['moving', 'fixed', 'moved ground-truth (fixed)', 'zeros']
ne.plot.slices(images, titles=titles, cmaps=['gray'], \
               do_colorbars=True);
```

If you run the preceding code snippet, you should obtain a figure as follows:

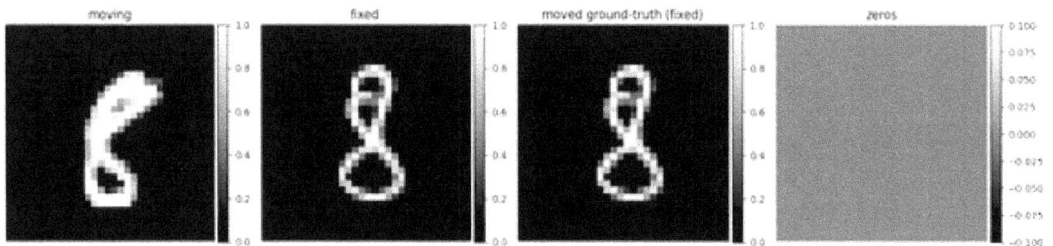

Figure 5.18: *Deep image registration with U-Net*

Now, let us train the model for 10 epochs (by invoking the model's **fit()** method), using the following code snippet:

```
nb_epochs = 10
steps_per_epoch = 100
hist = vxm_model.fit(train_generator, epochs=nb_epochs, \
                     steps_per_epoch=steps_per_epoch, verbose=2)
# Epoch 1/10
# 1/1 [==============================] - 0s 321ms/step
# 100/100 - 19s - loss: 0.0530 - vxm_dense_transformer_loss: 0.0506 -
# vxm_dense_flow_loss: 0.0481 - 19s/epoch - 194ms/step
# Epoch 2/10
# 1/1 [==============================] - 0s 31ms/step
# 100/100 - 14s - loss: 0.0234 - vxm_dense_transformer_loss: 0.0187 -
# vxm_dense_flow_loss: 0.0954 - 14s/epoch - 137ms/step
# Epoch 3/10
# 1/1 [==============================] - 0s 29ms/step
# 100/100 - 14s - loss: 0.0191 - vxm_dense_transformer_loss: 0.0144 -
# vxm_dense_flow_loss: 0.0941 - 14s/epoch - 135ms/step
# Epoch 4/10
# 1/1 [==============================] - 0s 29ms/step
# 100/100 - 13s - loss: 0.0175 - vxm_dense_transformer_loss: 0.0128 -
# vxm_dense_flow_loss: 0.0940 - 13s/epoch - 128ms/step
# Epoch 5/10
# 1/1 [==============================] - 0s 32ms/step
# 100/100 - 14s - loss: 0.0159 - vxm_dense_transformer_loss: 0.0113 -
# vxm_dense_flow_loss: 0.0924 - 14s/epoch - 137ms/step
# Epoch 6/10
# 1/1 [==============================] - 0s 31ms/step
# 100/100 - 14s - loss: 0.0151 - vxm_dense_transformer_loss: 0.0105 -
# vxm_dense_flow_loss: 0.0922 - 14s/epoch - 139ms/step
# Epoch 7/10
# 1/1 [==============================] - 0s 32ms/step
# 100/100 - 13s - loss: 0.0145 - vxm_dense_transformer_loss: 0.0099 -
# vxm_dense_flow_loss: 0.0924 - 13s/epoch - 129ms/step
# Epoch 8/10
# 1/1 [==============================] - 0s 29ms/step
# 100/100 - 14s - loss: 0.0137 - vxm_dense_transformer_loss: 0.0092 -
# vxm_dense_flow_loss: 0.0907 - 14s/epoch - 142ms/step
# Epoch 9/10
# 1/1 [==============================] - 0s 87ms/step
# 100/100 - 14s - loss: 0.0135 - vxm_dense_transformer_loss: 0.0089 -
# vxm_dense_flow_loss: 0.0912 - 14s/epoch - 139ms/step
# Epoch 10/10
# 1/1 [==============================] - 0s 50ms/step
# 100/100 - 13s - loss: 0.0131 - vxm_dense_transformer_loss: 0.0086 -
# vxm_dense_flow_loss: 0.0913 - 13s/epoch - 127ms/step
```

Once the network is trained, it is time to register/align images with **prediction**. We shall use images from the validation dataset for this purpose (ideally you should use the held-out test dataset, try it on your own). Generate (**moving, fixed**) image pairs from the validation data, to be input to the network, and run a forward pass on the network (using the **predict()** method), predicting the registered image (i.e., the moving image aligned to the fixed image) and the displacement fields.

Plot all the images, using the next code snippet, to visualize the alignment, along with the flow. Moreover, plot the loss with training epoch, to see how the **loss** function decreases over epochs during training phase.

```python
val_generator = vxm_data_generator(x_val, batch_size = 1)
val_input, _ = next(val_generator)
val_pred = vxm_model.predict(val_input)
# visualize
images = [img[0, :, :, 0] for img in val_input + val_pred] + \
        [np.dstack((val_input[0][0,:,:,0], val_input[1][0,:,:,0], \
            val_input[0][0,:,:,0]/2 + val_input[1][0,:,:,0]/2))] + \
        [np.dstack((val_input[1][0,:,:,0], val_pred[0][0,:,:,0], \
            val_input[1][0,:,:,0]/2 + val_pred[0][0,:,:,0]/2))]
titles = ['moving', 'fixed', 'moved', 'flow', 'before reg', \
                                          'after reg']
ne.plot.slices(images, titles=titles, cmaps=['gray'], \
                        do_colorbars=True, show=False)
ne.plot.flow([val_pred[1].squeeze()], width=5, show=False);
```

If you run the preceding code snippet, you should obtain a figure as follows:

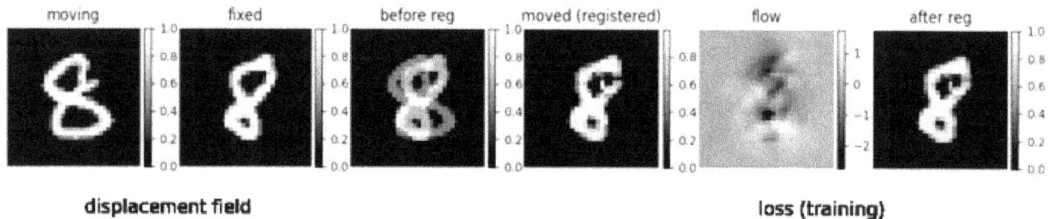

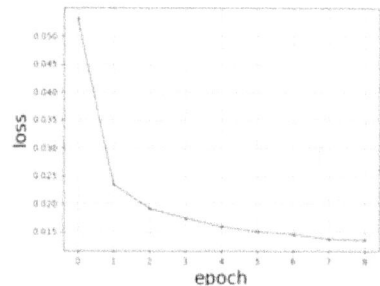

Figure 5.19: Image registration with VoxelMorph

Conclusion

In this chapter, we discussed about various feature extraction techniques and application of them in important image processing and computer vision problems such as image registration. You learnt how to implement extraction of features like SURF, BRISK, BRIEF with python libraries such as scikit-image, SimpleITK, cv2.

This chapter provided a detailed exploration of image feature extraction and its applications, with a focus on image registration. It began by introducing different types of feature detectors and descriptors, laying the groundwork for effective image alignment. Feature detection techniques were highlighted, including the Harris Corner detector and Shi-Tomasi Corner detector, implemented with OpenCV to extract prominent features in images.

The discussion then shifted to image registration, showcasing practical implementations using both classical and advanced techniques. Registration with ORB features was demonstrated using OpenCV and Scikit-image, while SURF features with OpenCV and DISK features with kornia illustrated additional robust methods for feature-based matching. The chapter also covered color channel alignment using the pystackreg library for precise registration of misaligned image channels.

Advanced registration techniques included deformable image registration with PyElastix, enabling flexible transformations for non-rigid alignment. The chapter further explored registration with SimpleITK, detailing methods using B-Splines for smooth, flexible transformations and Demons for intensity-based approaches. Finally, cutting-edge deep deformable image registration was introduced with VoxelMorph, leveraging TensorFlow/ Keras to achieve state-of-the-art results in medical and other complex image registration tasks.

By integrating traditional methods with deep learning approaches, this chapter provided readers with a comprehensive understanding of feature extraction and its applications, equipping them to tackle a variety of image registration challenges in research and practical settings.

Key terms

Harris Corner, Shi-Tomasi, ORB, SURF, DISK, B-Splines, Demons, VoxelMorph.

Questions

1. **Rotation invariance of ORB**: Show that the ORB is rotation invariant. For example, take the following image of the *Victoria Memorial Hall* and its rotated version as input images. Choose a single ORB feature (for example, the one on its fairy) detected in the original image (mark it red), show that the same feature is detected from the rotated image too. You should obtain a figure as follows:

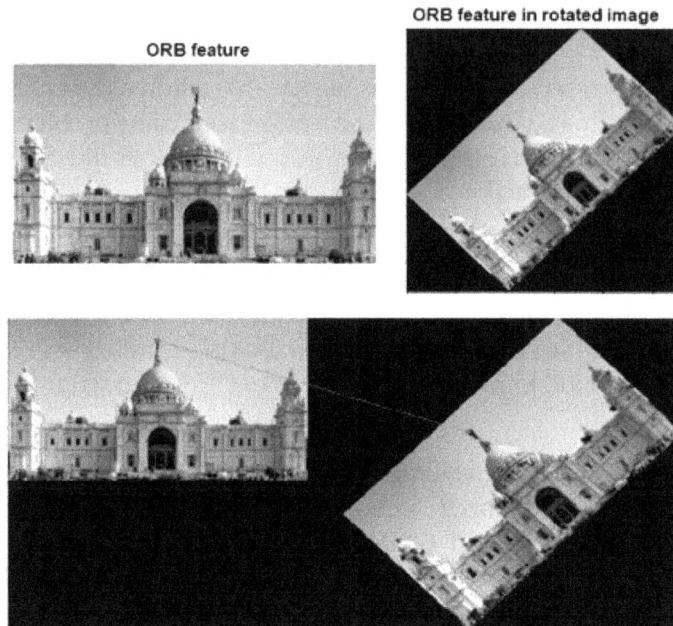

Figure 5.20: Rotation invariance of ORB features

Similarly, show that the **ORB** is **scale- invariant** too.

2. **Finding near-duplicate images (up to rotation/scaling)**: Use ORB features to find near-duplicate images, for example from the following images of the *Victoria Memorial Hall* and *Taj Mahal*. Notice that there are 2 unique images and all the other images are obtained by applying rotation/scaling/changing background.

Figure 5.21: Input images for near-duplicate image detection

Extract ORB feature descriptors (for example, 50 features) and concatenate the features to obtain a single vector from each image. Now, use a nearest-neighbor algorithm (for example, ball_tree from sklearn.neighbors.NearestNeighbors) to find the nearest descriptors from the images and display the top 4 (for example, $k = 4$) near-duplicate images found, as shown in the following figure. As can be seen, querying with a Victoria image (descriptor vector) fetches all the images obtained with rotation/scaling/changing the background of the original image (also report the **NN**-distances obtained).

query image

search result: near-duplicate images based on ORB descriptors (with NN-distances)

| 0.000 | 66.776 | 66.978 | 67.461 |

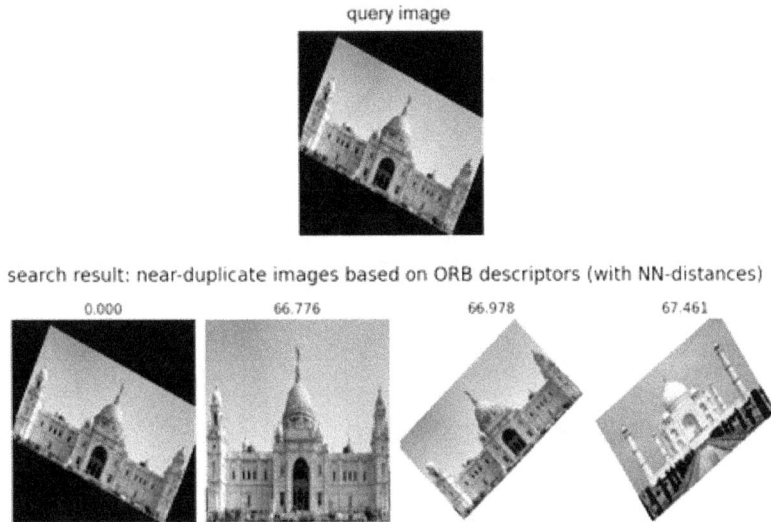

Figure 5.22: *Finding near-duplicate images with ORB features*

References

1. https://stackoverflow.com/questions/41692063/what-is-the-difference-between-image-registration-and-image-alignment

2. https://cs.brown.edu/courses/cs129/2012/asgn/proj1/

3. https://www.loc.gov/pictures/search/?q=Prokudin+negative&sp=3&st=grid

4. https://github.com/SuperElastix/elastix/releases/tag/5.1.0

5. https://in.mathworks.com/help/images/ref/imregdemons.html

6. https://www.cs.cmu.edu/~galeotti/methods_course/ITK_Registration.pdf

7. https://openaccess.thecvf.com/content_CVPR_2019/papers/Barath_MAGSAC_Marginalizing_Sample_Consensus_CVPR_2019_paper.pdf

8. https://stackoverflow.com/questions/37039224/attributeerror-module-object-has-no-attribute-xfeatures2d-python-opencv-2

9. https://dl.acm.org/doi/pdf/10.5555/3495724.3496919

Join our Discord space

Join our Discord workspace for latest updates, offers, tech happenings around the world, new releases, and sessions with the authors:

https://discord.bpbonline.com

CHAPTER 6
Applications of Image Feature Extraction

Introduction

As discussed in *Chapter 5, Image Feature Extraction and Its Applications: Image Registration*, image feature extraction involves identifying and encoding important elements of an image (edges, corners, blobs, textures, etc.) to create a simplified, informative representation. It plays a pivotal role in a wide range of computer vision applications, enabling the detection, recognition, and analysis of objects in both static and dynamic scenes. By isolating key visual attributes from images, feature extraction serves as the foundation for tasks such as stitching, recognition, and detection. This chapter delves into various practical applications of feature extraction techniques, highlighting their effectiveness in solving real-world problems across domains like multimedia, security, and surveillance.

Structure

This chapter covers the following topics:

- Panorama with opencv-python
- NMF for extracting face features with Nimfa

- Face recognition using LBPH with opencv-python

- Face feature extraction and recognition using Gabor filter banks

- Pedestrian detection with HOG vs HAAR-Cascade features with opencv-python

Objectives

This chapter explores diverse applications of image feature extraction techniques, focusing on their implementation and practical utility. Key topics include the creation of panoramas through image and video stitching using opencv-python, leveraging **non-negative matrix factorization** (**NMF**) for facial feature extraction, and implementing **Local Binary Patterns Histogram** (**LBPH**)-based face recognition with opencv-pthon. Advanced methods, such as facial feature extraction and recognition using **Gabor filter banks**, and a comparative analysis of **HOG** and **HAAR Cascade** features for pedestrian detection, are also covered. By the end of the chapter, you will gain hands-on experience and insights into applying these techniques effectively in various image processing and computer vision tasks.

Panorama with opencv-python

Image stitching (also called **image mosaicing**) refers to the image processing task of combining multiple overlapping images to create a (segmented) panorama image (alternatively called an **image mosaic**). There are three major components of image stitching:

- Register images so that corresponding features align accurately

- Determine overlap between adjacent images

- Blend the overlapping regions to create a coherent, artifact-free composite

In this section, we shall use the `stitching` module pipeline from `opencv-python` to perform image stitching, as illustrated in the following *Figure 6.1*. Using the `Stitcher` class, it is possible to configure and remove some steps, that is, adjust the stitching pipeline according to the particular needs. All building blocks from the pipeline are available in the `detail` namespace, and one can combine and use them separately.

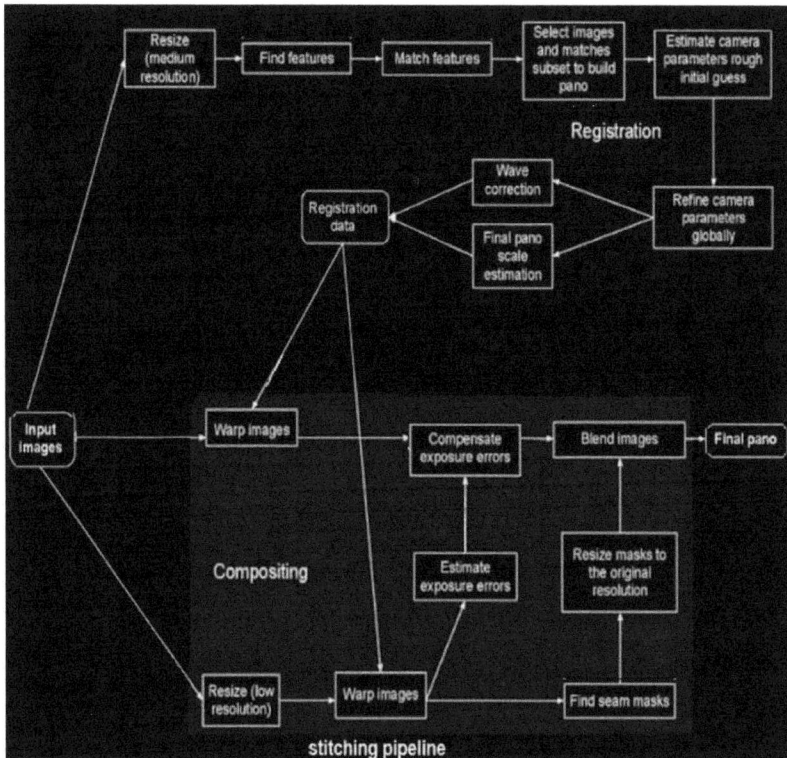

Figure 6.1: *Image stitching pipeline*

Image stitching

The following code demonstrates image stitching, here we stitch eleven images together to obtain a panorama image, using **opencv-python**'s **Stitcher.stitch()** method. Here are the steps involved:

1. **Create the stitcher object**: Use **cv2.createStitcher()** if you are using **OpenCV 3.x** or **cv2.Stitcher_create()** for **OpenCV 4.x**, to instantiate a **Stitcher** object. You can optionally pass the boolean parameter **try_use_gpu=True** if you have a GPU available, which can significantly accelerate the stitching process.

2. **Stitch the images**: Call the **stitch()** method on the **Stitcher** object, passing a list of input images. This method will attempt to align and combine the images into a single panoramic view and return the resulting panorama.

3. **Check the stitching status**: The **stitch()** method returns two values: a **status** code and the resulting panorama image. The status code indicates the success or failure of the stitching process. The possible status codes from the OpenCV documentation are:

   a. **OK = 0**: Stitching was successful.

b. **ERR_NEED_MORE_IMGS = 1**: Not enough keypoints were detected in the images, requiring additional input images.

c. **ERR_HOMOGRAPHY_EST_FAIL = 2**: The **RANSAC** algorithm for homography estimation (which robustly finds the best transformation between images by iteratively selecting point correspondences and rejecting outliers) failed, likely due to insufficient or poorly matched keypoints between the input images.

d. **ERR_CAMERA_PARAMS_ADJUST_FAIL = 3**: Failed to estimate camera parameters from the input images. In such cases, providing more images might improve keypoint detection and estimation.

4. **Handling black borders in the panorama**: Even after successful stitching, the output panorama image often has black borders caused by the perspective warping necessary to align the images. To remove these borders, you can use the **trim()** method from the **wand** library's **Image** class. Pass the parameters **color=Color('rgb(0,0,0)')** and **percent_background=0.0**, to trim the panorama image to its minimal bounding box, removing the black regions, as shown in the next code snippet.

By following these steps, you can successfully stitch images into a panorama and clean up any unnecessary background artifacts that may result from the stitching process. First let us load the images to be stitched and display them with **matplotlib.pylab**, using the following code snippet:

```python
import numpy as np
import glob
import matplotlib.pylab as plt
import cv2
print(cv2.__version__)
# 3.4.2
from wand.image import Image
from wand.color import Color

# grab the paths to the input images and initialize our images list
images = [cv2.imread(img) for img in glob.glob('images/Imgp_*')]
print('Number of images to stitch: {}'.format(len(images)))
# Number of images to stitch: 11
fig = plt.figure(figsize=(20, 15))
for i in range(len(images)):
    plt.subplot(3,4,i+1)
    plt.imshow(images[i])
    plt.axis('off')

fig.subplots_adjust(left=0, right=1, bottom=0, top=0.95, \
                                    hspace=0.05, wspace=0.05)
plt.suptitle('Images to stich', size=25)
plt.show()
```

If you run the preceding code snippet, you should obtain a figure like the next one, displaying all the images to be stitched as subplots:

Figure 6.2: *11 input images to stitch*

Now, run the image stitching with the **stitcher.stitch()** method, as explained, using the following code snippet:

```python
# initialize OpenCV's image sticher object & perform image stitching
stitcher = cv2.createStitcher()
(status, stitched) = stitcher.stitch(images)
# if status is 0, then image stitching is successful
if status == 0:

    plt.figure(figsize=(20,10))
    plt.imshow(cv2.cvtColor(stitched, cv2.COLOR_BGR2RGB))
    plt.axis('off'), plt.title('Stitched output image', size=20)
    plt.tight_layout()
    plt.show()

    stitched = Image.from_array(stitched)
    stitched.trim(color=Color('rgb(0,0,0)'), \
                percent_background=0.0, fuzz=0)
    stitched = np.array(stitched)

    # write the output stitched image to disk
    cv2.imwrite('images/output_panorama.jpg', stitched)
    plt.figure(figsize=(20,10))
    plt.imshow(cv2.cvtColor(stitched, cv2.COLOR_BGR2RGB))
```

```
    plt.axis('off')
    plt.title('Stitched output image (after trimming with wand)', \
                                                    size=20)
    plt.tight_layout()
    plt.show()
else: # stitching failed, not enough keypoints detected
    print("image stitching failed ({})".format(status))
```

If you run the preceding code snippet, you should obtain a figure, displaying the panorama images (with and without border artifacts) as follows:

Figure 6.3: Creating panorama image with opencv-python

Video stitching

A straightforward approach to video stitching is to stitch corresponding frames from the input videos sequentially. This approach assumes that the input videos:

- Have the same number of **Frames Per Second** (**FPS**).
- Have identical durations, i.e., the same number of frames.

Stitching two videos can be simply done by stitching individual frames from the videos, in a synchronized manner, with the assumption that the videos have the same FPS and length. The next code snippet demonstrates a basic video stitching pipeline using **opencv-python** and **imageio**, with the following steps:

1. **Ensure frame rate consistency**: Assert that the videos have same FPS. Read the left and right video frames sequentially with **imageio.get_reader()**.

2. **Read and resize frames**: Resize the left and right video frames to same size for consistency into a panoramic view.

3. **Stitch frames**: Use **Stitcher.stitch()** method to align and blend each pair of frames.

4. **Append stitched frames**: Append the output frame to the output video (opened with **imageio.get_writer()** function, using the same FPS as the input videos), if stitching is successful.

5. **Save final output**: After all frames are processed, close the writer and save the stitched video to disk.

Now refer to the next code snippet:

```python
import numpy as np
import datetime
import imutils
import time
import cv2
import imageio

stitcher = cv2.Stitcher_create()
total = 0

reader1 = imageio.get_reader('images/vid3.mp4')
reader2 = imageio.get_reader('images/vid4.mp4')
fps1 = reader1.get_meta_data()['fps']
fps2 = reader2.get_meta_data()['fps']

assert(fps1 == fps2)

writer = imageio.get_writer('video_stitched.mp4', fps = fps1)

for i, (left, right) in enumerate(zip(reader1, reader2)):
    # resize the frames
    left = imutils.resize(left, width=400)
    right = imutils.resize(right, width=400)
        # stitch the frames together to form the panorama
    (status, result) = stitcher.stitch([left, right])

    if status: continue

    # no homograpy could be computed
    if result is None:
        print("[INFO] homography could not be computed")
        break

    writer.append_data(cv2.resize(result, (800, 600)))

    plt.figure(figsize=(20,8))
    plt.subplots_adjust(0,0,1,0.95,0.05,0.05)
    plt.subplot(131), plt.imshow(left, aspect='auto')
    plt.axis('off')
    plt.title('Left Frame', size=20)
```

```
    plt.subplot(132), plt.imshow(right, aspect='auto')
    plt.axis('off'), plt.title('Right Frame', size=20)
    plt.subplot(133), plt.imshow(result, aspect='auto')
    plt.axis('off'), plt.title('Stitched Frame', size=20)
    plt.savefig('out_{:03d}.png'.format(i))
    plt.close()
writer.close()
```

If you run the preceding code snippet, you should obtain a figure as follows:

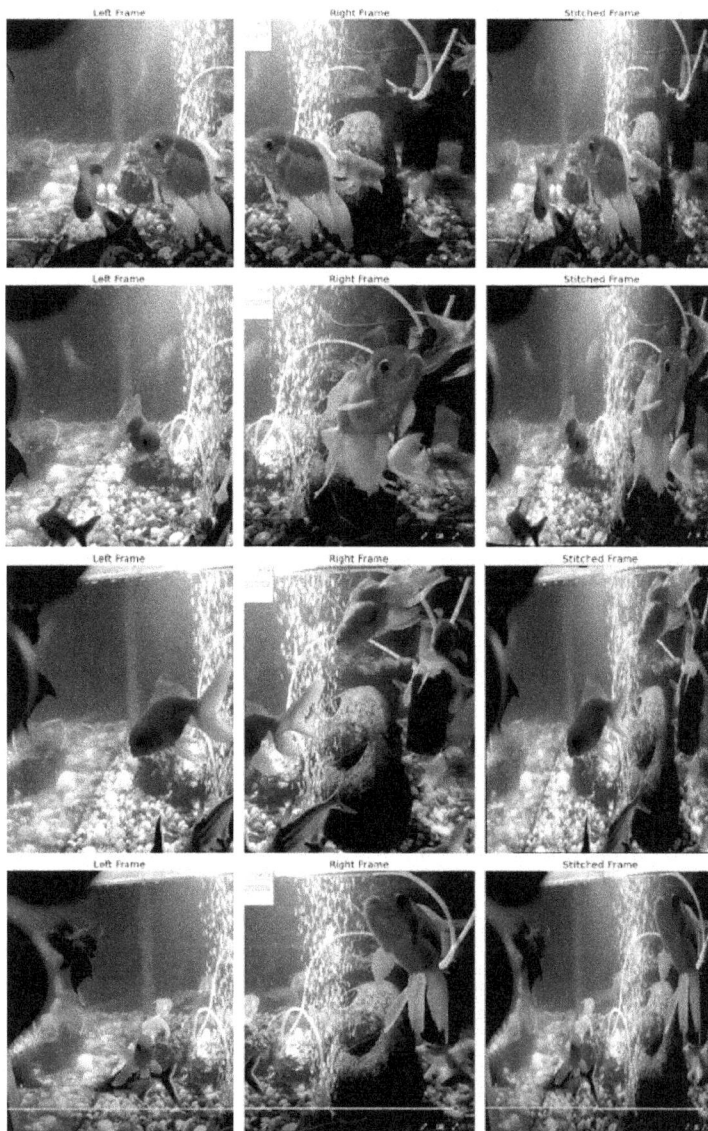

Figure 6.4: *Stitching video frames with opencv-python*

For advanced video stitching, consider:

- **Temporal consistency**: Apply smoothing or filtering techniques to avoid flickering or jitter between stitched frames over time.

- **Global motion estimation**: Track camera or scene motion across frames to maintain alignment continuity.

- **Multi-camera synchronization**: Handle slight desynchronization in multi-camera systems by aligning frames using timestamps or motion cues.

- **Exposure compensation over time**: Adjust for brightness/lighting variations that occur across the video duration.

- **Stitching failure handling**: Add fallback mechanisms (e.g., previous frame reuse or interpolation) when stitching fails temporarily.

The aforementioned points are specifically focused on ensuring smooth, coherent, and robust **video stitching** output over time.

NMF for extracting face features with Nimfa

NMF is a widely used unsupervised learning technique that decomposes (factorizes) a non-negative matrix (V) into two lower-rank non-negative matrices (W and H). This decomposition reveals latent structures in the data and is widely used in image analysis, especially face recognition. The key idea is that face images can be represented as additive combinations of sparse basis features.

Refer to the following figure for a mathematical definition of **NMF**:

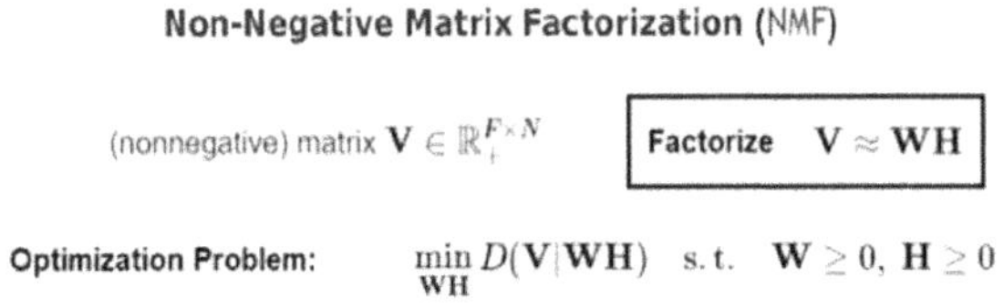

Non-Negative Matrix Factorization (NMF)

(nonnegative) matrix $\mathbf{V} \in \mathbb{R}_{+}^{F \times N}$ | Factorize $\mathbf{V} \approx \mathbf{WH}$ |

Optimization Problem: $\min_{\mathbf{WH}} D(\mathbf{V}|\mathbf{WH})$ s.t. $\mathbf{W} \geq 0,\ \mathbf{H} \geq 0$

Figure 6.5: Non-negative matrix factorization

The goal is to minimize the reconstruction error, typically measured using the **Frobenius norm**:

$$\min_{W,H} \|V - WH\|_F^2, \text{ so that } W, H \geq 0$$

This non-negativity constraint leads to a part-based, additive representation of the data, making it particularly useful for facial feature extraction.

The steps for NMF-based face feature extraction are as follows:

1. **Data preparation**: Collect a set of face images and represent each image as a matrix of pixels. The image matrix should be non-negative, and the dimensionality of the matrix should be the same for all images.

2. **Data normalization**: Standardize (normalize) the image data to have zero mean and unit variance. This step ensures that the NMF algorithm converges faster and produces better results.

3. **Component selection**: The number of components (or features) to extract is an important hyperparameter to choose in NMF. You can use techniques such as the elbow method or cross-validation to determine the optimal number of components.

4. **Applying NMF**: Apply NMF to the normalized image matrix to factorize it into two non-negative matrices

   i.   *W*: basis matrix, containing the feature vectors (part-based features)

   ii. *H*: coefficient matrix (weights for each basis vector), that represent each image as a linear combination of the features.

5. **Feature selection**: Identify the most significant (informative) basis vectors (features) in *W* using sparsity or thresholding to discard noisy or uninformative features.

6. **Feature extraction**: Extract the features from the original image matrix by multiplying it with the selected feature vectors from the matrix *W*.

7. **Final normalization**: Normalize the feature vectors to have zero mean and unit variance for downstream tasks.

The extracted features can be used for face recognition tasks, such as classification or clustering. Overall, NMF can be a powerful technique for face feature extraction.

Now, let us use the python library **nimfa**'s implementation of **NMF**, to extract features from the faces from the **CBCL** face database. Nimfa includes implementations of several factorization methods, initialization approaches, and quality scoring. Both dense and sparse matrix representation are supported. Let us walk through the code step by step:

1. Start by importing the required packages and modules:

```
from os.path import dirname, abspath
from os.path import join
from warnings import warn

import numpy as np
import nimfa
from matplotlib.pyplot import savefig, imshow, set_cmap, show, axis, \
                              figure, subplot
from PIL.Image import open, fromarray, new
from PIL.ImageOps import expand
```

2. Read face images from the **MIT-CBCL** database (download from the following link: **http://www.ai.mit.edu/courses/6.899/lectures/faces.tar.gz** and unzip); each face is a grayscale image of size 19×19.

3. Create a data matrix *V* by stacking 2429 flattened images along the columns. The matrix's shape is 361 (pixels) x 2429 (faces).

```
# print("Reading CBCL faces database")
dir = join('faces', 'train', 'face')
V = np.zeros((19 * 19, 2429))
for image in range(2429):
    im = open(join(dir, "face0%s.pgm" % str(image + 1).zfill(4)))
    V[:, image] = np.asarray(im).flatten()
```

Normalize the matrix , using the next code snippet.
```
# print("Data preprocessing")
V = (V - V.mean()) / np.sqrt(np.multiply(V, V).mean())
V = np.maximum(np.minimum((V + 0.25) * 0.25, 1), 0)
V.shape
#(361, 2429)
```

4. Use the following code snippet to visualize 225 randomly chosen faces from the matrix *V*:

```
indices = np.random.choice(range(2429), 225)
figure(figsize=(20,20))
for i in range(225):
    subplot(15,15,i+1)
    imshow(np.reshape(V[:,i],(19,19)), cmap='gray')
    axis('off')
show()
```

If you run the preceding code snippet, you should obtain a figure as follows:

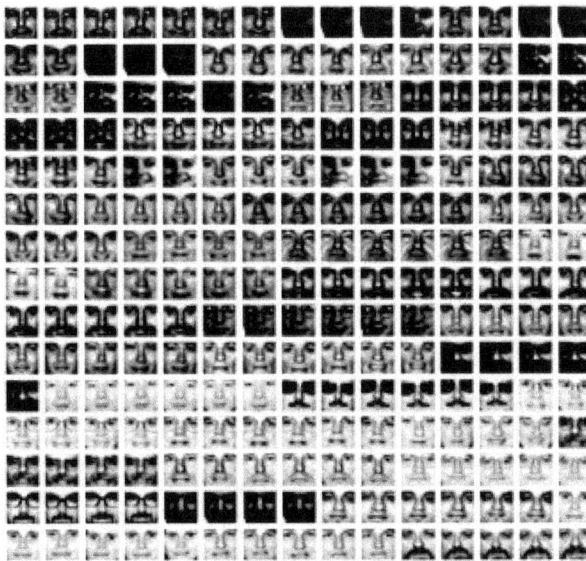

Figure 6.6: Input image samples from CBCL face dataset

5. Define the function **factorize()** that accepts a data matrix *V* as input argument and returns *basis* and *mixture* matrices of the fitted factorization model, using the **nimfa.Lsnmf()** function which implements the **alternating non-negative**

least squares matrix factorization using projected gradient (bound constrained optimization) method for each subproblem (**LSNMF**). It converges faster than the popular multiplicative update approach.

6. Compute 49 basis vectors (pass **rank =49** as argument of the function **nimfa. Lsnmf()**), experiment with different values of this parameter and observe the impact on the basis vector returned.

7. Invoke the function **factorize()** on the **CBCL** faces data matrix V to get the basis faces *W*, using the next code snippet:

```python
def factorize(V):
    lsnmf = nimfa.Lsnmf(V, seed="random_vcol", rank=49, \
                        max_iter=50, sub_iter=10, inner_sub_iter=10, \
                        beta=0.1, min_residuals=1e-8)
    print("Algorithm: %s\nInitialization: %s\nRank: %d" % \
                                (lsnmf, lsnmf.seed, lsnmf.rank))
    fit = lsnmf()
    sparse_w, sparse_h = fit.fit.sparseness()
    print("""Stats:
            - iterations: %d
            - final projected gradients norm: %5.3f
            - Euclidean distance: %5.3f
            - Sparseness basis: %5.3f, mixture: %5.3f""" %
    (fit.fit.n_iter,
    fit.distance(),
    fit.distance(metric='euclidean'),
    sparse_w,
    sparse_h))

    return fit.basis(), fit.coef()

W, _ = factorize(V)
W.shape
# (361, 49)
# Algorithm: lsnmf
# Initialization: random_vcol
# Rank: 49
# Stats:
#               - iterations: 50
#               - final projected gradients norm: 2.157
#               - Euclidean distance: 365.337
#               - Sparseness basis: 0.708, mixture: 0.467
blank = new("L", (133 + 6, 133 + 6))
for i in range(7):
    for j in range(7):
        basis = np.array(W[:, 7 * i + j])[:, 0].reshape((19, 19))
```

8. Plot the basis vectors. As can be seen from the next *Figure 6.7*, the basis images are sparse (representing parts of faces), that is, **NMF** computes part-phased features.

```
            basis = basis / np.max(basis) * 255
            basis = 255 - basis
            ima = fromarray(basis)
            ima = ima.rotate(180)
            expand(ima, border=1, fill='black')
            blank.paste(ima.copy(), (j * 19 + j, i * 19 + i))
figure(figsize=(7,7))
set_cmap('gray'), imshow(blank),axis('off')
show()
```

If you run the preceding code snippet, you should obtain a figure as follows:

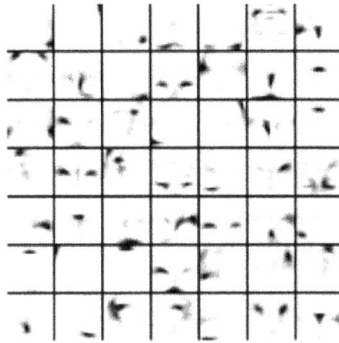

Figure 6.7: Sparse basis features obtained with NMF

Face recognition using LBPH with opencv-python

Face recognition is a biometric technology that identifies (or verifies) individuals by analyzing and comparing facial features from images or video. It works by detecting a face, aligning it, extracting unique features, and matching these features to a database of known faces. It is widely used in security, authentication, and surveillance applications. In this section we will explore how to use the **local binary patterns histogram** (**LPPH**) algorithm to implement a basic face recognition system. The process begins with extracting **local binary pattern** (**LBP**) features from face images by following these steps:

1. **Dividing a face into regions**: The face image is first divided into a grid of cells, for example, an 8x8 grid resulting in $R = 64$ regions. Each region captures local texture information, which is crucial for recognizing key facial features such as the eyes, nose, and mouth.

2. **Computing LBP histograms**: For each cell, a LBP histogram is computed. LBP encodes pixel-level texture by comparing each pixel with its neighbors, producing a binary pattern. The histograms from all the cells are then combined into a single feature vector, with spatial advanced features, as shown in the following figure:

A histogram formula of the LBP image

$$H_{i,j} = \sum_{x,y} I\left\{f_l(x,y) = i\right\} I\left\{(x,y) \in R_j\right\}$$

$$i = 0, \ldots, n-1$$
$$j = 0, \ldots, m-1$$

n: *number of different labels produced by the LBP operator*
m: *number of sub-regions*

$$I\{A\} = \begin{cases} 1, & A \text{ is true} \\ 0, & A \text{ is false} \end{cases}$$

binary indicator function

Figure 6.8: *Computing LBP histogram for a grayscale image*

3. **Spatial information encoding**: Although individual histograms discard spatial relationships, combining histograms from different cells retains some level of spatial encoding. This approach helps distinguish between various facial features by capturing their relative positions within the face.

   a. **Weighted histograms**: To enhance discriminative power, the histograms from different regions of the face are weighted differently:

      i. White regions (for example, eyes) are given a weight of 4x.

      ii. Light gray regions (for example, mouth and ears) are weighted 2x.

      iii. Dark gray regions (for example, cheeks and forehead) are weighted 1x.

      iv. Black regions (for example, nose and outer cheeks) are ignored, with a weight of 0x.

These weighted histograms are then concatenated to form the final feature vector. It provides higher discriminative power to more distinguishing features of the face, as shown in the following figure:

The original face image *(left)* followed by the weighting scheme for the **8x8** cells *(right)*

Figure 6.9: *Weighting scheme for LBPH*

Face recognition

To perform face recognition, the following steps are needed to be followed:

1. **Input and feature extraction**: When a new face is presented, LBP features are extracted following the same procedure used during training. The resulting histogram is weighted and concatenated just like the training data.

2. **Nearest neighbor classification**: The system compares the extracted histogram with those in the training set using the **k-NN** algorithm (typically with $k = 1$, to find the best match). The **chi-squared (χ^2) distance** is commonly used as the similarity metric, but other distance measures can be considered, too, as shown in the following figure:

Several possible dissimilarity measures

Histogram intersection: $D(\mathbf{S}, \mathbf{M}) = \sum_i \min(S_i, M_i)$

Log-likelihood statistic: $L(\mathbf{S}, \mathbf{M}) = -\sum_i S_i \log M_i$

Chi square statistic (χ^2): $\chi^2(\mathbf{S}, \mathbf{M}) = \sum_i \frac{(S_i - M_i)^2}{S_i + M_i}$

Euclidean distance: $d(\mathbf{S}, \mathbf{M}) = \sqrt{\sum_{i=1}^{n}(S_i - M_i)^2}$

S and **M** are two **LBP** histograms

Figure 6.10: Dissimilarity measures for LBPH-based face recognition

3. **Classification**: The system identifies the face by selecting the training face with the smallest χ^2 distance (or some other chosen metric). The label associated with the closest match is returned as the final classification.

Adaptability

One advantage of the **LBPH** method is that it can be updated incrementally. As new faces are added to the dataset, the model does not need to be retrained from scratch, unlike other methods such as **eigenfaces**. This makes LBPH a flexible and scalable solution for face recognition.

Let us implement a face recognition system with LBPH features using Python. We shall use **LFW** dataset from **scikit-learn**'s **datasets** module here. Start by importing the required libraries, modules and functions, as follows:

```
import cv2,os
import numpy as np
from PIL import Image
import pickle, time
import matplotlib.pylab as plt
from sklearn.datasets import fetch_lfw_people
from sklearn.model_selection import train_test_split
from sklearn.metrics import classification_report, confusion_matrix
```

Now follow the steps listed as follows:

1. Load the **LFW** dataset with the function **fetch_lfw_people()** from **sklearn. datasets**. Let us ensure that the extracted dataset will only retain faces of people that have at least **min_faces_per_person=70** different images.

2. The extracted face dataset (to be accessed by **lfw_people.data**) contains 1288 faces each of them of size 50 × 37, belonging to 7 different persons (check **lfw_people. target_names** and number of unique ids in **lfw_people.target**). We want to associate a face with an id, that is, the label we want to predict is the **id** of the person given his face.

3. Split the dataset randomly into *training* and *test* set with the function **train_test_ split()** from **sklearn.model_selection**, with 25% data in the *test* set (specified by the argument **test_size=0.25**), as done in the following code snippet:

```
lfw_people = fetch_lfw_people(min_faces_per_person=70, resize=0.4)

n_samples, h, w = lfw_people.images.shape

X = lfw_people.data
n_features = X.shape[1]
print(X.shape, h, w)
#   (1288, 1850) 50 37
y = lfw_people.target
print(np.unique(y))
# [0 1 2 3 4 5 6]

target_names = lfw_people.target_names
n_classes = target_names.shape[0]
print(target_names)
# ['Ariel Sharon' 'Colin Powell' 'Donald Rumsfeld' 'George W Bush'
#   'Gerhard Schroeder' 'Hugo Chavez' 'Tony Blair']
# print("Total dataset size:")
print("n_samples: %d" % n_samples)
# n_samples: 1288
print("n_features: %d" % n_features)
# n_features: 1850
print("n_classes: %d" % n_classes)
# n_classes: 7
```

```
X_train, X_test, y_train, y_test = train_test_split( \
                        X, y, test_size=0.25, random_state=42)

faces, ids = [], []
for i in range(X_train.shape[0]):
    faces.append(np.reshape(X_train[i,...], (h,w)))
    ids.append(y_train[i])
ids = np.array(ids)
```

4. With the *training* and *test* datasets prepared, we can now create an instance of the LBPH face recognizer using the function **cv2.face.LBPHFaceRecognizer_ create()**. This function accepts several parameters, which we will use with their default values:

    a. **radius**: Defines the radius for constructing the circular local binary pattern. A larger radius results in a smoother image while capturing more spatial information. The default value is 1.

    b. **neighbors**: Specifies the number of sample points used to build the circular local binary pattern. The default is 8, which strikes a balance between computational cost and accuracy. Increasing the number of neighbours improves detail but also increases computational requirements.

    c. **grid_x and grid_y**: These determine the number of cells in the horizontal and vertical directions, respectively. The default value of 8 is commonly used in studies. More cells produce a finer grid and result in a higher-dimensional feature vector.

    d. **threshold**: This value sets the limit for face prediction. If the distance to the nearest neighbour exceeds the threshold, the recognizer returns -1, indicating no match.

    Note: It is important to note that circular local binary pattern algorithm requires the input images to be in grayscale for both training and prediction.

5. Let us use the **train()** method to train the model using the following code snippet, which accepts the faces and the corresponding ids:

```
recognizer = cv2.face.LBPHFaceRecognizer_create()
recognizer.train(faces, ids)
recognizer.save('recognizer_training.yml')
```

6. Now, let us use the model's **predict()** method to recognize faces from the unseen **test** dataset, using the next code snippet:

```
# print("Predicting people's names on the test set")
y_pred = []
for i in range(X_test.shape[0]):
    pred = recognizer.predict(X_test[i,...].reshape((h,w)))
    y_pred.append(pred[0])
```

7. Display the **classification report** and the **confusion matrix** to evaluate how the face recognition worked on the test dataset:

```
print(classification_report(y_test, y_pred, target_names=target_names))
# Predicting people's names on the test set
#                    precision    recall  f1-score   support
#
#      Ariel Sharon       0.77      0.77      0.77        13
#      Colin Powell       0.98      0.90      0.94        60
#   Donald Rumsfeld       0.82      0.67      0.73        27
#     George W Bush       0.92      0.96      0.94       146
# Gerhard Schroeder       0.68      0.76      0.72        25
#       Hugo Chavez       0.82      0.60      0.69        15
#        Tony Blair       0.80      0.89      0.84        36
#
#          accuracy                           0.88       322
#         macro avg       0.83      0.79      0.80       322
#      weighted avg       0.88      0.88      0.87       322

print(confusion_matrix(y_test, y_pred, labels=range(n_classes)))
# [[ 10   0   1   1   0   1   0]
#  [  1  54   1   0   3   1   0]
#  [  1   0  18   6   1   0   1]
#  [  0   1   1 140   1   0   3]
#  [  0   0   1   1  19   0   4]
#  [  1   0   0   3   2   9   0]
#  [  0   0   0   2   2   0  32]]
```

8. Plot 12 faces from the **test** dataset, their *ground-truth* labels and the *predictions* by the face **recognizer**, using the function **plot_gallery()**, using the following code snippet:

```
def plot_gallery(images, titles, h, w, n_row=3, n_col=4):
    plt.figure(figsize=(1.8 * n_col, 2.4 * n_row))
    plt.subplots_adjust(bottom=0, left=.01, right=.99, \
                        top=.90, hspace=.35)
    for i in range(n_row * n_col):
        plt.subplot(n_row, n_col, i + 1)
        plt.imshow(images[i].reshape((h, w)), cmap=plt.cm.gray)
        plt.title(titles[i], size=12)
        plt.xticks(())
        plt.yticks(())
```

```
def title(y_pred, y_test, target_names, i):
    pred_name = target_names[y_pred[i]].rsplit(' ', 1)[-1]
    true_name = target_names[y_test[i]].rsplit(' ', 1)[-1]
    return 'predicted: %s\ntrue:      %s' % (pred_name, true_name)

prediction_titles = [title(y_pred, y_test, target_names, i) \
                                    for i in range(len(y_pred))]

plot_gallery(X_test, prediction_titles, h, w)
```

If you run the preceding code snippet, you should obtain a figure as follows:

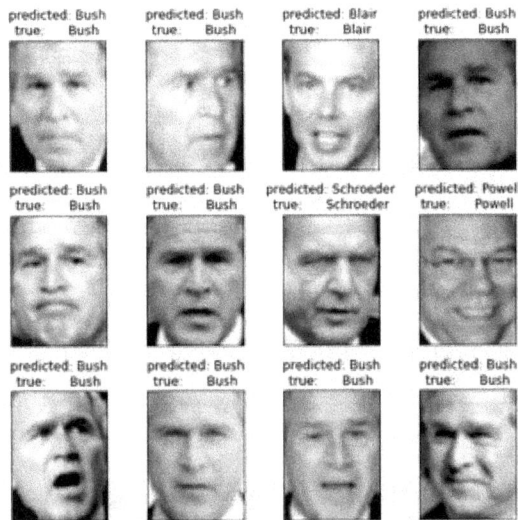

Figure 6.11: *Face recognition with LBPH*

As can be seen from the preceding figure, the face recognizer achieved a decent F_1 score on the **test** dataset, and the faces we have shown in *Figure 6.11* have been correctly recognized.

Finally, let us use an image from outside the dataset where two of the subjects are present simultaneously and use the recognizer to recognize the faces, using the next code snippet.

Before we **recognize** the face, we need to be able to **detect** the faces in the images first. Let us use the popular pretrained Haar feature-based cascade classifier from **opencv-python** (namely, **cv2.CascadeClassifier()**) for frontal face detection. Follow these steps:

1. Detect faces using **detector.detectMultiScale()** function, which detects objects of different sizes in the input image. The detected objects are returned as a list of rectangles:

   a. The parameter **scaleFactor=1.2** specifies how much the image size is reduced at each image scale.

b. The parameter `minNeighbors=5` specifies how many neighbors each candidate rectangle should have to retain it.

2. Once a face is detected, the **recognizer** is used to recognize the face, as shown in the next code snippet:

```python
detector = cv2.CascadeClassifier( \
                    "models/haarcascade_frontalface_default.xml")
im = cv2.imread('images/leaders.jpg')
img = cv2.cvtColor(im, cv2.COLOR_BGR2GRAY)
print(im.shape)
# (190, 265, 3)
all_faces = detector.detectMultiScale(img, scaleFactor=1.2, \
                                      minNeighbors=5)
for (x,y,w,h) in all_faces:
    cv2.rectangle(im,(x,y),(x+w,y+h),(225,0,0),2)
    id, conf = recognizer.predict(img[y:y+h,x:x+w])
    cv2.putText(im,str(target_names[id].rsplit(' ', 1)[-1]), \
                (x,y+h//5), cv2.FONT_HERSHEY_SIMPLEX, \
                0.5, (0, 255, 0), 1, cv2.LINE_AA) # Draw the text
plt.figure(figsize=(10,10))
plt.gray()
plt.imshow(cv2.cvtColor(im, cv2.COLOR_BGR2RGB)), plt.axis('off')
plt.show()
```

If you run the preceding code snippet, you should obtain a figure as follows:

***Figure 6.12**: Face detection/recognition with Haar Cascade/LBPH*

As can be seen from the preceding figure, the faces are recognized correctly by the **recognizer**.

Face feature extraction and recognition using Gabor filter banks

In this section, we shall learn how to use the Gabor filter banks extracted from face images for face recognition. As before, there are two steps: feature extraction and recognition.

Feature extraction with Gabor filter bank

Gabor filters are widely used for detecting edges and texture variations in an image. When a Gabor filter is applied to a specific feature, it produces a prominent response at the spatial location of that feature. This is particularly useful when working with convolution kernels in the spatial domain. Each Gabor filter consists of two components: a real part and an imaginary part, which represent orthogonal orientations. These components can be combined into a complex number or used separately, depending on the specific application, to capture different directional information, as illustrated in the following figure:

The Gabor Filter

Complex

$$g(x, y; \lambda, \theta, \psi, \sigma, \gamma) = \exp\left(-\frac{x'^2 + \gamma^2 y'^2}{2\sigma^2}\right) \exp\left(i\left(2\pi\frac{x'}{\lambda} + \psi\right)\right)$$

Real

$$g(x, y; \lambda, \theta, \psi, \sigma, \gamma) = \exp\left(-\frac{x'^2 + \gamma^2 y'^2}{2\sigma^2}\right) \cos\left(2\pi\frac{x'}{\lambda} + \psi\right)$$

Imaginary

$$g(x, y; \lambda, \theta, \psi, \sigma, \gamma) = \exp\left(-\frac{x'^2 + \gamma^2 y'^2}{2\sigma^2}\right) \sin\left(2\pi\frac{x'}{\lambda} + \psi\right)$$

where $x' = x\cos\theta + y\sin\theta$ and $y' = -x\sin\theta + y\cos\theta$.

Figure 6.13: Computing the Gabor kernels

Here, λ is the wavelength $= \frac{1}{f}$, where f is the frequency) of the sinusoidal wave, θ is the orientation, σ is the standard deviation of the Gaussian envelope, γ is the spatial aspect ratio, and φ is the phase offset.

The Gabor filter bank is created by varying the parameters λ and θ to capture different scales and orientations. This allows the filters to respond to various features in the image, such as edges and textures at different angles and frequencies. The Gabor filter's frequency and orientation characteristics closely resemble those of the human visual system.

With scikit-image

Let us now explore how to compute **Gabor filter banks** using the **filters** module from the library **scikit-image**. Gabor filters are computed at 5 scales and 8 orientations, which convolve each filter with the image to get 40 features (8 × 5 = 40); the function **build_filters()** defined in the following code snippet computes the filter bank using the function **skimage.filters.gabor_kernel()** (which expects frequency and orientation as parameters) and then we visualize the filters.

The different representations (response matrices) of the same image generate a feature vector. Hence, a feature vector may consist of mean/phase amplitude, local energy or orientation corresponding to maximum energy. Now, refer to the next code snippet:

```
from skimage.filters import gabor_kernel
from scipy.signal import convolve2d
# 5 scales and 8 orientations
def build_filters():
    freqs = []
     filters = []
     for freq in np.arange(0.1,0.6,0.12):
         for theta in np.arange(0, np.pi, np.pi / 8):
             kern = np.real(gabor_kernel(freq, theta=theta))
             filters.append(kern)
     return filters

filters = build_filters()

i = 1
plt.figure(figsize=(15,10))
plt.subplots_adjust(0,0,1,1,0.05,0.05)
for f in filters:
    plt.subplot(5,8,i), plt.imshow(f), plt.axis('off')
    i += 1
plt.show()
```

If you run the preceding code snippet, you should obtain a figure as follows, displaying the Gabor filter bank computed:

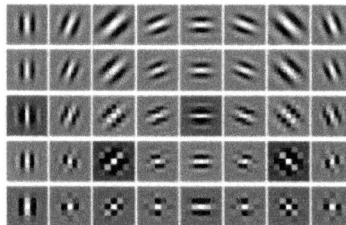

Figure 6.14: *Gabor kernels with scikit-image*

With opencv-python

Now, let us compute the Gabor filter bank again, but this time using the function **cv2.getGaborKernel()**. The next code snippet defines a function **build_filters()**, which returns a filter bank and subsequently defines another function **process()** that uses **cv2.filter2D()** to convolve the filters obtained with input *Lena* image and compute the maximum response of the filters:

```
import numpy as np
import cv2
import sys
def build_filters():
    filters = []
    ksize = 31
```

```
    for theta in np.arange(0, np.pi, np.pi / 16):
        kern = cv2.getGaborKernel((ksize, ksize), 4.0, theta, \
                                  10.0, 0.5, 0, ktype=cv2.CV_32F)
        kern /= 1.5*kern.sum()
        filters.append(kern)
    return filters
def process(img, filters):
    accum = np.zeros_like(img)
    for kern in filters:
        fimg = cv2.filter2D(img, cv2.CV_8UC3, kern)
        np.maximum(accum, fimg, accum)
    return accum
img_fn = 'images/lena.jpg'
img = cv2.imread(img_fn)
filters = build_filters()

res = process(img, filters)
plt.imshow(cv2.cvtColor(res, cv2.COLOR_BGR2RGB))
plt.show()
```

If you run the preceding code snippet, you should obtain a figure as follows:

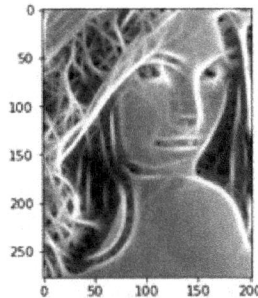

Figure 6.15: *Applying Gabor filter banks to Lena image*

Face recognition with Gabor features with opencv-python and scikit-learn

Once we know how to extract Gabor features from face images using the filter banks, we are ready to use it for face recognition. Let us use the **ORL** database of faces this time (download from the following link: **https://www.kaggle.com/datasets/tavarez/the-orl-database-for-training-and-testing** and extract the faces inside the **images/orl** folder), it contains 10 different images for each of 40 distinct subjects (the pictures were captured at different points in time, varying the lighting, facial expressions and facial details.

Let us start our implementation by importing the required libraries and reading the face images. Note that we shall use only 90 faces from the downloaded dataset belonging to first 9 persons.

```
import matplotlib.pyplot as plt
import numpy as np
import cv2
from glob import glob

faces = sorted(glob('images/orl/*_[1-9].jpg'))
len(faces)
# 90
```

Now follow the next steps to extract the Gabor features from the face images and create a dataset ready to be used by a supervised ML classification model:

1. Prepare filter bank kernels using the function **cv2.getGaborKernel()**, as before.

2. The images are processed using the real components of multiple Gabor filter kernels through the **cv2.filter2D()** function. The mean and variance of the filtered outputs are extracted as features, which are then used for classification, with the least squares error method employed for simplicity. Hence, there are 2 features generated for each of the 40 kernels, with a total of 80 features per face image, resulting in the dataset of size 90×80 (each column represents a feature).

3. The id/label of a person can be found from the last part of the file name, as shown in the next code snippet:

```
ksize = 5 #9
kernels = []   # Create empty list to hold all kernels to be
               # generated in a loop
sigma, gamma = 1, 0.5
for freq in np.arange(0.1,0.6,0.12):
    for theta in np.arange(0, np.pi, np.pi / 8):
        kernel = cv2.getGaborKernel((ksize, ksize), sigma, theta, \
                    1/freq, gamma, 0, ktype=cv2.CV_32F)
        kernels.append(kernel)
X = np.empty((0,2*len(kernels)))

y = []
for imfile in faces:
    im = cv2.imread(imfile, 0)
    label = int(imfile.split('_')[-1][0])
    features = []
    for kernel in kernels:
        # Now filter the image and add values to a new column
        fim = cv2.filter2D(im, cv2.CV_8UC3, kernel)
        features.append(np.abs(fim).mean())
        features.append(np.sum(fim**2)) #fim.var()
    X = np.append(X, np.array([features]), axis=0)
    y.append(label)
```

4. Plot the filters from the filter bank computed:

```
X.shape, len(y)
#((90, 80), 90)
plt.figure(figsize=(8,5))
plt.gray()
for i in range(len(kernels)):
    plt.subplot(5,8,i+1), plt.imshow(kernels[i]), plt.axis('off')
plt.show()
```

If you run the preceding code snippet, you should obtain a figure as follows:

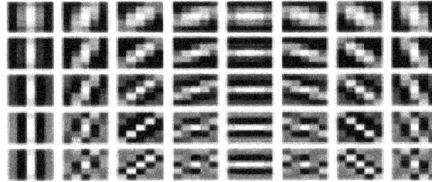

Figure 6.16: Gabor filter bank with opencv-python

5. Let us visualize how the Gabor features look like for a single face image, using the following code snippet:

```
plt.figure(figsize=(15,10))
im = cv2.imread(faces[0], 0)
label = int(imfile.split('_')[-1][0])
i = 0
plt.subplots_adjust(0,0,1,0.95,0.025,0.025)
for kernel in kernels:
    #Now filter the image and add values to a new column
    fim = cv2.filter2D(im, cv2.CV_8UC3, kernel)
    plt.subplot(5,8,i+1), plt.imshow(fim), plt.axis('off')
    i += 1
plt.show()
```

If you run the preceding code snippet, you should obtain a figure as follows:

Figure 6.17: Applying Gabor filter bank on a face

6. Once the dataset is generated using (mean and variance of) Gabor features, we can use our regular *train-test* splitting of the dataset with the function **train_test_split()** from **scikit-learn**'s **model_selection** module.

With random forest ensemble classifier

First, let us train a random forest ensemble classifier on the training dataset using the **sklearn.ensemble.RandomForestClassifier()**. The follow the next steps:

1. Let us use the classifier (trained on the training split) to predict the **label** (id) of a face from the test dataset, using the following code snippet.

2. Evaluate the performance of the classifier on the unseen *test* dataset, using **accuracy** and confusion matrix.

```
from sklearn.model_selection import train_test_split
from sklearn.ensemble import RandomForestClassifier
from sklearn.metrics import plot_confusion_matrix
import warnings
warnings.filterwarnings('ignore')

X_train, X_test, y_train, y_test, indices_train, indices_test = \
    train_test_split(X, y, range(len(y)), test_size=0.25, random_state=1)
clf = RandomForestClassifier(max_depth=2, random_state=1)
clf.fit(X_train, y_train)
y_pred = clf.predict(X_test)
print('accuracy: {}'.format(sum(y_pred==y_test) / len(y_test)))
# accuracy: 0.8260869565217391
plot_confusion_matrix(clf, X_test, y_test)
plt.show()
```

The following figure shows the *confusion matrix* obtained (on the unseen *test* dataset) with the random forest classifier:

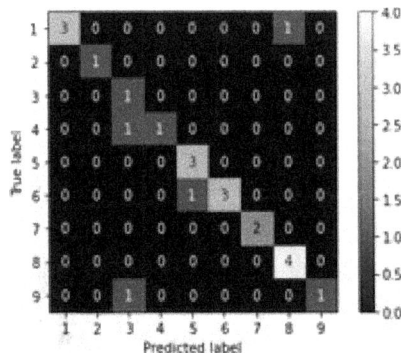

Figure 6.18: Confusion matrix with random forest classifier

As can be seen, we obtained 82.6% accuracy on the *test* dataset.

With 2-NN classifier

Now, let us use a different classifier, namely, a **2-nearest neighbors (2-NN) classifier** using the function **sklearn.neighbors.NearestNeighbors()**. Plot the test images, along with the *ground-truth* and the *predicted labels (ids)*, using the next code snippet:

```
from sklearn.neighbors import NearestNeighbors
neigh = NearestNeighbors(n_neighbors=2, radius=0.4)
neigh.fit(X_train)
nn_indices = neigh.kneighbors(X_test, 2, return_distance=False)
n = len(X_test)

plt.figure(figsize=(20,3))
plt.gray()
plt.subplots_adjust(0,0,1,0.95,0.05,0.05)
for i in range(n):
    im = cv2.imread(faces[indices_test[i]], 0)
    plt.subplot(2,n,i+1), plt.imshow(im), plt.axis('off')
    plt.title('True: {}'.format(y_test[i]), size=12)
    im = cv2.imread(faces[indices_train[nn_indices[i][0]]], 0)
    plt.subplot(2,n,i+n+1), plt.imshow(im), plt.axis('off')
    plt.title('NNbr: {}'.format(y[indices_train[nn_indices[i][0]]]), \
                                                            size=11)

plt.show()
```

If you run the preceding code snippet, you should obtain a figure as follows:

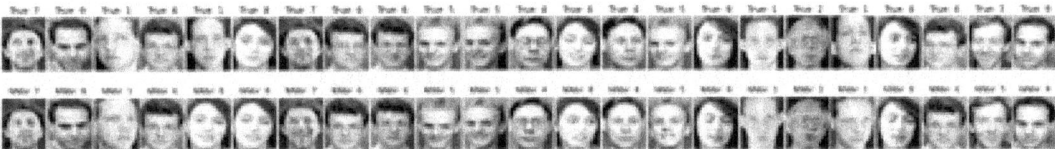

Figure 6.19: Ground-truth vs. predicted face label with 2-NN classifier

Pedestrian detection with HOG vs HAAR Cascade features with opencv-python

In this section, we shall explore how to use pretrained classifiers for people detection in an image using two different types of features extracted from the image, namely, HOG and HAAR.

Extracting HOG features

Histogram of Oriented Gradients (**HOG**) is a widely-used feature descriptor in computer vision and image processing, especially for object detection tasks. First introduced by *Navneet Dalal* and *Bill Triggs* for *pedestrian detection*, HOG has proven effective for identifying not only pedestrians but also other objects such as animals, faces, and text. It works by extracting gradient orientation histograms from an input image, which describe the local features of objects. The HOG descriptor can be computed using the following steps:

1. **Gradient calculation**: The gradient magnitudes and orientations are computed for each pixel in the image.

2. **Orientation binning**: The image is divided into small connected regions called cells, and for each cell, a histogram of gradient orientations is created.

3. **Block normalization**: Cells are grouped into larger blocks and the histograms are normalized within each block to account for variations in lighting and contrast.

Pedestrian detection with HOG NMS

To perform pedestrian detection using HOG-SVM, you first need to compute HOG descriptors, which capture gradient and edge information in localized regions of an image, making it ideal for detecting objects with distinct shapes, such as pedestrians. The HOG descriptors are extracted by sliding a fixed-size window (typically 64x128 pixels) across the image, and for multi-scale detection, this process is repeated at various scales of the image using a scale pyramid, where the image is progressively scaled down.

Classification with the SVM model

The HOG features are typically computed by sliding a fixed-size window, commonly 64x128 pixels, across the image. Since objects in the image may appear at different scales, the HOG computation is applied at multiple levels using a *scale pyramid*. The image is scaled down repeatedly, with a scaling factor between 1.05 and 1.2, until the window can no longer fit within the frame. For each window, the HOG features are extracted and passed to a binary **support vector machine** (**SVM**) classifier. The SVM, trained to distinguish between *pedestrians* and *non-pedestrians*, then predicts whether a window contains an object of interest. If a pedestrian is detected at any scale, the classifier returns a *bounding box* for that region.

The following figure shows a typical HOG object (pedestrian) detection workflow:

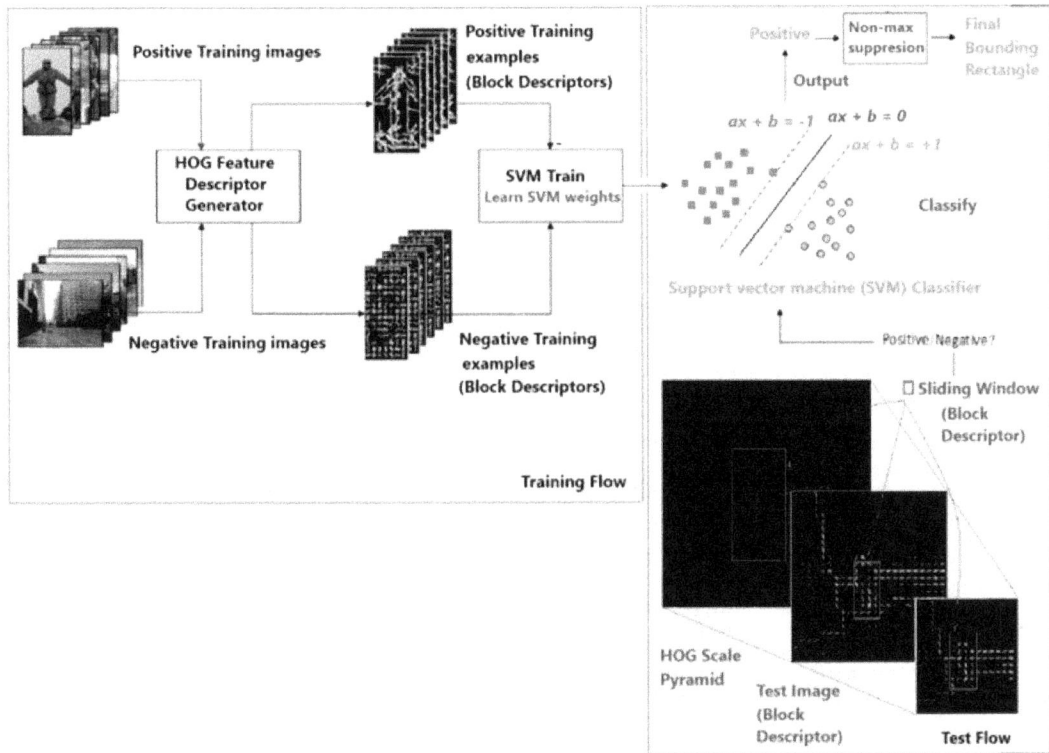

Figure 6.20: *Schematic for pedestrian detection with HOG-SVM classifier*

This method is more accurate than **Viola-Jones Haar-cascade** detection but comes with higher computational complexity due to the multi-scale analysis.

Computing Bounding-Boxes with HOG-SVM

In this section, we will explore how to use the **OpenCV** library in Python to detect pedestrians using **HOG-SVM**. The process involves computing HOG descriptors for each sliding window and using a pre-trained SVM classifier to predict the presence of a person within the image. The **detectMultiScale()** function in OpenCV simplifies this process by automatically handling multi-scale detection and applying **non-maximum suppression** (**NMS**) to eliminate redundant bounding boxes.

Let us start by importing the required libraries:

```
import numpy as np
import cv2
import matplotlib.pylab as plt
from imutils.object_detection import non_max_suppression
```

Follow the next steps, which explain the next python code snippet in details:

1. Create a **HOG** descriptor using default people (*pedestrian*) detector (with **cv2. HOGDescriptor()**).

2. Instantiate a pretrained **SVM** detector with the functions **cv2.HOGDescriptor_ getDefaultPeopleDetector()** and **setSVMDetector()**.

3. Given a pedestrian image, run detection on the image with the function **detectMultiScale()**, using a spatial stride (**winStride**) of 4 pixels (horizontal and vertical), a **scale** stride of 1.02, and zero grouping of rectangles (to demonstrate that **HOG** will detect at potentially multiple places in the *scale pyramid*; precisely it detects 69 bounding boxes as shown in the next figure, see the output of the next code snippet).

4. Draw bounding boxes on the image.

5. Next, use the function **non_max_suppression()** from **imutils.object_detection** module, in order to avoid detection of the same object at multiple times and scales. It will reduce the number of detections to 3.

6. You can also use **MeanShift** grouping to eliminate multiple detections of the same object (set the *boolean* argument **useMeanshiftGrouping=True** passed to the function **detectMultiScale()**).

```python
def draw_bounding_boxes(img, found_bounding_boxes, title):
    # copy the original image to draw bounding boxes on it for now,
    # as we'll use it again later
    img_with_raw_bboxes = img.copy()

    for (hx, hy, hw, hh) in found_bounding_boxes:
        cv2.rectangle(img_with_raw_bboxes, (hx, hy), \
                                    (hx + hw, hy + hh), (0, 0, 255), 2)
    img_with_raw_bboxes = cv2.cvtColor(img_with_raw_bboxes, \
                                    cv2.COLOR_BGR2RGB)
    plt.figure(figsize=(20, 12))
    plt.imshow(img_with_raw_bboxes, aspect='auto'), plt.axis('off')
    plt.title(title, size=20)
    plt.show()

img = cv2.imread("images/pedestrians.png")

hog = cv2.HOGDescriptor()
hog.setSVMDetector(cv2.HOGDescriptor_getDefaultPeopleDetector())

(found_bounding_boxes, weights) = hog.detectMultiScale(img, \
```

```
                  winStride=(4, 4), padding=(8, 8), scale=1.1, finalThreshold=0)
print(len(found_bounding_boxes)) # number of boundingboxes
# 69
draw_bounding_boxes(img, found_bounding_boxes, \
                        'Boundingboxes found by HOG-SVM without grouping')

(found_bounding_boxes, weights) = hog.detectMultiScale(img, \
          winStride=(4, 4), padding=(8, 8), scale=1.1, finalThreshold=0)
print(len(found_bounding_boxes)) # number of boundingboxes
# 69
found_bounding_boxes[:,2] = found_bounding_boxes[:,0] + \
                            found_bounding_boxes[:,2]
found_bounding_boxes[:,3] = found_bounding_boxes[:,1] + \
                            found_bounding_boxes[:,3]

found_bounding_boxes = non_max_suppression(found_bounding_boxes, \
                        probs = weights.ravel(), overlapThresh = 0.2)
found_bounding_boxes[:,2] = found_bounding_boxes[:,2] - \
                            found_bounding_boxes[:,0]
found_bounding_boxes[:,3] = found_bounding_boxes[:,3] - \
                            found_bounding_boxes[:,1]
print(len(found_bounding_boxes)) # number of boundingboxes
# 3

draw_bounding_boxes(img, found_bounding_boxes, \
            'Boundingboxes found by HOG-SVM after non-max suppression')

(found_bounding_boxes, weights) = hog.detectMultiScale(img, \
            winStride=(4, 4), padding=(8, 8), scale=1.01, \
            useMeanshiftGrouping=True)
print(len(found_bounding_boxes)) # number of boundingboxes
# 3
draw_bounding_boxes(img, found_bounding_boxes, \
            'Boundingboxes found by HOG-SVM with meanshift grouping')
```

If you run the preceding code snippet and draw bounding boxes on the extracted video frames after pedestrian detection, you should obtain figures like the following ones (results obtained without and with NMS suppression shown separately):

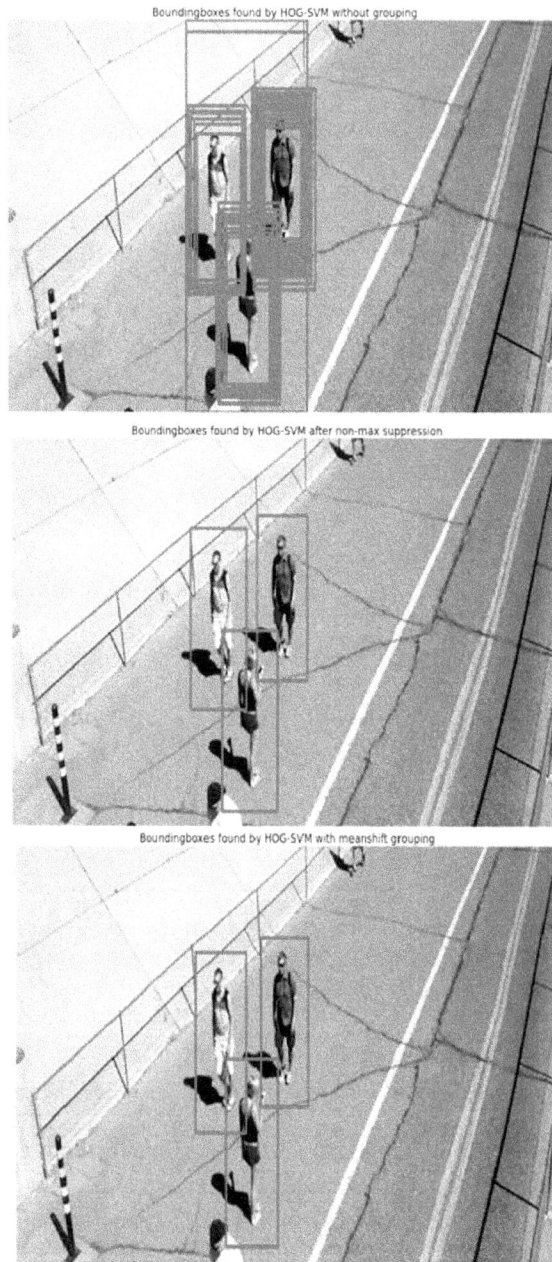

Figure 6.21: *HOG-SVM for pedestrian detection*

HAAR-like features for HAAR Cascade classifier

Haar-like features are effective in object detection, especially for tasks like object detection (for example, **face detection**, as demonstrated by the famous **Viola-Jones** algorithm).

These features operate by comparing the brightness of adjacent rectangular regions within an image, capturing key patterns such as edges, lines, and textures that are useful for distinguishing objects. To efficiently compute **Haar-like** features at various scales and locations, *integral* images are used, allowing for rapid calculation in constant time, which is a major advantage over other feature types.

Despite their speed, each Haar-like feature alone is weak, meaning it only provides limited classification accuracy. To accurately detect an object, such as a person, a large number of these features are generated across all possible positions and scales in the image. An **AdaBoost** *ensemble classifier* is then employed during training to sift through the vast number of features, selecting the most informative ones and combining them into a robust detection model. Once the model is trained, it uses these selected features to scan regions of an image, identifying objects like faces or other target items with high accuracy. This combination of fast feature computation and strong ensemble learning makes Haar-like features particularly powerful for real-time object detection tasks.

Computing Bounding Boxes with HAAR-Cascade classifier

Now, let us dive into the demonstration part. This time, first demonstrate the pedestrian detection task using a pretrained **HAAR-Cascade-AdaBoost** classifier:

1. Download the pre-trained model as an XML file from the following link: **https:// github.com/opencv/opencv/blob/master/data/haarcascades/haarcascade_ fullbody.xml**

2. Use the function **cv2.CascadeClassifier()** to perform the actual object detection and compare it with **HOG-SVM** detection, as shown in the next code snippet:

```
ped_cascade = cv2.CascadeClassifier('models/haarcascade_fullbody.xml')

img = cv2.imread("images/pedestrians.png")
gray = cv2.cvtColor(img, cv2.COLOR_BGR2GRAY)

peds = ped_cascade.detectMultiScale(gray, scaleFactor=1.01, minNbr=3)
print(len(peds)) # number of faces detected
# 3
img_haar = img.copy()
```

HAAR-cascade vs. HOG-SVM in pedestrian detection

Haar-cascade is faster but less accurate, while HOG-SVM offers better accuracy and robustness at the cost of higher computational demand.

Haar-cascade classifiers and HOG-SVM classifiers are both widely used for pedestrian detection, but they have distinct differences in performance and application. Haar-cascade classifiers are faster due to efficient feature computation using integral images, making them suitable for real-time detection tasks. However, they can struggle with accuracy, particularly in complex environments, and are sensitive to variations in lighting and pose.

In contrast, HOG-SVM classifiers provide higher accuracy by capturing detailed shape and texture information through gradient analysis. They are more robust to changes in lighting, pose, and background clutter, making them more reliable for pedestrian detection in complex scenes. However, HOG-SVM is computationally more intensive, leading to slower performance than Haar-cascade.

Now let us compare these two approaches using the next code snippet:

```python
(found_bounding_boxes, weights) = hog.detectMultiScale(img, \
                                    winStride=(4, 4), \
                                    padding=(8, 8), scale=1.01, \
                                    useMeanshiftGrouping=True)
print(len(found_bounding_boxes)) # number of bounding boxes
# 3
# copy original image to draw bounding boxes on it for now, as we'll
# use it again later
img_hog = img.copy()
for (hx, hy, hw, hh) in found_bounding_boxes:
    cv2.rectangle(img_hog, (hx, hy), (hx + hw, hy + hh), (0, 0, 255), 2)

for (x,y,w,h) in peds:
    img_haar = cv2.rectangle(img_haar,(x,y),(x+w,y+h),(0,0,255),2)

plt.figure(figsize=(15,7))
plt.subplots_adjust(0,0,1,0.95,0.05,0.05)
plt.subplot(121)
plt.imshow(cv2.cvtColor(img_haar, cv2.COLOR_BGR2RGB)), plt.axis('off')
plt.title('Pedestrian detection with HAAR-Cascade-AdaBoost', size=20)
plt.subplot(122)
plt.imshow(cv2.cvtColor(img_hog, cv2.COLOR_BGR2RGB)), plt.axis('off')
plt.title('Pedestrian detection with HOG-SVM-NMS', size=20)
plt.tight_layout()
plt.show()
```

If you run the preceding code snippet, you should obtain a figure like the following one, which shows pedestrian detection with HAAR-Cascade-AdaBoost vs HOG-SVM:

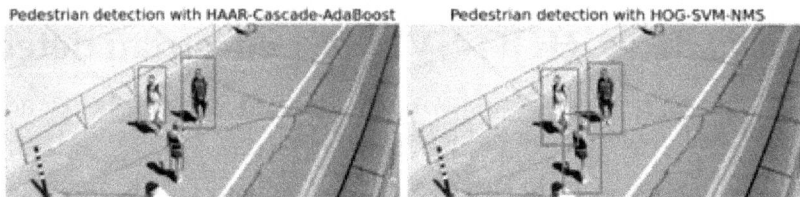

Figure 6.22: Pedestrian detection with Haar-Cascade vs. HOG-SVM

As can be seen from the preceding figure, both HAAR-Cascade-AdaBoost and HOG-SVM detected all persons in the pedestrian image. Try these person detectors on videos and compare the performances in terms of accuracy and time complexity.

Conclusion

This chapter continued to explore diverse techniques for feature extraction and their practical applications. It commenced with a detailed discussion on the creation of panoramas, including image stitching and video stitching (using OpenCV-Python), that demonstrates the practical applications of feature-based image alignment in producing seamless and immersive visual content. NMF is introduced as a tool for extracting face features, showcasing its utility in tasks related to facial image analysis. Face recognition techniques (with hand-crafted features) are covered extensively, employing LBPH features with OpenCV-Python. Additionally, the application of Gabor filter banks for face feature extraction and recognition further enriches the chapter, emphasizing the diversity of approaches available. The chapter concludes with a comparative analysis of pedestrian detection methods, pitting HOG against HAAR Cascade features with OpenCV-Python. The exploration of HOG NMS and the comparison of HAAR Cascade versus HOG SVM provide valuable insights into object detection strategies.

Key terms

Panorama, NMF, face recognition, LBPH, Gabor filter, HOG, HAAR Cascade, SVM.

Questions

1. **Feature extraction from deep neural nets**: The deep neural networks learn hierarchical representations, which allows them to capture both local and global features. Lower layers tend to focus on local details, while higher layers aggregate information to recognize more complex structures that may span the entire input.

   Use pretrained models (for example, torchvision models trained on **imagenet** dataset) to extract the deep features (*embeddings*) from the last layer prior to the classification layer. Use the following cats and dogs images to extract the deep features for each of them:

Figure 6.23: Cats and dogs input image for deep features instruction

For example, you can use the deep neural net architecture **ResNet50** to extract a 2048 dimensional vector *embedding* corresponding to each image. Next, use the dimension reduction technique **t-distributed_stochastict-distributed stochastic neighbor embedding** (**TSNE**) - feel free to use sklearn.manifold module's implementation, to reduce the embedding corresponding to each images to 2 dimensions and use scatterplot to visualize the images in the projected dimensions. Overlay the images on top, corresponding to their reduced 2D coordinates.

You should obtain a figure like the following one; the cats and dogs are clearly separated even in the low dimensional embedding, as can be seen:

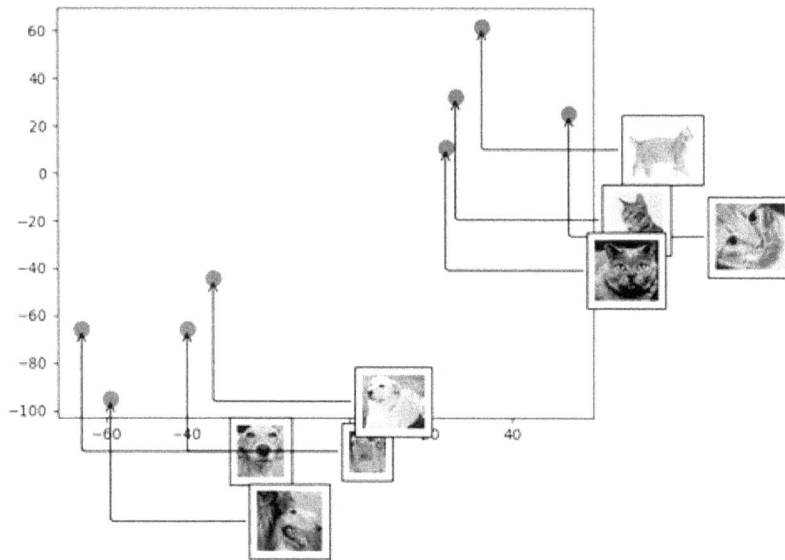

Figure 6.24: *Classifying cats and dogs images with ResNet embedding / T-SNE visualization*

2. **Semantic image search engine**: Use deep image features to search similar images. Download the Kaggle fast food dataset from the following link: **https://www. kaggle.com/datasets/utkarshsaxenadn/fast-food-classification-dataset**. The following figure shows a few sample images from the dataset (you may want to reduce the dataset, for example, create a small dataset with 81 pizzas, burgers and sandwiches, selected randomly, to start with):

Figure 6.25: *Fast food Kaggle dataset for image search engine*

Use a pretrained neural net (for example, **EfficientNet**) to obtain the embeddings for the images and use a nearest-neighbor algorithm (for example, ball_tree from sklearn.neighbors.NearestNeighbors) to find the nearest embeddings from the search images and display the top k (for example, k=5) similar images found, as shown in the following figure (along with the *NN-distance*: lower the distance, higher the similarity):

Figure 6.26: *Retrieving images using EfficientNet embeddings with image search*

You can use your code to recommend similar food items to customers. As you can see from *Figure 6.26*, querying with a burger image returns 5 most similar food-item images (by searching in the NN-embedding space), all but the last image are burger images. The last image returned is wrong; it is not a burger. Fine-tune the pre-trained model on the training dataset to improve the *accuracy* of the model, and test the accuracy (for example, with precision-5 metric) on the held-out *test* dataset.

References

1. https://www.youtube.com/watch?v=8_P257eFEqA

2. https://www.youtube.com/watch?v=ROgT1XDTX4Q

3. https://www.youtube.com/watch?v=kl6-NHxcn-k

4. https://www.youtube.com/watch?v=qRouVgXb1G4

5. https://www.youtube.com/watch?v=J5-xQJjn82s

6. https://www.youtube.com/watch?v=2qUIz-MCKX0

7. https://pyimagesearch.com/2018/12/17/image-stitching-with-opencv-and-python/

8. http://cbcl.mit.edu/software-datasets/FaceData2.html

9. https://youtu.be/TDmrzvtpwOM

Join our Discord space

Join our Discord workspace for latest updates, offers, tech happenings around the world, new releases, and sessions with the authors:

https://discord.bpbonline.com

CHAPTER 7
Image Classification

Introduction

In this chapter, as well as the succeeding one, we shall transition from low-level image processing tasks to the exciting realm of advanced computer vision, including image classification, object detection/recognition, and high-level image interpretation tasks. This chapter will provide a practical, in-depth exploration of various topics in computer vision, guiding you through more complex concepts step by step.

Image classification is a computer vision task that categorizes images by automatically assigning predefined labels to them based on their visual content. It is done by training machine-learning models to recognize image patterns or features, allowing them to categorize new images into predefined classes. The goal of the task is to teach machines to interpret and understand the content of an image and then assign a class label, from a set of predefined labels or categories. It goes beyond basic image processing since it focuses on high-level semantic understanding or categorization.

To classify images with classical supervised machine learning classification models, handcrafted features (like **HOG, SIFT**) are first extracted from images, and then the classification models (for example, **SVM, KNN, random forest**) used for classification. They learn statistical relationships between the (handcrafted) features and the corresponding class labels (in **training** phase), which enables the models to classify new (unseen) images based on similar feature patterns (in **test** phase). In contrast, the deep learning models, particularly **Convolutional Neural Networks** (**CNN**), can learn hierarchical features automatically from raw pixel data, eliminating the need for manual feature extraction. Popular CNN architectures include **LeNet-5**, **AlexNet**, **VGG16**, **residual networks** (**ResNet**), and **EfficientNet**, which have demonstrated high accuracy in various computer vision tasks. Deep learning has gained widespread popularity in the past decade due to its superior performance in image classification and related tasks.

Structure

This chapter focuses on the following topics:

- Classifying Fashion-MNIST images using machine learning models with scikit-learn
- Classifying Fashion-MNIST images using deep learning models with tensorflow/keras
- Image classification with pretrained models with tf.keras
- Image classification with custom classes using transfer learning with pytorch

Objectives

This chapter aims to provide a comprehensive understanding of image classification techniques, from traditional machine learning to state-of-the-art deep learning approaches. Through practical examples, you will learn to classify Fashion-MNIST images using machine learning models with `scikit-learn` and deep learning models with `tensorflow` and **keras**. Next you will learn how to use **pre-trained** models with `tensorflow`/`keras` for efficient classification tasks and implement **transfer learning** using `pytorch` to build custom classifiers for specific applications. By the end of the chapter, you will be equipped with the knowledge and skills to apply various image classification methods to diverse image datasets and problem domains.

Classifying Fashion-MNIST images using machine learning models with scikit-learn

Fashion-MNIST is a dataset that provides a more challenging alternative to the classic MNIST dataset, which consists of handwritten digits. Fashion-MNIST contains grayscale images of different types of clothing and accessories, with each of the images labeled with one of ten product types (classes). This dataset is often used for benchmarking image classification algorithms and offers a more realistic scenario for testing machine learning models.

In this section, we will explore how to perform image classification using the **Fashion-MNIST** dataset using `scikit-learn`, a powerful and accessible machine learning library in Python. We shall cover the theoretical aspects of image classification, the mathematical foundations behind classification algorithms, and provide practical examples with working code.

Understanding the Fashion-MNIST dataset

The **Fashion-MNIST** dataset is similar to the **MNIST** dataset of handwritten digits but consists of images of fashion items. Each image is a 28×28 pixel grayscale image, and there are 10 classes of clothing items, including:

- Ankle boot
- Bag
- Coat
- Dress
- Pullover
- Sandal
- Shirt
- Sneaker
- T-shirt/top
- Trouser

The dataset consists of 70,000 images, each image is labeled with its corresponding class.

This section explores how to perform image classification on the Fashion-MNIST dataset using `scikit-learn`. The goal is to predict the type of clothing or accessory in the image. You will learn:

- How to **train** a machine learning model on the images from a **training** split
- Use the model to **predict** the labels (classes) for the images from the held-out **test** split
- Evaluate the performance of the model (for example, how well it generalizes) on the unseen data using the **accuracy** metric.

Now follow the given steps to implement image classification with ML models:

1. Let us start the implementation by importing the following required libraries, modules, and functions, as done in the following code snippet:

    a. `urllib.request.urlretrieve`: Downloads files from the internet.

    b. `gzip`: Provides functionalities to work with `gzip` compressed files.

    c. `os`: Offers a way to interact with the operating system, such as checking file existence.

d. **numpy**: A fundamental package for numerical computations in Python, used here for array manipulations.

e. **scipy.stats.multivariate_normal**: Used for multivariate normal distributions.

f. **matplotlib.pyplot**: Used for creating visualizations and plots.

g. **warnings.simplefilter**: Configures warning filters to ignore **FutureWarnings**, the required libraries, modules, and functions.

Now, the following code snippets demonstrate how to train a few popular classification models on Fashion-MNIST training dataset and evaluate those models on the test dataset, by comparing the ground-truth labels with the ones predicted by the classification models:

```
%matplotlib inline
import gzip, os
import numpy as np
from scipy.stats import multivariate_normal
from urllib.request import urlretrieve
import matplotlib.pyplot as plt
import warnings
warnings.simplefilter(action='ignore', category=FutureWarning)
```

Here are the steps you need to follow:

1. **Data downloading**: Use the function **download()** to download the **Fashion-MNIST** dataset files from the specified URL. Invoke the function to obtain the training and test images. Here is the description of the function in details:

   a. **Purpose**: Downloads a file from the specified URL.

   b. **Parameters**:

      i. **filename**: The name of the file to be downloaded.

      ii. **source**: Base URL where the file is located. The default is the Fashion-MNIST dataset URL.

   c. **Functionality**: Constructs the full URL by appending filename to the base source URL and downloads it using **urlretrieve**.

2. **Data loading and preprocessing**: There are two stages here:

   a. **Preparing the dataset**: Before diving into classification, it is essential to load and prepare the Fashion-MNIST dataset. **scikit-learn** does not directly provide access to **Fashion-MNIST**, so we first need to download the data from the specified link provided (**http://fashion-mnist.s3-website.eu-central-1.amazonaws.com/**) and then process it for use with **scikit-learn** classification models.

b. **Feature extraction and preprocessing**: Before applying classification algorithms, we need to preprocess the data. For image classification, preprocessing typically involves:

  i. **Normalization**: It involves rescaling pixel values to a specific range (such as 0 to 1) to enhance the performance of machine learning algorithms.

  ii. **Flattening**: It implies converting 2D images into 1D vectors, since most traditional machine learning algorithms expect feature vectors as input.

c. Use the functions `load_fashion_mnist_images()` and `load_fashion_mnist_labels()` to load image and label data from the downloaded files, for each of the training and test data splits, along with performing the preprocessing required. The dataset comprises a total of 70000 images, split into 60000 training examples and 10000 test examples.

d. Now, let us understand the function `load_fashion_mnist_images()` in detail:

  i. **Purpose**: Loads the image data from a Fashion-MNIST file.

  ii. **Parameters**: This is `filename`, that is, the name of the file containing the image data.

  iii. **Functionality**: Checks if the file exists locally. If not, it downloads it. It also opens the file using `gzip` for reading and then reads the file into a **numpy** array, skipping the first 16 bytes of header information (`offset=16`). It reshapes the data to a 2D array where each row is a flattened 28×28 image (784 pixels), and normalizes the data to have values in between 0 and 1.

e. When loading the image data, you need to skip past the header of the compressed `.gz` file to access the actual pixel values. The offset parameter in `np.frombuffer` is used to specify how many bytes to skip from the start of the file before starting to read the data.

  i. **For images**: The header is 16 bytes long. Therefore, you use **offset=16** to start reading the pixel data immediately after the header.

  ii. **For labels**: The header is 8 bytes long. Therefore, you use **offset=8** to start reading the label data immediately after the header.

Now, refer to the next code snippet:

```python
# downloads a MNIST data file from zalandoresearch website
def download(filename, \
    source='http://fashion-mnist.s3-website.eu-central-1.amazonaws.com/'):
        print("Downloading %s" % filename)
        urlretrieve(source + filename, filename)

# Invokes download() if necessary, then reads in images
def load_fashion_mnist_images(filename):
    if not os.path.exists(filename):
        download(filename)
    with gzip.open(filename, 'rb') as f:
        data = np.frombuffer(f.read(), np.uint8, offset=16)
    data = data.reshape(-1,784)
    data = data / data.max() # normalization
    return data

def load_fashion_mnist_labels(filename):
    if not os.path.exists(filename):
        download(filename)
    with gzip.open(filename, 'rb') as f:
        data = np.frombuffer(f.read(), np.uint8, offset=8)
    return data

train_data = load_fashion_mnist_images('train-images-idx3-ubyte.gz')
train_labels = load_fashion_mnist_labels('train-labels-idx1-ubyte.gz')
test_data = load_fashion_mnist_images('t10k-images-idx3-ubyte.gz')
test_labels = load_fashion_mnist_labels('t10k-labels-idx1-ubyte.gz')
print(train_data.shape)
# (60000, 784) ## 60k 28x28 handwritten digits
print(test_data.shape)
# (10000, 784) ## 10k 28x28 handwritten digits
```

The 10 classes include items such as T-shirts/tops, trousers, pullovers, dresses, coats, sandals, shirts, sneakers, bags, and ankle boots, as follows:

```python
products = ['T-shirt/top', 'Trouser', 'Pullover', 'Dress', 'Coat', \
            'Sandal', 'Shirt', 'Sneaker', 'Bag', 'Ankle boot']
print(len(products))
#10
```

3. **Visualization**: The function **show_image(x, label)** displays an image given its 1D vector representation. The function also does the following things:

   a. Reshapes the flattened image x data back to a 28×28 pixel format.

   b. Uses **matplotlib.pylab imshow()** function to display the image in grayscale.

   c. Sets the title of the plot to the corresponding **label** description from products.

   d. Removes axis labels for clarity.

The next code snippet performs the following steps:

a. Iterates over the first 100 test images.

b. Visualizes the image using the function **show_image()** and the ground-truth labels with the image title.

c. Uses **plt.subplot()** to arrange these images in a 10×10 grid.

d. Applies **plt.tight_layout()** to adjust spacing and **plt.show()** to display the plot.

```python
def show_image(x, label):
    plt.imshow(x.reshape((28,28)), cmap=plt.cm.gray)
    plt.title(products[label], size=15)
    plt.axis('off')

plt.figure(figsize=(20,20))
for i in range(100):
    plt.subplot(10, 10, i+1)
    show_image(test_data[i,:], test_labels[i])
plt.tight_layout()
plt.show()
```

If you run the preceding code snippet, you should obtain a figure like the next one:

Figure 7.1: *Sample test images with labels from the Fashion-MNIST dataset*

Classification with machine learning models

A machine learning model is a mathematical or computational framework that learns patterns and relationships from data, enabling it to make predictions or decisions without explicit programming. Training and test datasets are crucial components in machine learning and statistical modeling. *Figure 7.2* shows the basic machine learning pipeline that we shall use. The two main phases in the pipeline are as follows:

- **Training**: During the training phase, a machine learning model learns patterns, relationships, and features from the labeled examples in the training dataset. The model adjusts its parameters based on the input features and their corresponding labels to reduce the gap between the predicted and actual outcomes (that is, class labels).

- **Evaluation**: The held-out test dataset, distinct from the training dataset, is used to evaluate the ability of the model to generalize on new, unseen examples (must not be used for training to avoid overfitting), by comparing the model-**predicted** labels against the **ground-truth** labels.

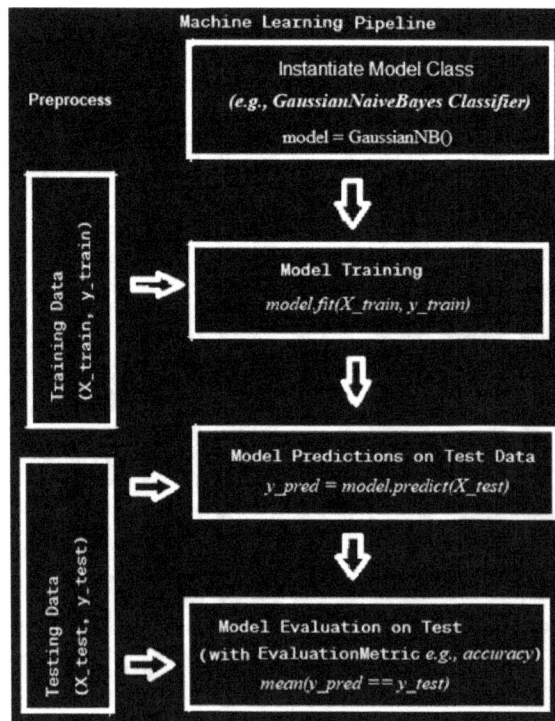

Figure 7.2: Machine learning pipeline

Using `scikit-learn`, we shall now navigate through the implementation of Fashion-MNIST images classification with a few classification models listed as follows and apply these models one-by-one to classify the image dataset:

- **Gaussian Naive Bayes**
- **Stochastic Gradient Descent (SGD)**
- **Random forest**

Gaussian Naive Bayes model

The **Gaussian Naive Bayes** model assumes that the likelihood of the features given the class $P(X|Y)$ follows a multivariate Gaussian (normal) distribution. The naive aspect refers to the assumption that the features are (conditionally) independent of each other, given the class.

For a feature vector $X = (x_1, x_2, \dots, x_n)$ and a class $Y = y$, the **probability density function** (**PDF**) of the multivariate Gaussian distribution is given by:

$$P(X \mid Y = y) = \frac{(2\pi)^{\frac{n}{2}}}{\mid \Sigma_y \mid^{1/2}} e^{-(X-\mu_y)^T \Sigma_y^{-1}(X-\mu_y)}$$

Where, μ_y is the mean vector for class y, Σ_y is the covariance matrix for class y, $\mid \Sigma_y \mid$ is the determinant of Σ_y.

Naive assumption: The naive part of Gaussian Naive Bayes comes from assuming that the features $x_1, x_2, \dots, x_n$ are conditionally independent given the class y. This simplifies the covariance matrix Σ_y to a diagonal matrix, with the variances of individual features on the diagonal.

During training, the model estimates the **parameters** (μ_y and Σ_y) for each class based on the training data.

During prediction, the model uses the **Bayes theorem** (as shown) to compute the **posterior probability** (for each of the class labels) and assigns the class with the highest probability as the predicted class:

$$P(Y \mid X) = \frac{P(X \mid Y)P(Y)}{P(X)}$$

Which implies:

$$P(Y = y \mid X) \propto P(X \mid Y = y)P(Y = y)$$

(up to a normalization constant)

Where $P(Y \mid X)$ is the **posterior probability** of class Y given the features X, $P(X \mid Y)$ is the **likelihood** of the features given the class, $P(Y)$ is the **prior** probability of class Y, and $P(X)$ is the probability of the features.

In summary, **Gaussian Naive Bayes** leverages Bayes theorem with the assumption of Gaussian distribution for feature likelihoods and naive independence to make predictions in a computationally efficient manner. The model is particularly useful for continuous feature spaces. Gaussian Naive Bayes is a **generative model** because it models the joint probability distribution P(X,Y) by learning P(X|Y) and P(Y), allowing it to generate data samples for each class.

The next code snippet shows how we can classify Fashion-MNIST images using a Gaussian Generative Model, specifically with the **Gaussian Naive Bayes classifier** (in this case, we have $n = 784$ dimensional feature vector X). Here is how it works:

1. **Import the modules**:

    a. First import the function **time** from the library **time**. This function is used to measure the time elapsed during training/prediction.

    b. Import the class **GaussianNB** from **sklearn.naive_bayes**. This is the Naive Bayes classifier based on Gaussian distributions. The underlying assumption is that the features are normally distributed.

2. **Train the model**:

    a. **start = time()** records the current time just before starting the training process. This is used to measure how long the training process takes.

    b. **GaussianNB(var_smoothing=1e-2)** instantiates a Gaussian Naive Bayes classifier (**GaussianNB** class) with the value of the **var_smoothing** parameter as 1×10^{-2}. This is a **regularization** parameter; it is used to avoid numerical instability (prevents division by zero) by adding a small value to the variance of each feature. This helps ensure that variance estimates do not become zero, which is particularly useful when working with features that may have very small variance.

    c. **clf.fit(train_data, train_labels)** trains the Gaussian Naive Bayes classifier (**clf**) on training data (**train_data**), using the training labels (**train_labels**).

    d. **end = time()** records the current time immediately after the training process is completed. Now **end - start** will give you the time taken to train the model.

3. **Visualize the learned means**:

    a. **plt.figure(figsize=(20,8))** creates a new figure with a size of 20 inches by 8 inches, suitable for displaying multiple images.

    b. Loop over each of the 10 product classes from the list of products.

    c. **plt.subplot(2,5,i+1)** creates a subplot in a 2×5 grid (2 rows and 5 columns) for each class, positioning each subplot according to $i + 1$.

d. **plt.imshow(np.reshape(clf.theta_[i], (28,28)), cmap=plt.cm.gray)** displays the **mean image** for class *i*. The mean image is obtained from **clf. theta_**, which contains the mean of the features (pixel values) for each class. **np.reshape(clf.theta_[i], (28,28))** reshapes this mean vector into a 28×28 pixel image. The **cmap=plt.cm.gray** argument sets the color map to grayscale.

e. **plt.axis('off')** hides the axis for each subplot to focus on the image itself.

f. **plt.title(products[i], size=20)** sets the title for each subplot to the name of the class from the products list, making it clear which class the displayed mean image corresponds to.

g. **plt.show()** displays the figure with all the subplots.

Now refer to the next code snippet:

```
from time import time
from sklearn.naive_bayes import GaussianNB

start = time()
clf = GaussianNB(var_smoothing=1e-2)
clf.fit(train_data, train_labels)
end = time()
print('Training Time: {} seconds'.format(end-start))
# Training Time: 0.954862117767334 seconds
plt.figure(figsize=(20,8))
for i in range(len(products)):
    plt.subplot(2,5,i+1)
    plt.imshow(np.reshape(clf.theta_[i], (28,28)), cmap=plt.cm.gray)
    plt.axis('off')
    plt.title(products[i], size=20)
plt.show()
```

If you run the preceding code snippet, you should obtain a figure as follows:

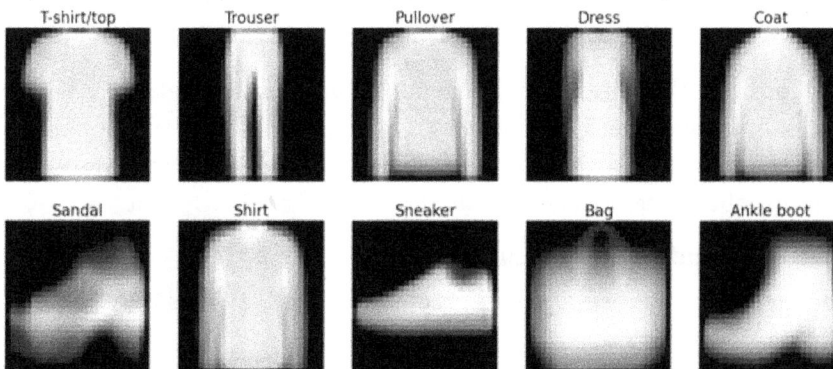

Figure 7.3: *Mean image for each class label from Fashion-MNIST with Gaussian Naïve Baysian classifier*

Now, predict the labels for the test images using the trained Gaussian Naive Bayes classifier, by computing $P(Y|X)$ that is, *Prob(label | image)* for each (test image, label) pair (using the **predict()** method) and measure the time taken to compute the label to be predicted. Compute the accuracy of prediction (proportion of test images for which the labels are correctly predicted by the model, that is, the predicted labels are identical to the ground-truth labels), using the next code snippet. Here is a detailed explanation of how it works:

1. **Measuring prediction time**:

    a. **start = time()**: Records the current time just before making predictions with the classifier. This helps in measuring how long it takes to make predictions on the test dataset.

    b. **test_predictions = clf.predict(test_data)**: Uses the trained Gaussian Naive Bayes classifier (**clf**) to predict the labels for the test dataset (**test_data**). The **predict** method returns an array of predicted labels for each test sample.

    c. **end = time()**: Records the current time immediately after making predictions.

    d. **print('Prediction Time: {} seconds'.format(end-start))**: Calculates the total time taken for prediction by subtracting start from end, and prints this time in seconds. This provides insight into the efficiency of the model during inference.

2. **Evaluating prediction accuracy**:

    a. **errors = np.sum(test_predictions != test_labels)**: Calculates the number of misclassified predictions. It compares the predicted labels (**test_predictions**) with the actual labels (**test_labels**) and counts the number of mismatches. **test_predictions != test_labels** produces a Boolean array where true indicates an incorrect prediction and **np.sum()** then counts the number of true values corresponding to the number of errors.

    b. **print("The GaussianNB (generative model) makes " + str(errors) + " errors out of 10000")**: Prints the total number of errors made by the Gaussian Naive Bayes classifier out of 10,000 test samples. The actual number of errors is inserted into the string to be output.

3. **Calculating and printing accuracy**:

    t_accuracy = sum(test_predictions == test_labels) / float(len(test_labels)):

    a. **test_predictions == test_labels**: Produces a Boolean array where **True** indicates a correct prediction and **False** indicates an incorrect one.

b. **`sum(test_predictions == test_labels)`**: Counts the number of correct predictions (the number of **True** values).

c. **`sum(test_predictions == test_labels) / len(test_labels)`**: Calculates the classifier's accuracy by dividing the number of correct predictions by the total number of predictions made.

d. **`t_accuracy`**: Stores the accuracy value, representing the proportion of correct predictions from all test samples.

In summary, the next code snippet evaluates the performance of the trained Gaussian Naive Bayes classifier on the **test** dataset:

```
start = time()
test_predictions = clf.predict(test_data)
end = time()
print('Prediction Time: {} seconds'.format(end-start))
# Prediction Time: 1.0611958503723145 seconds
errors = np.sum(test_predictions != test_labels)
print("The GaussianNB (generative model) makes " + str(errors) + \
                              " errors out of 10000")
# The generative model makes 3285 errors out of 10000
t_accuracy = sum(test_predictions == test_labels) / len(test_labels)
t_accuracy
# 0.6715
```

As can be seen from the preceding code, around 67% accuracy is obtained on the test dataset using the **`GaussianNB`** classifier, which is not good. Let us try a few more models to see if the accuracy improves.

Linear classifier with SGD training

The **`SGDClassifier`** in **`scikit-learn`** is an implementation of a linear classifier using SGD optimization. It is a variant of the traditional gradient descent algorithm that processes a single (randomly selected) training example at a time, updates the parameters (weights) using the gradient of the loss computed, making it particularly suitable for large datasets.

The goal of the classifier is to determine the optimal weights for a linear decision boundary that demarcates the classes in the input space. Let us go through the key mathematical concepts involved in **`SGDClassifier`**:

- **Linear model**: The **`SGDClassifier`** is based on a linear model that makes predictions using the following equation for binary classification (with two classes present):

   o **Decision function**: $f(x) = sign(w \cdot x + b)$

Here w is the weight vector, x is the input feature vector, b is the bias term, $w \cdot x + b$ represents the dot product and $sign(\cdot)$ is the sign function defined as follows:

$$sign(x) = \begin{cases} -1 & \text{if } x < 0 \\ 0 & \text{if } x = 0 \\ 1 & \text{if } x > 0 \end{cases}$$

The decision function outputs the sign of the linear combination of input features and weights, determining the predicted class.

o   **Loss function**: The optimization process involves minimizing a loss computing the prediction error (that is, the difference in between predicted and true labels). In the case of **SGDClassifier**, the loss function typically used for binary classification is the **hinge loss**. For a sample with the ground truth (true label) y and classifier-predicted score $f(x)$, the hinge loss is defined as:

$$L\big(y, f(x)\big) = \max\big(0, 1 - y \cdot f(x)\big)$$

- **Regularization**: To prevent overfitting, the **SGDClassifier** often includes a regularization term in the objective function. The regularization term encourages the model to use smaller weights. The two common types of regularization used are L_1 regularization (**Lasso**) and L_2 regularization (**Ridge**). The regularized objective function becomes:

$$J(w) = \text{Hinge Loss} + \alpha.\text{Regularization Term,}$$

Where α is the regularization strength, $J(w)$ being the **objective function**.

- **SGD**: The optimization is performed using SGD. The update rule for the weight vector in each iteration is:

$$w_{new} \leftarrow w_{old} - \eta \cdot \nabla J(w_{old})$$

Here η is the learning rate, $\nabla J(w_{old})$ is the gradient of the objective function with respect to the weights.

The gradient is computed based on a single randomly chosen training example (stochastic gradient). This randomness often helps the algorithm escape local minima and makes it computationally efficient for large datasets.

Since the problem we are trying to solve is a *multi-class classification* problem (with ten class labels) here, the **One-vs-All** (**OvA**) technique is used to train multiple binary classifiers, each focusing on distinguishing one class from the rest. The final class label is selected based on the binary classifier that outputs the highest confidence score among all classifiers.

Performing prediction with linear classifiers using SGD training in **scikit-learn** involves a series of steps, as shown in the following code snippet:

1. Start by importing **sklearn.linear_model.SGDClassifier**.

2. Initialize and train the **SGD classifier**. Create an instance of the **SGDClassifier** class and train it on your training data (with the **fit()** method). The default **loss** function is **hinge** (for **SGDClassifier** and also for **linearSVM** classifier), but you can adjust it based on your specific classification task. For example, here we shall use the modified Huber loss instead, which is a smoothed variant that combines both a quadratic and linear loss. It is defined as:

$$Huber(y, f(x)) = \begin{cases} \frac{1}{2}(1 - yf(x))^2, & if \ yf(x) \geq -1 \\ -4yf(x), & if \ yf(x) < -1 \end{cases}$$

The modified Huber loss works as follows:

a. When $y.f(x) \geq -1$, the loss is **quadratic** for predictions close to the boundary, i.e., the error grows quadratically.

b. When $y.f(x) < -1$ (meaning the classification is very wrong), the loss transitions to a **linear** penalty to avoid overly penalizing large error.

The following figure shows what the loss functions look like:

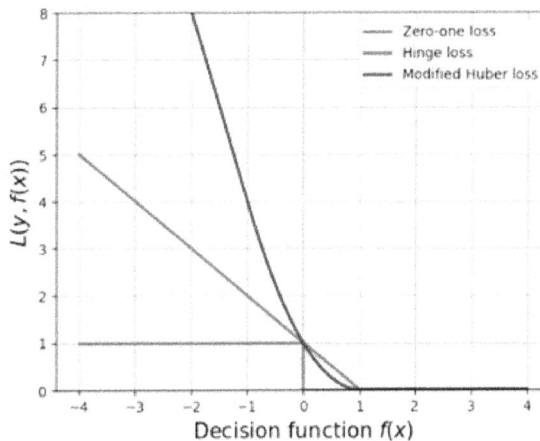

Figure 7.4: Loss functions

3. Measure the training time using the **time()** function and compute the difference in time:

```
from sklearn.linear_model import SGDClassifier
params = dict({"loss":"modified_huber","penalty":"12"})
clf = SGDClassifier(**params)
start = time()
clf.fit(train_data, train_labels)
end = time()
print('Training Time: {} seconds'.format(end-start))
#Training Time: 140.620023727417 seconds
```

4. **Make predictions**: Use the classifier (trained on the training dataset) to make predictions on your test set, using the method **predict()**, and also measure the time required to predict:

```
start = time()
pred_labels = clf.predict(test_data)
end = time()
print('Prediction Time: {} seconds'.format(end-start))
#Prediction Time: 0.07095885276794434 seconds
```

5. **Evaluate the model**: Assess the performance of your model using the accuracy metric. As can be seen from the following code snippet, the accuracy increased to 79.5%:

```
t_accuracy = sum(pred_labels==test_labels) / float(len(test_labels))
t_accuracy
#0.7958
```

6. This code snippet computes the **confusion matrix** using the function **confusion_matrix()** from the library **scikit-learn** for the classification model, and visualizes using the **heatmap()** function from the library **seaborn**.

   a. **cm = confusion_matrix(test_labels, pred_labels)**: Computes the **confusion matrix** from the true labels (**test_labels**) and the predicted labels (**pred_labels**). Here we have

      i. **test_labels**: The actual labels of the test dataset.

      ii. **pred_labels**: The labels predicted by the classifier for the test dataset.

   b. **cm**: Confusion matrix, a 2D array (or matrix/table) that summarizes the performance of a classification model, by showing the counts of **true positives (TP)**, **true negatives (TN)**, **false positives (FP)**, and **false negatives (FN)**. It summarizes the results of the model's predictions on a set of data, providing insight into the model's ability to correctly or incorrectly classify instances.

7. For multiclass classification problems with more than two classes, the confusion matrix is a square matrix where each row corresponds to the actual class, and each column corresponds to the predicted class. The element at position (i, j) in the table represents the number of samples with true label i and predicted label j. In other words, each element in the matrix shows how often the model predicted class j when the actual class was i.

8. The diagonal elements in the confusion matrix represent the number of correct predictions for each class, while the off-diagonal elements represent misclassifications, as shown in the next figure.

9. `pd.DataFrame(cm, range(10), range(10))` converts the confusion matrix array (`cm`) into a pandas `DataFrame` (`df_cm`) for easier manipulation and visualization.

10. `sns.heatmap(df_cm, annot=True, annot_kws={"size": 8}, fmt="g")` creates a heatmap using the library **seaborn** to visualize the confusion matrix. Here:

    a. `df_cm`: The `DataFrame` containing the confusion matrix.

    b. `annot=True`: Adds the numeric values from the confusion matrix to each cell in the heatmap.

    c. `annot_kws={"size": 8}`: Sets the font size of the annotations to 8.

    d. `fmt="g"`: Formats the annotations to be displayed as general integers (not in scientific notation).

```python
from sklearn.metrics import confusion_matrix
import pandas as pd
import seaborn as sns

cm = confusion_matrix(test_labels, pred_labels)
df_cm = pd.DataFrame(cm, range(10), range(10))
sns.set(font_scale=1.2)
sns.heatmap(df_cm, annot=True,annot_kws={"size": 8}, fmt="g")
plt.show()
```

If you run the preceding code snippet, you should obtain a figure like the next one:

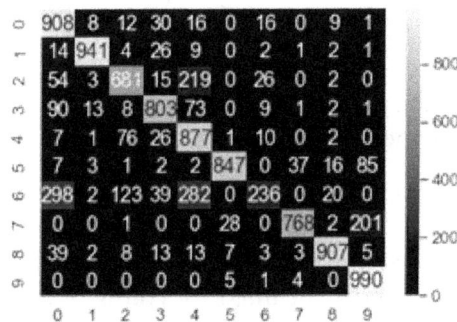

Figure 7.5: Confusion matrix for the linear classifier

By following these steps, you can effectively perform prediction with linear classifiers using **SGD** training in **scikit-learn**.

Random forest ensemble classifier

Random forest is an **ensemble learning** technique that creates several decision trees and combines (for example, using majority voting) their predictions to enhance accuracy and robustness. The basic building block of a random forest is decision tree (a supervised machine learning / classification model that makes decisions by recursively splitting data based on feature values, with each leaf node representing a final prediction or outcome). Here is how a random forest model is created:

1. **Bootstrap aggregating (Bagging)**: Random Forest employs a technique called **bagging**. Multiple decision trees are trained on different subsets of the training data, sampled with replacement (**bootstrapping**). Each tree sees a slightly different perspective of the dataset, introducing diversity.

2. **Feature randomization**: At each split in a decision tree, a random subset of the original features is considered. This prevents a single dominant feature from influencing all trees and contributes to the ensemble's diversity. The default number of features to consider at each split is the square root of the total number of features.

3. **Prediction aggregation (Voting)**: For classification, each tree predicts a class, and the final prediction is often determined by a **majority vote**.

4. **Decision tree training**: Given a dataset D with features X and labels Y, each decision tree T_i is trained on a bootstrapped sample D_i from D. At each split in a tree, a random subset of features is considered.

5. **Voting/averaging**: For classification, the final prediction $\hat{y}$ is determined by a majority vote:

$$\hat{y} = \underset{y}{argmax} \sum_{i=1}^{N} \mathbb{1}\{T_i(X) = y\}$$

6. **Ensemble effect**: The ensemble reduces overfitting and generalizes well to unseen data by aggregating the predictions of multiple diverse trees. The diversity comes from **randomization** and **bootstrapping**.

The model is less prone to **overfitting** compared to individual decision trees. Random forest combines the strengths of multiple decision trees through bagging and feature randomization to create a robust and accurate ensemble model. The diversity introduced by the individual trees, coupled with the majority voting or averaging mechanism, makes it a robust and widely used machine learning algorithm.

Let us use the following steps for classification with the random forest classifier from `scikit-learn`:

1. Create an instance of the **RandomForestClassifier** (imported from **sklearn. ensemble** module) and train it on the training split obtained earlier, using the method **fit()**. Measure the training time as earlier (compare with those of earlier models).

2. Adjust the **n_estimators** parameter, which represents the number of trees in the forest (for example, set **n_estimators=100**, as in the following code snippet):

```
from sklearn.ensemble import RandomForestClassifier
clf = RandomForestClassifier(n_estimators=100, max_depth=20, \
                                          random_state=0)

start = time()
clf.fit(train_data, train_labels)
end = time()
print('Training Time: {} seconds'.format(end-start))
# Training Time: 234.0610225200653 seconds
```

3. Use the classifier (trained on the training set) to make predictions on your test set, using the method **predict()**. Measure the prediction time.

```
start = time()
pred_labels = clf.predict(test_data)
end = time()
print('Prediction Time: {} seconds'.format(end-start))
# Prediction Time: 0.7255053520202637 seconds
```

4. Assess the performance of your model using relevant evaluation metrics such as **accuracy** and **classification report**.

    a. **classification_report**: A function from the **sklearn.metrics** module that generates a report showing the **precision, recall, F1-score**, and **support** for each class in a classification problem.

    b. **classification_report(test_labels,   pred_labels,   target_names=products)**: The arguments to the function are:

      i. **test_labels**: The true labels for the test dataset.

      ii. **pred_labels**: The predicted labels for the test dataset.

      iii. **target_names=products**: A list of class names to display in the report. This should match the class indices in **test_labels** and **pred_labels**.

    c. **Classification report output**: The **classification_report** function generates a report with the following evaluation metrics for each class:

      i. **Precision**: The ratio of correctly predicted positive observations to the total predicted positives. It answers the question: *Of all the samples that were predicted to be in class X, how many actually belong to class X?* Precision is calculated as:

$$Precision = \frac{TP}{TP + FP}$$

      ii. **Recall (sensitivity)**: The ratio of correctly predicted positive observations to all observations in the actual class. It answers the question: *Of all the samples that actually belong to class X, how many were correctly predicted to be in class X?* Recall is calculated as:

$$Recall = \frac{TP}{TP + FN}$$

iii. **F1-score**: The harmonic mean of precision and recall. It provides a single metric that balances both precision and recall. The F1-score is particularly useful when dealing with imbalanced datasets. It is calculated as:

$$F1\text{-}Score = \frac{2 \times Precision \times Recall}{Precision + Recall}$$

iv. **Support**: The number of actual occurrences of the class in the dataset. It indicates how many samples belong to each class.

By following these steps, you can effectively evaluate the random forest classifier from **scikit-learn**, on the test dataset, as shown in the following code snippet:

```
from sklearn.metrics import classification_report
print(classification_report(test_labels, pred_labels, \
                              target_names=products))
#                 precision    recall  f1-score   support
#
# T-shirt/top       0.82       0.86     0.84       1000
#      Trouser      1.00       0.96     0.98       1000
#     Pullover      0.77       0.79     0.78       1000
#        Dress      0.87       0.91     0.89       1000
#         Coat      0.76       0.82     0.79       1000
#       Sandal      0.97       0.96     0.96       1000
#        Shirt      0.72       0.59     0.65       1000
#      Sneaker      0.93       0.95     0.94       1000
#          Bag      0.95       0.97     0.96       1000
#   Ankle boot      0.96       0.95     0.95       1000
#     accuracy                          0.88      10000
#    macro avg      0.87       0.88     0.87      10000
#weighted avg       0.87       0.88     0.87      10000

t_accuracy = sum(pred_labels == test_labels) / float(len(test_labels))
t_accuracy
#0.8751
```

As can be seen from the preceding result, the test accuracy improved to 87%. The next code snippet plots the confusion matrix, which shows the correctly classified test images, for each individual class, along the diagonal:

```
cm = confusion_matrix(test_labels, pred_labels)
df_cm = pd.DataFrame(cm, range(10), range(10))
sns.heatmap(df_cm, annot=True,annot_kws={"size": 10}, fmt="g")
plt.show()
```

If you run the preceding code snippet, you should obtain a figure like the next one:

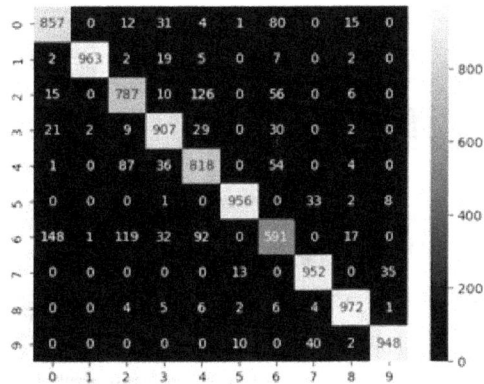

Figure 7.6: *Confusion matrix with random forest classifier*

The following code snippet plots a few of the test images classified wrongly by the model. The output is shown in the following figure, along with the true and predicted labels for each image.

```python
wrong_indices = pred_labels != test_labels
wrong_images, wrong_preds, correct_labs = test_data[wrong_indices], \
                pred_labels[wrong_indices], test_labels[wrong_indices]
print(len(wrong_preds))
# 1249
plt.figure(figsize=(20,20))
plt.gray()
j = 1
for i in np.random.choice(len(wrong_preds), 81):
    plt.subplot(9,9,j), plt.imshow(np.reshape(wrong_images[i],(28,28)))
    plt.axis('off')
    plt.title(products[wrong_preds[i]] + '->' + \
                                    products[correct_labs[i]])
    j += 1

plt.show()
```

If you run the preceding code snippet, you should obtain a figure as follows:

Figure 7.7: Fashion items wrongly classified with random forest classifier

Classifying Fashion-MNIST images using deep learning models with tensorflow/keras

The need for better performance and accuracy in image classification tasks drives the transition from traditional machine learning to deep learning models. As image data becomes more complex and voluminous, traditional models often fall short due to their reliance on manual feature engineering and limited capacity to capture intricate patterns. Deep learning models offer a more robust and scalable solution with their ability to automatically learn features and their hierarchical structure.

While traditional machine learning models have been valuable tools in the past, the advent of deep learning has provided a paradigm shift in how we approach image classification tasks. Error rates on the **ImageNet Large Scale Visual Recognition Challenge (ILSVRC)** demonstrated dramatic improvements with the advent of deep learning in 2012, and these improvements have continued since, as shown in the following figure. Human performance, in contrast, achieves an error rate of approximately 5%.

ImageNet Large Scale Visual Recognition Challenge (ILSVRC)

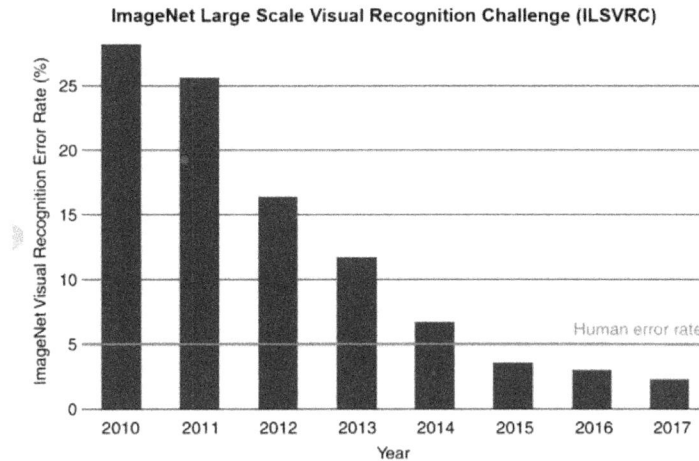

Figure 7.8: *ImageNet challenge visual recognition error rates*
Source: *https://www.researchgate.net/figure/Error-rates-on-the-ImageNet-Large-Scale-Visual-Recognition-Challenge-Accuracy_fig1_332452649*

Even for datasets such as Fashion-MNIST, which consist of relatively simple and low-dimensional image data, deep learning models still offer superior performance and efficiency, making them the preferred choice for achieving state-of-the-art results. In this section, we shall explore how to harness the power of deep learning with **tensorflow/ keras** to classify Fashion-MNIST images and achieve high levels of accuracy.

A neural network is generally considered a deep learning model when it has multiple hidden layers (deep architecture), employs non-linear activation functions, can learn hierarchical feature representations, requires substantial training data, and necessitates significant computational resources. First, let us understand the basic concepts and components of a deep convolutional neural network.

Convolution Neural Networks (**CNN**) are a type of deep neural network optimized for handling structured grid data, like images. They utilize convolution layers to autonomously learn and adaptively detect spatial patterns and feature hierarchies from the input data, benefiting from parameter sharing (thereby reducing the number of parameters), and increasing the field of view to capture broader contextual information. Now, let us go over the basic concepts and building blocks of CNN:

- **Convolution operation**: The core idea of a convolutional layer is to apply a set of filters (kernels) to the input image. Each filter is a small matrix that slides over the input image, performing element-wise multiplication and summing the results to produce a feature map. Mathematically, the convolution operation can be expressed as:

$$(I * K)(x, y) = \sum_{i=0}^{M-1} \sum_{j=0}^{N-1} I(x + i, y + j) \cdot K(i, j)$$

Where:

- o *I* is the input image.

- o *K* is the filter (kernel).

- o (x, y) denotes the position of the filter in the image.

- o *M* and *N* are the dimensions of the filter.

- **Activation function**: After convolution, an activation function (such as **ReLU**) is applied to introduce non-linearity into the model. The ReLU function is defined as:

$$ReLU(x) = max(0, x)$$

This function helps the model learn complex patterns.

- **Pooling layer**: Pooling layers reduce the spatial dimensions of the feature maps, helping decrease computation and control overfitting. The most common pooling operation is max pooling, which retains the maximum value in a defined window. Mathematically, for a 2×2 max pooling operation:

$$max\text{-}pool(x, y) = max\{I(x, y), I(x + 1, y), I(x, y + 1), I(x + 1, y + 1)\}$$

Where *I* is the feature map and (x, y) is the top-left corner of the pooling window.

- **Fully connected layers**: After several convolutional and pooling layers, the output is flattened and fed into fully connected (**dense**) layers. These layers perform classification based on the learned features.

- **Dropout layer**: A dropout layer is a type of regularization technique used in neural networks to prevent overfitting and improve the model's generalization to unseen data. It operates differently during training and testing phases as follows:

  - o **Training phase:** During training, each neuron (or unit) has a probability *p* (the **dropout rate**) of being dropped out (that is, the output is set to zero). For example, if the dropout rate is 0.5 (or 50%), then each neuron has a 50% chance of being dropped out during a particular forward pass. This dropout rate is applied independently for each neuron and each forward pass.

  - o **Testing phase:** During testing (or **inference**), dropout is not applied. All neurons are used, but their activations are scaled down by the dropout rate to account for the fact that they were only active part of the time during training. This scaling is done to maintain the balance of activations.

- **Forward pass**: Forward pass refers to the process of passing input data through the neural network to obtain an output or prediction. This involves computing the activations of each layer sequentially from the input layer to the output layer. The forward pass can be understood as a layer-by-layer transformation of the input, where each layer applies learned weights, biases, and activation functions to extract increasingly abstract features until the final output is produced. Here are the layers:

1. **Input layer**: The input data is fed into the input layer of the network.

2. **Hidden layers**: Each neuron in a hidden layer computes a weighted sum of its inputs and applies an activation function to produce an output.

   Mathematically, for a neuron j in layer l:

   $$z_j^{(l)} = \sum_i w_{ij}^{(l)} x_i^{(l-1)} + b_j^{(l)}$$

   Where, $w_{ij}^{(l)}$ are the weights, $x_i^{(l-1)}$ are the inputs from the previous layer, and $b_j^{(l)}$ is the bias term.

   The activation function $a_j^{(l)}$ is applied: $a_j^{(l)} = \sigma\left(z_j^{(l)}\right)$ where is the activation function (for example, **ReLU**, **sigmoid**).

3. **Output layer**: The final layer computes the output or prediction of the network. For a classification problem, this is typically a **softmax** activation function to produce class probabilities, as shown in the following figure:

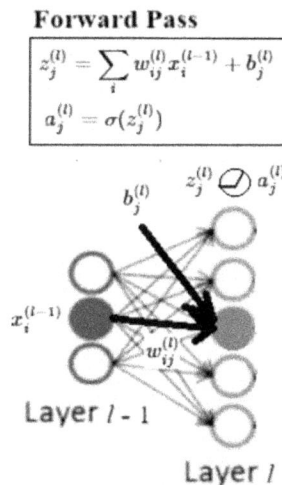

Figure 7.9: Forward propagation in a feedforward neural network

- **Backward pass**: Backward pass is the process of propagating the error backward through the network to update the weights and biases. This step involves calculating the gradients of the loss function with respect to each weight using the chain rule, as shown in the following *Figure 7.10*. The steps in the backward pass are as follows:

  1. **Compute loss**: Calculate the loss (or error) between the network's prediction and the actual target value using a loss function (for example, **cross-entropy loss** for classification).

  2. **Compute gradients**: Compute the gradient of the loss with respect to each weight and bias in the network using the **chain rule of partial derivatives**.

This involves propagating the gradients backward from the output layer to the input layer.

For each layer *l*: Compute the gradient of the loss function with respect to the activation values $\delta_j^{(l)}$:

$$\delta_j^{(l)} = \frac{\partial L}{\partial z_j^{(l)}} = \frac{\partial L}{\partial a_j^{(l)}} \cdot \frac{\partial a_j^{(l)}}{\partial z_j^{(l)}} = \frac{\partial L}{\partial z_j^{(l)}} \cdot \sigma'\left(z_j^{(l)}\right)$$

Where $\sigma'\left(z_j^{(l)}\right)$ is the derivative of the activation function.

Compute the gradients for the weights $w_{ij}^{(l)}$ and biases $b_j^{(l)}$:

$$\frac{\partial L}{\partial w_{ij}^{(l)}} = \frac{\partial L}{\partial z_j^{(l)}} \cdot \frac{\partial z_j^{(l)}}{\partial w_{ij}^{(l)}} = \delta_j^{(l)} \cdot x_i^{(l-1)}$$

$$\frac{\partial L}{\partial b_j^{(l)}} = \frac{\partial L}{\partial z_j^{(l)}} \cdot \frac{\partial z_j^{(l)}}{\partial b_j^{(l)}} = \delta_j^{(l)}$$

The next figure summarizes the math equations corresponding to the update of the weights in the neural network, in backward pass, with the backward propagation algorithm:

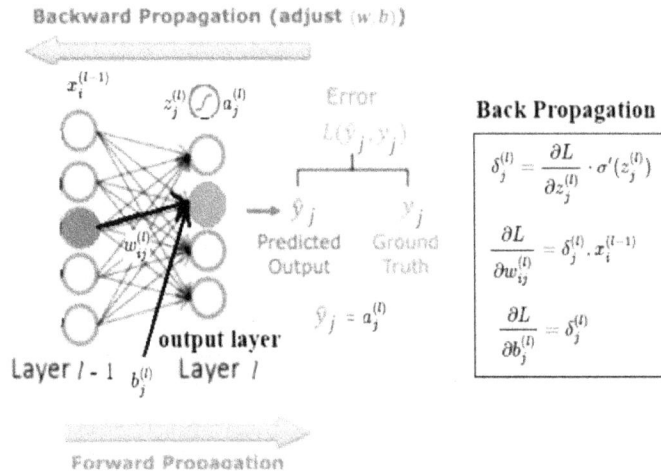

Figure 7.10: Math for neural-net weight update with backpropagation

- **Backpropagation**: Backpropagation is the algorithm used to perform the backward pass efficiently. It is an optimization algorithm that leverages the **chain rule for partial derivatives** to compute the gradients of the loss function with respect to the weights and biases. The steps in backpropagation are as follows:

  1. **Initialize gradients**: Start with the output layer and compute the gradient of the loss function with respect to the activations.

2. **Propagate gradients backward**: Use the chain rule to propagate these gradients backward through the network, layer by layer.

3. **Update weights and biases**: Use an optimization algorithm (for example, **Gradient Descent** or **Adam**) to update the weights and biases using the computed gradients. For example, in gradient descent, the weight-update equation is:

$$w_{ij} \leftarrow w_{ij} - \eta \cdot \frac{\partial L}{\partial w_{ij}}$$

Where, η is the learning rate.

- **Loss function and optimization**: The model is trained by **minimizing** a **loss function** L using optimization algorithms like **SGD** or **Adam**. For multi-class classification tasks (such as this one, since we have 10 class labels here), the common loss function is **categorical cross-entropy** (also called **softmax loss)**, defined as:

$$Loss = -\sum_{i=1}^{C} y_i \, log(p_i)$$

Where:

   o C is the number of classes.

   o y_i is the true label (one-hot encoded).

   o p_i is the predicted probability for class i.

The next python code snippet uses **tensorflow** and **keras** to build, train, and evaluate a CNN for classifying images from the Fashion-MNIST dataset. The code demonstrates the complete pipeline, including loading data, preprocessing, defining a CNN model, training, and evaluation.

Let us first import the required libraries using the following code snippet. The following list explains the purpose of each library, module, class or function used:

- **tensorflow as tf**: Imports TensorFlow for deep learning tasks.
- **fashion_mnist**: The dataset module from **Keras** that provides the Fashion-MNIST dataset.
- **Sequential**: A type of model in **Keras** where layers are stacked sequentially.
- **Conv2D**: Convolutional layer used for feature extraction from images.
- **MaxPooling2D**: Layer used for downsampling the feature maps.
- **Dropout**: Regularization layer to reduce overfitting.
- **Flatten**: Converts 2D matrices to 1D vectors.
- **Dense**: Fully connected layer used for classification.

- **to_categorical**: Converts integer labels to one-hot encoded vectors.

- **matplotlib.pyplot**: For plotting training and validation metrics.

- **device_lib**: Provides functions to list available devices like GPUs.

```python
import tensorflow as tf
from tensorflow.keras.datasets import fashion_mnist
from tensorflow.keras.models import Sequential
from tensorflow.keras.layers import Conv2D, MaxPooling2D, Dropout, \
                                    BatchNormalization, Flatten, Dense
from tensorflow.keras.utils import to_categorical
import matplotlib.pyplot as plt
from tensorflow.python.client import device_lib
```

Note that **graphics processing units (GPU)** are used for training deep neural networks, due to their ability to handle the massive parallelism and simultaneous computations required by deep learning algorithms efficiently, leading to significant speedups (otherwise, the training process can be very slow on CPUs). You are recommended to create a notebook in **Google colab (https://colab.research.google.com/)**, run the code in this section there using their GPU / TPU runtime, if you do not have GPU available on your local machine.

The function **get_available_gpus()** can be used to retrieve the names of available GPU devices, as shown in the next code snippet, where we have:

- **device_lib.list_local_devices()**: Lists all devices available to TensorFlow.

- **x.name for x in local_device_protos if x.device_type == 'GPU'**: Filters out only GPU devices.

Now, refer to the next code snippet:

```python
def get_available_gpus():
    local_device_protos = device_lib.list_local_devices()
    return [x.name for x in local_device_protos if x.device_type == 'GPU']
print(get_available_gpus())
# ['/device:GPU:0']
```

The following code snippet loads and preprocesses the Fashion-MNIST dataset, creates a CNN model using **keras Sequential API** (with **tf.keras.models)** and displays the summary of the model. Let us understand how it works in details (step-by-step):

- **tf.random.set_seed(221)** sets the random seed for TensorFlow's pseudo-random generator, to ensure that the sequence of random numbers is consistent across different runs of the code. This practice is crucial for achieving **reproducible** results.

- **fashion_mnist.load_data()** loads the Fashion-MNIST dataset, splitting it into training and test sets.

- **Reshape and normalize**: Here are the key functions:

  o `reshape((60000, 28, 28, 1))`: Reshapes the training images to be 4D tensors with shape (60000,28,28,1), where 60000 is the number of images, 28×28 is the image dimension, and 1 represents a single-color channel (grayscale).

  o `astype('float32') / 255`: Converts pixel values to `float32` and normalizes them to the range [0,1].

- **One-hot encoding**: One-hot encoding (**OHE**) is a method of converting categorical labels into a binary matrix representation. Each class label is represented by a binary vector where only one element is 1 (indicating the presence of the class), and all other elements are 0 (indicating the absence of the class).

- For Fashion-MNIST, there are 10 (product) classes. Thus, each label needs to be converted into a vector of length 10. Here are couple of example **OHE** vectors (from 10 possible unique vectors): class 0: [1,0,0,0,0,0,0,0,0,0], class 3: [0,0,0,1,0,0,0,0,0,0]. We need to convert the training and test labels to **OHE** representation in the following way:

  o `to_categorical(train_labels)`: Converts the class labels into a one-hot encoded format for the training labels.

  o `to_categorical(test_labels)`: Similarly converts the test labels.

- **Building the CNN model**: Here,

  o `Sequential([...])`: Defines a sequential model with layers stacked in the given order.

  o `Conv2D(64, (3, 3), activation='relu', input_shape=(28, 28, 1))`: First convolutional layer with 64 filters of size 3×3, with **ReLU** activation function and an input shape of 28×28 pixels with 1 channel.

  o `MaxPooling2D((2, 2))`: Applies **max-pooling** with a 2×2 window to reduce the dimensions of the feature maps.

  o `Dropout(0.2)`: Applies dropout with a rate of 0.2 (20%) after the max-pooling layer.

  o `Flatten()`: Flattens the 3D output from the last convolutional layer to 1D.

  o `Dense(256, activation='relu')`: Fully connected layer with 256 neurons and ReLU activation.

  o `Dense(10, activation='softmax')`: Output layer with 10 neurons for the 10 classes, uses the **softmax** activation function to produce class probabilities.

- **Model architecture overview**:

  The function **model.summary()** prints a detailed summary of the model's architecture, including the layers, their output shapes, and the number of parameters in each layer. This is particularly useful for understanding the structure of the model and verifying that it has been built as expected.

Refer to the next code snippet:

```python
# Reproducible output
tf.random.set_seed(1)

# Load and preprocess the Fashion-MNIST dataset
(train_images, train_labels), (test_images, test_labels) = \
                                        fashion_mnist.load_data()

# Reshape and normalize the images
train_images=train_images.reshape((60000,28,28,1)).astype('float32')/255
test_images=test_images.reshape((10000,28,28,1)).astype('float32')/255

# One-hot encode the labels
train_labels = to_categorical(train_labels)
test_labels = to_categorical(test_labels)

# Build the CNN model
model = Sequential([
    Conv2D(64, (3, 3), activation='relu', input_shape=(28, 28, 1)),
    MaxPooling2D((2, 2)),
    Dropout(0.2),
    Conv2D(256, (3, 3), activation='relu'),
    MaxPooling2D((2, 2)),
    Dropout(0.2),
    Flatten(),
    Dense(256, activation='relu'),
    Dropout(0.4),
    Dense(10, activation='softmax')
])

model.summary()
#Model: "sequential"
#_____
# Layer (type)                Output Shape              Param #
#================================================================
# conv2d (Conv2D)             (None, 26, 26, 64)          640
# max_pooling2d (MaxPooling2D) (None, 13, 13, 64)           0
# dropout (Dropout)           (None, 13, 13, 64)           0
# conv2d_1 (Conv2D)           (None, 11, 11, 256)       147712
# max_pooling2d_1 (MaxPooling2D) (None, 5, 5, 256)          0
# dropout_1 (Dropout)         (None, 5, 5, 256)            0
# flatten (Flatten)           (None, 6400)                 0
```

```
# dense (Dense)             (None, 256)             1638656
# dropout_2 (Dropout)       (None, 256)             0
# dense_1 (Dense)           (None, 10)              2570
#============================================================
#Total params: 1,789,578
#Trainable params: 1,789,578
#Non-trainable params: 0
#
```

The following figure shows the architecture of the model (dropout layers are not shown):

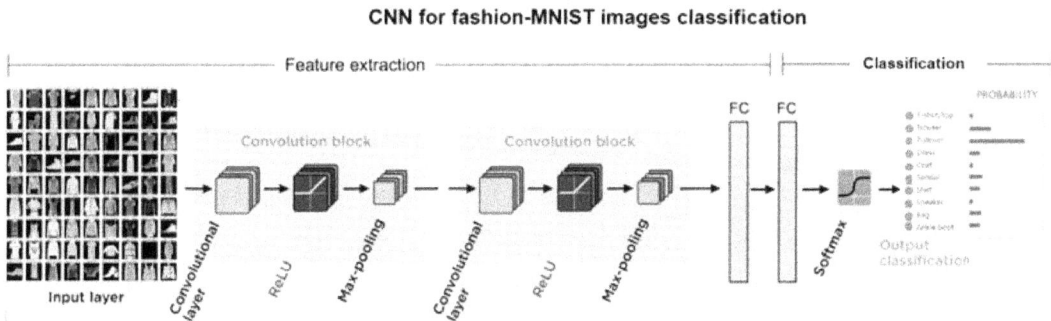

Figure 7.11: *Schematic diagram for Fashion-MNIST image classification with Keras sequential model*

Let us deep dive into the next steps:

- **Compiling the model**:
  - o **optimizer='adam'**: Specifies the **Adam** optimizer, which adapts learning rates during training.
  - o **loss='categorical_crossentropy'**: The loss function used for multi-class classification with **OHE** labels.
  - o **metrics=['accuracy']**: Metrics to monitor during training and evaluation, specifically **accuracy** in this case.

- **Training the model**:
  - o **model.fit()**: Trains the model on the training data.
  - o **train_images and train_labels**: Training data and labels.
  - o **epochs=5**: Number of epochs (iterations over the entire dataset) for training.
  - o **batch_size=64**: Number of samples per gradient update.
  - o **validation_split=0.2**: Fraction of training data to be used as validation data (20%).

- **Evaluating the model**:
  - o **model.evaluate()**: Evaluates the model's performance on the test dataset.

  o **test_images and test_labels**: Test data and labels.

  o **test_loss and test_accuracy**: Loss and accuracy of the model on the test set.

  o **print(f'Test accuracy: {test_accuracy:.4f}')**: Prints the test accuracy formatted to four decimal places.

• **Plotting training and validation accuracy**:

  o **plt.plot()**: Plots the training and validation accuracy over epochs.

  o **history.history['accuracy']**: Training accuracy recorded during training.

  o **history.history['val_accuracy']**: Validation accuracy recorded during training.

  o **plt.xlabel() and plt.ylabel()**: Label the x-axis and y-axis, respectively.

  o **plt.ylim([0, 1])**: Set the y-axis limits from 0 to 1.

  o **plt.legend(loc='lower right')**: Adds a legend to the plot.

  o **plt.show()**: Displays the plot.

The next code snippet complies the CNN model created previously, trains the model on training dataset and evaluates the model on the held-out test dataset. As can be seen, the accuracy on the held-out dataset with the deep learning model is more than 90.3%, higher than the one obtained with the classical machine learning models.

```
# Compile the model
model.compile(optimizer='adam',
              loss='categorical_crossentropy',
              metrics=['accuracy'])

# Train the model
history = model.fit(train_images, train_labels, epochs=5, batch_size=64, \
                                                validation_split=0.2)
#Epoch 1/5
#750/750 [==============================] - 13s 16ms/step - loss: 0.5117 -
#accuracy: 0.8145 - val_loss: 0.3266 - val_accuracy: 0.8827
#Epoch 2/5
#750/750 [==============================] - 11s 15ms/step - loss: 0.3381 -
#accuracy: 0.8767 - val_loss: 0.3064 - val_accuracy: 0.8877
#Epoch 3/5
#750/750 [==============================] - 9s 12ms/step - loss: 0.2940 -
#accuracy: 0.8932 - val_loss: 0.2921 - val_accuracy: 0.8899
#Epoch 4/5
#750/750 [==============================] - 12s 16ms/step - loss: 0.2659 -
#accuracy: 0.9023 - val_loss: 0.2563 - val_accuracy: 0.9066
#Epoch 5/5
#750/750 [==============================] - 13s 18ms/step - loss: 0.2428 -
```

```
#accuracy: 0.9091 - val_loss: 0.2494 - val_accuracy: 0.9068
#313/313 [==============================] - 2s 5ms/step - loss: 0.2633 -
#accuracy: 0.9030
# Evaluate the model
test_loss, test_accuracy = model.evaluate(test_images, test_labels)
print(f'Test accuracy: {test_accuracy:.4f}')
#Test accuracy: 0.9030

# Plot training and validation accuracy
plt.plot(history.history['accuracy'], label='accuracy')
plt.plot(history.history['val_accuracy'], label = 'val_accuracy')
plt.xlabel('Epoch')
plt.ylabel('Accuracy')
plt.ylim([0, 1])
plt.legend(loc='lower right')
plt.show()
```

If you run the preceding code snippet, you should obtain a figure like the next one:

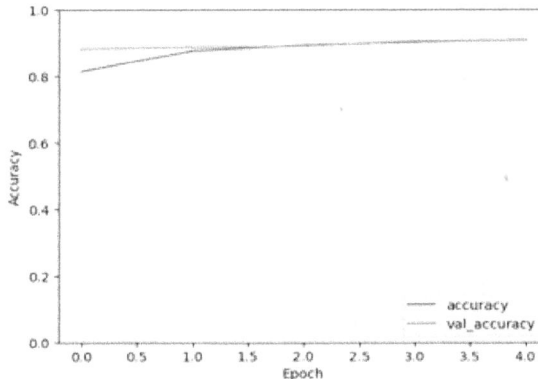

Figure 7.12: *Increase in training/validation accuracy w.r.t. number of training epochs*

Image classification with pretrained models with tf.keras

Pre-trained models are deep learning models that have previously been trained on a large dataset (for example, a few widely used **datasets** in **computer vision**: **ImageNet, CIFAR-10, CIFAR-100, MS COCO**). These models can be used as is, for classifying images into the categories they were trained on, or can be fine-tuned for specific image classification tasks. The strength of pre-trained models lies in their ability to capture high-level image features, making them highly versatile for various image classification tasks.

Pre-trained models can offer a powerful approach to image classification, significantly reducing the time and resources required to develop high-performing models. **Keras** provides an accessible interface to these models, making it easier for practitioners to leverage deep learning for their image classification tasks. Whether used directly or as a starting point for fine-tuning, pre-trained models in **keras** can accelerate the development of sophisticated image classification solutions.

Popular pre-trained models in tf.keras

tf.keras offers several state-of-the-art pre-trained models, including:

- **VGG16 and VGG19**: Models from the VGG team, known for their simplicity and depth.

- **ResNet50**: A model from *Microsoft*, known for its residual connections, which help in training very deep networks.

- **InceptionV3**: A model from *Google*, known for its efficiency and depth with fewer parameters.

- **MobileNet**: Also from Google, designed for mobile and embedded vision applications.

Using pretrained models for image classification

Image classification with pretrained models in **tf.keras** involves loading a pre-trained model, adapting it to your specific task, and making predictions. Before classification, images must be pre-processed to match the input format expected by the model. This typically involves resizing the image and scaling pixel values. In this example, we shall use several popular pre-trained models for image classification: **VGG16**, **VGG19**, **InceptionV3**, **ResNet50**, **MobileNet**, and **Xception**.

This following Python code snippet demonstrates how to use several pre-trained deep learning models from **tf.keras** for image classification. It involves loading multiple models, preparing images for prediction, making predictions, and visualizing the results. Here is a step-by-step explanation:

1. **Import libraries and functions**: The next code snippet imports necessary libraries including **keras**, **numpy** for numerical operations, several pre-trained models from **tf.keras.applications**(**vgg16**, **vgg19**, **inception_v3**, **resnet50**, **mobilenet**, **xception**), and functions for image processing and visualization, for example:

   a. **load_img**, **img_to_array**: Functions for image preprocessing.

   b. **decode_predictions**: Function to decode the predictions from the model into human-readable labels on the model you are using.

```
import numpy as np
from tensorflow.keras.applications
import vgg16, vgg19, inception_v3, resnet50, mobilenet, xception
from tensorflow.keras.preprocessing.image import load_img
from tensorflow.keras.preprocessing.image import img_to_array
from tensorflow.keras.applications.imagenet_utils import \
                                            decode_predictions

import matplotlib.pyplot as plt
import cv2
```

2. **Load pretrained models**: The following code snippet carries out the steps as defined:

   a. Loads several pretrained models (**VGG16, VGG19, InceptionV3, ResNet50, MobileNet, Xception**) with weights trained on **ImageNet** dataset.

   b. Instantiates the models from the corresponding list of model classes.

   c. Displays the summary of the **VGG16** model's architecture.

```
vgg16_model = vgg16.VGG16(weights='imagenet')
# Downloading data from https://storage.googleapis.com/tensorflow/keras-
# applications/vgg16/vgg16_weights_tf_dim_ordering_tf_kernels.h5
# 553467096/553467096 [==============================] - 33s 0us/step

vgg16_model.summary()
#Model: "vgg16"
#_____
# Layer (type)                 Output Shape              Param #
#================================================================
# input_1 (InputLayer)         [(None, 224, 224, 3)]     0
# block1_conv1 (Conv2D)        (None, 224, 224, 64)      1792
# block1_conv2 (Conv2D)        (None, 224, 224, 64)      36928
# block1_pool (MaxPooling2D)   (None, 112, 112, 64)      0
# block2_conv1 (Conv2D)        (None, 112, 112, 128)     73856
# block2_conv2 (Conv2D)        (None, 112, 112, 128)     147584
# block2_pool (MaxPooling2D)   (None, 56, 56, 128)       0
# block3_conv1 (Conv2D)        (None, 56, 56, 256)       295168
# block3_conv2 (Conv2D)        (None, 56, 56, 256)       590080
# block3_conv3 (Conv2D)        (None, 56, 56, 256)       590080
# block3_pool (MaxPooling2D)   (None, 28, 28, 256)       0
# block4_conv1 (Conv2D)        (None, 28, 28, 512)       1180160
# block4_conv2 (Conv2D)        (None, 28, 28, 512)       2359808
# block4_conv3 (Conv2D)        (None, 28, 28, 512)       2359808
# block4_pool (MaxPooling2D)   (None, 14, 14, 512)       0
# block5_conv1 (Conv2D)        (None, 14, 14, 512)       2359808
# block5_conv2 (Conv2D)        (None, 14, 14, 512)       2359808
# block5_conv3 (Conv2D)        (None, 14, 14, 512)       2359808
# block5_pool (MaxPooling2D)   (None, 7, 7, 512)         0
# flatten (Flatten)            (None, 25088)             0
```

```
# fc1 (Dense)                    (None, 4096)              102764544
# fc2 (Dense)                    (None, 4096)               16781312
# predictions (Dense)            (None, 1000)                4097000
#============================================================
#Total params: 138,357,544
#Trainable params: 138,357,544
#Non-trainable params: 0
#_____

vgg19_model = vgg19.VGG19(weights='imagenet')
#vgg19_model.summary()

inception_model = inception_v3.InceptionV3(weights='imagenet')
resnet_model = resnet50.ResNet50(weights='imagenet')
mobilenet_model = mobilenet.MobileNet(weights='imagenet')
xception_model = xception.Xception(weights='imagenet')
```

3. **Process and classify images**: Executes the following steps, using the next code snippet:

   a. Iterate through a list of image filenames (that you want to classify).

   b. For each image in the specified list, load the image (with the function **load_img()**) and resize to the input size expected by the models (224×224 pixels for most models). The **target_size** parameter for the function should match the input size expected by the model to be used.

   c. Convert the image from a **PIL** Image to a **numpy** array (with **img_to_array()** function) and adds an extra dimension to create a **batch** (using the function **np.expand_dims()**), as **tf.keras** models expect inputs in batch form.

   d. For each model, the image batch is preprocessed according to the requirements of that model. This typically involves scaling pixel values in a way that matches how the model was originally trained (use the method **preprocess_input()**).

   e. Classifying the image is as simple as calling the **predict()** method (running a **forward pass**) on the model with the preprocessed image as input. The model makes predictions on the input image, outputting the probabilities across all (1000) **ImageNet** classes.

4. **Decode predictions**: The predictions (probabilities) are decoded into human-readable class labels, with the top predictions (for example, **top**) being extracted for each model.

5. **Visualization**: For each of the input images, the following steps are executed:

a. The original image is resized for display and annotated with the top 5 predictions from each model, including the class labels and the associated probabilities.

b. The image is annotated with text showing the top prediction for each model, including the **label** and the **probability score**.

c. Uses **cv2.putText()** to add this information onto the image.

d. The annotated image is displayed using **matplotlib**, with the **axis** turned **off** for clarity, using the following code snippet:

```python
modules = [vgg16, vgg19, inception_v3, resnet50, mobilenet, xception]
models = [vgg16_model, vgg19_model, inception_model, resnet_model, \
                            mobilenet_model, xception_model]

for img in ['clock.jpg', 'bee.jpg', 'peacock.jpg', \
            'zebra.jpg', 'elephant.jpg', 'broccoli.jpg']:

    img = 'images/' + img
    # Load an image in PIL format
    original = load_img(img, target_size=(224, 224))
    numpy_image = img_to_array(original)
    image_batch = np.expand_dims(numpy_image, axis=0)

    labels = {}
    for i in range(len(modules)):
        module, model = modules[i], models[i]
        # prepare the image for the VGG model
        processed_image = module.preprocess_input(image_batch.copy())
        # get the predicted probabilities for each class
        predictions = model.predict(processed_image)
        labels[model.name] = decode_predictions(predictions)

    numpy_image = np.uint8(img_to_array(original)).copy()
    numpy_image = cv2.resize(numpy_image,(900,900))
    y = 40
    for model in models:
        cv2.putText(numpy_image, "{}: {}, {:.2f}".format( \
                    model.name, \
                    labels[model.name][0][0][1], \
                    labels[model.name][0][0][2]), \
                    (350, y), cv2.FONT_HERSHEY_SIMPLEX, 1, (255, 0, 0), 3)
        y += 35
    numpy_image = cv2.resize(numpy_image, (700,700))

    plt.figure(figsize=[10,10])
    plt.imshow(numpy_image)
    plt.axis('off')
    plt.show()
```

If you run the preceding code snippet, you should obtain a figure like the next one:

Figure 7.13: Image classification with pretrained popular deep learning models

Image classification with custom classes using transfer learning with pytorch

Pretrained models alone cannot classify custom classes they weren't originally trained on. To adapt them, **transfer learning** is used—this involves reusing a pretrained model's learned features and fine-tuning it on the new, task-specific dataset. In this section, we shall demonstrate how to implement **transfer learning** with **pytorch,** to perform image classification with custom classes. We shall use a **pretrained model** as **feature extractor** and train a new classifier (for example, the popular **ResNet** model) on top of it. Make sure you have **pytorch** installed (**pip install torch**), before we start.

Understanding transfer learning

Transfer learning is a powerful technique in deep learning that involves starting from a **pretrained model** and adapting it to a **new**, but **related** task. For image classification, this means leveraging the knowledge a model has gained from a large and diverse dataset like ImageNet and applying it to classification of images into custom categories.

Transfer learning typically involves two main steps:

1. **Feature extraction**: In feature extraction, the pre-trained model's layers are **frozen** except for the final layer(s), which are replaced with new ones tailored to the new task.

2. **Fine-tuning**: In fine-tuning, a part of the model, typically the last part (seldom the entire model) is then trained on the new dataset, allowing the model to adjust its weights to the new task.

`PyTorch`, a popular deep learning library, offers an accessible and efficient way to implement transfer learning. This section will demonstrate transfer learning with PyTorch for image classification with custom classes. The merits of transfer learning are as follows:

- **Efficiency**: Training a deep learning model from scratch requires significant computational resources and time. Transfer learning allows you to leverage existing models to achieve high performance with less computational effort.

- **Data requirements**: Deep learning models generally require large amounts of data to train. Transfer learning enables you to achieve high performance with smaller datasets.

Setting up the environment

You need to run the codes in this section on **Google Colab**, use their **GPU / TPU** runtime to speed-up the training process needed for **transfer learning**. First, we need to prepare the dataset, as explained.

Uploading the Dataset

Follow the next steps for data uploading / extraction:

1. First download the compressed image dataset from **Kaggle** through the following link: **https://www.kaggle.com/amadeus1996/fruits-360-transfer-learning-using-keras/data.**

2. Upload the **.tar** file it to your Google Drive.

3. Mount your Google Drive, using the following commands:

```
from google.colab import drive
drive.mount("/content/drive")
```

4. Extract the contents of the **.tar** file) containing image data, using the following sequence of commands in a terminal shell (first uncomment them and then run):

```
!tar -xvf /content/drive/MyDrive/256_ObjectCategories.tar
```

5. Then use the following three commands to create subdirectories within images for each animal category:

```
!mkdir images/goat!mkdir images/elk!mkdir images/raccoon
```

6. Use the final three commands to copy images from specific folders in the extracted archive to their respective category directories:

```
!cp -r 256_ObjectCategories/085.goat/* images/goat
!cp -r 256_ObjectCategories/065.elk/* images/elk
!cp -r 256_ObjectCategories/168.raccoon/* images/raccoon
```

The dataset contains images of **goats**, **elks**, and **raccoons**—custom classes we aim to classify using image classification with **transfer learning**.

Using the pretrained ResNet-18 model

The **ResNet-18** model is a deep CNN that is part of the **ResNet** family (the architecture shown in the following figure). It is designed to address some of the challenges faced by very deep neural networks, such as **vanishing gradients** and degradation of performance with increasing depth. It incorporates **residual learning** to address training challenges associated with deep neural networks. Its use of **residual blocks** with **identity shortcuts** makes it easier to train and optimize, even though it has fewer layers compared to deeper models in the **ResNet** family. Its architecture balances performance and computational efficiency, making it a popular choice for various applications in computer vision. Refer to the following figure:

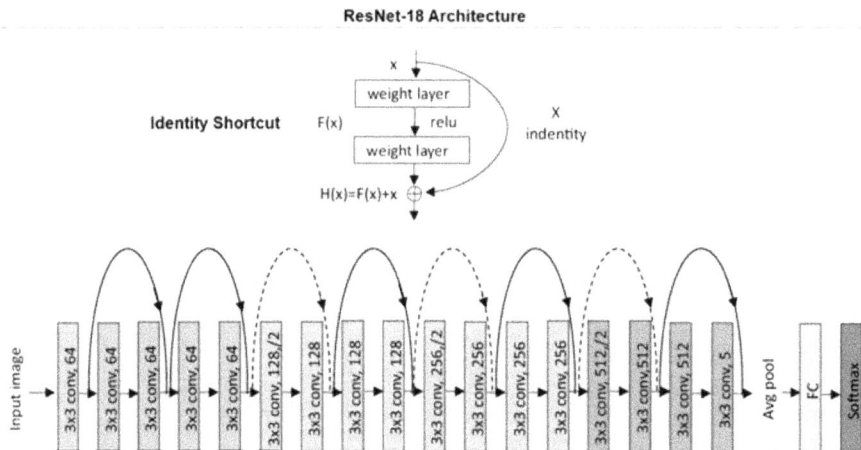

Figure 7.14: ResNet-18 model architecture

The following Python code snippet demonstrates how to use transfer learning with **pytorch** to classify a custom image dataset. The code effectively demonstrates how to leverage a pretrained **ResNet-18** model using **transfer learning** to classify images into custom categories with **pytorch**. Transfer learning allows for significant improvements in model performance with relatively small datasets by **fine-tuning** a model pretrained on a large and general dataset. The code can be broken down into the following key steps:

1. **Importing libraries:**

```python
import torch
import torch.nn as nn
import torch.optim as optim
from torch.optim import lr_scheduler
import torchvision
from torchvision import datasets, models, transforms
import numpy as np
import os, time, copy
from shutil import copyfile
import matplotlib.pyplot as plt
```

2. **Preparing dataset:**

   a. The function **create_training_validation_dataset()** organizes the image dataset into **training** and **validation** sets.

   b. It defines three classes (**'raccoon'**, **'goat'**, **'elk'**), corresponding to the new categories and creates separate directories for **training** and **validation** datasets (**images/train** and **images/valid**, respectively) for each class.

   c. It randomly splits the images for each class into **training** (80%) and **validation** (20%) sets, copying the images into the respective directories (using the function **copyfile()**).

Now, refer to the next code snippet:

```python
def create_training_validation_dataset():
    classes = ['raccoon', 'goat', 'elk']
    if not os.path.exists('images/train'):
        os.makedirs('images/train')

    for label in classes:
        if not os.path.exists(os.path.join('images/train', label)):
            os.makedirs(os.path.join('images/train', label))

    if not os.path.exists('images/valid'):
        os.makedirs('images/valid')

    for label in classes:
        if not os.path.exists(os.path.join('images/valid', label)):
            os.makedirs(os.path.join('images/valid', label))

    for label in classes:
        images = os.listdir(os.path.join('images/', label))
        train_indices = np.random.choice(len(images), \
                            int(0.8*len(images)), replace=False)
```

```
                valid_indices = list(set(range(len(images))) - \
                                set(train_indices))
            print(len(images), len(train_indices), len(valid_indices))
            for index in train_indices:
                copyfile(os.path.join('images/', label, images[index]),
                    os.path.join('images/train/', label, images[index]))
            for index in valid_indices:
                copyfile(os.path.join('images/', label, images[index]),
                    os.path.join('images/valid/', label, images[index]))

create_training_validation_dataset()
#140 112 28
#112 89 23
#101 80 21
```

3. **Data augmentation and normalization**:

   a. Apply transformations to the **training** dataset, such as **resizing**, random **cropping**, and horizontal **flipping**, in order to augment the data and help the model generalize better.

   b. Normalizes training and validation datasets using predefined **mean** and **standard deviation** values to match the pretrained model's requirements.

   c. Applies data **augmentation** and **normalization** for training, but just normalization for validation.

   d. **data_transforms**: A dictionary defining different image transformations for **training** and **validation** datasets.

4. **Loading dataset**:

   a. Uses **pytorch**'s **ImageFolder** to load images from the directory structure, applying the defined transformations (**data_transforms**).

   b. Creates **DataLoader** objects for both training and validation datasets to iterate over the data in batches.

   c. **data_dir**: The directory where the image data is stored.

   d. **DataLoader**: A dictionary mapping **train** and **valid** to **DataLoader** objects.

      i. **torch.utils.data.DataLoader**: A **pytorch** class for loading data in batches and managing shuffling and parallel data loading.

      ii. **batch_size=4**: Number of samples per batch.

      iii. **shuffle=True**: Shuffles the data at every epoch, which is generally used for training to ensure varied mini-batches.

      iv. **num_workers=4**: Number of subprocesses used for data loading. This speeds up data loading by utilizing multiple CPU cores.

5. **Setting up the computation device:**

   a. The training will be done on **GPU**. Otherwise, it will be too slow.

   b. **torch.device**: Determines the device to be used for computation.

   c. **"cuda:0"**: Uses the first GPU if available.

   d. **"cpu"**: Falls back to the CPU if no GPU is available.

   e. **device**: Stores the selected computation device. This ensures that the model and data are moved to the appropriate hardware (for example, GPU in this case) for training.

The following code snippet is part of a data preparation pipeline for training and validating a deep learning model using **pytorch**. It sets up image transformations for data augmentation, loads datasets from specified directories, creates data loaders for efficient data handling, calculates dataset sizes, and selects the appropriate computation device. This setup is crucial for training machine learning models efficiently and effectively.

```python
data_transforms = {
    'train': transforms.Compose([
        transforms.Resize(224),
        transforms.RandomResizedCrop(224),
        transforms.RandomHorizontalFlip(),
        transforms.ToTensor(),
        transforms.Normalize([0.485, 0.456, 0.406], \
                             [0.229, 0.224, 0.225])
    ]),
    'valid': transforms.Compose([
        transforms.Resize(256),
        transforms.CenterCrop(224),
        transforms.ToTensor(),
        transforms.Normalize([0.485, 0.456, 0.406], \
                             [0.229, 0.224, 0.225])
    ]),
}
data_dir = 'images'
image_datasets = {x: datasets.ImageFolder(os.path.join(data_dir, x), \
                      data_transforms[x]) for x in ['train', 'valid']}
dataloaders = {x: torch.utils.data.DataLoader(image_datasets[x], \
                      batch_size=8, shuffle=True, num_workers=4) \
                                    for x in ['train', 'valid']}
dataset_sizes = {x: len(image_datasets[x]) for x in ['train',
'valid']}
class_names = image_datasets['train'].classes

device = torch.device("cuda:0" if torch.cuda.is_available() else "cpu")
device
#device(type='cuda', index=0)
```

6. **Visualizing the image:**

a. The function **next(iter(dataloaders['train']))** retrieves the next batch of images (note that **batch_size** is 4 here) and their corresponding class labels from the training data loader: **inputs** variable is a batch of images, and **classes** variable contains the corresponding class indices.

b. **torchvision.utils.make_grid(inputs)**: Combines a batch of images into a single grid image, which is useful for visualizing multiple images at once.

c. The **plt.imshow()** function is designed to display a **pytorch tensor** as an image using **matplotlib**. It also handles image normalization and denormalization.

    i. **.numpy()** converts the **pytorch tensor** to a **numpy** array.

    ii. **.transpose((1, 2, 0))** changes the array shape from *(C,H,W)* i.e., (channels, height, width) to *(H,W,C)*, i.e, (height, width, channels) which is required for displaying an image with **matplotlib.pylab**.

    iii. **Denormalize image**: The **mean** and **std** (standard deviation) values are used to reverse the normalization applied to the images.

    iv. **np.clip()** ensures that pixel values are within the valid range [0,1] after denormalization.

```python
def imshow(inp, title=None):
    inp = inp.numpy().transpose((1, 2, 0))
    mean = np.array([0.485, 0.456, 0.406])
    std = np.array([0.229, 0.224, 0.225])
    inp = std * inp + mean
    inp = np.clip(inp, 0, 1)
    plt.imshow(inp)
    plt.axis('off')
    if title is not None:
        plt.title(title)

inputs, classes = next(iter(dataloaders['train']))
out = torchvision.utils.make_grid(inputs)

plt.figure(figsize=(10,5))
imshow(out, title=[class_names[x] for x in classes])
plt.show()
print(class_names, classes)
# ['elk', 'goat', 'raccoon'] tensor([2, 0, 2, 1])
```

If you run the preceding code snippet, you should obtain a figure like the next one:

['raccoon', 'elk', 'raccoon', 'goat']

Figure 7.15: Sample training images

7. **Training the model:**

Now, it is the time to train. The next python code snippet defines a function **train_model()** which will be used to **train** and **validate** a **pytorch** model (with **RestNet-18** backbone and pretrained **ImageNet** weights) over a specified number of epochs. The function handles both training and validation phases, updates the model weights, and tracks the best performing model, based on validation accuracy. Here is a detailed explanation of each part of the code:

a. The function **train_model()** accepts the following arguments:

   o **model**: The neural network model (with pretrained weights) to be trained (using **transfer learning**).

   o **criterion**: The **loss function** used to compute the loss.

   o **optimizer**: The **optimization algorithm** used to update model parameters.

   o **scheduler**: A **learning rate scheduler** to adjust the learning rate during training.

   o **num_epochs**: The number of **epochs** for which the model will be trained.

b. **Training initialization**: The variable **best_model_wts** is initialized to the current state dictionary of the pretrained model. It will be updated to hold the weights of the best performing model during training. The variable **best_acc** keeps track of the highest **validation accuracy** achieved.

c. **Training epochs**: It iterates through each epoch of training.

   o **if (epoch + 1) % 10 == 0:** It prints the current **epoch** number and the total number of epochs every epochs. This helps in monitoring the progress of training without cluttering the output.

   o **if phase == 'train':** It sets the model to training mode (using **model.train()**, which enables behaviors specific to training, such as

dropout and **batch normalization** updates and so on), otherwise to the evaluation mode (using `model.eval()`).

o   `inputs, labels = inputs.to(device), labels.to(device)`: It moves the data to the computation device (**CPU** or **GPU**).

o   `optimizer.zero_grad()`: Clears old gradients to prevent accumulation.

o   `with torch.set_grad_enabled(phase == 'train')`: Enables gradient calculation only if we are in the training phase.

o   `outputs = model(inputs)`: Performs a **forward pass** through the model.

o   `_, preds = torch.max(outputs, 1)`: Retrieves **predicted class labels** (corresponding to the **highest probability**).

o   `loss = criterion(outputs, labels)`: Computes the loss.

o   `if phase == 'train'`: It performs **backpropagation** and model **parameter update** through optimization only in the training phase.

    ▪ `loss.backward()`: Computes gradients.

    ▪ `scheduler.step()`: Updates the learning rate.

    ▪ `optimizer.step()`: Updates model parameters.

o   `running_loss` accumulates the loss for the **epoch** and `running_corrects` counts the number of correct predictions so far.

```python
def train_model(model, criterion, optimizer, scheduler, num_epochs=25):

    since = time.time()
    best_model_wts = copy.deepcopy(model.state_dict())
    best_acc = 0

    for epoch in range(num_epochs):

        if (epoch + 1) % 10 == 0:
            print('Epoch {}/{}'.format(epoch + 1, num_epochs))
            print('-' * 10)

        for phase in ['train', 'valid']:
            if phase == 'train':
                model.train()
            else:
                model.eval()
            running_loss, running_corrects = 0, 0
            for inputs, labels in dataloaders[phase]:
                inputs, labels = inputs.to(device), labels.to(device)
                optimizer.zero_grad() # zero the parameter gradients
```

```
                with torch.set_grad_enabled(phase == 'train'):
                    outputs = model(inputs)
                    _, preds = torch.max(outputs, 1)
                    loss = criterion(outputs, labels)
                    if phase == 'train':
                        loss.backward()
                        scheduler.step()
                        optimizer.step()
                running_loss += loss.item() * inputs.size(0)
                running_corrects += torch.sum(preds == labels.data)

            epoch_loss = running_loss / dataset_sizes[phase]
            epoch_acc = running_corrects.double() / dataset_sizes[phase]

            if (epoch + 1) % 10 == 0:
                print('{} Loss: {:.4f} Acc: {:.4f}'.format( \
                                        phase, epoch_loss, epoch_acc))
            if phase == 'valid' and epoch_acc > best_acc:
                best_acc = epoch_acc
                best_model_wts = copy.deepcopy(model.state_dict())

    time_elapsed = time.time() - since

    print('Training complete in {:.0f}m {:.0f}s'.format( \
                            time_elapsed // 60, time_elapsed % 60))

    print('Best val Acc: {:4f}'.format(best_acc))
    model.load_state_dict(best_model_wts)

    return model
```

d. **Model preparation**: sets up the model using the following steps:

   i. `models.resnet18(weights=models.ResNet18_Weights.DEFAULT)`: Loads the **ResNet-18** model with weights pre-trained on **ImageNet**.

   ii. **Freezing and unfreezing layers**: Freezes all the parameters corresponding to all the layers, except the last **fully connected** (**FC**) layer of the model by setting `requires_grad=False`. This means that the gradients for these parameters will not be computed during backpropagation, and thus they will not be updated during training. It also unfreezes the parameters of the final FC layer, allowing them to be updated during training. This is typically done to fine-tune the model for a new classification task with **transfer learning**.

   iii. `num_features = base_model.fc.in_features`: Gets the number of input features to the fully connected layer. This value corresponds to the number of output features from the preceding layer in the network.

    iv. `base_model.fc = nn.Linear(num_features, 3)`: Replaces the existing **FC** layer with a new one that has 3 output features. This is typically done to adapt the model to a new classification task with 3 classes, that is, to match the number of class labels in the custom dataset (3 in this case, namely, goat, elk and raccoon).

    v. Moves the model to the **GPU** if available.

e. **Training setup**: The following steps outline how the training process is set up for image classification using transfer learning:

    o Define a **loss** function (categorical **cross-entropy** loss, which is commonly used for multi-class classification tasks, measuring the difference between the **predicted class probabilities** and the **true class labels**) using the function `nn.CrossEntropyLoss()` and an **SGD** optimizer.

        i. `lr=0.01`: Sets the **learning rate** to 0.01.

        ii. `momentum=0.9`: Sets the **momentum** for the **SGD** optimizer. Momentum helps accelerate gradient vectors in the right directions, thus leading to **faster convergence**.

    o Implement a **learning rate scheduler** to adjust the learning rate over epochs.

        i. `lr_scheduler.StepLR`: LR scheduler that adjusts the learning rate by a specified factor at regular intervals.

        ii. `step_size=10`: Sets the number of epochs between each learning rate decay.

        iii. `gamma=0.5`: Sets the factor by which the learning rate will be decayed. For example, if the learning rate is 0.01, it will be reduced to 0.005 after 10 epochs.

Refer to the next code snippet:

```
torch.set_warn_always(False)
torch.manual_seed(121)   # set the random seed for reproducibility

base_model = models.resnet18\
    (weights=models.ResNet18_Weights.DEFAULT)
# Freeze all layers
for param in base_model.parameters():
    param.requires_grad = False
```

```
# Unfreeze last layer
for param in base_model.fc.parameters():
    param.requires_grad = True

num_features = base_model.fc.in_features
base_model.fc = nn.Linear(num_features, 3)
base_model = base_model.to(device)

criterion = nn.CrossEntropyLoss()
# Observe that all parameters are being optimized
optimizer = optim.SGD(base_model.fc.parameters(), lr=0.01, \
                                              momentum=0.9)

# Decay LR by a factor of 0.1 every 7 epochs
exp_lr_scheduler = lr_scheduler.StepLR(optimizer, step_size=10, \
                                              gamma=0.5)
```

o   Train the model for a specified number of **epochs** (50), adjusting the
model's **weights** based on the **loss** calculated on the **training** dataset
and evaluate the model's performance on the **validation** dataset. As
can be seen from the output of the following code snippet, the highest
validation accuracy reported is over 93%:

```
base_model = train_model(base_model, criterion, optimizer, \
                         exp_lr_scheduler, num_epochs=50)
#Epoch 10/50
#----------
#train Loss: 0.4501 Acc: 0.8327
#valid Loss: 0.2535 Acc: 0.9306
#Epoch 20/50
#----------
#train Loss: 0.4113 Acc: 0.8292
#valid Loss: 0.2905 Acc: 0.9167
#Epoch 30/50
#----------
#train Loss: 0.4864 Acc: 0.7972
#valid Loss: 0.2858 Acc: 0.9028
#Epoch 40/50
#----------
#train Loss: 0.4445 Acc: 0.8078
#valid Loss: 0.2868 Acc: 0.9028
#Epoch 50/50
#----------
#train Loss: 0.5053 Acc: 0.7829
#valid Loss: 0.2809 Acc: 0.9028
#Training complete in 5m 55s
#Best val Acc: 0.930556
```

8. **Model evaluation and visualization**: Here are the steps for evaluation of the model on the held-out **validation** dataset, along with supporting visualization:

o   Once the training is over, the best-performing model weights are saved and reloaded later when further evaluation or **inference** (the **mode** is changed to **evaluation**) is intended.

o   The model's predictions on the validation dataset are visualized with labels annotated using the function **visualize_model().** It shows images from the validation dataset, annotated by the predicted labels obtained by running a **forward pass** on the model with the image as input), as shown in the following code snippet. As can be seen from the following figure, all the 6 images are classified correctly by the model.

```python
torch.save(base_model.state_dict(), 'models/resnet18_trans_learn.pth')
base_model.load_state_dict(torch.load('models/resnet18_trans_learn.pth', \
                                        map_location='cpu'))
base_model.eval()

def visualize_model(model, num_images=6):

    model.eval()
    images_so_far = 0

    fig = plt.figure(figsize=(6,9))
    plt.subplots_adjust(0,0,1,0.925,0.05,0.08)

    with torch.no_grad():

        for i, (inputs, labels) in enumerate(dataloaders['valid']):
            inputs, labels = inputs.to(device), labels.to(device)
            outputs = model(inputs)
            _, preds = torch.max(outputs, 1)

            for j in range(inputs.size()[0]):
                images_so_far += 1
                plt.subplot(num_images//2, 2, images_so_far)
                plt.axis('off')
                plt.title('{}'.format(class_names[preds[j]]), size=15)
                imshow(inputs.cpu().data[j])

                if images_so_far == num_images:
                    plt.suptitle('predicted with Resnet-18 using transfer'
                                        'learning', size=15)
                    plt.show()
                    return

visualize_model(base_model)
```

If you run the preceding code snippet, you should obtain a figure like the next one:

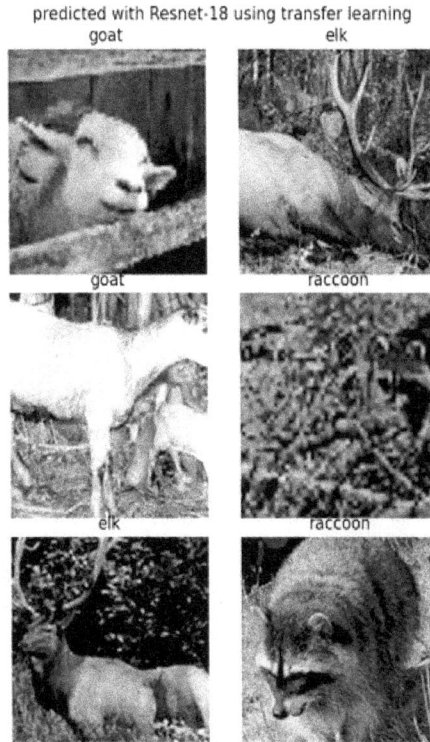

Figure 7.16: *Running inference with transfer learning*

9. **Testing with unseen images:**

Finally, let us classify a few unseen test images using the model and visualize the results obtained, using the following code snippet:

```python
from PIL import Image
import glob
import torch.nn.functional as F
from torch.autograd import Variable
loader =  transforms.Compose([
        transforms.CenterCrop(224),
        transforms.ToTensor(),
        transforms.Normalize([0.485, 0.456, 0.406], [0.229, 0.224, 0.225])
    ])
plt.figure(figsize=(20,25))
plt.subplots_adjust(0,0,1,0.925,0.05,0.08)
plt.suptitle('Test images predicted with Resnet18 using'
             'transfer learning', size=20)
i = 1
for img in glob.glob('images/test/*.jpg'):
```

```
    image = Image.open(img)
    image = loader(image).float()
    image = Variable(image, requires_grad=False)
    image = image.unsqueeze(0)
    out = base_model(image.to(device))
    y_prob = F.softmax(out, dim=1)
    prob, pred = torch.max(y_prob, 1)
    plt.subplot(5,3,i), plt.imshow(Image.open(img)), plt.axis('off')
    plt.title('{}, prob={:.4g}'.format(class_names[pred], \
                        round(prob.data.cpu().numpy()[0],3)), size=20)
    i += 1
plt.show()
```

If you run the preceding code snippet, you should obtain a figure as follows:

Figure 7.17: Classification with transfer learning (ResNet-18/ImageNet)

Once we finish running the code, the function **torch.cuda.empty_cache()** should be used to free up unused memory in the **GPU**:

```
torch.cuda.empty_cache()
```

Conclusion

This chapter provided a comprehensive overview of image classification techniques, starting with traditional machine learning models for classifying **Fashion-MNIST** images using **scikit-learn**, followed by deep learning approaches with **tensorflow** and **keras**. It explored the power of pre-trained models in **tensorflow** / **keras**, for efficient and accurate classification and demonstrated the versatility of transfer learning with **pytorch** for custom-class classification. By integrating these techniques, readers can apply a wide range of image classification methods to solve diverse real-world problems, from basic datasets to complex, domain-specific tasks.

Key terms

Image classification, pretrained model, transfer learning, VGG-16, ResNet.

Questions

1. Can the popular pretrained models (for example, models from **VGG**, **ReseNet** family) be used to classify **Fashion-MNIST** images? If yes, how? Use transfer learning and/or fine-tuning (for example, freeze last few layers of a model and train on Fashion-MNIST to update weights) to classify the images and compare the relative performances of the models against number of training epochs. You should obtain a figure like the one from **https://www.researchgate.net/figure/Comparison-of-the-accuracy-rate-in-the-Fashion-MNIST-dataset_fig5_351955214**, as shown:

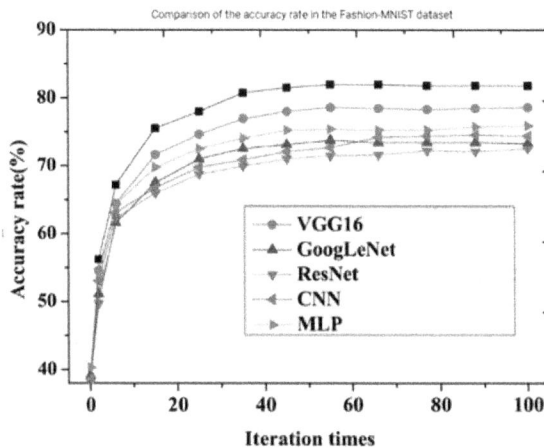

Figure 7.18: *Accuracy of deep learning models for Fashion-MNIST classification*
Source: *https://www.researchgate.net/publication/351955214_The_microscopic_visual_forms_in_architectural_art_design_following_deep_learning*

2. While transfer learning and fine-tuning with PyTorch, train the model by updating all the weight parameters of the **CNN** (without freezing any layer). Does the validation accuracy improve? Play with *hyperparameter tuning* (for example, change *epoch, learning rate, batch size* and so on) to observe the impact on *validation accuracy.*

References

1. https://developer.nvidia.com/cuda-downloads?target_os=Linux&target_arch=x86_64&Distribution=WSL-Ubuntu&target_version=2.0&target_type=runfile_local

2. https://www.researchgate.net/figure/Error-rates-on-the-ImageNet-Large-Scale-Visual-Recognition-Challenge-Accuracy_fig1_332452649

3. https://stackoverflow.com/questions/67905185/module-keras-engine-has-no-attribute-layer

4. https://ieeexplore.ieee.org/document/726791

5. https://www.deeplearningbook.org/

Join our Discord space

Join our Discord workspace for latest updates, offers, tech happenings around the world, new releases, and sessions with the authors:

https://discord.bpbonline.com

## CHAPTER 8

Object Detection and Recognition

Introduction

In the ever-evolving field of computer vision, **object detection and recognition** play a crucial role in enabling machines to interpret and understand visual data. These tasks form the backbone of many real-world applications such as autonomous driving, security surveillance, medical imaging, retail analytics, and human-computer interaction.

Object detection goes beyond simply identifying the presence of objects in an image—it also **localizes** them by drawing **bounding boxes** around each detected instance. For example, in a street scene, an object detection model can identify cars, pedestrians, and traffic signs while indicating their precise positions in the image. This dual task of **classification** and **localization** makes object detection a more complex and powerful technique than recognition alone. A few popular and very widely used object detection models include **Single Shot Multibox Detector (SSD)**, **Faster R-CNN**, **Mask R-CNN**, **You Only Look Once (YOLO)**, **RetinaNet**, and so on.

On the other hand, **object recognition** refers to the task of identifying and categorizing objects in an image or video. It involves determining what objects are present without necessarily providing precise locations. A key example is **face recognition**, which identifies a person from known identities, while **face verification** determines whether two face images belong to the same individual. A facial recognition system can identify specific individuals in an image, even without marking their exact positions. In contrast, **object detection** entails recognizing and determining the positions of multiple objects within an image or video by drawing bounding boxes around them. **Object localization** focuses on precisely locating a single object within an image, while **detection** extends this concept by handling multiple objects and assigning labels to each.

In the following sections, we will explore the principles and methodologies behind object detection and recognition, demonstrate how to implement them using Python, and review popular models and libraries. Whether you are a beginner seeking foundational knowledge or an experienced practitioner exploring advanced tools, this chapter will guide you through both the theoretical and practical aspects of these vital computer vision tasks.

Structure

In this chapter, we will cover the following topics:

- Object detection with pretrained deep learning models
- Custom object detection with transfer learning using YOLOv4 DarkNet
- Selective coloring with Mask R-CNN
- Face verification with DeepFace
- Barcode and QR code detection with Python

Objectives

In this chapter, we delve into key applications of object detection and recognition using Python and deep learning. You will learn how to perform object detection using pretrained models and how to build a custom object detector using **YOLOv4** with the **DarkNet** framework. The chapter also explores instance segmentation through selective coloring using **Mask R-CNN**. We introduce face verification using the **DeepFace** library, highlighting practical scenarios where determining whether two face images belong to the same person is crucial. Finally, you will learn how to detect **barcodes** and **QR codes** using specialized Python libraries. With a hands-on, application-oriented approach, this chapter will equip you with essential tools and techniques for solving real-world problems in visual recognition and detection.

Object detection with pretrained deep learning models

Object detection is a crucial area of computer vision that deals with identifying and localizing objects in images or videos. With the rise of deep learning, the accuracy and efficiency of object detection have significantly improved and pretrained models for object detection have become widely available, enabling developers to achieve impressive results often without building models from scratch.

As discussed earlier, object detection combines two fundamental tasks in computer vision:

- **Classification**: Recognizing what object is in the image.
- **Localization**: Identifying where in the image the object is located.

This task is challenging because it requires the system to not only detect objects but also draw bounding boxes around them. Here are a few state-of-the-art object detection models described as follows:

- **Faster R-CNN**: The **Faster R-CNN** model improves upon its predecessors, **R-CNN** (which used a multi-stage pipeline with external region proposals) and **Fast R-CNN** (which sped up detection by applying CNNs over the entire image), by introducing **Region Proposal Networks (RPNs)**. Region proposals are candidate bounding boxes likely to contain objects, refined and classified later, and traditional methods like selective search for generating region proposals, whereas RPNs generate these proposals nearly cost-free by sharing full-image convolutional features, making the system faster and more accurate, than traditional methods like selective search (**https://github.com/rbgirshick/py-faster-rcnn**).

- **YOLO**: The **You Only Look Once (YOLO)** model is a real-time, end-to-end object detection model that frames detection as a single **regression** problem, predicting bounding boxes and class probabilities simultaneously in one network pass (**https://github.com/AlexeyAB/darknet**). YOLO has multiple versions including YOLOv1, v2 (YOLO9000), v3, v4, v5, v6, v7, v8, and specialized variants like YOLO-NAS and YOLOX, each improving accuracy, speed, or usability. Compared to the R-CNN family, YOLO is significantly faster due to its single-stage architecture, while R-CNN variants are generally more accurate but slower because of their region proposal and refinement steps.

- **SSD**: The **SSD** model is an efficient model that eliminates the need for a separate object proposal generation step by predicting category scores and box offsets for a fixed set of default bounding boxes using small convolutional filters applied to feature maps (**https://github.com/balancap/SSD-Tensorflow**).

Here is a table comparing the key features of Faster R-CNN, YOLO, and SSD:

Feature	Faster R-CNN	YOLO	SSD
Architecture type	Two-stage (Region Proposal + Detection)	Single-stage (End-to-end regression)	Single-stage (End-to-end detection)
Speed	Slower (due to region proposals and two stages)	Faster (real-time detection)	Faster (real-time, but slightly slower than YOLO)
Region proposal	Uses RPN	Does not use region proposals; direct bounding box prediction	Uses default boxes and matching with object aspect ratios

Feature	Faster R-CNN	YOLO	SSD
Detection quality	High precision, better for small objects	Lower precision for small objects, but high speed	Balances speed and accuracy, good for medium objects
Application	Ideal for high accuracy in object detection, where speed is not the most important	Real-time applications like autonomous driving, surveillance	Suitable for real-time applications with good accuracy
Training complexity	Complex (needs two separate networks, RPN and detection)	Simple (end-to-end training)	Moderate (single network, but needs multiple default boxes)
Real-time performance	Not real-time (slower than YOLO and SSD)	Real-time (can process 30+ FPS)	Real-time (can process 30+ FPS)
Use case	High accuracy, particularly in fine-grained object detection	Fast detection for real-time applications	Balanced between speed and accuracy, often used in mobile devices and embedded systems
Popular variants	Faster R-CNN, Mask R-CNN (instance segmentation)	YOLOv3, YOLOv4, YOLOv5	SSD300, SSD512

Table 8.1: Comparison of Faster R-CNN, YOLO, and SSD

There are various pretrained deep learning models available for object detection, each with unique characteristics. This section demonstrates object detection using three popular (pretrained) models: **MobileNet-SSD** (with `caffe`/`opencv-python`), **YOLOv3** (with `gluoncv`/`mxnet`), and **YOLOv8** (with `ultralytics` framework). In the exercises you will be asked to demonstrate object detection in images using a **Faster R-CNN** pretrained model from `torchvision` / `pytorch`.

With MobileNet-SSD using opencv-python

One of the most efficient architectures for object detection tasks is **MobileNet-SSD**, which balances **speed** and **accuracy**, making it ideal for mobile and real-time applications on devices with limited computational resources, such as smartphones and IoT devices. Let us first explore the architecture of MobileNet-SSD, its advantages, and then we shall demonstrate how to use a pretrained model for object detection using `opencv-python`.

MobileNet-SSD architecture

The following bullet points break down its key components and how they work together:

- **MobileNet**: It is a lightweight deep neural network designed for mobile and embedded vision applications. Unlike heavy models such as **VGG** or **ResNet**, **MobileNet** uses **depth-wise separable convolutions**, which break down a regular convolution into two separate operations:

    o **Depthwise convolution**: Applies a single filter to each input channel (spatial convolution).

    o **Pointwise convolution**: Applies a 1×1 convolution to combine the outputs of depthwise convolution.

    o This architecture reduces computational costs significantly, making it suitable for resource-constrained devices.

- **SSD**: SSD is an object detection algorithm that predicts both object classes and bounding boxes in a single forward pass of the network. SSD divides the image into a grid, and for each grid cell, it predicts multiple bounding boxes and the probability of each class. Unlike Region Proposal Network used in other models like **Faster R-CNN**, **SSD** eliminates the need for separate region proposals, making it faster and more efficient.

- **MobileNet-SSD**: MobileNet-SSD combines the efficiency of **MobileNet** as a backbone feature extractor with the **SSD** detection head. This combination results in a lightweight, fast, and reasonably accurate object detection model that is particularly useful for embedded systems, real-time video processing, and applications with limited resources. The following figure shows the architecture of a **MobileNet -SSD** object detector:

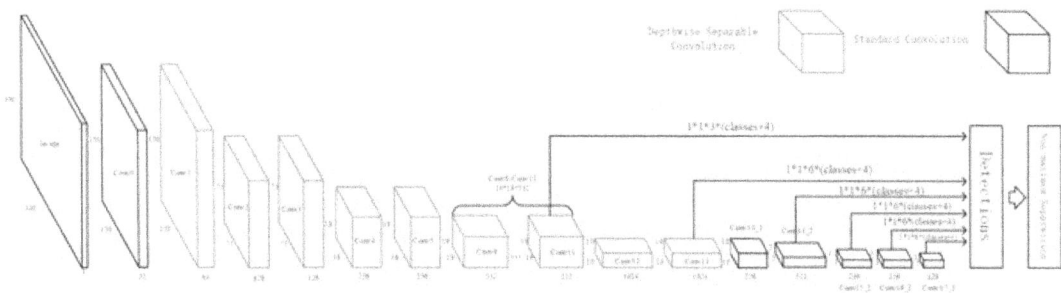

Figure 8.1: *MobileNet SSD architecture*
Source: https://www.mdpi.com/2078-2489/11/7/365

The next Python script uses a pretrained **MobileNet-SSD** model to perform object detection on an image. Here are the steps in details:

1. **Import the necessary packages**: At the very outset, import the following packages listed as follows (along with the purpose of using each of them), using the next code snippet:

    a. **openv-python (cv2)**: For image processing and model loading.

    b. **numpy**: For numerical computations.

    c. **imutils**: For image resizing.

    d. **Pillow (PIL)**: For handling image drawing and text overlay tasks.

```python
import cv2
from PIL import Image, ImageDraw, ImageFont
import imutils
import colorsys
import numpy as np
import matplotlib.pylab as plt
import time
```

2. **Model and configuration**: Define the path to the pre-trained **MobileNet-SSD** model and its **prototxt** file to be used. Also set a confidence threshold to filter out weak detections. The following explains each component:

    a. **prototxt**: This defines the architecture of the MobileNet-SSD model.

    b. **model**: This is the pre-trained MobileNet-SSD model trained on the COCO dataset.

3. **Labels and colors**: MobileNet-SSD can detect different object classes. The **labels** list defines a list of the class names, whereas the **colors** list defines a list of unique **Hue-Saturation-Value** (HSV) tuples, one for each class.

    a. **labels**: A list of class names that MobileNet-SSD can detect.

    b. **colors**: Generate a unique color for each class label using HSV tuples, making it easier to distinguish different objects in the image.

4. **Loading the model**: Load the pre-trained serialized MobileNet-SSD (**caffe**) model from the disk using **cv2.dnn.readNetFromCaffe()** function, from **opencv-python**. This loads both the model architecture and the pre-trained **weights** of the model.

5. **Preprocessing the input image**: Load the input image using **opncv-python**'s **imread()** function, resize it to a fixed **width** (while maintaining the **aspect ratio**, i.e., the **height** is automatically adjusted so the image does not look stretched or squished). Create a **4D blob** —a batch of images formatted as **(batch_size, channels, height, width)** for feeding into the deep neural network model,

using the function **cv2.dnn.blobFromImage()** which performs mean subtraction and resizes the image to 300×300 pixels (which is the input size expected by MobileNet-SSD).

6. **Running object detection**: Once the **blob** is created, pass it through the network (run a forward pass) and get the detections, using the **net.setInput()** and **net.forward()** methods.

7. **Processing the detections**: Loop over the detections to filter out weak ones based on the **confidence score**.

   a. **Confidence**: Filter out detections with a confidence score below 0.3.

   b. **Bounding box**: Calculate the bounding box coordinates for each detected object.

8. **Drawing bounding boxes and labels**: Once the valid detections are obtained, draw bounding boxes and labels on the image using **PIL** for better text rendering, it ensures smoother text rendering compared to **opencv-python**'s native **putText()** method.

9. **Displaying the output image**: Finally, display the image with the detected objects. *Figure 8.2* shows the annotated output image.

Now, refer to the next code snippet:

```
prototxt = 'models/MobileNetSSD_deploy.prototxt.txt'
model = 'models/MobileNetSSD_deploy.caffemodel'
conf = 0.3
labels = ["background", "aeroplane", "bicycle", "bird", "boat",
    "bottle", "bus", "car", "cat", "chair", "cow", "diningtable",
    "dog", "horse", "motorbike", "person", "pottedplant", "sheep",
    "sofa", "train", "tvmonitor"]

HSV_tuples = [(x/len(labels), 0.8, 0.8) for x in range(len(labels))]
colors = list(map(lambda x: colorsys.hsv_to_rgb(*x), HSV_tuples))

net = cv2.dnn.readNetFromCaffe(prototxt, model)
image = cv2.imread('images/dog_cycle.jpg')
image = imutils.resize(image, width=400)
(h, w) = image.shape[:2]
blob = cv2.dnn.blobFromImage(cv2.resize(image, (300, 300)), 0.007843, \
                                        (300, 300), 127.5)

net.setInput(blob)
detections = net.forward()
```

```python
for i in np.arange(0, detections.shape[2]):
    # extract the confidence
    confidence = detections[0, 0, i, 2]

    if confidence > conf:
        # extract the index of the class label from the `detections`,
        # compute(x, y)-coordinates of the bounding box for the object
        idx = int(detections[0, 0, i, 1])
        box = detections[0, 0, i, 3:7] * np.array([w, h, w, h])
        (startX, startY, endX, endY) = box.astype("int")

        # draw the prediction on the image
        label = "{}: {:.2f}%".format(labels[idx], confidence * 100)
        color = tuple([int(255*x) for x in colors[idx]])
        y = startY - 15 if startY - 15 > 15 else startY + 15
        pil_im = Image.fromarray(cv2.cvtColor(image,cv2.COLOR_BGR2RGB))
        thickness = (image.shape[0] + image.shape[1]) // 300
        font = ImageFont.truetype("arial.ttf", 15)
        draw = ImageDraw.Draw(pil_im)
        label_size = draw.textsize(label, font)

        if startY - label_size[1] >= 0:
            text_origin = np.array([startX, startY - label_size[1]])
        else:
            text_origin = np.array([startX, startY + 1])
        for i in range(thickness):
            draw.rectangle([startX + i, startY + i, endX - i, endY - i], \
                                                    outline=color)

        draw.rectangle([tuple(text_origin), tuple(text_origin + \
                                        label_size)],
                                        fill=color)
        draw.text(text_origin, label, fill=(0, 0, 0), font=font)
        del draw
        image = cv2.cvtColor(np.array(pil_im), cv2.COLOR_RGB2BGR)

plt.figure(figsize=(10,8))
plt.imshow(cv2.cvtColor(image, cv2.COLOR_BGR2RGB)), plt.axis('off')
plt.show()
```

If you run the preceding code snippet, you should obtain a figure as follows:

Figure 8.2: Detecting objects with pretrained MobileNet SSD

With Yolov3 using gluoncv and mxnet

In this section, we will demonstrate object detection using the powerful **YOLOv3** model with the `GluonCV` toolkit and `MXNet` framework, which offers a high-level, efficient, and flexible API with pre-trained state-of-the-art models for rapid prototyping and deployment. As described earlier, **YOLOv3** is one of the most popular end-to-end object detection models due to its balance between speed and accuracy. It processes images in real time, making predictions in a single pass through the neural network, hence the name **You Only Look Once**. We will now explore the YOLOv3 architecture, highlight its advantages, and demonstrate how to apply it to object detection tasks, with python code.

YOLOv3 architecture

YOLOv3 is the third iteration in the YOLO series of object detection models, designed to detect multiple objects within an image by predicting bounding boxes and class probabilities. It works by dividing the image into a grid and generating bounding box coordinates and class labels for each individual grid cell.

Unlike previous versions, YOLOv3 improves upon the following:

- **Multi-scale predictions**: YOLOv3 predicts boxes at three different scales, allowing it to detect both small and large objects.

- **Bounding box prediction**: It predicts four coordinates for each bounding box (x, y, width, and height) and uses **anchor boxes** to improve localization accuracy.

- **Feature extractor (Darknet-53)**: YOLOv3 uses **Darknet-53** (a 53-layer CNN built with residual connections and uses only 3×3 and 1×1 convolutions) as its backbone, which is deeper and more powerful compared to earlier versions (YOLOv2 uses Darknet-19).

The following figure shows the architecture of YOLOv3:

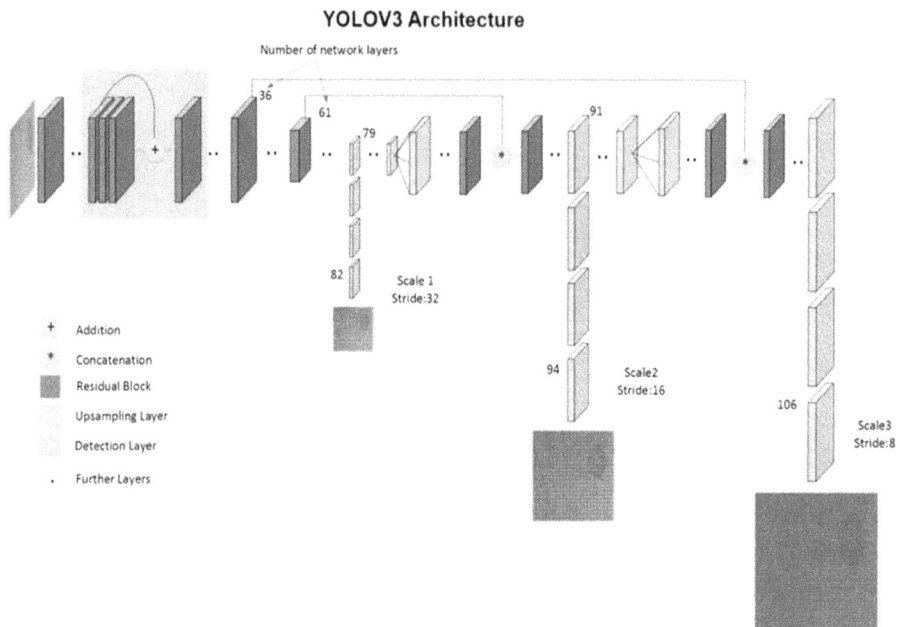

Figure 8.3: YOLOv3 architecture
*Source: https://www.researchgate.net/publication/340019698_*
Fabric_defect_detection_using_the_improved_YOLOv3_model

Advantages of YOLOv3

The advantages of YOLOv3 are:

- **Speed**: YOLOv3 is known for its speed, making it suitable for real-time object detection.

- **High accuracy**: While faster models may trade off some accuracy, YOLOv3 achieves a good balance between speed and precision.

- **Single-stage detection**: Unlike two-stage detectors (like Faster R-CNN), YOLOv3 makes predictions in a single forward pass, improving inference time.

GluonCV and **MXNet** are open-source libraries that facilitate deep learning in computer vision and general-purpose **GPU**-accelerated computing, respectively. The following points provide a clearer overview of their features and roles in the deep learning ecosystem:

- **MXNet**: Apache MXNet is a flexible, efficient, and scalable deep learning framework that supports fast model training and inference. It is designed to be both developer-friendly and performant, supporting a variety of programming languages including Python, C++, Scala, and R. MXNet is particularly known for its efficiency in both memory and computational speed, making it suitable for a wide range of deep learning tasks on devices ranging from mobile phones to distributed GPU clusters.

- **GluonCV**: GluonCV is a comprehensive toolkit for computer vision tasks, built on top of the MXNet deep learning framework. GluonCV provides pre-trained models for tasks like object detection, segmentation, pose estimation, and more. MXNet is a flexible and efficient deep learning framework that supports dynamic computational graphs, making it ideal for research and production applications.

Object detection with YOLOv3 with gluoncv

In the following demonstration, we will use a pre-trained YOLOv3 model available in GluonCV for detecting objects in an image. The next Python code snippet will allow us to load a pre-trained YOLOv3 model, process an input image with the model, and display the detected objects.

1. **Installing the required libraries**: To start, you need to install the **gluoncv** library and **mxnet** (if they are not already installed). They can be installed using **pip install**.

2. **Importing the necessary packages**: The next step is to import the required modules from **gluoncv** and **matplotlib**:

   a. **gluoncv's model_zoo**: Provides access to pre-trained models, including YOLOv3.

   b. **gluoncv's data.transforms.presets**: Includes utility functions to preprocess input images according to the model's requirements.

   c. **matplotlib.pylab**: Used for displaying the result images.

   Note: Dependency alert: GluonCV requires PyTorch versions ≥1.4.0 and <2.0.0. If your PyTorch version falls outside this range, you may need to upgrade using pip or conda.

```python
# !pip install gluoncv
# !pip install mxnet
from gluoncv import model_zoo, data, utils
from matplotlib import pyplot as plt
```

3. **Loading the pre-trained YOLOv3 model**: Load a pre-trained **YOLOv3** model with **Darknet-53** as the backbone (using **model_zoo.get_model()**), which has been trained on the **PASCAL VOC** dataset. Here **yolo3_darknet53_voc** refers to the YOLOv3 model with **Darknet-53** trained on the **VOC** dataset, which contains object categories.

```python
net = model_zoo.get_model('yolo3_darknet53_voc', pretrained=True)
```

4. **Preprocessing the input image**: Load the input image and apply YOLOv3-specific preprocessing using **gluoncv**'s preset transformation:

   a. **load_test()**: This function handles image loading and resizing, converting the image into the required input format for YOLOv3.

   b. **short=512**: Resizes the shorter side of the image to 512 pixels while maintaining the **aspect ratio** (i.e., the ratio of an image's **width** to its **height**).

   c. The preprocessed image is stored in the variable x, which will be used as input to the model. The original image (in its resized form) is stored in the variable img for visualization. As can be seen from the next code snippet, the preprocessed image **x** has a shape of (1, 3, 512, 512):

```
x, img = data.transforms.presets.yolo.load_test('images/dog_cycle.jpg', \
                                                    short=512)
print('Shape of pre-processed image:', x.shape)
# Shape of pre-processed image: (1, 3, 512, 683)
```

5. **Running object detection**: Pass the preprocessed image **x** to the model and run a **forward pass** (using the function **net()**), to get the **class IDs**, **scores** (**confidence**), and **bounding_boxs** of detected objects:

   a. **class_IDs**: Contains the predicted class IDs for each detected object.

   b. **scores**: Contains the confidence scores for the predictions.

   c. **bounding_boxes**: Contains the coordinates of the bounding boxes for each detected object.

6. **Visualizing the results**: Finally, we visualize the detected objects by drawing bounding boxes and class labels on the image:

   a. **utils.viz.plot_bbox()**: This utility function from the library **gluoncv** is used to draw the bounding boxes and labels on the image.

   b. **img**: The original image on which the bounding boxes are drawn.

   c. **bounding_boxes[0]**: The bounding boxes predicted by **YOLOv3**.

   d. **scores[0]**: The confidence scores for each bounding box.

   e. **class_IDs[0]**: The class IDs of the detected objects.

   f. **net.classes**: The list of object classes that YOLOv3 was trained on.

   g. **linewidth=6**: Sets the width of the bounding box lines.

   h. **fontsize=20**: Sets the font size for the class labels.

7. **Displaying the output**: Use **matplotlib.pylab** to display the image with bounding boxes. This will show the image with detected objects, each enclosed by a bounding box and labeled with its **predicted class** and **confidence score**.

```
class_IDs, scores, bounding_boxes = net(x)

plt.figure(figsize=(10,10))
utils.viz.plot_bbox(img, bounding_boxes[0], scores[0], class_IDs[0], \
                            class_names=net.classes,ax=plt.gca(), \
                            linewidth=6, fontsize=20)
plt.axis('off')
plt.show()
```

If you run the preceding code snippet, you should obtain a figure as follows:

Figure 8.4: Detecting objects using YOLOv3 with gluoncv

With YOLOv8 using ultralytics

In this section, we shall dive into **YOLOv8**, one of the cutting-edge models in the YOLO family, implemented through the **ultralytics** package. YOLOv8 improves upon its predecessors by delivering faster inference, better accuracy, and a more streamlined interface. This makes it suitable for both real-time and high-performance object detection tasks.

We will explore the architecture of YOLOv8, walk through the installation process, and explain how to train, evaluate, and use the model for object detection in images. To demonstrate its practical use, we will break down a Python code example step-by-step.

YOLOv8 architecture

YOLOv8 is one of the latest iterations of the YOLO series, continuing the tradition of being one of the fastest and most accurate object detection models. YOLOv8 has been designed with significant enhancements in:

- **Accuracy**: YOLOv8 features better object localization and classification than previous versions.

- **Speed**: With optimizations, YOLOv8 is faster, especially when using GPUs.

- **Flexibility**: It supports various input image sizes and can be deployed in both CPU and GPU environments efficiently.

Ultralytics YOLOv8 model types

The **ultralytics** package provides several **YOLOv8** model sizes, ranging from **YOLOv8n** (**nano**) for speed to **YOLOv8x** (**extra-large**) for accuracy. These model sizes allow users to choose between **fast inference** or **greater precision** based on their use case, as shown in the next figure:

Model	Size	Parameters (M)	FLOPs (B)	Speed (ms)	Accuracy (mAP)	Use case
YOLOv8n	Nano	~ 3.2M	~ 8.7B	Fastest (~2ms)	Lower	Real-time, edge devices, mobile application
YOLOv8s	Small	~ 11.2M	~ 28.6B	Fast (~3ms)	Moderate	Drones, embedded systems, speed-critical tasks
YOLOv8m	Medium	~ 25.9M	~ 78.9B	Balanced (~5ms)	Good	General object detection with balanced speed and accuracy
YOLOv8l	Large	~ 43.7M	~ 165.2B	Slower (~5ms)	High	Industrial automation, security cameras
YOLOv8x	Extra-Large	~68.2M	~ 257.8B	Slowest (~12ms)	Highest	High-precision applications, research, medical imaging

Table 8.2: Speed vs. accuracy tradeoff for ultralytics YOLOv8 models

Advantages of YOLOv8

The advantages of YOLOv8 are listed as follows:

- **End-to-end model handling**: It includes training, validation, and prediction all in one API.

- **Lightweight**: The model **YOLOv8n** (**nano**) offers **high-speed** object detection with **low memory** requirements.

- **Ease of use**: The model can be quickly deployed on various platforms, including mobile and edge devices.

Object detection using YOLOv8 with python

Now, let us demonstrate how to use YOLOv8 for object detection using the **ultralytics** package. The next Python code snippet will be used to demonstrate object detection with YOLOv8. Let us understand how it works:

1. **Check for GPU availability**: The function `torch.cuda.is_available()` returns **True** if the system has a **CUDA**-enabled **GPU**, otherwise **False**.

2. **Loading the YOLOv8 model**: Import the YOLO module from the **ultralytics** library and load the **YOLOv8n** (**nano**) model. The **yolov8n.pt** file is the pre-trained model that is designed for lightweight and fast object detection. When you call **YOLO("yolov8n.pt"),** the **ultralytics** library checks if **yolov8n.pt** exists in the cache. If not, it automatically downloads the pretrained weights from the official **Ultralytics** model hub. Then it loads the pre-trained **YOLOv8n** model, which is optimized for speed and efficient inference.

3. **Training the YOLOv8 model**: The model is trained on the **COCO8** dataset (a tiny sample version of the **COCO** dataset provided by **Ultralytics**) for 100 epochs using the method **model.train()**, with images resized to 640×640 pixels. The **data** argument to this function points to the dataset **YAML** file which contains the dataset configuration. The **device** argument ensures the model runs on a **GPU** if available, otherwise, it defaults to the CPU (you must train on GPU to avoid very slow training: Use **Google Colab** if you don't have a locally configured **CUDA**-enabled **GPU** or an **NVIDIA** graphics card, as it provides free access to powerful GPUs / TPUs for running deep learning models). Here is the list of input arguments to the function:

    a. **data="coco8.yaml"**: This specifies the path to the dataset configuration file. The **coco8** dataset is a small subset of the COCO dataset, often used for quick testing.

    b. **epochs=100**: Sets the number of epochs for training the model. An epoch is one complete pass through the entire dataset.

    c. **imgsz=640**: Resizes images to 640×640 pixels during training to standardize input size for better accuracy.

    d. **device=0**: Runs training on GPU if available (0 refers to the first GPU). If no GPU is available, it runs on the CPU.

The training process involves:

    a. Loading the dataset as specified in the YAML file.

    b. Training the model for the specified number of epochs.

    c. Logging the training results, including metrics such as loss and accuracy.

Refer to the next code snippet:

```
import torch
print(torch.cuda.is_available())
# True
from ultralytics import YOLO
# Load model
```

```
model = YOLO("yolov8n.pt")

# Train the model
train_results = model.train(
    data="coco8.yaml",  # path to dataset YAML
    epochs=100,  # number of training epochs
    imgsz=640,  # training image size
    device=0 if torch.cuda.is_available() else "cpu",  # device to run on,
                                # i.e. device=0 or device=0,1,2,3 or device=cpu
)
```

Refer to the following figure to see how the training process progresses:

```
                 from  n    params  module                                       arguments
  0                  -1  1       464  ultralytics.nn.modules.conv.Conv             [3, 16, 3, 2]
  1                  -1  1      4672  ultralytics.nn.modules.conv.Conv             [16, 32, 3, 2]
  2                  -1  1      7360  ultralytics.nn.modules.block.C2f             [32, 32, 1, True]
  3                  -1  1     18560  ultralytics.nn.modules.conv.Conv             [32, 64, 3, 2]
  4                  -1  2     49664  ultralytics.nn.modules.block.C2f             [64, 64, 2, True]
  5                  -1  1     73984  ultralytics.nn.modules.conv.Conv             [64, 128, 3, 2]
  6                  -1  2    197632  ultralytics.nn.modules.block.C2f             [128, 128, 2, True]
  7                  -1  1    295424  ultralytics.nn.modules.conv.Conv             [128, 256, 3, 2]
  8                  -1  1    460288  ultralytics.nn.modules.block.C2f             [256, 256, 1, True]
  9                  -1  1    164608  ultralytics.nn.modules.block.SPPF            [256, 256, 5]
 10                  -1  1         0  torch.nn.modules.upsampling.Upsample         [None, 2, 'nearest']
 11             [-1, 6]  1         0  ultralytics.nn.modules.conv.Concat           [1]
 12                  -1  1    148224  ultralytics.nn.modules.block.C2f             [384, 128, 1]
 13                  -1  1         0  torch.nn.modules.upsampling.Upsample         [None, 2, 'nearest']
 14             [-1, 4]  1         0  ultralytics.nn.modules.conv.Concat           [1]
 15                  -1  1     37248  ultralytics.nn.modules.block.C2f             [192, 64, 1]
 16                  -1  1     36992  ultralytics.nn.modules.conv.Conv             [64, 64, 3, 2]
 17            [-1, 12]  1         0  ultralytics.nn.modules.conv.Concat           [1]
 18                  -1  1    123648  ultralytics.nn.modules.block.C2f             [192, 128, 1]
 19                  -1  1    147712  ultralytics.nn.modules.conv.Conv             [128, 128, 3, 2]
 20             [-1, 9]  1         0  ultralytics.nn.modules.conv.Concat           [1]
 21                  -1  1    493056  ultralytics.nn.modules.block.C2f             [384, 256, 1]
 22        [15, 18, 21]  1    897664  ultralytics.nn.modules.head.Detect           [80, [64, 128, 256]]
Model summary: 225 layers, 3,157,200 parameters, 3,157,184 gradients, 8.9 GFLOPs

Transferred 355/355 items from pretrained weights
Freezing layer 'model.22.dfl.conv.weight'
AMP: running Automatic Mixed Precision (AMP) checks with YOLOv8n...
AMP: checks passed

train: Scanning C:\My Books\BPB\Part2\Chapter_05\datasets\coco8\labels\train.cache... 4 images, 0 backgrounds, 0 corrup
val: Scanning C:\My Books\BPB\Part2\Chapter_05\datasets\coco8\labels\val.cache... 4 images, 0 backgrounds, 0 corrupt: 1

Plotting labels to runs\detect\train3\labels.jpg...
optimizer: 'optimizer=auto' found, ignoring 'lr0=0.01' and 'momentum=0.937' and determining best 'optimizer', 'lr0' and 'momentum' automaticall
optimizer: AdamW(lr=0.000119, momentum=0.9) with parameter groups 57 weight(decay=0.0), 64 weight(decay=0.0005), 63 bias(decay=0.0)
Image sizes 640 train, 640 val

Using 8 dataloader workers
Logging results to runs\detect\train3
Starting training for 100 epochs...

      Epoch    GPU_mem   box_loss   cls_loss   dfl_loss  Instances       Size

      1/100     0.635G      1.069      3.506      1.513         21        640: 100%|██████████| 1/1 [00:01<00:00,  1.20
                 Class     Images  Instances      Box(P          R      mAP50  mAP50-95): 100%|██████████| 1/1 [00:00<0

                   all          4         17      0.619      0.877      0.888      0.615
```

Figure 8.5: Training YOLOv8 with ultralytics

4. **Evaluating the model**: Once the model is trained, it is to be evaluated on the validation dataset to measure its performance. The **`model.val()`** method runs evaluation on the validation dataset and returns a dictionary of performance evaluation metrics such as **precision**, **recall**, **F1-score, mAP50** (mean average precision at an **IoU** threshold of 0.50: it assesses the model's accuracy in detecting objects with at least 50% overlap with the ground truth), **speed metrics** (including **inference time, non-maximum suppression** time) etc. These metrics help to gauge how well the model has learned to detect objects.

5. **Performing object detection on an image**: Here, we use the trained **YOLOv8** model to perform object detection on an input (test) image. The model processes the image and outputs predictions, including bounding boxes, confidence scores, and class labels for detected objects.

   a. `model("images/dog_cycle.jpg")`: Performs object detection on the specified image and returns the detection results.

   b. `results[0].show()`: Displays the image with bounding boxes and class labels drawn around the detected objects. YOLOv8 automatically handles visualization using its built-in methods.

The detection process includes:

   a. Preprocessing the input image (resizing, normalization, and so on.).

   b. Running the image through the YOLOv8 model to predict bounding boxes and class labels.

   c. Drawing bounding boxes and displaying the results on the original image.

Let us now use the model (trained previously) for **inference**: use it to detect objects in a test image, run a **forward pass** on the model with the test image as input, as shown in next code snippet:

```
# Evaluate model performance on the validation set
metrics = model.val()
# Perform object detection on an image
results = model("images/dog_cycle.jpg")
results[0].show()
```

The following figure shows the annotated image obtained with detected objects. If you run the preceding code snippet, you should obtain a figure as follows:

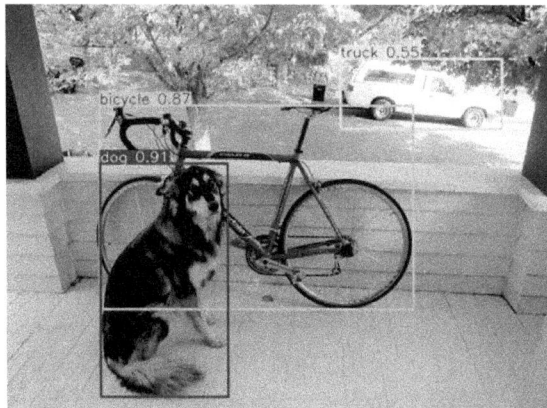

Figure 8.6: Detecting objects using YOLOv8 with ultralytics

Custom object detection with transfer learning using YOLOv4 Darknet

Pretrained object detection models may not always suffice because they are trained on general datasets and may not recognize custom objects, making transfer learning a good choice to adapt the model to new, specific classes. In this section, we shall walk through the process of creating a custom object (**raccoon**) detector using **transfer learning** with YOLOv4 in **Google Colab** (create a notebook at **https://colab.research.google.com/** and follow the steps listed as follows). **YOLOv4** is again a highly efficient end-to-end object detection model, offering an excellent trade-off between speed and accuracy. Follow the steps listed, to setup the environment, train the model and test it on unseen images, using a dataset for **raccoon detection**:

1. **Setting up the environment**: Start by cloning the YOLOv4 repository and setting up dependencies in Google Colab (Google Colab is to be used to train the model on GPU). YOLOv4 is implemented in the **Darknet** framework, which we will need to build from source.

2. **Cloning the Darknet repository**: Run the following command to clone the official YOLOv4 Darknet GitHub repository:

```
# run in google colab (you could run on WSL too)
!git clone https://github.com/AlexeyAB/darknet/
%cd darknet/
```

Using the preceding commands, first clone the Darknet repository into the current working directory and then navigate to the **Darknet** directory.

3. **Installing dependencies**: Change the `Makefile` to enable GPU and `opencv` and run make to create the darknet executable:

```
!apt install libopencv-dev python-opencv ffmpeg
```

4. **OpenCV** will help in image augmentation and other preprocessing tasks. Now, let us modify the Darknet `Makefile` to enable GPU, CUDNN, and OpenCV:

```
!sed -i 's/OPENCV=0/OPENCV=1/g' Makefile
!sed -i 's/GPU=0/GPU=1/g' Makefile
!sed -i 's/CUDNN=0/CUDNN=1/g' Makefile
# %cat Makefile
```

5. **Build Darknet**: After making these changes, build the Darknet framework (using the command `make` as shown). This process will compile Darknet with OpenCV, GPU, and CUDNN support, significantly speeding up training and inference.

```
!make
```

6. **Downloading/preparing the dataset**: In this step, we shall set up our dataset for custom object detection. Start with a dataset of raccoon images, which are annotated with bounding boxes for training **YOLOv4** model. The (compressed) dataset can be downloaded from this book's GitHub repository (**https://github. com/sandipan/Book-BPB600/blob/main/Chapter08/images/raccoons.zip** , download it and unzip). There are images containing one or more instances of the custom object (**raccoon**).

Each image has a corresponding **text** file with the same name, specifying the **bounding boxes** for the objects exactly in the format as the YOLOv4 Darknet model accepts, which looks like **[class, x, y, width, height]**.

In this annotation,

a. The first two coordinates *(x, y)* represent the **center** of the **bounding box**.

b. The next two represent the **width** and **height** of the bounding box, respectively.

Here we are providing you the annotated images (along with the ground-truth labels and bounding boxes for the objects to be detected) for training images. In the exercise section, you will explore how to annotate and extract bounding box coordinates from your own images manually/automatically/semi-automatically using tools available on the internet.

Since we shall use **Google Colab** for the training of the **YOLOv4 Darknet** model, we need to upload the annotated images to the **Google Drive** as shown in the following figure:

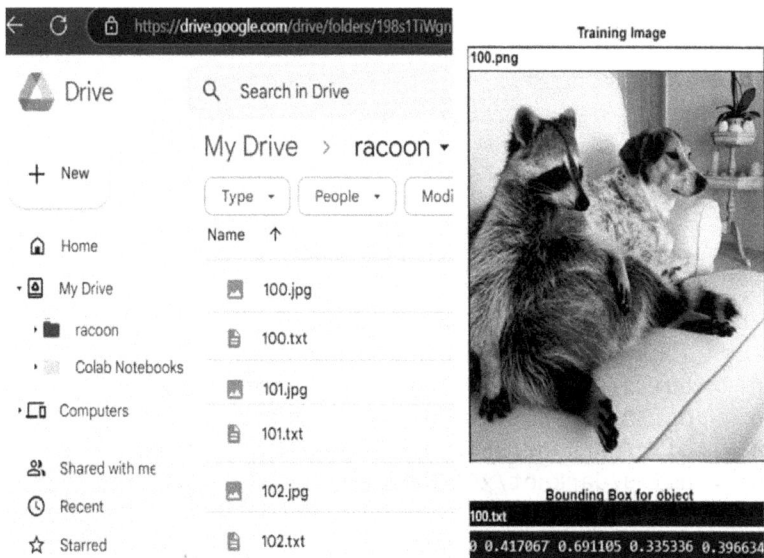

Figure 8.7: Uploading images to Google Drive

As can be seen from the preceding figure, the google drive contains a folder named **raccoon**, inside which all the images and the corresponding ground-truth annotation texts (with bound box coordinates) are uploaded. One such image, the ground-truth class (id 0, there is only one custom class **raccoon** that we want to detect) and the corresponding annotation bound box (normalized) coordinates is shown on the right in *Figure 8.8*.

7. **Defining classes**: Since we are detecting raccoons, we need to create a file listing the object classes (in our case, just one class). Let us create a file for class labels, as shown:

```
all_classes = """Raccoon"""

file = """text_file = open("build/darknet/x64/data/obj.names", "w");
                    text_file.write(all_classes);text_file.close()"""

exec(file)
%cat build/darknet/x64/data/obj.names
# Raccoon
```

This creates the **obj.names** file that lists all object classes, in this case, **Raccoon**.

8. **Defining data file**: We need to create a file **build/darknet/x64/data/obj.data** (using the following command), which specifies the information regarding the data (for example, the number of classes, paths for the training and validation data), and the location where the model checkpoints will be saved), as shown:

```
obj_data = """
classes= 1
train  = build/darknet/x64/data/train.txt
valid  = build/darknet/x64/data/valid.txt
names = build/darknet/x64/data/obj.names
backup = build/darknet/x64/backup/
"""

file = """text_file = open("build/darknet/x64/data/obj.data", "w");
          text_file.write(obj_data);text_file.close()"""

exec(file)

%cat build/darknet/x64/data/obj.data
classes= 1
train  = build/darknet/x64/data/train.txt
valid  = build/darknet/x64/data/valid.txt
names = build/darknet/x64/data/obj.names
backup = build/darknet/x64/backup/
```

Here the training and validation text files (**train.txt** and **valid.txt**, respectively) list the names of the **training** and **validation** set images, whereas **backup** represents the location for saving the model checkpoints while training. It also specifies that we have a single object class (**classes=1**) to be detected.

Loading pre-trained weights for transfer learning

YOLOv4 supports **transfer learning**, which allows us to **fine-tune** the model, which was pre-trained on a large dataset (like **COCO: Common Objects in Context**). This significantly reduces the training time required (to train from scratch) for custom datasets. Now, let us follow the next steps:

1. **Download the pre-trained weights**: We need to download the pre-trained model **yolov4.conv.137** and copy it to the right folder (**build/darknet/x64**), using the following command in the terminal. These weights will be used to initialize the network for training.

```
!wget -P build/darknet/x64/
#https://github.com/AlexeyAB/darknet/releases/download/darknet_
yolo_v3_optimal/yolov4.conv.137
```

2. **Mounting Google Drive for data**: Since our dataset is stored in Google Drive, we need to mount it directly into colab to access your training images and labels.

```
# Load the Drive helper and mount
from google.colab import drive

# This will prompt for authorization.
drive.mount('/content/drive')
# Mounted at /content/drive
```

Now that the files in the Google Drive becomes accessible from colab, copy the images/text annotations to the right path (**build/darknet/x64/data/obj/**), as expected by the model:

```
%cp -r "/content/drive/MyDrive/racoon/." build/darknet/x64/data/obj/
```

This command copies the images/corresponding annotations from Google Drive to the Colab folder, as shown in the following figure:

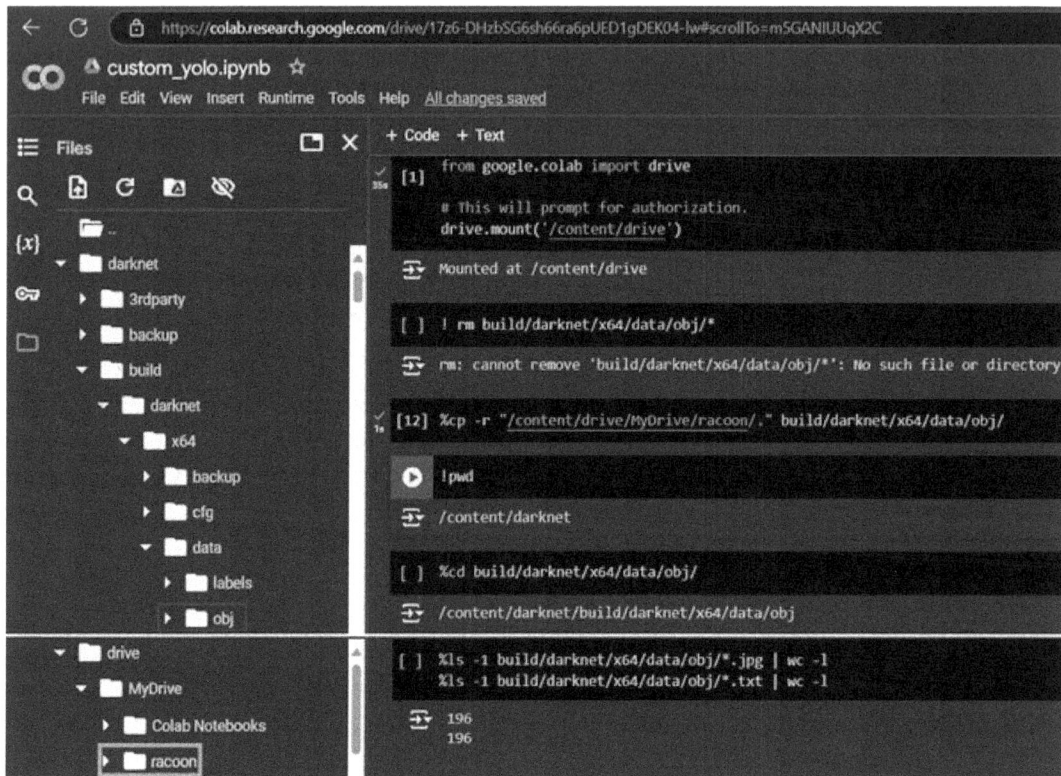

Figure 8.8: Copying images/annotations from google drive to Google Colab

Verify whether there are exactly same number of images and annotations (`.txt`) files (196 in total), using the following commands:

```
%ls -1 build/darknet/x64/data/obj/*.jpg | wc -l
#196
%ls -1 build/darknet/x64/data/obj/*.txt | wc -l
#196
```

3. **Preparing image lists**: To train **YOLOv4**, we need two text files (**train.txt** and **valid.txt**) that list the paths to training and validation images. Let us randomly split our dataset, each image has an 80% chance of being assigned to the **training** dataset and a 20% chance of being assigned to the **validation** dataset, determined by a random number generator seeded for reproducibility, as shown in the next code snippet:

```
import os, fnmatch
import numpy as np

train_file = open("build/darknet/x64/data/train.txt", "w")
valid_file = open("build/darknet/x64/data/valid.txt", "w")
listOfFiles = os.listdir('build/darknet/x64/data/obj/')
pattern = "*.jpg"

np.random.seed(24) # for reproducibility
for f_name in listOfFiles:
  if fnmatch.fnmatch(f_name, pattern):
    if np.random.rand(1) < 0.8:
      train_file.write("build/darknet/x64/data/obj/"+f_name+"\n")
      #print ("data/obj/"+f_name)
    else:
      valid_file.write("build/darknet/x64/data/obj/"+f_name+"\n")

train_file.close()
valid_file.close()
```

This script randomly splits the image files into **train.txt** and **valid.txt**.

4. **Verifying data**: To verify the number of images in each dataset, you can count the lines in the **train.txt** and **valid.txt** files, as shown:

```
# Count number of files
!wc -l build/darknet/x64/data/train.txt
#151
!wc -l build/darknet/x64/data/valid.txt
#45
```

Configuring YOLOv4 for custom training

YOLOv4 needs to be configured to match the number of object classes in your dataset. We will start by copying the default configuration file and then editing it for our custom training task. Follow the given series of preparation steps, as outlined:

1. **Editing the YOLOv4 configuration file**: Copy the default **yolov4.cfg** file to **yolov4_train.cfg** and make necessary changes for your custom training:

```
%cp cfg/yolov4.cfg cfg/yolov4_train.cfg
!sed -i 's/batch=1/batch=8/g' cfg/yolov4_train.cfg
!sed -i 's/subdivisions=1/subdivisions=2/g' cfg/yolov4_train.cfg
!sed -i 's/classes=80/classes=1/g' cfg/yolov4_train.cfg
!sed -i 's/filters=255/filters=18/g' cfg/yolov4_train.cfg
!sed -i 's/max_batches = 500200/max_batches = 2000/g' cfg/yolov4_train.cfg
!sed -i 's/steps=400000,450000/steps=1800,2200/g' cfg/yolov4_train.cfg
```

2. As can be seen from the preceding code, here is how the hyperparameter values are changed:

a. **batch**: Set to 8 (small value) for faster convergence (and also because the number of **training** images is small). As an exercise, check with 3 different values, namely, 16, 8 and 4 and observe the impact on training.

b. **subdivisions**: Set to 2, to reduce GPU memory load.

c. **classes**: Set to 1 for raccoon detection (need to change the number of classes to 1, becuase we are interested to detect a single object here, as opposed to 80 in the original config file).

d. **filters**: Set to 18, calculated as (classes + 5) × 3 = (1 + 5) × 3.

e. **max_batches**: Set to 2000 (recommended to be at least **2000*number_of_classes**), the model checkpoints stored at batches 500, 1000 and 2000 respectively.

f. **steps**: Set to 1800 and 2200 for learning rate decay.

Total number of images we have is 196, out of which 151 of them are used for training and the remaining are used for validation. A relevant portion of the config file (with few of the hyperparameters) to be used for training the YOLOv4 model are:

```
[net]
# Training
batch=8
subdivisions=2
width=416
height=416
channels=3
momentum=0.949
decay=0.0005
angle=0
saturation = 1.5
exposure = 1.5
hue=.1

learning_rate=0.0013
burn_in=1000
max_batches = 2000
policy=steps
steps=1800,2200
scales=.1,.1

[convolutional]
batch_normalize=1
size=3
stride=1
pad=1
filters=1024
activation=leaky

[convolutional]
size=1
stride=1
pad=1
filters=18
activation=linear

[yolo]
mask = 6,7,8
anchors = 12, 16, 19, 36, 40, 28, 36, 75, 76, 55, 72, 146, 142, 110, 192, 243, 459, 401
classes=1
```

Figure 8.9: *YOLOv4 config file*

Now we can start training the model on our annotated images, initializing it with the pretrained weights, using the following line of code.

3. **Training the model**: Now we are ready to train the custom YOLOv4 model. Execute the following command to begin training:

```
!./darknet detector train build/darknet/x64/data/obj.data
cfg/yolov4_train.cfg build/darknet/x64/yolov4.conv.137 -dont_show
```

This command trains the model using the dataset, configuration file, and pre-trained weights. A few iterations of training are shown in the following figure:

```
 157: 2.931075, 11.303170 avg loss, 0.000001 rate, 0.728067 seconds, 1256 images, 0.468906 hours left
Loaded: 0.000043 seconds
v3 (iou loss, Normalizer: (iou: 0.07, obj: 1.00, cls: 1.00) Region 139 Avg (IOU: 0.000000), count: 1, class_loss = 1.018232, iou_loss = 0.000000, total_loss =
v3 (iou loss, Normalizer: (iou: 0.07, obj: 1.00, cls: 1.00) Region 150 Avg (IOU: 0.417630), count: 17, class_loss = 6.139600, iou_loss = 1.145177, total_loss
v3 (iou loss, Normalizer: (iou: 0.07, obj: 1.00, cls: 1.00) Region 161 Avg (IOU: 0.411019), count: 28, class_loss = 10.493891, iou_loss = 0.373770, total_loss
 total_bbox = 9959, rewritten_bbox = 0.030124 %
v3 (iou loss, Normalizer: (iou: 0.07, obj: 1.00, cls: 1.00) Region 139 Avg (IOU: 0.000000), count: 1, class_loss = 0.936943, iou_loss = 0.000000, total_loss =
v3 (iou loss, Normalizer: (iou: 0.07, obj: 1.00, cls: 1.00) Region 150 Avg (IOU: 0.314127), count: 9, class_loss = 3.739927, iou_loss = 0.210741, total_loss =
v3 (iou loss, Normalizer: (iou: 0.07, obj: 1.00, cls: 1.00) Region 161 Avg (IOU: 0.287626), count: 24, class_loss = 9.388246, iou_loss = 0.113463, total_loss
 total_bbox = 9992, rewritten_bbox = 0.030024 %

 158: 5.293634, 10.702217 avg loss, 0.000001 rate, 0.735152 seconds, 1264 images, 0.467945 hours left
Loaded: 0.000077 seconds
v3 (iou loss, Normalizer: (iou: 0.07, obj: 1.00, cls: 1.00) Region 139 Avg (IOU: 0.000000), count: 1, class_loss = 0.974290, iou_loss = 0.000000, total_loss =
v3 (iou loss, Normalizer: (iou: 0.07, obj: 1.00, cls: 1.00) Region 150 Avg (IOU: 0.420950), count: 2, class_loss = 1.465065, iou_loss = 0.082233, total_loss =
v3 (iou loss, Normalizer: (iou: 0.07, obj: 1.00, cls: 1.00) Region 161 Avg (IOU: 0.426132), count: 14, class_loss = 6.191417, iou_loss = 0.112925, total_loss
 total_bbox = 10008, rewritten_bbox = 0.029976 %
v3 (iou loss, Normalizer: (iou: 0.07, obj: 1.00, cls: 1.00) Region 139 Avg (IOU: 0.000000), count: 1, class_loss = 0.833702, iou_loss = 0.000000, total_loss =
v3 (iou loss, Normalizer: (iou: 0.07, obj: 1.00, cls: 1.00) Region 150 Avg (IOU: 0.265348), count: 4, class_loss = 2.123889, iou_loss = 0.073504, total_loss =
v3 (iou loss, Normalizer: (iou: 0.07, obj: 1.00, cls: 1.00) Region 161 Avg (IOU: 0.373428), count: 17, class_loss = 7.014144, iou_loss = 0.157483, total_loss
 total_bbox = 10029, rewritten_bbox = 0.029913 %

 159: 3.107751, 9.942770 avg loss, 0.000001 rate, 0.732459 seconds, 1272 images, 0.467027 hours left
Loaded: 0.000057 seconds
v3 (iou loss, Normalizer: (iou: 0.07, obj: 1.00, cls: 1.00) Region 139 Avg (IOU: 0.000000), count: 1, class_loss = 0.746195, iou_loss = 0.000000, total_loss =
v3 (iou loss, Normalizer: (iou: 0.07, obj: 1.00, cls: 1.00) Region 150 Avg (IOU: 0.651219), count: 4, class_loss = 1.993922, iou_loss = 0.248510, total_loss =
v3 (iou loss, Normalizer: (iou: 0.07, obj: 1.00, cls: 1.00) Region 161 Avg (IOU: 0.436553), count: 15, class_loss = 6.250632, iou_loss = 0.148269, total_loss
 total_bbox = 10048, rewritten_bbox = 0.029857 %
v3 (iou loss, Normalizer: (iou: 0.07, obj: 1.00, cls: 1.00) Region 139 Avg (IOU: 0.469531), count: 2, class_loss = 1.421023, iou_loss = 0.721031, total_loss =
v3 (iou loss, Normalizer: (iou: 0.07, obj: 1.00, cls: 1.00) Region 150 Avg (IOU: 0.335029), count: 18, class_loss = 6.406221, iou_loss = 0.543491, total_loss
v3 (iou loss, Normalizer: (iou: 0.07, obj: 1.00, cls: 1.00) Region 161 Avg (IOU: 0.368685), count: 35, class_loss = 12.614141, iou_loss = 0.308021, total_loss
 total_bbox = 10103, rewritten_bbox = 0.029694 %
```

***Figure 8.10**: Training iterations with YOLOv4*

It may take around 30 mins – 1 hour to finish 2000 batches and in the end, the final model weights are stored in a file (**`yolov4_train_final.weights`**) on the **`backup`** folder provided.

4. **Model selection/testing the model/prediction**: Now, let us use the model (just trained) for prediction:

   a. Since the batch size 8 and subdivision size 2 resulted in higher accuracy (in terms of **Intersection Over Union** or **IOU** measure), the corresponding model is selected as the best fit model.

   b. The final model checkpoint is saved (**`yolov4_train_final.weights`**) can be used for prediction (with an unseen image **`racoons.jpg`**, you need to upload it to **`colab`** first) with the following command.

c. The annotated output is saved as **predictions.jpg** in the same directory. If you want to save the results in a specific file, you can redirect the output to a file.

```
!./darknet detector test build/darknet/x64/data/obj.data cfg/yolov4_train.cfg
                        build/darknet/x64/backup/yolov4_train_final.weights
                        -dont_show /content/raccoons.jpg
# Predictions
# Raccoon: 79%
# Raccoon: 75%
# Raccoon: 99%
```

If you run the preceding code snippet, you should have the racoons objects detected as shown in the next figure:

Figure 8.11: Custom object detection with YOLOv4

As can be seen from the preceding figure, all the 3 raccoons in the test image are detected by the model, with confidence 79%, 75% and 99%, even though couple of them were *partially occluded*.

Selective coloring with Mask R-CNN

Mask R-CNN is a powerful deep learning model for **instance segmentation**, which not only detects objects in an image but also generates high-quality **pixel-level segmentation masks** for each individual object instance. It builds on the object detection capabilities of **Faster R-CNN** and extends them to include precise segmentation. Let us first get acquainted with the key terminology and components:

- **Object detection**: Identifies and locates objects within an image by predicting bounding boxes and class labels.

- **Instance segmentation**: A more fine-grained task that creates pixel-wise masks for each detected object, distinguishing even overlapping instances of the same class.

- **Backbone network**: Typically, a deep CNN (e.g., **ResNet-50** or **ResNet-101** with **FPN**) used to extract rich hierarchical features from the input image.

- **Region Proposal Network (RPN)**: Generates candidate object regions (region proposals) from the backbone features.

- **RoIAlign**: A key improvement over the earlier **RoIPool**, **RoIAlign** precisely preserves spatial locations using bilinear interpolation, which is crucial for pixel-level tasks like mask prediction.

- **Bounding box and mask prediction**: The model simultaneously predicts object classes, refines bounding boxes, and produces a binary mask (segmentation) for each object.

This model is an extension of **Faster R-CNN** model, adding a branch for predicting object masks in parallel with bounding box recognition. In this section, we shall use the **Mask R-CNN** model to detect objects in an image and generate instance segmentation masks. Then these masks will be used to selectively color the detected objects while leaving the background in grayscale.

Here we shall use the library **mrcnn**, which is an implementation of the **Mask R-CNN** model in **keras** and **tensorflow**, used for object detection and instance segmentation with support for training, inference, and visualization. You can install the **mrcnn** library by cloning the official Mask R-CNN GitHub repository and installing its dependencies, here's how:

```
# clone the repository
git clone https://github.com/matterport/Mask_RCNN.git
cd Mask_RCNN

# install required packages
pip install -r requirements.txt

# install the library
python setup.py install
```

The following Python code snippet performs selective coloring of the objects detected in an image using **Mask R-CNN**. Here is a step-by-step explanation of how the selective coloring is achieved:

1. **Load Mask R-CNN model and weights**: As usual, begin by importing the necessary libraries such as mrcnn, **numpy**, and **matplotlib**. Then, download the pre-trained Mask R-CNN weights trained on the **COCO** dataset (which contains 80 object classes) and save them in the location specified by **COCO_MODEL_PATH**. These weights will be used to initialize the model for inference or fine-tuning.

```
from mrcnn import utils, visualize
import mrcnn.model as modellib
from mrcnn.config import Config

import os
import numpy as np
```

```
COCO_MODEL_PATH = "models/mask_rcnn_coco.h5"
if not os.path.exists(COCO_MODEL_PATH):
    utils.download_trained_weights(COCO_MODEL_PATH)
# Downloading pretrained model to models/mask_rcnn_coco.h5 ...
# ... done downloading pretrained model!
```

2. If you want to train the Mask R-CNN model, we need to provide a configuration object for training on MS COCO.

    a. The configuration class must derive from the base **Config** class and override values specific to the COCO dataset.

    b. Give the configuration class a recognizable name (for example, **CocoConfig**, as in the next code snippet).

    c. Depending on the memory available for GPU and the number of images it can fit, adjust **IMAGES_PER_GPU**.

    d. Specify the number of GPUs available as **GPU_COUNT**.

    e. Specify the number of classes (including background) as **NUM_CLASSES** (COCO has 80 classes + 1 **Background** class)

3. Since, we shall use the model for **inference**, we do not need to train and hence let us define the class **InferenceConfig**:

    a. Set batch size to 1 since we will be running inference on one image at a time (in general, **Batch_SIZE = GPU_COUNT * IMAGES_PER_GPU**), as shown in the next code snippet:

```
class CocoConfig(Config):
    NAME = "coco"
    IMAGES_PER_GPU = 1
    NUM_CLASSES = 81

class InferenceConfig(CocoConfig):
    GPU_COUNT = 1
    IMAGES_PER_GPU = 1
    BATCH_SIZE = 1
```

    b. Let us display the **config** file, using the next code snippet:

```
config = InferenceConfig()
config.display()
# Configurations:
# BACKBONE                       resnet101
# BACKBONE_STRIDES               [4, 8, 16, 32, 64]
# BATCH_SIZE                     1
# BBOX_STD_DEV                   [0.1 0.1 0.2 0.2]
```

```
# COMPUTE_BACKBONE_SHAPE          None
# DETECTION_MAX_INSTANCES         100
# DETECTION_MIN_CONFIDENCE        0.7
# DETECTION_NMS_THRESHOLD         0.3
# FPN_CLASSIF_FC_LAYERS_SIZE      1024
# GPU_COUNT                       1
# GRADIENT_CLIP_NORM              5.0
# IMAGES_PER_GPU                  1
# IMAGE_MAX_DIM                   1024
# IMAGE_META_SIZE                 93
# IMAGE_MIN_DIM                   800
# IMAGE_MIN_SCALE                 0
# IMAGE_RESIZE_MODE               square
# IMAGE_SHAPE                     [1024 1024    3]
# LEARNING_MOMENTUM               0.9
# LEARNING_RATE                   0.001
# LOSS_WEIGHTS                    {'rpn_class_loss': 1.0,
#                                  'rpn_bbox_loss': 1.0,
#                                  'mrcnn_class_loss': 1.0,
#                                  'mrcnn_bbox_loss': 1.0,
#                                  'mrcnn_mask_loss': 1.0}
# MASK_POOL_SIZE                  14
# MASK_SHAPE                      [28, 28]
# MAX_GT_INSTANCES                100
# MEAN_PIXEL                      [123.7 116.8 103.9]
# MINI_MASK_SHAPE                 (56, 56)
# NAME                            coco
# NUM_CLASSES                     81
# POOL_SIZE                       7
# POST_NMS_ROIS_INFERENCE         1000
# POST_NMS_ROIS_TRAINING          2000
# ROI_POSITIVE_RATIO              0.33
# RPN_ANCHOR_RATIOS               [0.5, 1, 2]
# RPN_ANCHOR_SCALES               (32, 64, 128, 256, 512)
# RPN_ANCHOR_STRIDE               1
# RPN_BBOX_STD_DEV                [0.1 0.1 0.2 0.2]
# RPN_NMS_THRESHOLD               0.7
# RPN_TRAIN_ANCHORS_PER_IMAGE     256
# STEPS_PER_EPOCH                 1000
# TOP_DOWN_PYRAMID_SIZE           256
# TRAIN_BN                        False
# TRAIN_ROIS_PER_IMAGE            200
# USE_MINI_MASK                   True
# USE_RPN_ROIS                    True
# VALIDATION_STEPS                50
# WEIGHT_DECAY                    0.0001
```

4. Create the Mask R-CNN model object in inference mode (using **mode="inference"**), using the **config**. Load weights trained on **MS COCO** (with the method **load_weights()**).

```
model = modellib.MaskRCNN(mode="inference", model_dir='.', \
                                     config=config)
model.load_weights(COCO_MODEL_PATH, by_name=True)
```

5. The next code snippet lists the COCO class names; there are 81 classes in the list. Index of the class in the list is its ID. For example, you can get the ID of the **teddy bear** class using **class_names.index('teddy bear')**.

```
class_names = ['BG', 'person', 'bicycle', 'car', 'motorcycle', 'airplane',
            'bus', 'train', 'truck', 'boat', 'traffic light',
            'fire hydrant', 'stop sign', 'parking meter', 'bench', 'bird',
            'cat', 'dog', 'horse', 'sheep', 'cow', 'elephant', 'bear',
            'zebra', 'giraffe', 'backpack', 'umbrella', 'handbag', 'tie',
            'suitcase', 'frisbee', 'skis', 'snowboard', 'sports ball',
            'kite', 'baseball bat', 'baseball glove', 'skateboard',
            'surfboard', 'tennis racket', 'bottle', 'wine glass', 'cup',
            'fork', 'knife', 'spoon', 'bowl', 'banana', 'apple',
            'sandwich', 'orange', 'broccoli', 'carrot','hot dog','pizza',
            'donut', 'cake', 'chair', 'couch', 'potted plant', 'bed',
            'dining table', 'toilet', 'tv', 'laptop', 'mouse', 'remote',
            'keyboard', 'cell phone', 'microwave', 'oven', 'toaster',
            'sink', 'refrigerator', 'book', 'clock', 'vase', 'scissors',
            'teddy bear', 'hair drier', 'toothbrush']

len(class_names)
# 81
```

6. **Selective coloring (color splash effect)**: The key to selective coloring lies in the **color_splash()** function. This function accepts an **image** and a segmentation **mask** (produced by the **Mask R-CNN** model) as input and selectively applies color only to the detected objects, leaving the rest of the image in grayscale. Let us understand how the function works step-by-step:

   a. **Grayscale conversion**: The image is first converted to grayscale, using the function **skimage.color.rgb2gray()**. However, it is not converted into a single channel, but into a -channel grayscale image, using the function **skimage.color.gray2rgb()**, ensuring it maintains the same shape as the original RGB image.

   b. **Mask creation**: Use the mask returned by Mask R-CNN to determine where the detected objects are located. Sum the **mask** along the instance dimension (**axis=-1**), collapsing all detected object masks into a single layer. This mask is binary, where pixels corresponding to any detected object have a value of **True** and the background has a value of **False**.

   c. **Object detection with Mask R-CNN**: When an image is passed to the model, it performs detection and returns the following information in the results dictionary:

    i.   **ROIs**: The bounding boxes of detected objects.

    ii.   **masks**: A Boolean mask indicating the location of each detected object.

    iii.   **class_ids**: The class IDs corresponding to the detected objects.

    iv.   **scores**: Confidence scores for the detected objects.

    d.   **Selective coloring**: The function then selectively keeps the original color values in the regions where the mask is **True** (that is, where objects are detected), and applies the grayscale version where the mask is **False** (that is, background):

```
def color_splash(image, mask):
    gray = skimage.color.gray2rgb(skimage.color.rgb2gray(image)) * 255
    mask = (np.sum(mask, -1, keepdims=True) >= 1)
    return np.where(mask, image, gray).astype(np.uint8) \
                                      if mask.shape[0] > 0 else gray
```

7. **Visualization of the color splash**: The function **show_image()** displays the output image obtained (with color splash effect). It plots the following three images side by side:

    a.   **original image**: The input image in full color.

    b.   **mask**: A binary mask highlighting the detected objects.

    c.   **splash**: The result of the selective coloring, where the detected objects remain in color while the rest is grayscale.

The function allows **selective object-coloring** based on specific object classes. For example, if you want to highlight only **bus**, it checks which detected objects match the **label 'bus'** and zeroes out the **mask** for other objects, as shown in the *Figure 8.12*.

```
def show_image(image, mask_rcnn_res, class_names, label='all'):

    if label != 'all':
        class_names = np.array(class_names)
        idx = np.where(class_names[mask_rcnn_res['class_ids']] != \
                                                              label)

        mask_rcnn_res['masks'][...,idx] = 0

    mask = np.zeros(image.shape[:2])
    for i in range(mask_rcnn_res['masks'].shape[2]):
        mask += mask_rcnn_res['masks'][...,i]
    splash = color_splash(image, mask_rcnn_res['masks'])

    plt.figure(figsize=(20,10))
    plt.gray()
```

```
plt.subplots_adjust(0,0,1,0.95,0.05,0.05)
plt.subplot(131), plt.imshow(image), plt.axis('off')
plt.title('original image', size=20)
plt.subplot(132), plt.imshow(mask), plt.axis('off')
plt.title('mask r-cnn objects{}detected'.format( \
        '' if label == 'all' else ' (' + label + ') '), size=20)
plt.subplot(133), plt.imshow(splash), plt.axis('off')
plt.title('selective coloring of the objects detected', size=20)
plt.show()
```

This ensures that only the specified object class (for example, bus) will remain in color, while all other objects and the background will appear in grayscale.

8. **Execution on an example image**: Finally, the code loads a sample image and runs the **Mask R-CNN** model to detect objects (using `model.detect()`).

The detected objects are visualized with the selective color splash effect, specifically focusing on the `'bus'` class as defined in the `show_image()` call, as shown in the following code snippet. The next figure (*Figure 8.12*) shows the output image with color splash, along with the input image and mask obtained with the Mask R-CNN model.

```
image = skimage.io.imread('images/bus.jpg')
results = model.detect([image], verbose=1)
show_image(image, results[0], class_names, 'bus')
# Processing 1 image
# image                   shape: (340, 510, 3)          min:      0.00000
# max:    255.00000   uint8
# molded_images           shape: (1, 1024, 1024, 3)     min:   -123.70000
# max:    150.10000   float64
# image_metas             shape: (1, 93)                min:      0.00000
# max: 1024.00000   float64
# anchors                 shape: (1, 261888, 4)         min:     -0.35390
# max:      1.29134   float32
```

If you run the preceding code snippet, you should obtain a figure like the next one:

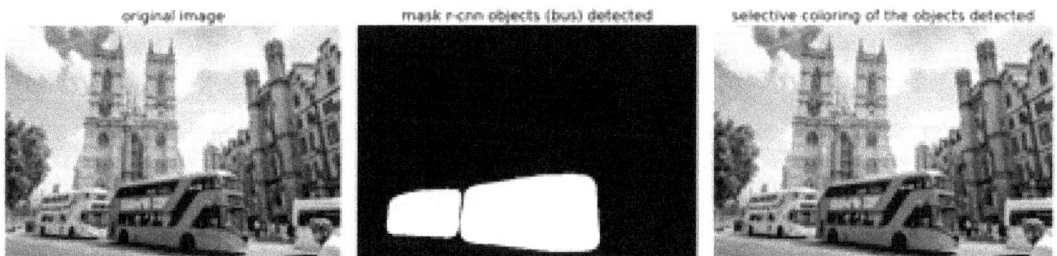

Figure 8.12: Selecting coloring with Mask R-CNN

Face verification with DeepFace

Face verification involves determining whether two images belong to the same person or not, by comparing their facial features. **Face verification** and **face recognition** are closely related but distinct tasks in facial analysis.

The different between face verification and face recognition are as follows:

- **Face verification** determines whether two images belong to the same person, producing a binary output (match or no match). It compares two inputs using similarity metrics like cosine or Euclidean distance and is simpler, often used in applications like smartphone unlocking or online authentication.

- In contrast, **face recognition** identifies a person in an image from a known set of identities, requiring a database of embeddings and solving a classification problem. It outputs the identity (or "unknown") and is used in tasks like security surveillance, tagging in photo libraries, and identifying individuals in public spaces.

- While verification involves **pairwise** comparison, recognition involves **one-to-many** matching, making it more complex.

- Both tasks typically rely on deep learning-based feature extractors trained on large-scale face datasets such as **VGGFace2** or **MS-Celeb-1M**.

In this section, we will learn how face verification works using the **DeepFace** framework, explore its underlying mathematical foundation, and demonstrate an implementation using a pretrained **VGGFace2** model, including detailed steps and Python code.

Face embeddings

DeepFace uses a deep convolutional neural network to extract face embeddings, which are high-dimensional vectors representing facial features. These embeddings encode discriminative features, such as the shape of facial landmarks, texture, and other unique traits.

Mathematically, the embedding $f(x)$ of an input image x is produced as: $f(x) = CNN(x; \theta)$, where θ are the learned weights of the network.

Similarity metrics

Two embeddings, $f(x_1)$ and $f(x_2)$, are compared using distance metrics:

- **Cosine distance**: $d_{cosine} = 1 - \dfrac{f(x_1) \cdot f(x_2)}{\|f(x_1)\| \|f(x_2)\|}$
- **Euclidean distance**: $d_{euclidean} = \| f(x_1) - f(x_2) \|$

Low distances indicate higher similarity.

Let us now implement face verification with Python. The implementation consists of loading a pretrained **VGGFace2** model, detecting faces in images, extracting embeddings, and verifying matches using similarity metrics.

Let us go through the following Python code step-by-step to explain how it works in detail:

1. **Importing required libraries:** Start by importing the required libraries, modules and functions using the next code snippet:

    a. The library **opencv_python (cv2)** is used for reading images and detecting faces using **Haar cascades**.

    b. **Keras/TensorFlow** are used for working with deep learning models (**VGGFace2** in this case).

```python
import numpy as np
import matplotlib.pyplot as plt
import cv2
import time
from tensorflow.keras.models import Model, Sequential
from tensorflow.keras.layers import Convolution2D, LocallyConnected2D,\
                                    MaxPooling2D, Flatten, Dense, Dropout
from tensorflow.keras.preprocessing.image import load_img, save_img, \
                                    img_to_array
from tensorflow.keras.preprocessing import image
import os
```

2. **Confirm GPU availability**: The following code snippet ensures the **GPU** is available for model inference, so that the inference is not too slow:

```python
import tensorflow as tf
tf.config.list_physical_devices('GPU')
# [PhysicalDevice(name='/physical_device:GPU:0', device_type='GPU')]
```

3. Define the model architecture using **tf.keras sequential API**:

```python
model = Sequential()
model.add(Convolution2D(32, (11, 11), activation='relu', \
                                name='C1', input_shape=(152, 152, 3)))
model.add(MaxPooling2D(pool_size=3, strides=2, padding='same', \
                                            name='M2'))
model.add(Convolution2D(16, (9, 9), activation='relu', name='C3'))
model.add(LocallyConnected2D(16, (9, 9), activation='relu', name='L4'))
model.add(LocallyConnected2D(16, (7, 7), strides=2, activation='relu',\
                                            name='L5'))
model.add(LocallyConnected2D(16, (5, 5), activation='relu', name='L6'))
model.add(Flatten(name='F0'))
model.add(Dense(4096, activation='relu', name='F7'))
model.add(Dropout(rate=0.5, name='D0'))
model.add(Dense(8631, activation='softmax', name='F8'))
```

4. **Inputs and outputs**:

    a. **Input layer**: `model.layers[0].input` defines the input for the neural network.

    b. **Output layer**: `model.layers[-3].output` takes the output of the third-last layer, which represents the face embeddings (a compact numerical representation of the face).

5. **Model summary**: Displays the architecture of the loaded model.

```
deepface_model = Model(inputs=model.layers[0].input, \
                       outputs=model.layers[-3].output)
deepface_model.summary()
# Model: "model"
#
# _____
# Layer (type)                    Output Shape              Param #
#===============================================================
# C1_input (InputLayer)           [(None, 152, 152, 3)]     0
# C1 (Conv2D)                     (None, 142, 142, 32)      11648
# M2 (MaxPooling2D)               (None, 71, 71, 32)        0
# C3 (Conv2D)                     (None, 63, 63, 16)        41488
# L4 (LocallyConnected2D)         (None, 55, 55, 16)        62774800
# L5 (LocallyConnected2D)         (None, 25, 25, 16)        7850000
# L6 (LocallyConnected2D)         (None, 21, 21, 16)        2829456
# F0 (Flatten)                    (None, 7056)              0
# F7 (Dense)                      (None, 4096)              28905472
#
# ===============================================================
# Total params: 102,412,864
# Trainable params: 102,412,864
# Non-trainable params: 0
#
# _____
```

6. Load the pretrained weights for **VGGFace2_DeepFace** model, with the following line of code:

```
model.load_weights("models/VGGFace2_DeepFace_weights_val-0.9034.h5")
```

7. **Haar cascade classifier for face detection:** Before we can verify a face against another one, we need to first detect the faces. **OpenCV**'s pre-trained Haar cascade XML file is used here to detect faces in images. Check if it is located in its library directory, using the following code snippet. If the Haar cascade file is missing, the code raises an error.

```
opencv_home = cv2.__file__
folders = opencv_home.split(os.path.sep)[0:-1]
path = folders[0]
for folder in folders[1:]:
    path = path + "/" + folder
```

```
detector_path = path+"/data/haarcascade_frontalface_default.xml"

if os.path.isfile(detector_path) != True:
    raise ValueError("Confirm that opencv is installed on your
            environment! Expected path ", detector_path," violated.")
else:
    detector = cv2.CascadeClassifier(detector_path)
    print("haarcascade is okay")
# haarcascade is okay
```

8. The next code snippet defines a function **detect_face()** which will perform the **detection** of faces prior to **verification**, here is how the function works step-by-step:

   a. **Read image**: Uses **cv2.imread()** to load the input image.

   b. **Face detection**: Uses the **Haar Cascade** classifier (**detector.detectMultiScale()**) to detect faces in the image:

      i. **1.2** is the scale factor (shrinks image by 20% in each scale step).

      ii. **5** is the minimum number of neighboring rectangles that must be detected for a region to be considered a face.

   c. **Crop detected face**: Extracts the bounding box coordinates (x, y, w, h) of the first detected face. A margin is calculated (currently set to 0) and used to adjust the crop, ensuring it remains within image bounds.

   d. **Resize face**: Rescales the cropped face to the target size of 152×152 pixels.

   e. **Convert to array**: Converts the resized face into a numerical array using **image.img_to_array()** from **tensorflow.keras.preprocessing** module.

   f. **Normalize pixels**: Divides pixel values by 255 to scale them between 0 and 1.

   g. **Return preprocessed face**: The resulting array is ready to be passed as input to the face verification neural network.

```
def detect_face(img_path, target_size=(152, 152)):

    img = cv2.imread(img_path)
    faces = detector.detectMultiScale(img, 1.2, 5)

    if len(faces) > 0:
        x,y,w,h = faces[0]
        margin = 0
        x_margin = w * margin / 100
        y_margin = h * margin / 100
```

```
        if y-y_margin > 0 and y+h+y_margin < img.shape[1] and \
            x-x_margin > 0 and x+w+x_margin < img.shape[0]:
            detected_face = img[int(y-y_margin):int(y+h+y_margin), \
                                int(x-x_margin):int(x+w+x_margin)]
        else:
            detected_face = img[int(y):int(y+h), int(x):int(x+w)]

        detected_face = cv2.resize(detected_face, target_size)

        img_pixels = image.img_to_array(detected_face)
        img_pixels = np.expand_dims(img_pixels, axis = 0)

        img_pixels /= 255    # normalize in [0, 1]

        return img_pixels
    else:
        raise ValueError("Face could not be detected in ", img_path,\
                    ". Please confirm that the picture is a face photo.")
```

8. **Compute the similarity/distance metrics**:

    a. **Cosine distance** is computed using the function **find_cosine_distance()**, as **1 - cosine similarity**. It compares the angle between two vectors in the embedding space, where values closer to 0 indicate higher similarity.

    b. **Euclidean distance** computed using the function **find_euclidean_ distance()** measures the straight-line distance between two points in embedding space, again, lower the distance means higher the similarity.

```
def find_cosine_distance(source_representation, test_representation):
    a = np.matmul(np.transpose(source_representation), \
                            test_representation)
    b = np.sum(np.multiply(source_representation, \
                            source_representation))
    c = np.sum(np.multiply(test_representation, test_representation))
    return 1 - (a / (np.sqrt(b) * np.sqrt(c)))

def find_euclidean_distance(source_representation,test_representation):
    euclidean_distance = source_representation - test_representation
    euclidean_distance = np.sum(np.multiply(euclidean_distance, \
                                            euclidean_distance))
    euclidean_distance = np.sqrt(euclidean_distance)
    return euclidean_distance

def l2_normalize(x):
    return x / np.sqrt(np.sum(np.multiply(x, x)))
```

9. Verify faces with the function **verify_face()** defined as follows, which accepts the following input arguments:

a. **dataset**: A list of image **pairs** along with their **ground-truth** labels (`True` for matches, `False` for non-matches).

b. **threshold**: A cosine distance value; if the distance between two images is below this threshold, they are considered a match.

10. Listed are the detailed steps explaining how the function **verify_face()** works:

a. **Extract embeddings**: **Detects** faces from input image pairs and computes **embeddings** for both images.

b. **Compute distances**: Calculates the **Euclidean distance** (alternatively you can compute the cosine distance too, but the **threshold** for matching will likely be different) between the embeddings.

c. **Match prediction**: If the **cosine distance** is **below** the **threshold**, the images are classified as a **match**. Otherwise, they are classified as **not matching**.

d. **Print results**: Outputs similarity scores and predictions.

Now, refer to the following code snippet:

```python
def verify_face(dataset, threshold=0.5):

    for case in dataset:

        img1_path = case[0]
        img2_path = case[1]
        target = case[2]

        print(f"{img1_path} and {img2_path}")
        img1 = detect_face(img1_path)
        img2 = detect_face(img2_path)

        fig = plt.figure()
        fig.add_subplot(1,2,1)
        plt.imshow(img1[0][:, :, ::-1]), plt.axis("off")
        fig.add_subplot(1,2,2)
        plt.imshow(img2[0][:, :, ::-1]), plt.axis("off")
        plt.show(block=True)

        img1_embedding = deepface_model.predict(img1)[0] # 4096 dim
        img2_embedding = deepface_model.predict(img2)[0] #  4096 dim

        euclidean_l2_distance = find_euclidean_distance( \
                                    l2_normalize(img1_embedding), \
                                    l2_normalize(img2_embedding))
        print("Euclidean L2 distance: ", euclidean_l2_distance)
        print("Actual: ", target, end = '')

        verified =  euclidean_l2_distance <= threshold
        # verified =  cosine_distance < threshold # 0.16

        print(" - Predicted: ", verified)
        print("--------------------------------------------------------")
```

11. **Run the verification**

   a. **dataset**: Contains pairs of image file paths and their ground truth labels.

   b. Call the function **verify_face()** with the **dataset** as input, evaluate each pair (there are five such face-image pairs to be verified, as shown) and print similarity scores along with the predictions:

```
dataset = [
          # face image-pairs of same persons, expecting matches
(True)
       ['images/fcr/mom/mom1.png', 'images/fcr/mom/mom2.png', True],
       ['images/fcr/dad/dad1.png', 'images/fcr/dad/dad2.png', True],

             # face-pairs of different persons, expecting mismatches
(False)
       ['images/fcr/mom/mom1.png', 'images/fcr/dad/dad1.png', False],
       ['images/fcr/mom/mom1.png', 'images/fcr/me/me.png'  , False],
       ['images/fcr/dad/dad1.png', 'images/fcr/me/me.png'  , False]
]
verify_face(dataset, 0.66)
# images/fcr/mom/mom1.png   and   images/fcr/mom/mom2.png
```

If you run the preceding code snippet, you should obtain the next results. Note that the first two face image pairs will result in **matches** (belong to **same person**'s **faces**), where the last three pairs result in **mismatches** (belong to **different person**'s faces).

Refer to the following figure, resulting in a match in verification, the verifier correctly decides that the face image pairs belong to the same person. The output is then provided.

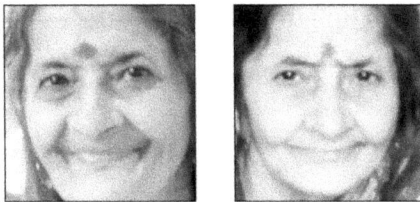

Figure 8.13: Match in face verification

Output:

```
# 1/1 [==============================] - 79s 79s/step
# 1/1 [==============================] - 0s 149ms/step
# Euclidean L2 distance:   0.6139698
# Actual:  True - Predicted:  True
# -------------------------------------------------
# images/fcr/dad/dad1.png   and   images/fcr/dad/dad2.png
```

Refer to the following figure, resulting in a match again (true positive):

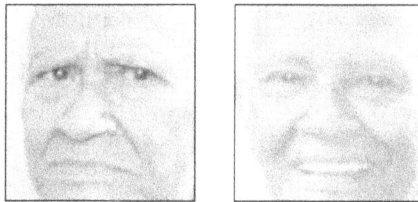

Figure 8.14: Match in face verification

Output:

```
# 1/1 [==============================] - 0s 174ms/step
# 1/1 [==============================] - 0s 176ms/step
# Euclidean L2 distance:   0.6548197
# Actual:   True - Predicted:   True
# -------------------------------------------------
# images/fcr/mom/mom1.png   and   images/fcr/dad/dad1.png
```

Refer to the following figure, resulting in a mismatch (true negative):

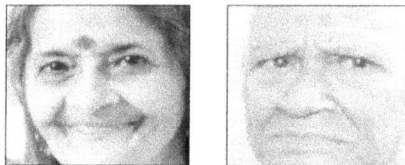

Figure 8.15: Mismatch in face verification

Output:

```
# 1/1 [==============================] - 0s 176ms/step
# 1/1 [==============================] - 0s 158ms/step
# Euclidean L2 distance:   0.7342232
# Actual:   False - Predicted:   False
# -------------------------------------------------
# images/fcr/mom/mom1.png   and   images/fcr/me/me.png
```

Refer to the following figure, resulting in a mismatch again:

Figure 8.16: Mismatch in face verification

Output:

```
# 1/1 [==============================] - 0s 166ms/step
# 1/1 [==============================] - 0s 459ms/step
# Euclidean L2 distance:  0.8190897
# Actual:  False - Predicted:  False
# ------------------------------------------------
# images/fcr/dad/dad1.png  and  images/fcr/me/me.png
```

Refer to the following figure, resulting in a mismatch again:

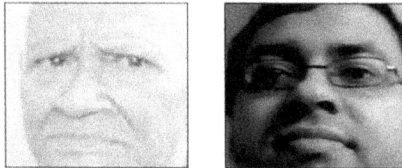

Figure 8.17: *Mismatch in face verification*

Output:

```
# 1/1 [==============================] - 0s 168ms/step
# 1/1 [==============================] - 0s 164ms/step
# Euclidean L2 distance:  0.8458919
# Actual:  False - Predicted:  False
# ------------------------------------------------
```

As can be seen from the preceding outputs, the face-pairs belonging to the same person were verified as **True** and different persons were verified as **False**.

In summary, the preceding code builds a face verification pipeline using a pretrained **VGGFace2** model. The key steps include:

1. Face **detection** (**OpenCV Haar cascade**).
2. Face **preprocessing** (resizing, normalizing).
3. **Embedding** extraction.
4. Similarity computation using **cosine** and **Euclidean** distances.

It demonstrates how to verify faces based on learned embeddings and interpret similarity metrics.

Barcode and QR code detection with Python

Barcodes and **quick response (QR)** codes have become indispensable tools for fast, efficient, and reliable data storage and retrieval in various industries, from retail and logistics to healthcare, manufacturing and advertising. These codes enable quick and error-free input of information simply by scanning a visual pattern using a camera or scanner. With the growing popularity of computer vision in automation and data processing, detecting and decoding these codes using Python has become highly accessible with the use of libraries like **pyzbar** and **qrcode**.

In this section, we shall understand the basics of barcodes and QR codes, explain the Python libraries that can be used to detect and decode them, and walk through practical examples for detecting and processing these codes in images and real-time video streams.

Understanding barcode and QR code

Bar codes and QR codes are both types of data encoding methods used to store information in a visual format that can be scanned and read by machines. Here are few details about them.

Bar codes:

- **Definition**: A barcode is a system for visually encoding data in a machine-readable format. Traditional barcodes are linear or one-dimensional (1D), meaning they store information along a single axis using varying line widths and spacings. This limits the amount of data they can represent. Common types of barcodes include:

  o **Universal Product Code** (**UPC**): widely used in retail for product identification.

  o **European Article Number** (**EAN**): A variation of UPC used internationally.

  o **Code 128**: A high-density barcode used for shipping and tracking.

- **Use cases**: Commonly used in retail for tracking inventory, pricing at point-of-sale, and more. Typically, barcodes encode product numbers, serial numbers, or other identifying information.

- **Capacity**: Limited data capacity, typically encoding numbers or a few characters.

QR codes:

- **Definition**: A QR code is a **two-dimensional** (**2D**) barcode that can store data both vertically and horizontally, it can hold significantly more data than traditional barcodes. It can hold significantly more data than traditional barcodes and supports a wider variety of content types, such as URLs, contact details (vCards), text, and even binary data like images or documents.

- **Use cases**: Used for a wide range of applications, including marketing, product labeling, ticketing, and personal identification. QR codes can encode URLs, contact information, texts, and much more.

- **Capacity**: Much higher data capacity compared to barcodes. A QR code can store up to a few kilobytes of data.

The key differences are:

- **Dimensionality**: Barcodes are 1D while QR codes are 2D.

- **Data capacity**: QR codes can store more data than barcodes.

- **Data types**: QR codes can encode various types of data, whereas barcodes are more limited.

- **Error correction**: QR codes have error correction capabilities, allowing them to be scanned even if they are partially damaged or obscured.

The following table summarizes the similarities and differences between **barcodes** and **QR codes**:

Aspect	Barcode (1D)	QR Code (2D)
Structure	Linear (horizontal only)	Matrix (horizontal + vertical)
Data capacity	Low (typically numeric or limited characters)	High (can store thousands of characters)
Encoded data types	Mainly numeric or limited alphanumeric	Text, numbers, URLs, vCards, binary data
Read direction	One direction (horizontal)	Two directions (horizontal and vertical)
Error correction	None or very minimal	Built-in error correction (can recover partially damaged code)
Scanning speed	Fast	Fast
Use cases	Retail, inventory, logistics	Mobile payments, marketing, ticketing, personal ID
Ease of scanning	Requires correct orientation	Can be scanned from any angle
Visual size	Smaller in appearance but longer for more data	More compact for large data
Popularity in mobile	Less commonly used	Widely adopted in smartphones
Requires internet?	No	No (but often links to online resources)
Machine readable?	Yes	Yes

Table 8.3: Similarities and differences between the barcodes and QR codes

Encoding, detection, decoding using Python libraries

Python offers several libraries that simplify the task of barcode and QR code detection. These libraries handle the complex image processing and decoding needed to detect and interpret codes. The most commonly used Python libraries for this purpose are:

- **opencv-python**: A comprehensive library for image processing and computer vision.

- **pyzbar**: A wrapper for the **ZBar** library that can detect and decode both barcodes and QR codes.

- **python-barcode**: A library can be used to create / generate **US** barcodes.

- **qrcode**: A library is popular for generating QR codes.

- First install the preceding libraries with **pip**. If they are not already installed. Next import all the libraries required, using the next code snippet:

```
#! pip install python-Levenshtein
#! pip install python-barcode
#! pip install qrcode
#! conda install pyzbar
# Install Microsoft Visual C++ 64 bit (on 64 bit windows 64 bit python)
# Link: https://www.microsoft.com/en-us/download/details.aspx?id=40784
from PIL import ImageFont, ImageDraw, Image
from pyzbar import pyzbar
import cv2
import numpy as np
import barcode
import qrcode
from barcode.writer import ImageWriter
import matplotlib.pylab as plt
```

Adding barcode/QR code to an image

This code snippet demonstrates how to generate a barcode and a QR code, and then add them to an existing image, which is the cover page of the book *Image Processing Masterclass with Python*. Here is a detailed breakdown of the code:

1. **Generate a barcode**:

   a. **barcode.get('ean13', str('123456789012'), writer=ImageWriter())** creates an **EAN-13** barcode for the number **'123456789012'** using the **ImageWriter** to output an image file.

   b. **bar1.save('images/bar1')** saves the generated barcode image to the specified path.

```
import barcode
bar1 = barcode.get('ean13', str(9789389898644), writer=ImageWriter())
bar1.save('images/bar1.png')
```

2. **Generate a QR code**: A **qrcode.QRCode** object is created with specific parameters such as version, error correction level, box size, and border. **qr.add_data(u'...')** adds data to the QR code. The data is a Unicode string, indicating the code can handle non-ASCII characters. Here is the list of parameters the function accepts:

a. **version**:

    i. Ranges from 1 to 40, controlling QR code size (for example, version 1 is a 21×21 matrix, version 2 is 25×25, version 3 is 29×29, and so on).

    ii. When set to **None**, the size is automatically adjusted based on the amount of data using the **fit=True** parameter.

b. **fill_color and back_color**:

    i. These parameters change the color of the QR code and its background.

    ii. Accept **RGB** color tuples when using the default image factory.

c. **error_correction levels**: This defines how much error correction is applied to the QR code, allowing it to still be scanned even if parts are damaged. The available levels are:

    i. **ERROR_CORRECT_L**: Corrects up to 7% errors.

    ii. **ERROR_CORRECT_M (default)**: Corrects up to 15% errors.

    iii. **ERROR_CORRECT_Q**: Corrects up to 25% errors.

    iv. **ERROR_CORRECT_H**: Corrects up to 30% errors.

d. **box_size**: Specifies the size of each individual box (square) in the QR code, in terms of pixels.

e. **border**: Defines the thickness of the border around the QR code, measured in boxes. The default is 4, which is the minimum allowed according to the QR code specification.

f. **qr.make(fit=True)**: This method configures the size of the QR code to automatically fit the data being encoded.

g. **qr1 = qr.make_image(fill_color="black", back_color="white")** generates an image from the QR code with specified colors.

h. **qr1.save('images/qr1.png')** saves the generated QR code image to the specified path.

```
qr = qrcode.QRCode(
    version=1,
    error_correction=qrcode.constants.ERROR_CORRECT_L,
    box_size=10,
    border=4,
)
qr.add_data(u'''বই: Image Processing MasterClass (BPB)
            সন্দীপন দে''')
qr.make(fit=True)
qr1 = qr.make_image(fill_color="black", back_color="white")
qr1.save('images/qr1.png')
```

3. **Load and copy the original image**:

   a. `im_orig = Image.open('images/book_cover.png')` loads the original image (a book cover).

   b. `im = im_orig.copy()` creates a copy of the original image to work on, preserving the original.

4. **Load barcode and QR code images**: `bar1 = Image.open('images/bar1.png')` and `qr1 = Image.open('images/bar2.png')` load the previously saved barcode and QR code images.

5. **Paste barcode and QR code onto the book cover**:

   a. `im.paste(bar1.resize((262,140)).rotate(10),  (550,10,812,150))` resizes the barcode, rotates it by 10 degrees, and pastes it onto the copied book cover image at the specified coordinates.

   b. `im.paste(qr1.resize((100,100)).rotate(-10),  (400,860,500,960))` does the same for the QR code, but rotates it by -10 degrees and places it at a different location on the cover.

6. **Save the modified image**:

   `im.save('images/book_cover_barcode.png')` saves the modified book cover, now with a barcode and QR code added, to the specified path.

```
im_orig = Image.open('images/book_cover.png')
im = im_orig.copy()
bar1 = Image.open('images/bar1.png')
qr1 = Image.open('images/qr1.png')
im.paste(bar1.resize((262,140)).rotate(10), (550,10,812,150))
im.paste(qr1.resize((100,100)).rotate(-10), (400,860,500,960))
im.save('images/book_cover_barcode.png')
```

The preceding code effectively demonstrated how to use Python for image processing tasks such as generating barcodes and QR codes, manipulating images (resizing, rotating), and combining multiple images.

Detect barcode or QR code

The following code snippet demonstrates how to detect and annotate barcodes and QR codes in an image using Python libraries such as **opencv-python (cv2)**, **pyzbar**, and **PIL**. Here is a step-by-step explanation on how the code works:

1. **Load the input image**: `im_bar = cv2.imread('images/book_cover_barcode.png')` loads the image file into memory.

2. **Convert image color space**: `cv2_im_rgb = cv2.cvtColor(im_bar, cv2.COLOR_BGR2RGB)` converts the image from BGR (Blue, Green, Red — the default color space in OpenCV) to RGB color space.

3. **Convert OpenCV image to PIL image**: `pil_im = Image.fromarray(cv2_im_rgb)` converts the RGB image (a NumPy array) into a PIL image object, which allows for more sophisticated image manipulations and drawing operations.

4. **Detect barcodes**: `barcodes = pyzbar.decode(im_bar)` uses the `pyzbar` library to detect and decode any barcodes in the original image (keep in mind that it uses the original BGR image).

5. **Process each detected barcode**: The code iterates over each detected barcode, performing following operations for each:

   a. Extracts the barcode's bounding box (`barcode.rect`) and decodes its data (`barcode.data.decode("utf-8")`) and type (`barcode.type`).

   b. Constructs a text string with the barcode data and type.

   c. Draws the bounding box, polygon (if the barcode is not perfectly rectangular), and the text annotation onto the **PIL** image using `ImageDraw.Draw(pil_im)` and `ImageFont.truetype` for custom font styling.

6. **Convert PIL image back to OpenCV image**: `im_out = cv2.cvtColor(np.array(pil_im), cv2.COLOR_RGB2BGR)` converts the modified PIL image (which is in RGB) back to a NumPy array and then to BGR color space for OpenCV compatibility.

7. **Save the annotated image**: `cv2.imwrite('images/book_cover_barcode_detected.png', im_out)` saves the annotated image to a file. Throughout this process, the code also prints the number of detected barcodes and information about each barcode (type and data) to the terminal. This script is useful for applications that require barcode scanning and processing directly from images, such as inventory management, retail checkout systems, and document tracking.

```python
im_bar = cv2.imread('images/book_cover_barcode.png')
cv2_im_rgb = cv2.cvtColor(im_bar, cv2.COLOR_BGR2RGB)
pil_im = Image.fromarray(cv2_im_rgb)
barcodes = pyzbar.decode(im_bar)
print('Number of barcodes found: {}\n'.format(len(barcodes)))
# loop over the detected barcodes
i = 1
for barcode in barcodes:
    (x, y, w, h) = barcode.rect

    barcodeData = barcode.data.decode("utf-8")
    barcodeType = barcode.type

    text = u"{} ({})".format(barcodeData, barcodeType)

    draw = ImageDraw.Draw(pil_im)
    font = ImageFont.truetype("images/kalpurush.ttf", size=50,
                              layout_engine=ImageFont.Layout.RAQM)
```

```
        draw.line(barcode.polygon,width=15)
        draw.polygon(barcode.polygon, outline='#0000ff')
        draw.rectangle(((x, y), (x + w, y + h)), outline='#ff0000', width=10)
        draw.text((x - 200, y + h + 1), text, font=font, fill=(0,255,0,255),
                        stroke_width=2)

        print("{}. Found barcode\n\ntype: {} \ndata:\n{}\n"\
                        .format(i, barcodeType, barcodeData))
        i += 1

im_out = cv2.cvtColor(np.array(pil_im), cv2.COLOR_RGB2BGR)
cv2.imwrite('images/book_cover_barcode_detected.png', im_out)
# Number of barcodes found: 2
# 1. Found barcode
# type: QRCODE
# data:
# বই: Image Processing MasterClass (BPB)
# সন্দীপন দে

# 2. Found barcode
# type: EAN13
# data:
# 9789389898644
# True
plt.figure(figsize=(20,10))
plt.subplot(131), plt.imshow(im_orig), plt.title('original', size=20)
plt.axis('off')
plt.subplot(132), plt.imshow(cv2.cvtColor(im_bar, cv2.COLOR_BGR2RGB))
plt.title('with barcode / qrcode added', size=20), plt.axis('off')
plt.subplot(133), plt.imshow(cv2.cvtColor(im_out, cv2.COLOR_BGR2RGB))
plt.title('barcode / qrcode detected', size=20), plt.axis('off')
plt.tight_layout()
plt.show()
```

If you run the preceding code snippet, you should obtain a figure as follows:

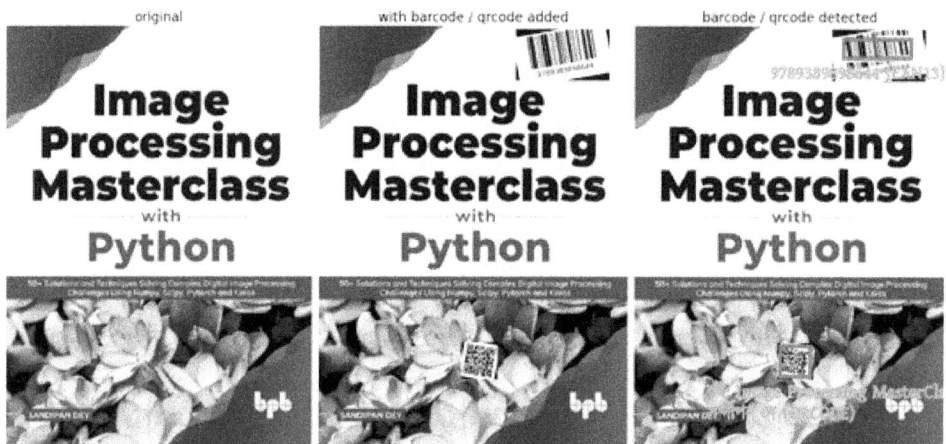

Figure 8.18: *Detecting and extracting Bar/QR code*

Conclusion

This chapter covers various approaches to object detection, and recognition using state-of-the-art deep learning models. It begins with running inference using pretrained **MobileNet-SSD** model (with `opencv-python`), which is lightweight and well-suited for mobile applications. It then explores object detection with **YOLOv3**, leveraging the `gluoncv` and `mxnet` libraries to demonstrate YOLO's efficiency in detecting multiple objects in real-time. Additionally, the latest **YOLOv8** model is introduced through the `ultralytics` API, highlighting its streamlined approach for rapid object detection.

The chapter also delves into custom object detection, showing how transfer learning with **YOLOv4** allows the model to be fine-tuned for specialized detection tasks. **Mask R-CNN** is then explored for instance segmentation, explaining how it can be used to apply selective color effects to detected objects. Finally, the chapter provides an overview of barcode and QR code detection, outlining how libraries like `pyzbar` can be used to detect and decode these codes in images, emphasizing practical real-world applications.

Key terms

Object detection, YOLOv3/v4/v8, MobileNet, Mask R-CNN

Questions

1. **Face recognition with keras_vggface**: Build a simple celebrity face recognition system using the Keras VGGFace model. You need to load a pretrained VGGFace model, process an input image of a celebrity, and use the function decode_predictions() to identify the face.

   Hint: Here are the key steps:

   a. Install and import required libraries, e.g, keras_vggface, keras_applications etc.

   b. Load the VGGFace model using VGGFace(model='vgg16', include_top=True).

   c. Preprocess an input face image, resize it to 224×224, convert it to a numpy array, expand dimensions, and preprocess using the method keras_vggface.utils.preprocess_input().

   d. Predict the face identity by passing the image through the model and use decode_predictions() to get the top predicted identities.

   e. Display the image and the predicted name(s), e.g., print the top 5 predictions with their confidence scores.

   For example, with SRK face image as input, first crop the image and predict the celebrity's name to obtain the output as shown:

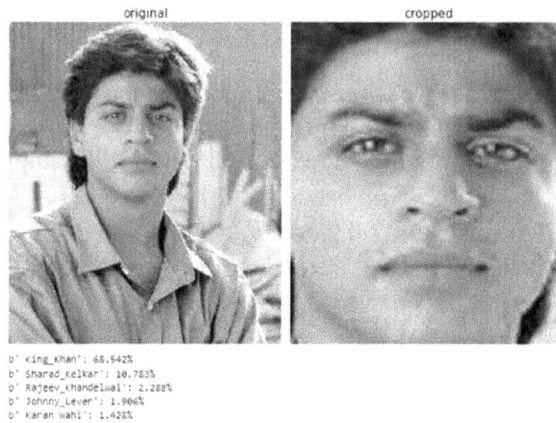

```
b' King_Khan': 65.542%
b' Sharad_Kelkar': 10.783%
b' Rajeev_Khandelwal': 2.288%
b' Johnny_Lever': 1.906%
b' Karan_Wahi': 1.428%
```

Figure 8.19: Celebrity Face Recognition with keras VGGFace

2. Explore the following online annotation tools:

    a. **labelImg (https://github.com/HumanSignal/labelImg)**

    b. **VIA (https://www.robots.ox.ac.uk/~vgg/software/via/)**

    c. **labelme (http://labelme.csail.mit.edu/Release3.0/)**

    d. **imagetagger (https://github.com/bit-bots/imagetagger)**

Learn how to use them to manually annotate images and extract the bounding boxes corresponding to the custom objects you want to detect with **YOLOv4 Darknet** model, and prepare the training dataset (make sure that the annotation text format is same as the model accepts). Also, use roboflow (**https://app.roboflow.com/**) to automatically/semi-automatically annotate custom images (for example, try the raccoon), as shown in the following figure:

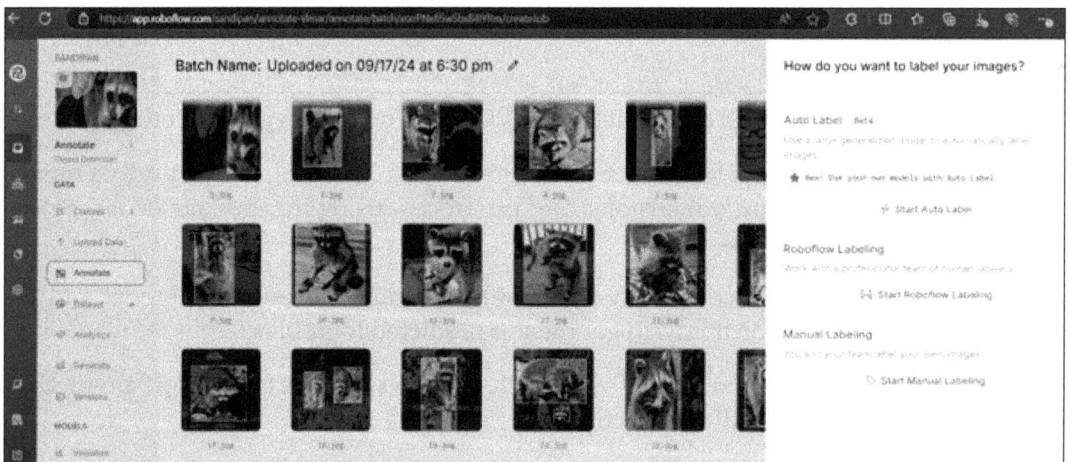

Figure 8.20: Using roboflow to automatically annotate images

3. For the following raccoon image and the given annotation text corresponding to the bounding box for the object (for **YOLOv4 Darknet** model), write code to draw bounding box. For the given input image, you should obtain the annotated output image shown side-by-side.

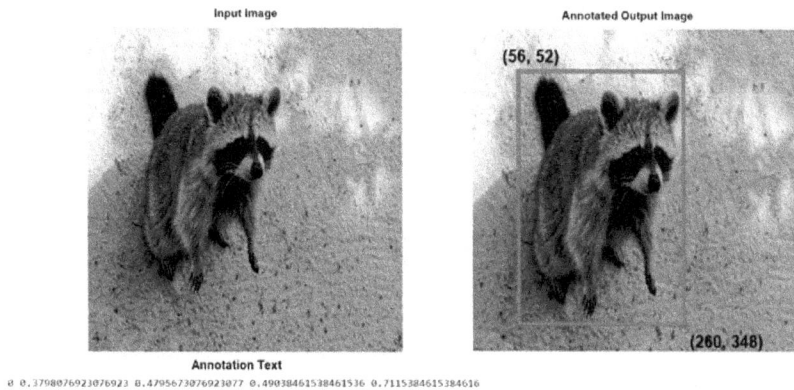

Figure 8.21: *Visualizing image with bounding box from an input image and annotation text*

4. **Intersection over Union (IoU)**: **IoU** is a widely used metric for assessing the performance of an object detection model. It measures how well the predicted bounding box (by the model) matches the ground-truth (true) bounding box. IoU is calculated as the ratio of the intersection area between the predicted and ground-truth bounding boxes to the total area covered by both boxes. The formula to compute IoU is as follows:

$$IoU = \frac{Area\,of\,Overlap}{Area\,of\,Union}$$

Where we have

- **Area of overlap**: The region where the predicted bounding box intersects with the ground truth bounding box.

- **Area of union**: The total area covered by both the bounding boxes combined.

In object detection, the IoU helps in determining the correctness of a detected object.

- **High IoU (close to 1)**: The prediction is very close to the ground truth.

- **Low IoU (close to 0)**: The prediction is far from the ground truth.

- **Thresholding**: Typically, An IoU threshold (such as 0.5) is commonly used to determine whether a detection is classified as a **true positive** (**TP**) or a **false positive** (**FP**). When the IoU of a predicted bounding box and a ground truth box is above the threshold, it is considered a true positive. If it is below the threshold, it is a false positive.

- **IoU** is used to compute evaluation metrics like precision, recall, and the **mean Average Precision** (**mAP**), which are commonly used to measure the performance of the models.

In this exercise, you will complete the implementation of the following function compute_iou() which accepts two bounding boxes as arguments and returns the IOU of these two bound boxes computed:

```python
def compute_iou(box1, box2):
    """
    Computes Intersection over Union (IoU) between box1 & box2.
    Arguments:
    box1, box2 -- List or tuple containing coordinates of the
    bounding boxes in the format: (x_min, y_min, x_max, y_max)
    Returns:
    iou -- Intersection over Union (IoU) value
    """

    iou = None
    ### ***Your Code Here*** ###

    return iou

# Example usage
box1 = [50, 50, 150, 150]   # Ground truth bounding box
box2 = [100, 100, 200, 200]   # Predicted bounding box

# test your implementation
iou_value = compute_iou(box1, box2)
# print(f"IoU: {iou_value}") # uncomment to print
# IoU: 0.14285714285714285  # you should obtain this IOU value
```

5. **Car License Plate Detection with YOLOv5 and Tesseract OCR**: Implement a complete pipeline for car license plate detection and recognition using pretrained (fine-tuned) **YOLOv5** model and **Tesseract OCR** (an open-source optical character recognition engine that extracts text from images by detecting character shapes using a neural network-based recognition pipeline). Here is a step-by-step guide for your implementation:

- **Download Dataset**: Use the Car Plate Detection dataset from **Kaggle**: **https://www.kaggle.com/datasets/andrewmvd/car-plate-detection** (with annotations in the **PASCAL VOC** format)

- **Set Up YOLOv5**:
   o Clone YOLOv5: !git clone **https://github.com/ultralytics/yolov5**
   o Install requirements: !pip install -r yolov5/requirements.txt

- **Prepare the Dataset**:
   o Convert XML annotations to **YOLO** format (.txt files).

o Split into training and validation sets.

o Create a data.yaml file with 1 class: ['licence'].

- **Train YOLOv5** using **Transfer Learning**:

  o Download a pretrained checkpoint (e.g., yolov5m6.pt) from the following link: **https://github.com/ultralytics/yolov5/releases**

  o Fine-tune it on your dataset: !python train.py --img 1280 --batch 4 --epochs 20 --data bgr.yaml --weights yolov5m6.pt

- **Detect License Plates**: Run inference on test images using your fine-tuned model: !python detect.py --source /path/to/image --weights best.pt

- **Apply OCR using Tesseract**

  o Install OCR tools: !sudo apt install tesseract-ocr, !pip install pytesseract

  o Crop detected plate regions and extract text: use the function pytesseract.image_to_string()

- Display the final image showing detected plates and recognized text. you should obtain a figure like the following:

Figure 8.22: *Car license-plate detection and extracting digits & letters with YOLO-V5 + tesseract*

6. **Object Detection Using Faster R-CNN with PyTorch:** Demonstrate object detection in an image using the pre-trained **Faster R-CNN** model from the torchvision. models.detection module in pytorch. Your solution should load an image, perform inference, and visualize the detected objects with bounding boxes and class labels, using appropriate thresholding and color coding. For an input image on the left, you should come up with the detected objects on the right, using Faster R-CNN pretrained model, as shown in the next figure:

Figure 8.23: *Object detection using pretrained faster R-CNN with pytorch*

References

1. https://app.roboflow.com/sandipan/racoon-detection-with-yolov4/

2. https://developer.nvidia.com/cuda-downloads

3. https://sandipanweb.wordpress.com/2022/01/17/custom-object-detection-with-transfer-learning-with-pre-trained-yolo-v4-model/

4. https://ieeexplore.ieee.org/document/7485869

5. https://arxiv.org/pdf/2004.10934

6. https://arxiv.org/pdf/1512.02325

7. https://www.youtube.com/watch?v=CgLp7cW5QJU

8. https://www.youtube.com/watch?v=Wq_vAWQ0Y_w

9. https://www.youtube.com/watch?v=xr_wpaGxlTk

10. https://www.youtube.com/watch?v=w5nHj1e5nfI

11. https://www.youtube.com/watch?v=2xNXWy7ubKs

Join our Discord space

Join our Discord workspace for latest updates, offers, tech happenings around the world, new releases, and sessions with the authors:

https://discord.bpbonline.com

## CHAPTER 9

Application of Image Processing and Computer Vision in Medical Imaging

Introduction

Medical imaging refers to the techniques and processes used to create visual representations of the interior of a body for clinical analysis and medical intervention. The rapid advancement of imaging technologies has significantly transformed the field of medical diagnostics, enabling earlier detection, more accurate analysis, enhanced environmental monitoring, and improved patient outcomes. This chapter explores the diverse applications of image processing and computer vision techniques in medical imaging, demonstrating how these tools can assist in interpreting complex medical data and automating key clinical tasks.

This chapter covers key tasks in medical image processing, including loading and visualizing specialized formats such as **DICOM** and **NIfTI** using libraries like **pydicom**, **nibabel**, and **itk**, along with 3D visualization of MRI data through tools like **matplotlib**, **vedo**, and **visvis** to better understand anatomical structures. It also explores image enhancement techniques using filters, morphological operations, and **CT** reconstruction with the inverse Radon transform. Advanced segmentation methods are introduced, such as graph cuts for brain **MRI**, and deep learning models like **XceptionNet**, highlighting the essential role of image processing in improving clinical decision-making and diagnostic accuracy.

Structure

In this chapter, we will cover the following topics in medical image processing:

- Medical image processing:
  - o Loading and displaying medical images of different formats and modalities with pydicom, nifti, itk libraries
  - o 3D visualization of a head MRI image with matplotlib, vtk, vedo and visvis
  - o Applying filters with medpy and itk
  - o Morphological filtering with the library itk
  - o Computation tomography reconstruction with inverse Radon transform using scikit-image
  - o Segmentation of brain MRI images with graph cut algorithms with medpy
  - o Pneumonia classification from chest X-ray using XceptionNet with tensorflow

Objectives

This chapter explores image processing techniques in medical imaging, covering visualization, filtering, segmentation, and machine learning applications to enhance medical diagnostics. It discusses usage of the key libraries like **pydicom**, **medpy** and deep learning models such as **XceptionNet** for improved analysis and patient outcomes. By bridging fundamental concepts and practical implementations, this chapter provides a robust foundation for addressing challenges in medical imaging through innovative image processing techniques. By the end of this chapter, you will master key image processing techniques and deep learning applications for analyzing and enhancing medical images to improve diagnostic accuracy and outcomes.

Medical image processing

The application of image processing in the medical domain has revolutionized the way healthcare professionals diagnose, treat, and manage diseases. With advancements in technology, image processing techniques have become indispensable tools in medical imaging, enabling the extraction of valuable information from images that are often invisible to the human eye. This section explores the various applications of image processing in the medical field, highlighting its impact on improving patient care and outcomes.

Medical image processing plays a vital role in modern healthcare by enabling the visualization, analysis, and interpretation of complex medical data. It involves the analysis and manipulation of medical images for various purposes, including diagnosis, treatment planning, and research. It encompasses a range of techniques from basic image enhancement to complex feature extraction and pattern recognition. The primary goal is to improve the visibility of important features within an image, facilitating a more accurate and efficient diagnosis. Key applications of image processing in the medical field include diagnostic imaging for enhanced anomaly detection, image segmentation for analyzing anatomical structures, 3D reconstruction for surgical planning, **computer-aided diagnosis (CAD)** for improved diagnostic accuracy, and telemedicine for remote patient care through secure image transmission.

To start with, let us define a few of terms that will be used frequently in this section:

- **Pixel vs. Voxel:**

  o **Picture element (pixel)** refers to the smallest unit of a 2D image, representing a single point in a flat image, like a slice from an MRI or CT scan.

  o **Volume element (voxel)** is the 3D equivalent of a pixel, representing a value in a 3D space, like a cube in a volumetric scan, such as a full 3D MRI or CT scan, containing depth information.

  o Pixels are 2D, while voxels extend this concept into three dimensions.

- **Modalities**: Different medical imaging modalities are used to visualize various aspects of the human body. Each modality is specialized for capturing specific types of tissue or abnormalities. Common modalities include:

  o **X-ray**: Utilizes ionizing radiation to capture 2D images of dense structures like bones.

  o **Computed tomography (CT)**: Produces detailed cross-sectional 3D images by combining multiple X-ray images, commonly used for diagnosing internal injuries and cancer. A **CT slice** is like looking at one thin layer of the body, and stacking slices together gives a 3D view—great for bone, lung, and organ imaging.

  o **Magnetic resonance imaging (MRI)**: Uses strong magnetic fields and radio waves to generate detailed 3D images of soft tissues such as the brain, muscles, and ligaments. An **MRI slice** is also a 2D layer, but it shows more soft tissue detail than CT and does not use radiation.

  o **Ultrasound**: Employs high-frequency sound waves to produce real-time images, commonly used for fetal imaging and examining soft tissues like the heart.

  o **Positron emission tomography (PET)**: Shows metabolic and functional processes in the body using radioactive tracers, often combined with CT for cancer detection.

These modalities vary in resolution, contrast, and the type of tissue they are best suited to visualize, depending on the clinical requirement.

This section covers a range of techniques essential for processing medical images across various formats and modalities, such as **Digital Imaging and Communications in Medicine (DICOM)**, **Neuroimaging Informatics Technology Initiative (NIfTI)**, and **Insight Segmentation and Registration Toolkit (ITK)**. We shall start from a few classical image processing techniques and then proceed to application of recent advanced deep learning models (using `tensorflow` and `pytorch`) for medical image analysis.

The key topics include loading and displaying medical images, 3D visualization of head MRI images, and applying advanced filters. Morphological filtering and CT reconstruction with inverse Radon transform further enhance image quality for diagnostic purposes. Segmentation technique such as graph cut is explored to extract meaningful structures from medical scans. Additionally, deep learning models like **XceptionNet** for pneumonia classification demonstrate the power of artificial intelligence in radiographic image analysis.

This chapter will equip you with essential tools and techniques to address a wide range of image processing tasks in the medical domain, with hands-on implementations in Python.

Loading and displaying medical images of different formats and modalities with python libraries

Medical imaging is a cornerstone of modern diagnostics and treatment planning, providing crucial insights into the human body's anatomy and pathology. Advances in imaging modalities such as **MRI**, **CT**, **USG**, and **PET** have revolutionized clinical practices across radiology, oncology, neurology, and other fields. To work effectively with this wealth of data, it is essential to have robust tools and libraries capable of handling diverse image formats and modalities.

Medical images are typically stored in specialized formats that encode not only pixel data but also vital metadata such as patient information, image acquisition parameters, and spatial orientations. Among these formats, **DICOM**, **NIfTI**, and **ITK** are widely used in different imaging domains. The complexity of these formats, along with the specific requirements of different modalities (for example, MRI, CT, or PET), necessitates the use of specialized libraries for reading, manipulating, and visualizing such data.

In this section, let us explore how to efficiently load, process, and display medical images from different formats and modalities using Python libraries such as `pydicom` (for DICOM images), `nibabel` (for NIfTI images), and `SimpleITK` (for ITK-compatible image data). These libraries provide seamless interfaces for handling medical image data, allowing researchers and clinicians to extract, manipulate, and visualize both image pixels and associated metadata:

- **pydicom** is a widely-used Python package for working with **DICOM** files, which are the standard format for storing medical imaging information. It enables easy extraction of pixel data, metadata, and complex attributes such as affine transformations or slice locations.

- **nibabel** focuses on formats like **NIfTI** and **Analyze**, commonly used in neuroimaging for storing 3D and 4D datasets, making it ideal for handling volumetric brain scans, fMRI data, and other similar datasets.

- **SimpleITK** and the broader **ITK** ecosystem support various medical image formats, including **NIfTI** and **DICOM**, while providing additional tools for image registration, segmentation, and analysis.

In this section, we shall cover the fundamental techniques for:

- Loading medical images in different formats and accessing image metadata and pixel arrays.

- Visualizing 2D and 3D medical images for interpretation and manual review.

- Handling image **modalities** such as **MRI**, **CT**, and **PET** across the **DICOM**, **NIfTI**, and **MetaImage** formats.

By the end of this section, you will be equipped with practical knowledge of how to work with medical imaging data across various formats and modalities, leveraging Python's extensive libraries to streamline workflows in medical image analysis.

DICOM format

DICOM is the standard format for storing, transmitting, and managing medical images and related metadata. It ensures interoperability between medical imaging devices, workstations, and healthcare systems. Each DICOM file contains both pixel data (images from modalities like MRI, CT, and X-rays) and metadata, such as patient details, image acquisition parameters, and spatial orientation. DICOM files use a structured tag system for metadata, supporting rich information for diagnostics and integration into **picture archiving and communication systems** (**PACS**).

DICOM's key features include:

- Interoperability across devices and systems.

- Rich metadata storing patient, study, and imaging details.

- Support for 2D, 3D, and 4D images from various modalities.

- Integration with PACS for image storage and retrieval.

However, DICOM files can be large and complex, requiring specialized tools for handling, processing, and ensuring privacy. Despite these challenges, DICOM remains a critical standard in modern healthcare.

The next Python code demonstrates how to load and display medical images stored in the DICOM format. The code leverages the **pydicom** library to read DICOM files and **matplotlib** to visualize them. Here is a detailed explanation of how this code works, step by step:

1. **Installing required libraries**: The **pydicom** library is used for reading and handling DICOM files in Python. Use **pip** to install the library, which provides functionality to extract metadata and pixel data from DICOM files. You can also use it to manipulate and visualize the images.

2. **Importing necessary modules**:

    a. **glob**: This module allows you to find all file paths that match a specified pattern. It is used here to search for DICOM files in the directory.

    b. **pydicom**: This module is used to read DICOM files, which contain both metadata (for example, patient information, scan parameters) and image pixel data.

    c. **matplotlib.pyplot**: Used for visualizing the medical images. **plt.imshow()** will display each slice of the MRI as an image.

3. **Setting up the plotting environment**:

    a. **plt.figure(figsize=(10,20))**: This command creates a new figure for plotting, with dimensions of 10 units wide and 20 units tall. The large size accommodates displaying multiple images in a grid layout.

    b. **plt.gray()**: This sets the colormap to grayscale, which is suitable for most medical images like MRI and CT scans that are typically represented in grayscale.

    c. **plt.subplots_adjust(0,0,1,0.95,0.01,0.01)**: Adjusts the spacing of the subplots to remove unnecessary padding between images. This creates a more compact display for a large number of images.

4. **Loading DICOM files**:

    a. **glob()**: This function finds all DICOM files in the specified directory that match the given pattern ('MR*'), as shown in the next code snippet. It returns a list of file paths that match the pattern. In this case, it looks for MRI scan slices, which typically start with the prefix MR.

    b. **pydicom.read_file(dfile)**: This reads each DICOM file into a **pydicom** dataset object. The dataset contains both the image data and metadata like patient information and scan parameters.

    c. **mr_scan = [...]**: This list comprehension iterates through all matching DICOM files, reading them into a list called **mr_scan**. Each element in **mr_scan** is a **pydicom** object representing an MRI slice.

5. **Ordering slices by slice location**: DICOM files from medical imaging (especially in MRI or CT) usually contain a series of image slices that represent cross-sections of a body part. These slices need to be displayed in the correct order based on their position along a particular axis (for example, head to feet).

   a. `slice.SliceLocation`: Each DICOM file contains metadata that specifies the position of the slice (typically the `SliceLocation` attribute). This information helps ensure the slices are displayed in the correct order.

   b. `sorted(mr_scan, key=lambda slice: slice.SliceLocation)`: This sorts the `mr_scan` list by the `SliceLocation` attribute, ensuring the slices are ordered from the top of the scan (for example, top of the head) to the bottom (such as, base of the neck). Now, the list **mr_scan_ordered** contains the slices in the correct order, using the following code snippet:

```
#! pip install pydicom
from glob import glob
import pydicom

mr_scan = [pydicom.read_file(dfile) \
                    for dfile in sorted(glob('images/dicom/MR*.dcm'))]
mr_scan_ordered = sorted(mr_scan, \
                        key=lambda slice: slice.SliceLocation)
```

6. **Displaying the slices**:

   a. `dicom_file.pixel_array`: This extracts the image data from the DICOM file as a NumPy array. DICOM images store the pixel values in this array format. The `pixel_array` attribute gives direct access to this image data.

   b. `plt.subplot(4,8,i)`: This divides the figure into a grid of 4 rows and 8 columns. The variable **i** keeps track of the current subplot, starting at 1 and incrementing with each loop iteration. This allows for displaying up to 32 slices in the grid.

   c. `plt.imshow()`: This command displays the image (the slice) in the current subplot. The **mr** variable holds the pixel data extracted from the DICOM file.

   d. `plt.axis('off')`: This removes the axes and labels from the plot, making the images easier to view without cluttering the display with unnecessary axis ticks and labels.

   e. `plt.suptitle()`: Adds a title to the entire figure, giving context to the displayed images. In this case, the title is **Full head MRI scan DICOM files** with a font size of 15.

   f. `plt.show()`: Finally, this command renders and displays the plot. The entire set of MRI slices will be shown in a grid format.

```
plt.figure(figsize=(12,4))
plt.gray()
plt.subplots_adjust(0,0,1,0.95,0.01,0.01)
i = 1
for dicom_file in ct_scan_ordered:
  plt.subplot(4,8,i), plt.imshow(dicom_file.pixel_array )
  plt.axis('off')
  i += 1
plt.suptitle('Full head MRI scan DICOM files', size=15)
plt.show()
```

If you run the preceding code snippet, you will get a figure like the following one which visualizes the DICOM files corresponding to a full head MRI scan:

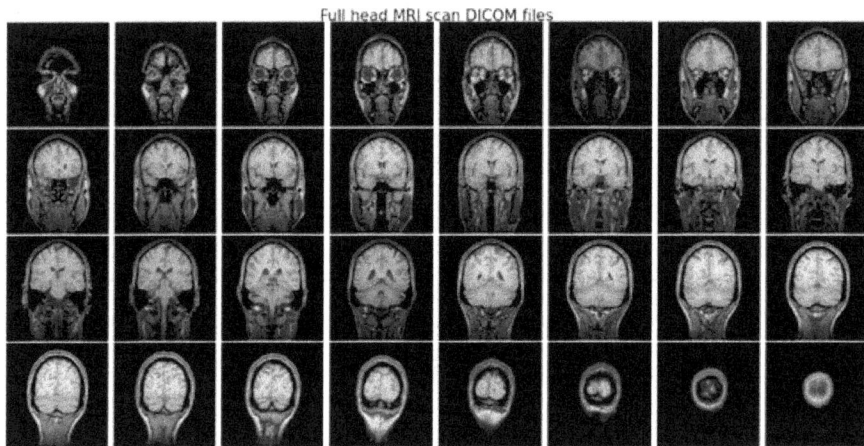

Figure 9.1: *Full head MRI scan DICOM files*

NIfTI format

NIfTI is a widely used file format in neuroimaging for storing 3D and 4D medical imaging data, particularly for modalities like MRI and fMRI. It efficiently handles volumetric data and includes a compact header with image metadata such as dimensions and an affine transformation matrix for mapping voxel data to real-world coordinates. NIfTI files can be compressed and are compatible with many neuroimaging analysis tools like FSL and SPM. While primarily used in brain research, NIfTI's focus on volumetric data makes it less versatile for other medical imaging modalities.

The next Python code snippet uses the **nibabel** library to load and visualize a medical image stored in the NIfTI format, which is commonly used for storing MRI and other types of 3D medical images. Here is a detailed explanation of how the code works step by step:

1. **Importing and loading the NIfTI image**:

    a. **nibabel**: This is a Python package used to handle neuroimaging file formats like **NIfTI** (**.nii, .nii.gz** files), as well as other formats like **Analyze** and **DICOM**. It is commonly used for loading, manipulating, and saving 3D or 4D medical imaging data.

    b. **nifti = nib.load('images/201_t2w_tse.nii.gz')**: This loads the NIfTI file from the given path. The file **201_t2w_tse.nii.gz** is a compressed NIfTI file (the **.gz** extension indicates **gzip** compression). The function **nib.load()** reads the image and returns a **Nifti1Image** object, which contains the image data and metadata such as voxel dimensions, orientation, and affine transformations.

2. **Inspecting the NIfTI image data and metadata**:

    a. **print(nifti)**: This prints basic information about the NIfTI object, including metadata such as the affine transformation matrix and file structure.

    b. **nifti.shape**: Returns the shape of the image, which tells you how many voxels (3D pixels) there are in each dimension. For instance, the given MRI brain scan has a shape like (256, 256, 27), meaning there are 256 voxels in the x and y axes (each slice is 256×256) and 27 slices in the z-axis (depth).

    c. **nifti.header.get_data_shape()**: This is another way to obtain the shape of the image, using the NIfTI file's header. The header stores metadata about the image, such as data type, dimensions, and scaling factors.

3. **Converting the NIfTI image to a NumPy array**:

    a. **nifti.get_fdata()**: This function extracts the image data from the NIfTI object and returns it as a NumPy array. The **get_fdata()** method converts the data into a floating-point array, which is convenient for further analysis and visualization. NIfTI images are typically stored in 3D (or 4D) arrays.

    b. **print(image_array.dtype, image_array.shape)**: This prints the data type (for example, **float64**) and shape of the extracted image array. For example, the shape is (256, 256, 27) for the given 3D brain MRI, which means there are 27 slices of 256×256 voxels.

```
#!pip install nilabel
import nibabel as nib
nifti = nib.load('images/201_t2w_tse.nii.gz')
print(nifti.shape) # get the image shape
# (256, 256, 27)
print(nifti.header.get_data_shape()) # get image shape another way
# (256, 256, 27)
image_array = nifti.get_fdata()
print(image_array.dtype, image_array.shape)
# float64 (256, 256, 27)
```

4. **Creating a grid of subplots for visualization**:

   a. **plt.subplots(3, 9, figsize=(12, 4))**: This command creates a grid of subplots using **matplotlib**. In this case, it creates a 3×9 grid (27 subplots in total). Each subplot will be used to display one slice from the 3D MRI volume.

   b. **figsize=(12, 4)**: Specifies the figure size in inches (width 12, height 4) to ensure the grid is large enough for all the subplots.

   c. **plt.subplots_adjust()**: Adjusts the spacing between the subplots to reduce padding. This helps maximize the use of space, removing excess margins between images.

5. **Displaying the slices**:

   a. **slice_counter = 0**: This variable keeps track of which slice (in the z-axis) of the 3D image to display. The slices are indexed along the third axis (**image_array[:,:,slice]**).

   b. The nested loops iterate through the rows and columns of the grid to fill each subplot with an MRI slice.

   c. **axis[i][j].imshow(image_array[:,:,slice_counter], cmap="bone")**: This displays the current slice as a 2D image using **imshow()**. The slice is extracted from the **NumPy** array **image_array** by taking a cross-section along the z-axis (**[:,:,slice_counter]**). **cmap='bone'** option applies a grayscale colormap with a bluish tint, commonly used in medical imaging to enhance contrast and detail.

   d. **axis[i][j].axis('off')**: Hides the axes and ticks for each subplot to provide a clean display of the images.

Now, refer to the following code snippet:

```python
fig, axis = plt.subplots(3, 9, figsize=(12, 4))
plt.subplots_adjust(0,0,1,0.9,0.01,0.01)
slice_counter = 0
for i in range(3):
    for j in range(9):
        if slice_counter < image_array.shape[-1]:
            axis[i][j].imshow(image_array[:,:,slice_counter, cmap='bone')
        slice_counter+=1
        axis[i][j].axis('off')
plt.suptitle('Full head MRI scan NIfTI files', size=15)
plt.show()
```

If you run the following code snippet, you will get a figure like the following one which visualizes the NIfTI files corresponding to a full head MRI scan:

Full head MRI scan NIfTI files

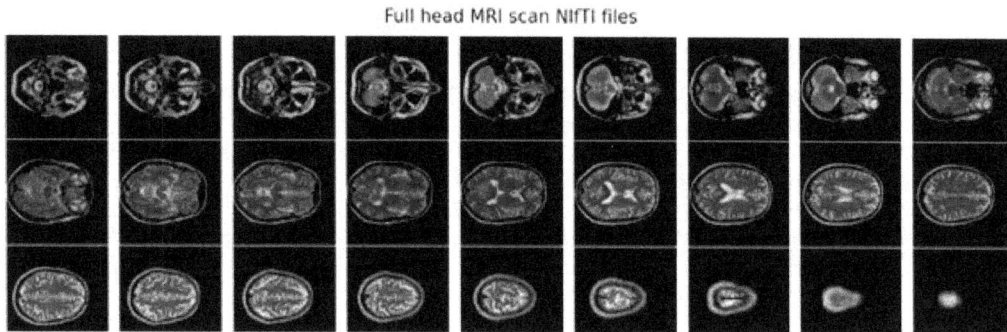

Figure 9.2: Fill head MRI scan NIfTI files

RAW or MetaImage format

The **MetaImage** format is used for storing medical images, particularly in 3D and 4D imaging like CT and MRI scans. It consists of two files:

- A **.mhd** (Metaimage header) file that contains metadata (image dimensions, data type, voxel spacing).

- A **.raw** file that holds the uncompressed pixel data in a binary format.

The format is called RAW because the image data is stored without compression, making it easy to process large datasets quickly. It is commonly used in medical research due to its simplicity, flexibility, and compatibility with libraries like **SimpleITK** and **itk**, though the lack of compression results in larger file sizes.

The following Python code reads and displays medical images using the **SimpleITK** library, which is commonly used for handling medical image formats such as DICOM, NIfTI, and MetaImage. Here is how the code works:

1. **Loading the image**:

   a. The function **load_itk()** is defined in the next code snippet, it reads a medical image file (in this case, a **.mhd** file) using **SimpleITK's ReadImage()** function.

   b. **SimpleITK** handles a variety of medical image formats, with the ability to read both image data (for example, pixel values) and metadata (such as, origin and spacing).

   c. The loaded image (**itkimage**) is then converted to a NumPy array using **sitk.GetArrayFromImage()**. This converts the medical image into a format that can be easily manipulated in Python.

   d. The array is reordered to have axes in the order z, y, x (**axial, coronal, sagittal** planes), which is more suitable for visualization and manipulation.

Note: To successfully load a MetaImage using `SimpleITK.ReadImage()`, both the `.mhd` and `.raw` files must be located in the same directory. If the `.raw` file is missing or not found at the expected path, the image loading will fail. Make sure to keep them together when using this function.

2. **Retrieving metadata (origin and spacing):**

   a. **Origin:** The code extracts the origin of the scan using `itkimage.GetOrigin()`. The origin defines the spatial position of the image's starting point (the coordinate of the first voxel) in the real world. This is useful for aligning the image with physical coordinates.

   b. **Spacing:** The spacing is retrieved using `itkimage.GetSpacing()`. Spacing represents the physical distance between adjacent voxels along each axis (z, y, x). This metadata is essential for converting between voxel space (discrete coordinates in the image) and real-world space (millimeters or other units).

```
#!pip install SimpleITK
import SimpleITK as sitk
import numpy as np
import matplotlib.pylab as plt

def load_itk(filename):
    itkimage = sitk.ReadImage(filename)
    ct_scan = sitk.GetArrayFromImage(itkimage)
    origin = np.array(list(reversed(itkimage.GetOrigin())))
    spacing = np.array(list(reversed(itkimage.GetSpacing())))
    return ct_scan, origin, spacing

ct, _, _ = load_itk('images/chest_ct.mhd')

print(ct.shape)
#(112, 256, 256)
```

3. **Visualizing the CT scan:** After loading the CT scan (a volumetric image) into the `ct` NumPy array, the code proceeds to visualize it slice-by-slice using `matplotlib`.

   a. The `ct.shape[0]` indicates the number of slices in the scan (along the z-axis).

   b. A for loop iterates over each slice of the CT scan, and for each slice, `plt.imshow(ct[i])` displays the 2D cross-sectional image.

   c. The figure is displayed in a 7×16 grid, meaning 7 rows and 16 columns of subplots, with `plt.axis('off')` used to hide axis labels.

This workflow is typical for handling 3D medical image data, such as CT or MRI scans, where you need to process and visualize slices or perform further analysis:

```
plt.figure(figsize=(14,7))
plt.gray()
plt.subplots_adjust(0,0,1,0.95,0.01,0.01)
for i in range(ct.shape[0]):
    plt.subplot(7,16,i+1), plt.imshow(ct[i]), plt.axis('off')
plt.suptitle('Chest CT-scan mhd (raw) files', size=15)
plt.show()
```

If you run the preceding code snippet, you should obtain a figure like the next one:

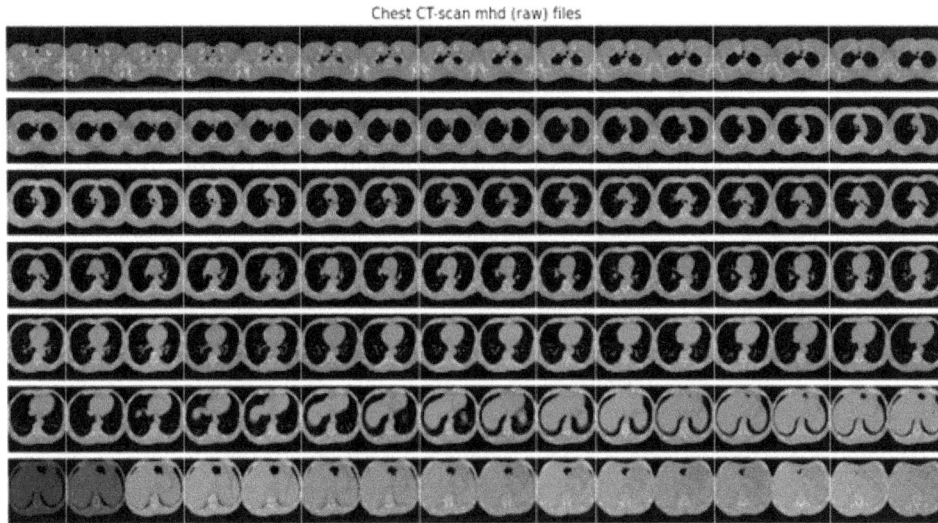

Figure 9.3: Chest CT scan .mhd (.raw) files

3D visualization of a head MRI image with matplotlib, vedo and visvis

In this section, you will learn how to visualize a head MRI image in 3D using various python libraries.

With matplotlib

The next Python code visualizes a 3D head MRI image using **matplotlib**'s 3D plotting capabilities. Here is how the code works in detail (step-by-step):

1. **Loading the MRI image**:

   a. The function **load_itk(filename)** is responsible for loading the MRI image from a file.

   b. It uses **SimpleITK** (imported as **sitk**), to read the image using the function **sitk.ReadImage(filename)** and converts it into a NumPy array (3D array for voxel intensities) using **sitk.GetArrayFromImage()**. This allows for easier manipulation and visualization.

c. The image is reshaped so that its axes align correctly: (z, y, x). The axes represent depth (z-axis), height (y-axis), and width (x-axis) of the image.

d. The function also extracts the spatial origin (physical coordinate of the first voxel, using the function **itkimage.GetOrigin()**) and voxel spacing (distance between adjacent pixels/voxels in each direction in physical units, using the function **itkimage.GetSpacing()**) of the MRI data.

2. **3D plotting function**: Creates a 3D surface plot of the volumetric image using the *Marching Cubes* algorithm, here is how it works in details:

a. The function takes in the 3D array **ct** (the CT scan dataset) and a threshold value (1150 in this case). This threshold defines the intensity level for rendering the 3D surface.

b. It uses the function **measure.marching_cubes()** from the **skimage** library, which is used to extract a 3D surface from a 3D array of scalar values (such as the CT image data). The marching cubes algorithm generates a surface (a mesh of triangles) by detecting contours at the specified threshold value in the volumetric data. It returns

i. **verts**: Vertices of the triangles in 3D space.

ii. **faces**: The indices of vertices forming triangular faces.

3. **Rendering the 3D surface**: Once the vertices and faces are computed, the next step is to render the 3D surface:

a. **Poly3DCollection** from **mpl_toolkits.mplot3d.art3d** is used to create a collection of polygons from the vertices and faces.

b. This creates a translucent (**alpha = 0.1**) surface by assembling the triangular faces into polygons.

c. **face_color = [0.5, 0.5, 1]**: Defines a light blue color.

d. **ax.add_collection3d(mesh)**: Adds the mesh to the 3D axis.

e. The axes limits are then set to match the dimensions of the image data (since the CT image could be non-cubic).

f. Finally, **plt.show()** is called to display the rendered 3D visualization of the CT scan.

4. **Understanding the visualization process**:

a. **Thresholding**: The threshold value (1150 in this example) is critical in defining which parts of the CT image will be visualized. In CT data, voxel intensities are measured in Hounsfield Units (HU), which correspond to different tissue densities. Selecting an appropriate threshold allows for the isolation of specific anatomical structures, such as bone, soft tissue, or air-filled spaces.

b. **Marching cubes algorithm**: This algorithm extracts a 3D surface from a volumetric dataset by identifying where the voxel intensities cross the threshold. The result is a set of triangular surfaces that can be visualized as a mesh.

c. **3D plot**: The generated surface is plotted using `Poly3DCollection` and displayed interactively using `matplotlib's` 3D plotting features.

Refer to the next code snippet:

```python
from mpl_toolkits.mplot3d.art3d import Poly3DCollection
import numpy as np
from skimage import measure
import pydicom
import matplotlib.pylab as plt
import SimpleITK as sitk

def load_itk(filename):
    itkimage = sitk.ReadImage(filename)
    ct_scan = sitk.GetArrayFromImage(itkimage)
    origin = np.array(list(reversed(itkimage.GetOrigin())))
    spacing = np.array(list(reversed(itkimage.GetSpacing())))
    return ct_scan, origin, spacing

def plot_3d(image, threshold=-300):
    verts, faces, _, _ = measure.marching_cubes(image, threshold)
    fig = plt.figure(figsize=(10, 10))
    ax = fig.add_subplot(111, projection='3d')
    mesh = Poly3DCollection(verts[faces], alpha=0.1)
    face_color = [0.5, 0.5, 1]
    mesh.set_facecolor(face_color)
    ax.add_collection3d(mesh)
    ax.set_xlim(0, image.shape[0])
    ax.set_ylim(0, image.shape[1])
    ax.set_zlim(0, image.shape[2])
    ax.set_title(f'3D plot with Marching Cubes algorithm'
                    '(level={threshold})', size=15)
    plt.show()

ct, _, _ = load_itk('iamges/FullHead.mhd')
plot_3d(ct, 1150)
```

If you run the preceding code, you should obtain a 3D visualization as shown in the following figure:

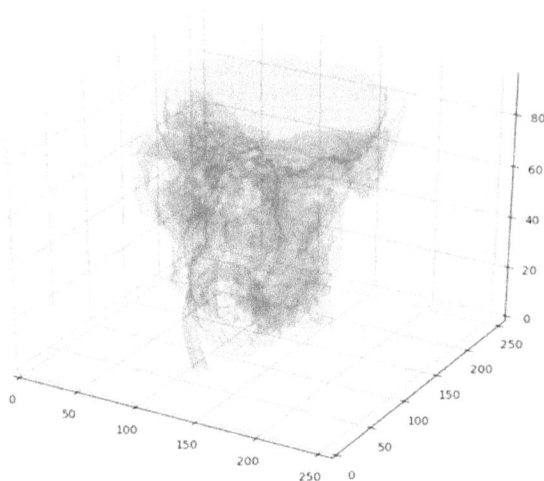

Figure 9.4: 3D visualization of the full head mhd file with matplotlib

With the library visvis

The next Python code utilizes the **visvis** library, along with **measure.marching_cubes_lewiner()** from the **skimage** library, to visualize a 3D medical image, specifically a CT scan. Here is a detailed breakdown of how the code accomplishes this task:

1. First, import the **visvis** library (if not installed, first install it using **pip**), which is a visualization library for Python. It provides tools for 2D and 3D plotting and is particularly useful for visualizing volumetric data such as medical images.

2. Use the function **load_itk()** (defined earlier) to read the medical image file in metaimage (**.mhd**) format. This function returns the image data (**ct**), along with the origin and spacing of the image.

3. Use the **marching_cubes_lewiner()** function from the module **skimage.measure** to run the marching cubes algorithm on the loaded CT image data, along with the following input parameters:

   a. **ct**: The 3D volumetric data (the **CT scan**) from which we want to extract a surface mesh

   b. **1150**: This is the threshold value used to determine the surface of the volume. It helps to extract the iso-surface (represents all points within the volume that have the same intensity value) at this particular intensity level. In medical imaging, this value may correspond to a specific tissue type or density (for example, bone), and returns the following outputs:

      i. **verts**: The vertices of the mesh that represent the iso-surface.

      ii. **faces**: The **faces** that connect the vertices to form the 3D surface.

iii. **normals**: The **normals** of the faces, which can be used for lighting calculations.

iv. **values**: The original voxel **values** at the vertices.

4. **Visualizing the 3D mesh**:

a. The function **vv.mesh()** creates a 3D mesh visualization using the extracted vertices, **faces**, **normals**, and **values** as parameters, to render the iso-surface of the CT scan.

b. Finally, the function **vv.use()** function sets up the current visualization environment, and **Run()** starts the event loop, allowing the user to interact with the 3D visualization (for example, by rotating, zooming etc.) and activates the visualization window.

```
import visvis as vv
ct, _, _ = load_itk('FullHead.mhd')
verts, faces, normals, values = measure.marching_cubes_lewiner(ct, \
                                                                1150)
vv.mesh(verts, faces, normals, values)
vv.use().Run()
```

If you run the preceding code, it should pop up a window with a 3D visualization as shown in the following figure:

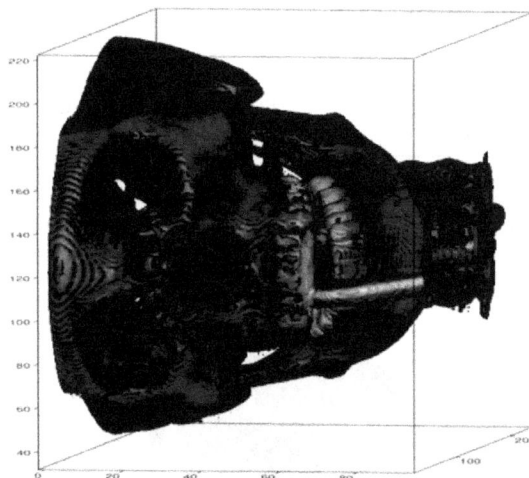

Figure 9.5: 3D visualization of the full head mhd file with the library visvis

With the library vedo

The next Python snippet code utilizes the **vedo** library, which is specifically designed for scientific visualization - particularly 3D graphics - to render a medical image in 3D. Here is a step-by-step explanation of how this code does the 3D visualization:

1. First, import the library **vedo** (install it with **pip**, if not already installed), which is a powerful tool for 3D visualization in Python. It offers a high-level interface for rendering and interacting with 3D geometries.

2. Use the function **measure.marching_cubes()** from the library **skimage** to read the data and extract a 3D surface mesh from the volumetric data (in this case, a CT image stored in the variable **ct**), with the same parameter values as in the last section, with the vertices of the mesh that define the surface (**verts**) and the faces that connect these vertices to form the polygonal mesh (**faces**) returned as output.

3. **Creating the polygonal mesh**: Create a **Mesh** object from the extracted vertices and faces using the **Mesh** class in **vedo**. The **Mesh** object will represent the 3D structure defined by the vertices and faces extracted from the medical image.

   a. The **.c('jet')** method sets the color map for the mesh to the **'jet'** colormap, which is a widely used colormap for visualizing scalar fields. This enhances the visual distinction of different regions of the mesh based on intensity.

   b. The **method.alpha(1.0)** sets the transparency of the **Mesh** to fully opaque (1.0 means no transparency).

   c. Finally, the **method.show()** renders the mesh in a 3D viewer. This opens an interactive window where users can manipulate the view (e.g., by rotating, zooming, panning etc.).

```
from vedo import *
verts, faces, _, _ = measure.marching_cubes(ct, 1150)
Mesh([verts, faces]).c('jet').alpha(1.0).show()
```

If you run the preceding code, it should pop up a window with a 3D visualization as shown in the following figure:

Figure 9.6: 3D visualization of the full head mhd file with the library vedo

Applying filters with medpy and itk

As explained earlier, medical image processing is a key tool in the diagnosis and analysis of diseases. By applying various filters, we can extract features, enhance images, and blend labels with scans to gain insights. This section discusses the application of **gradient**, **sigmoid**, and **overlay** filters to medical images using **medpy**, **itk**, and other libraries like **scipy**. It demonstrates how to work with 3D medical images (for example, with CT and MRI modalities) and applies these filters for visualization and analysis.

Applying gradient filter with scipy and medpy

Gradient filters are used to detect edges and features in images by computing the change in intensity values between neighboring pixels. In this section, we will use the function **generic_gradient_magnitude()** from the module **scipy.ndimage.filters**, with popular operators **Prewitt** and **Sobel**, to compute the gradient of an image, as shown in the next code snippet. Here is the detailed code breakdown:

1. **Loading the image**: Use the **load()** function from **medpy** to load the compressed medical image **b0.nii.gz** (in **NIfTI-1** format), which typically denotes the baseline (non-diffusion-weighted) image in diffusion MRI (**dMRI**) studies. The function returns both the image data (representing a 3D volume) and its header.

2. **Gradient magnitude calculation**: The function **generic_gradient_magnitude()** calculates the gradient magnitude of the image. First apply the *Prewitt* operator, which is a simple edge detection filter. The Prewitt operator detects edges by convolving the image with two 3×3 kernels that approximate the gradient of intensity in the x and y directions:

   G_x = [[-1, 0, 1], [-1, 0, 1], [-1, 0, 1]], G_y = [[1, 1, 1], [0, 0, 0], [-1, -1, -1]], and the edge magnitude is computed as $\sqrt{|G| = G_x^2 + G_y^2}$. The result is stored in **data_output**.

3. **Visualization**: The filtered image is displayed using **matplotlib.pylab**. Compare the original image and the result after applying the gradient filter.

4. **Sobel filter application**: An alternative to the *Prewitt* filter is the *Sobel* filter, which is more sensitive to edges. The *Sobel* operator detects edges by convolving the image with two 3×3 kernels that approximate the gradient of intensity in the x and y directions:

   G_x = [[-1, 0, 1], [-2, 0, 2], [-1, 0, 1]], G_y = [[1, 2, 1], [0, 0, 0], [-1, -2, -1]], and the edge magnitude is again computed as $\sqrt{|G| = G_x^2 + G_y^2}$. Apply this filter in a similar way to *Prewitt* and display the output side by side for comparison.

5. **Gradient filter visualization**: The comparison between **Prewitt** and **Sobel** filters helps us visualize the edges in the medical images more clearly. Sobel is generally more sensitive to noise but provides more distinct edge detection. Prewitt is simpler but may miss fine details.

6. **Example output**:

   a. **Prewitt filter output**: Displays more basic edges.

b. **Sobel filter output**: Captures finer details and is more robust for medical image analysis.

Now, refer to the following code snippet:

```python
import scipy
from scipy.ndimage.filters import generic_gradient_magnitude, prewitt, sobel
from medpy.io import load, save
from medpy.core import Logger

data_input, header_input = load('images/b0.nii.gz')
# prepare result image
data_output = scipy.zeros(data_input.shape, dtype=scipy.float32)

# apply the gradient magnitude filter
generic_gradient_magnitude(data_input, prewitt, output=data_output)

plt.figure(figsize=(20,7))
plt.bone()
plt.subplot(131), plt.imshow(data_input), plt.axis('off')
plt.title('original', size=20)
plt.subplot(132), plt.imshow(data_output), plt.axis('off')
plt.title('otuput gradient prewitt', size=20)

# alternative to prewitt is sobel
generic_gradient_magnitude(data_input, sobel, output=data_output)

plt.subplot(133), plt.imshow(data_output), plt.axis('off')
plt.title('otuput gradient sobel', size=20)
plt.tight_layout()
plt.show()
```

If you run the preceding code snippet, you will obtain a figure like the following one:

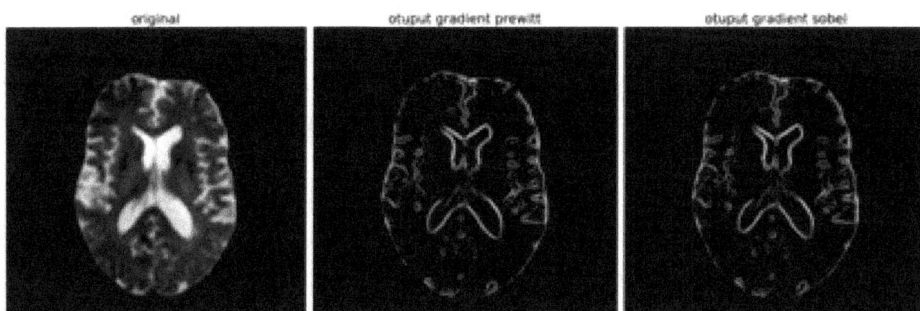

Figure 9.7: *Computing the gradients from the NIfTI image with scipy/medpy*

Applying sigmoid filter with ITK

A *sigmoid* filter is commonly used to enhance the contrast of an image, particularly in medical imaging, where specific intensity ranges are targeted for analysis. The library **itk** provides a powerful **sigmoid** filter that is highly customizable through its **alpha** and **beta** parameters, as shown in the next code snippet. Here is the detailed code breakdown:

1. **Reading the image**: Use python-style template instantiation using **itk. ImageFileReader[ImageType]** (to select the correct C++ class), to read a *brain proton density* image slice (an MRI image that displays a cross-sectional view of the brain based on the concentration of hydrogen protons, providing contrast primarily between tissues with different proton densities) in PNG format.

2. **Sigmoid filter setup**: A **SigmoidImageFilter** is applied to the input image. This filter adjusts pixel intensities by mapping values between a specified range (in this case, from 0 to 1), improving contrast.

3. **Alpha and beta values**: The filter's response can be tuned by changing the **alpha** (*contrast*) and **beta** (midpoint *intensity*) values. Higher **alpha** (α) results in more contrast. Compare the outputs obtained with different values of the parameter **alpha**.

4. **Sigmoid filter visualization**: The **sigmoid** filter significantly enhances areas of interest in medical images by improving contrast. This is particularly useful when trying to highlight specific tissue types or abnormalities in CT or MRI scans.

Now, refer to the next code snippet:

```python
PixelType = itk.UC
Dimension = 2

ImageType = itk.Image[PixelType, Dimension]

reader = itk.ImageFileReader[ImageType].New()
reader.SetFileName('images/BrainProtonDensitySlice6.png')
input = reader.GetOutput()

sigmoidFilter = itk.SigmoidImageFilter[ImageType, ImageType].New()
sigmoidFilter.SetInput(input)
sigmoidFilter.SetOutputMinimum(0)
sigmoidFilter.SetOutputMaximum(1)

beta = 128
plt.figure(figsize=(20,7))
plt.subplots_adjust(0,0,1,0.9,0.05,0.05)
plt.subplot(1,3,1), plt.imshow(itk.GetArrayFromImage(input))
plt.axis('off'), plt.title('input', size=15)
i = 2
for alpha in [1.2, 1.5]:
    sigmoidFilter.SetAlpha(alpha)
    sigmoidFilter.SetBeta(beta)
    output = sigmoidFilter.GetOutput()
    plt.subplot(1,3,i), plt.imshow(itk.GetArrayFromImage(output))
    plt.axis('off')
    plt.title(r'$\alpha$={}'.format(alpha), size=15)
    i += 1
plt.suptitle('Applying Sigmoid Filter on an Image with itk', size=20)
plt.show()
```

If you run the preceding code snippet, you will obtain a figure like the following one (sigmoid filter with different values of):

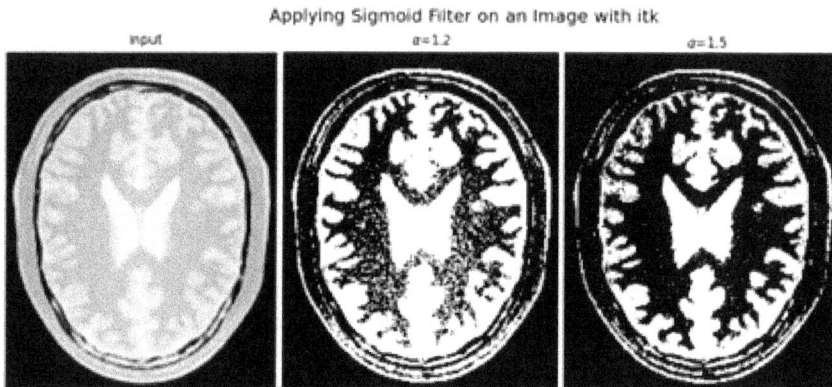

Figure 9.8: *Applying a sigmoid filter on a brain proton density slice image with ITK*

Applying overlay filter with ITK and opencv-python

Overlay filters are used to blend medical images with their corresponding labels (for example, segmentation masks), enhancing visualization and aiding to the interpretation of anatomical structures. This is crucial when working with annotated medical images, such as tumor segmentation or organ delineation, as demonstrated with the next code snippet. Here is the detailed code breakdown:

1. **Loading image and label data**: Load a 3D medical image corresponding to a multi-parametric MRI scan of prostate and the associated label files using the library **nibabel**. Here the labels represent the *segmentation masks* (for example, prostate boundaries).

```python
import nibabel as nib
import itk
import cv2
import numpy as np

prostate_images = nib.load('images/prostate_00.nii.gz').get_fdata()
prostate_images = (255*prostate_images / prostate_images.max()).astype(np.uint8)
prostate_labels = nib.load('images/label_prostate_00.nii.gz').get_fdata() \
                                                    .astype(np.uint8)
print(prostate_images.shape, prostate_labels.shape)
# (320, 320, 15, 2) (320, 320, 15)
```

2. **Label conversion**: The segmentation mask (label image) is converted into an **itk. LabelMap**. This step prepares the labels for overlay on the original image.

3. **Overlay filter application**: The **LabelMapOverlayImageFilter** blends the label map with the corresponding medical image. The function **SetOpacity(0.5)** blends the label with 50% *opacity* for clear visualization.

4. **Overlay filter visualization**: The output provides a clear understanding of the anatomical structure (*image*) and its annotated label (*segmentation*), making it easier to analyze. This is especially important in tasks like tumor detection, where overlaying segmentation results on scans improves clarity.

Now, refer to the following code snippet:

```
LabelType = itk.ctype("unsigned long")
LabelObjectType = itk.StatisticsLabelObject[LabelType, Dimension]
LabelMapType = itk.LabelMap[LabelObjectType]

i = 8
converter = itk.LabelImageToLabelMapFilter[ImageType, \
                                            LabelMapType].New()
converter.SetInput(itk.GetImageFromArray(prostate_labels[...,i]))

RGBImageType = itk.Image[itk.RGBPixel[PixelType], Dimension]
overlayFilter = itk.LabelMapOverlayImageFilter[LabelMapType, \
                                            ImageType, RGBImageType].New()
overlayFilter.SetInput(converter.GetOutput())
overlayFilter.SetFeatureImage(itk.GetImageFromArray( \
                                            prostate_images[...,i,0]))
overlayFilter.SetOpacity(0.5)

plt.figure(figsize=(20,7))
plt.gray()
plt.subplot(131), plt.imshow(prostate_images[...,i,0]), plt.axis('off')
plt.title('input (prostate CT)', size=20)
plt.subplot(132), plt.imshow(prostate_labels[...,i]), plt.axis('off')
plt.title('label', size=20)
plt.subplot(133)
plt.imshow(cv2.rotate(itk.GetArrayFromImage(overlayFilter.GetOutput()) \
                                cv2.ROTATE_90_COUNTERCLOCKWISE))
plt.axis('off'), plt.title('overlayed label (with itk)', size=20)
plt.tight_layout()
plt.show()
```

If you run the preceding code snippet, you will obtain a figure like the following one:

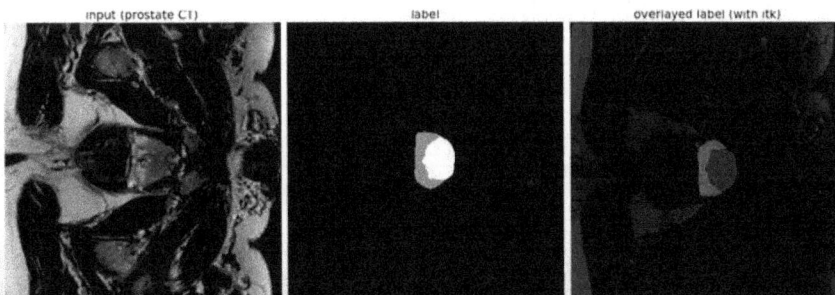

Figure 9.9: *Applying overlay filter to display label overlay on a NIfTI image with itk/opencv*

Morphological filtering with the library ITK

Morphological filtering is a powerful technique used in image processing to extract and analyze structural information from images. It is particularly effective in the realm of medical imaging, where it can assist in highlighting features of interest, such as organs and tissues, and suppressing noise. *Morphological* operations are based on the shape of objects within an image, using set theory to define operations like **dilation, erosion, opening**, and **closing**. These operations are often applied to binary or grayscale images and can be used for various tasks, including segmentation, noise reduction, and feature extraction.

Morphological operations rely on a **structuring element** (**SE** - a small shape or template) that is used to probe and transform the image. The two fundamental operations are:

- **Dilation**: This operation increases the size of the *foreground* objects in a binary image. Formally, for a binary image A and a structuring element B, dilation can be defined as:

$$A \oplus B = z \in Z^n \mid (B_z \cap A \neq \Phi)$$

  Here, B_z is the translation of the structuring element B by the point z.

- **Erosion**: This operation decreases the size of the *foreground* objects in a binary image. It is defined as:

$$A \ominus B = z \in Z^n \mid (B_z \subseteq A)$$

  In essence, erosion removes pixels on object boundaries.

Additionally, **hole filling** can be considered to be a morphological operation where small gaps or holes within objects are filled. This is important in medical imaging to ensure continuous structures, particularly when dealing with binary masks representing anatomical regions.

The following Python code illustrates how to implement morphological operations using the library **itk**. The next code snippet applies *dilation* and *erosion* to a grayscale medical image and fills holes in a binary medical image. Let us understand the code step-by-step in detail:

1. Begin by importing the required libraries, including **itk** (for image processing) and **matplotlib** (for visualization), with the following lines of code:

```
#! pip install itk
import itk
import matplotlib.pylab as plt
```

2. **Dilation and erosion**:

   a. **Setting up the image and structuring element**: The input and output image paths are defined, along with the radius for the structuring element. The pixel type is set to *unsigned char* (8-bit), and the image dimension is set to 2 (for a 2D image). A structuring element of a specified radius is created using a ball shape.

b. **Reading the input image**: An **ITK** image reader (**ImageFileReader**) is instantiated, which reads the specified input image file (a CT slice).

c. **Erosion operation**: ITK uses C++-style templates, exposed in Python via square brackets. A grayscale erosion filter (implemented by the template class **itk.GrayscaleErodeImageFilter**) is instantiated with three template arguments:

   i.   **ImageType** — the input image type, example: **itk.Image[itk.UC, 2]** (*unsigned char*, 2D)

   ii. **ImageType** — the output image type, it's often the same as the input, but **ITK** allows different types if needed.

   iii. **StructuringElementType** — the type of morphological structuring element.

It applies the *erosion* operation to the input image using a *circular SE* of *radius 2*,

   i.   Defined using a dimension-specific type alias for **ITK** 's **FlatStructuringElement** class using Python-style template syntax, enabling the creation of a flat morphological structuring element.

   ii. Created using the **ITK** factory method **StructuringElementType. Ball()**, via its Python interface.

Note: Understanding the ITK factory method

In **ITK**, objects such as filters and readers are created using the factory method **.New()**, rather than standard constructors. This approach returns a smart pointer, ensuring efficient memory management and allowing **ITK** to dynamically manage object creation at runtime.

The output of this operation is stored in **output_erosion**, using the next code snippet:

```
itk.auto_progress(2)

input_image = "images/cthead15.png"
output_image = "images/output.png"
radius = 5
PixelType = itk.UC
Dimension = 2

ImageType = itk.Image[PixelType, Dimension]
ReaderType = itk.ImageFileReader[ImageType]
reader = ReaderType.New()
reader.SetFileName(input_image)
```

```
StructuringElementType = itk.FlatStructuringElement[Dimension]
structuringElement = StructuringElementType.Ball(radius)
input = reader.GetOutput()
GrayscaleFilterType = itk.GrayscaleErodeImageFilter[ImageType, \
                                    ImageType, StructuringElementType]
grayscaleFilter = GrayscaleFilterType.New()
grayscaleFilter.SetInput(input)
grayscaleFilter.SetKernel(structuringElement)
output_erosion = grayscaleFilter.GetOutput()
```

d. **Dilation operation**: Similar to *erosion*, a grayscale *dilation* filter (**GrayscaleDilateImageFilter**) is instantiated to apply dilation to the input image, producing another output image.

e. The method **SetInput()** sets the input image for the **grayscaleFilter**, whereas the method **SetKernel()** specifies the structuring element that the filter will use during the morphological operation.

f. **Writing the output image**: The output of the erosion operation is written to the specified output file using an **ITK** image writer (**ImageFileWriter**).

```
GrayscaleFilterType = itk.GrayscaleDilateImageFilter[ImageType, \
                            ImageType, StructuringElementType].New()
grayscaleFilter = GrayscaleFilterType.New()
grayscaleFilter.SetInput(input)
grayscaleFilter.SetKernel(structuringElement)
output_dilation = grayscaleFilter.GetOutput()

WriterType = itk.ImageFileWriter[ImageType]
writer = WriterType.New()
writer.SetFileName(output_image)
writer.SetInput(output_erosion)
writer.Update()
```

If you run the preceding code snippet and display the input image along with the output images obtained by applying morphological erosion and dilation operations side-by-side, you should obtain a figure like the following one:

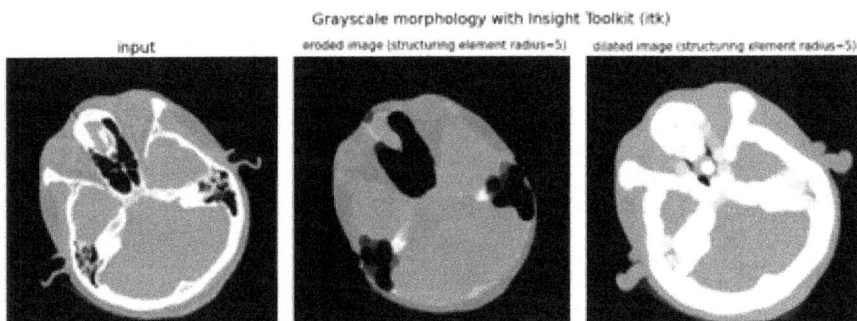

Figure 9.10: Applying grayscale dilation/erosion on a ct image with itk

3. **Hole filling**: Again, read a binary image, and instantiate a voting binary iterative hole-filling filter (**VotingBinaryIterativeHoleFillingImageFilter**). This filter fills small holes in binary images based on *majority voting* from neighboring pixels.

   a. The method **SetRadius()** sets the radius of the neighborhood that the filter considers around each pixel during the voting process. The radius determines how many pixels in each dimension are examined. A larger radius considers a wider neighborhood, which may result in more aggressive hole filling.

   b. The method **SetMajorityThreshold()** sets the minimum number of neighboring foreground pixels required to change a background pixel to foreground. For example, if the threshold is set to 10, any background pixel surrounded by 10 or more foreground neighbors will be filled in.

   c. The method **SetBackgroundValue()** defines which pixel value is treated as background in the binary image. Typically, this is set to 0, meaning pixels with a value of 0 are considered background and candidates for hole filling.

   d. The method **SetForegroundValue()** specifies the pixel value that represents the foreground (usually 1 or 255), which is the value assigned to filled pixels.

   e. The method **SetMaximumNumberOfIterations()** sets the maximum number of iterations the filter will perform. The filter iteratively applies the voting rule until all fillable holes are processed or this iteration limit is reached, helping to avoid excessive computation or infinite loops.

   f. The input image and the results of the hole-filling operation with different radii values are displayed using **matplotlib.pylab**.

Now, refer to the following code snippet:

```
import itk
import matplotlib.pylab as plt

PixelType = itk.UC
Dimension = 2

ImageType = itk.Image[PixelType, Dimension]
reader = itk.ImageFileReader[ImageType].New()
reader.SetFileName('images/BinaryThresholdImageFilter.png')
input = reader.GetOutput()

radius = 5
binaryFilter = itk.VotingBinaryIterativeHoleFillingImageFilter[\
                                                ImageType].New()

binaryFilter.SetInput(input)
```

```
plt.figure(figsize=(20,7))
plt.gray()
plt.subplots_adjust(0,0,1,0.9,0.05,0.05)
plt.subplot(1,3,1), plt.imshow(itk.GetArrayFromImage(input))
plt.axis('off'), plt.title('input', size=15)
i = 2
for radius in [3, 5]:
    binaryFilter.SetRadius(radius)
    binaryFilter.SetMajorityThreshold(10)
    binaryFilter.SetBackgroundValue(0);
    binaryFilter.SetForegroundValue(255);
    binaryFilter.SetMaximumNumberOfIterations(20);
    output = binaryFilter.GetOutput()
    plt.subplot(1,3,i), plt.imshow(itk.GetArrayFromImage(output))
    plt.axis('off'),  plt.title('radius={}'.format(radius), size=15)
    i += 1
plt.suptitle('Iterative Hole Filling with itk', size=20)
plt.show()
```

If you run the preceding code snippet, you should obtain a figure as follows:

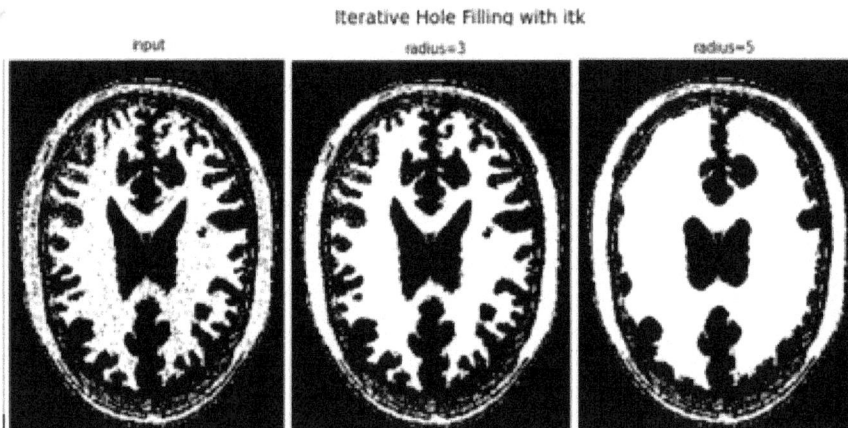

Figure 9.11: Iterative hole filling with itk

Computed tomography reconstruction with inverse Radon transform using scikit-image

Computed tomography (**CT**) is a critical medical imaging technique that generates cross-sectional images of the human body. It works by capturing multiple X-ray images from different angles around the body and then reconstructing them to form a detailed internal view. The reconstruction process is mathematically complex, as it involves converting 2D projections (*sinograms*) into 3D images. One of the most commonly used techniques in CT image reconstruction is the *inverse Radon transform*.

The theory behind CT reconstruction is grounded in the *Radon transform*. This transform converts a 2D object (image) into a set of 1D projections. These projections are acquired by integrating the image along parallel lines at various angles. The *inverse Radon transform,* often referred to as *filtered back-projection,* is the process of reconstructing the original image from its sinograms. Now, let us try to understand the underlying mathematical details:

- **Radon transform**: The Radon transform converts an image into its projection data by integrating along lines at different angles. Mathematically, for a function $f(x,y)$ representing the original image, the *Radon Transform* $R_f(\theta, t)$ for an angle θ is given by:

$$R_f(\theta, t) = \int_{-\infty}^{\infty} f(x\cos\theta + y\sin\theta)dx$$

   Where θ is the *projection angle, t* is the *position* of the line at that *angle*. The result is a *sinogram,* which represents the projections of the image at different angles.

- **Inverse Radon transform**: To reconstruct the image from the *sinogram,* the *inverse Radon transform* is used. A simple form of this process, called *back-projection,* involves smearing each projection back across the image domain. However, back-projection alone leads to blurred reconstructions. To counter this, a filtering step is applied before back-projection, known as **filtered back projection** (**FBP**). Mathematically, the *inverse* of the *Radon transform* is given by:

$$f(x,y) = \int_0^{\pi} R_f(\theta, x\cos\theta + y\sin\theta)d\theta$$

   Filtering is applied in the *Fourier domain* using a *high-pass filter* (for example, *ramp filter*). This ensures that high-frequency components (edges) in the image are enhanced, leading to sharper reconstructions.

The following Python code demonstrates how to perform CT reconstruction using the *Radon transform* and *inverse Radon transform* implementations provided by the `skimage` library. Let us walk through the following code snippet and explain each step:

1. **Start by importing the necessary libraries**:

   a. The functions `radon()` and `iradon()` from the module `skimage.transform` are used to apply the *Radon* and *inverse Radon transforms,* respectively.

   b. The function `imread()` from `skimage.io` loads the CT image.

   c. The library `numpy` is used for numerical operations, and `matplotlib` is used for visualizing the images.

2. **Load CT image**: The CT image is loaded using `imread()`, which reads the image stored in the `'images/cthead15.png'` file. The second argument `as_gray=1` converts the image to grayscale.

3. **Set the range of projection angles**: The *for* loop sets two different increments for the projection angles ($d\theta$ = 5° and 1°). The variable θ contains the set of angles from 0° to 180° at intervals defined by $d\theta$. The smaller the angle step, the more detailed the reconstruction.

4. **Apply radon transform (generate sinogram)**: The **radon()** function computes the *Radon Transform* of the image **im**, resulting in a *sinogram*. The sinogram is the collection of all 1D projections of the image at different angles specified by θ.

5. **Visualize sinogram**: Visualize the *sinogram* using **pcolor()**. The sinogram represents the 1D projections of the image, and the **inferno** color map enhances the contrast.

6. **Reconstruct image with simple back projection (laminogram)**: The function **iradon()** is used to reconstruct the original image from the *sinogram* without applying any filter. This process is called **simple back projection**, and the result is a blurred image called a **laminogram**.

7. **Reconstruct image with filtered back projection (FBP)**: Here, the function **iradon()** reconstructs the image using FBP with a **ramp** filter. The **ramp** filter removes low-frequency components and enhances edges, producing a much sharper and clearer image compared to **simple back-projection**.

8. Finally, ensure that the layout of the subplots is properly spaced using **plt.tight_layout()** and display the final figure with all the images (input CT image, *sinogram*, *laminogram*, and *filtered back projection*).

Now, refer to the following code snippet:

```python
from skimage.transform import radon, iradon
from skimage.io import imread
import numpy as np
import matplotlib.pylab as plt
import warnings
warnings.filterwarnings('ignore')

im = imread('images/cthead15.png', 1)
for dθ in [5, 1]:
  θ = np.arange(0., 180., dθ)
    plt.figure(figsize=(20,6))
    plt.gray()
    plt.subplot(141), plt.imshow(im, aspect='auto'), plt.axis('off')
    plt.title('input CT image', size=20)
    sinogram = radon(im, theta=θ)
    plt.subplot(142), plt.pcolor(sinogram, cmap='inferno')
    plt.title(f'sinogram (radon), with {len(θ)} θs', size=20)
    recons_im = iradon(sinogram, theta=θ, filter_name=None)
    plt.subplot(143), plt.pcolor(recons_im), plt.axis('off')
```

```
    plt.title('laminogram (recons. iradon)', size=20)
    recons_im = iradon(sinogram, theta=θ, filter_name='ramp')
    plt.subplot(144), plt.pcolor(recons_im), plt.axis('off')
    plt.title('filtered backproj (recons. iradon)', size=20)
    plt.tight_layout()
    plt.show()
```

If you run the preceding code snippet, you should obtain a figure as follows:

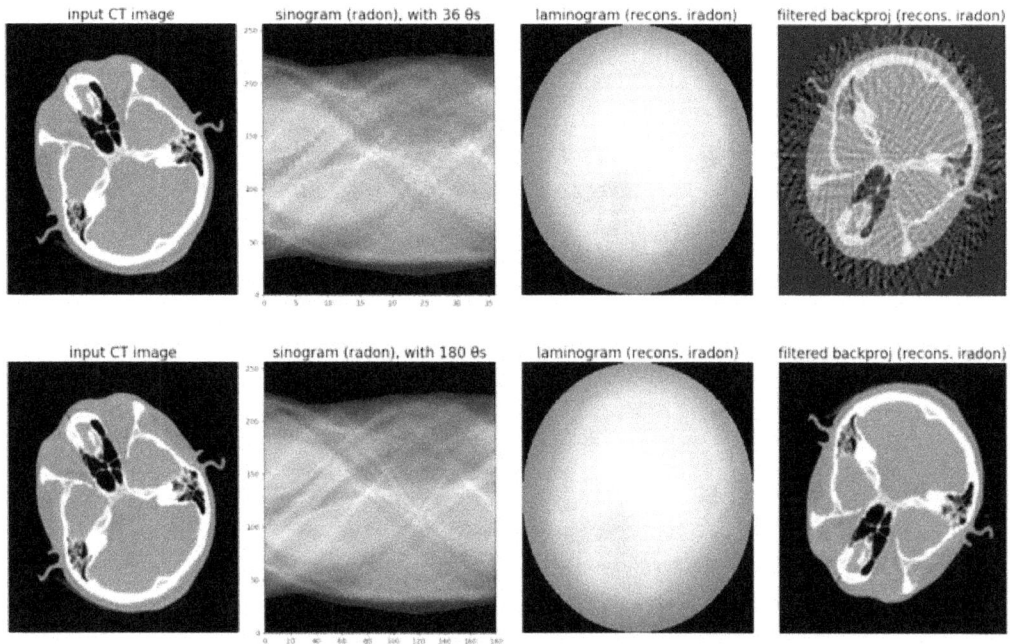

Figure 9.12: CT reconstruction using inverse Radon transformation with scikit-image

Segmentation of brain MRI images with graph cut algorithms with medpy

In medical image processing, segmentation is the process of partitioning an image into distinct regions, typically corresponding to different anatomical structures or tissue types. For brain MRI images, segmentation is crucial for identifying tumors, lesions, and specific brain structures. One powerful method for segmentation is the *graph cut* algorithm, which models the problem as a graph where nodes represent pixels or regions, and edges represent relationships between them (for example, intensity differences). The goal is to find a *minimum cut* through the graph that best separates the *foreground* from the *background*.

This section focuses on using the graph cut algorithm for segmenting brain MRI images using the **medpy** library in Python. The process involves the following key components that form the foundation of the graph-based segmentation approach:

- **Graph representation of the image**: In the graph cut method, the image is represented as a graph $G = (V, E)$, where V is the set of nodes (each node corresponds to a *pixel* or *voxel* in the image) and E is the set of edges connecting the nodes. Each node is connected to its neighboring nodes, and there are two special nodes called *source* and *sink*, representing the *foreground* and *background*, respectively.

- **Energy minimization**: The segmentation problem is formulated as an *energy minimization* problem, where the objective is to find a labeling of nodes (*foreground* or *background*) that minimizes a predefined energy function. The *total energy* consists of two terms:

  o **Data term $D(p)$**: Measures how well the label assigned to a pixel p (*foreground* or *background*) agrees with the observed intensity or prior knowledge (e.g., markers).

  o **Smoothness term $S(p, q)$**: Encourages neighboring pixels p and q to be assigned the same label, particularly if their intensities are similar. The total energy is given by:

$$E(L) = \sum_p D(p) + \sum_{(p,q)} S(p, q)$$

Where we have

- L is the label assignment over pixels (*foreground* or *background*).

- $D(p)$ is the data term for pixel p, which can be based on *markers* (user-defined seeds) or intensity values.

- $S(p, q)$ is the *smoothness* term between neighboring pixels p and q, which encourages consistent labeling between similar pixels (encouraging spatial coherence). The goal is to *minimize* this *energy* to find the optimal labeling for the image.

- **Min-cut/Max-flow**: The segmentation problem is solved using the *max-flow / min-cut* algorithm. The algorithm finds the *minimum cut* that separates the *source* (*foreground*) from the *sink* (*background*), which corresponds to the optimal segmentation. This method efficiently finds the globally optimal solution by minimizing the energy function.

Now, let us segment a few example MRI images using the implementation of the graph cut segmentation algorithm from the **medpy** library in Python, as shown in the following code snippet. Here are the detailed steps:

1. **Importing required libraries**: First, import the necessary libraries, using the following code snippet. The **medpy** library provides tools for loading a medical

image and applying the *graph cut segmentation*. The **split_marker()** function is used to separate the *marker* image into *foreground* and *background* regions.

```
from medpy import graphcut, filter
from medpy.graphcut.wrapper import split_marker
from medpy.core import ArgumentError, Logger
from medpy.io import load, save
import scipy
import numpy as np
import matplotlib.pylab as plt
import logging, os
```

2. **Graph cut segmentation with labeling**: The **graphcut_label()** function performs segmentation of an image using the graph cut algorithm, first by generating a graph from labeled regions and applying the *minimum-cut* algorithm to separate *foreground* from *background* based on image intensity and boundary terms. It relies on the following images passed as arguments: a *region* image that provides initial labels (e.g., superpixels or labeled regions), an *additional* image that serves as intensity reference and a *marker* image to indicate known foreground and background voxels. Here is how the function works:

   a. First it initializes a **Logger** class to monitor the progress of the algorithm.

   b. The input images are loaded as follows:

      i. **b0.nii.gz**: The main region image to be segmented,

      ii. **b1000.nii.gz**: An auxiliary image providing additional intensity information,

      iii. **b0markers.nii.gz**: A *marker* image containing manually labeled *foreground* and *background* regions, it guides the graph construction and segmentation process.

   c. The **boundary_term** is chosen as **boundary_stawiaski**, based on the **Stawiaski** method, which computes the smoothness cost between neighboring pixels. The boundary function serves as an edge detector in the original image. Conceptually, it serves as an edge detector by calculating local contrast and assigning higher weights (energy penalties) to edges between dissimilar pixels, discouraging segmentation across strong boundaries.

   d. The **split_marker()** function separates the *marker* image into two parts:

      i. **fgmarkers_image_data**: The *foreground markers*.

      ii. **bgmarkers_image_data**: The *background markers*. These markers provide hard constraints for the segmentation algorithm and guide the segmentation process by indicating which regions of the image are known to be foreground and background.

e. The function **graphcut.graph_from_labels()** generates the graph from the labeled image data and markers. The graph represents the relationship between pixels based on intensity differences (boundary term). The additional image data is used as input to the boundary term function to influence edge weights.

f. The **maxflow()** function computes the *maximum flow* in the graph, which corresponds to the *minimum cut* in the graph. This step solves the *energy minimization* problem, producing a binary segmentation by separating the *foreground* from the *background*.

g. The segmentation results are applied to the region image. Each pixel is labeled as either foreground (1) or background (0) based on the result of the graph cut. The **filter.relabel_map()** function updates the image labels accordingly.

h. Finally, the segmented image is displayed alongside the original image and the marker image.

```python
def graphcut_label(region, additional, marker):

    logger = Logger.getInstance()
    logger.setLevel(logging.INFO)
    boundary_term = graphcut.energy_label.boundary_stawiaski
    logger.info('Selected boundary term: stawiaski')

    region_image_data, reference_header = load(region)
    badditional_image_data, _ = load(additional)
    markers_image_data, _ = load(marker)
    markers_image_data = np.squeeze(markers_image_data)
    region_image_data_orig = region_image_data.copy()

    fgmarkers_image_data, bgmarkers_image_data = split_marker(\
                                        markers_image_data)

    # check if all images dimensions are the same
    if not (badditional_image_data.shape \
            == region_image_data.shape \
            == fgmarkers_image_data.shape \
            == bgmarkers_image_data.shape):
        logger.critical('Not all images are of same shape.')
        raise ArgumentError('Not all images are of same shape.')

    # recompute the label ids to start from id = 1
    region_image_data = filter.relabel(region_image_data)
```

```
            gcgraph = graphcut.graph_from_labels(region_image_data,
                                    fgmarkers_image_data,
                                    bgmarkers_image_data,
                                    boundary_term = boundary_term,
                                    boundary_term_args = \
                                    (badditional_image_data))
                            # second is directedness of graph , 0)

        del fgmarkers_image_data
    del bgmarkers_image_data

    maxflow = gcgraph.maxflow()
    # apply results to the region image
    mapping = [0] # no region with id 1 exists in mapping
                    # entry used as padding
    mapping.extend([0 \
        if gcgraph.termtype.SINK == gcgraph.what_segment(int(x) - 1) \
        else 1 for x in scipy.unique(region_image_data)])
    region_image_data = filter.relabel_map(region_image_data, \
                                            mapping)

    plt.figure(figsize=(20,7))
    plt.gray()
    plt.subplot(141), plt.imshow(region_image_data_orig)
    plt.axis('off'), plt.title('input', size=20)
    plt.subplot(142), plt.imshow(badditional_image_data)
    plt.axis('off'), plt.title('additional', size=20)
    plt.subplot(143), plt.imshow(markers_image_data)
    plt.axis('off'), plt.title('marker', size=20)
    plt.subplot(144), plt.imshow(region_image_data), plt.axis('off')
    plt.title('output graphcut segmentation', size=20)
    plt.tight_layout()
    plt.show()
graphcut_label('b0.nii.gz', 'b1000.nii.gz', 'b0markers.nii.gz')
```

If you run the preceding code, you should obtain a figure like the following one:

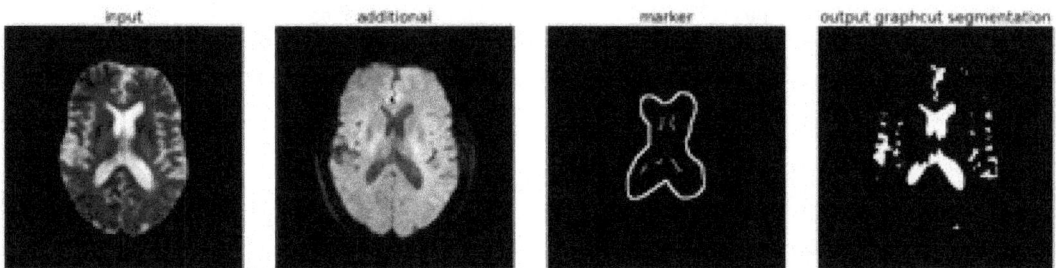

Figure 9.13: Applying graph cut segmentation to a brain MRI image with medpy

3. **Graph cut voxel segmentation**: The `graphcut_voxel()` function defined in the next code snippet performs graph-cut segmentation on a 3D voxel-based medical image, where segmentation is computed over the entire volume rather than slice-by-slice.

    a. **Graph construction**: The function `graphcut.graph_from_voxels()` generates a graph from voxel data, where the boundary term, defined by **boundary_difference_power**, is based on voxel intensity differences. The graph is constructed in 3D, and a *sigma* parameter controls the influence of intensity variations, effectively tuning the *smoothness* of the segmentation.

    b. **Segmentation via max-flow**: The same *max-flow* algorithm is used to compute the *minimum cut* and segment the 3D voxel image into *foreground* and *background* Regions, based on intensity gradients and marker constraints.

Now, refer to the next code snippet:

```python
def graphcut_voxel(input, marker):
    logger = Logger.getInstance()
    logger.setLevel(logging.INFO)
    boundary_term = graphcut.energy_voxel.boundary_difference_power
    badditional_image_data, reference_header = load(input)
    markers_image_data, _ = load(marker)
    markers_image_data = np.squeeze(markers_image_data)
    fgmarkers_image_data, bgmarkers_image_data = \
                                    split_marker(markers_image_data)
    # check if all images dimensions are the same
    if not (badditional_image_data.shape == \
            fgmarkers_image_data.shape == bgmarkers_image_data.shape):
        raise ArgumentError('Not all images are of same shape.')
    # extract spacing if required
    spacing = header.get_pixel_spacing(reference_header)
    sigma = 10
    gcgraph = graphcut.graph_from_voxels(fgmarkers_image_data, \
                                    bgmarkers_image_data, \
                                    boundary_term = boundary_term,\
        boundary_term_args = (badditional_image_data, sigma, spacing))
    maxflow = gcgraph.maxflow()
    # reshape results to form a valid mask
    result_image_data = scipy.zeros(bgmarkers_image_data.size, \
                                    dtype=scipy.bool_)
    for idx in range(len(result_image_data)):
        result_image_data[idx] = 0 \
            if gcgraph.termtype.SINK == gcgraph.what_segment(idx) else 1
    result_image_data = result_image_data.reshape(\
                                    bgmarkers_image_data.shape)
    return result_image_data, badditional_image_data, markers_image_data
```

c. **Visualization and Output**: To visualize the segmentation output effectively, we need to blend the result mask with the original volumetric image to create a clear overlay, with the next code snippet. Here are the details steps explaining how the code works:

i. The **graphcut_voxel()** function is called with a volumetric image and its corresponding marker image, returning a binary segmentation mask (**result_image_data**), along with the original intensity image (**badditional_image_data**).

ii. An empty RGB image is created where the *red* and *blue* channels are filled with the mask (highlighting segmentation in *magenta*).

iii. This mask is *blended* with the grayscale image (converted to RGB) using a 40% mask and 60% image mix.

iv. The result is a composite image that clearly shows where the segmentation aligns with anatomical structures, making visual inspection easy and intuitive.

Now, refer to the next code snippet:

```
result_image_data, badditional_image_data, markers_image_data = \
                        graphcut_voxel('images/b1000.nii.gz', \
                                    'images/b0markers.nii.gz')

# save resulting mask
result_image_data_out = np.zeros((result_image_data.shape[0], \
                            result_image_data.shape[1], 3))
result_image_data_out[..., 0] = result_image_data_out[..., 2] \
                            = 255*result_image_data
output = (0.4 * result_image_data_out + \
        0.6 * gray2rgb(badditional_image_data)).astype(np.uint8)

plt.figure(figsize=(20,7))
plt.gray()
plt.subplot(131), plt.imshow(badditional_image_data)
plt.axis('off'), plt.title('input', size=20)
plt.subplot(132), plt.imshow(markers_image_data)
plt.axis('off'), plt.title('marker', size=20)
plt.subplot(133), plt.imshow(output), plt.axis('off')
plt.title('output graphcut voxel segmentation', size=20)
plt.tight_layout()
plt.show()
```

If you run the preceding code snippet, you should obtain a figure like the following one:

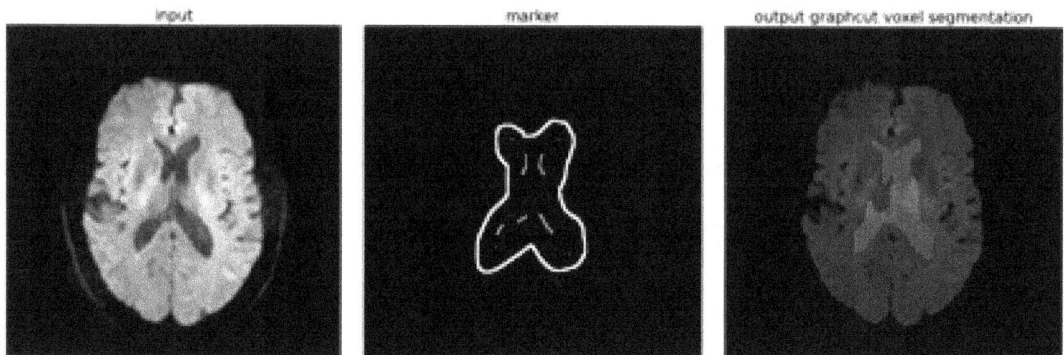

Figure 9.14: Graph cut voxel segmentation with medpy

Graph cut segmentation is a powerful tool for segmenting complex medical images such as brain MRI. By formulating the problem as a graph, it leverages global optimization techniques to produce highly accurate segmentation results. The **medpy** library provides an efficient implementation of graph cut segmentation for both 2D and 3D medical images, making it a valuable tool for medical image analysis.

Pneumonia classification from chest X-ray using XceptionNet with tensorflow

Pneumonia, a severe infection that inflames the air sacs in one or both lungs, is a leading cause of illness and death worldwide. Chest X-ray images are commonly used to diagnose pneumonia, and automated approaches like deep learning can significantly improve the speed and accuracy of diagnoses. In this section, we will discuss the application of **XceptionNet**, a powerful CNN, for pneumonia classification using chest X-ray images. This task is carried out using a publicly available *Kaggle* dataset (**chest-xray-pneumonia**), and let us demonstrate the full workflow in Python using the TensorFlow framework, explaining how to use XceptionNet for pneumonia detection. The following is a detailed list of steps to be executed:

1. **Setup Kaggle account**: For this problem, we shall use a publicly available dataset from **Kaggle** (a platform for data scientists and machine learning practitioners to access widely available public datasets, participate in competitions, share code, and collaborate within a global community). Go to **https://www.kaggle.com/** and create a new account, if you do not already have one.

2. We shall use *Google Colab* to demonstrate the python code, we need to be able to access the *kaggle* public dataset **chest-xray-pneumonia** from inside colab. We shall use the **kaggle public API** for this purpose.

3. The first step is to create a new *token* from your profile, as shown in the following figure. It will get downloaded to your local machine as **kaggle.json** file. Now you need to upload the **.json** file to *Google Colab*, to be able to use *Kaggle API*.

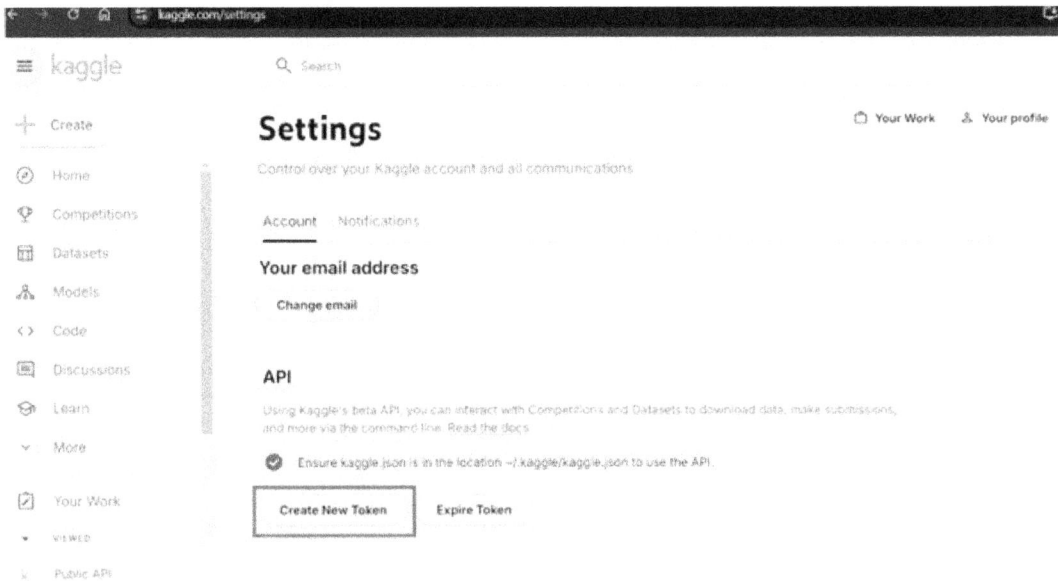

Figure 9.15: Creating a Kaggle API token

4. Start by creating a new notebook (for example, **pneumonia_classification. ipynb**) on *Google Colab*. You can use the **files.upload()** function from **google. colab** module to upload the *Kaggle API token* (the **kaggle.json** file which contains the credentials to access Kaggle datasets) from the local machine to *Google Colab*, as shown in the following code snippet:

```
# import function to upload files (upload kaggle.json)
from google.colab import files
# Upload Kaggle key
files.upload()
```

5. If you run the preceding command from inside the notebook in Colab, an Open file dialog control should open from which you can choose the **json** file from the right path from your local machine, as shown in the following figure:

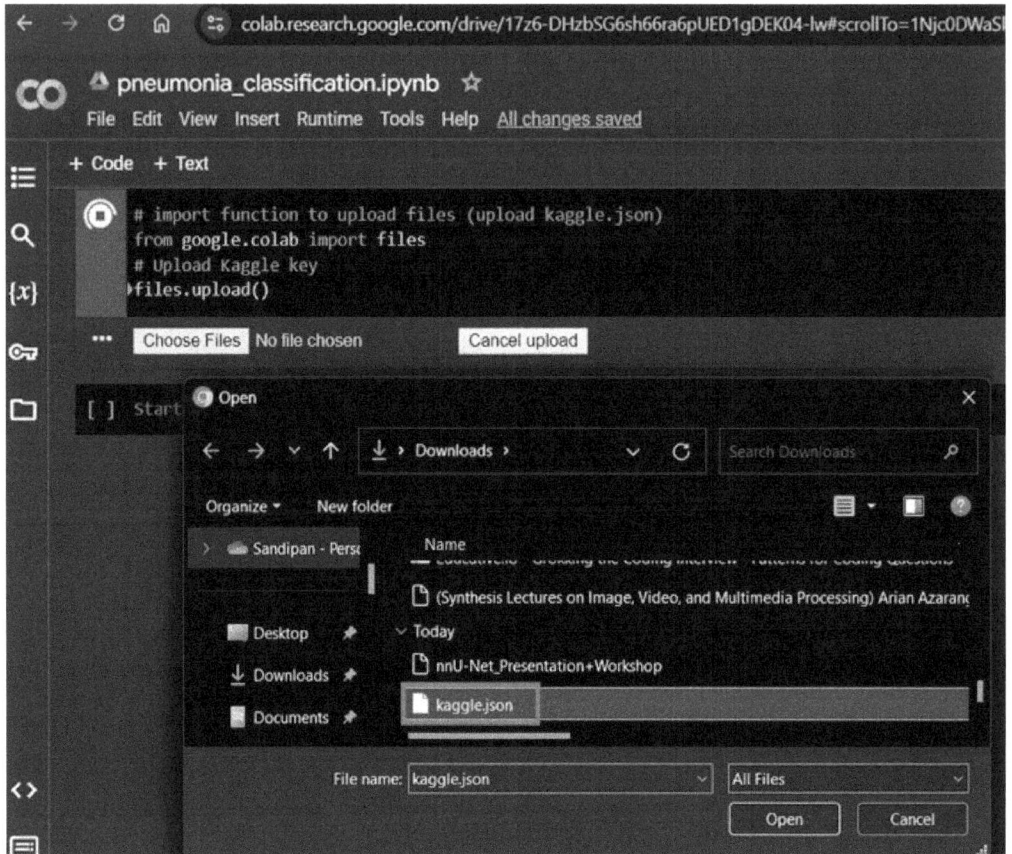

Figure 9.16: Uploading Kaggle json (token) to Google Colab

6. Install the **Kaggle CLI** in the Colab environment (using the following line of code, with **pip**), which allows you to download datasets from *Kaggle* directly. The **-q** flag runs the installation in quiet mode, meaning it does not show detailed installation logs.

```
!pip install -q Kaggle
```

7. Run the following commands to:

   a. Create a hidden **.kaggle** directory to store the *Kaggle API key*, using the following shell command: **!mkdir ~/.kaggle**.

   b. Copy the uploaded **kaggle.json** file to the **.kaggle** directory, using the following shell command: **!cp kaggle.json ~/.kaggle/**.

   c. Change the permission of the **kaggle.json** file to ensure it is only readable by the user (security measure), using the following command: **!chmod 600 ~/.kaggle/kaggle.json**

```
! mkdir ~/.kaggle
! cp kaggle.json ~/.kaggle/
! chmod 600 ~/.kaggle/kaggle.json
```

8. Run the next commands in the console to:

    a. Download the Chest X-ray Pneumonia dataset using the *Kaggle CLI*. The dataset ID **paultimothymooney/chest-xray-pneumonia** is used to identify the dataset.

    b. Unzip the downloaded dataset into the current working directory. It will create a folder **chest_xray** and extract the **zip** file inside the folder (as shown in the following figure). This makes the files (X-ray images) accessible for further processing.

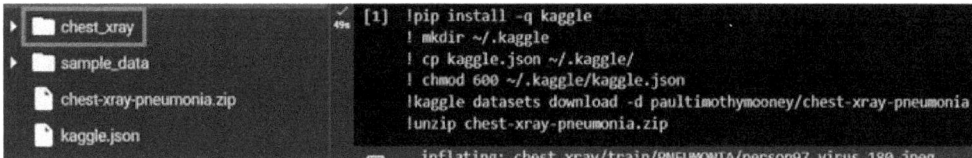

Figure 9.17: Downloading chest x-ray pneumonia Kaggle dataset in colab

The commands to be run are as follows:

```
!kaggle datasets download -d paultimothymooney/chest-xray-pneumonia
!unzip chest-xray-pneumonia.zip
```

9. Use the following *magic* command in Google Colab that ensures that the environment is using **tensorflow version 2.x**. It switches the **tensorflow** version if needed, making sure you are working with **tensorflow 2.x** instead of an older version like **tensorflow 1.x**. This command is specific to Colab and helps in managing **tensorflow** versions easily.

```
%tensorflow_version 2.x
```

10. Let us import the required Python libraries, modules and functions, using the following code snippet:

```
import tensorflow as tf
from tensorflow import keras
from keras.preprocessing.image import img_to_array, array_to_img
from keras import backend as K
from sklearn.utils import class_weight
from sklearn.metrics import confusion_matrix

from PIL import Image
import cv2
import numpy as np
```

```
from IPython.display import display
import matplotlib.pyplot as plt
import matplotlib.cm as cm
import pathlib, gc
```

11. Define the following constants, for example:

   a. **IMG_HEIGHT**, **IMG_WIDTH**: These define the target *height* and *width* to which each chest X-ray image will be resized (150×150 pixels).

   b. **BATCH_SIZE**: Specifies the number of images that will be processed in a single step (or *batch*) by the neural network. A larger batch size allows for more parallel computation, while a smaller batch size can be more memory-efficient.

   c. **RESCALE**: The constant **1./255** is to convert from **uint8** to **float32** in range [0,1].

```
RESCALE      = 1./255
BATCH_SIZE   = 64
IMG_HEIGHT, IMG_WIDTH = 150, 150
IMG_SHAPE    = (IMG_HEIGHT, IMG_WIDTH, 3)
TARGET_SIZE = (IMG_HEIGHT, IMG_WIDTH)
SHUFFLE_BUFFER_SIZE = 6000
```

12. The **reset_graph()** function defined in the following code snippet will be used to reset the current **tensorflow** computation graph and clear any allocated resources to avoid memory issues or conflicts when running multiple models or sessions in sequence. The following list explains what it does:

   a. **Deletes the existing model (if provided)**: If a model is passed as an argument, it attempts to delete it, freeing up memory associated with that model. If this deletion fails for any reason, it returns **False** without proceeding.

   b. **Clears the current TensorFlow graph session**: This clears the current **tensorflow** backend session (with the function **clear_session()**), which removes any leftover states or computations in memory, resetting the graph.

   c. **Runs garbage collection**: It calls Python's garbage collector (the function **gc.collect()**) to clean up any unreferenced objects in memory, helping to free up system resources.

   d. **Returns True**: If everything goes smoothly, it returns **True**, indicating the graph and resources have been successfully reset.

13. Call the function **reset_graph()** to ensure that the environment is clean before starting new model training or inference to avoid memory leakage and conflicts from previous models or graphs.

```
def reset_graph(model=None):
    if model:
        try:
            del model
        except:
            return False
    K.clear_session()
    gc.collect()
    return True

reset_graph()
```

14. The next code snippet sets up the directories in preparation for training a deep learning model:

   a. **pathlib.Path** is used to define the file paths for the *training, testing,* and *validation* datasets.

   b. The dataset consists of three subsets: **train, test**, and **validation**; each located in the **chest_xray/** directory. These paths will later be used to load the images.

15. It also calculates dataset related statistics (for example, **train_data_count, test_data_count, val_data_count, TOTAL_IMAGE_COUNT** and so on).

```
root_dir = "./"
dataset_root_dir = r"chest_xray/"
# input dir
train_dir  = pathlib.Path(dataset_root_dir + r"train")
test_dir   = pathlib.Path(dataset_root_dir + r"test")
val_dir    = pathlib.Path(dataset_root_dir + r"val")
# output dir
output_dir  = root_dir + r"data/output/"
output_figures_dir  = output_dir + "figures"

temp = root_dir
for d in output_figures_dir.split('/'):
    temp += d + "/"
    if not os.path.exists(temp):
        os.mkdir(temp)

train_data_count  = len(list(train_dir.glob('*/*.jpeg')))
test_data_count   = len(list(test_dir.glob('*/*.jpeg')))
val_data_count    = len(list(val_dir.glob('*/*.jpeg')))

TOTAL_IMAGE_COUNT  = train_data_count + test_data_count \
                                      + val_data_count
STEPS_PER_EPOCH = np.ceil(TOTAL_IMAGE_COUNT/BATCH_SIZE)
```

16. Preprocess the images using the function **preprocess_image()** defined in the following code snippet:

    a. **tf.image.decode_jpeg(img, channels=3)**: This function decodes the input JPEG-encoded image file into a 3-channel (RGB) image *tensor*.

    b. **tf.image.resize(img, [IMG_HEIGHT, IMG_WIDTH])**: Resizes the image to the specified *height* and *width* (150×150 in this case).

    c. **img /= 255.0**: Normalizes the image data to a range between 0 and 1. Image pixel values are typically in the range [0,255], so dividing by 255 scales them to the range [0,1], which helps with the training process, as neural networks work better with normalized data.

17. Load *train/test* images and labels, using the functions **load_image_train()**, and **load_image_test()**, respectively.

    a. The functions accept an input image and return the preprocessed image and the corresponding label.

    b. **tf.io.read_file(file_path)**: Reads the image from the input image path.

    c. The function **get_label()** returns 1 for *pneumonia* and 0 for *normal* class.

    d. **tf.strings.split(file_path, '/'):** Splits the file path string into components using '/' as the delimiter. This is used to identify whether the file belongs to a **NORMAL** or **PNEUMONIA** class based on its directory.

Now, refer to the next code snippet:

```python
def preprocess_image(img):
    img = tf.image.decode_jpeg(img, channels=3)
    img = tf.image.resize(img, [IMG_HEIGHT, IMG_WIDTH])
    img /= 255.0  # Normalize to [0, 1] range
    return img
def get_label(file_path):
    parts = tf.strings.split(file_path, '/')
    return parts[-2] == CLASS_NAMES
def decode_img(img):
    img = tf.image.decode_jpeg(img, channels=3)
    img = tf.image.convert_image_dtype(img, tf.float32)
    return tf.image.resize(img, (IMG_HEIGHT, IMG_WIDTH), \
                    method=tf.image.ResizeMethod.NEAREST_NEIGHBOR)

def load_image_train(file_path):
    label = get_label(file_path)
    img = tf.io.read_file(file_path)
    img = decode_img(img)
    return img, label
```

```
def load_image_test(file_path):
    label = get_label(file_path)
    img = tf.io.read_file(file_path)
    img = decode_img(img)
    return img, label
```

18. Create the *training* batches, using the following code snippet:

    a. **tf.data.Dataset.list_files(str(train_dir/'*/*.jpeg'))**: Creates a **tensorflow** dataset from all the JPEG files found in the training directory. The path includes ***/*.jpeg** to ensure it finds all JPEG images in the nested folders.

    b. **.map(load_image_label)**: Maps each file path in the dataset to the **load_ image_train()** function, which loads and preprocesses the images along with their corresponding labels.

    c. **.batch(BATCH_SIZE)**: Groups the images and labels into batches of size 64 (as defined earlier). This allows efficient training with multiple images at once.

19. This process is repeated for the *validation* and *test* datasets as well, as shown in the next code snippet:

```
train_dir_ = str(train_dir/'*/*')
val_dir_ = str(val_dir/'*/*')
test_dir_ = str(test_dir/'*/*')

train_dataset = tf.data.Dataset.list_files(train_dir_)
train_dataset = train_dataset.shuffle(SHUFFLE_BUFFER_SIZE)
train_dataset = train_dataset.map(load_image_train, \
                    num_parallel_calls=tf.data.experimental.
                    AUTOTUNE)
train_dataset = train_dataset.batch(BATCH_SIZE)

val_dataset = tf.data.Dataset.list_files(val_dir_)
val_dataset = val_dataset.shuffle(SHUFFLE_BUFFER_SIZE)
val_dataset = val_dataset.map(load_image_test)
val_dataset = val_dataset.batch(val_data_count)

test_dataset = tf.data.Dataset.list_files(test_dir_)
test_dataset = test_dataset.shuffle(SHUFFLE_BUFFER_SIZE)
test_dataset = test_dataset.map(load_image_test)
test_dataset = test_dataset.batch(test_data_count)
train_dataset, val_dataset, test_dataset
```

Now, we shall use the popular *XceptionNet* model (pretrained on *ImageNet*) and will apply *transfer learning* by training the parameters corresponding to the added layers on top of it. **XceptionNet** is a deep convolutional neural network based on *depth-wise separable convolutions*, which improves efficiency and performance over standard convolutions. As shown in *Figure 9.18* (by default the input image size is 299×299×3, although here we shall use different input shape), its structure consists of:

- **Entry flow**: Initial convolutional layers followed by *residual* connections and *separable* convolutions that down sample the input.

- **Middle flow**: A series of repeated *depth-wise separable* convolution blocks, each with *residual* connections, focusing on feature extraction.

- **Exit flow**: Final set of *separable* convolutions followed by *global average pooling* and fully connected layers for classification. This design allows for efficient learning with fewer parameters while maintaining high accuracy.

Refer to the following figure:

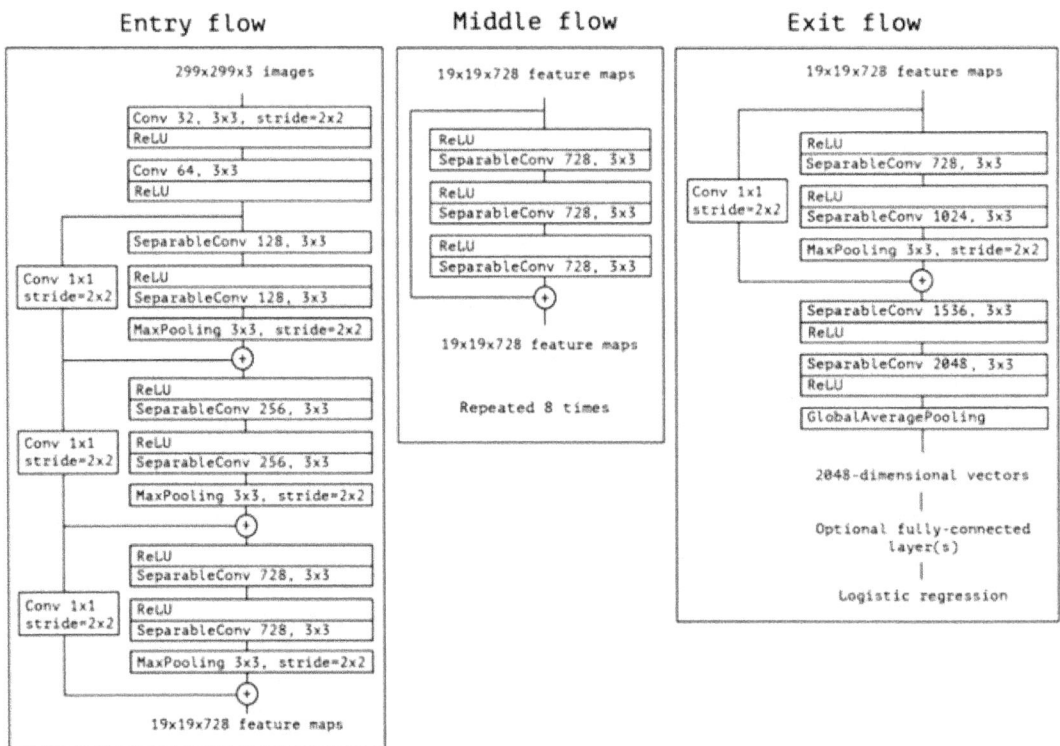

Figure 9.18: *XceptionNet architecture*
Source: *https://www.researchgate.net/figure/ception-architecture-35_fig4_350331747*

Now, let us deep dive into our python implementation, with the following detailed code-breakdown:

1. Let us build the **XceptionNet** model, using the next code snippet:

    a. The function **tf.keras.applications.Xception()** loads the pre-trained **XceptionNet** model, which has already been trained on the ImageNet dataset. The **include_top=False** argument means that the final classification layer (the **top**) is excluded, as we want to add our own custom layers for pneumonia classification.

    b. **input_shape=(IMG_HEIGHT, IMG_WIDTH, 3)**: Specifies the input shape of the images, which is (150,150,3) — 150×150 pixels with 3 color channels (RGB).

    c. **weights='imagenet'**: Uses weights pre-trained on the **ImageNet** dataset.

    d. **base_model.trainable = False**: Freezes the base model, meaning its pre-trained weights will not be updated during training. This allows the network to use pre-learned features from ImageNet while we train only the newly added layers.

2. Add custom layers on top the neural net:

    a. The function **models.Sequential()** creates a sequential model, meaning the layers are stacked one after the other in sequence.

    b. **base_model**: The pre-trained **XceptionNet** model is the first layer of this new model.

    c. **layers.GlobalAveragePooling2D()**: Reduces each feature map to a single number by averaging all the values in that map. This reduces the spatial dimensions and allows the network to focus on the most important global features.

    d. **layers.Dense(1, activation='sigmoid')**: Adds a fully connected layer with 1 output neuron (for **binary classification**). The *sigmoid* activation function is used to produce a probability between and , where values closer to indicate *normal* and values closer to indicate *pneumonia*.

Now, refer to the next code snippet:

```
inputs = tf.keras.Input(shape=IMG_SHAPE)
x = keras.applications.xception.Xception(
    input_tensor = inputs, # pass input to input_tensor
    include_top = False,
    weights = 'imagenet'
)
x.trainable = False
```

```
# flat the base model with x.output
x = tf.keras.layers.BatchNormalization()(x.output)
x = tf.keras.layers.Flatten()(x)
x = tf.keras.layers.Dense(2, activation='softmax')(x)
model = tf.keras.Model(inputs, x)
```

Next, let us train this model on the *training* dataset of chest X-rays, adjust for class-imbalance, and track the performance, using the next code snippet. Follow the next steps:

1. **Set the learning rate and optimizer**:

   a. `INITIAL_LEARNING_RATE = 1e-4`: Sets the learning rate to 0.0001. The learning rate controls how much to adjust the weights of the model with respect to the gradient.

   b. `optimizer = tf.keras.optimizers.Adam(learning_rate=INITIAL_LEARNING_RATE)`: Initializes the **Adam** optimizer, an adaptive optimization algorithm that adjusts the learning rate based on momentum and **Root Mean Square Propagation** (**RMSProp** is an adaptive optimization algorithm that adjusts the learning rate for each parameter by maintaining a moving average of squared gradients to improve convergence stability). It improves performance with minimal tuning.

2. **Define the loss function and evaluation metrics:**

   a. Use more generic *categorical cross-entropy* (using `loss = 'categorical_crossentropy'`) as the `loss` function, which is suitable for multi-class classification problems. You could use `'binary_crossentropy'` as well, since we have a binary classification problem (try on your own).

   b. Use accuracy (`metrics = ['accuracy']`) as a performance metric during *training* and *validation*.

3. **Compile the model**: Use `model.compile()` to compile the model with the specified `loss` function (`categorical_crossentropy`), optimizer (**Adam**), and evaluation metric (`accuracy`). After this step, the model will be ready for training.

4. **Calculate class weights**:

   a. Extract the class labels corresponding to the *maximum prediction probability* (with `np.argmax()`) from the **train_dataset** by iterating over it and finding the class with the highest probability.

   b. Computes class weights to handle *class-imbalance* using the method `class_weight.compute_class_weight()`. The `balanced` option adjusts the weights inversely proportional to class frequencies.

   c. Convert the computed class weights into a dictionary that maps each class to its weight.

5. **Train the model**:

   a. Set the initial number of epochs (**INITIAL_EPOCH**) to 10, meaning the model will train over 10 full passes of the dataset.

   b. Begin training the model with **model.fit()**, using the following arguments to the function:

      i. **train_dataset**: Training data used for fitting the model.

      ii. **class_weight = classweights**: The class weights to handle *class-imbalance*.

      iii. **shuffle = True**: Shuffles the training dataset each epoch for better generalization.

      iv. **validation_data = val_dataset**: Provides the validation dataset for performance evaluation.

      v. **epochs = INITIAL_EPOCH**: Number of epochs to train the model.

      vi. **verbose = 1**: Displays detailed progress during training.

6. **Plot learning curves**: Plot the *training* and *validation* **accuracy** and **loss** over the **epochs** based on the **history** object returned from **model.fit()** using **plot_learning_curves(history)**, as shown in the next code snippet:

```python
INITIAL_LEARNING_RATE = 1e-4
optimizer = tf.keras.optimizers.Adam(learning_rate=\
                                    INITIAL_LEARNING_RATE)
loss = 'categorical_crossentropy'
metrics = ['accuracy']
model.compile(
    loss=loss,
    optimizer=optimizer,
    metrics=metrics
)
y_labels = np.argmax(next(iter(train_dataset))[1].numpy(), axis=1)
classweights = class_weight.compute_class_weight(\
                        class_weight = "balanced", \
                        classes = np.unique(y_labels), \
                        y = y_labels)
classweights = dict(zip(np.unique(y_labels), classweights))

INITIAL_EPOCH = 10
history = model.fit(
        train_dataset,
        class_weight = classweights,
        shuffle = True,
        validation_data = val_dataset,
        epochs = INITIAL_EPOCH,
        verbose = 1
    )
plot_learning_curves(history)
```

If you run the preceding code to train the model, you should get the following plots showing how the *training* and *validation* **loss** decreases, and how the *training* and *validation* **accuracy** changes over the training epochs:

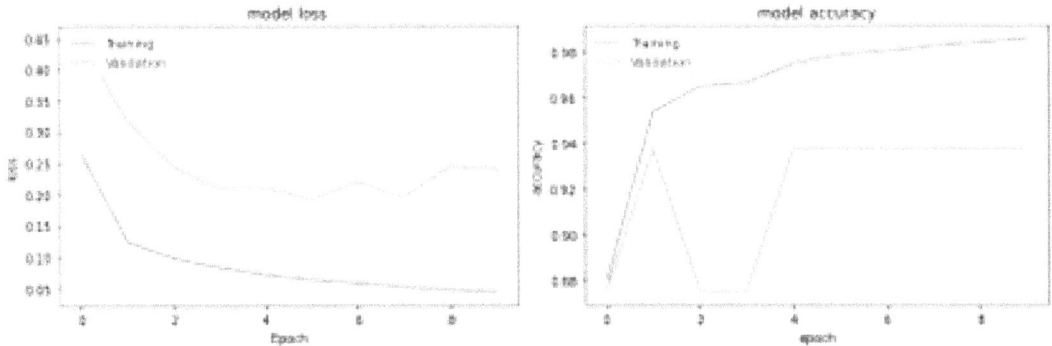

Figure 9.19: *Training/validation loss and accuracy with epochs*

The next code snippet evaluates the model's performance on the (held-out) *test* dataset, calculating the **loss** and **accuracy**, then prints these **metrics**. It helps assess how well the model generalizes to unseen data. Again, follow the next steps:

1. **Extract test data**: Retrieve the next batch of data from the test dataset (**test_dataset**), which contains images (**x_test**) and their corresponding labels (**y_test**), using **next(iter(test_dataset))**, a python *iterator* (use a python *generator* instead for lazy evaluation and efficient memory handling).

2. Evaluate the trained model on the *test* dataset using the function **model.evaluate()**, the function accepts the following arguments:

    i. **x_test.numpy()**, **y_test.numpy()**: The test images and labels are converted to NumPy arrays to be passed into the evaluate function.

    ii. **verbose=0**: Suppresses the output of the evaluation process (silent mode). If set to 1, it would show a progress-bar during evaluation. The function returns a **list (score)**, where:

        a. **score[0]** represents the **loss** on the *test* dataset (*categorical cross-entropy* in this case).

        b. **score[1]** represents the **accuracy** on the *test* dataset.

Now, refer to the next code snippet:

```
x_test, y_test = next(iter(test_dataset))
score = model.evaluate(x_test.numpy(), y_test.numpy(), verbose=0)
print('Model Loss: {}, Accuracy: {}'.format(score[0], score[1]))
```

If you run the preceding code snippet, you should get an output as follows:

```
- - - - - - - - - - - - - - - - - - - - - - - - - - - - - - - - - - - - - - - - - - - - - - - - - - - -

Derived Report
- - - - - - - - - - - - - - - - - - - - - - - - - - - - - - - - - - - - - - - - - - - - - - - - - - - - -
Precision     : 79.58%
Recall        : 97.95%
F1-Score      : 87.82%
- - - - - - - - - - - - - - - - - - - - - - - - - - - - - - - - - - - - - - - - - - - - - - - - - - - - -
Report for Model File:  ./data/output/models/2022-03-28_20-14-38/epoch_03-val_loss_0.21.hdf5
- - - - - - - - - - - - - - - - - - - - - - - - - - - - - - - - - - - - - - - - - - - - - - - - - - - - -

              precision   recall  f1-score  support

    NORMAL       0.94       0.58     0.72      234
    PNEUMONIA    0.80       0.98     0.88      390

    accuracy                         0.83      624
    macro avg    0.87       0.78     0.80      624
 weighted avg    0.85       0.83     0.82      624

- - - - - - - - - - - - - - - - - - - - - - - - - - - - - - - - - - - - - - - - - - - - - - - - - - - - -
```

Figure 9.20: Performance of the model on the (unseen) test images

The next code snippet makes *predictions* on the *test* data, extracts the *predicted* and *true* class labels, and generates a *confusion matrix* that compares the two. It saves the matrix as an image file at the specified location (**confusion_matrix_file**). The confusion matrix visually shows the performance of the model by illustrating the *true positives, false positives, true negatives,* and *false negatives* for each class. Follow the next steps:

1. **Make predictions on the test data**:

    a. Use the trained model to *predict* the class labels for the *test* dataset (**x_test**), with the function **model.predict()**.

    b. Convert the test data to a NumPy array (using the function **numpy()**) to be fed into the model.

    c. The output **y_pred** will be an array of probabilities for each class.

2. **Extract predicted class labels**: Extract the index of the highest probability using the function **np.argmax()**, along the given axis:

    a. **axis=1**: extract the index of the maximum value along the columns (**classes**) for each image,

    b. The result **y_pred_classes** is the *predicted* class label for each image in the *test* dataset.

3. **Extract true class labels y_true**:

```
from sklearn.metrics import confusion_matrix
y_pred = model.predict(x_test.numpy())
y_pred_classes = np.argmax(y_pred, axis = 1)
y_true = np.argmax(y_test.numpy(), axis = 1)
```

Now, use the function **sklearn.metrics.confusion_matrix(y_true, y_pred)** or the function **sklearn.metrics.ConfusionMatrixDisplay(model, x_test, y_test)** to display the confusion matrix as shown in the following figure:

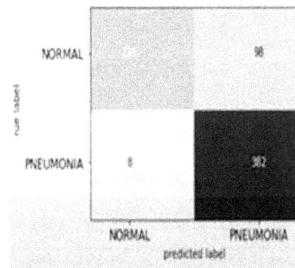

Figure 9.21: *Confusion matrix (on test dataset) for pneumonia classification*

Finally, let us implement a **Gradient-weighted Class Activation Mapping** (**Grad-CAM**) to gain intuitive visual insights into the decision-making process of a deep learning model, using the next code snippet. The purpose of Grad-CAM is to highlight the regions of an image that were most important for the model's decision. Let us break down the code step-by-step:

1. The function **get_img_array(img_path, size)** converts an image into a form that the model can process:

   a. **keras.preprocessing.image.load_img(img_path, target_size=size)**: Loads an image from the specified path (**img_path**) and resizes it to a specified target size (**size**). The result is a **PIL** image (**img**).

   b. **keras.preprocessing.image.img_to_array(img)**: Converts the **PIL** image into a NumPy array with pixel values.

   c. **np.expand_dims(array, axis=0)**: Adds an extra dimension to the image array so that it becomes a *batch* of size 1.

   d. Returns the processed image array.

2. The function **make_gradcam_heatmap(img_array, model, last_conv_layer_name, pred_index=None)** generates the **Grad-CAM** heatmap for a given image array:

   a. Create the gradient model using **tf.keras.models.Model()**, this model maps the input image **(model.inputs)** to the output of the *last convolutional layer* (obtained with **model.get_layer(last_conv_layer_name))** and the final prediction **(model.output)** of the model. This allows to calculate gradients with respect to the convolutional layer's output.

b. Use **tensorflow**'s automatic differentiation tool **tf.GradientTape()** to record operations for calculating the *gradient* of the model's *prediction* with respect to the activations of the last convolutional layer.

c. If **pred_index** is not provided, we choose the index of the top *predicted class* for the image, using **tf.argmax()**. The predicted class is the one with the highest score.

d. Compute the *gradient* of the top predicted class with respect to the last convolutional layer's output, using the function **tape.gradient()**.

e. Take the average of the gradients for each feature map, using **tf.reduce_mean()**. This gives a measure of how important each channel in the feature map is to the model's prediction.

f. Compute the weighted sum to compute the heatmap, by multiplying each channel of the last convolutional layer by its corresponding *pooled gradient* to create the *class activation heatmap*, followed by a successive normalization, to have the heatmap between and for better visualization.

3. The function **save_and_display_gradcam()** generates and saves the **Grad-CAM** heatmap superimposed on the original image:

a. Loads a *test* image from **x_test** using the index **id**, then expands its dimensions to create a *batch*.

b. Uses the model to *predict* the class probabilities for the image and prints both the *predicted* and *actual* classes.

c. Calls the **make_gradcam_heatmap()** function to create a heatmap based on the last convolutional layer (**last_conv_layer_name**).

d. Applies the **"jet" colormap**, which converts the heatmap to RGB colors for better visualization.

e. The heatmap is blended with the original image using an *alpha* transparency factor. The value **255 * img** converts the original image to the same range as the heatmap.

Now, refer to the next code snippet:

```
def get_img_array(img_path, size):
    img = keras.preprocessing.image.load_img(img_path, \
                                         target_size=size)
    return np.expand_dims(keras.preprocessing.image.img_to_array(img),\
                                         axis=0)
```

```python
def make_gradcam_heatmap(img_array, model, last_conv_layer_name, \
                                          pred_index=None):
    grad_model = tf.keras.models.Model([model.inputs], \
            [model.get_layer(last_conv_layer_name).output, model.output])
    with tf.GradientTape() as tape:
        last_conv_layer_output, preds = grad_model(img_array)
        if pred_index is None:
            pred_index = tf.argmax(preds[0])
        class_channel = preds[:, pred_index]
    grads = tape.gradient(class_channel, last_conv_layer_output)
    pooled_grads = tf.reduce_mean(grads, axis=(0, 1, 2))
    last_conv_layer_output = last_conv_layer_output[0]
    heatmap = last_conv_layer_output @ pooled_grads[..., tf.newaxis]
    heatmap = tf.squeeze(heatmap)
    heatmap = tf.maximum(heatmap, 0) / tf.math.reduce_max(heatmap)
    return heatmap.numpy()


def save_and_display_gradcam(id, alpha=0.4):
    img = x_test[id].numpy()
    img_array = np.expand_dims(img, axis=0)
    preds = model.predict(img_array)
    last_conv_layer_name = "conv_7b_ac"
    heatmap = make_gradcam_heatmap(img_array, model, \
                                      last_conv_layer_name)
    heatmap = np.uint8(255 * heatmap)
    jet = cm.get_cmap("jet")
    jet_colors = jet(np.arange(256))[:, :3]
    jet_heatmap = jet_colors[heatmap]
    jet_heatmap = keras.preprocessing.image.array_to_img(jet_heatmap)
    jet_heatmap = jet_heatmap.resize((IMG_WIDTH, IMG_HEIGHT))
    jet_heatmap = keras.preprocessing.image.img_to_array(jet_heatmap)
    superimposed_img = jet_heatmap * alpha + 255 * img
    superimposed_img = keras.preprocessing.image.array_to_img(\
                                          superimposed_img)
    superimposed_img.save(cam_path)
    display(Image(cam_path))

save_and_display_gradcam(10)
```

If you run the preceding code snippet, you should get a figure as follows:

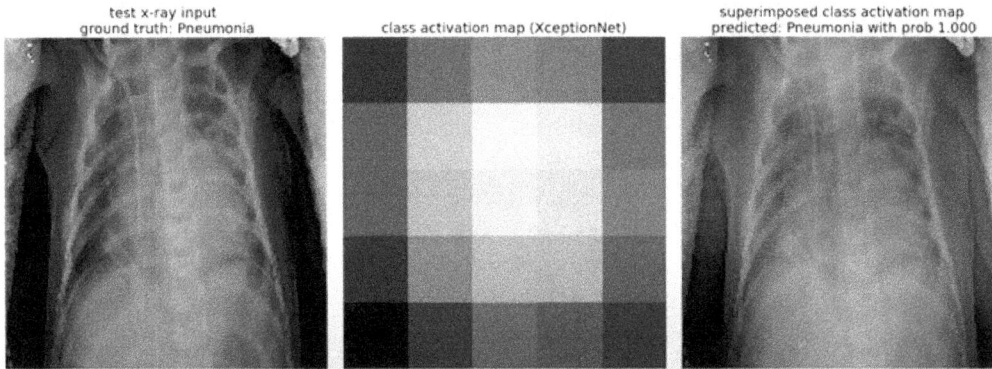

Figure 9.22: *Superimposing class activation map with on a pneumonia positive x-ray image with Grad-CAM*

The following figure shows a few chest X-ray test images with *ground-truth* (*true*) vs. *predicted* labels. The code to produce the following visualization is left as an exercise; it should be pretty straightforward.

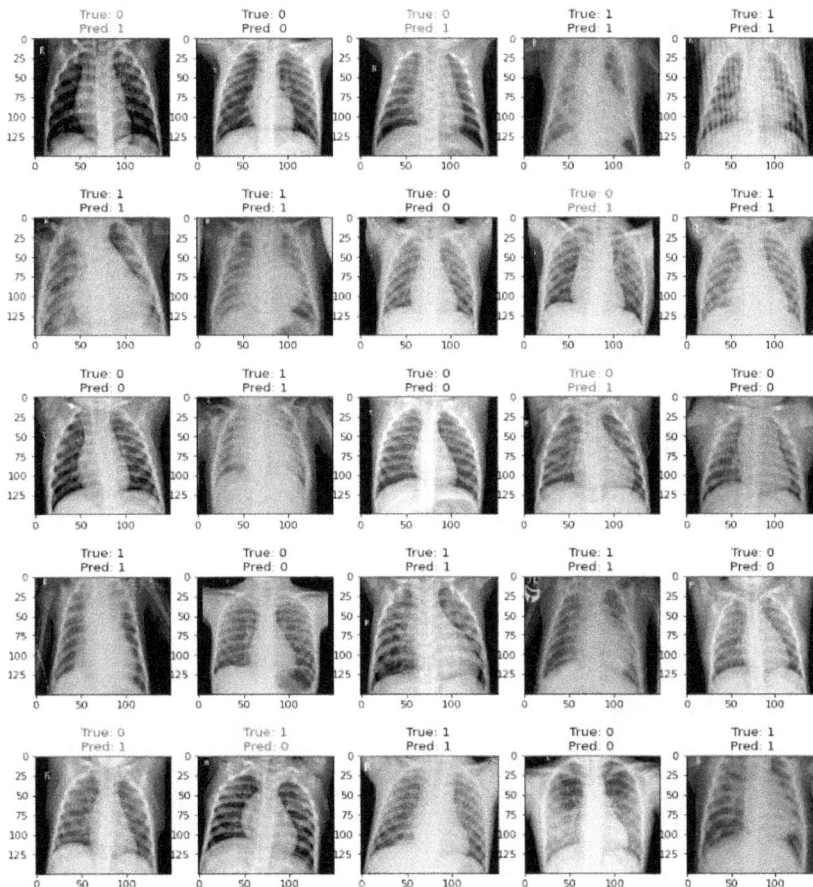

Figure 9.23: *Sample test chest X-ray images with GT/prediction for pneumonia*

Conclusion

This chapter explores the diverse applications of image processing and computer vision in medical imaging, focusing on key challenges and solutions. It addresses the processing of various image formats such as DICOM and NIfTI, 3D visualization of MRI scans using tools like `matplotlib, visvis` and `vedo`, and the application of filters and morphological operations with libraries like `medpy` and `itk`. Advanced techniques, including CT reconstruction via the inverse Radon transform, segmentation of brain MRI images with graph cut, and deep learning models like **XceptionNet** for disease detection, are explored, highlighting the impact of these technologies on improving diagnostic accuracy.

Questions

1. Convert medical images in **DICOM** format to **NIfTI** format (Hint: use the library dicom2nifti).

2. Use the visualization toolkit (the python library vtk) to load and render a full-head MRI scan stored in the metaImage (.mhd) format. You can follow the steps:

    i. Load the 3D .mhd file representing a full-head MRI scan using vtkMetaImageReader.

    ii. Render the volume using either volume rendering (vtkGPUVolumeRayCastMapper) or slicing (vtkImageReslice or vtkImageViewer2).

    iii. Display the 3D image in an interactive window with appropriate orientation and grayscale mapping.

    Hints:

    • Use vtkRenderWindowInteractor for interactivity.

    • Apply a vtkPiecewiseFunction and vtkColorTransferFunction to control opacity and grayscale lookup.

If you visualize FullHead.mhd, it should be rendered as follows:

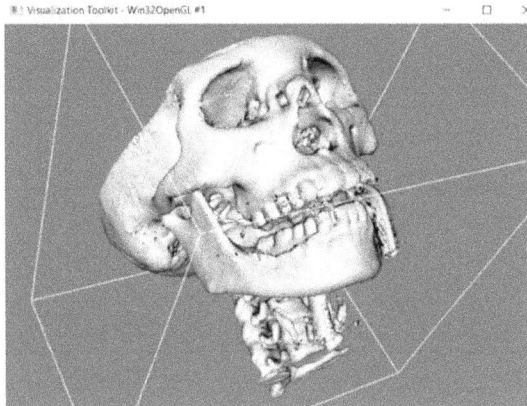

Figure 9.24: *Rendering of head image*

References

1. https://www.researchgate.net/publication/28359596_Interactive_Liver_Tumor_Segmentation_Using_Graph-cuts_and_Watershed

2. https://github.com/mateuszbuda/brain-segmentation-pytorch/tree/master

3. https://arxiv.org/pdf/1610.02391

4. https://github.com/MIC-DKFZ/nnUNet/blob/master/documentation/inference_example_Prostate.md

5. https://www.nature.com/articles/s41592-020-01008-z

6. https://link.springer.com/chapter/10.1007/978-3-319-24574-4_28

7. http://medicaldecathlon.com/

8. https://ieeexplore.ieee.org/document/8099678

9. https://www.youtube.com/watch?v=_eYIh7fxucM

10. https://www.youtube.com/watch?v=EzTsOSJRGwE

11. https://www.youtube.com/watch?v=hcqnEkfs6u8

12. https://www.youtube.com/watch?v=eCaXIPKz7yc

13. https://www.youtube.com/watch?v=bU-KxXNUQ80

14. https://github.com/divamgupta/image-segmentation-keras

15. https://www.youtube.com/watch?v=pFKARAl-wzA

16. https://www.youtube.com/watch?v=eW6LWmkigrc

Join our Discord space

Join our Discord workspace for latest updates, offers, tech happenings around the world, new releases, and sessions with the authors:

https://discord.bpbonline.com

CHAPTER 10

Application of Image Processing and Computer Vision in Medical Imaging and Remote Sensing

Introduction

In this chapter, we explore advanced applications of computer vision techniques in two critical domains: **medical imaging** and **remote sensing**. We continue to explore computer vision models for medical imaging, by addressing challenges such as disease detection and anatomical structure segmentation using state-of-the-art deep learning models. These solutions demonstrate how computer vision can aid in diagnostics and treatment planning. In the realm of computer vision and image processing in remote sensing, we first focus on the segmentation of **FloodNet** images using **VGG-UNet**, the monitoring and management of flood-prone areas. We also examine the landcover classification problem with **Fastai**'s **ResNet101** applied to the **EuroSAT** dataset, showcasing how satellite imagery can be leveraged to understand and manage natural resources and environmental changes.

Through these examples, this chapter provides a well-rounded view of how modern image processing and machine learning techniques contribute to solving real-world problems across healthcare and environmental monitoring. It highlights the pivotal role of computer vision in extracting actionable insights from complex image datasets, thereby enhancing decision-making and planning.

Structure

This chapter covers the following topics:

- Medical image processing
- Computer vision and image processing in remote sensing

Objectives

By the end of this chapter, you will be able to apply deep learning and computer vision techniques to solve real-world problems in medical imaging and remote sensing. You will understand how models like U-Net, nnUNet, CovidNet, and ResNet101 are used for tasks such as disease detection, organ and tumor segmentation, environmental monitoring, and landcover classification. Through hands-on examples with libraries such as TensorFlow, **pytorch**, **fastai**, and **keras_segmentation**, you will gain practical skills in building and evaluating image analysis pipelines that contribute to healthcare diagnostics and natural resource management.

Medical image processing

This chapter builds upon *Chapter 9, Application of Image Processing and Computer Vision in Medical Imaging*, by further exploring advanced techniques in medical image analysis through the lens of image processing and computer vision. It delves into state-of-the-art semantic segmentation methods, including **nnUNet** for prostate image segmentation and **UNet** for detecting brain tumors, highlighting how these models effectively extract clinically relevant structures from complex medical scans. Furthermore, the chapter examines deep learning applications such as **Covid-Net** for identifying **COVID-19** in chest radiographs, showcasing the transformative role of artificial intelligence in modern diagnostic imaging.

COVID-19 detection from radiographs with Covid-Net with tensorflow

The global COVID-19 pandemic has highlighted the importance of rapid and accurate virus detection, especially in medical imaging. Among the diagnostic tools available, radiographs such as **chest X-rays** (**CXR**) and **CT scans** have played a pivotal role in identifying COVID-19-related lung abnormalities. Leveraging deep learning models such as **COVID-Net**, a convolutional neural network (**CNN**) designed specifically for detecting COVID-19 from medical imaging, has provided a powerful solution for automating this process.

In this section, we will explore how to use a pretrained COVID-Net model for detecting COVID-19 from chest CT scans. The following code example demonstrates the complete workflow: loading the model, preprocessing the input images, running inference, and visualizing the results using Grad-CAM. This serves as a practical introduction to applying deep learning for medical image classification and interpreting model outputs to gain insights into decision-making processes. The key steps involved are outlined as follows:

1. **Importing the required libraries**: Let us start by importing the required libraries, as usual. Note that we shall use **tensorflow** version **1.15** here. We shall use Google Colab for the implementation, and use the GPU runtime for faster execution create a new notebook. Copy-paste and run the following code on Colab:

```
# run in google colab
import os
import cv2
import numpy as np
#!pip install tensorflow==1.15
import tensorflow as tf
import matplotlib.pyplot as plt
#!pip install gdown
```

2. **Downloading the dataset**: The dataset used in this example is from **Kaggle**'s **COVIDx-CT** dataset. This dataset includes CT scans images labeled as **Normal**, **(Non-COVID-19) Pneumonia**, or **COVID-19**, making it a suitable choice for training and testing a model designed to detect COVID-19 from CT images. The dataset can be downloaded using the **Kaggle CLI**, by running the following commands in the console:

```
! pip install kaggle
! mkdir ~/.kaggle
! cp kaggle.json ~/.kaggle/
! chmod 600 ~/.kaggle/kaggle.json
! kaggle datasets download hgunraj/covidxct
!unzip covidxct -d covidxct
%cd kaggle/input/covidxct/
! unzip val_COVIDx_CT-2A.txt.zip
% cd ../
```

The dataset consists of CT scan images and corresponding labels that indicate the class of the image. This labeling is essential for supervised learning tasks, where the model learns to classify images based on the ground-truth provided.

3. **Downloading the pretrained model**: To save time and computational resources, we use a pretrained model called **COVID-Net CT-2 S**. The model files are hosted on Google Drive and can be downloaded using their respective IDs.

```
# Model name
MODEL_NAME = 'COVID-Net CT-2 S'
# Model location
MODEL_DIR = 'kaggle'
META_NAME = 'model.meta'
```

```
CKPT_NAME = 'model'
# Model IDs in Google Drive
MODEL_IDS = {
    'COVID-Net CT-2 L': (
        '1YQxVRYJ37nPSCtjUU9WWlXWRWYvZkKPl',
        '1EgelTN_fyku2m2fALqpJvfjkuQ7Wqqdg',
        '12BhWk_KiQ-hX--Qb7ASdPQTUOfOPccQE'),
    'COVID-Net CT-2 S': (
        '1zKTSxAhRrFhJxUnCcAf73WEZ7OcqvMre',
        '1CSYekjpU1qYXxuOkjL0fBuzBIkvFXAqw',
        '12uiQc5QePuqg2ErRF8llrL1vD9aFIiiJ')
}
!gdown --id {MODEL_IDS[MODEL_NAME][0]}
!gdown --id {MODEL_IDS[MODEL_NAME][1]}
!gdown --id {MODEL_IDS[MODEL_NAME][2]}
```

These files contain the *architecture, checkpoint (weights),* and *metadata* necessary for running the model on new images.

The pretrained model we will use here is **COVID-Net CT-2 S**, which is a deep learning model designed for COVID-19 detection and severity assessment from chest CT scans. Here is what it does:

1. **COVID-19 detection**: It classifies whether a given CT scan slice shows signs of COVID-19 infection.

2. **Severity assessment**: In addition to binary detection (COVID-positive or negative), the model is trained to estimate the *severity* of infection (e.g., *mild, moderate,* or *severe*), making it useful for clinical triage and monitoring disease progression.

3. **Model variant -S**: The "S" in **CT-2 S** refers to the *small* variant of the model, which has a more compact architecture. It is optimized for faster inference and lower computational cost, making it suitable for deployment in resource-constrained environments. **COVID-Net CT-2 S** is part of the broader **COVID-Net** initiative and was trained on the **COVIDx-CT** dataset, which contains CT scan images labeled with expert annotations for presence and severity of COVID-19. The key components of **COVID-Net CT-2** are:

   a. Convolutional layers that automatically extract features from CT scan images.

   b. Residual connections inspired by the **ResNet** architecture, which allow for training deeper networks without encountering the *vanishing gradient* problem. Final dense layers that classify the input image into one of the three categories: *Normal, (Non-COVID-19) Pneumonia,* or *COVID-19.*

   c. COVID-Net models are tailored to handle medical imaging, where specific structures in the image are crucial for accurate classification.

4. **Loading the model**: To load the model, **tensorflow**'s low-level API is used. The model is saved as a *MetaGraph* (**.meta**) file that defines the *computation graph*, and a *checkpoint* (**.ckpt**) file that contains the trained *weights*. The function load_graph() defined in the next code snippet creates a new **tensorflow** *graph* and *session*, and loads a saved model's meta graph from the specified **.meta** file using **import_ meta_graph()**. It returns the *graph*, *session*, and *saver* object for further use.

The **create_session()** function defined in the following code snippet sets up and configures a **tensorflow** *session* to execute the computation graph. Here is how the code works in details:

a. **tf.ConfigProto()**: This line creates a configuration object (**config**) that allows customization of various settings for the TensorFlow session. These settings help control how **tensorFlow** interacts with system resources like CPUs, GPUs, memory, etc.

b. **config.gpu_options.allow_growth = True**: By default, **tensorFlow** allocates all available GPU memory when it starts a session. This can sometimes lead to memory waste, if not all of it is needed. The **allow_growth = True** setting allows TensorFlow to allocate GPU memory dynamically, meaning it will only allocate as much memory as the model requires and gradually grow as more is needed. This ensures better GPU memory management.

c. **tf.Session(config=config)**: This line creates a **tensorflow** session (**sess**) with the configuration defined earlier. A session in **tensorflow** is used to run operations or computations defined in the computational graph (for example, loading data, making predictions, and so on). The session is what actually executes the computations in the graph on the available hardware (CPU or GPU).

Note: In TensorFlow 1.x, sessions are essential for running operations within the computational graph—such as loading data, making predictions, and executing other computations on available hardware (CPU or GPU). However, beginning with TensorFlow 2.x, eager execution is enabled by default. This means computations are executed immediately as they are called in Python, eliminating the need for explicitly managing sessions in most use cases.

Important: If you are running this code, ensure you are using TensorFlow 1.x, as it depends on manual session handling, which is not compatible with TensorFlow 2.x without modification.

The session object (**sess**) is returned, allowing other parts of the code to interact with and use this session for running **tensorflow** operations (such as *inference* or model *training*), as shown in the next code snippet:

```python
def load_graph(meta_file):
    graph = tf.Graph()
    with graph.as_default():
        # Create session and load model
        sess = create_session()
        # Load meta file
        print('Loading meta graph from ' + meta_file)
        saver = tf.train.import_meta_graph(meta_file, \
                                        clear_devices=True)
    return graph, sess, saver

def create_session():
    config = tf.ConfigProto()
    config.gpu_options.allow_growth = True
    sess = tf.Session(config=config)
    return sess
```

d. Once the graph is restored from the meta file, the pretrained weights are loaded using the checkpoint **ckpt** using the function **load_ckpt()**:

```python
def load_ckpt(ckpt, sess, saver):
    # Load weights
    if ckpt is not None:
        print('Loading weights from ' + ckpt)
        saver.restore(sess, ckpt)
```

e. The following code snippet defines the locations of *data* and key *tensor variables* for running *inference* on the *pretrained* COVID-19 detection model:

```python
# Data location
IMAGE_DIR = 'kaggle/input/covidxct/2A_images'
LABEL_FILE = 'kaggle/input/covidxct/val_COVIDx_CT-2A.txt'
# Tensor names
IMAGE_INPUT_TENSOR = 'Placeholder:0'
TRAINING_PH_TENSOR = 'is_training:0'
FINAL_CONV_TENSOR = 'resnet_model/block_layer4:0'
CLASS_PRED_TENSOR = 'ArgMax:0'
CLASS_PROB_TENSOR = 'softmax_tensor:0'
LOGITS_TENSOR = 'resnet_model/final_dense:0'
# Class names, in order of index
CLASS_NAMES = ('Normal', 'Pneumonia', 'COVID-19')
```

f. The next code snippet creates the full paths for the model's meta and checkpoint files, loads the TensorFlow graph and session (**sess**) from the meta file (**meta_file**), and restores the model's weights from the checkpoint (**ckpt**):

```
# Create full paths
meta_file = os.path.join(MODEL_DIR, META_NAME)
ckpt = os.path.join(MODEL_DIR, CKPT_NAME)
# Load metagraph and create session
graph, sess, saver = load_graph(meta_file)
# Load checkpoint
with graph.as_default():
    load_ckpt(ckpt, sess, saver)
```

This process restores the complete model, which is now ready for inference.

5. **Preprocessing CT images**: Before feeding images to the model, they need to be preprocessed. The CT scan images are grayscale, and they are resized to the input dimensions expected by the model (for example, 512×512 pixels). Bounding boxes are applied to focus the model on specific regions of interest.

```
def load_and_preprocess(image_file, bbox=None, width=512, \
                                                 height=512):
    # Load and crop image
    image = cv2.imread(image_file, cv2.IMREAD_GRAYSCALE)
    if bbox is not None:
        image = image[bbox[1]:bbox[3], bbox[0]:bbox[2]]
    image = cv2.resize(image, (width, height), cv2.INTER_CUBIC)
    # Convert to float in range [0, 1] and stack to 3-channel
    image = image.astype(np.float32) / 255.0
    image = np.expand_dims(np.stack((image, image, image), \
                                        axis=-1), axis=0)
    return image
```

6. The **load_labels()** function is responsible for loading image file names, their associated class labels, and bounding boxes from a label file. This information is then used for model inference and visualization in subsequent parts of the code. Here is a breakdown of how the function works:

a. The function takes an argument, **label_file**, which is the path to a text file that contains image labels, classes, and bounding boxes for the images.

b. It returns three lists:

    i. **fnames**: List of image file names.

    ii. **classes**: List of corresponding class labels for each image.

    iii. **bboxes**: List of bounding boxes for each image.

```
def load_labels(label_file):
    fnames, classes, bboxes = [], [], []
    with open(label_file, 'r') as f:
        for line in f.readlines():
            fname, cls, xmin, ymin, xmax, ymax = \
                                line.strip('\n').split()
            fnames.append(fname)
            classes.append(int(cls))
            bboxes.append((int(xmin), int(ymin), \
                                int(xmax), int(ymax)))
    return fnames, classes, bboxes
```

7. Use the next lines of code to select the first image from the dataset, retrieve the corresponding class label (**cls**) and bounding box (**bbox**) and preprocess the image. Then load image filenames, classes, and bounding boxes from the label file (**LABEL_FILE**).

```
idx = 0
image_file = os.path.join(IMAGE_DIR, filenames[idx])
cls, bbox = classes[idx], bboxes[idx]
image = load_and_preprocess(image_file, bbox)
filenames, classes, bboxes = load_labels(LABEL_FILE)
```

8. **Running inference**: Once the model is loaded and the images are preprocessed, we can run *inference* and visualize the results using *Grad-CAM*, which highlights the areas in the image that the model considered *important* for its *classification*.

    The **run_inference()** function is responsible for performing inference on one or more images using a pre-trained model loaded in a **tensorflow** session. It processes the images in batches, runs them through the model, and returns the *predicted* class *labels* along with their corresponding *confidence scores*, as shown in the next code snippet:

```
def run_inference(graph, sess, images, batch_size=1):
    # Create feed dict
    feed_dict = {TRAINING_PH_TENSOR: False}
    # Run inference
    with graph.as_default():
        classes, confidences = [], []
        num_batches = int(np.ceil(images.shape[0]/batch_size))
        for i in range(num_batches):
            # Get batch and add it to the feed dict
            feed_dict[IMAGE_INPUT_TENSOR] = \
                    images[i*batch_size:(i + 1)*batch_size, ...]
            # Run images through model
            preds, probs = sess.run([CLASS_PRED_TENSOR, \
                        CLASS_PROB_TENSOR], feed_dict=feed_dict)
```

```
                      # Add results to list
                      classes.append(preds)
                      confidences.append(probs)
              classes = np.concatenate(classes, axis=0)
              confidences = np.concatenate(confidences, axis=0)
              return classes, confidences
```

9. **Grad-CAM overview**: Grad-CAM is a technique that helps visualize the regions of the image that are most influential in the model's decision-making process. This is particularly useful in medical imaging, as it can reveal whether the model is focusing on clinically relevant areas (e.g., regions affected by COVID-19) and provides insights into why the model classifies an image as *positive* for COVID-19. The **make_gradcam_graph()** function defined in the next code snippet augments the existing TensorFlow graph by adding operations to compute the gradient of the predicted class score with respect to the feature maps of the final convolutional layer:

```
def make_gradcam_graph(graph):
    with graph.as_default():
        # Get required tensors
        final_conv = graph.get_tensor_by_name(FINAL_CONV_TENSOR)
        logits = graph.get_tensor_by_name(LOGITS_TENSOR)
        preds = graph.get_tensor_by_name(CLASS_PRED_TENSOR)
        # Get gradient
        top_class_logits = logits[0, preds[0]]
        grads = tf.gradients(top_class_logits, final_conv)[0]
        # Comute per-channel average gradient
        pooled_grads = tf.reduce_mean(grads, axis=(0, 1, 2))
    return final_conv, pooled_grads
```

10. **Generating Grad-CAM heatmap**: Let us compute the Grad-CAM heatmap using the gradients and convolutional layer activations. The heatmap highlights regions in the image that are most influential in the model's decision-making process.

The function **run_gracam()** defined in the following code block generates the Grad-CAM heatmap — for the given input image — using the activations from the final convolutional layer (**final_conv**), used to determine which parts of the image the model focused on — the gradient values (**pooled_grads**, computed with respect to the predicted class), to be used to weigh the importance of each channel in the final convolutional layer — on top of the **tensorflow** session (**sess**) that runs the model and its computations:

```
def run_gradcam(final_conv, pooled_grads, sess, image):
    with graph.as_default():
        final_conv_out, pooled_grads_out, \
        class_pred, class_prob = sess.run(
```

```
            [final_conv, pooled_grads, CLASS_PRED_TENSOR, \
                                      CLASS_PROB_TENSOR],
            feed_dict={IMAGE_INPUT_TENSOR: image, \
                       TRAINING_PH_TENSOR: False})
    final_conv_out = final_conv_out[0]
    class_pred = class_pred[0]
    class_prob = class_prob[0, class_pred]
    # Compute heatmap as gradient-weighted mean of activations
    for i in range(pooled_grads_out.shape[0]):
        final_conv_out[..., i] *= pooled_grads_out[i]
    heatmap = np.mean(final_conv_out, axis=-1)
    # Convert to [0, 1] range
    heatmap = np.maximum(heatmap, 0)/np.max(heatmap)
    # Resize to image dimensions
    heatmap = cv2.resize(heatmap, (image.shape[2], \
                                   image.shape[1]))
    return heatmap, class_pred, class_prob
```

11. The following code snippet first sets up the required elements for **Grad-CAM**, extracting the final convolutional layer and computing gradients and then runs Grad-CAM on the input image, generating a **heatmap** that shows the important regions for the classification, along with the *predicted class* (**class_pred**) and its *confidence score* (**class_prob**):

```
final_conv, pooled_grads = make_gradcam_graph(graph)
heatmap, class_pred, class_prob = run_gradcam(final_conv, \
                                    pooled_grads, sess, image)
```

12. **Visualizing predictions**: After obtaining the **heatmap**, we can overlay it on the original CT scan image, as done in the following code snippet:

```
# Show image
fig, ax = plt.subplots(1, 2, figsize=(9, 5))
plt.subplots_adjust(0,0,1,0.9,0.05,0.05)
plt.subplots_adjust(hspace=0.01)
ax[0].imshow(image[0]), ax[0].axis('off')
ax[0].set_title('input CT image', size=10)
ax[1].imshow(image[0]), ax[1].axis('off')
ax[1].set_title('Covid-Net CT classification', size=10)
ax[1].imshow(heatmap, cmap='jet', alpha=0.4)
plt.suptitle('Predicted Class: {} ({:.3f} confidence), True Class:'
             '{}'..format(CLASS_NAMES[class_pred], \
             class_prob, CLASS_NAMES[cls]), size=12)
```

```
print('**DISCLAIMER**')
print('Do not use this prediction for self-diagnosis. '
    'You should check with your local authorities for '
    'the latest advice on seeking medical assistance.')
plt.show()
```

If you run the preceding code snippet, you should obtain a figure like the following one. This will allow medical professionals to interpret the model's decision and verify if the highlighted regions correspond to actual COVID-19 abnormalities.

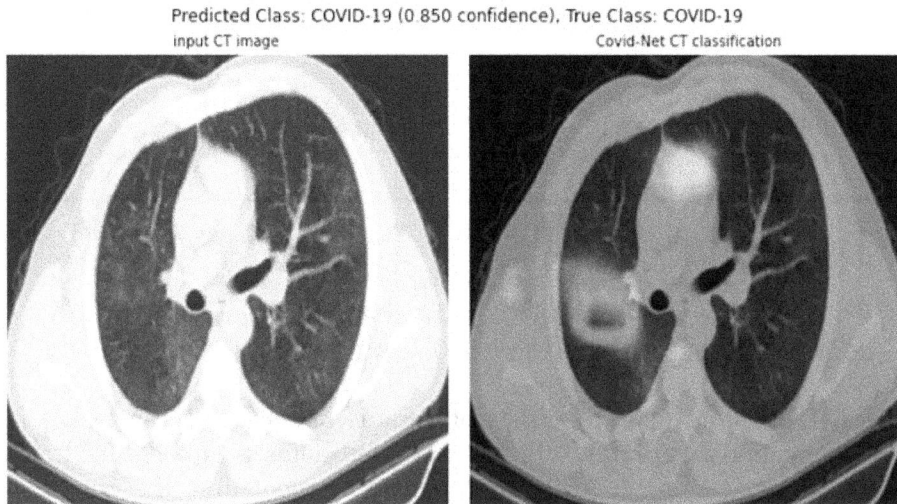

Figure 10.1: CT image classification with Covid-Net and overlaying class activation

Prostate image segmentation with nnUNet with Medical Decathlon dataset

Prostate cancer is one of the most common malignancies affecting men worldwide. Accurate segmentation of the prostate gland in medical images is crucial for effective diagnosis, treatment planning, and monitoring. Deep learning models, particularly CNNs, have demonstrated significant success in medical image segmentation tasks. This section explores the application of **nnUNet**, a robust and flexible framework for biomedical image segmentation, to the task of prostate image segmentation using the **Medical Decathlon** dataset.

The **nnUNet** framework (as shown in *Figure 10.2*) leverages **U-Net** architecture, which consists of an *encoder-decoder* structure. The encoder captures *context* through down-sampling, while the decoder enables precise *localization* via up-sampling. Refer to the following figure:

nn-UNet architecture

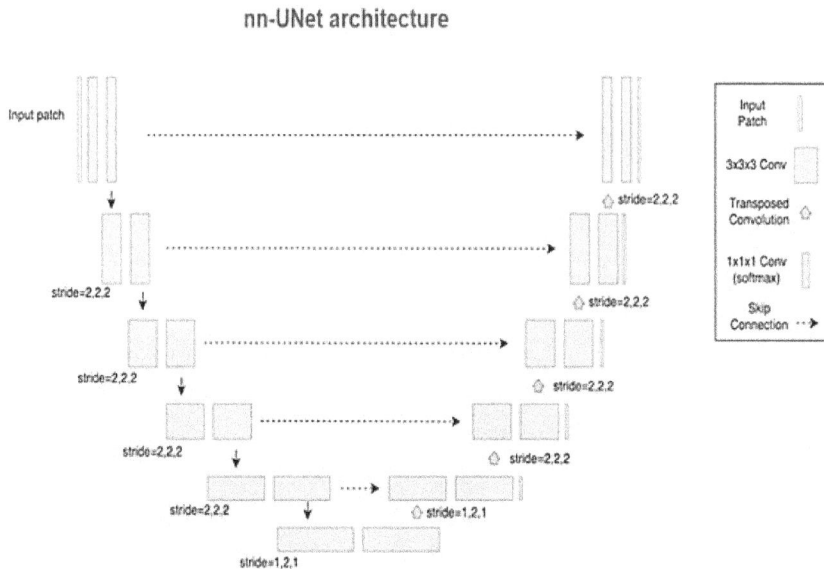

Figure 10.2: *nnU-Net architecture*
Source: *https://www.researchgate.net/figure/figure-supplement-1-*
Diagram-of-the-nnU-net-architecture-used-for-HiippUnfold-This-119_fig2_366312394

The **Medical Decathlon** dataset consists of various medical imaging tasks, including prostate segmentation. It provides diverse annotated datasets suitable for training and validating machine learning models. For prostate segmentation, the dataset includes *multi-modal MRI scans* that capture detailed information about the prostate anatomy.

Let us now explore how to use a pretrained **nnUNet** model for prostate image segmentation, using the library **nnunet**. Use Google Colab to run this example (create a new notebook and copy paste the code). Follow the given steps:

1. Start by importing essential libraries. Here the library **nibabel** is used for loading and saving **NIfTI** images, **glob** helps to retrieve file paths, **matplotlib** is used for visualization, and **skimage.color** assists in converting label images to RGB format. Install the library **nnunet** with **pip**, if not already installed.

```
# run in colab
#! pip install nnunet
import nibabel as nib
from glob import glob
from skimage import color
import matplotlib.pylab as plt
```

2. Copy the prostate dataset (**Task05_Prostate.tar**) from the **Medical Decathlon** dataset (as shown in *Figure 10.3*), shared by the following (*Google Drive*) *link*: **https:// drive.google.com/drive/folders/1HqEgzS8BV2c7xYNrZdEAnrHk7osJJ–2**, to your google drive and rename to **Task05_Prostate.tar**:

Figure 10.3: Copying the prostrate (Medical Decathlon) dataset from Google Drive

3. **Mount** the Google Drive to the Google Colab environment, enabling access the prostate dataset from Colab, by running the following code snippet:

```
from google.colab import drive
drive.mount('/content/drive/')
```

4. Extract the contents of the prostate segmentation dataset from the **.tar** file stored on Google Drive:

```
!tar xvf drive/MyDrive/Task05_Prostate.tar
```

5. **nnUNet commands**: Run the following commands on shell, one by one, as explained:

    a. **nnUNet_convert_decathlon_task**: Converts the prostate dataset into the **nnUNet** format.

    b. **nnUNet_download_pretrained_model**: Downloads a pretrained model specifically *fine-tuned* for *prostate segmentation*.

    c. **nnUNet_print_pretrained_model_info**: Prints details about the downloaded pretrained model.

    d. **nnUNet_predict**: Runs *inference* on the *test* images using the specified model and outputs the segmented images to the designated directory (**output_dir**, specified by **-o** switch).

```
!nnUNet_convert_decathlon_task -i Task05_Prostate
!nnUNet _download_pretrained_model Task005_Prostate
!nnUNet _print_pretrained_model_info Task005_Prostate
!nnUNet _predict -i $nnUNet_raw_data_base/nnUNet_raw_data/Task005_
Prostate/imagesTs/ -o output_dir -t 5 -m 3d_fullres
```

6. Use the **glob** function to collect the paths of the original *input test* images and the *segmented* output images from their respective directories (**Task05_Prostate/ imagesTs/** and **output_dir**, respectively).

7. Load a *test* image and its corresponding *segmented* output using the function **nibabel.load()**.

8. Create a figure to display the images. The original prostate MRI slices are shown using a **bone colormap**, which enhances the contrast of bone structures.

9. Visualize the segmented output image using the **label2rgb()** function from **skimage.color** module. This function assigns different colors (for example, red, blue and green) to differently labeled regions, for clear visualization against the background of the original image. The **alpha** parameter controls the transparency of the overlay, as shown in the next code snippet:

```python
nifiles = glob('Task05_Prostate/imagesTs/*.nii.gz')
nifiles_seg = glob('output_dir/*.nii.gz')
i, j = 1, 10
nifti = nib.load(nifiles[i]).get_fdata()
nifti_seg = nib.load(nifiles_seg[i]).get_fdata()
plt.figure(figsize=(20,7))
plt.subplots_adjust(0,0,1,0.95,0.05,0.05)
plt.subplot(131), plt.imshow(nifti[...,j,0], cmap='bone')
plt.axis('off')
plt.title('Prostate input 0', size=20)
plt.subplot(132), plt.imshow(nifti[...,j,1], cmap='bone')
plt.axis('off')
plt.title('Prostate input 1', size=20)
plt.subplot(133)
plt.imshow(color.label2rgb(nifti_seg[...,j], \
                           nifti[...,j,0] / nifti[...,j,0].max(), \
                           colors=[(255,0,0),(0,0,255),(0,255,0)], \
                           alpha=0.01, bg_label=0, bg_color=None))
plt.axis('off'), plt.title('Segmented output with UNet', size=20)
plt.show()
```

If you run the preceding code snippet, you should obtain a figure as follows, with the input image channels (0 and 1) shown on the left, along with the overlayed output color-coded segmentation labels on the right, displayed side-by-side:

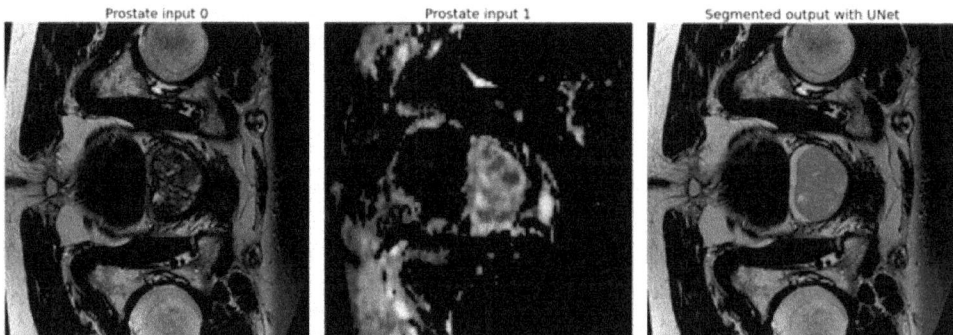

Figure 10.4: Semantic segmentation with U-Net

Binary semantic segmentation of brain tumors using U-Net with pytorch

Binary semantic segmentation in medical imaging, particularly in brain images, plays a crucial role in diagnosing and understanding various neurological conditions, such as tumors, lesions, and other abnormalities. This process involves classifying each pixel in an image as belonging to one of two classes: the *region of interest* (for example, a *tumor*) or the *background*. This chapter explores the methodologies, challenges, and applications of binary semantic segmentation in brain imaging, providing insights into the latest advancements and hands-on Python code examples.

U-Net: a convolution neural network

As seen previously, CNNs are the backbone of most image processing tasks. In binary semantic segmentation, CNNs can be adapted to classify each pixel in an image. **U-Net**, a type of CNN designed specifically for medical image segmentation, has shown significant success in this area.

U-Net architecture

U-Net's architecture is symmetric, with a contracting path to capture context and a symmetric expanding path for precise localization. This design is particularly effective for medical image segmentation tasks. Here are the key components:

- The U-Net model consists of four levels of blocks in the **encoding** and **decoding** paths.

- Each block in the **encoding** path contains two *convolutional* layers with **batch-normalization** and **ReLU** activation (**Rectified Linear Unit**, an activation function in neural networks defined as $f(x) = max(0, x)$), followed by a *max-pooling* layer.

- In the **decoding** path, *up-convolutional* layers replace *max-pooling*. The number of filters increases progressively through the blocks: 32, 64, 128, and 256 filters, while the bottleneck layer uses 512 filters.

- **Skip connections**: Link the *encoding* layers to their corresponding *decoding* layers to preserve spatial information.

- The input is a 3-channel brain **MRI** (**Magnetic Resonance Imaging**) slice representing pre-contrast, **FLAIR** (**Fluid-Attenuated Inversion Recovery**), and post-contrast sequences.

- The output is a single-channel probability **map** that identifies abnormal regions, which can be converted into a binary segmentation mask using a thresholding technique, as demonstrated in the following figure:

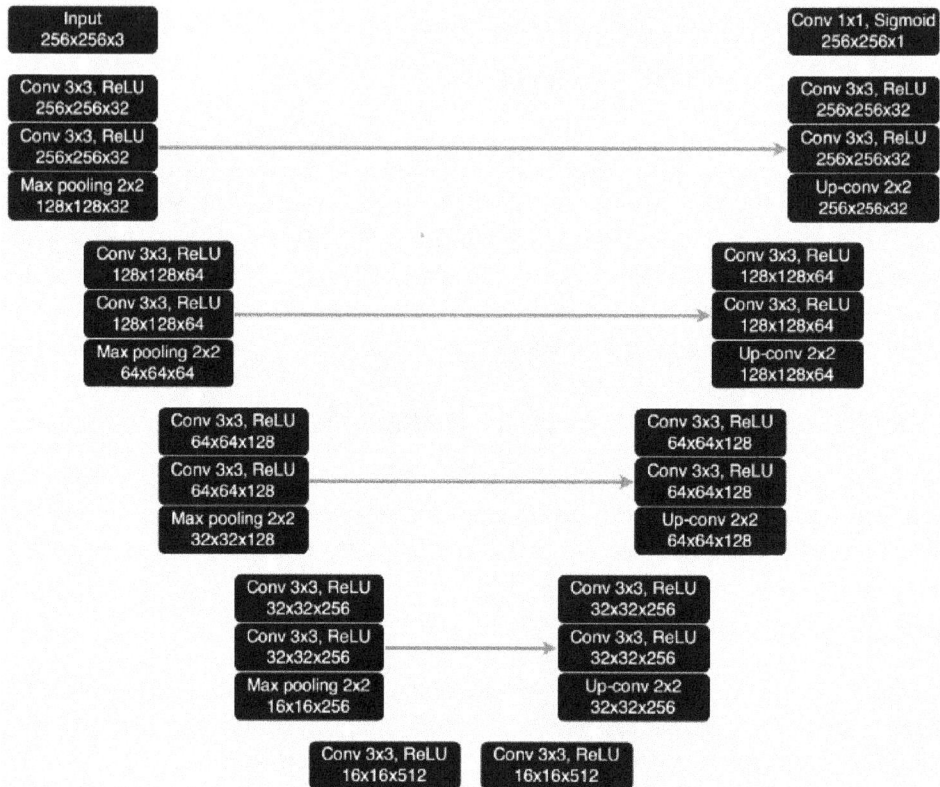

Figure 10.5: U-Net architecture

The following Python code demonstrates brain tumor segmentation on brain MRI images (you can download the images from the *brain MRI segmentation dataset* from *kaggle*: **https:// www.kaggle.com/datasets/mateuszbuda/lgg-mri-segmentation**) using a pretrained U-Net model from **pytorch hub**, showcasing how deep learning can be applied to extract tumor regions from medical scans. Let us break down the key steps involved:

1. **Loading the pretrained U-Net model**:

    Here, the **torch.hub.load()** function loads a pretrained **U-Net** model from a repository. The U-Net architecture is widely used for medical image segmentation, especially for tasks like brain tumor segmentation. The parameters for this model are:

    a. **in_channels=3**: The input consists of 3 channels, which corresponds to the RGB image.

    b. **out_channels=1**: The output will have a single channel, which will contain the *probability map* of the *tumor* (regions with a higher probability correspond to abnormal tissue).

c. **init_features=32**: This is the number of *convolutional filters* used in the first layer. The number of filters doubles at each down-sampling stage of the U-Net model.

d. **pretrained=True**: This indicates that the model has been *pretrained*, meaning the weights have already been optimized using a relevant dataset, allowing it to produce accurate predictions without further training.

2. **Preprocessing the input image**: Before feeding an MRI image into the pretrained U-Net model for brain tumor segmentation, it is essential to preprocess the input so that it aligns with the model's requirements. This involves loading, transforming, and formatting the image, explained as follows:

a. **Loading the image**: The MRI image is loaded from the file system using the **PIL** library and converted to an RGB format (using the function **convert('RGB')**), ensuring it matches the model's expected input (3 channels).

b. **Preprocessing**: The input image is transformed into a tensor using **transforms.ToTensor()**, which normalizes pixel values to the range [0,1]. This is necessary because the neural network expects input images as tensors with values in a normalized range.

c. **Batching the input**: After converting the image to a tensor, the **unsqueeze(0)** function adds a *batch* dimension. This is because models in PyTorch expect inputs in the shape **[batch_size, channels, height, width]**.

3. **Handling GPU acceleration**: If a GPU is available, both the input image tensor and the model are moved to the GPU using **to('cuda')**. This allows for faster computation, leveraging GPU acceleration for the *forward pass* during *inference*.

4. **Performing inference (segmentation)**: Once the MRI slices have been preprocessed and the model is ready, we move on to the inference step to obtain the tumor segmentation. In this stage, the model is used to *predict* the presence of tumor regions in the image without updating any weights. The key steps are as follows:

a. **Disabling gradients**: The **torch.no_grad()** context ensures that *no gradients* are computed during *inference*. This reduces memory consumption and speeds up the process since gradient calculations are not required for *prediction*.

b. **Model prediction**: The model takes the input *batch* and performs a *forward pass*, generating the output, which is a single-channel image representing a *probability map*. The values in the output range between 0 and 1, where higher values indicate a higher *likelihood* of a tumor being present in that region of the MRI slice.

5. **Post-processing the output**: After obtaining the raw prediction from the model, post-processing is necessary to convert it into a usable and visually interpretable format. The following steps outline how the output is normalized, binarized, and prepared for side-by-side visualization along with the input image:

   a. **Normalizing the input image**: The input image is converted to a NumPy array and normalized by dividing all pixel values by the maximum pixel value. This ensures that the pixel values range from 0 to 1.

   b. **Converting the predicted mask**: The model's output is a single-channel probability map. The function `torch.round()` is used to round the output values to either 0 or 1, converting the *probability map* into a *binary mask* (1 indicates the *tumor* region, and 0 represents *normal* tissue).

   c. The `function.squeeze()` removes unnecessary dimensions from the output tensor.

   d. The result is converted to a NumPy array using `.cpu().numpy()`, which first moves the data back to the CPU (if it is on GPU).

   e. **Colorizing the predicted mask**: The `gray2rgb()` function from `skimage.color` converts the grayscale single-channel mask into a 3-channel mask for better visualization, where the tumor region can be displayed with distinct colors.

6. **Storing results**: Finally, the normalized input image and the predicted binary mask are stored in the **inputs** and **pred_masks** lists, respectively. These lists are used to store results for all images in the directory **images/brain_mri/*.tif,** allowing batch processing of multiple MRI slices.

```python
import torch
import numpy as np
from PIL import Image
from torchvision import transforms
from glob import glob
from skimage.color import gray2rgb

model=torch.hub.load('mateuszbuda/brain-segmentation-pytorch', \
                     'unet', in_channels=3, out_channels=1, \
                     init_features=32, pretrained=True)

inputs, pred_masks = [], []
for f in glob('images/brain_mri/*.tif'):
    input_image = Image.open(f).convert('RGB')
    preprocess = transforms.Compose([
                    transforms.ToTensor(),
                    transforms.Normalize,
```

```
    ])
    input_tensor = preprocess(input_image)
    input_batch = input_tensor.unsqueeze(0)

    if torch.cuda.is_available():
        input_batch = input_batch.to('cuda')
        model = model.to('cuda')
    with torch.no_grad():
        output = model(input_batch)

    in_img = np.array(input_image)
    in_img = in_img / in_img.max()
    pred_mask = gray2rgb(torch.round(output[0]).squeeze()\
                                        .cpu().numpy())

    inputs.append(in_img)
    pred_masks.append(pred_mask)
```

7. Iterate over the lists of input images and predicted masks obtained here, display the images (4 of them) along with the predicted (binary) tumor masks, using the following code snippet, to obtain a figure like *Figure 10.6*:

```
import matplotlib.pylab as plt

plt.figure(figsize=(10,5))
for i in range(len(inputs)):
    plt.subplot(2,4,i+1), plt.imshow(inputs[i]), plt.axis('off')
    plt.subplot(2,4,i+5), plt.imshow(pred_masks[i]), plt.axis('off')
plt.suptitle('brain images and predicted tumor masks', size=15)
plt.tight_layout()
plt.show()
```

If you run the preceding code snippet, you should obtain a figure as follows:

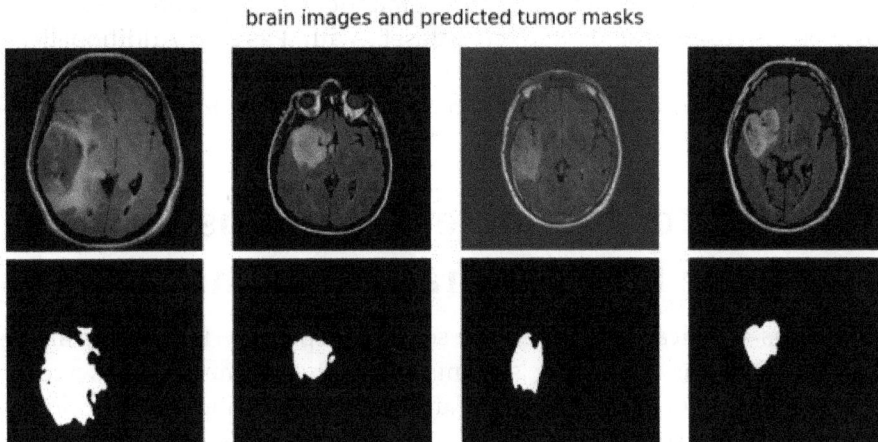

Figure 10.6: Predicting brain tumor masks with the pretrained U-Net model

Computer vision and image processing in remote sensing

Remote sensing, which involves gathering information about the Earth's surface through satellite or aerial imagery, has become a critical tool for environmental monitoring (for example, deforestation, desertification, and the effects of climate change on glaciers and ice caps), agriculture (such as, crop monitoring, soil properties analysis, and management of water resources), urban planning (for example, by providing detailed land use and land cover maps, monitoring urban sprawl, and assessing infrastructure development), disaster management (that is, early warning systems, damage assessment, planning recovery efforts etc.), and many other fields. Image processing plays a pivotal role in enhancing, interpreting, and analyzing remote sensing data, enabling the extraction of valuable information for various applications. Leveraging modern computer vision and image processing techniques has dramatically enhanced the ability to interpret and analyze remote sensing data at scale.

In this section, we will explore the three key applications of computer vision in remote sensing:

- **Segmentation of FloodNet images using VGG-UNet with `keras_segmentation`**: FloodNet is a dataset focused on flood event detection and segmentation. We will use the VGG-UNet architecture, combining VGG16 as a feature extractor with a U-Net decoder to perform pixel-level segmentation of flood-affected areas.

- **Landcover classification with `Fastai ResNet101` using the EuroSAT dataset**: The EuroSAT dataset contains satellite images labeled by different land cover classes. Using the library **Fastai**, we will employ a ResNet101-based model to classify these land cover types with high accuracy.

- **Satellite image segmentation using `Fastai` and `Weights & Biases` with the FloodNet dataset**: We will perform semantic segmentation of satellite images, once again using the FloodNet dataset, with **Fastai**. Additionally, we will integrate **Weights & Biases** (`wandb`) to seamlessly track training metrics, visualize model performance, and monitor progress over time for improved experiment management.

Segmentation of FloodNet images using VGG-UNet with the library keras_segmentation

Flood detection is a critical task in remote sensing, especially in disaster management, urban planning, and early warning systems. Semantic segmentation, which involves pixel-wise classification of an image, plays an essential role in identifying flood-affected regions from satellite imagery. This section presents a deep learning-based approach for flood segmentation using the **VGG-UNet** model and the **FloodNet** dataset. The model leverages a combination of VGG-16 backbone (as encoder) and a U-Net-style decoder, to perform accurate flood region segmentation.

As explained earlier, *semantic segmentation* refers to the task of classifying every pixel in an image into one of several predefined categories. Mathematically, semantic segmentation can be formulated as a multi-class classification problem at the pixel level. Given an input image $I \boxtimes R^{H \times W \times C}$, where H is the height, W is the width, and C is the number of channels (for example, RGB), the goal is to predict a segmentation mask $M \boxtimes R^{H \times W \times K}$, where K is the number of classes (such as, *flooded* and *non-flooded*, on case of binary segmentation).

VGG-UNet architecture

VGG-UNet is a hybrid architecture (illustrated in *Figure 10.7*) that integrates the VGG-16 convolution neural network with the U-Net architecture:

- VGG-16 acts as a feature extractor (*encoder*) by applying a series of convolutional layers, reducing the spatial resolution while increasing the depth of features.

- The U-Net *decoder* uses *transposed convolutions* to *up-sample* these features back to the original resolution, allowing *pixel-wise classification*. The core idea of U-Net is to enable precise localization by combining low-level features from earlier layers with high-level features from deeper layers. This is achieved using *skip connections*, which concatenate corresponding feature maps from the *encoder* and *decoder* paths.

- The architecture is adequate for segmentation tasks, particularly for medical imaging and remote sensing. Its success lies in combining semantic information from deep layers with spatial information from shallow layers.

Refer to the following figure:

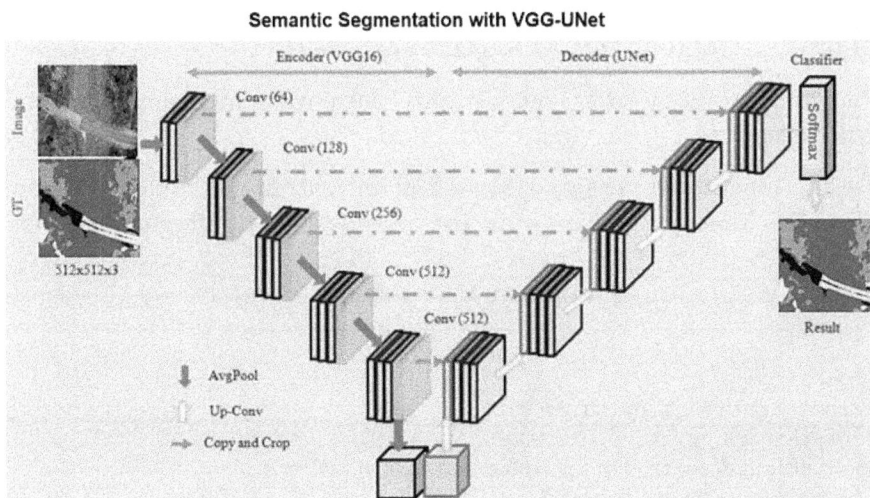

Semantic Segmentation with VGG-UNet

Figure 10.7: *Schematic diagram of semantic segmentation with VGG-UNet encoder decoder*
Source: *https://www.researchgate.net/figure/Block-diagram-of-implemented-VGG-UNet_fig1_363529612*

FloodNet dataset

The FloodNet dataset comprises aerial images and their corresponding segmentation masks, annotated with the following 10 semantic classes:

- Background
- Building flooded
- Building non-flooded
- Road flooded
- Road non-flooded
- Water
- Tree
- Vehicle
- Pool
- Grass

It is designed for the *EarthVision 2021* challenge and provides a unique opportunity for applying deep learning models for flood detection. The dataset is split into *train* and *test* sets, and images are resized to 512×512 pixels for the experiments.

Now, let us demonstrate the segmentation of FloodNet images using the VGG-UNet model with the **keras_segmentation** library (install it with **pip**, if not already installed). The following code needs to be run in Google Colab; it illustrates the entire pipeline, from dataset preparation to segmentation results. Here are the steps you need to follow:

1. First, get the publicly available dataset **FloodNet Challenge @ EARTHVISION 2021 - Track 1** from the following google drive link: **https://drive.google.com/drive/folders/1sZZMJkbqJNbHgebKvHzcXYZHJd6ss4tH** (copy to your Google Drive)

2. Map your Google Drive to your Google Colab environment and access the dataset, as done earlier.

3. Use the function **resize_and_save()** defined in the following code snippet, to resize the (*train* and *test*) images (corresponding to different class labels) from the FloodNet dataset to the size 512×512, and save them locally in Google Colab environment in the required format for training the model:

```
# run in colab
import numpy as np
import matplotlib.pylab as plt
from skimage.io import imread
from skimage.color import label2rgb
import os
#!pip install keras_segmentation
from keras_segmentation.models.unet import vgg_unet
```

```
RESIZE = (512,512)
temp_root="/content/drive/MyDrive/FloodNet Challenge"
          "@ EARTHVISION 2021 - Track 1"
local_root = "/content/512_Images"
def resize_and_save(path, resize=RESIZE, samples='all'):
    if len(os.listdir(os.path.join(local_root, path))) == 0:
        print(f"{path} --> Saving...\n")
        if samples == 'all':
            samples = len(os.listdir(os.path.join(temp_root, path)))
        for img_name in tqdm(os.listdir(os.path.join( \
                                     temp_root, path))[:samples]):
            img = cv2.imread(os.path.join(temp_root, path, img_name))
            img = cv2.resize(img, RESIZE)
            cv2.imwrite(os.path.join(local_root, path, img_name), img)
    else:
        print(f"{path} --> images are already saved")

os.makedirs("/content/512_Images/Train/Labeled/Flooded/image", \
                                                 exist_ok=True)
os.makedirs("/content/512_Images/Train/Labeled/Non-Flooded/image", \
                                                 exist_ok=True)
os.makedirs("/content/512_Images/Train/Labeled/Flooded/mask", \
                                                 exist_ok=True)
os.makedirs("/content/512_Images/Train/Labeled/Non-Flooded/mask", \
                                                 exist_ok=True)
os.makedirs("/content/512_Images/Train/Unlabeled/image", exist_ok=True)
os.makedirs("/content/512_Images/Test/image", exist_ok=True)
resize_and_save("Train/Labeled/Flooded/image")
resize_and_save("Train/Labeled/Non-Flooded/image")
resize_and_save("Train/Labeled/Flooded/mask")
resize_and_save("Train/Labeled/Non-Flooded/mask")
resize_and_save("Train/Unlabeled/image")
resize_and_save("Test/image")
```

4. Initialize the VGG-UNet model with 10 classes, corresponding to different types of flooded and non-flooded regions and input image size 512×512.

5. *Train* the model on the annotated images for 5 epochs (optionally split the training dataset into *train* and *validation* dataset, use the *validation* dataset for *model evaluation* while training), as shown in the following code snippet:

```
model = vgg_unet(n_classes=10,  input_height=512, input_width=512)
model.train(
    train_images  =  "512_Images/Train/Labeled/All/image",
    train_annotations = "512_Images/Train/Labeled/All/mask",
    #validate=True,
    #val_images =  "512_Images/Val/Labeled/All/image",
    #val_annotations = "512_Images/Val/Labeled/All/mask",
    checkpoints_path = "models/vgg_unet_1",
    epochs=5
)
```

6. Create a folder named **out** to store the predicted segmentation for the *test* images.

7. Use the next code snippet to iterate over the *test* images, generate and save *predicted segmentation masks* (obtained using the method **predict_segmentation()**) as files, for each image.

8. Visualize the original images, predicted masks, and overlayed images using the next code snippet, offering a clear view of how the model performs in segmenting flooded regions:

```python
folder = '512_Images/Test/image'
for f in os.listdir(folder):
    out = model.predict_segmentation(out_fname=os.path.join('out/', f))
for f in os.listdir(folder):
    test_img = imread(os.path.join('512_Images/Test/image/', f))
    test_mask = imread(os.path.join('out/', f), 1)
    test_img = test_img / test_img.max()
    test_mask = test_mask / test_mask.max()
    if len(np.unique(mask_san)) > 1:
        plt.figure(figsize=(20,10))
        plt.subplots_adjust(0,0,1,0.95,0.05,0.05)
        plt.subplot(131), plt.imshow(img_san), plt.axis('off')
        plt.title('input (test)', size=20)
        plt.subplot(132), plt.imshow(mask_san, cmap='jet')
        plt.axis('off')
        plt.title('predicted segmentation mask\n with PSP-UNet'
                  ' (trained only for 5 epochs)', size=20) #cividis
        plt.subplot(133), plt.imshow(label2rgb(mask_san, img_san))
        plt.axis('off'), plt.title('overlayed mask', size=20)
        plt.show()
```

If you run the preceding code snippet, you should obtain a figure as follows:

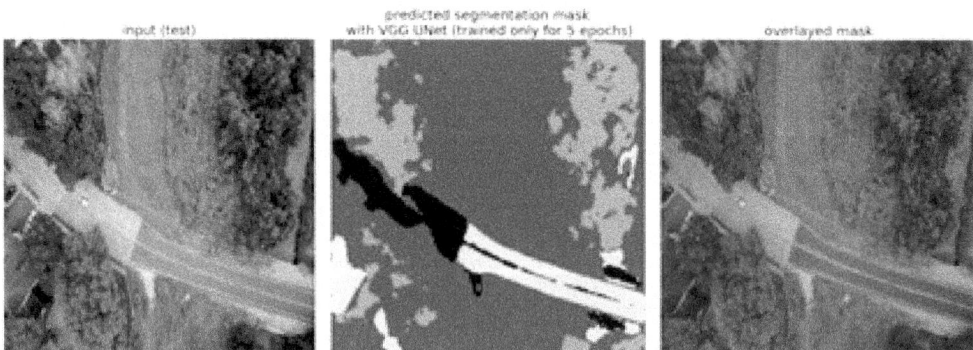

Figure 10.8: Segmenting a sample image from the FloodNet dataset using VGG-UNet

This section showcased the use of VGG-UNet for accurate flood segmentation in satellite images, which can aid to timely disaster management.

Landcover classification with Fastai ResNet101 with EuroSAT dataset

Landcover classification is crucial for understanding and managing Earth's surface features, particularly in agriculture, urban planning, and environmental monitoring. Remote sensing data, such as satellite images, provides valuable information for these tasks. In this section, we will focus on applying deep learning techniques for landcover classification using the **EuroSAT** dataset and the **ResNet101** architecture.

Deep learning, particularly CNNs, has proven highly effective for image classification tasks. *ResNet101* is a popular CNN architecture that introduces residual connections to solve the problem of *vanishing gradients*, allowing for the training of deeper networks. Ee will demonstrate *landcover classification* using the **Fastai** library, which simplifies the application of state-of-the-art deep learning techniques.

We shall use **ResNet101** that is *pretrained* on **ImageNet** and *fine-tune* it on the **EuroSAT** dataset, using the **Fastai** library. It provides efficient tools for *transfer learning, data augmentation*, and *model interpretation*, allowing for high performance with minimal effort.

Residual networks

The **ResNet** architecture, proposed by *He et al.* (2016), introduces *residual connections* that bypass certain layers, enabling the training of deeper networks. This helps mitigate the *vanishing gradient* problem by allowing gradients to flow more easily through the network during *backpropagation*. The key idea is that each block learns a *residual function F* such that the output is computed as: *output = activation(input + F(input, W))*, where *F(Input, W)* is the *residual function* learned by the block, and *W* denotes the trainable parameters. This formulation helps in training deeper networks by allowing the model to learn only the residual (or difference) from the identity mapping. **ResNet101** has 101 layers and leverages these *residual connections* to achieve high performance while maintaining efficient training.

EuroSAT dataset

The *EuroSAT* dataset is based on *Sentinel-2* satellite images covering 10 classes of *land use* and *land cover*. These include *residential areas, industrial areas, forests, agricultural areas, water bodies*, and more. The dataset provides RGB and multi-spectral images, with a resolution of 10 meters per pixel, making it suitable for classification tasks in remote sensing.

Let us now walk through the following code demonstration, explaining each step   in detail to understand the implementation thoroughly. Again, run the code on Google Colab (**https://colab.research.google.com/**). Follow the given steps:

1. Use the *magic* command **%reload_ext autoreload**, as shown in the following code block, to ensure that if any external libraries or code files are modified, they are reloaded into the session. Install **Fastai** with **pip**.

2. Import the necessary libraries:

   a. **fastai.vision**: Contains tools for image classification.

   b. **error_rate**: A metric for evaluating model performance, defined as 1-*accuracy*.

   c. **zipfile, urllib, os**: Utilities for downloading and unzipping the dataset.

```
# run in colab
# !pip install fastcore==1.3.19 Fastai==2.2.5
# import the required libraries
%reload_ext autoreload
%autoreload 2
from fastai.vision import *  # import the vision module
from fastai.metrics import error_rate  # import evaluation metric
import zipfile # import module to unzip the data
import urllib.request
import os # import module to access file paths
```

3. Download the compressed EuroSAT dataset from the public URL provided in the next code snippet, save it as **2750.zip**, and then extract the compressed file, as shown in the following code snippet:

```
url = 'http://madm.dfki.de/files/sentinel/EuroSAT.zip'
urllib.request.urlretrieve(url,"2750.zip")
zf = zipfile.ZipFile("2750.zip")
zf.extractall()
```

4. Define the current working directory (**data_path**) and set the **path** to point to the folder where the dataset is located.

5. Generate *data augmentation* transformations with the function **get_transforms()**. In this case, it applies random *vertical flips* but disables *warping* (*perspective distortions*) to the images to create variations in the *training* data, as can be seen from the next code snippet.

6. The method **ImageDataBunch.from_folder()** loads the images from folders. It accepts the following arguments:

   a. **train = "."**: Indicates that all images are in the same folder, and a *validation* set will be created by splitting the data.

   b. **valid_pct=0.2**: Reserves 20% of the data for *validation*.

   c. **ds_tfms = tfms**: Applies the *data augmentation* transformations.

   d. **size=224**: Resizes the images to 224×224 pixels.

   e. **bs=32**: Sets the *batch* size to 32.

7. The method **.normalize(imagenet_stats)** normalizes the images based on the *mean* and *standard deviation* of the **ImageNet** dataset.

8. The method `.show_batch()` displays a *batch* of 5x5 images with their respective labels.

9. The function `cnn_learner()` creates a *learner* object (`learn`) using a *pretrained* ResNet101 model (`models.resnet101`), where `metrics=error_rate` sets the evaluation metric to *error rate*.

10. `learn.summary()` prints a summary of the model architecture.

```
data_path = os.getcwd()
path = datapath4file(data_path+'/2750')
tfms = get_transforms(flip_vert=True, max_warp = 0.)
data = ImageDataBunch.from_folder(path, train = ".",
                                  valid_pct=0.2, ds_tfms = tfms,
                                  size=224, bs = 32)
                     .normalize(imagenet_stats)
# data.show_batch(rows=5, figsize=(15,15))
learn = cnn_learner(data, models.resnet101, metrics=error_rate)
# print(learn.summary())
```

11. The method `learn.lr_find()` runs the *learning rate finder* to identify an *optimal learning rate*.

12. The `Fastai` library provides a **learning rate finder** (**LR finder**), which helps determine the best learning rate for training deep learning models. The function `learn.recorder.plot(suggestion=True)` plots the learning rate graph and suggests a suitable learning rate, it runs an *LR range test* and suggests an *optimal learning rate* using a method based on *gradient* behavior:

```
learn.lr_find()
learn.recorder.plot(suggestion=True)
#Min numerical gradient: 1.20E-03
#Min loss divided by 10: 6.92E-03
```

Running these lines of code generates a figure as follows:

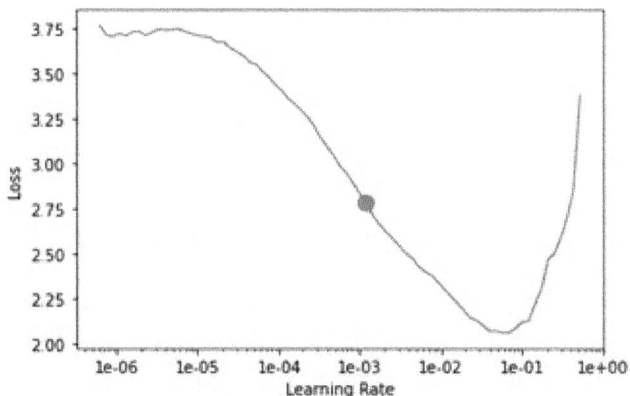

Figure 10.9: Finding the optimal learning rate with Fastai

As we can see from the preceding figure,

    a. **Before the optimal LR**: The loss remains high (too small LR, slow learning).

    b. **Optimal LR**: The loss drops steeply.

    c. **After the optimal LR**: The loss spikes up (*unstable training* due to too high LR).

13. Next, set the *learning rate* to the *optimal* value found (**lr = 1.20E-03**).

14. *Train* the model for epochs using the **one-cycle** policy, which adjusts the learning rate dynamically during training, using the function **learn.fit_one_cycle()**, as can be seen in the following code snippet:

```
lr = 1.20E-03
learn.fit_one_cycle(6, slice(lr))
```

The next table lists the training / validation loss, error rate and time taken to run each epoch. If you run the preceding code you will get a table like the following one:

epoch	train_loss	valid_loss	error_rate	time
0	0.353621	0.196879	0.065741	04 46
1	0.271100	0.150675	0.048519	04 54
2	0.169197	0.119906	0.032778	04 55
3	0.133454	0.077560	0.026296	04 55
4	0.090694	0.074163	0.023704	04 55
5	0.093963	0.064720	0.020926	04 55

Figure 10.10: Drop in training /validation loss with epochs

15. The function **learn.freeze()** freezes the weights of the earlier layers so that only the final layers are *fine-tuned*.

16. The function **learn.lr_find()** runs the learning rate finder again for *fine-tuning* the final layers:

```
learn.freeze()
learn.lr_find()
```

17. **ClassificationInterpretation.from_learner(learn)** creates an interpretation object to analyze the model's performance.

18. **interp.top_losses()** finds the samples with the highest losses, that is, where the model performs worst:

```
interp = ClassificationInterpretation.from_learner(learn)
losses,idxs = interp.top_losses()
len(data.valid_ds)==len(losses)==len(idxs)
# True
```

19. Plot a *confusion matrix*, which visually represents the performance of the model by showing how many samples were correctly and how many are incorrectly classified for each class:

```
interp.plot_confusion_matrix(figsize=(6,6), dpi=100)
```

If you run the preceding code snippet, you should obtain a confusion matrix plot like the next one:

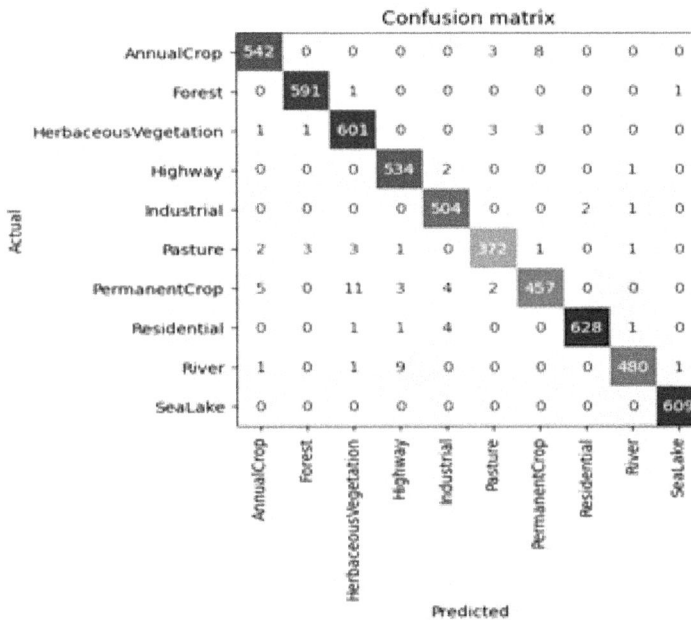

Figure 10.11: Confusion matrix for the multi-class classification of the EuroSAT landcover dataset

20. List the most confused class pairs, that is, where the model makes the most mistakes in distinguishing between two classes.

```
interp.most_confused(min_val=5)
# [('PermanentCrop', 'HerbaceousVegetation', 11),
# ('River', 'Highway', 9),
# ('AnnualCrop', 'PermanentCrop', 8),
# ('PermanentCrop', 'AnnualCrop', 5)]
```

21. **learn.export()** exports the trained model for later use.

22. **learn.show_results()** displays a sample images from the *validation* set along with the **predicted** and **true** labels.

```
learn.export()
learn.show_results(rows=6, figsize=(15,15))
```

Run the preceding code snippet to obtain a figure as follows:

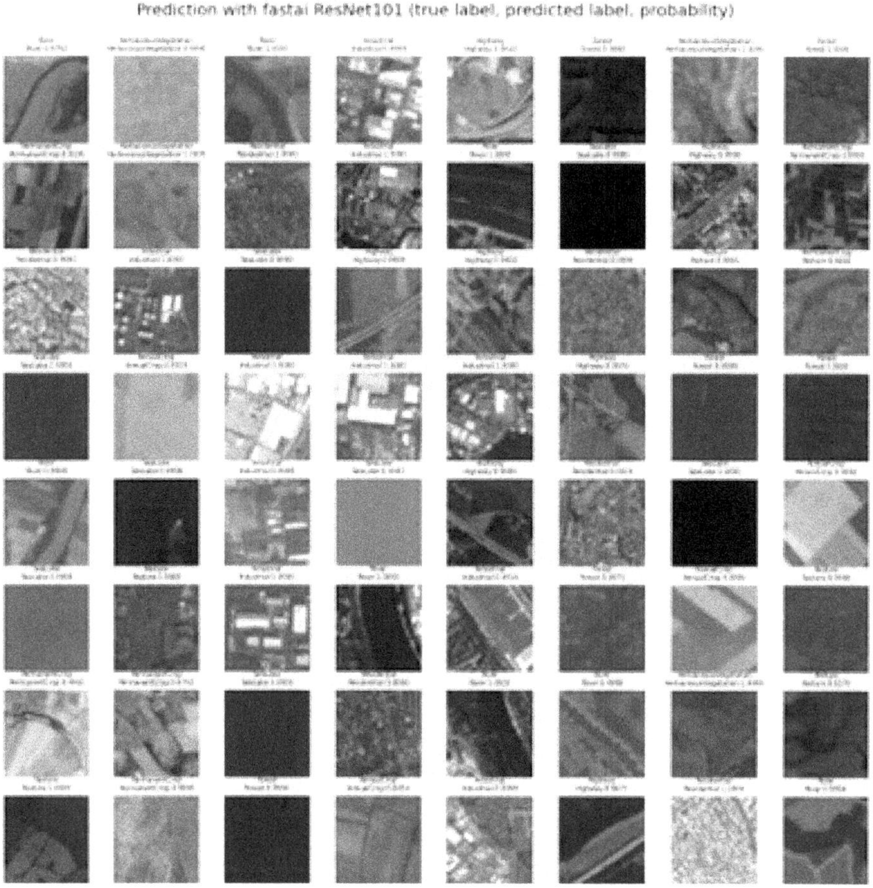

Figure 10.12: GT vs. predicted landcover class labels of EuroSat test dataset with RestNet101

In this section, we demonstrated the application of **ResNet101** for *landcover classification* using the **EuroSAT** dataset. We utilized the library `Fastai` to load the data, apply data augmentation, and fine-tune the pretrained model. The EuroSAT dataset offers a wide variety of land cover types, making it an ideal dataset for training deep learning models to recognize different surface features. Through this example, we have shown how CNNs, specifically ResNet101, can effectively classify satellite images, which has broad applications in remote sensing and environmental monitoring.

Satellite image segmentation using Fastai and wandb with SN7 dataset

Satellite image segmentation is a crucial task in the field of remote sensing and **geographic information systems** (**GIS**). Segmentation helps in identifying different land cover types, such as *buildings, water bodies, roads, vegetation,* and so on, which can be applied in urban planning, agriculture, and environmental monitoring. In this section, we will walk through an implementation of binary satellite image segmentation (that is, categorize the surface features of the Earth into two distinct classes, namely, *building* and *land*) using the **SN7** dataset, the **Fastai** library, and *Weights and Biases* (**wandb**) for experiment tracking.

The **SpaceNet 7 (SN7)** dataset focuses on multi-temporal urban development, specifically on building footprint extraction from multi-spectral satellite imagery over time. This task is challenging due to the large variations in lighting, shadows, and resolution between satellite images.

We shall use a **U-Net** architecture with a **ResNet34** encoder, leveraging *transfer learning* again to *fine-tune* the model on our satellite data. We shall again use Google Colab for running the following implementation. Follow these steps:

1. Let us start by importing the necessary libraries, as shown in the next code snippet:

    a. **Fastai.vision.all** contains tools for vision-related deep learning tasks.

    b. **wandb** is to be used for experiment tracking and visualizing metrics.

    c. **rasterio**, **geopandas**, and **shapely** handle the satellite image format, such as geospatial data processing and geometries.

```python
# run in colab
import os
#!pip install rasterio geopandas shapely wandb -Uqq
from Fastai.vision.all import *
from tqdm import tqdm
from pdb import set_trace
from pprint import pprint
import wandb
from Fastai.callback.wandb import *
import rasterio
from rasterio.plot import reshape_as_image
import rasterio.mask
from rasterio.features import rasterize
import pandas as pd
import geopandas as gpd
from shapely.geometry import mapping, Point, Polygon
from shapely.ops import cascaded_union
warnings.filterwarnings("ignore")
path = Path('/content/train')
Path.BASE_PATH = path
```

2. Our data resides on **AWS cloud**. The next part is a setup for downloading data from AWS. It writes *AWS credentials* to a configuration file for secure access to the **SN7** dataset.

3. You must use your own *AWS credentials*, that is, **aws_access_key_id** and **aws_secret_access_key** to be able to access the dataset, refer to this article for the same: **https://docs.aws.amazon.com/keyspaces/latest/devguide/access.credentials.html**

```
text = '''
[default]
aws_access_key_id = XXXXXXXXXXXXXX
aws_secret_access_key = XXXXXXXXXXXXXXXXX
'''

path = "/content/config/awscli.ini"
with open(path, 'w') as f:
    f.write(text)
!cat /content/config/awscli.ini

!export AWS_SHARED_CREDENTIALS_FILE=/content/drive/My\
                                    Drive/config/awscli.ini
path = "/content/config/awscli.ini"
os.environ['AWS_SHARED_CREDENTIALS_FILE'] = path
print(os.environ['AWS_SHARED_CREDENTIALS_FILE'])
```

4. First, install the Python library corresponding to **AWS CLI** in Colab (with **pip**)

5. The next **AWS CLI** commands download and extract the **SN 7** dataset from an **AWS S3** bucket:

```
!pip install awscli
!aws s3 cp s3://spacenet-dataset/spacenet/SN7_buildings/tarballs/
SN7_buildings_train.tar.gz .
!aws s3 cp s3://spacenet-dataset/spacenet/SN7_buildings/tarballs/
SN7_buildings_train_csvs.tar.gz .
!aws s3 cp s3://spacenet-dataset/spacenet/SN7_buildings/tarballs/
SN7_buildings_test_public.tar.gz .
!mv SN7_buildings_train.tar.gz drive/MyDrive
!tar xvf SN7_buildings_train.tar.gz
!tar xvf SN7_buildings_train_csvs.tar.gz
!tar xvf SN7_buildings_test_public.tar.gz
```

6. Use GPU runtime for faster execution in Colab. Verify if **pytorch** can execute on GPU, using the next code snippet:

```
try:
    print(torch.cuda.get_device_properties(0))
except:
    print("No CUDA device available.")
```

7. Next, define several key hyperparameters, using the following code snippet:

    a. **BATCH_SIZE**: The number of images processed in each training *batch*.

    b. **TILES_PER_SCENE**: Number of image *tiles* per scene.

    c. **ARCHITECTURE**: The architecture used for the *encoder* (**ResNet34**).

    d. **EPOCHS**: The number of training *epochs*.

e. **CLASS_WEIGHTS**: Weights assigned to each class for handling *class-imbalance*. Buildings are given more weight since there are fewer *building* pixels compared to *land* pixels.

f. **LR_MAX**: The maximum *learning rate* used in the training loop.

g. **ENCODER_FACTOR**: This factor scales down the learning rate for the *encoder*.

```
BATCH_SIZE = 12 # 3 for xresnet50, 12 for xresnet34 -Tesla P100 (16GB)
TILES_PER_SCENE = 16
ARCHITECTURE = xresnet34
EPOCHS = 40
CLASS_WEIGHTS = [0.25,0.75]
LR_MAX = 3e-4
ENCODER_FACTOR = 10
CODES = ['Land','Building']
# Weights and Biases config
config_dictionary = dict(
    bs=BATCH_SIZE,
    tiles_per_scene=TILES_PER_SCENE,
    architecture = str(ARCHITECTURE),
    epochs = EPOCHS,
    class_weights = CLASS_WEIGHTS,
    lr_max = LR_MAX,
    encoder_factor = ENCODER_FACTOR
)
```

8. Define the function **generate_mask()** in the following code snippet, to generate a binary **mask** from a shapefile, vector file (**shp** or **geojson**) and the corresponding raster satellite image.

   a. **rasterio.open(raster_path)**: Reads the satellite image.

   b. **gpd.read_file(shape_path)**: Reads the building footprint shapefile.

   c. **poly_from_utm()**: This function converts building polygons to the image's coordinate system.

   d. **rasterize**: Converts vector geometries (*polygons*) into *rasterized masks* (pixel-wise classification).

9. The **save_masks()** function iterates through all the satellite images in each scene directory and invokes the **generate_mask()** function to generate *binary masks* for each image. These masks represent the presence of buildings or other objects of interest in the image. If the mask already exists, the function skips that image; otherwise, it creates the mask and saves it in a **binary_mask** folder within the same scene. The binary masks are crucial for training the segmentation model, as they serve as the *ground-truth labels* for each satellite image.

```python
def generate_mask(raster_path, shape_path, output_path=None, \
                                        file_name=None):
    #Load raster
    with rasterio.open(raster_path, "r") as src:
        raster_img = src.read()
        raster_meta = src.meta
    #Load o shapefile Json
    train_df = gpd.read_file(shape_path)
    #Verify crs
    if train_df.crs != src.crs:
        print(" Raster crs : {}, Vector crs : {}."
                "\n Convert vector and raster to the same CRS." \
                .format(src.crs,train_df.crs))
    #Function that generates the mask
    def poly_from_utm(polygon, transform):
        poly_pts = []
        poly = cascaded_union(polygon)
        for i in np.array(poly.exterior.coords):
            poly_pts.append(~transform * tuple(i))
        new_poly = Polygon(poly_pts)
        return new_poly

    poly_shp = []
    im_size = (src.meta['height'], src.meta['width'])
    for num, row in train_df.iterrows():
        if row['geometry'].geom_type == 'Polygon':
            poly = poly_from_utm(row['geometry'], src.
            meta['transform'])
            poly_shp.append(poly)
        else:
            for p in row['geometry']:
                poly = poly_from_utm(p, src.meta['transform'])
                poly_shp.append(poly)
    if len(poly_shp) > 0:
        mask = rasterize(shapes=poly_shp, out_shape=im_size)
    else:
        mask = np.zeros(im_size)

    # Save or show mask
    mask = mask.astype("uint8")
    bin_mask_meta = src.meta.copy()
    bin_mask_meta.update({'count': 1})
    if (output_path != None and file_name != None):
        os.chdir(output_path)
        with rasterio.open(file_name, 'w', **bin_mask_meta) as dst:
            dst.write(mask * 255, 1)
        else:
            return mask
```

```
def save_masks():
  for scene in tqdm(path.ls().sorted()):
    for img in (scene/'images_masked').ls():
      shapes = scene/'labels_match'/(img.name[:-4]+\
                            '_Buildings.geojson')
      if not os.path.exists(scene/'binary_mask'/img.name):
        if not os.path.exists(scene/'binary_mask'):
          os.makedirs(scene/'binary_mask')
        generate_mask(img, shapes, scene/'binary_mask', img.name)
save_masks()
```

10. The function **get_masked_images()** retrieves a list of satellite images from a specified directory (**Path**) that contain both the satellite image and the corresponding **mask** (labeled data). It returns the first **n** pictures from every scene. These images will later be used to train the segmentation model.

```
def get_masked_images(path:Path, n=1)->list:
  files = []
  for folder in path.ls():
    files.extend(get_image_files(path=folder, \
                                 folders='images_masked')[:n])
  return files

masked_images = get_masked_images(path, 1)
sample_scene = (path/'L15-0683E-1006N_2732_4164_13')
```

If you plot the preceding sample scene, along with its *ground-truth mask* side-by-side, you should get a figure as follows:

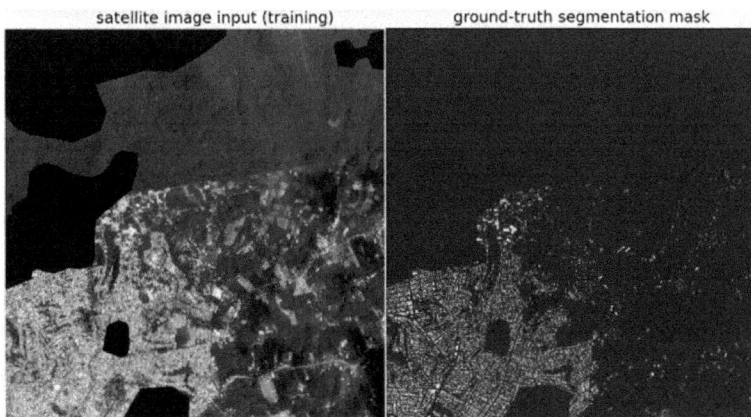

Figure 10.13: *A sample training image from SN7 dataset and the corresponding GT segmentation mask*

11. The next function **cut_tiles()** splits large images into *smaller tiles*, which makes training more efficient and helps the model focus on *localized regions*:

```python
def cut_tiles(tile_size:int):
    "Cuts large images & masks into equal tiles & saves them to disk"
    masked_images = get_masked_images(path, 5)
    for fn in tqdm(masked_images):
        scene = fn.parent.parent
        if not os.path.exists(scene/'img_tiles'):
            os.makedirs(scene/'img_tiles')
        if not os.path.exists(scene/'mask_tiles'):
            os.makedirs(scene/'mask_tiles')
        # Create mask for current image
        img = np.array(PILImage.create(fn))
        msk_fn = str(fn).replace('images_masked', 'binary_mask')
        msk = np.array(PILMask.create(msk_fn))
        x, y, _ = img.shape
        # Cut tiles and save them
        for i in range(x//tile_size):
            for j in range(y//tile_size):
                img_tile = img[i*tile_size:(i+1)*tile_size,
                               j*tile_size:(j+1)*tile_size]
                msk_tile = msk[i*tile_size:(i+1)*tile_size,
                               j*tile_size:(j+1)*tile_size]
                Image.fromarray(img_tile)
                    .save(f'{scene}/img_tiles/{fn.name[:-4]}_{i}_{j}.
                    png')
                Image.fromarray(msk_tile)
                    .save(f'{scene}/mask_tiles/{fn.name[:-4]}_{i}_{j}.
                    png')
TILE_SIZE = 255
cut_tiles(TILE_SIZE)
```

If you run the given code, you should obtain smaller tiles cut from the scenes, as shown:

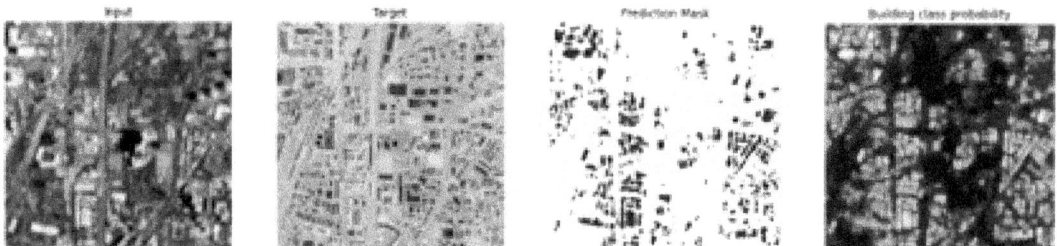

Figure 10.14: Prediction mask for a sample tile cut from an original scene

12. Define the **DataBlock** object, which organizes the dataset for training, defines how images and their segmentation masks are processed, with the following arguments:

   a. **ImageBlock()** defines input images, and **MaskBlock** defines the binary segmentation masks.

b. **get_items** specifies how to get input images.

c. **get_y** specifies how to get the corresponding *mask* for each image.

d. **splitter** defines how to split the dataset into *training* and *validation* sets.

e. **batch_tfms** applies batch-level transformations like *normalization* and *augmentation*.

f. The *augmentation* applied (as the list **tfms**) uses the following classes:

    i. **Dihedral** for random horizontal and vertical flips,

    ii. **Rotate** for rotations up to 180 degrees,

    iii. **Brightness** for adjusting brightness by ±20%,

    iv. **Contrast** for modifying contrast by ±20%,

    v. **Saturation** for changing saturation by ±20%, and

    vi. **Normalize.from_stats** to normalize the data using *ImageNet* statistics.

These transformations help improve the model's robustness to variations in orientation, lighting, and color during training.

13. Next, configure the data loading pipeline for *training* and *validation*:

a. Build **DataLoaders** from the tiles **DataBlock**, by loading the *image* and *mask* pairs, applying necessary transformations, and *batching* the data for model training.

b. The **vocab** attribute specifies the categories (*land, building*) that the model should predict in the segmentation task. This setup is crucial for handling the training data pipeline efficiently, which is key for training a segmentation model.

```
tfms = [Dihedral(0.5),              # Horizontal and vertical flip
        Rotate(max_deg=180, p=0.9), # Rotation in any direction
        Brightness(0.2, p=0.75),
        Contrast(0.2),
        Saturation(0.2),
        Normalize.from_stats(*imagenet_stats)]

# Independent variable is Image, dependent variable is Mask
tiles = DataBlock( \
        blocks = (ImageBlock(), MaskBlock(codes=CODES)),
        get_items=get_undersampled_tiles, # Collect undersampled tiles
        get_y=get_y,                       # Get dependent variable: mask
        splitter=FuncSplitter(valid_split), # Split into train / valid
        batch_tfms=tfms # Transforms (GPU): augmentation,normalization
    )

dls = tiles.dataloaders(path, bs=BATCH_SIZE)
dls.vocab = CODES
```

The next code block sets up the learning configuration for a **U-Net** model using the library **Fastai**. It sets up a U-Net segmentation model with *weighted cross-entropy loss* to handle *class-imbalance*, using the *Adam optimizer* and specific metrics for evaluation. It also includes functionality to save the best model during training based on the *Dice coefficient*.

14. **weights = Tensor(CLASS_WEIGHTS).cuda()**: Converts the **CLASS_WEIGHTS** (which is a list of weights for each class) into a **pytorch** *tensor* and moves it to the GPU (if available), using **.cuda()**. These weights will be used to give different importance to classes during training, which can be particularly useful in cases of class-imbalance (for example, when one class is much more prevalent than another).

15. **loss_func = CrossEntropyLossFlat(axis=1, weight=weights)**: Creates a **loss** function using *cross-entropy* loss.

    a. **axis=1**: Indicates that the class dimension is the second dimension (that is, the model outputs *probabilities* for each class across pixels).

    b. **weight=weights**: Applies the class weights defined earlier to adjust the *loss* calculation for each class based on its importance. This **loss** function will help the model learn to prioritize (give more importance to) the *underrepresented class* (e.g., *building*) during training.

16. **learn = unet_learner(dls, ...)**: Initializes a U-Net model learner with the provided configurations, along with the following parameters:

    a. **dls**: The **DataLoaders** object containing the *training* and *validation* datasets.

    b. **ARCHITECTURE**: Specifies the model architecture to use (in this case, **xResNet34**).

    c. **loss_func**: Sets the custom weighted **cross-entropy** loss function created earlier.

    d. **opt_func=Adam**: Specifies the optimizer to use for training (**Adam** optimizer).

    e. **metrics=[Dice(), foreground_acc]**: Defines custom evaluation metrics to monitor during training.

    f. **Dice()**: Measures the **Dice** coefficient, a metric for evaluating the *overlap* between *predicted* and *true* segmentation masks. It ranges from 0 (no overlap) to 1 (perfect match), making it a useful metric to evaluate segmentation accuracy.

       Mathematically, the **Dice** coefficient is computed as $\frac{2|A \cap B|}{|A|+|B|}$, where A is the set of predicted pixels, B is the set of ground-truth pixels, and $|\cdot|$ denotes the number of pixels in the set.

g. **foreground_acc**: It is a custom metric to evaluate the model's performance by calculating the accuracy only on the *foreground* (non-background) pixels (the *building* class in this case).

h. **self_attention=False**: Indicates that *self-attention* layers are not used in this model.

i. **cbs=[SaveModelCallback(...)]**: Includes *callbacks* for model *training*, such as *saving* the *best model* based on the *Dice* metric.

```
weights = Tensor(CLASS_WEIGHTS).cuda()
loss_func = CrossEntropyLossFlat(axis=1, weight=weights)

learn = unet_learner(dls,                # DataLoaders
              ARCHITECTURE,              # xResNet34
              loss_func=loss_func,       # Weighted cross entropy loss
              opt_func = Adam,           # Adam optimizer
              metrics = [Dice(), foreground_acc], # Custom metrics
                  self_attention = False,
                  cbs = [SaveModelCallback(
                          monitor='dice',
                          comp=np.greater,
                          fname='best-model'
                      )]
                  )
```

The next code snippet integrates **Weights & Biases** (**W&B**) for experiment tracking and logging during the training of a deep learning model. Follow these steps (17-22):

17. First install the **wandb** library with **pip** in Colab.

18. **wandb.login()**: Prompts to log in to a W&B account. This is necessary to authenticate and enable logging of training metrics, configurations, and results to the W&B dashboard.

19. **wandb.init(project="spacenet7", config=config_dictionary)**: Initializes a new W&B run for tracking, it accepts the following parameters:

    a. **project="spacenet7"**: Names the project in which the current run will be logged. This helps organize different experiments under the same project.

    b. **config=config_dictionary**: Passes a configuration dictionary containing *hyperparameters* and settings for the experiment. This information is logged to W&B for reference.

20. **learn.unfreeze()**: Unfreezes the layers of the model, allowing all parameters to be updated during training. This is usually done after initial training with frozen layers to *fine-tune* the model further.

21. **`learn.fit_one_cycle(...)`**: Starts the training of the model using the *one-cycle training policy*, with the following parameters:

    a. **EPOCHS**: Number of training epochs.

    b. **`lr_max=slice(lr_max/ENCODER_FACTOR, lr_max)`**: Specifies the *learning rate schedule*. It uses a slice to gradually increase the learning rate up to a maximum value (**`lr_max`**) and then decrease it, optimizing training stability and performance.

    c. **`cbs=[WandbCallback()]`**: Includes the *W&B callback* to log metrics and other training information to the *W&B dashboard* during training.

22. **`wandb.finish()`**: Finalizes the current W&B run. This command stops the logging and uploads any remaining metrics or results to the W&B server.

```
#!pip install wandb --upgrade
# Log in to your W&B account
wandb.login()
wandb.init(project="spacenet7", config=config_dictionary)
learn.unfreeze()
learn.fit_one_cycle(
    EPOCHS,
    lr_max=slice(lr_max/ENCODER_FACTOR, lr_max),
    cbs=[WandbCallback()]
)
wandb.finish()
```

23. Retrieve the *predicted probabilities* (**probs**), *ground truth targets* (**targets**), *predicted classes* (**preds**), and *associated losses* (**losses**) for the *validation* dataset (**dls.valid**), while decoding the predictions and including the loss in the output, using the next line of code:

```
probs,targets,preds,losses = learn.get_preds(dl=dls.valid, \
                        with_loss=True, with_decoded=True, \
                        act=None)
```

If you plot the original image and the **Fastai**-predicted segmentation masks side-by-side for the sample image given here, you should obtain a figure as follows:

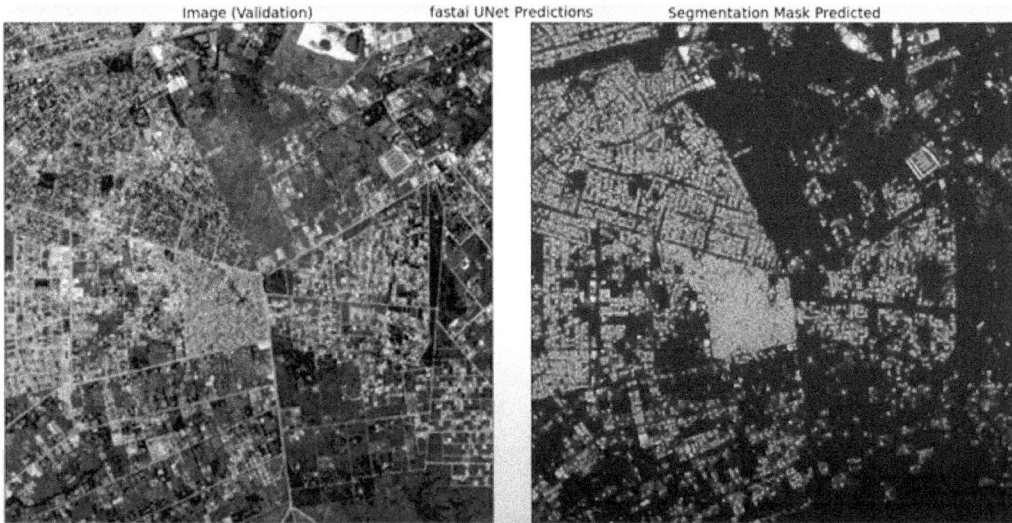

Figure 10.15: *Segmenting a sample image from SN7 dataset with Fastai/U-Net*

Conclusion

This chapter explores the diverse applications of image processing in medical imaging and remote sensing, focusing on key challenges and solutions in both domains. Deep learning models like **XceptionNet** and **Covid-Net** for disease detection, are examined. The chapter also covers prostate segmentation using **nnUNet** and brain tumor detection with **U-Net**, highlighting the impact of these technologies on improving diagnostic accuracy.

In remote sensing, the chapter explores the segmentation of **FloodNet** images using **VGG-U-Net**, landcover classification with **Fastai**'s **ResNet101** on the **EuroSAT** dataset, and satellite image segmentation using **Fastai** and **wandb** with the **FloodNet** dataset. These techniques demonstrate the power of image processing for environmental monitoring and resource management, offering valuable insights into both healthcare and remote sensing applications.

Key terms

U-Net, Covid-Net, VGG-Unet, Fastai, nnUNet, FloodNet, Resnet101

Questions

1. Understand how the *optimal learning rate finder* works in Fastai (refer to the *arxiv paper [17]*). Can you implement it on your own, to find the best learning rate for a deep learning model on a given training dataset?

2. **Brain tumor detection** using *transfer learning* with Mask R-CNN with **Medical Decathlon** dataset: Download the dataset Task01_BrainTumour.tar from the Google Drive from **http://medicaldecathlon.com/**. In this exercise problem, you will learn how to perform *custom object detection and instance segmentation* using *transfer learning* with the *Mask R-CNN* model. Start by randomly selecting 2000 images from the training dataset along with the labels and create *annotation jsons* from the labels (for example, define a function to create *annotations* and *bounding boxes*) You should obtain annotated images as shown:

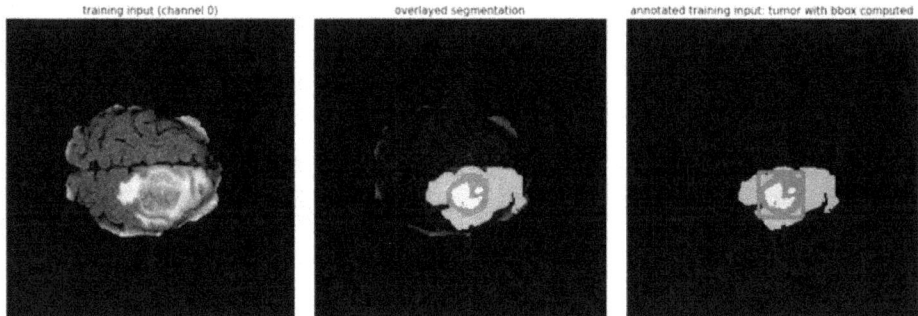

Figure 10.16: Brain tumor detection using transfer learning with Mask R-CNN

Partition the annotated images into two sets: *training* and *validation*. Define a function load_image_dataset() to load the *train* and *validation* images along with *annotations*. There should be only 1 class corresponding to *tumor*, that we want to detect. Define a function display_image_samples() to display images with annotations, you should obtain a figure as follows:

Figure 10.17: Displaying an annotated brain tumor image

Train the model (for example, for 10 epochs) on the annotated images, by *freezing* all the layers except the *head* layers. After training is over, use the model for *inference*, to *predict* the *tumor* region (along with the *bounding box*) of a *test* image (from the held-out dataset), and overlay on top the actual label (use the color_spalsh() function from *Chapter 8, Object Detection and Recognition*). You should obtain a figure as follows, for the given *test* image:

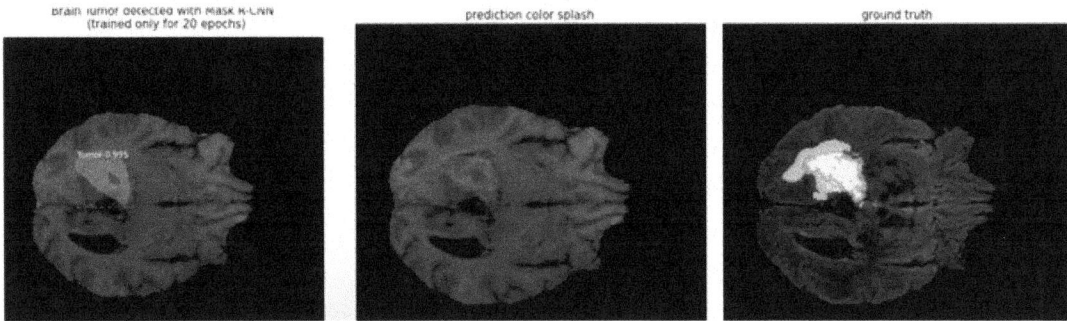

Figure 10.18: Overlaying GT annotation/prediction mask for tumor with Mask R-CNN

3. Implement a function to compute the **Intersection over Union** (**IoU**) of the model on the test images, from the previous question, to evaluate the model. Remember that the IoU measures the overlap between the predicted bounding box and the ground truth bounding box. It is defined as the area of overlap divided by the area of union between the predicted and ground truth boxes.

References

1. **https://github.com/mateuszbuda/brain-segmentation-pytorch/tree/master**

2. **https://arxiv.org/pdf/2003.09871**

3. **https://arxiv.org/pdf/1610.02391**

4. **https://www.nature.com/articles/s41592-020-01008-z**

5. **https://link.springer.com/chapter/10.1007/978-3-319-24574-4_28**

6. **http://medicaldecathlon.com/**

7. **https://ieeexplore.ieee.org/document/8099678**

8. **https://github.com/chrieke/awesome-satellite-imagery-datasets**

9. **https://www.youtube.com/shorts/UWFxyZYHIio**

10. **https://www.youtube.com/watch?v=pFKARAl-wzA**

11. **https://www.youtube.com/watch?v=AwjAp_6K958**

12. **https://www.youtube.com/watch?v=J87VNteZ6RI**

13. **https://www.youtube.com/watch?v=X3uuRQ7UolI**

14. **https://www.youtube.com/watch?v=XBAB7m_ckuY**

15. **https://www.youtube.com/watch?v=Uji-tBivDeo**

16. **https://www.youtube.com/watch?v=eW6LWmkigrc**

17. **https://arxiv.org/pdf/1506.01186**

Join our Discord space

Join our Discord workspace for latest updates, offers, tech happenings around the world, new releases, and sessions with the authors:

https://discord.bpbonline.com

## CHAPTER 11

Miscellaneous Problems in Image Processing and Computer Vision

Introduction

In the previous chapters, we have explored a wide range of image processing and computer vision problems, including image restoration, segmentation, feature extraction, classification, and object detection, and their applications across various domains. In this chapter, we turn our attention to a diverse set of miscellaneous yet fascinating problems in image processing and computer vision. Our focus will extend to cutting-edge deep learning techniques applied to creative and analytical tasks such as deep generative art (e.g., deep dreaming and style transfer), pseudo-colorization of black-and-white images, and visualization of image features using dimensionality reduction methods. We will also delve into the realm of 3D computer vision, learning how to generate point clouds from images. Additionally, this chapter will guide you through implementing a basic virtual reality (VR) application using a webcam, and demonstrate techniques to embed videos into images, as well as add subtitles to videos using Python libraries. Finally, we will explore the exciting domain of image synthesis from text using generative AI, leveraging OpenAI's DALL-E model to transform natural language descriptions into vivid, realistic images. We will also examine how generative AI techniques can be used to seamlessly blend multiple cloned objects into an image, completing our journey through these engaging and unconventional image processing challenges.

Structure

This chapter covers the following topics:

- Deep dreaming with pytorch
- Neural style transfer with perceptual losses
- Image colorization with pretrained pytorch models
- Visualizing VGG16 features in 2D with t-SNE and classifying with SVM
- Creating point cloud from images
- Augmented reality with opencv-python
- Embedding and playing video clips with moviepy
- Generating images from text with GAN-CLS
- Image editing with seamless cloning
- Image generation and editing with Dall-E

Objectives

By the end of the chapter, you should be able to apply deep learning techniques for creative image transformations using deep dreaming and neural style transfer, perform image colorization with pretrained PyTorch models, and visualize high-dimensional image features using t-SNE for classification with SVM. You will also learn to generate 3D point clouds from 2D images, build basic augmented reality applications with OpenCV, and manipulate video content by embedding clips or adding subtitles using MoviePy. Additionally, you will be equipped to synthesize images from text using models like GAN-CLS and DALL-E, and perform seamless image editing through advanced cloning techniques.

Deep dreaming with pytorch

Deep Dream is a computer vision program (created by *Google*) that uses a convolutional neural network to find and enhance (amplify) patterns in images with algorithmic pareidolia, creating a dreamlike hallucinogenic appearance in the deliberately over-processed images.

However, after enough reiterations, even imagery initially devoid of the sought features will be adjusted enough that a form of pareidolia results, by which psychedelic and surreal images are generated algorithmically. Deep Dream uses gradient ascent optimization — similar to the reverse of backpropagation— not to train the model, but to modify the input image so that certain neuron activations are maximized. The network weights remain fixed throughout; only the pixel values of the input image are updated, making this process more akin to feature visualization than training.

Deep Dream's CNN must first be trained. The training process is based on repetition and analysis. For example, in order for Deep Dream to understand and identify cats, the neural network must be fed examples of millions of cat images. In this section, we shall use a **VGG16** deep neural net model (the architecture shown in the following figure), pre-trained on the **ImageNet** dataset.

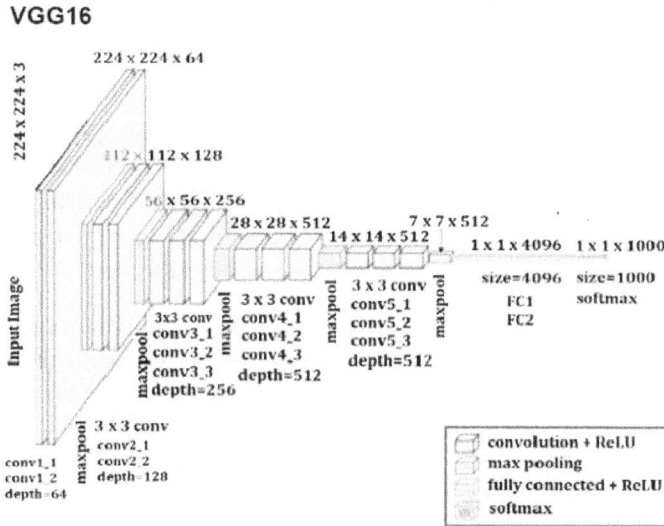

Figure 11.1: VGG16 architecture

Deep dreaming is a gradient ascent process that tries to maximize the L_2 norm of activations of a particular **Deep Neural Net** (**DNN**) layer. Mathematically, the objective is to optimize the input image I to maximize the activation $Aa_l(I)$ of a particular layer l in the network. The most common objective function is:

$$\text{maximize} \max_I \|a_l(I)\|_2^2$$

This is done using gradient ascent, where the image is updated iteratively as:

$$I_{t+1} = I_t + \eta \cdot \nabla_I \|a_l(I_t)\|_2^2$$

Where we have:

- I_t is the input image at iteration t,
- η is the learning rate (step size),
- $a_l(I_t)$ are the activations at layer l given the image I_t,
- $\nabla_I \|a_l(I_t)\|_2^2$ is the gradient with respect to the input image.

Here are a few simple practical tricks that can be useful for getting visually appealing output images:

- **Jitter:** Offset image by a random jitter (a small random shift to the image) before computing gradients.

- **Gradient normalization:** Normalize the magnitude of gradient before applying updates to prevent exploding updates.

- **Octave scaling:** Apply the optimization across multiple scales (octaves).

Guided Deep Dream is a variant of Deep Dream that directs the image modification process using a separate **guide image**, also referred to as a control image. Instead of merely amplifying features in the original image, it adjusts the *input* so that its neural activations at a chosen layer resemble those of the *guide*, effectively maximizing the filters activated by the guide. This is achieved through gradient ascent on the input image, allowing the output to blend stylistic or structural elements from both images. Here, the difference between the two activations is minimized using gradient ascent on the source image: $I_{new} = I + \eta \cdot \nabla_l loss(A_l(I), A_l(G))$. Additionally, **looped hallucinations** can be created by iteratively feeding the output image back as the input for the next round of dreaming, leading to progressively intensified and evolving visual patterns.

Now, let us proceed to implement Guided Deep Dream using Python. To do so, carefully follow the step-by-step procedure outlined, which will guide you through preparing the images, selecting neural network layers, and applying gradient-based optimization to synthesize the final dream-like output:

1. Let us start by importing the required libraries.

```python
import torch
from torchvision import transforms, models
from torch.autograd import Variable
from IPython.display import clear_output
from PIL import Image
import scipy.ndimage as ndimage
import numpy as np
import matplotlib.pylab as plt
```

2. Use the function **show_image_tensor()** in the following code snippet to display an image tensor provided as input to the function. Prior to plotting the image, it reshapes the tensor and de-normalizes it, converts it to a NumPy array and scales the pixel values in between [0,255]. The function **clear_output(wait=True)** clears the current cell output in jupyter notebooks, updating it smoothly after the next output appears—useful for dynamic displays in loops.

```python
def show_image_tensor(img):
    mean = np.array([0.485, 0.456, 0.406]).reshape([1, 1, 3])
    std = np.array([0.229, 0.224, 0.225]).reshape([1, 1, 3])
    img = img[0].transpose(1, 2, 0)
    img = std * img + mean
    img = np.clip(np.uint8(img*255), 0, 255)
    plt.figure(figsize=(15,15))
    plt.imshow(img), plt.axis('off'), plt.title('Guided Deep Dream', size=20)
    plt.show()
    clear_output(wait=True)
```

3. Define the function **step_next()** that implements a basic gradient ascent step, by applying the first two tricks described previously. The function accepts the input image (**img**), the **model** (pretrained VGG16) and the control image (**guide**), as input parameters.

   It also accepts an **objective_func**, which is used to compute the L_2 distance between the activations and the features extracted from the guide image, and the argument **end_layer** that specifies the layer in the pretrained model at which the activation maximization will be done. Along with that, optional parameters such as **learning_rate** can be passed to the function, when required.

4. Apply a small random cyclic shift (jitter) to the input image in both x and y directions (with **np.roll()**) to encourage spatial diversity during optimization.

5. Convert the images to **tensors** and send them to GPU, if available.

6. Invoke the function **forward()** on the input and the control image to run forward propagation through the model layers up to the **end_layer**, generating the activation values and guide features, respectively.

7. The backpropagation needs to be performed on the images themselves, and that is why we need to define a couple of variables with **requires_grad=True**, to enable gradient computation.

8. Use the function **objective_func()** to maximize the dot-products between activations of the current image, and their best matching correspondences in the features from the guide image.

9. Compute the L_2 distance between the activation values and guide features. Run back propagation with the function **backward()**.

10. **Perform gradient ascent**: Update the input image with gradient along with a proper learning rate.

11. Show the updated image at every **show_every** interval.

   Now, refer to the next code snippet:

```
def forward(model, x, end):
    layers = list(model.features.children())
    last = len(layers)
    for index in range(min(end, last)):
        model = layers[index]
        x = model(x)
    return x

def objective_func(activations, guide_features):
    x, y = activations.data[0].cpu().numpy(), \
                        guide_features.data[0].cpu().numpy()
```

```
      ch, w, h = x.shape
      x, y = x.reshape(ch, -1), y.reshape(ch, -1)
      sim = x.T.dot(y)
      diff = y[:, sim.argmax(1)]
      diff = torch.Tensor(np.array([diff.reshape(ch, w, h)]))
      return diff

def step_next(img, model, guide, end_layer=30, distance=objective_func,
              max_jitter = 30, learning_rate = 0.05, num_iterations = 20,
              show_every = 10):
    mean = np.array([0.485, 0.456, 0.406]).reshape([3, 1, 1])
    std = np.array([0.229, 0.224, 0.225]).reshape([3, 1, 1])

    for i in range(num_iterations):

        shift_x, shift_y = np.random.randint(-max_jitter, \
                                             max_jitter + 1, 2)
        img = np.roll(np.roll(img, shift_x, -1), shift_y, -2)

        model.zero_grad()
        img_tensor = torch.Tensor(img)
        guide_tensor = torch.Tensor(guide)

        if torch.cuda.is_available():
            img_tensor = img_tensor.cuda()
            guide_tensor = guide_tensor.cuda()

        img_variable = Variable(img_tensor, requires_grad=True)
        guide_variable = Variable(guide_tensor, requires_grad=True)

        act_value = forward(model, img_variable, end_layer)
        guide_features = forward(model, guide_variable, end_layer)

        diff_out = distance(act_value, guide_features)
        act_value.backward(diff_out)

        ratio = np.abs(img_variable.grad.data.cpu().numpy()).mean()
        learning_rate_eff = learning_rate / ratio
        img_variable.data.add_(img_variable.grad.data * learning_rate_eff)

        img = img_variable.data.cpu().numpy()  # b, c, h, w
        img = np.roll(np.roll(img, -shift_x, -1), -shift_y, -2)
        img[0, :, :, :] = np.clip(img[0, :, :, :], -mean / std, \
                                  (1 - mean) / std)

        if i == 0 or (i + 1) % show_every == 0:
            show_image_tensor(img)

    return img
```

12. Finally, it is time to put the preceding implementations together in the function **deep_dream()**. Let us implement the gradient ascent using the function **step_next()** through different scales called **octaves**.

13. Load the pretrained **vgg16** model from **torcvision.models** and print the model structures. Note that including the non-linear **ReLU** activation layers, there are 30 layers in the network.

```
def deep_dream(model, base_img, end_layer=30,
                    octave_n=6, octave_scale=1.4, control=None,
                    distance=objective_func):

    octaves = [base_img]
    for i in range(octave_n - 1):
        octaves.append(ndimage.zoom(octaves[-1], (1, 1, 1.0 / octave_scale, \
                                        1.0 / octave_scale), order=1))

    detail = np.zeros_like(octaves[-1])
    for octave, octave_base in enumerate(octaves[::-1]):
        h, w = octave_base.shape[-2:]
        if octave > 0:
            h1, w1 = detail.shape[-2:]
            detail = ndimage.zoom(detail, (1, 1, 1.0 * h / h1, 1.0 * w / w1),
                                        order=1)
        input_oct = octave_base + detail
        out = step_next(input_oct, model, control, end_layer=end_layer,
                                        distance=distance)
        detail = out - octave_base

model = models.vgg16(pretrained=True)
# model # print the model structure
```

14. Use **torchvision.transforms** module to compose the transforms to the image, first converting the images to **pytorch tensors** and then normalizing the tensors, with **transforms.Normalize()** function, which accepts the mean and the standard deviation of the RGB color channels to be used for normalization.

15. Read the input and guide images with **PIL** library's **Image.open()** method and apply the composed transformation.

16. Note that by default, the image data format is **batches, channel, height, width (BCHW)** dimensions of the input image, respectively. The function **unsqueeze()** creates an additional dimension for batch as the first (0th) dimension.

```
img_transform = transforms.Compose([
    transforms.ToTensor(),
    transforms.Normalize([0.485, 0.456, 0.406], [0.229, 0.224,
    0.225])
])
input_img = np.array(Image.open('images/bbt.jpg'))
guide_img = np.array(Image.open('images/cat.jpg'))
input_tensor = img_transform(input_img).unsqueeze(0)
guide_tensor = img_transform(guide_img).unsqueeze(0)
```

The following figure shows the input image (from the TV show *The Big Bang Theory*) and the control (guide) image (of a cat) that we are going to use:

Figure 11.2: *Input and guide images for guided deep dreaming with pytorch*

17. Use GPU if available (check availability with the function **torch.cuda.is_ available()**).

18. The function **model.cuda()** by default sends the model to the current device (GPU, for example, if available).

19. We want to update the image but do not want to change the model parameters (keep them fixed). That is what is done by having **param.requires_grad = False** in the next code snippet:

```
if torch.cuda.is_available():
    model = model.cuda()
for param in model.parameters():
    param.requires_grad = False
```

20. Now, we are all set to invoke the **deep_dream()** function implemented previously, with the loaded model, the input and the control image, along with the layer where the activation maximization will happen. The complexity of the details generated in the output depends on which layer's activations we try to maximize. Higher layers produce complex features, while lower ones enhance edges and textures, giving the image an impressionist feeling.

21. The following line of code first uses one of the initial layers of VGG16 (the layer 8), leading to produce edge-like features in the output, and then it uses one of the deep layers of VGG16 (the layer 26), leading to produce complex features from the guide image (for example, eyes of cat) in the output, as shown in the following figure.

22. Use GPU (for example, run on Google Colab) to speed up the execution of the code.

```
deep_dream(model, input_tensor.numpy(), 8, control=guide_tensor.numpy())
# Layer 8
deep_dream(model, input_tensor.numpy(), 26, control=guide_tensor.numpy())
# Layer 26
```

If you run the preceding code, you should obtain a figure as follows:

Figure 11.3*: Guided deep dream with pytorch*

Neural style transfer with perceptual losses

Neural style transfer (**NST**) is a deep learning technique that applies the artistic style of one image to another while preserving its content structure. Unlike traditional methods that rely on *pixel-wise loss*, NST uses *perceptual losses* computed from high-level feature maps of a pre-trained convolutional neural network, such as VGG19. The key components of the SNT loss function include *content loss*, which measures the difference between high-level feature maps of the content image and the stylized image, and *style loss*, which uses Gram matrices of deep feature maps to capture texture and style patterns from the style image. Additionally, *total variation loss* is sometimes used to encourage spatial smoothness and remove noise.

Perceptual losses are preferred over traditional pixel-wise losses because they better capture high-level semantics, ensuring that the generated image maintains both meaningful content and style structure. This approach, introduced by *Gatys et al.* (2016), has been further improved for real-time applications using feed-forward neural networks and advanced loss functions.

Using pre-trained pytorch model

In this section, we will discuss how to implement NST using deep learning. The goal is to blend the **content** of one image with the **style** of another, producing a new image that inherits the structural elements of the content image and the aesthetic qualities of the style image. Before diving into the deep learning model, let's clarify the following key concepts:

- NST works by combining a **content** image (*C*) and a **style** image (*S*).
- The algorithm generates a third image G that merges the content of C with the style of S. Unlike most deep learning applications that train a model by adjusting

weights, NST optimizes the image pixels directly to minimize a composite loss function.

- NST typically uses a **pre-trained CNN** (e.g., VGG16 or VGG19) for feature extraction—a classic example of **transfer learning**, where a model trained on one task (e.g., image classification) is repurposed for a different task (style transfer).

- **Loss functions in NST**: NST relies on a **meta-loss function** composed of the following components:

  o **Content loss**: The earlier layers of a CNN detect low-level features (e.g., edges), while the deeper layers capture high-level features. The **middle layers** are ideal for capturing **image content**, making them a good choice for measuring content similarity. To compute content loss, we compare the feature activations of the content image $a^{(C)}$ and the generated image $a^{(G)}$ at a chosen hidden layer:

  $$\mathcal{L}_{\text{content}}(C,G) = \frac{1}{4n_C n_W n_H} \sum_{all\ entries} (a^{(C)} - a^{(G)})^2$$

  Here, n_W, n_H, and n_C are width, height, and number of channels in the chosen hidden layer, respectively. The content loss measures how different $a^{(C)}$ and $a^{(G)}$ are. Minimizing this loss ensures that G retains the content structure of C.

  o **Style loss**: To capture style, we first need to compute the Gram matrix $\mathcal{G}$, by computing the matrix of dot products from the unrolled features, and measures the **correlation** between different filter responses, effectively capturing texture and stylistic patterns. The style loss for the hidden layer l can be represented as the following:

  $$\mathcal{L}^l_{\text{style}}(S,G) = \frac{1}{4n_C^2 (n_W n_H)^2} \sum_{i=1}^{n_C} \sum_{j=1}^{n_C} (\mathcal{G}^{(S)}_{ij} - \mathcal{G}^{(G)}_{ij})^2$$

  $$\mathcal{L}^l_{\text{style}}(S,G) = \sum_l \lambda^l \mathcal{L}^l_{\text{style}}(S,G)$$ $\mathcal{G}$:Gram matrix
  l: layer

  We want to minimize the distance between the Gram matrices for the images S and G. The overall weighted style loss (which we want to minimize) is represented as shown in the preceding formula, by summing the style loss across the layers l. Here, λ^l represents the weights for layer l. Bear the following in mind:

    ▪ The style of an image can be represented using the Gram matrix of a hidden layer's activations. However, we get even better results combining this representation from multiple different layers. This is in contrast to the content representation, where usually using just a single hidden layer is sufficient.

- ▪ Minimizing the style cost will cause the image G to follow the style S of the image.

- **Overall loss (Perceptual loss)**: A cost function that minimizes both the style and the content cost is the following:

$$\mathcal{L}_{\text{total}}(G) = \alpha\mathcal{L}_{\text{content}}(C, G) + \beta\mathcal{L}_{\text{style}}(S, G)$$

This loss function is also called **perceptual loss** function [3], and it depends on high-level features from a pretrained loss network and not on low-level per-pixel loss.

Sometimes, to encourage spatial smoothness in the output image G, a total variation regularizer $TV(G)$ is also added to the RHS convex combination of perceptual loss. The next figure shows the architecture of the neural net and how it is typically trained:

- o Here, the loss network (Φ) is a pre-trained VGG16 on the ImageNet dataset.

- o The content representation is taken from the layer **relu3_3**.

- o The style representations are taken from layers **relu1_2, relu2_2, relu3_3** and **relu4_3**.

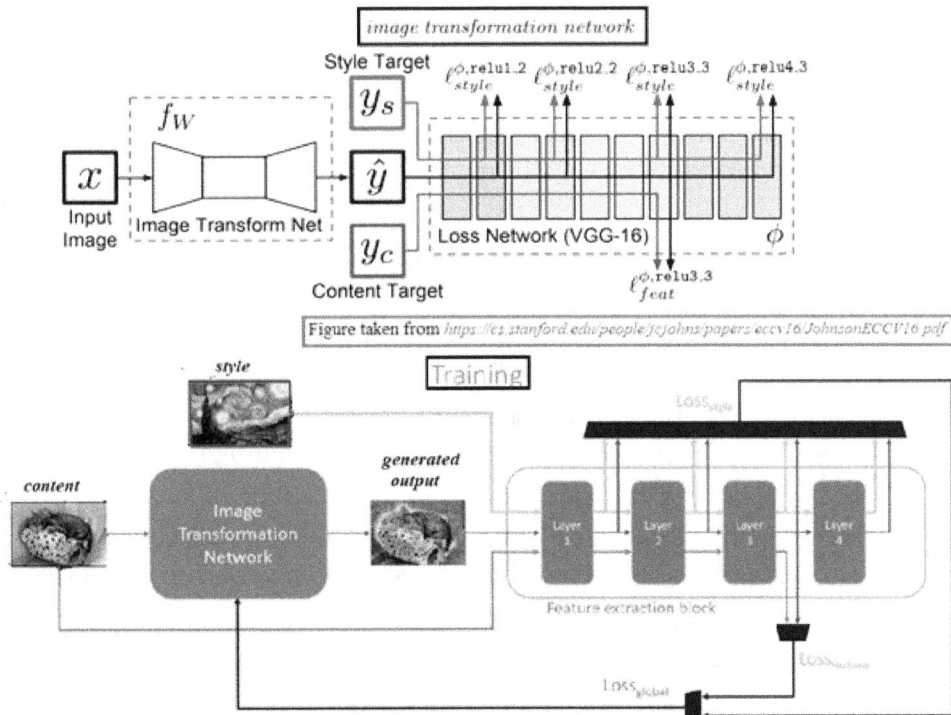

Figure 11.4: *Image transformation network for NST*
Source: *https://cs.stanford.edu/people/jcjohns/papers/eccv16/JohnsonECCV16.pdf*

In this section, however, we shall not use transfer learning (it will be particularly slow, if we use a content and a style image and run backpropagation to obtain the stylized image with iterative updates by bringing the perceptual loss down).

Instead, we shall use a few pretrained PyTorch models, each trained to apply a specific style image, for example, candy, wave, and so on.

Since each neural net model is already trained and dedicated to a particular *style* image, we shall no longer need the style images. We just need to provide a *content* image input to the pretrained neural net (with the specific style) and run inference for the particular style transfer (which will be fast). This approach enables real-time artistic style transfer using deep learning. Now, follow the next steps:

1. Let us start by importing the additional required libraries, modules, functions and classes, using the following code snippet:

```
import cv2
import torch.nn.functional as F
import torchnet as tnt
import torchfile
from skimage.io import imread
import os, time
```

2. The function **forward()** in the next code snippet applies a forward pass through the pretrained model, given the preprocessed input image **x** and the model parameters **params**.

3. The inner function **g()** extracts the *weight* and *bias* values corresponding to a layer from the pretrained model, by the name of the network layer.

4. The function **stylize()** preprocesses the input image with the transform **tr** and runs forward pass on the pretrained model with the image as input. We have a pretrained model corresponding to each style. Hence, running forward pass with the corresponding pretrained model with the input image will output a stylized image with the corresponding style.

5. The function **tnt.transform.compose()** creates a series of transformations (for example, rescaling, transposing, creating a tensor, adding new dimension etc.) to be applied on the input image.

6. The function **load_params()** loads the pretrained **torch** model from disk as a Python dictionary and converts the values to **torch** tensors to **torch** variables.

    Now, refer to the next code snippet:

```
def forward(x, params):
    def g(f, y, name, stride=1, padding=0):
        return f(y, params['%s.weight'%name], params['%s.bias'%name], \
                 stride, padding)
```

```
        x = F.relu(g(F.conv2d, x, 'c1', 1, 4))
        x = F.relu(g(F.conv2d, x, 'c2', 2, 1))
        x = F.relu(g(F.conv2d, x, 'c3', 2, 1))
        for i in range(1, 6):
            x += g(F.conv2d, F.relu(g(F.conv2d, x, 'r%d.c1'%i, padding=1)), \
                                    'r%d.c2'%i, padding=1)
        x = F.relu(g(F.conv_transpose2d, x, 'd1', 2, 1))
        x = F.relu(g(F.conv_transpose2d, x, 'd2', 2, 1))
        return g(F.conv2d, x, 'd3', 1, 4).clamp(0,255)

tr = tnt.transform.compose([
        lambda x: cv2.resize(x, (0,0), fx=0.5, fy=0.5),
        lambda x: x.transpose(2, 0, 1).astype(np.float32),
        torch.from_numpy,
        lambda x: x.contiguous().unsqueeze(0),
    ])

def stylize(im, params):
    return forward(Variable(tr(im)), params)

def load_params(filename, verbose=False):
    params = torch.load(filename)
    for k,v in sorted(params.items()):
        params[k] = Variable(v)
    return params
```

7. Next, initialize the styles array (**'candy'**, **'wave'** and so on) and the corresponding pre-trained models.

8. Load the input image using the function **imread() from the module skimage.io**.

9. For each of the pre-trained models do the following

    a.   Load the parameters using **load_params()** function.

    b.   Run a forward pass through the model using the **stylize()** function.

    c.   Use the transformation to convert the stylized output obtained to a NumPy array as a post-processing step.

    d.   Compute the time taken to stylize the image (how long inference took) using **time.time()** function.

    e.   Finally, plot the input image and the output stylized images.

Now, refer to the next code snippet:

```
styles = ['wave', 'candy', 'feathers']
model_path = 'models/'
models = ['wave.pth', 'candy.pth', 'feathers.pth']

tr_backward = tnt.transform.compose([
        lambda x: x.byte().numpy(),
        lambda x: x.transpose(1,2,0),
```

```
    ])
im = imread('images/victoria.jpg')

def plot_image(im, title):
    plt.imshow(im), plt.axis('off')
    plt.title(title, size=20)

plt.figure(figsize=(20,15))
plt.subplot(2,2,1), plot_image(im, 'Input Image')

for k in range(len(models)):
    params = load_params(os.path.join(model_path, models[k]))
    start = time.time()
    stylized = stylize(im, params)
    output = tr_backward(stylized.data[0])
    end = time.time()
    print("Neural style transfer took {:.4f} seconds" \
                                        .format(end - start))
plt.subplot(2,2,k+2)
plot_image(output, 'Neural Style Transfer Output with Style: ' + \
                                                    styles[k])
plt.tight_layout()
plt.show()
# Neural style transfer took 1.6850 seconds
# Neural style transfer took 1.6790 seconds
# Neural style transfer took 1.6181 seconds
```

If you run the preceding code snippet, you should obtain a figure as follows:

Figure 11.5: NST with PyTorch pretrained models

Real-time style transfer with pytorch ONNX model

Open Neural Network Exchange (ONNX) is an open standard format for representing machine learning models. The **torch.onnx** module can export PyTorch models to ONNX. The model can then be consumed by any of the many runtimes that support ONNX [7].

In this section, we shall explore how to import a pretrained **onnx** model using the library **onnxruntime**, with the following code snippet. ONNX Runtime is a cross-platform accelerator for machine learning model inference and training. Follow these steps to implement the real-time style transfer:

1. Use **pip** to install **onnxruntime** first, if not already installed. Import the library.

2. Load the input (*content*) image and preprocess it: for example, resize with **cv2. resize()** (note that here the input content image size needs to be 224×224), convert to **BCHW** format, by prepending the batch dimension and so on, in order to make it ready to be consumed by the model as input.

3. Load the pre-trained **onnx** model to apply the mosaic style, by running prediction (a forward pass) on the network with the input *content* image.

4. Finally, post-process the output obtained from the neural net obtain the final stylized image.

   Now, refer to the next code snippet:

```
#!pip install onnxruntime
import onnxruntime

content_image = plt.imread('images/me.jpg')
x = cv2.resize(content_image, (224,224))
x = np.array(x).astype('float32')
x = np.transpose(x, [2, 0, 1])
x = np.expand_dims(x, axis=0)
ort_session = onnxruntime.InferenceSession('models/mosaic-9.onnx')
ort_inputs = {ort_session.get_inputs()[0].name: x}
ort_outs = ort_session.run(None, ort_inputs)
img_out_y = ort_outs[0].squeeze()
result = np.clip(img_out_y, 0, 255)
result = result.transpose(1,2,0).astype("uint8")
stylized_image = Image.fromarray(result)
```

If you plot the input content and the output stylized images side-by-side, you should get the next figure:

Figure 11.6: Real-time style transfer with pytorch onnx model

Fast style transfer for arbitrary styles with TensorFlow Hub

As discussed earlier, two images are similar in *content* if their high-level features (as extracted by an image recognition system) are close in Euclidean distance. In contrast, two images are similar in *style* if their low-level features exhibit similar spatial statistics (typically measured using the Gram matrix to capture feature correlations). Here are some key points to consider:

- **Traditional NST** implementations rely on an iterative optimization procedure that updates a generated image to match a content image and a fixed style image. While this approach is effective, it is computationally expensive and does not learn a reusable representation of the painting style. To address this limitation, a separate style transfer network $T(\cdot)$ is used:

  o Typically implemented as a CNN with an **encoder–decoder** architecture.

  o Learns a transformation from a content image to a stylized image using a fixed *style* image with perceptual loss objective.

  o The parameters of the network are trained by minimizing the objective using a corpus of photographic images as content.

  o After training, the network can instantly produce a stylized output $\hat{x} = T(c)$, given a content image c. This enables **real-time inference**, but requires a separate model to be trained for each unique style.

  o The resulting network can artistically render an image dramatically faster, but a separate network must be learned for each painting style (as we have seen in the last couple of implementations).

- However, training a new network for each painting style is inefficient and wasteful because painting styles common visual patterns, color distributions, and compositional semantics.

- A trick to eliminate this waste is to build a **style transfer network** as a typical encoder/decoder architecture but specialize the conditional instance normalization parameters specific to each painting style.

- Along with this, to perform stylizations for unseen painting styles (never previously observed), an additional **style prediction network** $P(\cdot)$ is used. It takes as input an arbitrary style image s and predicts the embedding vector $\tilde{S}$ of normalization constants for the style transfer network $T(.)$, which transforms the photograph into a stylized representation.

- The *content* and *style* losses are derived from the distance in representational space of the VGG image classification network. The style prediction network largely follows the **Inception-v3** architecture. The following figure illustrates the architecture of the model [1]:

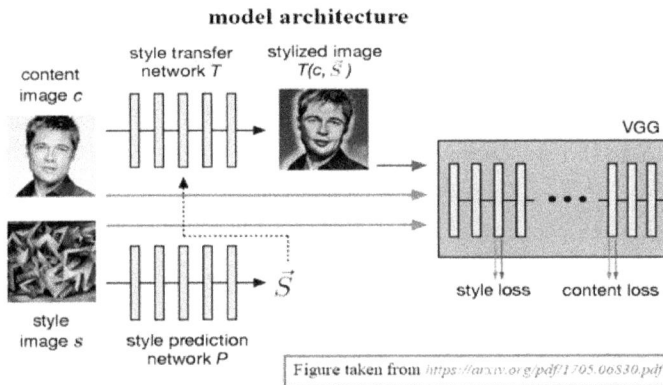

Figure 11.7: *Model architecture for fast style transfer*
Source: https://arxiv.org/pdf/1705.06830.pdf

In this section, we shall use a pretrained model again, this time from TensorFlow Hub (**magenta**). However, this time we can use arbitrary style input image to the network along with the content input image, to obtain arbitrary stylizations. Let us walk through the steps to demonstrate fast style transfer, using a pretrained neural net:

1. Let us start by importing the required libraries (for example, **tensorflow2)** and all relevant dependencies, using the following code snippet:

```
import tensorflow as tf
import tensorflow_hub as hub

print("TF Version: ", tf.__version__)        # 2.8.0
print("TF-Hub version: ", hub.__version__)   # 0.9.0
print("Eager mode enabled: ", tf.executing_eagerly())  # True
print("GPU available: ", tf.test.is_gpu_available())   # False
```

2. Load the pretrained model with **tensorflow_hub** module, using the following code snippet:

```
hub_handle = 'https://tfhub.dev/google/magenta/arbitrary-image-
stylization-v1-256/2'
hub_module = hub.load(hub_handle)
```

3. Load and preprocess an image using the **load_image()** function:

   a. Convert the image to **float32** NumPy array.

   b. Add batch dimension.

   c. Normalize to range [0,1].

4. **Content_image**, **style_image**, and **stylized_image** all are expected to be 4-D Tensors in BHWC format, with shapes **[batch_size, image_height, image_width, 3]**.

```
def load_image(image_path, image_size=(256, 256), preserve_aspect_ratio=True):
    img = plt.imread(image_path).astype(np.float32)[np.newaxis, ...]
    img = img / img.max()
    img = tf.image.resize(img, image_size, preserve_aspect_ratio=True)
    return img

content_image = load_image('images/me.jpg', (512,512))
style_image = load_image('images/bharatmata.png')
```

5. Finally, run *inference* and obtain the predicted stylized image by invoking the **hub_module()** function with the input content and style images using the following code block:

```
start = time.time()
outputs = hub_module(tf.constant(content_image), tf.constant(style_image))
stylized_image = outputs[0]
print('Time taken to run inference: {}'.format(time.time() - start))
# Time taken to run inference: 5.438430309295654
```

If you run prediction with the following given content image, along with the following two different style images (namely, *abstraction* and *Bharatmata),* and plot the input content, style and output stylized images, you should obtain an output figure as follows:

Figure 11.8: Fast neural style transfer with pretrained model from TensorFlow Hub

Image colorization with pretrained pytorch models

In this section, you will learn how to automatically obtain a photorealistic color image, given a black and white (grayscale) image, using couple of different pretrained **pytorch** models. Typically, computer vision pipelines that employ **self-supervised learning** involve performing two tasks, a *pretext task* and a *real (downstream) task*. A self-supervised model learns useful representations by generating its own training labels from the input data. **Image colorization** fits this approach well, as the model can be trained to predict the color channels (chrominance) from the grayscale input (luminance) using full-color images during training, but only grayscale images at inference. Image colorization is a classic pretext task in self-supervised learning, where the objective is to reconstruct plausible color information for grayscale images.

Since the mapping between grayscale and color is inherently ambiguous and non-deterministic (for example, a car could be red, blue, or green), multiple valid colorizations can exist for the same input. Therefore, the task is under-determined, and the model must learn priors about the world to select realistic outputs. For objects that can plausibly exhibit multiple colors, the network may average these possibilities, producing a neutral (for example, greyish) output. Recent research has improved diversity in results using latent variables and variational autoencoders.

With DeOldify

For a given image of pixels, automatic colorization can be naively seen as regression from $\mathbb{R}^N$ to $\mathbb{R}^{N\times 3}$ (involves predicting RGB values from luminance). But using a *luminance-chrominance* color space (designed to extract separately, the *luminance*: the intensity and *chrominance*: the color information, encoded in the 1st component and the other two components, respectively), the problem can be simplified to a regression from $\mathbb{R}^N$ to $\mathbb{R}^{N\times 2}$.

There exist several different luminance-chrominance color spaces, for example, CIELAB (**Commission Internationale de l'Éclairage Lab*** – a perceptually uniform color space where **L*** represents lightness, and **a*** and **b*** represent color-opponent dimensions), YUV (**Luminance (Y) and Chrominance (U, V)** – a color space that separates brightness (**Y**) from color components (**U, V**) for efficient encoding in video and image compression) and so on.

Let u be a gray-scale image of size N. Directly derive the first component in the YUV space, $u_Y = u$ and learn a transformation $F: R^N \rightarrow R^{2\times N}$ s.t., $(\hat{u}_U, \hat{u}_V) = F(u_Y)$, where $\hat{u}_U$ and $\hat{u}_V$ are the estimated second and third components in the YUV space. The under-determined structure of this problem leads to an infinity of solutions, which models well the ambiguous feature of the automatic colorization problem. The goal is to pick a realistic solution among all possible ones. Here are a few key aspects of DeOldify:

- DeOldify builds up on the idea of linking colorization with classification but in the context of *transfer learning*.

- It is an end-to-end CNN based method. The original method is presented in three different versions: *video, stable* and *artistic*.

- Uses **GAN** to colorize the image. The generator adds color to grayscale input, whereas the critic (discriminator) criticizes the coloring generated and classifies as *fake* or *real*.

- The method uses a pretrained **ResNet** (ResNet34 is used for video/stable where ResNet101 is used for artistic) as a backbone (corresponds to the encoding part) for the architecture of its network and the loss function used for optimization during training involves the intermediary feature-maps of a pretrained VGG network.

- The loss function is inspired by the feature reconstruction loss used in style transfer.

- The whole network is a **U-Net**, a classical architecture for segmentation problems.

- The *generator* is a pretrained U-Net that has been modified to include **spectral normalization** and **self-attention**.

- The method achieves strikingly good results. More surprisingly, it also yields very good results on videos in terms of temporal consistency while simply proceeding frame by frame without adding any temporal stabilization process.

The following figure shows the architecture of the network [4]:

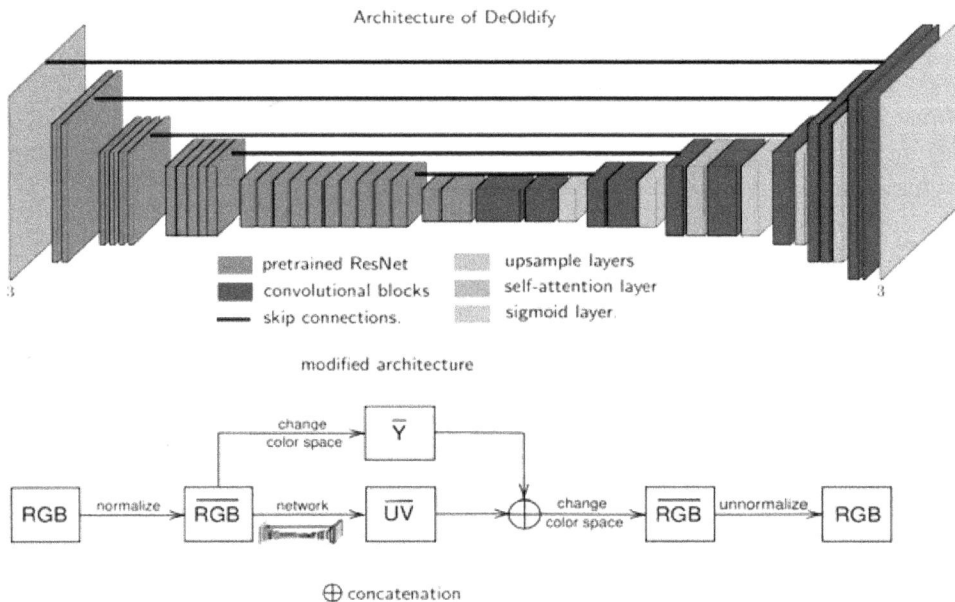

Figure 11.9: *Architecture of the DeOldify model*
Source: https://www.ipol.im/pub/art/2022/403/article_lr.pdf

- The network predicts the normalized components U and V from R, G, and B, and the unnormalization process is applied after converting the image back to RGB (since pre-trained **ResNet/VGG** requires their input images in RGB).

The model additionally uses the following technologies:

- **Self-attention layer**: Enhances the network's ability to model long-range spatial dependencies by allowing any pixel to influence any other. Its residual implementation allows optional integration. Refer to the following figure:

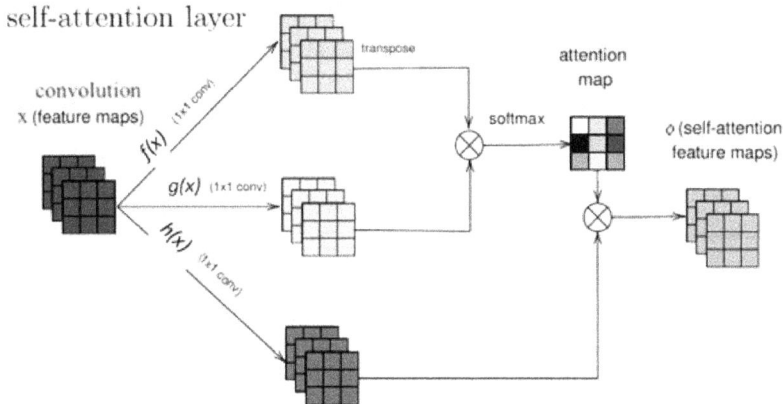

Figure 11.10: *Schematic for a self-attention layer*

- **Conventional training**: The loss function used for training is inspired by the feature reconstruction loss defined as follows, as an ℓ_1 loss (less sensitive to outliers):

$$\ell(x, y) = \lambda_0 \|x - y\|_1 + \sum_{j \in J} \lambda_j \|\phi_j(x) - \phi_j(y)\|_1$$

ϕ : pretrained VGG network
x : input image
feature maps of layer j

- **Progressive training**: During training, the image size is progressively increased. The underlying idea is that training first on small images will make the network learn large-scale image structures and as the resolution of the training images is increased, the network will learn smaller and smaller structures.

- **Spectral normalization**: Added to all convolution layers except the convolution of the last upsampling layer to stabilize network training. It provides more stable results.

- **Post-processing**: During inference, the predicted color image is converted to YUV and only the chrominance components U and V are kept. Then those components are concatenated with the luminance component Y derived from the original gray-scale image and the obtained image is converted back to RGB.

- **NoGAN training**: Combines supervised classifier training with *adversarial training*. A binary classifier is trained to detect *real* vs. *generated* colorizations. This discriminator is later reused in the GAN framework. Rather than relying on adversarial loss from the beginning, intermediate generator models are periodically evaluated, allowing refinement without full adversarial cycles.

The GAN framework encourages the generator learn what colors make an image appear realistic. If it repeatedly assigns unrealistic hues (e.g., all clothes as brown), the critic catches on. Over time, both models improve, producing increasingly plausible colorizations. So, the simple intuition is that GANs are effectively learning the loss function for you. Now, let us explore how to colorize a grayscale image using a pretrained **DeOldify** model [6], follow the next steps:

1. Start by cloning the required repository and navigating to the required folder.

```
!git clone https://github.com/jantic/DeOldify.git DeOldify
%cd DeOldify
```

2. Let us first set the device we want to load the pretrained (**pytorch**) model on, the choices for the device are CPU, GPU0, …, GPU7 (depending on the number of GPUs, if you have any), using **deoldify.device**.

3. Import everything from **deoldify.visualize** module to visualize the output colorized model.

```
#!pip install ffmpeg-python
#!pip install yt_dlp
from deoldify import device
from deoldify.device_id import DeviceId
device.set(device=DeviceId.CPU)
from deoldify.visualize import *
```

4. Invoke the function **get_image_colorizer()** to obtain an instance of the **artistic** version of the **colorizer**, with the following line of code:

```
colorizer = get_image_colorizer(artistic=True)
```

5. Finally, use the **get_transformed_image()** method from **colorizer** object to obtain the output colorized image. The method accepts the grayscale input image filename, along with the **render_factor** and the **watermarked** parameters.

   a. The default value of the **render_factor** parameter is carefully chosen to be and it should work okay for most scenarios. This determines the resolution at which the color portion of the image is rendered.

   b. A lower resolution will render faster, and colors also tend to look more vibrant. Older and lower quality images in particular will generally benefit by lowering the render factor.

c. Higher render factors are often better for higher-quality images, but the colors may get slightly washed out.

d. The **watermarked** boolean parameter, selected **True** by default, places a watermark icon of a palette at the bottom left corner of the image. This is intended to be a standard way to convey to others viewing the image that it is colorized by AI.

6. Plot the input grayscale image along with the output colorized image side-by-side.

```
render_factor = 35
imfile = '../images/butterfly.jpg'
out_img_deoldify = colorizer.get_transformed_image(imfile, \
                    render_factor=render_factor, watermarked=False)

plt.figure(figsize=(15,7))
plt.gray()
plt.subplots_adjust(0, 0, 1, 0.95, 0.05, 0.05)
plt.subplot(121), plt.imshow(plt.imread(imfile)), plt.axis('off'), \
plt.title('original', size=20)
plt.subplot(122), plt.imshow(out_img_deoldify), plt.axis('off'), \
plt.title('colorized (DeOldify)', size=20)
plt.rcParams.update({'font.size': 15,})
plt.text(475, 20, 'render_factor: ' + str(render_factor), color='white', \
                            backgroundcolor='black')
plt.show()
```

If you run the preceding code snippet, you should obtain a figure as follows:

Figure 11.11: Image colorization with DeOldify

With CIC

Colorful Image Colorization (**CIC**) is another fully automatic approach, leading to vibrant and realistic colorizations for a grayscale image. This colorization task is treated as a powerful pretext task for self-supervised feature learning, acting as a cross-channel encoder [2]. Let us look over the following points:

- The colorspace used is CIELAB color space. Given an input grayscale image with an intensity channel X (L), the objective is to learn a mapping to the two associated color channels Y (ab).

- The network architecture is shown in the following figure. Each **conv** layer refers to a block of 2 or 3 repeated **convolution** and **ReLU** layers, followed by a **BatchNorm** layer. The net has no pooling layers, only spatial down-sampling or up-sampling is used between **conv** blocks if needed.

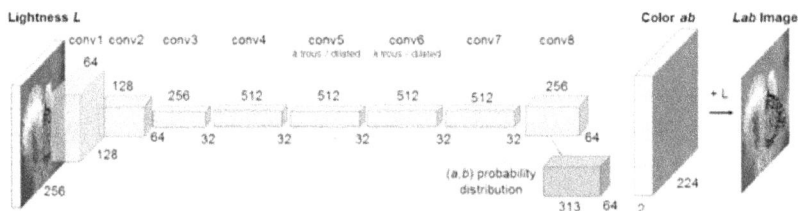

Figure 11.12: *Network architecture for CIC*
Source: https://arxiv.org/pdf/1603.08511.pdf

- The naive L_2 loss is not robust to the inherent ambiguity and multimodal nature of the colorization problem (leading to averaging effect, favoring grayish, desaturated results). Hence, multinomial classification (*cross entropy*) loss is used instead. The problem is treated as multinomial classification (at the scale of the pixels).

- The ab output space is quantized into bins with grid size 10 and $Q = 313$ values are kept, the ones that are in-gamut. For a given input X, a mapping $\hat{Z} = G(X)$ is learned as a probability distribution over possible colors, where Q is the number of quantized ab values and Z is the vector converted from the ground-truth color Y, using a soft-encoding scheme.

- The 5-nearest neighbors to $Y_{h,w}$ in the output space are selected and weighted proportionally to their distance from the ground-truth using a Gaussian kernel with $\sigma = 5$.

- The class imbalance problem is addressed by reweighting the loss of each pixel at train time based on the pixel color rarity.

- Finally, the probability distribution $\hat{Z}$ is mapped to color values $\hat{Y}$ (in ab space) with function $\hat{Y} = H(\hat{Z})$.

- **Class probabilities to point estimates**: The mode of the predicted distribution for each pixel (providing a vibrant but sometimes spatially inconsistent result) or mean can be chosen (producing spatially consistent but desaturated results).

- The metrics **perceptual realism** (assessed via **Amazon Mechanical Turk** or **AMT**, which is a crowdsourced evaluation method where human annotators assess the realism of generated images or videos) and **semantic interpretability** (with

VGG classification) are used for model evaluation. It is tested by feeding the fake colorized images to a VGG classifier. If the classifier performs well, that means the colorizations are accurate.

- The model often produces good colorizations with legacy black and white photos, even though the low-level image statistics of the legacy photographs are quite different from those of the modern-day photos.

Here we shall just use a pretrained CIC model for colorization of a grayscale image using the following code snippet. Follow the next steps, to obtain a colorized grayscale image with CIC:

1. Start by cloning the required repository and navigating to the required folder.

```
!git clone https://github.com/richzhang/colorization.git
!pip install requirements.txt
%cd colorization
```

2. Import everything from the **colorizers** module. Load the **eccv16()** and **siggraph17()** colorization models, with the *pretrained* weights.

3. Move the models to *GPU* if available.

4. Load and preprocess the input grayscale image and move to GPU, if one is available, using the next code snippet:

```
from colorizers import *
colorizer_eccv16 = eccv16(pretrained=True).eval()
colorizer_siggraph17 = siggraph17(pretrained=True).eval()
if torch.cuda.is_available():
    colorizer_eccv16.cuda()
    colorizer_siggraph17.cuda()
img = load_img(imfile)[...,:3]
(tens_l_orig, tens_l_rs) = preprocess_img(img, HW=(256,256))
if torch.cuda.is_available():
    tens_l_rs = tens_l_rs.cuda()
```

5. Invoke the colorizer models with the preprocessed inputs. Colorizers output 256×256 *ab* maps.

6. Post-process, resize and concatenate to original *L* channel, move them to CPU.

7. Plot the input grayscale image and the output colorized images, obtained using both the previous models.

```
out_img_eccv16 = postprocess_tens(tens_l_orig, \
                              colorizer_eccv16(tens_l_rs).cpu())
out_img_siggraph17 = postprocess_tens(tens_l_orig, \
                              colorizer_siggraph17(tens_l_rs).cpu())
```

```
plt.figure(figsize=(20,7))
plt.subplots_adjust(0, 0, 1, 0.95, 0.05, 0.05)
plt.subplot(131), plt.imshow(img), plt.axis('off')
plt.title('original', size=20)
plt.subplot(132), plt.imshow(out_img_eccv16), plt.axis('off') plt.
title('colorized (ECCV 16)', size=20)
plt.subplot(133), plt.imshow(out_img_siggraph17), plt.axis('off')plt.
title('colorized (SIGGRAPH 17)', size=20)
plt.show()
```

If you run the preceding code snippet, you should obtain a figure as follows:

Figure 11.13: Image colorization with ECCV 16 vs. SIGGRAPH 17 pretrained CIC models

Visualizing VGG16 features in 2D with t-SNE and classifying with SVM

In this section, we shall learn how to extract features from images with a pretrained deep neural network model, VGG16, and visualize them in 2D using a dimension reduction technique called t-SNE. We will use the images from the *dogs-vs-cats* dataset from *Kaggle*. We shall see the VGG16 features preserve the semantic similarity in between the images in the sense that the images from the same class (category) will appear nearer in 2D space, as opposed to the images from different classes, which will be further apart, in general. Now follow these steps for the demonstration:

1. Let us start by downloading the image dataset from the following link: **https://www.kaggle.com/c/dogs-vs-cats.**

    a. First you need to create a Kaggle account, if you do not already have one.

    b. Login to your Kaggle account, create an API token and download it as **JSON** file.

    c. Use Google Colab:

        i. Navigate o **https://colab.research.google.com/** and open it in your browser.

ii. Create a notebook, upload the Kaggle API token **JSON** file.

iii. You need to install the **kaggle** package, if not already done.

iv. Type in the following commands, and run to download the dataset:

```
! pip install kaggle
! mkdir ~/.kaggle
! cp kaggle.json ~/.kaggle/
! kaggle competitions download -c dogs-vs-cats
! unzip dogs*.zip
! unzip train.zip
```

A **zip** file will get downloaded, unzip it, it will create couple of **zip** files **train.zip** and **test.zip**. Uncompress the **train.zip** images; it will create image files with names starting with *cat* (**cat*.jpg**) and *dog* (**dog*.jpg**), for cats and dogs images, respectively. The training archive contains ~25K images of dogs and cats.

2. Run all of the following codes in the Colab notebook created, set the runtime type to **GPU** to speed up processing.

3. Let us start by importing the libraries required, using the following code snippet:

```
import tensorflow
import tensorflow.keras
from tensorflow.keras.preprocessing import image
from tensorflow.keras.applications.imagenet_utils import \
                    decode_predictions, preprocess_input
from tensorflow.keras.models import Model
from tensorflow.keras.applications import VGG16
from tensorflow.keras.preprocessing import image
from sklearn.model_selection import train_test_split
from sklearn.svm import SVC
from sklearn.metrics import classification_report, \
                    confusion_matrix, ConfusionMatrixDisplay
from sklearn.manifold import TSNE
import matplotlib.pylab as plt
from matplotlib.offsetbox import OffsetImage, AnnotationBbox
import numpy as np
import pandas as pd
from glob import glob
from random import choices
```

4. Now let us load the VGG16 model, pretrained on the **imagenet** images using the next code snippet. Here we will use the pretrained VGG16 model, from the module **tensorflow.keras.applications**. The following figure shows the architecture, the different layers of the deep neural network:

VGG-16 (Keras)

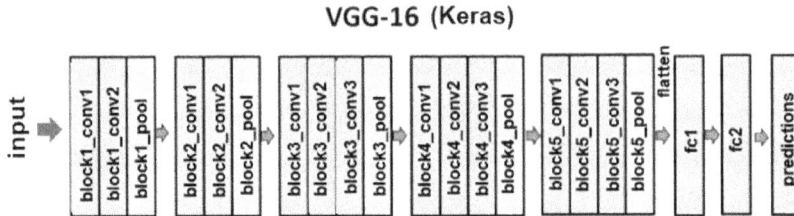

Figure 11.14: VGG-16 architecture (Keras)

a. Instantiate a VGG16 model pretrained **imagenet** day using **VGG16()**.

b. Note the parameter **include_top** is set to **True**, which will include the last two fully-connected (**fc**) layers; we shall use the last one as feature extractor.

c. **Use Model() to create a keras** model that takes the same input as the original VGG16 model but outputs the activations from the 2nd fully connected layer. Use the function **model.get_layer()** to extract the features (a vector of dimension 4096) corresponding to the layer by name (**fc2**), as done in the following code snippet:

```
model = VGG16(weights='imagenet', include_top=True)
feat_extractor = Model(inputs=model.input, \
                       outputs=model.get_Layer("fc2").output)
# feat_extractor.summary()
```

5. Read the image filenames by walking through the **train** folder, filtered by the file extension (for example, only **jpg** images) using the function **glob()** from the library **glob**.

6. Use **np.random.choices()** function to select n = 1024 cats and n = 1024 dogs images randomly from all the images. Store the corresponding ground-truth labels (class names) in the variable **labels**. Here we are choosing only 2048 ranomly sampled images for demonstration purpose.

```
n = 1024
np.random.seed(1)
labels = ['cat']*n + ['dog']*n
images = np.random.choice(glob('train/cat*.jpg'), n, replace=False).tolist() +
         np.random.choice(glob('train/dog*.jpg'), n, replace=False).tolist()
len(images)
# 2048
```

7. Load the images chosen using **load_img()** function (resized to 224×224×3, specified by the **target_size**). Create a batch of size 2048 and run a *forward pass* through the pre-trained VGG16 network to extract the features for all the images from the **fc2** layer (a feature vector of length 4096 for each of 2048 images), using the **predict()** function, as shown in the following code block:

```
x = np.zeros((len(images),224,224,3))
for i in range(len(images)):
    x[i] = image.load_img(images[i], target_size=(224,224))
feats = feat_extractor.predict(x)
print(feats.shape)
# (2048, 4096)
```

8. Now, let us introduce a popular *unsupervised* and *non-parametric* dimension-reduction algorithm called **t-SNE**, often used to visualize high dimensions feature vectors in 2D:

   a. The algorithm preserves local structure (neighborhoods) and minimizes *KL divergence* between high and low-dimensional pairwise affinities. The optimization uses gradient updates, as shown in the following *Figure 11.15*.

   b. Perplexity is a key hyperparameter that determines the number of nearest neighbors considered.

   c. The algorithm simulates attractive and repulsive forces in a particle system to place similar data points near each other.

The following figure shows the mathematical model for **t-SNE**:

t-Distributed Stochastic Neighbor Embedding (*t-SNE*)

high-dimensional pairwise similarities

$$p_{ij} = \frac{\exp\left(-\|x_i - x_j\|^2 / 2\sigma^2\right)}{\sum_{k \neq l} \exp\left(-\|x_k - x_l\|^2 / 2\sigma^2\right)}$$

Gaussian

low-dimensional map

$$q_{ij} = \frac{\left(1 + \|y_i - y_j\|^2\right)^{-1}}{\sum_{k \neq l}\left(1 + \|y_k - y_l\|^2\right)^{-1}},$$

Student t-distribution $df = 1$

gradient descent cost function

$$C = KL(P\|Q) = \sum_i \sum_j p_{ij} \log \frac{p_{ij}}{q_{ij}}.$$

Kullback-Leibler divergence

$$\frac{\delta C}{\delta y_i} = 4 \sum_i (p_{ij} - q_{ij})(y_i - y_j)\left(1 + \|y_i - y_j\|^2\right)^{-1}$$

$$y^{(t)} = y^{(t-1)} + \eta \frac{\delta C}{\delta y} + \alpha(t)\left(y^{(t-1)} - y^{(t-2)}\right) \quad Perp(P_i) = 2^{H(P_i)}, \quad H(P_i) = -\sum_j p_{j|i} \log_2 p_{j|i}$$

gradient update

Shannon entropy

Figure 11.15: t-SNE for non-parametric dimension reduction caption
Source: https://www.jmlr.org/papers/volume9/vandermaaten08a/vandermaaten08a.pdf

9. Here, we shall use the function **TSNE()** from the module **sklearn.manifold** for reducing the dimension of the feature vectors from 4096 to 2 (set **n_components=2**), using the following code snippet. Let us use random initialization of embedding, set **perplexity** to 3 (try different values of this hyperparameter and see the impact on dimension reduction) and **learnung_rate** to **auto**:

```
tsne = TSNE(n_components=2, learning_rate='auto', init='random', perplexity=3)
       .fit_transform(np.array(feats))
df = pd.DataFrame({'tsne-2d-one': tsne[:,0], 'tsne-2d-two': tsne[:,1], \
       'label': labels})
df.head()
```

The following figure shows the **DataFrame**, with each data point as a 2D **t-SNE** representation on an image, along with the ground-truth label.

	tsne-2d-one	tsne-2d-two	label
0	15.748092	9.109365	cat
1	19.970919	-15.171882	cat
2	33.246052	10.163391	cat
3	11.935716	-7.471368	cat
4	34.340569	-4.774371	cat

Figure 11.16: DataFrame with 2D t-SNE features and the class label

Now, let us explore whether we can classify the cats and dogs correctly using these 2-D features using the following code snippet. Here is a detailed explanation of the code:

1. Split the sample images into *train* and *test* dataset (with the **train_test_split()** function from the module **sklearn.model_selection**).

2. Train a support vector machine classifier (instantiate **SVC()** from **sklearn.svm**) with **linear** *kernel* on the train dataset (with train labels).

3. Use the model to *predict* the classes for the unseen *test* images using the classifier object's **predict()** method.

4. Display the *confusion matrix* and the *classification report* to evaluate the classifier.

5. As can be seen, the accuracy is quite high on the small test samples (92%).

   Now, refer to the next code snippet:

```
X = df.values
X = X[:, :2]
y = df.label.values
X_train, X_test, y_train, y_test = train_test_split(X, y,
                                    test_size=0.33, random_state=42)
clf = SVC(kernel="linear").fit(X_train, y_train)
y_pred = clf.predict(X_test)
cm = confusion_matrix(y_test, y_pred, labels=clf.classes_)
disp = ConfusionMatrixDisplay(confusion_matrix=cm,
                              display_labels=clf.classes_)
disp.plot()
plt.show()
print(classification_report(y_test, y_pred))
```

If you run the preceding code snippet, you should obtain a figure as follows:

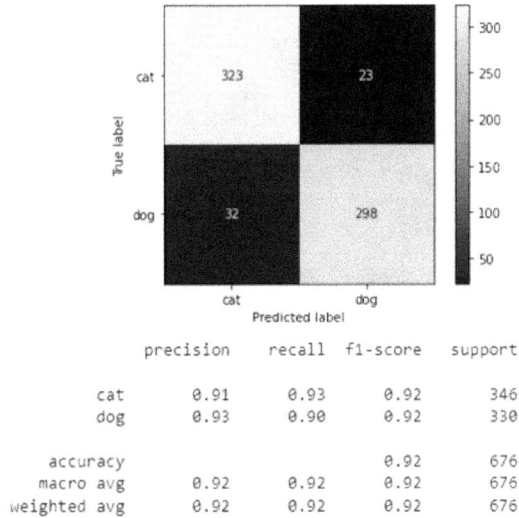

```
              precision    recall  f1-score   support

         cat       0.91      0.93      0.92       346
         dog       0.93      0.90      0.92       330

    accuracy                          0.92       676
   macro avg       0.92      0.92      0.92       676
weighted avg       0.92      0.92      0.92       676
```

Figure 11.17: *Add a caption*

6. Finally, plot the 2D points obtained by applying **t-SNE** to the **VGG16** feature vectors. Use different colors for the points as per their class labels. Plot a few of the images corresponding to the 2D points on the plot using **AnnotationBbox()**, as shown in the following code snippet.

7. Notice how the points are well-separated in 2D. The points corresponding to the cat images lie on one side and those corresponding to dogs lie on the other side.

8. Plot the decision surface and the decision boundary using the **SVC** classifier trained (left as an exercise). You should obtain a figure like the following *Figure 11.18*.

Now, refer to the following code snippet:

```python
plt.figure(figsize=(20,20))
ax = plt.gca()
sns.scatterplot(x="tsne-2d-one", y="tsne-2d-two", hue="label", \
    palette=sns.color_palette("hls", 10), data=df, legend="full", alpha=0.7)

artists = []
x, y = np.atleast_1d(df['tsne-2d-one'].values, df['tsne-2d-two'].values)
for i, row in df.iterrows():
    if random() > 0.95: # plot images 5% of the times
        ab = AnnotationBbox(OffsetImage( \
        cv2.resize(plt.imread(images[i]), (50,50)), zoom=1), \
        (row['tsne-2d-one'],row['tsne-2d-two']), xycoords='data', frameon=False)
        artists.append(ax.add_artist(ab))
ax.update_datalim(np.column_stack([x, y]))
ax.autoscale()
```

Refer to the following figure:

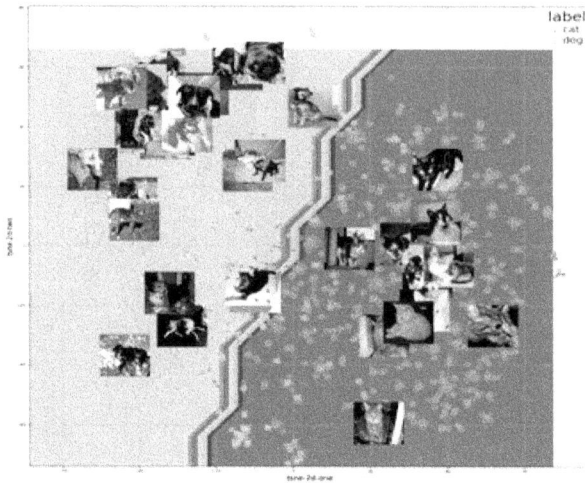

Figure 11.18: *Decision surface/boundary for the binary cat vs. dog classifier with SVC*

Creating point cloud from images

A **point cloud** is a discrete set of data points in space. The points may represent a 3D shape or object. Each point position has its set of cartesian coordinates *(x, y, z)*. Compared to 2D images, 3D point cloud data provides rich geometric, shape, and scale information. It is less affected by variations in lighting and occlusion, making it highly valuable for scene understanding. 3D point cloud semantic segmentation is widely used in applications such as autonomous driving, robotics, and augmented reality. In the context of self-driving cars, for instance, it helps the vehicle interpret and understand its surrounding environment.

In this section, you will learn how to create **point cloud** from images. We shall approach this in two steps:

1. Create a **depth map** (dense prediction) **RGB-D** image from given input **RGB** image.

2. Generate a **point cloud** from the **depth map**.

Creating depth map with vision transformers

Dense prediction or **depth-map** denotes the distance of a scene point from the camera. In this section, we will use a pre-trained **vision transformer** architecture, specifically **Monocular Depth Estimation (MiDaS)**, which is highly effective for generating dense depth predictions. This architecture excels at disambiguating complex visual content and producing fine-grained depth estimates. The following *Figure 11.19* shows the architecture of the deep learning model [10]:

Vision Transformers for Dense Prediction

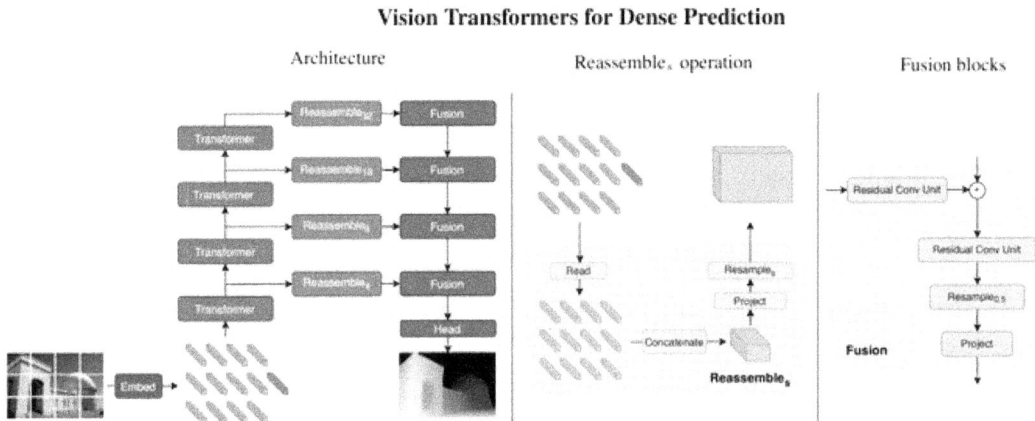

Figure 11.19: *Vision transformers for dense prediction*
Source: https://arxiv.org/pdf/2103.13413.pdf

Here is a brief explanation of the preceding figure:

- The input image is transformed into *tokens* (orange) by extracting *non-overlapping patches* followed by a linear projection of their flattened representation (for example, with *DPT-Large*).

- The image embedding is augmented with a *positional embedding* and a patch-independent *readout token* (red) is added.

- The tokens are passed through multiple *transformer* stages and are reassembled into an image-like representation (feature maps) at multiple resolutions (green).

- *Fusion modules* (purple) progressively fuse and up sample the representations to generate a fine-grained prediction.

- *Fusion blocks* combine features using *residual convolutional* units and upsample the feature map.

Now let us deep dive into the actual implementation, with the following key steps to be followed:

1. Start by importing the required libraries and modules, as usual.

```
import open3d as o3d
import torch
import cv2
from glob import glob
import matplotlib.pylab as plt
```

2. **MiDaS (https://pytorch.org/hub/intelisl_midas_v2/)** estimates relative inverse depth from a single image. It depends on the library **timm**, so it needs to be installed first.

3. Read the **JPEG** images from the folder **images/pcl/input** one by one, traversing the folder using the function **glob.glob()**.

4. Load a pretrained model (for example, **MiDaS v3 - Large**, which offers higher accuracy but slower inference speed).

5. Load and apply appropriate image transforms (for example, resizing and normalization) depending on whether a large or small model is used.

6. Move the model and tensors to **GPU,** if available, for faster processing.

7. Generate the depth map prediction and resize it back to the original image resolution.

8. Save the resulting depth-map using **plt.imsave()**.

Now, refer to the following code snippet:

```python
#! pip install timm
model_type = "DPT_Large"

for filename in glob('images/pcl/input/*.jpg'):
  img = cv2.imread(filename)
  img = cv2.cvtColor(img, cv2.COLOR_BGR2RGB)

  midas = torch.hub.load("intel-isl/MiDaS", model_type)

  device = torch.device("cuda") if torch.cuda.is_available() else \
                                   torch.device("cpu")
  midas.to(device)
  midas.eval()

  midas_transforms = torch.hub.load("intel-isl/MiDaS", "transforms")

  transform = midas_transforms.dpt_transform
  input_batch = transform(img).to(device)

  with torch.no_grad():
      prediction = midas(input_batch)
      prediction = torch.nn.functional.interpolate(
          prediction.unsqueeze(1),
          size=img.shape[:2],
          mode="bicubic",
          align_corners=False,
      ).squeeze()

  output = prediction.cpu().numpy()
  img = img / img.max()
  output = cv2.normalize(output, None, 0, 1, norm_type=cv2.NORM_MINMAX, \
                                           dtype=cv2.CV_32F)
  plt.imsave('images/pcl/col_{}'.format(filename.split('/')[-1]), img)
  plt.imsave('images/pcl/depth_{}'.format(filename.split('/')[-1]),
  output)
```

Creating point cloud from depth map with Open3D

Let's now learn how to create **point cloud** from **depth map** images using the **Open3D** library. This process involves combining color and depth data to produce a 3D spatial representation of a scene. Let us go through the steps:

1. The first step is to combine an RGB image and its corresponding depth image (obtained for a given input image in the last section), using the function **RGBDImage. create_from_color_and_depth()** from **open3d.geometry** module. This creates an RGB-D image where depth is encoded as an additional channel.

2. Let us visualize the **depth maps** for a couple of RGB images, using the following code snippet:

```
for imf in ['victoria', 'whale']:
    im = plt.imread("images/pcl/col_{}.jpg".format(imf))
    color_raw = o3d.io.read_image("images/pcl/col_{}.jpg".format(imf))
    depth_raw = o3d.io.read_image("images/pcl/depth_{}.jpg".format(imf))
    rgbd_image = o3d.geometry.RGBDImage.create_from_color_and_depth(color_raw,
                                                                    depth_raw)

    plt.figure(figsize=(15,10))
    plt.subplots_adjust(0,0,1,0.95,0.05,0.05)
    plt.subplot(121), plt.title('input color image', size=20), plt.imshow(im)
    plt.subplot(122)
    plt.title('depth-map image obtained with deep learning model', size=20)
    plt.imshow(rgbd_image.depth, cmap='nipy_spectral'), plt.axis('off')
    plt.show()
```

If you run the preceding code snippet, you should obtain a figure as follows:

Figure 11.20: *Creating point cloud from depth map with Open3D*

3. With an **RGB-D** image created, let us now compute the **point cloud** from it. The point cloud to be computed is also called 2.5D **point cloud**, since it is estimated from a 2D depth image, rather than full 3D sensors like *LIDAR*. Here are the steps to compute the point cloud:

   a. **Depth camera calibration**: First let us calibrate (estimate the **intrinsic parameters** of) the depth camera to compute the camera matrix and then use it to compute the point cloud. Here, we shall use built-in intrinsic parameters from Open3D for common devices like *PrimeSense*. The calibration matrix M is a 3×3 matrix, shown in *Figure 11.21*.

   b. **Computation of the point cloud**: Transforming the depth pixel (u, v) from the depth image *2D* coordinate system to the depth camera *3D* coordinate system (x, y, z), using the following formulae shown in *Figure 11.21*, where $depth(x, y)$ is the depth value at (x, y) obtained from the depth image [9]:

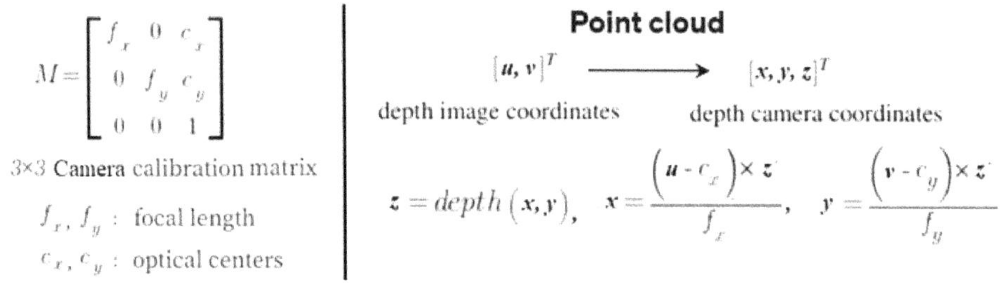

$$M = \begin{bmatrix} f_x & 0 & c_x \\ 0 & f_y & c_y \\ 0 & 0 & 1 \end{bmatrix}$$

3×3 **Camera** calibration matrix

f_x, f_y : focal length

c_x, c_y : optical centers

Point cloud

$$[u, v]^T \longrightarrow [x, y, z]^T$$

depth image coordinates   depth camera coordinates

$$z = depth(x, y), \quad x = \frac{(u - c_x) \times z}{f_x}, \quad y = \frac{(v - c_y) \times z}{f_y}$$

Figure 11.21: *Computing point cloud from depth-map*

4. Let us print the camera intrinsic parameters obtained using the function **o3d.camera.PinholeCameraIntrinsic()**. As can be seen, the focal length of the camera for both x and y axis is 525 and the optical center is located at (319.5,239.5).

```
camera_intrinsic = o3d.camera.PinholeCameraIntrinsic( \
           o3d.camera.PinholeCameraIntrinsicParameters.PrimeSenseDefault)
print(camera_intrinsic.intrinsic_matrix)
# [[525.     0.   319.5]
#  [  0.   525.   239.5]
#  [  0.     0.     1. ]]
```

5. Create the **point cloud** from the input **RGBD** image and the camera intrinsic matrix, using the factory (static) method **create_from_rgbd_image()** from the class **o3d.geometry.PointCloud**, as done in the following code snippet. Given depth value d at (u, v) image coordinate, the corresponding 3D point (x, y, z) is computed as shown in *Figure 11.21*.

6. **Post-processing**: Flip the returned point cloud (using a *reflection matrix*). Otherwise, it will be upside down.

7. Visualize the point cloud created from RGBD images, as shown in *Figure 11.22*.

```
pcd = o3d.geometry.PointCloud.create_from_rgbd_image(rgbd_image, camera_intrinsic)
pcd.transform([[1, 0, 0, 0], [0, -1, 0, 0], [0, 0, -1, 0], [0, 0, 0, 1]])
vis = o3d.visualization.Visualizer()
vis.create_window()
vis.add_geometry(pcd)
o3d.visualization.ViewControl.set_zoom(vis.get_view_control(), 0.5)
vis.run()
```

If you run the preceding code snippet, you should obtain a figure as follows:

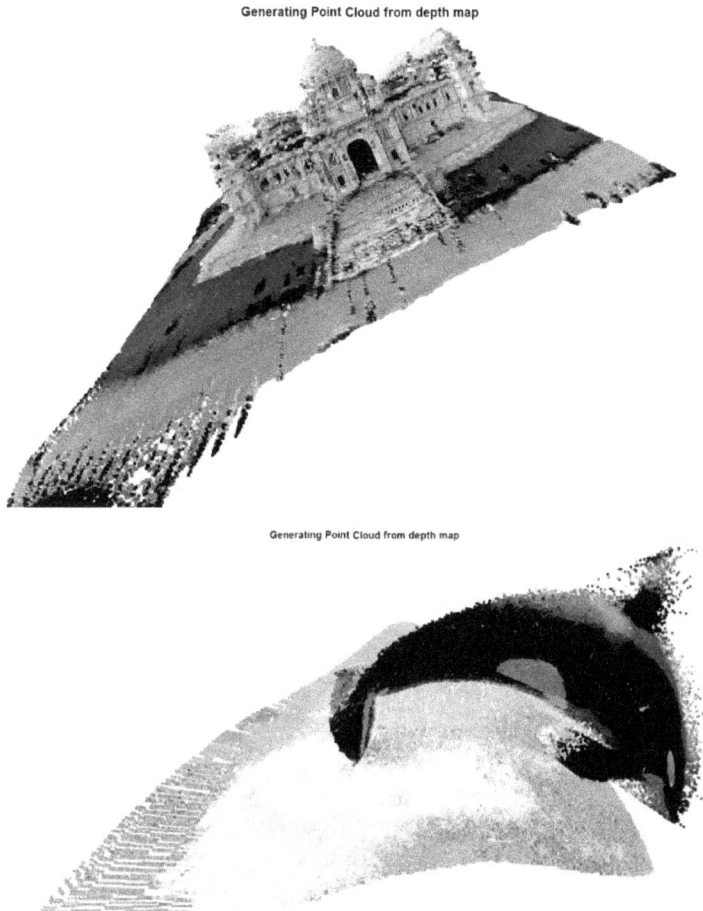

Figure 11.22: Generating point clouds with Open3D

Augmented reality with opencv-python

Augmented reality (**AR**) aims at integrating virtual information (for example, text, graphics and so on) with real-world objects, to enhance the environment. It adds value to the user's interaction with the real world, as opposed to a simulation, as done in case of **virtual reality** (**VR**). AR uses the existing real-world environment and adds additional virtual information; in other words, it presents users with virtual objects in their natural environment. For example, users, who are looking at their smartphone/tablet screen, will be able to see enhanced information about the things they are looking at using AR-enhanced apps.

In this section, we will use **opencv-python** to create (real-time) AR-enhanced frames obtained from a webcam (for example, laptop camera). A 3D horse model object will be added to the video frames on top of the surface of a book (to be used as *marker* image - a predefined, recognizable image used as a reference point to place virtual objects within the camera frame) according to the position and orientation of the book. Here are the key steps to create an AR-enhanced *webcam* environment:

1. Start capturing video frames with webcam (with **opencv-python**).

2. Hold the front surface of the book (which corresponds to the *marker* image) in front of the camera (in different poses) so that it can be detected.

3. Enhance the webcam environment by adding a projection of a 3D *object* model on top of the surface of the book.

Now, let us carefully go through the following detailed steps, to setup the *marker* image and load the 3D model object for AR:

1. Start by importing the libraries required for the implementation.

```
import numpy as np
import cv2
import matplotlib.pylab as plt
from IPython.display import display, Image
```

2. Specify the *marker* image file (a book cover JPEG image) and the *3D object model* (a **Wavefront OBJ** file), using the next line of code:

```
marker, model3d = 'images/book_cover.jpg', 'models/horse.obj'
```

The following figure shows the image of the cover page of the book, to be used as *marker* in the video frames and the 3D *horse* object model (to be rendered and projected onto the frames), to be used to create the AR-enhanced environment:

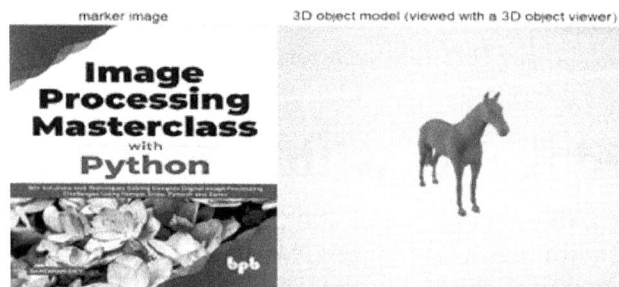

Figure 11.23: Marker image and 3D object model to be used for AR

3. The class **OBJ** defined in the following code snippet loads a **Wavefront OBJ** file when instantiated (the constructor **init()** implements a simplified version of an OBJ file parser).

4. As can be seen from the Wavefront OBJ file format (a widely-used plain text file format that represents 3D geometry) shown in *Figure 11.24*, a 3D model OBJ file contains different sections such as **vertices** (v), **vertex normals** (vn), **texture coordinates** (vt), **faces** (f) and so on, that need to be processed separately and stored. The lines starting with '**#**' indicate comments and they will be ignored while parsing the OBJ file.

5. The class OBJ will be used to load the 3D horse model object. Part of the file's contents are shown in the following figure (it shows how the *obj* file looks when opened with a text editor):

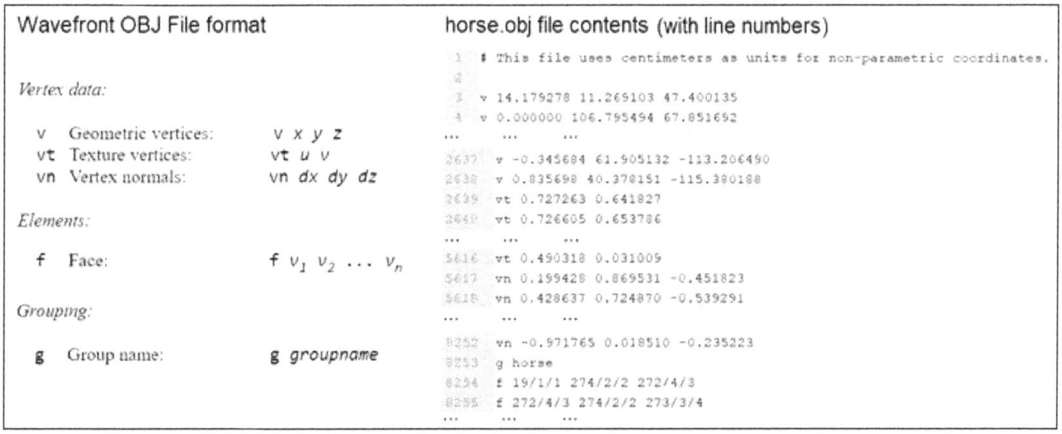

Wavefront OBJ File format			horse.obj file contents (with line numbers)
			1 # This file uses centimeters as units for non-parametric coordinates.
Vertex data:			2
			3 v 14.175278 11.269103 47.400135
v	Geometric vertices:	v *x y z*	4 v 0.000000 106.795494 67.851652
vt	Texture vertices:	vt *u v*	... ...
vn	Vertex normals:	vn *dx dy dz*	2637 v -0.345684 61.905132 -113.206490
			2638 v 0.835698 40.378151 -115.380188
Elements:			2639 vt 0.727263 0.641827
			2640 vt 0.726605 0.653786
f	Face:	f *v₁ v₂ ... vₙ*	... ...
			5616 vt 0.490318 0.031005
			5617 vn 0.199428 0.869531 -0.451823
			5618 vn 0.428637 0.724870 -0.539291
Grouping:			... ...
			8252 vn -0.971765 0.018510 -0.235223
g	Group name:	g *groupname*	8253 g horse
			8254 f 19/1/1 274/2/2 272/4/3
			8255 f 272/4/3 274/2/2 273/3/4
			... ...

Figure 11.24: Contents of the object model file

Now, refer to the next code snippet:

```python
class OBJ:
    def __init__(self, filename, swapyz=False):
        self.vertices = []
        self.normals = []
        self.texcoords = []
        self.faces = []
        for line in open(filename, "r"):
            if line.startswith('#'): continue
            values = line.split()
            if not values: continue
            if values[0] == 'v':
                v = list(map(float, values[1:4]))
                if swapyz:
                    v = v[0], v[2], v[1]
```

```
                self.vertices.append(v)
        elif values[0] == 'vn':
            v = list(map(float, values[1:4]))
            if swapyz:
                v = v[0], v[2], v[1]
            self.normals.append(v)
        elif values[0] == 'vt':
            self.texcoords.append(map(float, values[1:3]))
        elif values[0] == 'f':
            face = []
            texcoords = []
            norms = []
            for v in values[1:]:
                w = v.split('/')
                face.append(int(w[0]))
                if len(w) >= 2 and len(w[1]) > 0:
                    texcoords.append(int(w[1]))
                else:
                    texcoords.append(0)
                if len(w) >= 3 and len(w[2]) > 0:
                    norms.append(int(w[2]))
                else:
                    norms.append(0)
            self.faces.append((face, norms, texcoords))
```

Creating the AR environment consists of the following steps:

a. Recognize the reference flat surface (*marker* image).

b. Estimate the *homography* (to transform the surface coordinate system to the target frame coordinate system).

c. Compute the *3D projection matrix* (from the *homography* and the *camera parameters*).

d. Project the 3D model object onto the video frame (pixel space) and draw it.

Before projecting the 3D object on a video frame, we must find and grab the reference flat (book) surface (corresponding to the *marker* image) inside the video frame. We shall implement the recognition of the target book surface using feature extraction and matching (using **ORB** rotation-invariant fast feature detector and descriptor). From the matched points, we can estimate the *projective transformation matrix*. These are precisely done in the steps 6.*a* and 6.*b*, respectively, as described.

Let us start implementing the preceding steps *a-d*, by following the next steps:

1. Define the function **render()**, which renders (projects) the loaded 3D **obj** model into the current video **frame**.

   a. We want to render the model in the middle of the reference surface (**marker**). To do so, model points must be displaced by half the width and height of the marker image.

    b. Since the actual size of the model with respect to the rest of the frame may be unknown, we may have to scale it (using the **scale_matrix**, set to be identity matrix, to start with) to have the desired size.

    c. The feature points (**feature_pts**) used to detect the *marker* image inside the video frame will be highlighted in red circles.

2.   The 3D **obj** model is already loaded, just project the corresponding **points** on top of the video **frame** with the right **projection** matrix (with matrix multiplication, using the function **cv2.perspectiveTransform()**).

3.   Once the projection is done, fill the faces of the projected horse model with a color (for example, use the color *cremello* or *palomino*), using the function **cv2.fillConvexPoly()**, which fills the convex polygon defined by the given input points (**dst**) with the given color (specified by BGR values) and draws on the input **frame**.

Now, refer to the next code snippet:

```
def render(frame, obj, projection, marker, feature_pts):

    for pt in np.reshape(feature_pts.astype('int32'), (-1,2)):
        frame = cv2.circle(frame, pt, 1, (0,0,255), 2)

    vertices = obj.vertices
    scale_matrix = np.eye(3) # * 3
    h, w = marker.shape

    for face in obj.faces:
        face_vertices = face[0]
        points = np.array([vertices[vertex - 1] for vertex in face_vertices])
        points = np.dot(points, scale_matrix)
        points = np.array([[p[0] + w / 2, p[1] + h / 2, p[2]] for p in points])
        dst = cv2.perspectiveTransform(points.reshape(-1, 1, 3), projection)
        cv2.fillConvexPoly(frame, np.int32(dst), (135,181,222))

    return frame
```

4.   Define the function **compute_projection_matrix()**to to compute the 3D projection matrix, given the *camera calibration matrix A* (**camera_parameters**) and the estimated *homography matrix H*, as shown in the next code snippet. *Figure 11.25* shows the math required to compute the 3D projection matrix (we need to ensure that the rotation basis vectors computed for the final matrix are orthonormal):

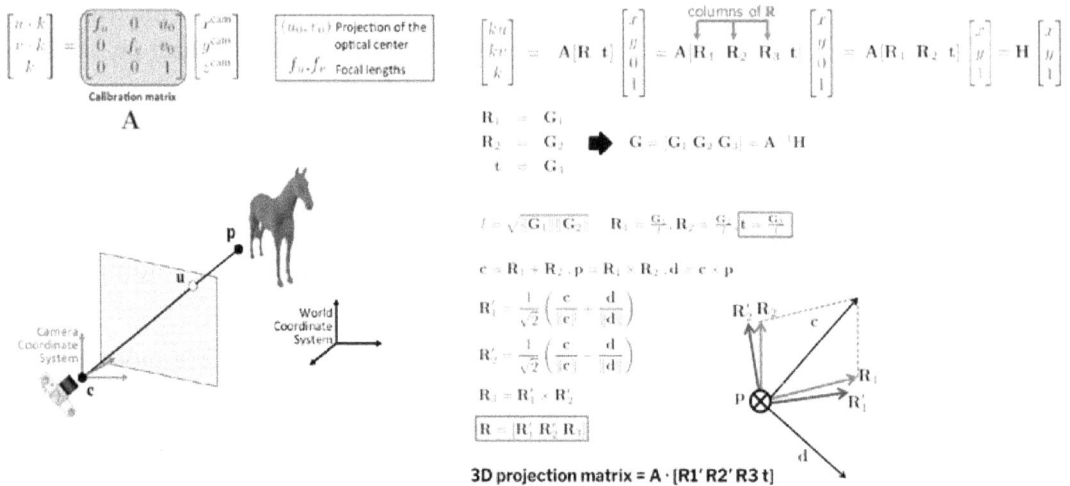

Figure 11.25: Computing the 3D projection matrix given the camera calibration and homography matrix
Source: https://bitesofcode.wordpress.com/2018/09/16/augmented-reality-with-python-and-opencv-part-2/

5. The function computes the rotations along the x and y axis, as well as the translation, and then it normalizes the vectors as shown in the preceding figure.

6. Next, it computes the orthonormal basis and the 3D projection matrix from the reference surface (**world coordinates**) to the current frame (**camera coordinates**).

```python
def compute_projection_matrix(A, H):

    H = H * (-1)
    R_t = np.dot(np.linalg.inv(A), H)
    R_1, R_2, R_3 = R_t[:, 0], R_t[:, 1], R_t[:, 2]
    l = np.sqrt(np.linalg.norm(R_1, 2) * np.linalg.norm(R_2, 2))
    R_1, R_2, t = R_1 / l, R_2 / l, R_3 / l
    c = R_1 + R_2
    p = np.cross(R_1, R_2)
    d = np.cross(c, p)
    R_1 = np.dot(c / np.linalg.norm(c, 2) + d / np.linalg.norm(d, 2), 1 \
                                                     / np.sqrt(2))
    R_2 = np.dot(c / np.linalg.norm(c, 2) - d / np.linalg.norm(d, 2), 1 \
                                                     / np.sqrt(2))
    R_3 = np.cross(R_1, R_2)
    projection = np.stack((R_1, R_2, R_3, t)).T
    return np.dot(A, projection)
```

Finally, the next code snippet defines the function **add_augmented_reality()** which creates the AR environment (combines all the steps described previously), by adding the projected 3D model object (**model3d**) on top of the reference book surface (**marker**) on the webcam video frames. Here is a detailed breakdown of the code step-by-step:

1. First, let us load the 3D model from **.obj** file using the **OBJ** class constructor (specifies axis swap with **swapyz=True**). Load the gray-scale **marker** image (of the front page of the book - the target surface image) with **cv2.imread()** function. This is the reference surface that will be searched for in the video stream.

2. Instantiate **oriented BRIEF (ORB)** keypoint detector using the function **cv2.ORB_create()**. Extract features (*keypoints*) and compute the corresponding descriptors for the **marker** image, using the method **detectAndCompute()**.

3. Instantiate a *Brute-Force descriptor matcher* object based on hamming distance, using **cv2.BFMatcher()**.

4. Start capturing video from the webcam with **cv2.VideoCapture()** and read frames iteratively in real-time (until we have finished reading a total of **max_num_frames**). This is the time when you need to hold the surface corresponding to the marker image (here, the front surface of the book) facing toward the camera in different poses.

5. Read the *current frame*, extract the keypoints and descriptors, and match the descriptors with the *marker* descriptors computed earlier to recognize and detect the book surface inside each frame. Sort them in the order of their distance (the lower the distance, the better the match).

6. If enough matches are found (number of matches must be greater than **min_matches**, the minimum number of matches needed for valid recognition, chosen to be 10 here), estimate the **homography** matrix (for projective transformation from the **src_pts** belonging to the reference *marker* and the **dst_pts** belonging to the *current frame*) using the function **cv2.findHomography()** with the *RANSAC* algorithm, to keep the good matches (*inliers*) providing the correct estimation and filtering out the remaining bad matches (*outliers*), specified with the **mask** returned.

7. Compute the 3D projection matrix using the function **compute_projection_matrix()** (from the **homography** matrix and **camera_parameters**) and project the 3D model object on the identified reference surface in the frame (to AR-enhance), using the function **render()** defined earlier. Draw keypoints corresponding to the good matches on the frame with red circles.

8. Save the current input frame to input path ("images/ar/input/") and the AR-enhanced output frame to the output path ("images/ar/output/").

9. The following **camera_parameters** (camera calibration matrix) defined in the next code block works well; it can be tweaked or even can be estimated for better projection.

Now, refer to the next code snippet:

```python
min_matches = 10
camera_parameters = np.array([[800, 0, 320], [0, 800, 240], [0, 0, 1]])

def add_augmented_reality(marker, model3d, max_num_frames=100):
    obj = OBJ(model3d, swapyz=True)
    marker = cv2.imread(marker, 0)
    orb = cv2.ORB_create()
    kp_marker, des_marker = orb.detectAndCompute(marker, None)
    bf = cv2.BFMatcher(cv2.NORM_HAMMING, crossCheck=True)

    cap = cv2.VideoCapture(0)
    display_handle=display(None, display_id=True)
    num_frames = 0
    try:
        while True:
            ret, frame = cap.read()
            if not ret:
                print("Unable to capture video")
                return
            in_frame = frame.copy()
            kp_frame, des_frame = orb.detectAndCompute(frame, None)
            matches = bf.match(des_marker, des_frame)
            matches = sorted(matches, key=lambda x: x.distance)
            if len(matches) > min_matches:
                src_pts = np.float32([kp_marker[m.queryIdx].pt \
                                    for m in matches]).reshape(-1, 1, 2)
                dst_pts = np.float32([kp_frame[m.trainIdx].pt \
                                    for m in matches]).reshape(-1, 1, 2)
                homography, mask = cv2.findHomography(src_pts, dst_pts, \
                                            cv2.RANSAC, 5.0)
                if homography is not None:
                    try:
                        projection = compute_projection_matrix( \
                                        camera_parameters, homography)
                        frame = render(frame, obj, projection, marker, \
                                        dst_pts[mask])
                    except Exception as err:
                        print(err)
                        pass
                cv2.imwrite('images/ar/input/frame_{:03d}.jpg' \
                                .format(num_frames), in_frame)
                cv2.imwrite('images/ar/output/frame_{:03d}.jpg' \
                                .format(num_frames), frame)
                out_frame = np.concatenate((in_frame, frame), axis=1)
                _, out_frame = cv2.imencode('.jpeg', out_frame)
                display_handle.update(Image(data=out_frame.tobytes()))
```

```
                if num_frames > max_num_frames: break
                num_frames += 1
            else:
                print("Not enough matches found: {}/{}" .format(len(matches), \
                                            min_matches))

    except KeyboardInterrupt:
        pass
    finally:
        cap.release()
        display_handle.update(None)
```

10. Invoke the function **add_augmented_reality()** with the reference surface image and the 3D model obj path.

11. The ORB keypoints corresponding to good matches are shown as small red dots in the output.

    Refer to the next line of code, that does the job:

```
add_augmented_reality(marker, model3d)
```

The following figure shows an input video frame and the corresponding AR-enhanced output frame, obtained by running the preceding line of code:

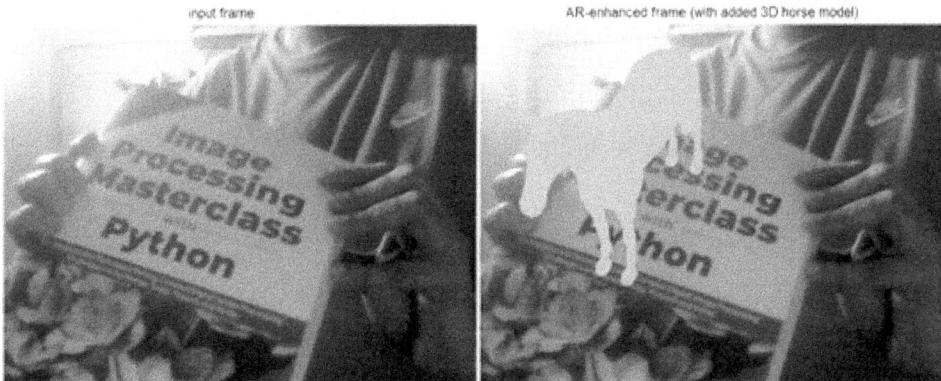

Figure 11.26: Matching ORB keypoints and enhancing frame with AR

The next figure shows a few AR-enhanced frames obtained applying the AR on a few frames from the webcam:

Figure 11.27: *AR-enhanced frames*

Since we are using real-time videos, the performance of surface object (book) detection can be enhanced with object tracking, which we are not doing here; it is left as an exercise for the user.

Embedding and playing video with moviepy

In this section, we will explore how to use **moviepy** library functions to embed video clips at different regions of an image and create a composite video clip to display all the clips together. Follow the given steps to achieve the same:

1. Let us start by importing the required libraries using the following code snippet:

```python
# ! pip install moviepy
from moviepy.editor import *
from moviepy.video.tools.segmenting import findObjects
from moviepy.video.tools.subtitles import SubtitlesClip
import cv2
import numpy as np
import matplotlib.pylab as plt
from glob import glob
```

2. Load the image containing the regions where we want to show the video clips. Display the image.

```
image = "images/screen.png"
plt.figure(figsize=(10,10))
plt.imshow(cv2.cvtColor(cv2.imread(image), cv2.COLOR_BGR2RGB)),
plt.axis('off')
plt.title('Original image', size=25)
plt.show()
```

If you run the preceding code snippet, you should obtain a figure as follows. The image contains 5 regions, hence we can embed 5 different video clips in these regions and play them simultaneously.

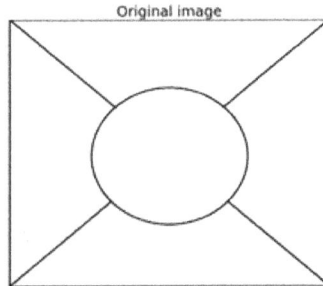

Figure 11.28: Cover image to embed movie parts inside

3. Locate the regions in the image using the **findObjects()** function from the **video. tools.segmenting** module of **moviepy**; it accepts an input **ImageClip** object instantiated with the input image (containing multiple regions) and returns a list of regions, each representing a separate object on the screen (as can be seen from the output of the following code snippet, it found regions, as expected).

4. Let us find the path of 5 video files that we want to embed inside the 5 regions found, using the **glob.glob()** function from the video input path.

```
im = ImageClip(image)
regions = findObjects(im)
print(len(regions), im.size)
# 5, (930, 773)
video_files = sorted(glob('images/vid/in/V*.mp4'))[:5]
```

Add subtitles

We can add subtitles to the composite video if we want to. Let us create a dummy subtitle **.srt** file in the output folder using the following function: **create_subtitle_file()**:

```
def create_subtitle_file():
    with open('images/vid/out/subtitles.srt', 'w') as f:
        for i in range(20):
            f.write('{}\n00:00:{:02d},000 --> 00:00:{:02d},000\nComposite video
                    subtitle {}\n\n'.format(i+1, i, i+1, i+1))
create_subtitle_file()
```

Now, let us deep dive into next code snippet (which actually does the video embedding) and understand how it works step-by-step:

1. Let us load 5 video files; the frame rate of the videos we used are different (the first couple of them is 60 fps, where the remaining are 20 fps).

2. Let us first create 5 short video clips (by instantiating **VideoFileClip** objects) of same duration (for example, first 20 seconds, using the method **subclip()**) and having the same frame rate (20 frames per second, using the method **set_fps()**) from the videos, save the video clips in the output folder, as shown in the following code snippet.

3. Fit each video clip into its corresponding region obtained earlier.

4. Instantiate a **SubtitlesClip** object from the subtitles **.srt** file created earlier, so that we can add subtitle to the composite output video.

5. Instantiate a **CompositeVideoClip** object and combine the video clips with the subtitles. Scale the video down (with **resize()**, to speed up) and save the composite video in the output folder.

6. Append the composite video file to the list of video files.

7. Note that this particular composition takes quite some time, so be patient till it creates the output video.

Now, refer to the next code snippet:

```python
frame_rate = 20
n_secs = 20
clips = [VideoFileClip(vf, audio=False).subclip(0, n_secs).set_fps(frame_rate) \
                                            for vf in video_files]

comp_clips = [c.resize(r.size)
                .set_mask(r.mask)
                .set_pos(r.screenpos)
                for c,r in zip(clips,regions[:len(clips)])]

generator = lambda txt: TextClip(txt, font='Georgia-Regular', \
                        fontsize=24, color='white')
subtititles = SubtitlesClip("images/vid/out/subtitles.srt", generator)

cc = CompositeVideoClip(comp_clips + [subtititles.set_pos(('center','bottom'))], \
                        size=im.size)
cc.resize(0.6).write_videofile("images/vid/out/composition.mp4", fps=frame_rate)
for i in range(len(clips)):
    clips[i].write_videofile('images/vid/out/Vid_{:02d}.mp4'.format(i))
    clips[i].reader.close()

video_files += ["images/vid/out/composition.mp4"]
```

8. We can double check whether the output video clips have the same frame rate using the attribute **.fps (=20.0)**, find the duration of a clip with **.duration**

and compute the total number of frames **(=400)** in each of the clips created by multiplying them (as shown in the following code block).

9. The following code block finds the minimum number of frames in the clips:

```python
video_clips = sorted(glob('images/vid/out/V*.mp4'))
min_len = np.inf
for c in video_clips:
    clip = VideoFileClip(c)
    num_frames = int(clip.fps * clip.duration)
    print(clip.fps, num_frames)
    # 20.0 400
    min_len = min(min_len, num_frames)
    clip.reader.close()
print(min_len)
# 400
```

10. Select a random **index**. Use **opencv-python** to capture the videos and extract the particular frame **index** (by calling the **.set()** method with **cv2.CAP_PROP_POS_FRAMES** and **index** argument) from the input video clips and the output composite video.

11. Plot the frame at the chosen index for each of the video clips and also the output composite video clip, and display them, as done in the following code block.

12. Extract the frame dimension, frame rate and frame count for a video, using **VideoCapture.get()** method using arguments **cv2.CAP_PROP_FRAME_WIDTH, cv2.CAP_PROP_FPS** and **cv2.CAP_PROP_FRAME_COUNT,** respectively. As can be seen from the output of the next code snippet, the **fps** is 20.0 and total number of frames is 400 for the output composite video.

13. The frame 230 was shown from the input and the output composite video clips and as can be seen from *Figure 11.29*, the subtitle is added to the output clip.

```python
index = np.random.choice(min_len, 1)[0]
print(index)
# 230
plt.figure(figsize=(20,10))
plt.subplots_adjust(0,0,1,0.95,0.05,0.05)
i = 1
for vid in video_clips:
    cap = cv2.VideoCapture(vid)
    cap.set(cv2.CAP_PROP_POS_FRAMES, index)
    _, frame = cap.read()
    plt.subplot(2,3,i), plt.axis('off')
    plt.imshow(cv2.cvtColor(frame, cv2.COLOR_BGR2RGB), aspect='auto')
    i += 1
    cap.release()
```

```
plt.suptitle('Frame {} from the video clips'.format(index), size=25)
plt.show()
cap = cv2.VideoCapture('images/vid/out/composition.mp4')
width  = cap.get(cv2.CAP_PROP_FRAME_WIDTH)
height = cap.get(cv2.CAP_PROP_FRAME_HEIGHT)
fps = cap.get(cv2.CAP_PROP_FPS)
total_frames = cap.get(cv2.CAP_PROP_FRAME_COUNT)
cap.set(cv2.CAP_PROP_POS_FRAMES, index)
_, frame = cap.read()
plt.figure(figsize=(20,15))
plt.imshow(cv2.cvtColor(frame, cv2.COLOR_BGR2RGB)), plt.axis('off')
plt.title('Frame {} from the composite video clip'.format(index),
size=25)
plt.show()
```

If you run the preceding code snippet, you should obtain a figure as follows:

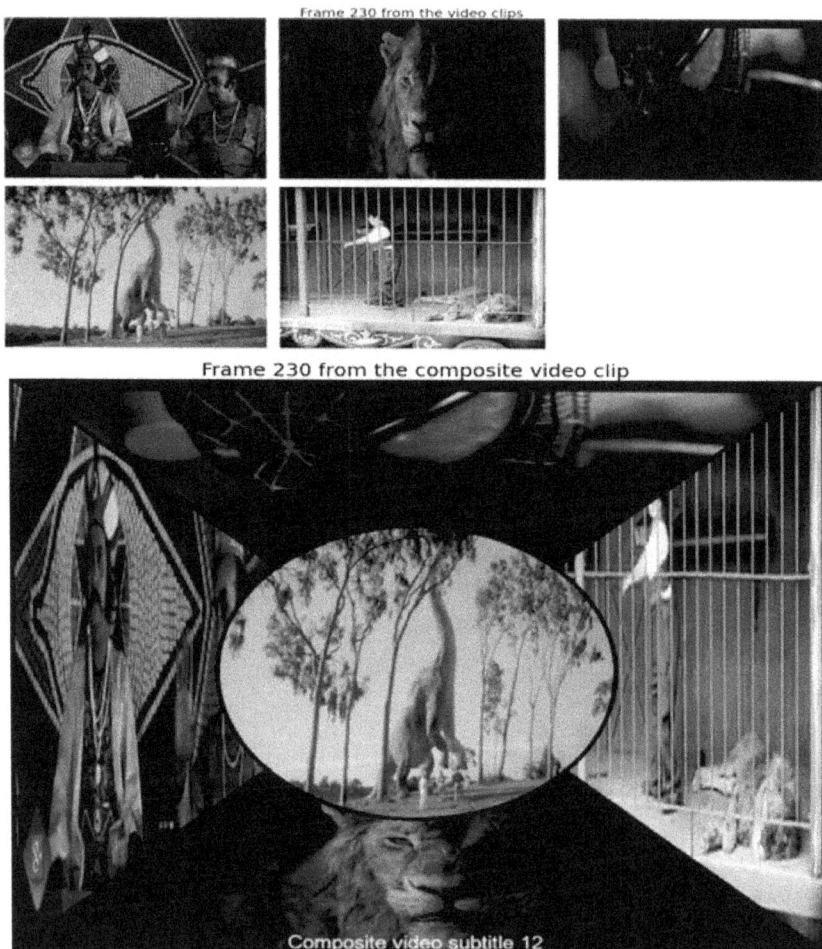

Figure 11.29: Embedding video clips with moviepy

Generating images from text with GAN-CLS

In this section, you will learn how to generate images of birds from given text descriptions using a generative deep learning model called **Generative Adversarial Network with Conditional Latent Space (GAN-CLS)**. This model is an enhanced version of **Deep Convolutional Generative Adversarial Network (DC-GAN)** that incorporates **textual input** instead of just class labels, allowing it to generate images that visually match a given sentence [14]. It has been trained on the **Caltech-UCSD Birds** dataset (along with five text descriptions per image).

GAN-CLS is an example of **generative AI**, a class of machine learning models that can create new content—such as images, text, or audio—based on learned data patterns. In this case, it generates images that correspond to textual descriptions.

The system is built around a **conditional GAN framework**, where both the **generator** and **discriminator** are conditioned on encoded text features. The text is processed using a hybrid character-level convolutional-recurrent neural network, which converts the sentence into a meaningful feature vector that captures its visual essence. The model solves two key sub-problems:

- Learning a text feature representation that captures the essential visual details.
- Using these features to synthesize a realistic image of a bird.

The main distinction of this model from the conditional GANs is that this model conditions on text descriptions instead of class labels.

Generator Network (G)

The generator starts by:

- Sampling a random noise vector **z** from a standard normal distribution.
- Encoding the input text **t** into a feature vector using a text encoder $\phi(t)$.
- Compressing $\phi(t)$ and concatenating it with **z**.
- Feeding this combined input into a **deconvolutional neural network** that outputs a synthetic image.
- This process is called **feed-forward inference**, where the generator learns to produce images that look like real birds described by the input text.

Matching-Aware Discriminator (D)

The discriminator is trained with three types of inputs:

- Real images paired with matching text (should be classified as *real*).
- Fake images generated by G with any text (should be classified as *fake*).
- Real images paired with *mismatched* text (should also be classified as *fake*).

- By doing so, the discriminator not only checks for visual realism but also for how well the image matches the description. This **matching-aware mechanism** helps the generator learn to better align images with text.

MSGAN: Preventing Mode Collapse

To address a common GAN issue called **mode collapse**—where the generator only learns to produce a few types of outputs—**Mode-Seeking GAN (MSGAN)** introduces a regularization term in the loss function. This encourages the generator to create more diverse images by exploring more possible outputs that still match the text.

The following figure shows the GAN-CLS model architecture, along with the algorithm:

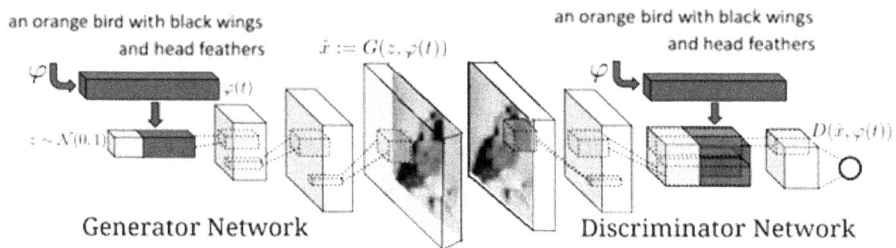

Figure 11.30: GAN-CLS algorithm for text-to-image generation
Source: http://proceedings.mlr.press/v48/reed16.pdf

Imagine describing a bird in a sentence—like *a small bird with a red head and yellow belly*. GAN-CLS takes this description and tries to **visualize it as an image**, almost like a digital artist painting what you describe. It does this through two networks:

- The **generator** tries to paint the bird from your description.

- The **discriminator** critiques the painting, saying either:

   o This looks real and matches the description, or

   o This is fake, or

   o This image doesn't match what was described.

Over time, the generator improves its skills by trying to fool the discriminator, learning to paint more realistic and better-matching bird images. MSGAN adds another layer of creativity by encouraging the generator not to repeat itself and instead produce more varied images from different text inputs.

This entire system is a prime example of **generative AI**, where machines are not just analyzing data, but creating entirely new content that didn't exist before—bridging natural language and visual imagination.

Now, let us start the demonstration, here we shall use a pretrained generator model. For faster inference, run the following code on *GPU* (for example, on Google Colab, mount your Google Drive first, upload the pretrained models to *gdrive* and then access them from Colab). Now follow the next steps carefully:

1. Start by importing the required libraries, modules, and functions for text-to-image synthesis.

```
import tensorflow as tf
print(tf.__version__)
# 2.8.0
from tensorflow.keras.utils import array_to_img
import nltk
from nltk.tokenize import word_tokenize
import gensim
```

2. First download the **word2vec** pre-trained Google News corpus (with 3 billion running words) word vector model (3 million English word vectors with -dimensions), for example, from the following repository: **https://github.com/mmihaltz/word2vec-GoogleNews-vectors** and unzip it to extract the **.bin** file (~ 3.4 GB) inside the **models** folder. It will be used to extract the latent embedding vectors corresponding to the input text descriptions that the generator model will use to generate the corresponding image later.

3. Use the function **load_word2vec_format()** from **gensim.models.KeyedVectors** module to load the in binary **word2vec** format file.

4. Load the pretrained generator model (download it from here: **https://github.com/AloneTogetherY/text-to-image-synthesis/tree/master/trained_model**)   to generate bird images from text descriptions.

```
nltk.download('punkt')
model = gensim.models.KeyedVectors.load_word2vec_format( \
                    'models/GoogleNews-vectors-negative300.bin', binary=True)
gen_model = tf.keras.models.load_model('models/bird_model.h5')
gen_model.compile()
```

5. The function **create_sent_vector()** accepts a **sentence** (text description) and returns the corresponding *embedding* as a 300 dimensional vector, as shown in the following code snippet. The embedding is computed as an average of the **word2vec** embeddings for the words present in it.

6. The function **generate_word_vectors_from_desc()** accepts a text description (**text_desc**) corresponding to the image of the bird we want to generate, replicates it **n_samples** times and converts them to latent embeddings. This is done because we want the generator to generate **n_sample** images for the given input text.

```python
def create_sent_vector(sent):
    result_array = np.empty((0, 300))
    for word in word_tokenize(sent):
        result_array = np.append(result_array, [model[word]], axis=0)
    final = np.mean(result_array, axis=0).astype('float32')
    return final

def generate_word_vectors_from_desc(text_desc, n_samples):
    vectors = []
    for i in range(n_samples):
        v = create_sent_vector(text_desc)
        vectors.append(v)
    return np.asarray(vectors), np.asarray([])
```

7. The function **generate_latent_points()** defined in the following code snippet accepts the latent embedding dimension **latent_dim** for the generator input, and the number of samples **n_samples** the generator needs to output corresponding to the input text description **text_desc**.

8. It creates an input **x_input** of size **nsamples** × **latentdim**, by sampling from the standard normal distribution and also computes **n_samples** sentence-embedding-vectors **text_captions** using the function **generate_word_vectors_from_desc()**. They are returned and will be used as input to the generator model for image synthesis.

```python
def generate_latent_points(latent_dim, n_samples, text_desc):
    x_input   = tf.random.normal([n_samples, latent_dim])
    text_captions, labels = generate_word_vectors_from_desc( \
                                              text_desc, n_samples)
    return [x_input, text_captions]
```

9. Generate images by conditioning on the given **test_input** (created from the input text descriptions) by running a forward pass with the generator model. Plot the **n_sample** images generated. Note that the generator model needs to be run with **training=False**.

```
def generate_images(model, test_input, text_desc):
    plt.figure(figsize=[15, 3])
    plt.subplots_adjust(0,0,1,0.925,0.05,0.05)
    predictions = model(test_input, training=False)
    for i in range(predictions.shape[0]):
        plt.subplot(1, 9, i+1)
        plt.imshow(array_to_img(predictions.numpy()[i]))
    plt.suptitle('Generative adversarial text to image synthesis\nText: {}' \
            .format(text_desc), size=15) # Text to image synthesis with GAN
    plt.show()
```

10. Finally, invoke the function **generate_images()** with the pretrained generator **gen_model** and generate latent points from the input **text_desc**. The generated output images (yellow birds) from the given input text are shown:

```
desc = 'This bird is completely yellow' # 'This bird is green'
# desc = 'This bird has white breast with brown feathers'
# desc = 'This bird has white breast with blue feathers'
generate_images(gen_model, generate_latent_points(100, 9, text_desc), \
                                                    text_desc)
```

If you run the preceding code snippet, you should get 9 bird images generated as shown in the following image, corresponding to the text description:

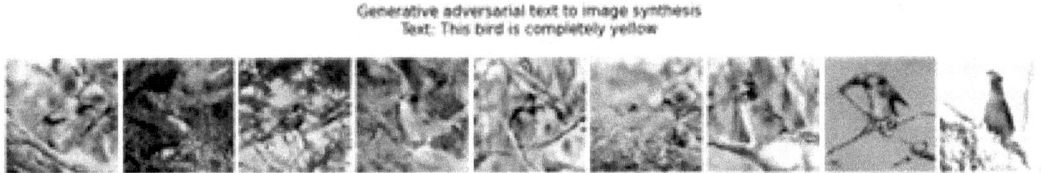

Figure 11.31: Text-to-image synthesis with GAN

11. This pretrained model was trained only for 960 epochs, hence mode collapse problems are likely to be visible [14]. To generate images with better quality, train the GAN-CLS model for many more epochs [11]. This is left as an exercise.

12. Also, note that you may need to remove stop-words from the input text; the corresponding **word2vec** embeddings are not likely to be present in the pretrained **word2vec** model. You may use other word embedding models, too.

Image editing with seamless cloning

In this section, we will explore how to seamlessly clone objects—like a person or any texture patch—from one image (source) into another (target) image using **Poisson blending**, a technique implemented in OpenCV. The main challenge is making the boundary of the source object look real and seamless on the target image, without destruction of the source object. **Poisson image editing** is a gradient domain editing and blending technique that can clone an object (texture) from a source image (captured by a mask image) with a target image seamlessly. Instead of simply copying pixel values, it focuses on **copying the gradient (intensity changes)** of the source object into the masked area of the target image. This method ensures that:

- The internal texture and shading of the source object are preserved.
- The boundary pixels align smoothly with the target image's surroundings.

In essence, it is a guided interpolation, since the cloned values of the source pixels are found by interpolating the values of the edge pixels into the target image's masked area, with the guidance provided by the gradient of the source image. The gradient of the source and output images in the masked region will be the same after seamless cloning is done. Moreover, the intensity of the target image and the output image at the masked region boundary will be the same .

Mathematically, it is an optimization (minimization) problem of an overdetermined system (as shown in the following *Figure 11.32*). The edge pixels act as constraints and their values are anchored to their values in the target image, while for each of the masked pixels in the target image, we have to solve two equations: setting its x and y gradients equal to the corresponding and gradients of the source image, respectively. Minimizing the error in the solution vector is a linear regression problem that may be solved by the normal equation with pseudo-inverse. Once the solution vector of pixels is obtained, it overwrites the masked portion of the target image, and the cloning process is complete.

The following figure shows how a source image patch g is integrated seamlessly with a target image f* (over the region Ω), with a new image patch f (over the region Ω) obtained as a solution with a poisson solver [13]:

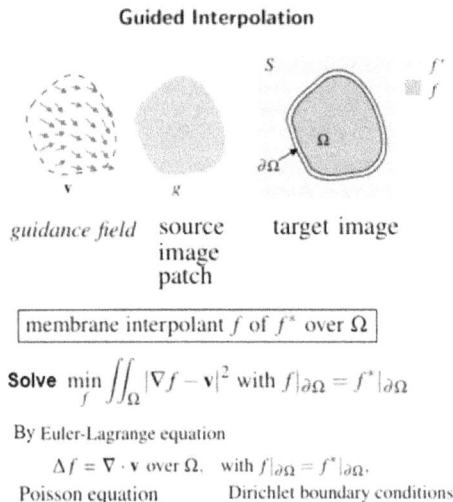

Guided Interpolation

guidance field   source image patch   target image

membrane interpolant f of f^* over Ω

Solve $\min_f \iint_\Omega |\nabla f - \mathbf{v}|^2$ with $f|_{\partial\Omega} = f^*|_{\partial\Omega}$

By Euler-Lagrange equation

$\Delta f = \nabla \cdot \mathbf{v}$ over Ω, with $f|_{\partial\Omega} = f^*|_{\partial\Omega}$.

Poisson equation   Dirichlet boundary conditions

Figure 11.32: Guided interpolation
Source: *https://www.cs.jhu.edu/~misha/Fall07/Papers/Perez03.pdf*

Let us start by importing the required libraries, note the version of **opencv-python** used. The function **plot_images()** plots the source, destination, mask and output images side-by-side with **matplotlib.pylab** module's **imshow()**.

```python
import cv2
print(cv2.__version__) # make sure the major version of OpenCV is >= 3
# 4.8.0
import numpy as np
import matplotlib.pylab as plt

def plot_images(src, dst, mask, output):
    plt.figure(figsize=(20,10))
    plt.subplot(131)
    plt.imshow(cv2.cvtColor(dst, cv2.COLOR_BGR2RGB), aspect='auto')
    plt.axis('off'), plt.title('Destination Image', size=20)
    plt.subplot(132), plt.imshow(cv2.cvtColor((0.6*src + 0.4*mask) \
                        .astype(np.uint8), cv2.COLOR_BGR2RGB), aspect='auto')
    plt.axis('off'), plt.title('Source Image (with mask)', size=20)
    plt.subplot(133), plt.imshow(cv2.cvtColor(output, cv2.COLOR_BGR2RGB), \
                                        aspect='auto'), plt.axis('off')
    plt.title('Output Image with Seamless Cloning', size=20)
    plt.tight_layout()
    plt.show()
```

Now follow the next steps for the demonstration of seamless cloning:

1. Here, we have a single destination image that has a waterfall, with spiderman standing in front of it. We also have 5 different source images, each with a mask corresponding to the spiderman's position in the image.

2. Now, we shall iteratively blend each of the source object (the spiderman) with the destination image, guided by the masked region in the source, using *seamless cloning,* as shown in the following figures 11.33 and 11.34.

3. We shall use **cv2.seamlessClone()** function, which accepts the source (**src**) and destination (**dst**) images, along with the **src_mask** and the parameter **center** which specifies where in the target image the masked object should be placed and blended.

4. Since the object to be blended is solid in each of the cases, **NORMAL_CLONE** is used. Note that the rough source masks also include backgrounds in the corresponding sources, which is nicely blended with the background in the corresponding location in the target image, something that simple copy-paste could not have done (try to change **NORMAL_CLONE** to **MIXED_CLONE** and explain which one works better here).

Now, refer to the next code snippet:

```python
# read source and destination images
from skimage.exposure import equalize_adapthist
dst = cv2.imread("images/1.jpeg")
centers = {2:(200,350), 3:(350,745), 4:(800,125), 5:(850,750), 6:(500,125)}
# read the mask image
for i in range(2,7):
    src = cv2.imread(f"images/{i}.jpeg")
    src =  equalize_adapthist(src.astype(np.uint8))
    src = (255*src/src.max()).astype(np.uint8)
    src_mask = cv2.imread(f"images/{i}_mask.jpg")
    # this is where the CENTER of the airplane will be placed
    center = centers[i]
    # clone seamlessly.
    output = cv2.seamlessClone(src, dst, src_mask, center, cv2.NORMAL_CLONE)
    # display result
    plot_images(src, dst, src_mask, output)
    dst = output
```

Refer to the following figure, which shows the blended images obtained by applying seamless cloning of each of the source images iteratively with the destination image:

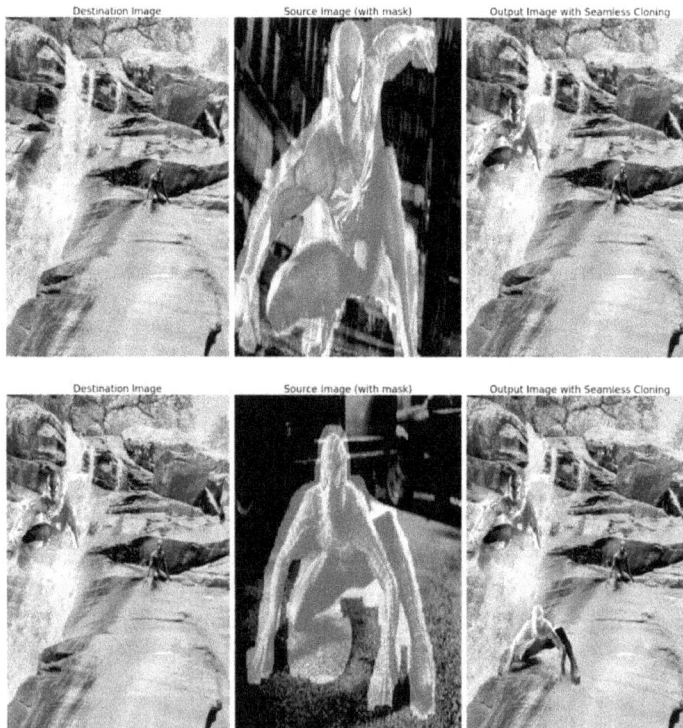

Figure 11.33: Inserting object (spiderman) into an image with seamless cloning

Again, refer to the next figure that shows the destination image with more source images are blended (with masks) into it, using seamless cloning:

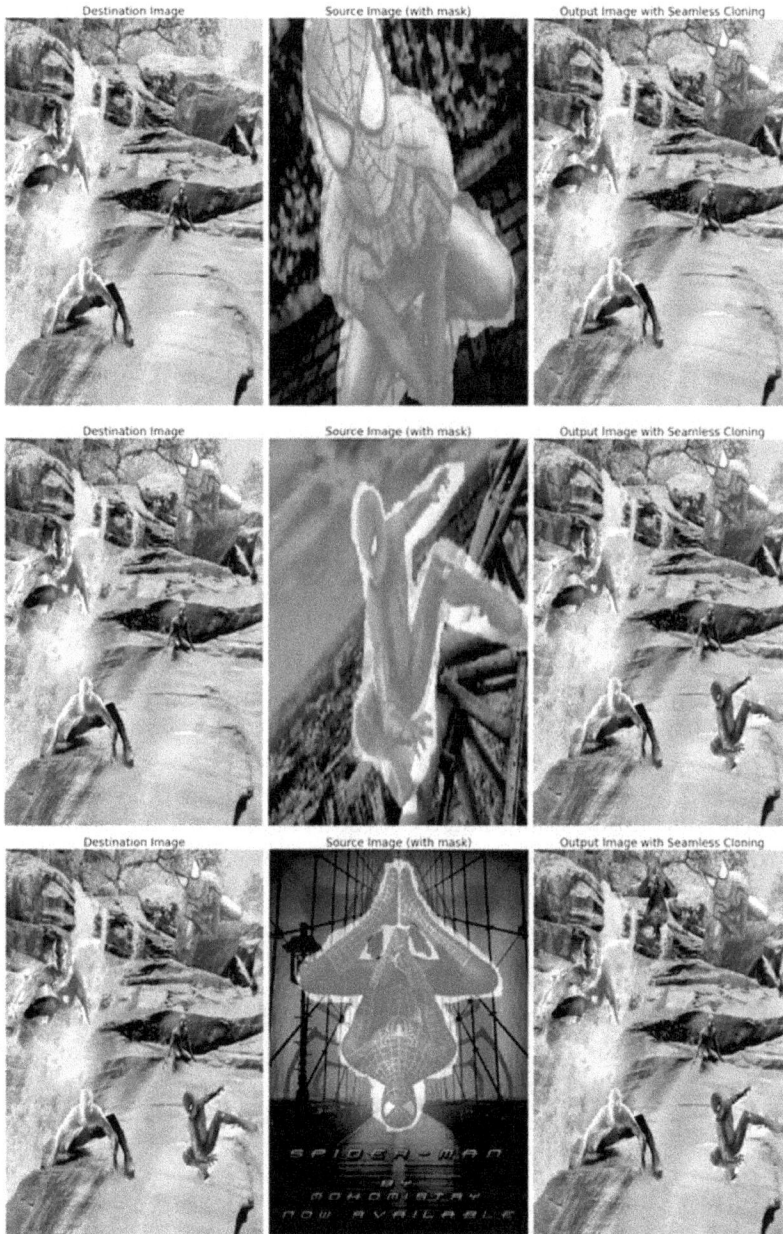

Figure 11.34: *Inserting object (spiderman) into an image with seamless cloning*

The following figure shows the final output image created after multiple blending and seamless cloning steps:

Figure 11.35: Image editing with seamless cloning with opencv-python

Image generation and editing with DALL-E

DALL-E is a **generative AI model** developed by OpenAI that creates and edits images from natural language prompts. It belongs to the class of **large language models (LLMs)** and uses a **decoder-only transformer architecture**, similar to GPT-3. The model was trained on hundreds of millions of *text–image pairs*, enabling it to generate high-quality images that correspond to the meaning and style described in the prompt.

DALL-E is capable of combining unrelated concepts, applying transformations to existing images, and rendering imaginative scenes that reflect textual input. It takes in both the prompt and image (if provided) as a single stream of up to 1,280 tokens and learns to generate each token one by one using *maximum likelihood estimation.*

OpenAI introduced the original DALL-E in early 2021, followed by **DALL-E 2** in 2022, which generates more realistic and detailed images with 4× greater resolution. **DALL-E 3**, released in late 2023, significantly improved *prompt understanding* and *image quality*, and is tightly integrated with **ChatGPT (GPT-4-turbo)**. This version supports **inpainting** (editing image regions via point-and-click), offering a conversational and intuitive way to generate or modify visual content.

Zero-shot text-to-image generation

Given an image description as prompt, DALL-E model can generate an image, without any additional task-specific training. This capability is called zero-shot reasoning. The model will produce a high-quality, contextually accurate image even if it has never seen the exact phrases in the prompt before.

How to use DALL-E 2 via the OpenAI API

To use the DALL-E 2 API for programmatic image generation, follow these steps:

1. **Create an OpenAI account:**

    Go to **https://platform.openai.com/signup** and sign up with your email address or log in with an existing Google or Microsoft account.

2. **Access the API keys:**

    After verifying your email and logging in, visit the API dashboard at **https://platform.openai.com/account/api-keys** to generate your secret API key, which you'll use in your code to authenticate API calls.

3. **Check Free credits:**

    OpenAI typically offers **free trial credits** (e.g., $5 worth) to new users for the first few months. These credits can be used across OpenAI's models, including DALL-E 2. You can view your credit balance at **https://platform.openai.com/account/usage**.

4. **Buy credits (if needed):**

    Once your free credits are exhausted, you can purchase additional credits from **https://platform.openai.com/account/billing**. Pricing is usage-based and transparent.

> **Note: As of now, DALL-E 3 is only accessible via the ChatGPT interface, not through the API.**

Now, let us use the DALL-E 2 APIs to demonstrate text-to-image-synthesis following the next steps:

1. Install the library **openai** with **pip**
2. Use your own API key to make the following example work.
3. Let us start by importing the required libraries and providing your own API key.

```python
# pip install openai==0.28

import openai  # OpenAI Python library to make API calls
import requests  # used to download images
import os  # used to access filepaths
from PIL import Image  # used to print and edit images

# set API key
openai.api_key = 'XXXXXX'  # use your own API key here, replace XXXXXX
```

4. Use the API **openai.Image.create()** which accepts the following arguments:

    a. The **prompt** text as the description of the image (be as specific as possible) to be generated, as shown (here, we want the model to generate a photo of the Victoria Memorial Hall in the winter season).

b. **n = 1**, that is, the number of images to be generated.

c. **size**, that is, the size of the image to be generated (here 1024×1024). The API allows you to generate images with a few predefined sizes.

d. **response_format="url"** specifies that the output can be downloaded from a **url** which will be returned.

e. **style = 'natural'** specifies that we want a natural image (as opposed to, for example, a digital art).

```python
prompt = "Photo of Victoria Memorial Hall in the winter. \
        A yellow taxi is standing in front with snows over it. \
        On the right, a boy is taking selfie."
# call the OpenAI API
generation_response = openai.Image.create(
    prompt=prompt,
    n=1,
    size="1024x1024",
    response_format="url",
    style = 'natural'
)

generated_image_name = "opeani_generated_image.png"  generated_
image_filepath = os.path.join('images/', generated_image_name)
generated_image_url = generation_response["data"][0]["url"]
# extract image URL from response
generated_image = requests.get(generated_image_url).content
# download image

with open(generated_image_filepath, "wb") as image_file:
    image_file.write(generated_image)  # write the image to the file

display(Image.open(generated_image_filepath))
```

The following figure shows the output generated with the API using the preceding **prompt**:

Figure 11.36: Text-to-image generation using DALL-E OpenAI API

Editing an image with mask

This DALL-E training procedure not only allows it to generate an image from scratch, but also to regenerate specific parts or regions (defined by a mask) of an existing image, in a way that is consistent with the text prompt. This process is called **inpainting**.

The DALL-E training process enables the model to understand which parts of an image to leave unchanged and which part to regenerate based on a **mask** and a **new prompt**. The mask image defines the area to edit: **the transparent (or black) region** in the mask is the area DALL-E will regenerate, while everything else in the image stays as it is.

The following code snippet demonstrates how the taxi in the image generated previously can be replaced by a cat using appropriate mask and a re-written prompt, while keeping the other parts of the image intact.

The following figure shows the mask to be used to regenerate a part of the image, with the transparent part to be regenerated by the model. Generating such a mask from a binary one requires some effort; the task is left as an exercise for the reader.

Figure 11.37: Creating a mask for editing an image generated with DALL-E

Note the prompt now mentions a big orange cat. The API to be used for editing the image (that is, to regenerate the region corresponding to the transparent part in the mask) is `openai.Image.create_edit()`, which accepts the input image to be edited along with the mask (with the transparent region to be edited) and the prompt.

Let us generate one such image of size 1024×1024, using the next code snippet, the URL of the generated image result is being returned. The output image is shown in *Figure 11.38*:

```python
prompt = "Photo of Victoria Memorial Hall in the winter. \
         A big orange cat is sitting in front. \
         On the right, a boy is taking selfie."

response = openai.Image.create_edit(
  image=open("images/openai_generated_image.png", "rb"),
  mask=open("images/openai_mask.png", "rb"),
  prompt=prompt,
  n=1,
  size="1024x1024"
)
image_url = response.data[0].url
with open('images/openai_edited_image.png','wb') as f:
    f.write(requests.get(image_url).content)

display(Image.open(('images/openai_edited_image.png')))
```

The following figure shows the output generated with the API using the preceding prompt:

Figure 11.38: Image editing with DALL-E OpenAI API

Conclusion

In this chapter, we explored a few more advanced techniques in computer vision and image processing, including deep generative art, image pseudo-colorization, text-to-image synthesis, and seamless cloning. Till now, we have been mostly dealing with 2D image processing, but in this chapter, we learned a few 3D image processing / computer vision techniques, for example, generating 3D point clouds and loading/projecting 3D objects. By now, you should also be able to implement basic AR applications with your webcam. You also learned how to use advanced GAN models for image synthesis from the text, as well as NLP methods (with the **gensim** library), such as how to create sentence embeddings from text sentences, which is a crucial part of solving the text-to-image synthesis problem. Along with **opencv-python**, we learned how to use other libraries such as **moviepy** (which is an important library for video/movie editing). Finally, we learned how to use generative AI models for text-to-image translation and for image editing using the cutting-edge **DALL-E 2** model from **OpenAI**.

Key terms

Artistic style transfer, DeOldify, CIC, Deep Dream, Poisson blending, Augmented reality, Vision transformer, GAN-CLS, MSGAN

Questions

1. **Controlled** vs. **uncontrolled deep dream**: Modify the deep dream code with PyTorch to work without any control (guide) image, that is, just maximizing the activation at the specific layer of the **VGG16** pretrained network (pretrained on **ImageNet**).

   Show that with the following input image of Disney cartoons (Mickey & Donald) the unguided vs. guided deep dream output will be like the ones shown in the following figure, when you use the following flower image as the control image (for the guided deep dream), VGG16 pretrained weights and maximize the activation for layer 26. Try changing the activation layer to be considered for gradient ascent and observe the impact on the output, for example, what happens when shallower vs. deep layer is chosen?

Figure 11.39: Guided vs. unguided deep-dreaming with VGG-16

2. Deep Dream with **GoogleNet** (Inception V3): Instantiate the inception_v3 class torch-vision.models with pre-trained weights and modify the deep dream code to use inception_v3 instead of Vgg16 (the base architecture shown in the following figure).

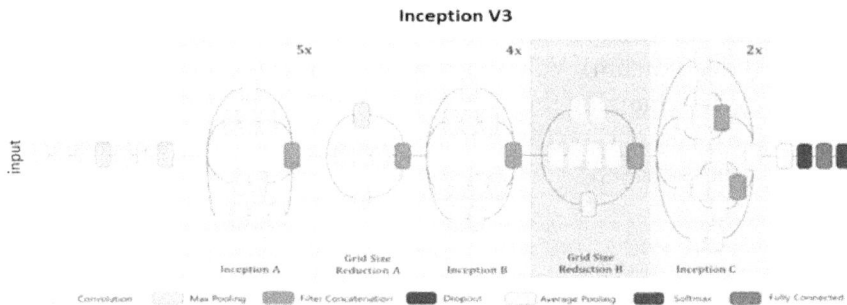

Figure 11.40: Inception V3 model architecture

Perform deep-dreaming at the layers Inception A, B, C, D, E (you may need to use pytorch *hooks*). You may use the following code snippet to obtain the corresponding layer numbers:

```
model = models.inception_v3(pretrained=True)
l = list(model.modules())
for x in [248, 229, 190, 159, 128, 97, 84, 62, 40]:
    print(x, l[x]._get_name())
# 248 InceptionE
# 229 InceptionD
# 190 InceptionC
# 159 InceptionC
# 128 InceptionC
# 97 InceptionC
# 84 InceptionB
# 62 InceptionA
# 40 InceptionA
```

You should obtain an output like the following figure, with an input image of a sky:

Figure 11.41: *Deep dreaming with GoogleNet*

3. Compare and show the output of the colored images obtained using different colorization algorithms for the same grayscale images. You should obtain a figure like the following one for the given input images (hint: you may want to implement couple of Python functions get_deoldify_output() and get_cic_output()):

Figure 11.42: *Comparing image colorization models*

4. Tune the render_factor hyperparameter of the **DeOldify** algorithm (for example, change from 20 to 40) and observe the impact on the color image generated, starting from the following input grayscale image given.

You should obtain a figure like the following one, for different values of render_ factor, in increasing order:

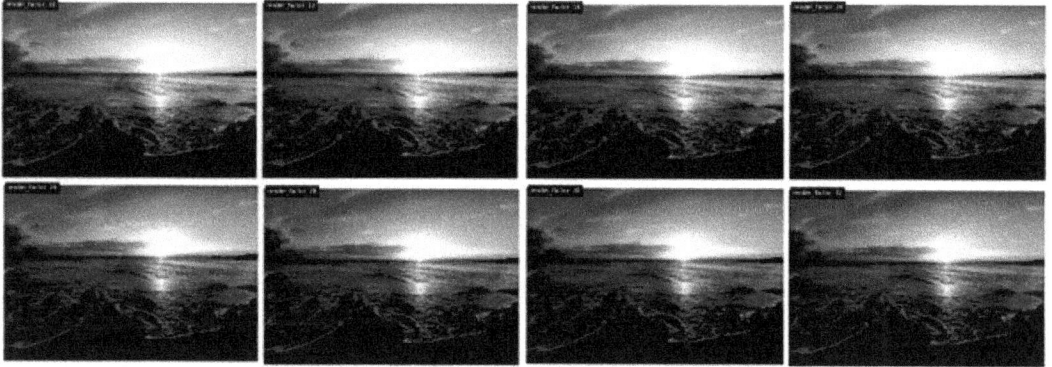

Figure 11.43: *Hyperparameter tuning with image colorization model DeOldify*

Compare the colorized output images obtained using different versions (artistic, stable and so on) the **DeOldify** colorizer outputs. Extract frames from a black-and-white (grayscale) video and colorize with different versions.

Now, start with a color image (ground-truth). Convert it to a grayscale image and automatically color the image using the preceding algorithms. Compute the Raw accuracy (as defined here: **https://arxiv.org/pdf/1603.08511.pdf**), defined by the percentage of predicted pixel colors within a thresholder L_2 distance (choose a threshold between 0 to 150) of the ground truth in *ab* color space (convert RGB to Lab).

5. Use the library neural-style to obtain stylized image with NST starting with a content and a style input image. Note that it uses iterative updates to modify the output image, so you should run on GPU, otherwise it will be very slow. (hint: use the following commands to setup the library and download the models)

```
#!pip install neural-style
#!neural-style -download_models models/
!neural-style -style_image starry_night.jpg -content_image metro.png
            -output_image output.png -model_file nin_imagenet.pth
            -gpu 0 -backend cudnn -num_iterations 1000 -seed 123
            -content_layers relu0,relu3,relu7,relu12
            -style_layers relu0,relu3,relu7,relu12 -content_weight 10
            -style_weight 500 -image_size 512 -optimizer adam
```

You should obtain an output as shown in the following figure with the given content (metro rail) and style (*Van Gogh's starry night*) image. Note the command line arguments used, many of them are hyperparameters to the model (for example, content_weight, style_weight, optimizer), tweak them to observe the impact on the generated image. Refer to the following figure:

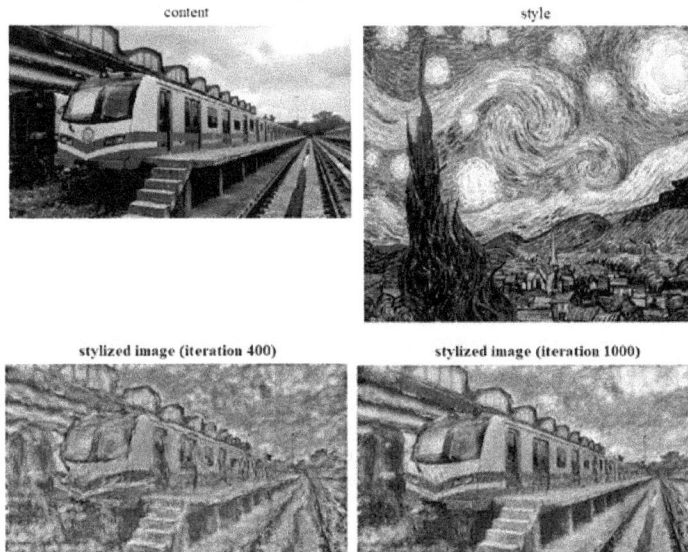

Figure 11.44: NST with the library neural-style

Next, use it to combine multiple style images with a content image, and you should obtain a figure like the following, once you start with the inputs shown:

Figure 11.45: NST - combining multiple styles with neural-style

Refer to this paper **https://arxiv.org/pdf/1703.06953.pdf** (that introduces a **CoMatch** Layer which learns to match the second order feature statistics with the target styles) and this pytorch implementation **https://github.com/zhanghang1989/ PyTorch-Multi-Style-Transfer** to implement **MSGNet**. Start with an image of a train as content and the candy style image to obtain the following output image with artistic style transfer, shown in the next figure:

Figure 11.46: Artistic style transfer with MSGNet

Finally, use **MSGNet** for much faster inference and better-quality stylized output image, with multiple style images.

6. **Image-to-Video Generation Using a Diffusion Model**: Implement a pipeline that transforms a single static image into a short video using a pretrained diffusion model. Use the 🤗 **Hugging Face** diffusers library and the Stable Video Diffusion (**SVD**) model from Stability AI. Your implementation should do the following:

   - Load a pretrained SVD model suitable for converting still images into videos.

   - Preprocess a sample image (e.g., a photo of your choice or a classic image like Lena).

   - Generate a sequence of frames using the model.

   - Export the resulting frames as a video file (e.g., .mp4).

   Hints:

   - Use the DiffusionPipeline class from diffusers to load the model.

   - The model accepts 16-bit float tensors and is designed to run on CUDA-enabled devices.

   - Use utility functions like load_image() and export_to_video() to streamline your pipeline.

   Optional challenges:

   - Try different image resolutions and observe how it affects the output.

   - Vary the number of output frames and frame rate (fps) to create different video lengths and speeds.

   - Replace the image with a custom input and adjust resizing appropriately.

References

1. https://arxiv.org/pdf/1705.06830.pdf

2. https://arxiv.org/pdf/1603.08511.pdf

3. https://cs.stanford.edu/people/jcjohns/papers/eccv16/JohnsonECCV16.pdf

4. https://www.ipol.im/pub/art/2022/403/article_lr.pdf

5. https://www.researchgate.net/publication/329610370_Hands-on_Image_Processing_in_Python

6. https://github.com/jantic/DeOldify

7. https://github.com/onnx/models/tree/main/vision/style_transfer/fast_neural_style

8. https://www.jmlr.org/papers/volume9/vandermaaten08a/vandermaaten08a.pdf

9. https://cs.gmu.edu/~xzhou10/doc/kinect-study.pdf

10. https://arxiv.org/pdf/2103.13413.pdf

11. https://github.com/AloneTogetherY/text-to-image-synthesis

12. https://bitesofcode.wordpress.com/2018/09/16/augmented-reality-with-python-and-opencv-part-2/

13. https://www.cs.jhu.edu/~misha/Fall07/Papers/Perez03.pdf

14. http://proceedings.mlr.press/v48/reed16.pdf

15. https://arxiv.org/pdf/1903.05628.pdf

16. https://www.youtube.com/watch?v=cwe0nBqkDWk

17. https://www.youtube.com/watch?v=98ZYF9M-4Js

18. https://www.youtube.com/shorts/hpaaT5yaaeE

19. https://www.youtube.com/watch?v=bxzuCmcHlO4

20. https://www.youtube.com/watch?v=d2CSrDKs6Jw

21. https://www.youtube.com/watch?v=XBTaE32-wL4

22. https://www.youtube.com/watch?v=eL33bEyy88o

23. https://www.youtube.com/watch?v=4-_Fc5S4rNE

24. https://www.youtube.com/watch?v=qdDlW4g9Yik

25. https://www.youtube.com/watch?v=QFml23buJqQ

26. https://www.youtube.com/watch?v=23nHljrSh3I

27. https://www.youtube.com/watch?v=8mWaFrCFdCw

28. https://arxiv.org/abs/2102.12092

Join our Discord space

Join our Discord workspace for latest updates, offers, tech happenings around the world, new releases, and sessions with the authors:

Index

E

F

N

www.ingramcontent.com/pod-product-compliance
Lightning Source LLC
Chambersburg PA
CBHW061737210326
41599CB00034B/6708